South Africa, Greece, Rome

How have the histories of ancient Greece and Rome intersected with that of South Africa? This book canvasses architecture, literature, visual arts and historical memory. Some of the most telling manifestations of classical reception in South Africa have been indirect: for example, neoclassical architecture or retellings of mythical stories. Far from being the mere handmaiden of colonialism (and later apartheid), classical antiquity has enabled challenges to the South African establishment, and provided a template for making sense of cross-cultural encounters. Though access to classical education has been limited, many South Africans, black and white, have used classical frames of reference and drawn inspiration from the ancient Greeks and Romans. While classical antiquity may seem antithetical to post-apartheid notions of heritage, it deserves to be seen in this light. Museums, historical sites and artworks, up to the present day, reveal juxtapositions in which classical themes are integrated into South Africa's pasts.

GRANT PARKER teaches Classics and African Studies at Stanford University, California, and is currently Extraordinary Professor in the Department of Ancient Studies, Stellenbosch University, South Africa. His research focuses on Roman imperial culture, classical reception, collective memory, and the history of collecting.

Frontispiece A whole and a headless monument to the 'triumph of the Dutch language' together with other Afrikaner monuments, Burgersdorp, Cape. 29 September 1990. Photograph by David Goldblatt.

South Africa, Greece, Rome

Classical Confrontations

EDITED BY GRANT PARKER

CAMBRIDGE
UNIVERSITY PRESS

CAMBRIDGE
UNIVERSITY PRESS

University Printing House, Cambridge CB2 8BS, United Kingdom

One Liberty Plaza, 20th Floor, New York, NY 10006, USA

477 Williamstown Road, Port Melbourne, VIC 3207, Australia

4843/24, 2nd Floor, Ansari Road, Daryaganj, Delhi – 110002, India

79 Anson Road, #06–04/06, Singapore 079906

Cambridge University Press is part of the University of Cambridge.

It furthers the University's mission by disseminating knowledge in the pursuit of
education, learning and research at the highest international levels of excellence.

www.cambridge.org
Information on this title: www.cambridge.org/9781107100817
DOI: 10.1017/9781316181416

First published 2017

Printed in the United Kingdom by TJ International Ltd. Padstow Cornwall

A catalogue record for this publication is available from the British Library.

Library of Congress Cataloging-in-Publication Data
Names: Parker, Grant Richard, 1967– editor.
Title: South Africa, Greece, Rome : classical confrontations / edited by Grant Parker.
Description: Cambridge : University Printing House, 2017. | Includes bibliographical
references and index.
Identifiers: LCCN 2017029297 | ISBN 9781107100817 (alk. paper)
Subjects: LCSH: South Africa – Civilization – Classical influences. | Civilization, Classical.
Classification: LCC DT1752 .S67 2017 | DDC 700/.482922110968–dc23
LC record available at https://lccn.loc.gov/2017029297

ISBN 978-1-107-10081-7 Hardback

Contents

v

Colour plates are to be found between pp. 298 and 299

Plates

Illustrations

Contributors

JONATHAN ALLEN, Associate Professor, Department of Political Science, Northern Michigan University

JOHN ATKINSON, Professor emeritus, School of Languages and Literature, University of Cape Town

PHILIP R. BOSMAN, Associate Professor, Department of Ancient Studies, Stellenbosch University

JO-MARIE CLAASSEN, Associate Professor emerita, Department of Ancient Studies, Stellenbosch University

KATHLEEN M. COLEMAN, James Loeb Professor of the Classics, Harvard University

NIKOLAI ENDRES, Professor, Department of English, Western Kentucky University

FEDERICO FRESCHI, Executive Dean of the Faculty of Art, Design and Architecture, University of Johannesburg

JOHN HILTON, Senior Research Associate, School of Religion, Philosophy and Classics, University of KwaZulu-Natal, Durban

SAMANTHA MASTERS, Lecturer, Department of Ancient Studies, Stellenbosch University

PETER MERRINGTON, independent scholar

GRANT PARKER, Associate Professor, Department of Classics, Stanford University, and Extraordinary Professor, Department of Ancient Studies, Stellenbosch University

ELIZABETH RANKIN, Professor emerita, School of Humanities: Art History, University of Auckland

ROY SARGEANT, independent scholar

ROLF MICHAEL SCHNEIDER, Professor emeritus, Institut für Klassische Archäologie, Ludwig Maximilian University, Munich

ELKE STEINMEYER, Senior Lecturer, School of Religion, Philosophy and Classics, University of KwaZulu-Natal, Durban

ANNA TIETZE, Lecturer, Michaelis School of Fine Art, University of Cape Town

DEON H. VAN ZYL, independent scholar

DAVID WARDLE, Professor, School of Languages and Literature, University of Cape Town

Preface

South African engagements with ancient Greece and Rome, in their many facets, form the subject matter of this book. The contributors' collective aim is to explore the country's past in relation to classical antiquity – a loaded term, to be sure, used here as shorthand for Greaco-Roman antiquity, broadly conceived. Conversely, the book offers a range of South African interpretations of classical antiquity. Between these covers we have sought to contribute to the cultural histories of both South Africa and of classics. With 'confrontations' in the subtitle we emphasise the inequalities and tensions involved in those histories.

The challenges of such a bifocal project should not be underestimated. Despite the recent growth of interest in the classical tradition, often under the mantra of reception, it remains hard to persuade northern-hemisphere and especially US classicists that Southern Africa has anything significant to offer. By the same token, most (South) Africanists currently writing would probably be surprised to hear that classical antiquity deserves their attention. For intellectual and political reasons, there remains much bridge-building to do.

At the time when work on this volume neared completion, a heated debate raged at the University of Cape Town, my alma mater, about the presence of a prominent statue of Cecil John Rhodes, a major figure in the essays that follow. On 9 April 2015 the statue was removed to an undisclosed location by the university administration, following weeks of student protests which converged under the hashtag #RhodesMustFall. Other universities witnessed similar exchanges; statues elsewhere in the country were defaced or otherwise contested. While much of the discussion involved wider issues about education and the economy, there is no doubt that the symbolic power of monuments – even of traditional, figurative ones – came dramatically to the fore. In the intervening months 'Fallist' activism has moved on to a FeesMustFall campaign throughout the country's campuses. Nevertheless, the original RhodesMustFall initiative would suggest that the classical tradition continues to play a role in South African public history. Confrontations indeed.

I warmly thank all the contributors for their patience in the lengthy gestation of this project, and for dialogue through its twists and turns. For their wise counsel I especially thank Jonathan Allen, John Atkinson,

Kathleen Coleman and John Hilton among contributors, as well as John Allison, Henri (Jatti) Bredekamp, Jacob Dlamini, Michael Onyebuchi Eze, Yusuf Gabru, Jonathan Jansen, Michael Lambert, Carmel Schrire, Richard Whitaker and Betine van Zyl Smit. I treasure the memory of spirited conversations on the subject with the late Robert Shell. Rolf Michael Schneider deserves special thanks for his input over several years, ranging from its most practical aspects to its most abstract considerations. His enthusiasm for the topic has been an inspiration.

Several Stanford units have provided interlocutors and other kinds of support: the Center for African Studies (CAS), the Center for the Comparative Study of Race and Ethnicity, the Department of Classics and the Stanford Archaeology Center. I am especially grateful to CAS for sponsoring a workshop series, 'Memory and heritage in South Africa', and to Lindsay Moira Weiss for co-convening it. I have learnt much from audiences at the University of the Free State, Stellenbosch University, Duke University and the University of North Carolina – Chapel Hill.

In the latter stages of this book's preparation the assistance of Raleigh Browne, Lori Joe, Kristin Kueter and Dan-el Padilla Peralta has been invaluable; earlier on Sander Gonzalez, Jocelyn Hickox, Susan Lape, Matthew Loar, Sandy Rowoldt Shell, Linda van de Vijver and Lydia Zodda came to the rescue. My long-standing debts to Richard Parker, Robert Pryor and Martin Rollo are enormous. I am grateful for John Filmalter, Russell Scott and Paul Weinberg for providing original photography, and to Kenney Mencher for his sketch. Michael Sharp deserves special thanks for supporting this project through thick and thin, and I am grateful also to Marianna Prizio and her Cambridge University Press colleagues, as well as to the anonymous reviewers.

Over several years, so many people have discussed elements of this project with me, in seminar settings or informally, so many have helped materially, so many librarians, archivists and others have contributed, that I cannot name everyone. Let me at least say that I am most grateful to all of them, and at the same time humbled by a sense that there remains so much more to do in this broader topic – especially in relation to the evolving conversation about heritage and public history. This project has, in part, been one of collecting, and I trust that the process will continue in other formats: see https://exhibits.stanford.edu/SAGR

*

All URLs were functioning as of 9 March 2016.

PART I

———

Prologue

1 | The Azanian Muse: Classicism in Unexpected Places

GRANT PARKER

On 12 February 1991 a meeting took place at Cape Town's airport, then known as D. F. Malan Airport in memory of the first apartheid-era prime minister, between leaders of the African National Congress and President F. W. de Klerk's ruling National Party. One year earlier, Nelson Mandela, the African National Congress (ANC) leader, had been released from lengthy imprisonment and the organisation itself unbanned. The purpose of the meeting was to clear the way for formal talks about the transition to democracy, talks which had at the time stalled as a result of violent exchanges involving both the black population and the security forces. The meeting ultimately produced the D. F. Malan Accord, an agreement on the terms of engagement that did much to make possible the first democratic election of April 1994. This was uncharted territory and the mood was tense. Sceptics on each side questioned the entire exercise of negotiating a democratic solution to the country's political impasse, which had long been marked by violence. There was no guarantee of a peaceful outcome.[1]

During a tea break, one member of the African National Congress delegation, Chris Hani, initiated a conversation with Gerrit Viljoen, who was at the time Minister of Constitutional Development and De Klerk's right-hand man (Fig. 1.1). Hani was Chief of Staff of the ANC's armed wing, Umkhonto we Sizwe ('Spear of the Nation'). The subject of their conversation was Sophocles' tragedy *Philoctetes*, about which Hani raised some detailed points of interpretation. Together with Pallo Jordan, also of the ANC delegation, Hani and Viljoen fell into deep discussion. According to De Klerk, Viljoen was 'impressed' by their 'enthusiasm and depth of knowledge'.[2] The fact that an ancient, scholarly topic arose in a high-voltage political meeting certainly occasioned surprise at the time, all the more because it was initiated by a guerrilla who grew up among the country's poorest. Indeed, Hani had spent his early years in the rural Eastern Cape, his parents minimally

---

[1] Sparks 1994: 131.

[2] F. W. de Klerk, private communication, 1 April 2010: for recollections of the incident I thank the former President, as well as former Minister Pallo Jordan (private communications, 19 and 21 August 2010).

Figure 1.1 Gerrit Viljoen alongside President F. W. de Klerk and Adriaan Vlok (Minister of Law and Order), in the second round of talks with the ANC. Viljoen is seated opposite Nelson Mandela, who led the ANC delegation, and Alfred Nzo. Pretoria, 6 August 1990.

educated.[3] Despite the two leaders' differences of allegiance and background, Sophocles' play provided common ground and, in particular, an icebreaker.

Gerrit Viljoen (1926–2009) was the son of a professor of Greek, and had had a stellar academic career: having studied initially at the University of Pretoria, he took the Classical Tripos (first class) at Cambridge and then a doctorate in classical philology at Leiden. He became professor of Greek at the University of South Africa (1957), then rector of the newly formed Rand Afrikaans University, now known as the University of Johannesburg (1967), before taking political office in 1978. His academic research focused on Greek lyric poetry, especially the *Odes* of Pindar.[4] Viljoen was an establishment figure par excellence, and at one stage chaired the influential and partly secret Afrikaner organisation, the Broederbond (1974–80).[5] Having initially been the senior constitutional expert on de Klerk's team, Viljoen resigned in 1992 for health reasons, and left politics completely. He died in 2009.

---

[3] Hani's autobiographical essay of 1991 is reproduced in Houston and Ngculu 2014: 55–56; compare Smith and Tromp 2009 and MacMillan 2014.

[4] Kriel 2009: vii–x; Louw and van Rensburg 1997. Viljoen's Leiden dissertation appeared as *Pindaros se Tiende en Twaalfde Olimpiese Odes* (Viljoen 1955). Given the aristocratic character of Pindar's poems, it is tempting to argue that their particular inflection of antiquity resonated with the Broederbond's exclusivist style of Afrikaner nationalism.

[5] Smith 2009 and Giliomee 2003: esp. 583–84.

Figure 1.2 Chris Hani, with fellow ANC leaders Tony Yengeni and Willie Hofmeyr, on Church Square, Cape Town (1991). In the background is the Slave Lodge, which functioned at the time as the SA Cultural History Museum: see also Figs 1.13, 9.9 and 9.11.

Hani (1942–93), on the other hand, had studied Latin and English at the historically black University of Fort Hare and then at Rhodes University, both in the Eastern Cape (Fig. 1.2).[6] While fighting against apartheid in exile, he maintained scholarly habits, reading voraciously. His original choice to study Latin was linked to the fact that it was a requirement for entry into the legal profession. Hani's popularity in South Africa was enormous following his return from exile in 1991. However, he would not live to see the first democratic election, since he was assassinated at his home near Johannesburg by a white supremacist in April 1993. As we shall see, the relation between classical antiquity and South Africa's emerging elite had many facets, involving no less a figure than Mandela himself during his Robben Island imprisonment. Translated ancient texts were among the library books available to prisoners, even to political prisoners on Robben Island. Such ancient works, typically in Penguin translations, were considered by the authorities to be innocuous and innocent of the subversiveness they sought to quell (Fig. 1.3).[7]

---

[6] I thank Mr Steven Fourie, Registrar of Rhodes University, for making available Hani's academic record, covering the years 1959–61 (copy dated 22 April 2010). Cf. Lambert 2011: 110–15.

[7] See the publication accompanying an exhibit at Cape Town's South African Museum: Kathrada and Deacon 1996. Cf. Coombes 2003: 61.

Figure 1.3 Books from the prison library: *Esiqithini: the Robben Island exhibition*, South African Museum, Cape Town (1996). Penguin edition translations of Greek tragedies are pictured alongside Indian sacred texts, which are inscribed with A. M. Kathrada's name on the cover. Photograph by Matthew Willman.

In itself, the airport episode amounts to little, and is hard to document following the deaths of the two main protagonists. Nonetheless, it should at the very least attune us to the element of surprise: whereas classical antiquity is very widely attested as a source of social hierarchy and division, its role as a bridge-builder – or, to put it differently, a safety-valve – is much less known. The Hani/Viljoen exchange is thus emblematic of the scope and nature of the current volume, which seeks to excavate distinctively South African contexts of classical antiquity, to explore the often surprising afterlives of ancient Greek and Roman texts, ideas, styles and artefacts. To be sure, classical antiquity has been part of the colonial legacy, during both the Dutch- and the British-ruled periods of South African history, roughly 1652–1806 and 1806–1910, respectively. Several of the essays that follow make the colonial connection clear. Recent scholarship has shown the small but influential role classics played in the formation of the Indian Civil Service, both at the East India Company College at Haileybury (founded 1806) and later at Balliol College, Oxford.[8] But clearly neither of these characterisations tells the whole story. For one thing, Hani's undoubted attachment to ancient literature casts into question

---

[8] Vasunia 2008.

any assumption that classical antiquity has been merely the handmaid of colonialism or of apartheid. Classicism has been evident in some unexpected places, and it has been part of the lives not merely of those whose elite education enabled them to learn Latin at a young age. In the spectrum of South African interactions with ancient Greece and Rome presented below, it will be as important to show some familiar, mainstream instances of classicism alongside less expected and less canonical ones. What is more, the episode coincides with a critical period in South African history, namely the transition to democracy that started in earnest when, opening Parliament on 2 February 1990, De Klerk unexpectedly announced the unbanning of the ANC and the release of Mandela. In one sense the Viljoen/Hani moment looks forward to the post-1994 period of ANC-led majority government, and to a time when, amid the restructuring of school and university curricula, university departments of ancient studies have had to define and defend their turf anew in a changing landscape. Most departments have been reduced in the number of instructors, through attrition, redeployment and retrenchment; others have been closed down or amalgamated out of existence. Historically white universities face the challenge of how to appeal to the new student demographic. This is now much more racially diverse, containing a high percentage of non-native speakers of English or Afrikaans, the established languages for teaching Latin and Greek especially, and of first-generation university attenders, who gravitate naturally to the professional tracks rather than the humanities. In another sense the episode also looks back upon a time in which ancient Greece and Rome held a place of some prominence, if one thinks beyond the figure of Viljoen himself to the country's Roman–Dutch juristic tradition and to some of its most prominent buildings, including the Union Buildings in Pretoria. Far from being a one-sided, unchanging set of material, classical antiquity has fulfilled very different social roles at different times. At that critical point in South Africa's history, Sophocles played a minor but revealing role.

1. The Muse in Azania

The muse herself needs no introduction. As the collective symbols of artistic and other kinds of creativity, the muses go all the way back to the earliest Greek literature. Best known is the invocation of the muse that begins Homer's *Odyssey*: 'Tell me, Muse, of the man of many turns...' (1.1). They appear sometimes singly and sometimes in groups of different sizes, linked initially with Pieria and nearby Mount Olympus. These god-desses were a source of inspiration for poets, intellectuals and others.[9]

In this essay the muse is a metaphor for classicism, namely the ideas, forms, artefacts and texts of the ancient Greeks and Romans. The notion of the classical is by no means without its complications, particularly as it relates to the intellectual and aesthetic histories of idealised forms.[10] It has aesthetic and ethical implications. Another element at the edges of the current collection is the relative role of other traditions of antiquity, including Egyptian and Phoenician.[11] For present purposes, however, we may take the term 'classical' to denote the cultural productions of ancient Greece and Rome. Unless otherwise specified, the term 'antiquity' in the pages that follow refers to those particular ancient cultures. Their special status in Western European civilisation is a large topic in its own right, involving the history of the Christian church as well as the deployment of ancient symbols as a source of legitimacy on the part of several post-ancient polities. While this special status of 'classical' antiquity in Europe is well established, its role in Africa, including South Africa, is much less obvious. That role is explored in the current volume.

It is only recently that colonial and postcolonial receptions of antiquity have begun to receive attention.[12] Some such studies have emphasised the role of classics in the scholarly background of metropolitan-trained colonial elite. Others have shown that, in its (post)colonial manifestations, antiquity has sometimes been a source of social power for upwardly mobile people, in the colonies as indeed in the motherland; that it has been no monolith, with classical material deployed sometimes in subversive ways that challenge rather than reinforce the colonial establishment. Such themes will be apparent in the current collection.

Azania needs rather more explanation. This is the ancient name for the Horn of Africa, attested first in the anonymous *Periplus of the Erythraean Sea* (sections 16–19), a captain's manual of around AD 40–70. In ancient topography it denotes the land immediately adjacent to the north-west

---

[9] Bottini 2006.   [10] Porter 2006, esp. 1–67.

[11] There are special problems in comparing the reception of Egypt and Phoenicia in South Africa. Most significantly, both are better known through the Hebrew Bible, especially the Pentateuch, than in any more direct sense. To take a concrete example, obelisks may be considered a link with Egypt, for example in early twentieth-century commemorations of the Anglo-Boer War and of the Great Trek. But the link is an indirect one, since obelisks were first imported by Roman emperors and have since then been widely deployed as a symbol of power. See further Cornelius 2003. Furthermore, scholarly accounts of the Phoenicians emphasise how little is known of them, e.g. Markoe 2001.

[12] Notably Goff 2005; Hardwick and Gillespie 2007; Greenwood 2010.

Indian Ocean, today's Somalia, Kenya and Tanzania.[13] Later, the term would be found also in Claudius Ptolemy's *Geography*, a second-century AD text representing both the culmination of ancient geography and also, as we shall see, an important point of departure for early modern European geography, following its translation into Latin in 1406.[14] Much later, the name 'Azania' would be revived in the attempt to find an anti-colonial alternative to the term 'South Africa', which was officially used after the Act of Union in 1910. In practice, use of the name 'Azania' marked the split of an Africanist faction away from the African National Congress in 1959. This faction became the Pan Africanist Congress under the leadership of Robert Sobukwe (1924–78).[15] A small number of political organisations continue to use the name Azania today: an act of continued defiance against the dominance of the ANC and its partners in government. Consequently, the ancient name is far from obscurantist and pedantic: for some, it signals the failure of the ANC since the 1950s to constitute a single, unified organisation. This would be the only apparent explanation for the fact that the term continues to raise hackles in South Africa today, even though both the Pan Africanist Congress and Azanian People's Organisation (AZAPO) have had only negligible popular support, as reflected in the elections since 1994. Beyond this narrowly political use, the name has been a symbol of African pride, by implication invoking the glories of Egypt and Ethiopia as alternatives to the seeming monopoly of Greece and Rome. Other factors too might have determined its use: in general, the desire to make the point that South Africa is part of the African continent; and specifically to signal Kenyan and Tanzanian support for the struggle against apartheid. Nonetheless, the choice of the name is problematic if its main aim is to decolonise minds: as the chapters here show, the classical tradition in South Africa has been associated with colonialism in various forms. The name 'Azania' has emerged at a particular moment; as will be very apparent, the reasons for invoking antiquity and circumstances in doing so have been remarkably different, and it is questionable whether the preference for 'Azania' over 'South Africa' as a name constitutes any meaningful stand against colonialism in itself.

To gain some perspective on the range of South Africa's classical traditions, it might have seemed obvious to focus on Greek and Latin pedagogy. Indeed, some attempt will be made to do so in the paragraphs immediately following: at the very least, engagement with the languages themselves provides a basis of sorts and can be easily measured. The story has already

---

[13] Hilton 1993.   [14] Berggren and Jones 2000: 52.   [15] Lodge 1983: 67–90; Kondlo 2009.

been told.[16] However, in the present volume as a whole, pedagogy is more a matter of historical setting than a central focus. Here the emphasis will be, rather, on cultural productions that have involved Greek and Roman antiquity in a central way. The book seeks variously to address the question, *How have ancient Greece and Rome intersected with South African histories?* The plural 'histories' is advisedly used, so to include not only politics and cultural productions but also the more modest *petits récits* ('small narratives') of individuals rather than institutions.[17] The overarching question of the book subsumes two related concepts, namely tradition and reception. As used here, both are conceived broadly.[18] The question is also intended to emphasise that South African receptions of antiquity deserve to be explicitly located in that country's history, particularly of the nineteenth and twentieth centuries. Several smaller but still fundamental questions follow, for example: Who has been involved in classical reception, and to what ends? Is it possible to identify instances in which classical pasts have displaced other pasts? Between these covers we canvass a broad range of artefacts, styles, texts and ideas. While the case-study format is well suited to such diversity and breadth, the present essay seeks to identify some unifying themes and phenomena.

2.   Authority

It is already evident that Graeco-Roman antiquity has been implicated in various kinds of authority. As a next step it will be necessary to consider the educational role classical antiquity has played, particularly in an institutional sense.

In classical antiquity the extent of Africa was not known, and there was no awareness of the southern end of the African continent. Herodotus is pointedly vague when, in the course of describing Nilotic geography, he

---

[16]   Smuts 1960 and 1976, to which Lambert 2011 adds a critical edge. For African contexts: Dominik 2007 and Hilton 2007: 11–40. See now also Murray (2014) on women's classical education.

[17]   Cultural history was substantially established as a field in the mid- to late nineteenth century by Jakob Burckhardt 1990. On *petits récits* see Jean-François Lyotard 1984: 60.

[18]   Some classicists have argued for the concept of reception as preferable to that of tradition, on the grounds that tradition implies uncritical celebration: e.g. Hardwick 2003. However, since Hobsbawm and Ranger 1983, this is not the case: it has become axiomatic, at least in the historical disciplines generally, that the notion of tradition deserves some measure of scepsis, and that the term has lost its supposed innocence.

comes to the area south of Elephantine.[19] The question of Africa's southern extent is, for Herodotus and later geographers, tied up with that of the source of the Nile and its annual inundation.[20] Later ancient writers would also be concerned with this set of questions. In antiquity and well beyond, the southern part of Africa would remain quite literally Europe's 'terra incognita'.[21] It is in these circumstances that Pliny the Elder, composing his *Natural History* in the second half of the first century AD, could refer to a Greek proverb according to which Africa always produces something new.[22]

One factor in the persistence of this idea is the ongoing authority of ancient maps, particularly Claudius Ptolemy's *Geography* (second century AD): apart from some theoretical discussion, the bulk of the work (books 2–7) comprises a list of some 8100 toponyms, together with their coordinates. This work, written in ordinary *koine* Greek and translated into Latin only in 1406, was the point of departure for western map-making from around that time well into the fifteenth century, amid many exploratory voyages. The Ptolemaic schema played an important role in the evolution of western cartography in this so-called Age of Discovery. One divergence that would emerge was that the Indian Ocean proved to be not an inland sea, which Ptolemy had indicated (Fig. 1.4), and this meant that India could be reached from western Europe by rounding the Cape.[23] Martin Waldseemüller' *Universalis Cosmographia* (originally 1507, Fig. 1.5) famously used the name 'America' but it is also one of the first to show Africa's southern limit. In both respects Waldseemüller was responding to voyages undertaken by Iberian explorers, yet the tradition of Claudius Ptolemy continued to provide the larger framework.

The southern end of Africa was less significant to European science in itself than it was as a key point on the sea-route to India. In this context Portuguese explorers were the first Europeans to round the Cape: first

---

[19] Elephantine is located at the first cataract, in an area that roughly coincides with the southern border of the modern state of Egypt.

[20] Herodotus offers a series of competing theories on the inundation, of which he clearly states his favourite, namely that the sun is driven by storms from its original path onto the inland regions of Africa ('Libya'): *Histories* 2.24, cf. 2.25–27.

[21] Romm 1992: 16, 35, 122.

[22] 'vulgare Graeciae dictum semper aliquid novi Africam adferre': Pliny, *Natural History* 8.42, apparently referring to Aristotle, *Historia animalium* 606b20. See in detail van Stekelenburg 2003 and Ronca 1992. Van Wyk Smith 2009 sketches a broad context, but its main theses require caution.

[23] Grafton 1992. For the history of cartography as a long-term, changing balance of continuity and change, see the cautionary remarks of Woodward 2007.

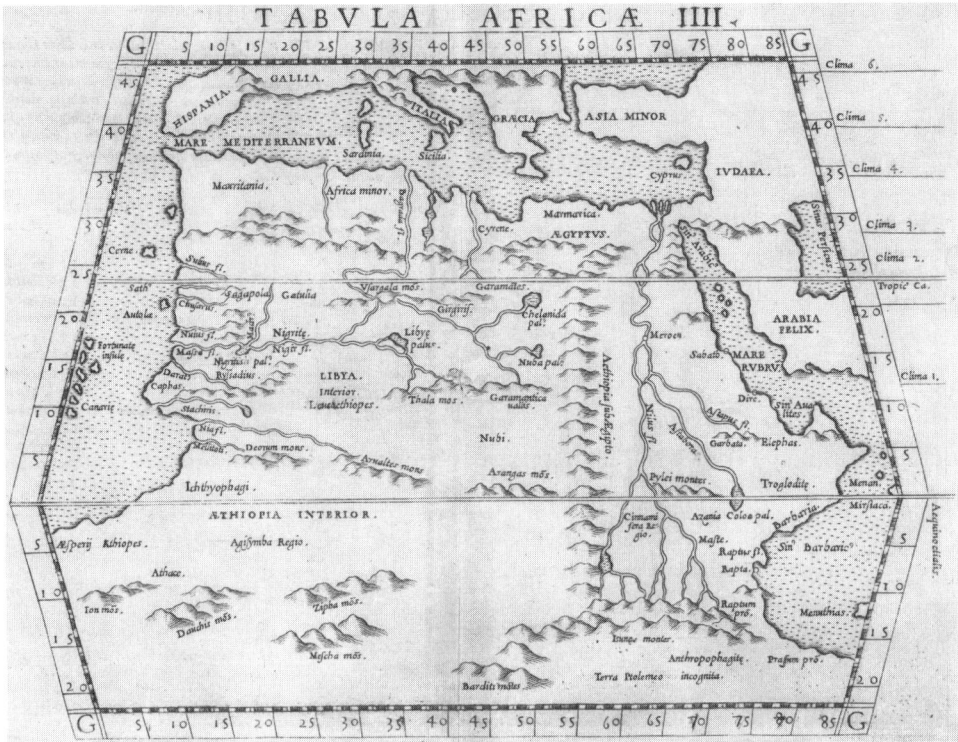

Figure 1.4 Ptolemy, Tabula Africae IIII (Venice 1561). Copperplate, 18 × 24 cm.

Bartholomew Dias in 1487 and later Vasco da Gama in 1497–98.[24] The inscriptions the early Portuguese seafarers left behind in southern Africa were in vernacular Portuguese rather than scholarly Latin.[25] A telling contrast emerges here, which may be considered emblematic of the limited role of ancient Greece and Rome in early colonialism: on the one hand, maps produced in the European metropolis reveal a classicising tendency, with their use of a Ptolemaic paradigm and sometimes Latin, whereas on the other hand the travellers themselves show a preference for the vernacular, in part by virtue of the limits of their education.

The classical framework had dimensions beyond the science of maps. In the sixteenth century, classical mythology was creatively amended to accommodate a new figure: Adamastor. This character, invented by Camões as a personification of the 'Cape of Storms' ('Cabo tormentoso' by its Portuguese name), is carefully aligned with classical mythology as 'one

---

[24] Dias' contribution was to show how it was possible to round the Cape, and thus reach the Indian Ocean by sea: Axelson 1961.

[25] The early inscriptions also make use of French and English: Schoonees 1991.

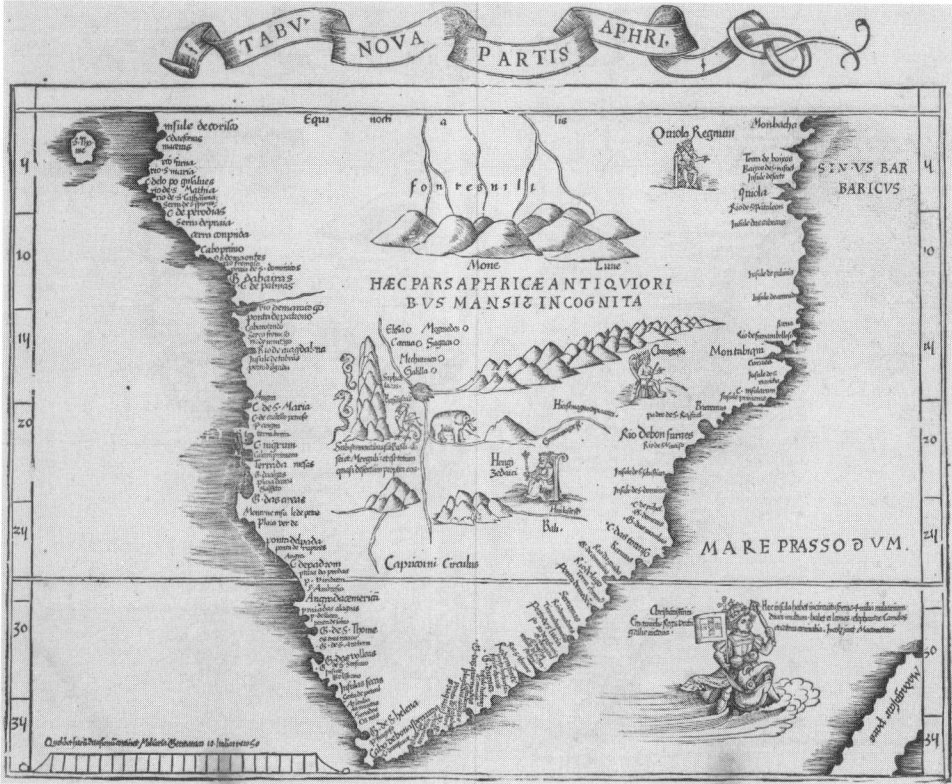

Figure 1.5 Tabula novae partis Aphricae. Woodcut map (Lyons 1535) based on Martin Waldseemuller, *Universalis Cosmographia* (1507), 30 × 42 cm. Border and ornament are by Hans Holbein and Graf. The reissued map includes three kings on their thrones, an elephant, a cockatrice and two serpents, while the King of Portugal rides a bridled sea monster.

of those rugged Titans' (Canto 5.51). Having fallen in love with the nymph Thetis, he is thwarted by her mother Doris. Adamastor's curse threatens all Europeans who round the Cape, Dias having been the first victim. The curse, with its prophecy of the fate that Portuguese seafarers can expect, marks the Cape of Storms as forbidden territory and in a dire prophecy warns potential travellers that nature's secrets are not to be desecrated without retribution:

> I am the vast, secret promontory
> you Portuguese call the Cape of Storms,
> which neither Ptolemy, Pompey, Strabo,
> Pliny, nor any authors knew of.
> Here Africa ends. Here its coast

Figure 1.6 Cyril Coetzee, *T'kama-Adamastor* (1999): oil on canvas, 8.64 m × 3.26 m. Photograph by Russell Scott. (A black and white version of this figure will appear in some formats. For the colour version, please refer to the plate section.)

> concludes in this, my vast inviolate
> plateau, extending southwards to the Pole
> and, by your daring, struck to my very soul.[26]

The figure of Adamastor is thus created in a classical frame, even if that frame had to be specifically enlarged to accommodate it. Following Camões, many literary and visual artists have taken up this mythical figure, so that Adamastor has even become a symbol of the violence accompanying colonialism. This is seen, for example, in Cyril Coetzee's large mural, *T'kama Adamastor* (1999) as well as literary works of Roy Campbell, André P. Brink and Douglas Livingstone (see Fig. 1.6, Plate 1 and Coleman, this volume).[27] The idea that antiquity can be brought into creative dialogue with colonial history is seen also in the New Zealand artist, Marian Maguire, in various etchings and lithographs (Figs 1.7–8).

Furthermore, some of the earliest European descriptions of the south-western Cape and its hinterland are in Latin. This is not surprising, given the status of Latin as a scholarly language of early modern Europe. The first such writer, Willem ten Rhyne (1647–1700), spent only a few weeks at the Cape on his way to Java in 1673, yet his 'Short account of the Cape of Good Hope' (1686) initially reveals his keen interest in botanical matters, elsewhere in evidence, whereas the final two-thirds are devoted to a description of the indigenous Khoi people ('Hottentotti'). By contrast,

---

[26] Canto 5.50 translated by Landeg White. On Adamastor's curse see further Ferreira 2008 and Van Wyk Smith 1988.

[27] Coetzee's mural is located in the William Cullen Library of the University of the Witwatersrand, Johannesburg: see Vladislavić 2000. On Campbell see Crewe 1999.

Figure 1.7 Marian Maguire, 'A New Zealander by Parkinson and Ajax by Exekias play draughts', from *The Odyssey of Captain Cook* (2005). Lithograph, 520 × 700 mm.

Figure 1.8 Marian Maguire, 'Athena, as Justice, in a New Zealand landscape of 1870'. From the series A Taranaki Dialogue (2010). Etching, 150 × 235 mm.

Jan Willem van Grevenbroek (1644–1725) arrived at the age of forty, and then spent the rest of his long life at the Cape, the first ten years as a senior administrator under Governor Simon van der Stel. His lengthy letter on the

Figure 1.9 *De Promontorio Bonae Spei. The Cape of Good Hope: a Latin oration delivered in the Hamburg Academy, 10 April 1767.* By Gysbert Hemmy from Africa. Translated and edited by K. D. White, with additional notes by G. S. Nienaber and D. H. Varley. Cape Town: South African Public Library, 1959.

Cape of Good Hope was composed in highly wrought literary Latin, with many poetic touches. The Neolatin tradition from and about the Cape is not substantial, but its products are historically significant in themselves as the earliest accounts of the South African hinterland. Whereas these works stemmed mostly from armchair European travellers, there is in one instance a Cape-born writer. From the later eighteenth century two works survive of Gysbert Hemmy, born at the Cape to a German merchant family. One is a legal treatise on the admissibility of slaves' evidence against their masters, 'On the testimony of Aethiopians, Chinese and other pagans', whereas the other is a speech, 'On the Cape of Good Hope', delivered in 1767 at the Johanneum, a school in Hamburg whose humanistic tradition goes back to the time of Martin Luther (Fig. 1.9).[28] It is in this period that the Cloete Cellar of Groot Constantia Estate received an elaborate classicising pediment, depicting the mythological scene of Zeus abducting Ganymede (Fig. 1.10).

One area in which Latin had particular purchase in early Cape history is law. Whereas civil law replaced Roman-Dutch law in many parts of

[28] The Latin title is *Dissertatio juridica inauguralis de testimoniis Aethiopum, Chinensium aliorumque paganorum in India orientali* (1770), translated by Hewett 1998. On the speech, see Kytzler 2000 and Van Stekelenburg 2003.

Figure 1.10 Cloete Cellar (1781) of Groot Constantia Estate, Constantia, near Cape Town, designed by the architect Louis Thibault and sculptor Anton Anreith. The pediment depicts The Rape of Ganymede, in which Zeus changes himself into an eagle in order to abduct the youth. Photograph by Paul Weinberg.

the world around the time of Napoleon, Roman-Dutch law would prove a lasting legacy of the Dutch occupation. It endures to the present day, even though in effect much attenuated by the use of case law. Along with Roman-Dutch law came Latin as the medium of legal discourse. Slavery was practised at the Cape from the early Dutch settlement, from the 1660s up to abolition in 1834, and the law governing it used Roman precedent in one important respect: that slaves were property, and therefore unable to enter into legal contracts such as marriage. From a recent study it emerges that the reception of Roman law at the Cape reveals detailed knowledge, including chapter-and-verse citation, with the original Latin used more than translations. Roman law was used in both prosecution and defence, by both slaves and their masters; by the same token, Graeco-Roman precedent was used on both sides of the debate around abolition.[29]

Beyond texts there is also another use of antiquity visible when, for example, a brass bell installed by governor Simon van der Stel at the Castle of Good Hope, South Africa's oldest building complex still standing (Fig. 1.11), carried a Latin inscription: 'With the blessing of the Lord of

[29] Hilton 2007a and 2011; cf. Hilton 2013.

Figure 1.11 Castle of Good Hope, Cape Town. Built in 1666–79 by the Dutch East India Company, the Castle is the country's oldest extent colonial building. See also Fig. 18.1 below.

the earth exalted on high, Claudius Fremy's foundry produced me in Amsterdam in the year 1697.'[30] In this literal sense, Latin was present at the Cape from the end of the seventeenth century, and remains up to the present.

During the Dutch occupation there were few institutions of learning in the colony, but the situation changed substantially with the arrival of the

---

[30] Barker 2003: 117. The Latin text reads 'Claudii Fremii me fecit Amstelodami anno 1697. Benedicat et super exaltet eum in caelos'.

British around the time of the Napoleonic Wars.[31] Whereas the first British occupation lasted for only the years 1795–1803, the second was more enduring and had greater impact. Having begun with the Battle of Blaauwberg in 1806, it lasted in its full political sense until the Act of Union in 1910. Under British rule the introduction of church-run schools brought instruction in Latin for the first time. Over the decades this would be largely restricted to the colonial elite, including its young women: the most significant exceptions were Lovedale and later Fort Hare, where Mandela, Hani and others studied (see Claassen, this volume).[32]

When institutions were established to provide education for the sons, and later daughters, of the colonists, Latin had a place of some significance. This is in keeping with European traditions of the period. The British astronomer John Herschel (1792–1871) spent the years 1834–38 at the Cape for the purpose of observing the skies, and during that period he was visited by Charles Darwin. Herschel's sojourn catalysed educational reform at the Cape and was subsequently marked with the erection of a small obelisk at his former Cape home, where now a school is named in his memory.[33]

The discovery of diamonds in the Hopetown/Kimberley area along the Orange River (1866–71), followed by gold farther inland on the Reef (1886), precipitated drastic changes at levels of the region's society and economy. Those who emerged in the late nineteenth century as the mineral magnates, namely Cecil John Rhodes, Alfred Beit and other 'Randlords', started converting their financial gains into cultural capital. They did so in style. Johannesburg, the centre of the gold industry, was a brand new city, and in that environment the occasional but visible use of classical motifs asserted a past that was not necessarily otherwise apparent. In this way Johannesburg, perhaps even more than older cities such as Cape Town, Port Elizabeth and Durban, acquired many noble buildings in the classical or Palladian styles. (See Freschi, this volume.)

Rhodes' engagement with antiquity had many facets (see Hilton, this volume), including the commissioning of an ambitious series of translations from Greek and Latin texts (see Wardle, this volume). In a sense this is ironic, given that he was himself no great scholar, and his command of Greek and Latin was only barely adequate for the purposes of his Oxford

---

[31] Greek and Latin books make two appearances around the year 1800, but they do not appear to lend themselves to wider conclusions: Dick 2013: 40, 47.

[32] Smuts 1960, 1976; Murray 2014.

[33] Herschel's prominence in science was such that his activities elicited an extended satire by the American naturalist John Locke, composed in the style of Lucian (second century AD): see Hilton 2005.

Figure 1.12 Houses of Parliament, Cape Town. Originally built 1875–84 according to designs by Charles Freeman and Henry Greaves, the complex was extended in the 1920s by Herbert Baker. Photograph by Paul Weinberg.

degree. His close association with the architect Herbert Baker (1862–1946) resulted in significant architectural activity, both in the Transvaal and in Cape Town (Fig. 1.12). After Rhodes' death in 1902, Baker designed the Union Building, which marked the establishment of the Union of South Africa, amalgamating the four provinces (1910, Fig. 2.13). Baker's classical designs may be considered a link with not only Britain but also with other colonies such as India and New Zealand.

Latin became a prerequisite for certain positions in the legal profession, and consequently for legal training. This stipulation did not necessarily represent a conscious effort to exclude blacks, very few of whom had access to Latin in high school, but it did largely have that effect. The Latin requirement for law was dropped in 1994, very soon after the ANC's accession, and by that point most South African departments of classics enrolled the largest number of their students via the juristic route. In Dutch Reformed and other seminaries, Greek was part of the theological curriculum. In 1958 the Classical Association of South Africa was founded, providing a forum for discussion about classical material.[34] Its activities, in research, teaching and community outreach, are visible in the Association's journals, *Acta Classica* and *Akroterion*.

3.　The Struggle with Greek and Latin

Some of the contexts in which elements of antiquity present themselves are surprising, to say the least. For one, many of the names of the slaves from the later seventeenth to the early nineteenth centuries were classical. Explanations for this practice differ: one scholar has seen this custom as degrading, consistent with the naming of pets, whereas another sees a direct connection with ancient Roman naming practice.[35] Either way, the legacy of slave names is very evident in the Cape Town telephone directory today, with names such as Cupido, Hector and Adonis abundantly in evidence (Fig. 1.13, cf. 1.14).

Further, apart from the episode with which this introduction began, there are three poignant moments in the struggle against apartheid, all of them located in prisons and known through the memoirs of leading political figures. The most famous episode involves Mandela himself, who participated in a production of *Antigone* in December 1974, ten years into what would be a 27-year-long imprisonment. The production took place on Robben Island, in B Section Hall. Some thirty prisoners of B Section attended the performance, along with a handful of warders. Copies were obtained through the prison library, and the performances themselves were sanctioned by the prison authorities.[36] Frank Anthony was another of the prisoners taking part.[37]

In his memoir Mandela writes of this in the context of his admiration for ancient Greek plays, which he found 'enormously elevating' (441). Mandela was especially interested in, and even inspired by, the heroic temperament of Greek tragic heroes:

---

[34]　The early history of the association is traced in a series of articles by Henderson 2004, 2005, 2006, 2007, 2008, 2010, 2013, 2014.

[35]　Shell 1994: 242; contrast Hilton 2004.

[36]　These are the recollections of fellow inmate Ahmed Kathrada, who attended the performance (personal correspondence May 2007 and telephonic interview 17 August 2010). In his memoir Kathrada (2004: 259) attributes this version of *Antigone* to Jean Anouilh (1960 [1943]); nonetheless, there is no question about the presence on Robben Island of English translations of Sophocles' Greek.

[37]　Bartlett 2006; Pirro 2011: 105.

Figure 1.13 Gavin Younge and Wilma Cruise, *Slave Memorial* (2008), Church Square, Cape Town: 'Sc[h]ipio' recalls the Roman general and statesman Publius Cornelius Scipio Africanus. See also Figs 1.2 and 9.11. Photograph by Paul Weinberg.

What I took out of them was that character was measured by facing up to difficult situations and that a hero was a man who would not break down even under the most trying circumstances. (441)

The sentiment is not as narrowly gendered as it seems, for it applies to Antigone, a heroine 'who symbolized our struggle; . . . a freedom fighter . . . [who] defied the law on the ground that it was unjust'. (442) When Mandela offered to take part in the production, he was asked to play the part of Creon. Mandela's subsequent reflection on the play focuses on his role in the ANC and the struggle against apartheid: he says of Creon that 'his inflexibility and blindness ill become a leader, for a leader must temper justice with mercy'. (442) In this way Mandela distances himself from Creon's self-righteous inflexibility in the play. Not surprisingly given the nature of the memoir, Mandela's comment is made very much under the spotlight of historical evaluation. The self-criticism it conveys is certainly characteristic of *Long Walk to Freedom*. From the play he quotes lines 194–97:

Figure 1.14 'Love and Beauty: Sartjee the Hottentot Venus'. Prints H163-MA1955-541 Photograph: Museum Africa, Johannesburg.

Of course you cannot know a man completely, his character, his principles, sense of judgment, not till he's shown his colours, ruling the people, making laws. Experience, there's the test.[38]

Mandela's status seems to hinge more on the struggle against apartheid and the democratic transition, whereas his presidency (1994–99) came towards

[38] Mandela 1994a: 441, quoting lines 194–97 in the translation by Fagles, Sophocles 1982: 67. This corresponds to Sophocles, *Antigone*, lines 175–77 in the original Greek. Fagles' version, though quoted in Mandela's memoir, actually postdates the Robben Island performance by nearly a decade.

the end of a distinguished political career. The memoir was thus published around his accession; presumably much of it was written down between his release from prison and the first democratic election (26–29 April 1994), and thus reflects his concerns about the prospect of taking power for the first time. Given the time at which *Long Walk to Freedom* was composed, Mandela's leadership was certainly under scrutiny: to a degree that is hard to conceive in retrospect, members of the liberation movement and indeed of the ANC were suspicious of the process of negotiations which led to his release.

While this revival of an ancient Greek play was significant, it is also somewhat isolated. It is clear that Shakespeare was pre-eminently the 'common culture and text' of Robben Islanders, more so than the Bible or any other text (Fig. 1.15).[39] In this context the many references among prisoners to Julius Caesar should be seen: it was in his Shakespearean form that he was known.

Second, Albie Sachs, then an ANC cadre and later a Constitutional Court justice, recollects a period in 1963 when he was arrested under State of Emergency legislation, and held in solitary confinement in various Cape Town prisons. Among these was the Caledon Square Police Station in the city centre. Sachs recalls with vividness and gentle self-mocking the point at which he contemplates his cell, which even at the time seemed to him a 'mere temporary staging-post':

On the walls are the names of others who have been here as political prisoners. Someone has written up slogans in Latin: must be a teacher – who could it be? Yes, of course, here is his name, Achmat Osman. He was here for one day only. SIC TRANSIT NOX DOLORIS. Not very spirited that – 'Thus passes a night of sorrow.' I think I will add a bit, though it is not easy to write on the wall with a ballpoint. I scratch the words SED SIC ADVINIT NOVA DIES – 'But thus arrives a new day.' Or should it be 'advenit' and not 'advinit'? I am sure Achmat will not mind my making the addition, even if my grammar is weak. Here he has written another one: VAE TYRANNIS and there VAE TYRANNIBUS. Obviously he too was not sure which was the right word. Well, no inspector [of education] will tick him off for poor work here, 'Cursed by the tyrants' – I think that is what it means. VITAS LIBERTAS. 'Long live liberty.' That is more like it. Trust old Achmat to hurl defiance at them – in Latin.[40]

Latin plays a curious role here: it is a source of bonding and even conversation between prisoners occupying the cell at different times. Whereas graffiti are very common in jail cells, here the status of Latin makes for

---

[39] Sampson 1999: 231.   [40] Sachs: 1996: 199, cf. Dick 2013: 135.

JULIUS CÆSAR [Act 2

Fierce fiery warriors fight upon the clouds,
In ranks and squadrons and right form of war, 20
Which drizzled blood upon the Capitol;
The noise of battle hurtled in the air;
Horses did neigh, and dying men did groan,
And ghosts did shriek and squeal about the streets.
O Cæsar, these things are beyond all use, 25
And I do fear them!
Cæs. What can be avoided,
Whose end is purpos'd by the mighty gods?
Yet Cæsar shall go forth; for these predictions
Are to the world in general as to Cæsar.
Cal. When beggars die there are no comets seen: 30
The heavens themselves blaze forth the death of princes.
Cæs. Cowards die many times before their deaths:
The valiant never taste of death but once.
Of all the wonders that I yet have heard,
It seems to me most strange that men should fear, 35
Seeing that death, a necessary end,
Will come when it will come.

Re-enter Servant.
What say the augurers?
Serv. They would not have you to stir forth to-day.
Plucking the entrails of an offering forth,
They could not find a heart within the beast. 40
Cæs. The gods do this in shame of cowardice.
Cæsar should be a beast without a heart,
If he should stay at home to-day for fear.
No, Cæsar shall not. Danger knows full well
That Cæsar is more dangerous than he: 45
We are two lions litter'd in one day,
And I the elder and more terrible;
And Cæsar shall go forth.
Cal. Alas, my lord,
Your wisdom is consum'd in confidence.
Do not go forth to-day. Call it my fear 50
That keeps you in the house, and not your own.
We'll send Mark Antony to the Senate House,
And he shall say you are not well to-day.
Let me, upon my knee, prevail in this.
Cæs. Mark Antony shall say I am not well; 55
And for thy humour I will stay at home.

Enter DECIUS.
Here's Decius Brutus, he shall tell them so.
Dec. Cæsar, all hail! Good morrow, worthy Cæsar.
I come to fetch you to the Senate House.
Cæs. And you are come in very happy time, 60
980

To bear my greeting to the senators
And tell them that I will not come to-day.
Cannot, is false; and that I dare not, falser;
I will not come to-day. Tell them so, Decius.
Cal. Say he is sick.
Cæs. Shall Cæsar send a lie? 65
Have I in conquest stretch'd mine arm so far,
To be afeard to tell greybeards the truth?
Decius, go tell them Cæsar will not come.
Dec. Most mighty Cæsar, let me know some cause,
Lest I be laugh'd at when I tell them so. 70
Cæs. The cause is in my will: I will not come.
That is enough to satisfy the Senate.
But for your private satisfaction,
Because I love you, I will let you know:
Calphurnia here, my wife, stays me at home.
She dreamt to-night she saw my statua, 75
Which, like a fountain with an hundred spouts,
Did run pure blood; and many lusty Romans
Came smiling and did bathe their hands in it.
And these does she apply for warnings and portents
And evils imminent, and on her knee 80
Hath begg'd that I will stay at home to-day.
Dec. This dream is all amiss interpreted;
It was a vision fair and fortunate.
Your statue spouting blood in many pipes, 84
In which so many smiling Romans bath'd,
Signifies that from you great Rome shall suck
Reviving blood, and that great men shall press
For tinctures, stains, relics, and cognizance.
This by Calphurnia's dream is signified. 90
Cæs. And this way have you well expounded it.
Dec. I have, when you have heard what I can say—
And know it now: the Senate have concluded
To give this day a crown to mighty Cæsar.
If you shall send them word you will not come, 95
Their minds may change. Besides, it were a mock
Apt to be render'd, for some one to say
'Break up the Senate till another time,
When Cæsar's wife shall meet with better dreams'.
If Cæsar hide himself, shall they not whisper 100
'Lo, Cæsar is afraid'?
Pardon me, Cæsar; for my dear dear love
To your proceeding bids me tell you this,

[handwritten: 16·12·99 NRDMandela]

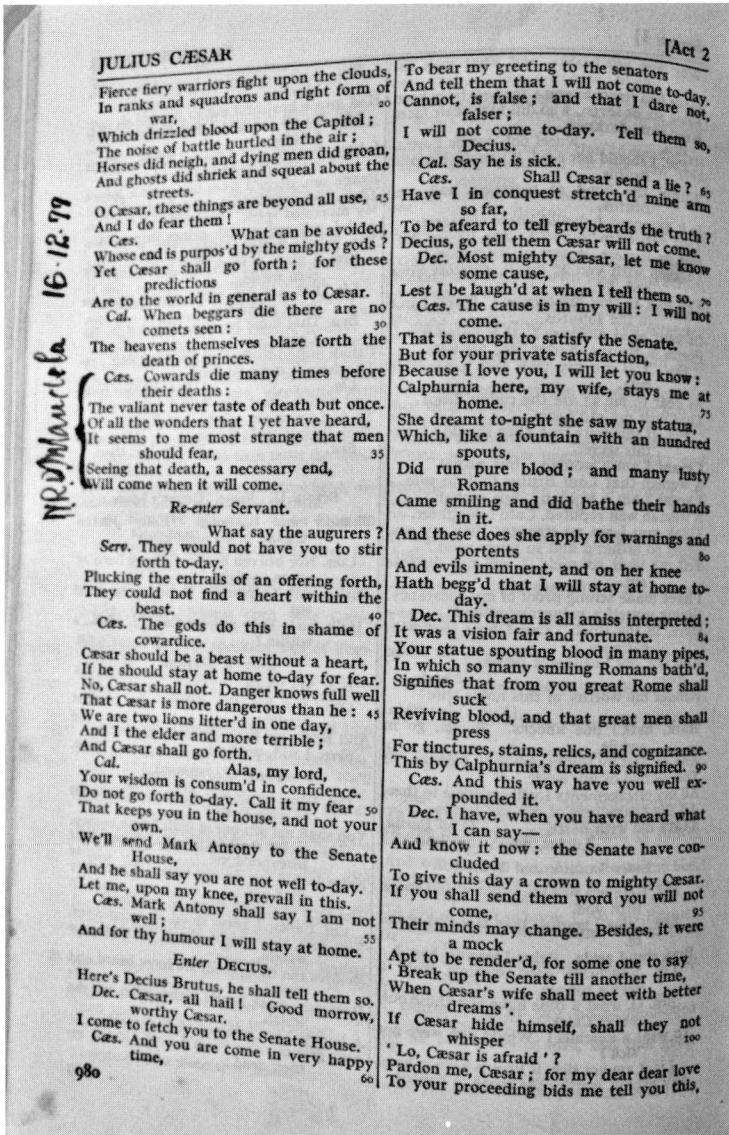

Figure 1.15 The so-called Hindu Bible: copy of William Shakespeare's *The Complete Works* disguised as an Indian religious text, belonging to Sonny Venkatrathnam. Lines from *Julius Caesar* (p. 980) were marked by Nelson Mandela together with his signature and the date, and other prisoners made their own selections.

comic relief, in Sachs' retelling. There is a pointed contrast between Sachs' attentiveness to his friend's feelings ('I am sure Achmat will not mind') with the bullying ways or *kragdadigheid* of the apartheid state. A lawyer, Sachs, gently pokes fun at himself and also at his comrade, a teacher,

Osman, for they both fumble for the correct form of the inflected ancient language. Sachs includes an incorrect translation of his own: 'Vae tyrannis' means 'Woe to the tyrants', 'Long live liberty' would be 'Vivat libertas' in Latin. Both of these he would certainly have been able to check in the process of publishing his book. Rather, Sachs prefers to play along in a game of faltering Latin. If this is a correct characterisation of Sachs' own attitudes in the quotation above, how to explain Osman's use of Latin in his graffiti? Presumably it was a source of pride in the fact that he knew Latin, whereas his jailors did not. That simple assertion, even if it was not understood by its immediate target, could provide an affirmation of self-worth on the part of Osman, a mixed-race person (a 'coloured' in the still prevalent terminology of apartheid) in the face of racial segregation governing all possible spheres of life.

Third, the dynamics of power around Latin emerge in the memoir and notebooks of Ahmed Kathrada (1929–2017), particularly when he writes of the stark social relations of Robben Island. Along with Mandela, Kathrada was one of the accused at the Rivonia Trial (1963–64), and would share his incarceration in B Section at close quarters: sentenced to life imprisonment at the Rivonia Trial, he was released in 1989. He attended the 1974 performance of *Antigone*. Kathrada writes thus about a third political prisoner, Don Davids, who had recently been moved to B Section because of perceived insolence towards one of the warders. Neverthless, Davids used the privilege of being able to pursue studies by correspondence.

When the officer in charge of our studies came to announce the results of the final exams, no one was more surprised than Don to learn that his credits included Latin, a subject he had not taken.

Don pointed out the error, but the warders were having none of it, insisting that the results were accurate. Don stood his ground. Finally, quite exasperated by this reluctant student, the study officer blurted out in Afrikaans: 'Don Davids, do you want the Latin, or do you not want the Latin?'

Don sheepishly whispered, 'I'll take the Latin', and walked away.

To 'take the Latin' in this instance is the line of least resistance, conformity to an authoritarian state. The scholarly activities of Robben Island prisoners are a theme in all accounts, often (as here) contrasting with the lack of education or sophistication on the part of some of the warders. A number of the prisoners will have taken Latin as part of a law degree. Despite the off-putting aspect of authoritarianism revealed in the anecdote, there are several references to ancient authors in Kathrada's memoir: all of them are epigraphs to chapters and exhibit timeless wisdom that offsets the pettiness and humiliation of day-to-day life on Robben Island. This applies also at a stylistic level, where the epigraphs vary the texture when seen against the specificities of Kathrada's life and career. Thus Sophocles, Horace and Marcus Aurelius are quoted, as are Confucius, Yeats, Lenin, Emerson, Einstein and others.[41] Most quoted is Howard Fast's *Spartacus*, which was initially self-published by its author in 1951 but would become a major success both as a novel and as film (1960). Kathrada himself took courses in ancient history via the University of South Africa, in fact beginning during Gerrit Viljoen's last years as head of Classics there (1957–67).[42]

4. Practices of Classicism

From this rich array a number of aspects of the classical deserve to be brought out, so as to illustrate particular ways in which South Africans have engaged with antiquity.

First, and perhaps most obviously, antiquity has been invoked as a political symbol and source of authority: Greece and Rome have been fundamental elements of the social order. This is well indicated by the Fourth Raadsaal in Bloemfontein and Durban City Hall (Figs 1.16–17).[43] There is a classical element in both private and public architecture, involving the British Empire's most prominent architects: Edward Lutyens and especially Sir Herbert Baker. Whereas Baker's Union Buildings in Pretoria are best known, Johannesburg has a number of grandiose private homes in its northern suburbs (see Freschi, this volume). It is in such public contexts that we find the most obvious connection between classics and political power.

That said, it is equally true that classical antiquity has not been the mere handmaid of power. Rather, a few significant cases reveal that ancient Greece and Rome have provided some space for critique. The deployment of classical themes in political cartoons may be considered a late manifestation of this phenomenon (Figs 1.18–21 and Plate 2). More significantly for current purposes, recent scholarship on South African adaptations of Greek drama clearly illustrate the trend.[44] Antigone has proven one of the most frequent and politically significant myths taken up by South African dramatists. This is not surprising, given the overt clash between human and

---

[41] Kathrada 2006. For other South African readings of Marcus Aurelius – soldier, philosopher and emperor – see Wardle below and Bredenkamp 2007.

[42] Kathrada 2004: 236.   [43] Claassen 2009.   [44] Van Zyl Smit 2003.

Figure 1.16 Fourth Raadsaal, Bloemfontein, built in the 1880s as the legislature of the Republic of the Orange Free State, now housing the Free State Provincial Legislature.

divine authority in the play, and its valorisation of a protagonist who speaks truth to power, even at the cost of her own life. *Antigone* on Robben Island is in a sense consistent with a long tradition of Antigones, as is Fugard's play, *The Island* (1973, Fig. 1.22).[45] The myths of Medea and Electra have also been creatively explored in South Africa (Figs 1.23–24).[46]

Whereas the late apartheid and post-apartheid periods provide obvious evidence on this score, one less obvious but no less interesting figure is the Afrikaans author N. P. van Wyk Louw (1906–70). On the one hand he embodied the Afrikaner establishment, as one of the most distinguished Afrikaans authors of his time and the holder of a university chair in Afrikaans and Nederlands. He was a member of the Broederbond, and was quoted in an inscription on the Afrikaans Taalmonument (language monument) at Paarl. Yet he was also a decidedly moderate voice within Afrikanerdom, and clashed publicly with the then prime minister,

[45] Fugard 2002: 128–47; Goff 2007.
[46] Van Zyl Smit 2014 and 2007: 73–91; and compare Steinmeyer in this volume.

Figure 1.17 The City Hall, opened on 12 April 1910, and the Cenotaph, unveiled on 7 March 1926, Durban, Natal. 1980. Photograph by David Goldblatt.

H. F. Verwoerd, in the early 1960s. His play *Germanicus* (1957), drawing on Tacitus' *Annals*, clearly explores alternatives to autocracy, took issue with the hard-line nationalism of his time.[47] It is true that his creative use of antiquity might have contributed to his status as 'obscure and elitist in the eyes of the masses'.[48] Nonetheless, it offers an instructive contrast with his older contemporary, Gerard Moerdyk (1890–1958), who, in keeping with his training and travels, was deeply indebted to classical forms even though

[47] For a cautious interpretation of the politics of the play, see Jo-Marie Claassen's introduction to her translation of *Germanicus* (2013).

[48] Brink 2003: 210.

Figure 1.18 Zapiro (Jonathan Shapiro), 'Protection of Information bill', Cartoon 100720tt. President Jacob Zuma depicted as the emperor Nero, and South African civil society as early Christians suffering persecution. *The Times*, 20 July 2010.

he chose not to acknowledge those debts explicitly (see Rankin and Schneider, this volume).

The classical scholar, Afrikaans poet and public intellectual, T. J. Haarhoff presents a compelling case: a solid supporter of General Smuts, he was a prolific classical scholar who exhibited an ongoing concern with the question of cross-cultural encounter and was quite explicit about the links between antiquity and modernity.[49] Thus his work, *The Stranger at the Gate: aspects of exclusiveness and co-operation in ancient Greece and Rome, with some reference to modern times* (1934), was dedicated 'to the spirit of racial co-operation'. In such a case it is a moot point whether the deep impetus to publish scholarly writing is related to the social issues of the day, or alternatively to antiquity per se. Indeed, any glimpse at Haarhoff's output over some four decades suggests that Roman antiquity and South African modernity were mutually constitutive interests, at the very least in the way in which he presented them. Haarhoff merits comparison with two contemporaries, the statesman Jan Hendrik Hofmeyr and the philosopher Martin Versfeld, in so far as they deployed antiquity as moderate critiques of imperialism and nationalism (see Allen, this

[49] Parker 2010; cf. Whitaker 1997; Lambert 2011.

Figure 1.19 Zapiro (Jonathan Shapiro), 'From the Ancient Games to the Modern Paralympics', Cartoon 120913tt. *The Times*, 12 September 2013.

volume). Haarhoff was in some senses ahead of his time; but it is clear that his purview was limited to Anglo-Afrikaner relations, to the exclusion of other races.[50] Smuts himself presents a complex case, if we try to reconcile his intcllcctual lifc with his political and racial attitudes.[51]

The same principle of encoding the present is visible in the different context of the novelist, Mary Challans, who published very successfully under the name of Mary Renault. Born in Britain, she emigrated to South Africa in 1948. Antiquity provided the setting for the majority of her works, and as such – like the very South African environment she chose to inhabit – was a safe haven in which she and her partner, Julie Mullard, could pursue an alternative lifestyle, or was at least an environment freer from the homophobic prejudices that characterised her British origins (see Endres, this volume). On this view, Cape Town especially

---

[50] As it happens, Haarhoff's two successors as head of Classics at the University of the Witwatersrand provide divergent points of comparison. Simon Davis, in whose appointment Haarhoff played a direct part, followed his senior colleague's footsteps in the theme of one of his books: *Race-Relations in Ancient Egypt: Greek, Egyptian, Hebrew, Roman* (1951). The book was not well received: Murray 1997: 250–51. By contrast to such cross-cultural topics, Davis' successor M. T. W. Arnheim published two books focusing on the aristocracy (1972, 1977). Like Haarhoff but with different leanings, Arnheim also wrote on the politics of the day, and it is impossible to overlook links between scholarly and popular works.

[51] Du Toit 2011.

Figure 1.20 Luciana Acquisto, President Zuma as Cupid: cartoon in the style of Zapiro, painted on a flower pot. The shower head refers to Zuma's political rape trial (2005), and 'I love' to his polygamy (compare Catullus 85, 'Odi et amo': 'I hate and I love'). Original artwork, University of Stellenbosch, 2010. (A black and white version of this figure will appear in some formats. For the colour version, please refer to the plate section.)

had a Mediterranean climate, and with it offered 'Mediterranean' freedom from sexual restraint (see Merrington, this volume).

The political freedoms offered by antiquity have often fallen into the category of liberal humanism. Several figures discussed here are heirs to this tradition. Hofmeyr, Haarhoff, Mandela and Hani have all, in different ways, been dialogic figures in South African history. Albeit merely in fleeting moments, and perhaps never fully realised, antiquity has seemed to offer the possibility of intergroup dialogue on equal terms.

Again, this concept was vaguely in play during the Hani/Viljoen conversation at Cape Town airport. Hani, in a brief autobiographical essay dated April 1991, reflected that his early Catholicism was the driving force behind his 'fascination with Latin studies and English literature':

Figure 1.21 Luciana Acquisto, Julius Malema as a hoplite (Greek citizen soldier). As leader of the ANC Youth League, Malema initially supported Jacob Zuma's ascendancy, but after his expulsion from the ANC outspokenly opposed him. Original artwork, University of Stellenbosch, 2010.

These studies . . . were gobbled up by me and I became an ardent lover of English, Latin and Greek literature, both modern and classical. My studies of literature further strengthened my hatred of all forms of oppression, persecution and obscurantism. The action of tyrants as portrayed in various literary works also made me hate tyranny and institutionalised oppression.[52]

In Hani's conception here, antiquity stands next to English literature, more broadly than specifically linked with liberal humanism. One might compare Anthony Sampson's point with regard to Robben Island, namely that the common frame of reference was in the first instance Shakespeare, rather than classical antiquity or, for that matter, the Christian Bible. In this regard *Julius Caesar* might be considered a point of intersection between ancient pasts and English literature, and indeed this play was itself a favourite in the prison.

---

[52] www.sahistory.org.za/people/thembisile-chris-hani.

Figure 1.22 John Kani and Winston Ntshona in *The Island*, performed at the Market Theatre, Johannesburg, 1986. Photograph by Ruphin Coudyzer.

Since its foundation in 1912 the ANC has had three major strands: liberal humanist (linked to Christianity, and seen for example in Chief Albert Luthuli); Africanist (Mbeki) and Communist (Hani and Zuma).[53] Mandela had ties with all three, but his engagement with Sophocles points

---

[53] Walshe 1970: 339–49. Turok 2010 explores the implications of this diverse legacy for the ANC's present and future.

Figure 1.23 Mark Fleishman's production of Euripides' *Medea*, performed at the Market Theatre, Johannesburg, 1994/95. Photograph by Ruphin Coudyzer.

most directly to the liberal humanist tradition, which also included Hani (though not in any exclusive way). The Lovedale/Fort Hare missionary tradition of education provided a strong link between liberal humanism and Christianity, one that was displaced by Bantu education.

More generally, it needs to be said – now with Michael Lambert – that ancient Greece and Rome have had a particular role in the making of colonial identities.[54] Classical education has been the badge of privilege in a context of unequal access. In such a case, classical studies on the part of South Africans within the country has resonated with the older tradition of colonial image making – the lens through which Africa and other seemingly exotic parts were represented on European maps. Consistent with this, classics has also been a source of upward mobility. Just as fourth-century CE Latin poet, Ausonius of Bordeaux, could rise from obscure provincial origins to some of Rome's highest political offices as a result of his eloquence and his teaching of rhetoric,[55] so did antiquity offer some South Africans the possibility of raising their social station. The critical

---

[54] Lambert 2011; for some concern about Lambert's characterisations, see the reviews by Atkinson 2012, Claassen 2012, Matthews 2012.

[55] Matthews 1975: 56–87.

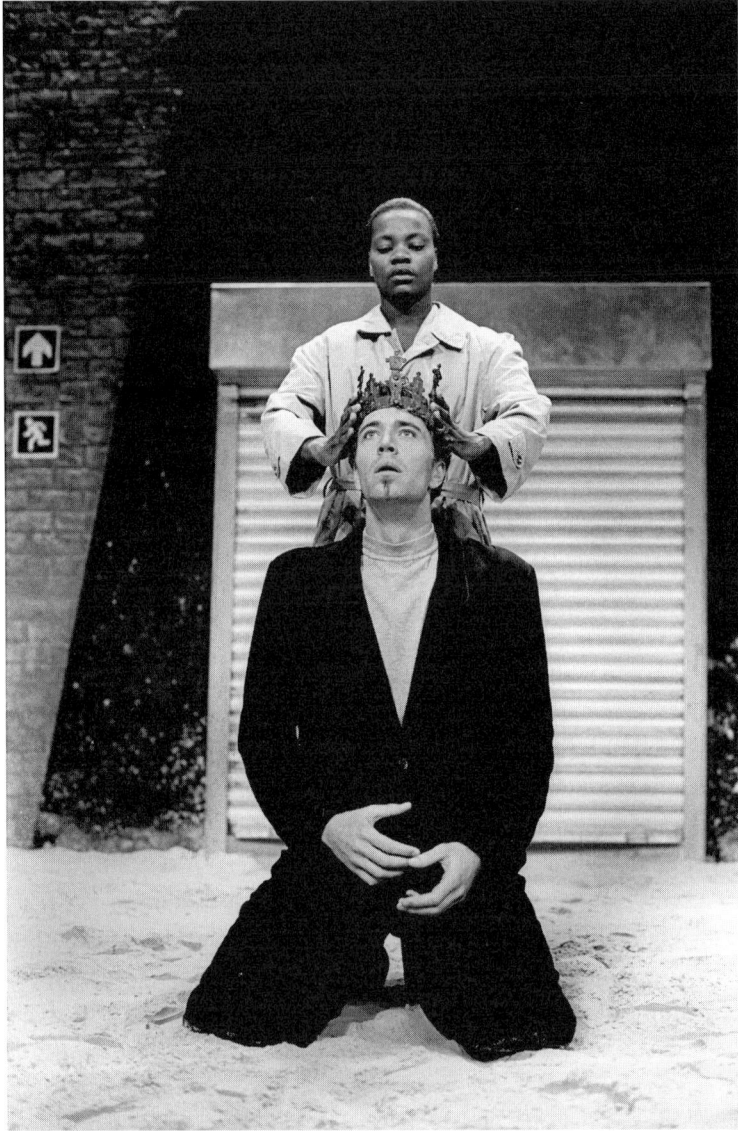

Figure 1.24 Mark Fleishman's production of Euripides' *Medea*, performed at the Market Theatre, Johannesburg, 1994/95. Photograph by Ruphin Coudyzer.

social division in the South Africa is a racial one: the Lovedale School was run by missionaries for African children, and for a substantial period offered Latin and Greek in its curriculum. Lovedale and the nearby and closely related institution, the University of Fort Hare, trained the genera-tion of Southern African leaders who began to make their mark around the middle of the twentieth century: among them Mandela, Oliver Tambo, A. C. Jordan (writer, scholar and father of Pallo Jordan), Seretse Khama and Robert Mugabe (leaders of Botswana and Zimbabwe respectively). For all of them, Latin was part of the curriculum of legal studies. Later on, the pernicious effects of Bantu education were sorely felt, so that academic standards dropped and studies were subject to disruption. Nonetheless, Chris Hani later began his classical studies at Lovedale and Fort Hare: though he began his university education there after the implementation of the highly restrictive Bantu Education Act of 1953 (no. 47), the Latin part of his curriculum reflects the missionary origins of the institutions.[56]

The strong connection of antiquity with political power has given antiquity a role – not necessarily a large one – in popular culture: a number of public symbols may ultimately connote political power, but are linked only in the loosest sense. Many are no more than a name, but even in such cases it is worth considering what image of antiquity emerges. Some are whole cloth imports from the consumer culture of Europe or the United States, such as 'Caesar's Palace' – first a nightclub, then a hotel and most recently an extensive casino complex in Johannesburg, this is named and inspired by the Las Vegas hotel which opened in the 1960s. In the Johannesburg version, there is palpable invocation of ancient Rome as a symbol of decadence, an association that is as old as antiquity itself and is today extremely widespread (Fig. 1.25).[57] Such popular instances of classicism are at the furthest remove from pedagogy, and have only the most indirect link with antiquity.

Other symbols have a distinctively South African history. On 15 August 1985, at a time when the National Party government was under strong domestic and international pressure to relent in its segregation policies, the then President P. W. Botha gave a speech which was advertised in advance as the decisive crossing of the Rubicon. This speech was delivered at a National Party conference in Durban. Expectations ran high that Botha, who had come to power in 1978 as a reformist, would announce a decisive break with apartheid's more oppressive measures. Media agencies organised live broadcasts domestically and overseas. But when the time came for the press conference, Botha was in an

---

[56] In 1954 H. F. Verwoerd, then Minister of Native Affairs and later Prime Minister, notoriously warned against 'blindly producing pupils trained on a European model. . . . [I]t is of no avail for [an aspirant black teacher] to receive a training which has as its aim absorption in the European community, where he cannot be absorbed'. Quoted by Clark and Worger 2004: 51.

[57] Classical forms and decorative elements are part of a stylistic mix that is focused on Tuscany. The complex as a whole draws variously on international heritage stereotypes: Hall and Bombardella 2005.

Figure 1.25 'The conqueror': bronze statue at Emperors' Palace Hotel Casino Convention and Entertainment Resort, Johannesburg. Photograph by Russell Scott.

uncompromising mood, defiantly warning critics not to dictate terms to his government. He would continue with his programme of reform, but not bow to external pressure. When the speech was delivered the phrase 'crossing the Rubicon' was indeed used, as promised, but Botha had omitted the crucial foregoing paragraph, so that its intended meaning was weakened or even inverted by Botha's uncompromising tone. That section of the speech, including the omitted paragraph, turns out to have been drafted by the Foreign Minister, Pik Botha (no relation), a moderate who had done much to arouse expectations of reform in his dealings with the international community. And so, far from making a decisive move towards reform, P. W. Botha in this speech displayed the truculence for which he had become famous. The repercussions would be drastic and immediate: tightening international financial strictures, and escalating domestic dissent, which caused Botha in 1986 to declare the State of Emergency conferring broad powers on the armed forces. In any account of the turbulent 1980s, this was a landmark moment.[58] By an historical

---

[58] On the Rubicon speech as a 'crossing suspended', see Giliomee 2012: 175–206; cf. Pottinger 1988: 330; O'Meara 1996: 330–32; Papenfus 2010: 387–99.

irony, a particular wine from Meerlust, a distinguished estate outside of Stellenbosch, is also called Rubicon. This predates P. W. Botha's speech and was never intended to contain any reference to it. The continuity of South Africa's wine culture from apartheid to the post-apartheid age, and its lack of explicit party-politics, may itself be considered symptomatic of the consumerism that has escalated in South Africa since the 1980s, and especially since the end of apartheid.

Exactly two months after P. W. Botha's 'Rubicon' speech, on 15 October 1985, one of the most notorious instances of premeditated state violence took place in Athlone, a 'coloured' or mixed-race suburb of Cape Town. In an area that had witnessed regular anti-apartheid protests on the part of schoolchildren, security police intervened with lethal force. On the back of a South African Railways truck several security policemen hid between large metal crates. Once the truck had driven close to the gathering, armed police emerged from above the crates and opened fire on the protesters. Three were killed: Jonathan Claasen (aged 21), Shaun Magmoed (15) and Michael Miranda (11).[59] Because of the strategy adopted by the security forces this episode became known as the 'Trojan Horse' incident (Fig. 1.26). It gained notoriety both because the video footage, captured by the American CBS network, was widely broadcast outside South Africa, and because the police involved were found, in an official inquiry, to have acted in an unreasonable way, but the Attorney General of the Cape declined to prosecute them. When this episode subsequently came before the Truth and Reconciliation Commission, one of the Commissioners, Pumla Gobodo-Madikizela, claimed in the public hearing that the term Trojan Horse 'conceals rather than reveals what it was all about'.[60]

One of the peculiarly South African inflections of Greece and Rome has been linked with the notion of a 'Mediterranean' climate. Since the widespread adoption of the Köppen climate classification system in the early decades of the twentieth century, the region's 'Mediterranean' identity has been defined by its distinctive vegetation. Receiving winter rainfall, it supports the 'Mediterranean triad' (wheat, grapes and olives) as well as fruit and vegetable crops. Dominated by the Cape Floristic Region with its characteristic *fynbos*, the huge number of species thereof is out of keeping with its small size. Yet the susceptibility of the area to wine and other crops was evident from early Dutch colonial times, particularly since the arrival of

[59] www.youtube.com/watch?v=3qxwdJoz1v0.
[60] www.justice.gov.za/trc/special/trojan/rasool.htm (near end).

Figure 1.26 Trojan Horse Memorial (2005), Athlone, Cape Peninsula, commemorating an incident in which three black youths were killed by policemen in a staged counterattack (1985). Photograph by Paul Weinberg.

the French Huguenots in 1688 and with them viticulture. In 1910, when the Union of South Africa was formed following the South African War, new factors were brought to bear in this asserted connection (see Merrington, this volume). For one thing, it was linked with Rhodes' vision of a Cape-to-Cairo rail, road and telegraph route.[61] The southwestern Cape, as opposed to the rest of the new country, was thus marked out as comprehensible, and inviting, for British tourists. In the post-war age of mass air transport, the Mediterranean-ness of the Cape has again received prominence in the Club Med chain of international resorts. At Langebaan, about 120 km north of Cape Town on the Atlantic coast, is the resort Club Mykonos, evoking in its name at least the idea of Mediterranean leisure. The 'Mediterranean' identity of the southwestern Cape is today part and parcel of its tourist branding.[62] The significance of this detail is apparent in the fact that international tourism has risen sharply since the end of apartheid.

Finally, it is necessary to take account of the variety of aspects involved in classical antiquity. Consider J. M. Coetzee, one of the most distinguished creative artists South Africa has produced, and one who has vigorously resisted attempts to characterise him as a South African writer. In 2002 he

[61] See the classic article by Merrington 2001.
[62] In the case of Cape Town, see Bickford-Smith 2009.

emigrated to Adelaide, later taking Australian citizenship. Yet Coetzee was born and grew up in South Africa, and the country's social relations have long provided the setting for his novels, whether explicitly or implicitly. In the wide range of themes and approaches Coetzee has deployed, classical antiquity plays an important part, with perhaps only Van Wyk Louw coming remotely close in this respect.

The point to note here is that antiquity, as invoked by Coetzee, has many different forms. A few examples will suffice. *Waiting for the Barbarians* (1980) conjures a discourse about civilisation and barbarism, spurred by Cavafy's poem of the same title, only to question it. While the novel defies any attempt to situate it historically, there are signs that it invokes both the fall of the Roman Empire in the West in the fifth century CE and the sack of Rome by the Gauls under Brennus around 387 BC. Antiquity thus provides a horizon of historical expectation. Readers are invited to supply concrete points of comparison from worlds with which they are more familiar, not only apartheid South Africa but potentially any setting where intergroup conflict is rife. It is perhaps this openness to historical recontextualisation that accounts for the success of the novella over three decades.

By contrast, two other novels bring out the pedagogical side of classical antiquity. In *Age of Iron* (1990) the protagonist, Mrs Curren, is a Latin teacher in Cape Town during the apartheid years – a fact that is not disclosed until the final stages of the novel. Having long opposed apartheid in the abstract, her sympathies are reconfigured and even reinvented when she witnesses the killing of her black servant's son, as well as other violence, and she becomes host to the homeless man who had been living in her driveway. It emerges towards the end of the novel that she is dying of cancer. The teaching of Latin comes to symbolise the vulnerability of white liberalism in South Africa, the liberal tradition embodied in Mrs Curren. More recently, *Elizabeth Costello* (2003), particularly the essay/chapter entitled 'The humanities in Africa', brings to bear the aesthetic and political questions surrounding the place of European (including ancient European) texts in an African setting. Typically of Coetzee, any hint of dogmatic utterance is quashed by the interplay of voices within the text. The very questions addressed by Coetzee are ones that have been considered by an official commission of inquiry recently undertaken by the South African Department of Education.[63]

The more philosophical dimensions of antiquity emerge in *Diary of a Bad Year* (2007). An aging writer, Senor C, falls in love with a young

---

[63] Sitas et al. 2011; cf. Jansen and Vale 2011.

neighbour, Anya, whom he employs as a typist. The novel is an amalgam of Senor C's musings on the most varied of subjects, with a diary at the bottom of each page documenting the emerging and ultimately disastrous relationship that develops between the two. Here we sense in the background Plato's *Phaedrus*, which explores the timeless character of beauty, a highly idealised quality that seems at some points to offer the possibility of withstanding the decline and fall of empires, and thus defying historical time. The philosophical side of antiquity is balanced, indeed marred, by a rather less admirable professorial one.

While these various kinds of ancient presence emerge from the novels, with their play of narrative voices, Coetzee has addressed the question of the classical more directly in his essay, 'What is a classic?'.[64] Given the subtlety of Coetzee's art, it is all the more tempting to seek his own opinions in the essay, which started life as a public lecture. At the same time this scholarly voice seems to compete with the voices heard in his novels, where several of his later fictional characters are aging white males who, as creative writers or scholars, invite comparison with the author himself. Coetzee's antiquity thus has many forms, and this alone should caution us to recognise the wide variety of South Africa's classical engagements.[65]

5.   Towards a Balance Sheet

To stand back from the aspects raised above is to have the chance to think somewhat more abstractly about classical receptions in South Africa, and in particular how classical antiquity may be compared with other pasts. Here the task is not so much to identify aspects of antiquity as to evaluate their place in the South African milieu, to the degree that this is possible.

In the most obvious sense, the phenomenon of translation needs to be considered from various points of view. Given that the post-war boom in South African classical studies coincided with the coming to power of Afrikaner nationalism, it is not surprising that the post-war decades witnessed a number of translations of ancient works into Afrikaans. Virgil's foundational epic was translated twice, into both verse and prose. Other poems by Virgil and Catullus were also translated into Afrikaans, apparently beginning with T. J. Haarhoff's *Die Liefde van Catullus* in 1933. This is no ordinary translation in that actual translations are interspersed

---

[64] Coetzee 2001: 1–16.   [65] Meskell and Weiss 2006.

with original poems, so as to tell a story of the love affair between the poet/lover and Lesbia. Afrikaans had not become an official language until 1925, at which point its divergences from the Dutch language were recognised. This is a complicated story in itself, given that the slaves of the Dutch played a substantial role in the evolution of the language, as a patois reflecting the fact that they came from far-flung parts of the Indian Ocean basin. However, when the Afrikaans language became a focal point of emerging Afrikaner identity, its slave origins were conveniently suppressed so it could become a symbol of colonial nation building. Translations into English are far less evident, for the obvious reason that it reflects no equivalent nation building impulse; it is only recently, in the post-apartheid age, that vernacular South African English has acquired a major translation of its own.[66] Drama is a slightly different matter in that many South African versions take great liberties with the original, so that the term 'translation' is not necessarily appropriate. Indeed, flexibility on many fronts, including the possibility of freedom from an original text, accounts for the longstanding and ongoing use of classical myth in South Africa.[67] Of a different order is a translation of Homer's epics into isiZulu – 'would be' is the strictly correct term to use here, given that the task of translating has been contemplated rather than undertaken at the current juncture. In the absence of existing African language translations of classical works, it is imperative to consider the linguistic and cultural preconditions that might make such an exercise possible. A discussion of this kind serves as a reminder that acts of translation are also acts of comparison.[68] The isiZulu word that denotes translation, *humusha*, has primary meanings of deceit and seduction, and is highly charged compared to its Greek and Latin equivalents.

More generally speaking, the relation between classical and other pasts is not easy to pinpoint.[69] Graeco-Roman antiquity has seldom, if ever, been part of the same conversations as African archaeology.[70] There are institutional reasons for this, in that in South Africa the academic disciplines of archaeology and classics have overlapped little in practice. Institutional

---

[66] Whitaker 2012, cf. Whitaker 2002: 523–53 and Hardwick 2008.

[67] See Steinmeyer, this volume. Scholarship on this rich topic goes back to Conradie 1976.

[68] Mackenzie 2009.

[69] The special status of ancient Egyptians and Phoenicians has briefly been touched on already.

[70] According to an influential article, the classical background of some major British archaeologists helped foster an essentialist approach to ethnic identity, in keeping with Herodotus, Caesar and Tacitus. 'Such classical authors had a tribal perception of society, with the result that archaeologists reared on these texts were at home with the social concepts of the ethnographers of Africa.' Hall 1984: 461.

practice can only go so far as a means of explanation, for it is itself the result
of ideas and attitudes. The exception that proves the rule is not South
African but lies immediately to the north of the Limpopo River, namely
Great Zimbabwe. Today it is widely agreed that the complex was built in
the period roughly 1200 to 1450, by indigenous Bantu speakers. However,
when it became known to Europeans at the end of the nineteenth century,
some propagated the view that Great Zimbabwe was built instead by
Phoenicians, or perhaps Arabs. This view, expressly denying African
agency, was promoted by the government of Ian Smith. An early propo-
nent was J. Theodore Bent, whose book, *The Ruined Cities of Mashonaland*,
appeared in 1891, following a season of excavation that had been sponsored by Cecil John Rhodes. Bent had excavated previously in Asia Minor
and the Persian Gulf, and had travelled extensively in Italy and Greece.
By contrast, the first excavation of a scientific nature was performed in
1905–6 by David Randall-MacIver, and from this point the African element was recognised. However, this new insight did not necessarily affect
popular opinion among white Rhodesians, hence the scope for the Smith
government to promote a different view. The Phoenicians in this popular
conception are not fully classical in the sense of ancient Greece and Rome,
but perhaps the telling point, for purposes of the time, was that the
Phoenicians were <u>not</u> sub-Saharan African. With this partial exception
and another, the question of the relation of classical antiquity to other
antiquities has been largely moot.[71]

The other exception concerns the collection and display of antiquities
in South African museums. Like Rhodes, the 'Randlord' Alfred Beit
associated his legacy with classical art, as is seen in the collection of
plaster casts bequeathed to the city of Cape Town upon his death.
The Beit Collection did not find a permanent home, however, and was
quietly dispersed, so that very few pieces are today still known (see Tietze,
this volume). Cape Town's major museums reflect a particularly haphazard approach to collecting antiquities: they certainly formed
a significant part of the early history of the South African Museum,
resulting in large measure from private donations of varied character
and quality. There was a strong tendency to the collection of everyday
items, many of them obtained in South African elite in the course of
Mediterranean travels. The antiquities were later moved to what was
known since 1966 as the South African Cultural History Museum
(SACHM), now the Slave Lodge. When in 2000 the SACHM and other

[71] Bent 1893; Randall-MacIver 1906. The scholarly landscape is mapped by Garlake 2002.

Cape Town museums underwent incorporation under the umbrella of Iziko Museums, most ancient Greek and Roman artefacts were withdrawn from display and made available to the Sasol Museum of Stellenbosch University on temporary loan. Some ancient Egyptian artefacts were allowed to remain in the Slave Lodge. The status of the entire display on the second floor of the Slave Lodge was undergoing review at the time of writing – a direct, if somewhat belated, response to sea-change in South African society over recent decades. There is much at stake in the choice of what to exhibit, and how, given the history of the extraordinarily varied history of the Slave Lodge since it was first built in 1679.[72] The fact that the Egyptian, Greek and Roman antiquities originally stood on prominent display in the ground floor is all the more pointed, given that in its new form, the museum now uses the very same rooms for its presentation of slavery at the Cape.

At a more abstract level, it is interesting to note that ancient Greece and Rome have been involved in a number of comparisons with other pasts. It is worth asking, however briefly, what is at stake with such comparisons. For one thing, it is clear that antiquity has frequently been invoked in the sense of cultural capital. In *An African Athens*, Philippe-Joseph Salazar describes South Africa's democratic formation in a classical Greek frame.[73] The ancient Greeks are invoked in terms of their democratic political system and particularly its deployment of rhetoric as an instrument of democracy. On the whole, Salazar compares South Africa's relation to the African continent with that of ancient Greece to modern Europe. South Africa, by this reckoning, has much to offer a new postcolonial order, in the best sense fulfilling the trends of decolonisation that began after World War II; whereas Athens was the 'school of Hellas', South Africa is in effect presented by Salazar as the 'school of Africa'. This is an unusual book, out of the Anglo-Saxon mainstream (Salazar trained at the Sorbonne and returned there after a South African spell in the 1980s and 90s). The book is the exception that proves the rule: little

---

[72] One of the country's oldest buildings, it was built by the Dutch as a residence for urban slaves (in which capacity it also functioned as a brothel) and later as an insane asylum. In the nineteenth and twentieth centuries it had a series of roles in governmental service, including as parliament, supreme court, post office and library. Its role as a museum began in 1960 when it became the SACHM and continued as the Slave Lodge from 2000 under the umbrella of Iziko Museums of Cape Town. A 'site of memory' par excellence, the changing history of the Slave Lodge closely reflects South Africa's changing political scene, and Greek and Roman antiquities have played an (admittedly small) place therein.

[73] Salazar 2002.

reference was made to the ancient Greeks in South Africa's political transition of the 1990s, at a time when there was much debate about the nature of democracy.[74]

It is not entirely obvious how to account for such an omission. It could be that, whereas Latin had been part of the school curriculum of several of the participants (more on the National Party side) and commentators, the Greeks had played a much smaller role. It could also be that the Victorian tradition of comparative anthropology, most readily associated with James Frazer, was considered tainted. In any case, one such Frazerian gesture sees Spartan and Zulu warfare compared.[75]

Finally, it is clear that much of what has been adduced here as evidence of South African classicism is indirect. Whereas in the eighteenth century northern European visitors to Italy and other Mediterranean lands encountered antiquity via its ruins, artefacts and historic locations,[76] there has been little or no South African equivalent. Only much later did a handful of travellers visit ancient sites and return with artefacts, which informed private collections and in some cases museums (see Masters, this volume). The post-apartheid period has seen heightened overseas air travel and thus greater ease of access: but by this time antiquity has lost much of its earlier prominence, and the law considerably limits the international acquisition of antiquities. By far the most of the contact South Africans have had with ancient Greece and Rome has been indirect, whether through translations, distinctive forms or other intermediaries. To take one highly visible example, the frieze of the Voortrekker Monument may have been conceived in South Africa but it was realised in Italy by Italian stonemasons. It is in this context that one should understand Gerard Moerdyk's public disavowal of classical influence, even when in practice antiquity did much to shape his architectural training and never ceased to provide a point of departure. The writer and artist Breyten Breytenbach (1939–), a dissident first in relation to

---

[74] In a speech held at Athens on 19 May 2005, former president F. W. de Klerk cited Heraclitus on the inevitability of change, and quoted Pericles's funeral oration on the nature of participatory democracy. However, this is not much of an exception to the general silence concerning antiquity because it was heard by a Greek rather than a South African audience, and well after the first democratic election. See De Klerk 2005.

[75] Ferguson 1918, recently reprinted in Wheeler 2007, cf. Gluckman 1940. And most floridly, Bryant (1967: 175): 'Blest with such unhampered freedom and unruffled peace, the Zulu gloried in the fullness of the joie de vivre, in a lovely climate and a beautiful land. Was this Utopia in actual being? Was it not Arcady refound?'

[76] Bignamini and Hornsby 2010.

apartheid and latterly in relation to the ANC-led government, has likewise had no truck with classical antiquity over the decades; yet his experimental theatre piece *Boklied* ('goat song') revisits ancient Greek dramatic tradition.[77] All its characters are poets, and the dialogue concerns the composition of poetry. Greek antiquity thus provides a point of reflection. Indeed, as recent scholarship has richly shown, theatrical deployment of classical mythology has been plentiful and varied, but few productions have taken the original Greek texts into account. It would have been unreasonable to expect anything else.

Again, Robben Island presents vestigial but fascinating material. Mission-educated prisoners in the early 1960s sometimes honoured fallen comrades with the following lines:

> And how can man die better
> than facing fearful odds
> for the ashes of his fathers
> and the temples of his gods?

This comes from 'Horatius' in George Macauley's very popular ballad, the *Lays of Ancient Rome*, composed in India in 1842.[78] The poem became a staple of British colonial education. In this, the first ballad, Horatius Cocles and his two companions heroically and successfully defend Rome by holding a bridge against Lars Porsenna's invading army of Etruscans.[79]

In all, popular manifestations of antiquity deserve some prominence in this account of classicism in South Africa. Though the term 'vernacular classicism' seems like an oxymoron, it is on the whole well suited to the dynamics of the country's classical engagements. It accords well with James Porter's recent reassessment of the very notion of the classical, in which mediated contact receives emphasis.[80] There can be no doubt that the mediated quality of classicism, the phenomenon of 'identifying with a prior identification',[81] is starkly seen in South Africa.

---

[77] Breyten Breytenbach, *Boklied* (1998). There is also a character called Isis, portrayed as a 'black woman who represents the interests of Africa's indigenous peoples and its women': see Viljoen 2004: 331. There is also a male figure Tereus, who represents Breytenbach's European connections. Jo-Marie Claassen writes of Breytenbach as an exile in the style of Ovid, despite himself (1999: 256).

[78] Lodge 2006: 4; cf. Mandela 1994a: 9.

[79] In the canonical account by Livy (*Ab Urbe condita* 2.10.2–11), Horatius had already become a paradigm (*exemplum*) of ancient Roman courage (*virtus*). According to Roman tradition, this episode took place around 510 BC.

[80] Porter 2006: esp. 44, 59–64.   [81] Porter 2006: 57.

6.   Remember Dido

What if Aeneas had stayed in Africa? What if Carthage instead of Rome had become the centre of the new empire? Would the African roots of this empire have made a difference to history's development? Would all transcultural communication possibly be less difficult, had Aeneas not shunned this encounter in the first place?[82]

With these bold questions the South African musician Hans Huyssen introduces a compact disc that combines Henry Purcell's seventeenth-century music with contemporary compositions from various parts of Africa, all arranged for small string ensemble. Following several African-composed pieces, the collection culminates with a suite comprising music from *Dido and Aeneas* (1688) and *The Fairy Queen* (1692). The final piece is a setting of Dido's lament – a landmark in western music, famous for its pathos. With this unusual combination Huyssen 'explores the common ground as well as characteristic differences' of particular kinds of African and European music, challenging the usual divisions into categories such as commercial, classical, modern and serious. All pieces are performed on period instruments of the European baroque period, a choice made so that its less smooth sound might invite comparison with traditional African instruments. The attempt to engender dialogue between African and European musical forms is not new, and has particular point in South Africa, where many 'classical' musicians have found the need to assert their role in the post-apartheid milieu. Of relevance here is Huyssen's 'hypothesis of an alternative ending to the chronicle of Dido and Aeneas'. Whereas the Aeneas story has typically been seen as one of the establishment of western power, here Huyssen opens a space for counter-factual history, inviting readers and listeners to consider alternatives to the grand narrative of western ascendancy. The experiment has several dimensions, artistic and political. The 'Rainbow nation' concept of South African society was already somewhat discredited by the time of Mbeki's accession in 1999 and with its demise came the end of the ANC's honeymoon period in government. Nonetheless, Huyssen's project expresses a comparable hankering for greater dialogue between the many cultural traditions present in South Africa, and more generally in the African continent.

As a rereading of Virgil, *Remember Dido* invokes at least two moments of twentieth-century history. As early as the 1920s T. J. Haarhoff, the Virgilian scholar, poet and public intellectual, sought a South African

---

[82] Huyssen 2006: page 4 of booklet.

setting for the *Georgics*: Haarhoff's concern was the Afrikaners' connection with the land, in which respect Haarhoff invoked the yeoman farmer of the ancient Roman world. The comparison underlies his Oxford BLitt thesis, which appeared first as *Vergil in the Experience of South Africa* and later *Vergil the Universal*. Virgil's poem, the *Aeneid*, is the only major classical work to have received two South African translations, both into Afrikaans. Closer to Huyssen's time, and perhaps also to his outlook, Nelson Mandela was in Tunis when, in June 1994, as newly elected president of South Africa, he addressed the Organisation of African Unity. In his speech Mandela heralded the end of apartheid and the decades-long struggle against it.[83] He did this by recalling the elder Cato's well-known determination to destroy Carthage, a goal that was realised in 146 BC:

And Carthage was destroyed. Today we wander among its ruins, (and) only our imagination and historical records enable us to experience its magnificence. Only our African being makes it possible for us to hear the piteous cries of the victims of the vengeance of the Roman Empire . . .

It is this very defeat which, in the light of South Africa's ending of apartheid, should give hope to African nations to shake off the shackles of colonialism. Mandela thus ends on an optimistic note:

We are certain that you will prevail over the currents that originate from the past, and ensure that the interregnum of humiliation symbolised by, among others, the destruction of Carthage, is indeed consigned to the past, never to return.

On the same lines, former president Thabo Mbeki in September 2010 addressed a summit meeting of African student leaders at the University of Cape Town, beginning with the injunction, 'Carthage must be rebuilt!'[84] Ideology apart, the underlying political reality is that nearby Algeria had provided a template and material support for the armed struggle against apartheid; Algeria, like other north African states, had supported the ANC in exile. Both Mandela and Mbeki's speeches were made in a framework of pan-Africanism, spearheaded by the Organisation of African Unity. Central to Mbeki's presidency (1999–2008) was the so-called 'African Renaissance', the goal of African renewal from out of the shadow of colonialism – renewal in all its economic, cultural and scientific dimensions.[85] Even after the departure of Mbeki from the political scene the notion of an 'African Renaissance' remains an attractive one: a recent

---

[83] Mandela 1994b.   [84] Mbeki 2005.

[85] See esp. the essays in Makgoba 1999. Some critics have found the initiative impossible on its own terms: e.g. Distiller 2006.

report suggests that it be used so as to engender a more dialogic and less essentialist definition of Africa, recognising that 'Africa has never been a bounded unit in ancient or more recent history'.[86] The very term 'African Renaissance' remains a problematic one: from an Africanist point of view the notion of 'Renaissance' retains an ultimately European frame of reference. Whereas the European Renaissance involved, in an important way, the rediscovery of ancient Greece, the ancient Greek element does not seem to have featured in the African Renaissance. Nonetheless, Carthage constitutes a variant on Rhodes' dream of a 'Cape-to-Cairo' corridor, adapted for the post-apartheid age. In each case, a Mediterranean city (an ancient one, in the case of Carthage) helped assert South Africa's place in the wider world.

The impetus to rebuild Carthage, or to remember Dido, is thus that to retell colonial history's grand narrative from the perspective of the victims and in so doing to challenge the worst excesses of colonialism. In the current context it serves as a reminder of the variety of South African receptions of antiquity, and of the indirect nature of those receptions. At the same time it articulates a counter-factual possibility, as we have seen with Huyssen. It is thus impossible to write about the classical tradition in South Africa without a sense of what might have been, particularly the power of a liberal humanistic tradition to prevail with greater force against intolerance, nor to feel concern for its future.[87]

Classicism has been an index, much more than might have been obvious, to South Africa's history and in particular to its cross-cultural encounters. This is, in part, a matter of colonial identity-formation, as Lambert has shown. But it is more than that too. In the earlier period of colonialism, Greek and Latin scientific discourse were part of the mapping of sub-Saharan Africa: this is true both of European cartography of the fifteenth and sixteenth centuries, such as Waldseemüller's world map, and of the earliest descriptions. The scientific tradition, especially of the Netherlands, did much to locate Southern Africa in European thought-worlds, particularly within the schema of Claudius Ptolemy. This did not mean that classical antiquity would play a large part in the Dutch colony, and it was not until British nineteenth century, and especially the imperial impulse of Rhodes and others, that Greece and Rome acquired a significant role in public symbols. While such symbols have tended to connote colonial authority and thus been largely the preserve of white South Africans, a small number of significant exceptions deserve notice,

---

[86] Sitas et al. 2011: 19.   [87] Sitas et al. 2011.

particularly those of the black elite who, like Nelson Mandela, were educated in the Lovedale/Fort Hare missionary tradition. Chris Hani was the
most eminent representative thereof in the late apartheid era.

Beyond any narrower notion of classicism, South African popular culture has thus produced a wide variety of engagements with Graeco-Roman
antiquity. It is in this sense that we might consider, for example, the
deployment of Greek myths in plays, in so many cases produced by and
for people who have had no overt classical learning whatever. The point is
not that playwrights and audiences have largely lacked Greek and Latin,
but that classical texts have played a role even without widespread knowledge of those languages. It is debatable how significant such exceptions
are in the overall scheme of things,[88] but there can be no doubt that they
reflect the multivalence of classical antiquity, and its openness to varied
deployment.

7.　Classical Engagements

Several broad points have emerged, and are presented here with a view to
connecting the essays that follow. Together these points offer a framework
within which to consider South African contexts of classical antiquity,
ranging in time from the Ptolemaic maps of ancient Rome and the early
modern seaborne empires to the democratic transition of the 1990s and to
contemporary theatre.

Ancient Greece and Rome have been the source of remarkably varied
forms of expression, and involved different modes of engagement. Thus,
individual essays in this volume address material objects (see Masters,
Tietze, Wardle below), styles and media (Freschi, Rankin/Schneider),
concepts (Allen, Van Zyl), literary texts (Merrington, Coleman), mythology (Steinmeyer, Sargeant) and historical consciousness (Hilton, Endres,
Parker above). Any definition of classicism in this context must recognise
its enormous variety, united only by a shared connection with ancient
Greece and Rome.

Engagements with antiquity have displayed different degrees of directness. Most direct are the most politically elite and most scholarly. On the
other hand, some of the most telling cases are emphatically indirect,
involving persons who have had no training in Latin and Greek, for
example Mandela's version of Sophocles on Robben Island. Vernacular

---

[88] Lambert's view (2011) is generally minimalist and pessimistic; see esp. 125–32.

classicism, to use an oxymoron that matches the title of the current essay, is one way to characterise some of the less official, less scholarly instances (Bosman).

Ancient Greece and Rome have had divergent political impact. Sometimes they have constituted symbols of authority, both in the law (see Van Zyl) and also architecture (Freschi, Hilton); by the same token there have been classical symbols of resistance or critique, none more so than Socrates (Allen). It remains an open question why the law – a legal tradition that can be traced back to Greece and Rome – has failed to curb the excesses of oppressive governments that have ostensibly promoted it.

Ancient Greece and Rome have also had divergent cultural impact. On the one hand, Greece and Rome have sometimes had exceptional status, implicitly or explicitly receiving pride of place at the expense of indigenous cultures throughout the modern period, a tendency that has changed since the end of apartheid (see Masters). On the other hand, there have been South African translations of texts that can be understood both in a narrowly linguistic sense and in a broader cultural sense. Some scholarly, philologically careful translations of Greek and Latin plays have been performed on South African stages (Sargeant). However, many performances have been loose adaptations, revealing greater freedom from the Greek or Latin original (Steinmeyer). Either way, classical antiquity has been a touchstone of cross-cultural interaction: both the Adamastor myth (Coleman) and the Voortrekker Monument (Rankin/ Schneider) draw on the classical to formulate their visions of South African history.

Finally, the stories outlined above show that several people have found something personally valuable in the art, literature or thought of the Greeks and Romans. This is as true of Cecil Rhodes on his deathbed, reading Marcus Aurelius' *Meditations*, as it is of Nelson Mandela in prison, sharing lines from Shakespeare's *Julius Caesar* with fellow inmates. Far from being the exclusive preserve of a racial elite that it has often seemed, classical antiquity has in fact shown enormous power to stimulate reflection and imagination.

PART II

Conceiving Empire

Since antiquity, imperial powers have made selective use of other empires in representing themselves. The connection between Britain and classical antiquity is a rich sphere of analysis. At a time when Johannesburg was being built, several of the British and pro-British elite expressed their new-found status, as well as their relation to the empire, by means of monumental architecture (**Freschi**). Rhodes, though no great scholar himself, was nonetheless fascinated with ancient Greece and especially Rome, and it was Marcus Aurelius' *Meditations* that he read on his deathbed. Rhodes' own direct involvement with antiquity should be considered alongside the manner of his memorialisation. Classicism not only reflects his own predilections and those of his circle but is also central to the memory of the man today. Indeed, the statues that have been at the centre of the RhodesMustFall protests of 2015–16 reflect the classical tradition (**Hilton**). Nor did the imperial impulse die with Rhodes in 1902. Around the time the Union of South Africa was formed in 1910, British-oriented settlers reinvented the Cape as 'Mediterranean', a concept that continues to resonate today especially in contexts of tourism (**Merrington**).

'Poetry in Pidgin': Notes on the Persistence of
Classicism in the Architecture of Johannesburg

FEDERICO FRESCHI

The psychic life of the metropolis is inseparable from the metropolitan form . . .
Metropolitan built forms are themselves a projective extension of the society's
archaic or primal fantasies, the ghost dances and the slave spectacles at its foundation. – Achille Mbembe[1]

Over the past few years I have watched, fascinated, the erection of an
extraordinary house at Number 90, First Road, Hyde Park in
Johannesburg (Fig. 2.1 and Plate 3). A bizarre parody of every classicising architectonic element *all'antica*, one's first view is of the considerable length of the perimeter wall, which comprises a series of bays
treated as miniature aediculae, each with oddly truncated Corinthian
columns supporting a continuous, massive entablature (Fig. 2.2).
The entablature in turn features an aggressively stepped frieze termi-
nating in dentils so oversized as to look more like crenellations,
surmounted by elaborate balustrades running the length of the wall.
Each bay is populated at its base and crown with a grotesque proliferation of ersatz classical statuary featuring every character in the
classical canon: Venuses (draped and nude) rub shoulders with
Demeters; Apollos with Neptunes; Atlantes with Discoboli; Cupids
with Bacchuses, and, on either side of the pediment surmounting the
elaborate portal, twin replicas of Michelangelo's *David* fix their defiant
gaze on the far horizon, stonily challenging the bemused passer-by to
let an involuntary exclamation of '*kitsch!*' pass his or her lips (Fig. 2.3).
Beyond the entrance the house itself develops the theme to a point of
Churrigueresque excess, every doorway, balcony and window sur-
round subject to the kind of decorative flourishes that Charles
Jencks, unwittingly quoting W. D. Howells in his *Italian Journeys* of
1883, might describe as 'frantically Baroque'.[2]

Indeed, it is easy to dismiss this project as a manifestation of egregious
vulgarity and suburban bad taste: the worst excesses of nouveau riche self-
aggrandisement bathetically masquerading as bourgeois sophistication.

[1] Mbembe 2008: 38.   [2] Jencks 1991: 58.

55

Figure 2.1 Architect unknown, Number 90, First Road, Hyde Park, Johannesburg, 2011. A newly built house in the upmarket Johannesburg suburb of Hyde Park, this project reveals the contemporary suburban taste for 'Tuscan' styling. (A black and white version of this figure will appear in some formats. For the colour version, please refer to the plate section.)

Figure 2.2 Architect unknown, Number 90, First Road, Hyde Park, Johannesburg, 2011. Perimeter wall, treated as a series of balustraded aediculae and populated with ersatz classical statuary.

Figure 2.3 Architect unknown, Number 90, First Road, Hyde Park, Johannesburg, 2011. The tympanum sculptures of the pediment above the portal.

Yet, for all its self-consciousness and artifice, there is something endearingly and quintessentially Johannesburg about Number 90, First Road's unabashed revelling in its own stylistic excesses (a point to which I shall return later in this essay), and it certainly led me to muse on the persistence of the classical tradition in Johannesburg architecture. It also put me in mind of Edwin Lutyens (1869–1944), who, with his contemporary and sometime rival Herbert Baker (1862–1946), was the last great master of official British imperial architecture in the early twentieth century, and, in that capacity, one of the last great classicists. Lutyens is best remembered in South Africa for his work on two of Johannesburg's most significant classical structures, the Rand Regiments Memorial (Fig. 2.4) and the Johannesburg Art Gallery (Figs 2.5–6), both designed during his brief visit to South Africa in 1910, and completed in 1911 and 1915, respectively. In explaining the rationale for the formal severity of these buildings he famously grumbled to Herbert Baker that,

... in old countries you can use rough materials, where you find men instinctively handling it from boyhood and unconsciously weaving texture into it. In a new country it is impossible to expect any help of that sort in the fabric of a building ... There is in Africa no tradition on which accidents can rely, and reliance can only

Figure 2.4 Edwin Lutyens, Rand Regiments' Memorial (now the National Anglo-Boer War Memorial), Saxonwold Memorial Park, Saxonwold, Johannesburg, 1911. On top is a bronze *Angel of Peace* by the Russian-born sculptor, Naoum Aronson.

remain with the best thought . . . as concerns her architecture . . . You get no great poetry in a pidgin language, though you may get poetic sentiment.[3]

Lutyens's misgivings notwithstanding, Johannesburg has since its inception – for better or worse – boasted an unbroken tradition of classical buildings. From the Beaux-Arts facades of the early banking houses (Fig. 2.7), hotels (Fig. 2.8) and Randlords' clubs (Fig. 2.9), via the English country house grandeur of its early schools (Fig. 2.10) to the elaborate

[3] Hussey 1950: 209.

Figure 2.5 Edwin Lutyens, Johannesburg Art Gallery, Joubert Park, Johannesburg, 1911–15. The entrance portico is in a severe Tuscan style that reflects Lutyens's unwillingness to bend to local architectural tastes and sentiment.

Figure 2.6 Edwin Lutyens, Johannesburg Art Gallery, Joubert Park, Johannesburg, 1911–15. The windowless ashlar walls of the gallery are relieved by pedimented niches flanked by engaged Tuscan columns.

Figure 2.7 Stucke & Bannister, Standard Bank Chambers, Johannesburg, 1906–8. A flamboyant example of Edwardian classicism, the Standard Bank Chambers was constructed using state-of-the-art steel-frame construction techniques imported from the United States.

neoclassicism of the University of the Witwatersrand campus (Fig. 2.11), to the columned porticoes in the rapidly expanding suburbs of the 1920s and 30s, and ultimately to the egregious proliferation of 'Tuscan' references in recent commercial projects and speculative housing clusters (Fig. 2.12), the classical sentiment has prevailed. Taken at face value, these various

Figure 2.8 Reid & Reid, Cosmopolitan Hotel, Jeppestown, Johannesburg, 1899.

Figure 2.9 Leck & Emley, Rand Club, Johannesburg, 1904.

Figure 2.10 John Ralston, Jeppestown High School (now Jeppe Boys' High School), Kensington, Johannesburg, 1908–11. Photograph 1980s.

classicisms seem little more than the parvenu ancestors of Number 90, First Road, but as I argue in this essay, they in fact create something of a palimpsest of the complexities and contradictions that constitute an ongoing aspect of Johannesburg's architectural imaginary. In effect, they are nothing less than a persistent 'poetry in a pidgin language', which at its

Figure 2.11 Emley & Williamson and Williamson & N. T. Cowin, Great Hall of the University of the Witwatersrand, Braamfontein, Johannesburg, 1922. The giant Corinthian portico of the University Great Hall dominates the north south axis of the campus, and is the centrepiece of its neoclassical architecture.

heart raises some important questions about history, time, space and belonging, and how they are enacted in the construction of Johannesburg's cosmopolitan identity.

1. The 'Peculiar but Strong' Hold of Classicism in South African Architecture

Of course, the persistence of the classical tradition in architecture is part of a much broader historical trend. As George Hersey notes in response to his own question, 'Why do we still use the classical orders?',

Graeco-Roman classicism was not only the architecture of the Greeks and Romans and of their empires, it was also the architecture, mutatis mutandis, of Romanesque Europe and of Byzantium, of the Renaissance and the Baroque, of Neoclassicism,

Figure 2.12 RHWL Architects, Montecasino, Fourways, Johannesburg, 2000. In this elaborate Mediterranean-themed casino and entertainment complex, the designers have sought to recreate the experience of a Tuscan town, including ersatz laundry hanging from supposed apartment balconies and fake pigeons on simulated trees.

the Baroque Revival, the Beaux-Arts, and fascism; and it is even, in a peculiar but strong way, a contributor to postmodernism.[4]

From the point of view of South African architectural history we can add to this taxonomy some further 'peculiar but strong' manifestations:

First, the gracious symmetry and restraint of Cape Dutch (or perhaps more correctly 'Cape Colonial'[5]) architecture, with its characteristic gables and delicate mouldings, is as much a vernacular response to climate and context as it is the colonist's nostalgic reiteration of the established traditions of the distant metropole – this is particularly evident in the gables of the late eighteenth centuries, which often featured self-consciously classical

[4] Hersey 1988: 1.
[5] Recent scholarship has problematised the seemingly self-evident 'Dutch' provenance of early Cape colonial architecture by pointing both to stylistic influences from Northern Europe (Schellekens 1997: 204–6), and to a diverse range of cultural and social influences in the early Cape Colony (Markell et al. 1995: 10–34). As Yvonne Brink notes, 'the "Cape Dutch" tradition only originated in the third decade of the 18th century, more than 80 years after the initial colonial settlement on the shores of Table Bay' (Markell et al. 1995: 29).

pediments and pilasters somewhat out of step with the steeply pitched thatched roofs and earth-hugging horizontality of the homesteads.

Second, the Mediterranean-inspired 'Union Classical Style' of the late nineteenth and early twentieth centuries, of which Herbert Baker's Union Buildings (Fig. 2.13) is the quintessential exemplar.[6] The Tuscan Doric colonnades, Palladian windows, and Cordova tiles that characterised this style were seen by South African architects – as I discuss more fully below – as an appropriate response to climate and context, and whose origins in the classical world are entirely self-evident.

Third, in Art Deco's decorative tropes of the machine age during the industrial boom of the 1930s, which, although expressing a 'popular enthusiasm for modernity and celebrat[ing] the present rather than the past',[7] was nonetheless concerned with a formality and grandeur that was entirely classical in scale and conception (Figs 2.14–15).

Fourth, in the sophisticated abstractions of the Modern Movement architecture advocated by the Transvaal Group[8] at the University of the Witwatersrand in the 1930s, which was to have such far-reaching effects. Their asymmetry and streamlined forms notwithstanding, these buildings have a rationality, clarity of purpose, and formal restraint that is worthy of the highest traditions of classicism.[9]

Indeed, one might well argue with Hersey that classicism has been the necessary condition of South African architecture from the earliest European settlement, being implicit in almost every style associated with its historical trajectory (and moreover continuing to thrive, albeit in a much bastardised form). The only exceptions, perhaps, are a short-lived Victorian flirtation with the Gothic, and those styles that have sought a more authentic response to climate and cultural context by evoking African vernacular traditions. Amongst these one might note Gerhard Moerdyk's (1890–1958) *volksargitektuur* (or 'people's architecture') of the 1930s, which sought to promote an Afrikaner architecture that was distinctly different from the classical tradition associated with British imperialism. For Moerdyk, this was achieved largely

[6] Harber 1992: 7–8.   [7] Doordan 2001: 24.

[8] The Transvaal Group comprised a group of young architects including Rex Martienssen (1905–42), Gordon McIntosh (1904–83), Norman Hanson (1909–90) and John Fassler (1910–71). Based at the University of the Witwatersrand's School of Architecture, these architects aggressively promoted the theories and practical applications of the European vanguard modernism in South Africa. Recognised by Le Corbusier as '*Le groupe Transvaal*' they thus placed Johannesburg architecture at the cutting edge of contemporary design. See Herbert 1975.

[9] It thus comes as no surprise that Rex Martienssen's doctoral thesis was on the subject of 'The idea of space in Greek architecture' (1956), published as *The Idea of Space in Greek Architecture with special reference to the Doric temple and its setting* (1964).

Figure 2.13 Herbert Baker, Union Buildings, Pretoria, 1909–12. Baker would later write that the two towers, linked by a semicircular colonnade, symbolised the union of South Africa's 'two races', namely British and Boers.

Figure 2.14 Burnet, Tait & Lorne, 44 Main Street, Johannesburg, 1938, headquarters of the Anglo-American corporation. The building is a fine example of stripped classicism with Art Deco decorative flourishes.

Figure 2.15 Burnet, Tait & Lorne, 44 Main Street, Johannesburg, 1938. The elaborate bronze work of the entrance portal and elsewhere on the building was designed by the British artist Walter Gilbert, who had also designed the gates at Buckingham Palace.

by superimposing decorative elements drawn from Great Zimbabwe over modernistic, streamlined forms built from regional materials (Fig. 2.16). In the best-known example of this style, the Voortrekker Monument (completed 1948), this highly selective reading of an African vernacular subsumed within the streamlined modernity of the overall design carried an important ideological message: it served to make a claim for the authenticity of the modern Afrikaner's uniquely African origins, and their consequently unequivocal claim to nationhood. Moerdyk's disavowal of classicism notwithstanding, it nonetheless continues to haunt his architecture both in its commitment to the heroic decorative tradition and in its symmetry, formality, and carefully considered relationships of part to whole.[10]

More successful in its attempts to pursue alternatives that emphatically renounce a debt to classicism is the work of Norman Eaton (1902–66). Eaton actively promoted a regionalist aesthetic, informed by his investigation of the vernacular building traditions of African rural settlements. As the architect put it, 'time and time again these Native ensembles have made me conscious of the same thing; of the

---

[10] See Rankin and Schneider below.

Figure 2.16 Gerhard Moerdijk, Merensky Library (now the Edoardo Villa Museum), University of Pretoria, Pretoria, 1936. The Merensky Library is the first example where Moerdijk's ideas – later to find their fullest expression in the Voortrekker Monument – are articulated.

quiet grace with which they grow out of and yield to the natural beauties of their surroundings'.[11] He also looked to Great Zimbabwe and Egypt for stylistic influences, and promoted the use of locally-fired, simple bricks that had long been associated with the Pretoria building industry. The resulting structures, both domestic and commercial, aimed to promote a sense of *genius loci* rooted in an atavistic sense of the land, and became an important progenitor of Pretoria Regionalism.[12] More recently the work of architects like Peter Rich

[11] Fisher 1997: 81.

[12] The dominant style of post-World War II suburban Pretoria, Pretoria Regionalism is characterised partly by its use of materials ('rustic brick, either directly as clinker or as whitewashed stock; low-pitched iron roofs; deep shaded eaves and verandas; sun-shy windows; [and] sensitivity to landscape and land features': Artefacts, *Pretoria regionalism* www.artefacts .co.za/main/Buildings/style_det.php?styleid=185), and partly by a self-conscious modernity inspired by contemporary Brazilian architecture. As with Moerdyk's *volksargitektuur* of the inter-World War period, there is an ideological component to this: As the nationalist agenda was increasingly being pushed after 1948, this insistence on the construction of an identity that was at once 'authentically' rooted in Africa and yet at the cutting edge of modernity was an important component of the imaginary of Afrikaner nationalism as both legitimately 'African' and part of a forward-looking community of nations.

and Kate Otten insists, in different ways, that solutions to architectural problems can and should be found in African vernacular traditions. The ArchiTravel online architecture guide describes Rich's style as 'a fusion of modernist influences ... and spatial modes derived from a local tribal vernacular',[13] while Otten's website characterises her style as 'a search for an African identity in architecture that reflects the uniqueness of our landscape, context and way of life'.[14]

These examples notwithstanding, it is clear that an overwhelming proportion of South African architectural history owes a debt, directly or indirectly, to the classical tradition. This is particularly true of Johannesburg, where the determined embrace of regionalism is something of a recent addition to the mainstream architectural scene – indeed, given Johannesburg's rapacious appetite for commercialism, the dominant tendency has always been towards emulating popular styles and tastes from elsewhere in pursuit of maximum return on investment, with little regard for the sustained development of an 'authentic' style. As Norman Hanson put it in 1952, 'it is in the nature of our cycles of building – developing quickly and proceeding feverishly – that superficialities and mannerisms, early acquired and retained, prevail'.[15] For Hanson, this in turn leads to 'the disease of "Façadism"[16] ... [which] at its worst, brings a rash of clichés, overworked motifs and meaningless "appliqué" work, no different in kind from the too easily despised nineteenth Century buildings'.[17] Unfortunately, fifty years later, this assessment still rings true and Hanson might indeed have been describing Number 90, First Road or any number of the gratuitously ornamented commercial buildings that continue to proliferate in Johannesburg's ever-expanding suburbs.

2. Building on the Memories and Souls of the Dead: Origins and Interpretations

Johannesburg's continued architectural engagement with classicism is thus clearly part of a much broader historical trajectory – from the Renaissance

---

[13] ArchiTravel Online Architecture Guide, *Peter Rich Architects* www.architravel.com/architravel/architects/peter-rich-architects/ (accessed 6 February 2017).

[14] *Kate Otten Architects* www.kateottenarchitects.com.   [15] Hanson 1952: 4.

[16] 'Façadism' has recently come to signify the practice demolishing a building but retaining its façade intact in order to build new structures behind or around it. Hanson is clearly using the term in its older sense, namely the practice or principle of being concerned with the outward appearance of a building to the exclusion of other considerations.

[17] Hanson 1952: 4.

to Postmodernism, each age has appropriated classicism for its own ends. Clearly, the embedded associations of classical architecture continue to exert an enduringly powerful hold over the Western imagination, and, moreover, also in the developing world. As various writers have shown,[18] there is an increasing global tendency, as Brian B. Taylor argues, to renounce 'prejudices against the colonial past and against historical references in general to build upon and elaborate historical forms and models, to proclaim a kind of "universal" validity for certain architectural vocabularies'.[19] That these vocabularies are largely classical is noted in discussions by both by Taylor, on noteworthy postmodern buildings in Thailand, and by Fan, on recent commercial projects in China. Taylor argues that in Thailand,

The rampant use of neo-classical fragments (Greek, Roman, and hybrid versions of these) in reinforced concrete to decorate buildings, is the result of a combination of factors: the architects' desire to be part of a 'global' trend characterised by Western classical decoration and a certain strata of Thai society that wishes to advertise their worldly success.[20]

Fan finds similarly materialistic reasons for the proliferation of classical forms in China's recent building boom: 'Applying a Graeco-Roman style', he suggests,

appears to be a more practical and effective way to signify an explicit, recognizable, Western connection … classical forms, with their distinctly Western appearance, have become an effective tool to promote sales in the popular longing for a Western lifestyle.[21]

Classicism in this context is thus prized for the commercial capital inherent in its exoticism and association with the perceived sophistication and glamour of the commercial and cultural capital cities of the West, and for the status that it is therefore seen to confer. Although this is driven largely by the rampant ideology of materialism that characterises China's recent emergence as a global economic superpower, Fan also notes that the implicit 'representational orthodoxy' of classicism has resulted in 'the most ornate classical designs in China's recent building boom [being] those for government buildings'.[22] This he attributes to a desire on the part of the Chinese government to evoke political authority by recreating 'the Western symbolism of "institution"', and in that way claiming credibility and legitimacy on a global platform.

[18] Taylor 1984; Greenhalgh 1990; Fan 2009: 64–74.   [19] Taylor 1984: 24.   [20] Taylor 1986: 20.
[21] Fan 2009: 67.   [22] Fan 2009: 69.

Indeed, part of the enduring appeal of classicism is precisely that it is fundamentally an authoritarian tradition. As Michael Greenhalgh notes, one of the main features of classicism is

an emphasis on morality, on Empire (in the widest sense – Papal and Imperial), on textual tradition and on a new aesthetic. It is certainly true that Classicism itself is an authoritarian tradition, peculiarly fitted to the expression of political and dynastic superiority.[23]

'Only rarely', he continues, 'has the ideal of Classicism been applied without some attendant ideology', and classicism is therefore 'not merely a range of styles, but rather a way of perceiving the world and using the arts to persuade others to see it in a similar fashion'.[24] For Christopher Hussey it is straightforward: 'The classical Orders, like those societies that have successfully employed them in their buildings, connote the authority of an autocrat, omniscient or benevolent or neither.'[25] The natural corollary of the implicit authoritarianism of classicism is its elitism. Indeed, this is, as Alexander Tzonis and Liane Lefaivre argue, implicit in the very term *classical*, which, they point out, 'means related to the social order of the *classici*, the highest rank of the hierarchical social structure of ancient Rome, juxtaposed to the lowest, that of the *proletarii*'.[26]

The persistence of classicism in architecture, irrespective of political, cultural or geographical context thus seems to arise out of a complex intersection of deeply embedded cultural associations on the one hand, and the aspirations of new urban elites everywhere to claim social legitimacy on the other – as we shall see, this is particularly the case for Johannesburg. The origins of the classical language of form are significant in this regard. As various writers have shown,[27] the classical orders originated in sacred architecture, and their authority thus comes not only from their subsequent history, but from their original use in the temple architecture of ancient Greece. As Roger Scruton notes, the Romans used the classical orders in all their important public buildings in order to retain a sacred presence within the functions of civic life.[28] In this way, they established what has been the enduring underlying principle of the use of classicism in significant public architecture: 'An interpenetration of the sacred and the secular, and thus the sanctifying of ordinary humanity, and the humanising of the divine.'[29]

---

[23] Greenhalgh 1990: 8.   [24] Greenhalgh 1990: 9.   [25] Hussey 1950: 166.
[26] Tzonis and Lefaivre 1987: 1.
[27] *Inter alia* Tzonis and Lefaivre 1987; Hersey 1988; Scruton 1994.   [28] Scruton 1994: 108.
[29] Ibid.

The origins of the term the *orders* of classical architecture – namely the formal canon as it relates to the decorative elements of classical architecture – is also telling with regard to the extent to which classicism and notions of moral didacticism are intertwined. As Ingrid D. Rowland notes, the term comes from the Italian *ordine*, and dates from the Renaissance, being first used by Angelo Colocci[30] and Raphael in a letter to Pope Leo X. 'Here for the first time in the history of architecture', she writes,

the varieties of classical columns – Doric, Ionic, Tuscan, Corinthian, and the Renaissance invention, Attic – take the name 'orders'. They have kept the name ever since, even though Vitruvius, Alberti, Francesco di Giorgio, Fabio Calvo, Cesare Cesariano, and indeed every writer on classical architecture before about 1519 used the rhetorical term *genus* or one of its derivatives to classify these architectural styles.[31]

The change from *genus* to *order* is significant, she notes, in that Italian Renaissance usage *ordine* denoted both a set of 'instructions', as well as the notion of a 'class of objects' (with further associations with the cohesive unity of contemporary religious orders). The usage quickly gained currency, she argues, partly because High Renaissance classicists like Bramante and Raphael were seeking stricter definitions for a formal vocabulary of architecture, and partly – particularly in the context of papal Rome – because,

'Order' is a classification whose connotations are more defined, more absolute than the loose kinship of *genus*, and this binding categorization fits the temperament of papal Rome, which deals by vocation with eternal verities. 'Order' in papal Rome is never an entirely neutral word, because order derives from God and serves to define the trace of God's presence.[32]

The 'correct' usage (i.e. canonically appropriate according to the dictates defined by Renaissance scholars) of the orders has thus by long tradition come to imply two things: first, a kind of failsafe formula for beauty, founded on the principles of harmony, proportion and exactitude of detail that had first been defined by the ancients. As Greenhalgh notes, for early theorists,

One useful property Classicism was believed to possess was its rationality, in that its main precepts can be expressed as a series of easily explained rules and models:

---

[30] Angelo Colocci (1467–1549), famed humanist and papal secretary of Pope Leo X, collaborated with Raphael on Leo X's commission to draw the most accurate reconstruction of Rome of the Caesars. He was also involved in the translation of Vitruvius' *De Architectura* into Italian. See Rowland 2006.

[31] Rowland 2006: 527.   [32] Ibid., 528.

if it could be understood by the mind, extrapolated into a system, subjected to rules and measurements, then it could be taught, and be passed on from generation to generation.[33]

This was certainly true for the great Renaissance architectural theorist, Leon Battista Alberti (1404–72), for whom beauty in architecture famously depended on 'that reasoned harmony of all the parts within a body, so that nothing can be added, taken away, or altered, but for the worse'.[34] That the model for this is the architecture of the Graeco-Roman world goes almost without saying, and lest there be any doubt that an objective standard for this kind of beauty exists, Alberti was quick to insist that this is not the case:

Yet some would ... maintain that beauty, and indeed every aspect of building, is judged by relative and variable criteria, and that forms of buildings should vary according to individual taste and must not be bound by any rule of art. A common fault this, among the ignorant – to deny the existence of anything they do not understand.[35]

Second, the use of the orders comes to establish the canon of a particular kind of beauty, rooted in notions of authority and legitimacy. For George Hersey (1988) this extends beyond the reach of papal Rome of the Renaissance or even indeed imperial Rome. He finds the didactic meanings of classical ornament implicit in its very point of origin, in a way that is both atavistic and somewhat sinister: he argues that the various ornamental elements of the classical orders derive from rituals of sacrifice in the Hellenistic world, and were preserved as part of the cultural memory of the ancient Greeks. 'For an inhabitant of the Hellenistic world', he writes,

The words 'Doric', 'echinus', or 'Ionic fascia' in Greek, did not have the purely workaday associations they have for us. They suggested bound and decorated victims, ribboned exuviae set on high, gods, cults, ancestors, colonies. Temples were read as concretions of sacrificial matter, of the things that were put into graves and laid on walls and stelai.[36]

He conjures the image of the primordial temple as an altar set in a grove of trees, festooned with the trappings of sacrifice – including fruits and flowers and the remains of sacrificial animals (and possibly even humans) – along with battle trophies and other votive objects. Although the formal rituals and settings changed, the imagery became part of a deeply embedded cultural language, eventually becoming – literally – cast in stone. According to Hersey, this not only explains common features like

---

[33] Greenhalgh 1990: 11.   [34] Quoted by Akkerman 2003: 83.   [35] Quoted by Hills 2005: 97.
[36] Hersey 1988: 149.

egg-and-dart and bead-and-reel ornament (whose avatars would have been votive objects) and animal imagery such as bucrania (animal sacrifices), but also the anthrophomorphic qualities of columns, which may stem from the image of sacrificial humans lashed to a support. He argues that this is further borne out in the terminology: the *torus* and *cavetto* mouldings at the base of Ionic and Corinthian columns derive from the names of types of rope, while a column base 'composed of toruses and cavetti often does resemble a set of tautened ropes'.[37] The fluting of the columns resembles the folds of a chiton, while the mouldings beneath the capital – the *trachelium* and *hypotrachelium* are derived from the word for throat. *Capital* itself, of course, derives from the Latin for head, while leafy bands and volutes that are commonly associated with the Ionic and Corinthian capitals could be read as coiled braids of hair or garlands worn around the head.[38] Even the shadows created by the *scotia*, or concave moulding at the base of the column, are redolent of primordial myth and ritual. Not only is Scotia the name of the 'goddess of darkness and underworld things' but,

Darkness or shadow was perceived by the ancients not as the mere absence of light but as a palpable substance, a vapor that was dark because it was dense with the tiny mote-like souls of the dead. So if we look again at the shadows cast by a scotia molding, we are to see them as thick with souls.[39]

In effect, Hersey's argument is a nuanced development of the theory, first advanced by Vitruvius, that classical ornament has its origin in the structural forms of primitive wooden structures translated over time into stone with no structural use. According to this theory, each of the component parts of the classical orders as we know them are derived from primordial structural members: Columns are the translation into stone of posts set into a platform, their fluting the grain of the timber marked with the cuts of the tool used to trim the log. The capitals are stylised representations of the transitional members that once supported the superstructure, the triglyphs of the frieze beam-ends, the mutules the ends of rafters and so on.[40] As we have seen, Hersey complicates this 'expression of structure' theory by taking it to a further metaphoric level: in this way, he reminds us of the deep-seated cultural and symbolic associations that architecture has; what Edwin Heathcote describes as 'the way in which ritual and symbolic elements transmute over time into practical features and then, once those practical uses too have been forgotten, hang around to haunt buildings as

---

[37] Hersey 1988: 21.   [38] Hersey 1988: 23, 28.   [39] Hersey 1988: 21.   [40] Hearn 2003: 98.

ghostly reminders of former uses'. Applying Hersey's reading of classical ornament to the everyday domestic environment, Heathcote argues that the disposition of the wall – from skirting to ceiling moulding – roughly corresponds to the base, shaft and capital of the classical column. In this way, the memory of classicism persists in even the most mundane of environments, and if Hersey's argument for the embedded ritualistic associations of classicism is applied, our houses are effectively 'built on the memories and souls of the dead'.[41]

These ideas bring into sharp focus the relationship between notions of cultural memory, and the complex ways in which architecture and architectural styles both reflect and construct social meanings. Given its deep-rooted and even – if Hersey and Heathcote are to be believed – atavistic relationship to the Western cultural imagination, then classicism is clearly more than a style but also a 'state of mind and a "world view"'.[42] As Greenhalgh notes,[43] the profligate use of styles in the contemporary environment means that meanings that architecture may once have had been considerably debased. Nonetheless, the persistence of classicism suggests more than just an appeal to history, but also to the notion of some deeply engrained moral and intellectual truth.

3. Great Towers to the Glory of the Sun: Classicism in Johannesburg

We return then to the question, what are the embedded truths for classicism in Johannesburg, and why does it persist in a social and cultural context where any currency that it may once have had has seemingly long been devalued? It seems to me that its persistence is about three closely intertwined things: first, it is fundamentally about history (both recorded and imagined); second, it is about climate and context; and third, it is about memory and identity. Underscoring all three of these things is Johannesburg's relative newness as a city – prior to the discovery of gold in 1886 there was very little in the way of human settlement on the veld on which Johannesburg subsequently arose. Yet, within a decade it had all the appearance and appurtenances of a fully formed town – as Winston Churchill described it in 1900,

We had marched for nearly 500 miles through a country which, though full of promise, seemed to European eyes desolate and wild, and now we turned a corner

---

[41] Heathcote 2010.   [42] Greenhalgh 1990: 11.   [43] Greenhalgh 1990: 17.

suddenly, and there before us sprang the evidence of wealth, manufacture and bustling civilization. I might have been looking from a distance at Oldham.[44]

Like other new cities born of the insatiable greed of the gold rush and the industrial revolution (for example, Manchester, San Francisco and Melbourne), Johannesburg experienced massive growth in a remarkably short space of time, with a concomitant boom in building and proliferation of architectural styles. As the corrugated iron shanties receded, the early townscape was initially dominated by the 'restless sky-line' of neo-Gothic spires and turrets decorated with fussy wrought-iron work.[45] It was not long, however, before buildings that needed to give the appearance of permanence and venerability – banks, stock exchange, clubs – were built in a faithful imitation of the flamboyant Beaux-Arts classicism then popular in European cities.

This is hardly surprising – classicism, was, after all not only the style associated with institutionalised respectability, but has, as Anthony Grafton et al. argue, always had

An obvious appeal to ruling elites or those aspiring to power and legitimacy, as a way of expressing authority, and is commonly invoked by individuals, groups, or governments wanting to restore order and inspire confidence after a period of insecurity or unrest, such as civil war or revolution.[46]

In the post-Anglo-Boer War context, those who made their fortunes quickly could claim through the architecture of their institutions and homes a mantle of respectability if they did not already have it. In this way, the erstwhile mining camp soon assumed a metropolitan character on the model of the European cities that it emulated – as Achille Mbembe puts it, 'Like every colonial town, [Johannesburg] found it hard to resist the temptation of mimicry, that is, of imagining itself as an English town and becoming a pale reflection of forms born elsewhere.'[47]

Formally decorated public buildings were an essential component of the invention of this identity. Indeed, as part of the unspoken recognition of the role of architecture as public art, ornament was, until the mid-twentieth century, an inevitable and necessary condition of important buildings. According to Christine Boyer, 'until the end of the nineteenth century builders of industrial cities were absorbed with picture making', that is, the construction of grandiose urban spaces and vistas, whose buildings and monuments were,

[44] Quoted by Chipkin 1993: 11.   [45] Greig 1978: 1.   [46] Grafton et al. 2010: 60.
[47] Mbembe 2008: 38.

Jewels of the city to be placed in scenographic arrangements and iconographically composed to civilize and elevate the aesthetic tastes and morals of an aspiring urban elite. This was an architecture of ceremonial power whose monuments spoke of exemplary deeds, national unity, and industrial glory.[48]

Johannesburg certainly did not lag in this regard. By the end of the first decade of the twentieth century it not only had a rationally designed urban grid with lavishly decorated buildings in the heart of its central business district,[49] but Edwin Lutyens – one of the most celebrated architects of his day and poised to become the architect laureate of the British Empire in all but official title – had been retained to design two of the most important symbols of 'ceremonial power': an art gallery and a triumphal arch.

Lutyens had come to Johannesburg at the behest of Florence, Mrs (later Lady) Lionel Phillips, who had conceived the idea of providing the booming mining town with an official art gallery. In this way she could not only 'uplift the colonial philistine' – as a contemporary London critic put it[50] – but also fulfil Cecil Rhodes's cultural ideals of British imperialist domination.[51] A competition for the design of the gallery not having yielded any results,[52] she was advised by Hugh Lane, Irish collector and connoisseur, to call upon Lutyens who had designed Lane's garden in Cheyne Walk.

Lutyens was simultaneously captivated and horrified by Johannesburg: 'No wonder the Boers fought for their country,' he wrote admiringly to his wife, 'Tonight the moon is a revelation. No wind so it is warm and oh so soft and all so gentle and a view to the mountains 30 miles away'.[53] Yet he could not fail to notice the incongruities and contradictions of the mining town, viewed from the Phillips's home, Villa Arcadia on Parktown ridge, where he was being accommodated: 'There is this villa decked land

---

[48] Boyer 1994: 33–34.

[49] Many of the early multi-storey buildings were built using the steel frame construction techniques pioneered in Chicago in the 1880s, and were fitted with generators and lifts. The earliest examples – Corner House (1903) and the Carlton Hotel (1904) – predate the use of similar technology in London: Chipkin 1993: 44.

[50] Carman 2006.   [51] Percy and Ridley 1985: 190.

[52] Herbert Baker had in fact been nominated as one of preferred candidates for the design of the Art Gallery, but due to internal wrangling both on the committee of the Transvaal Association of Architects and the Johannesburg Municipality, it was decided to appoint Lutyens as the chief architect (Greig 1978: 2). 'The town council etc. are all dead against Baker,' Lutyens wrote to his wife from Johannesburg, 'and they want to rope me in without Baker. This makes my position difficult – Baker is as good and generous as gold and I must be careful not to hurt him however advantageous to myself' (Percy and Ridley 1985: 208).

[53] Ibid.

standing above a squalid town with here and there big buildings,' he wrote to his wife upon his arrival on 12 December 1910,

> a sort of Birmingham without its smoke and every other block of buildings razed to the ground to appease some appalling angel. Then beyond miles of chimneys belching black smoke and weird cat's cradle erections ... the mines, mines of gold, the very heart of a modern world, and beyond the veldt wasting for hundreds of miles. They want me to go down a gold mine bit I don't want to go down their man-built holes and see the miners and the pthysis the dust gives 'em – though water jets and every modern contrivance possible to minimise the evil is adopted. Yet it is there and I don't like men digging for potatoes they may not eat and gold they may not spend.[54]

Nonetheless, he could not help but be excited by the possibilities that limitless wealth and the imperialist agenda being promoted by his hosts evoked: 'Rather than not,' he concluded, 'be let build marble cathedrals and great towers to the glory of the sun'.[55]

To this end he enthusiastically set about offering 'to go over the whole town plan of Johannesburg',[56] as well as to work on a number of other projects: the designs for the University of Cape Town; the town plan of Pretoria; the design of the Rand Regiments Memorial; the Art Gallery, Joubert Park and Parade Ground; the Johannesburg cathedral; and Lionel Phillips's garden. In the end only two of these projects were executed by Lutyens: the great triumphal arch of the Rand Regiments Memorial (1911)[57] and the Johannesburg Art Gallery (begun in 1912, with subsequent additions in 1929). Both the built projects reflect his conviction that it was necessary to insist on formal severity and strict classicism when building in a country that was not part of European civilisation.[58] As we have seen, this was due to his conviction that since there were no creditable craft traditions outside of Europe on which happy accidents of form could rely,[59] one had to insist on the rationality, clarity and exactitude of the

---

[54] Ibid.   [55] Ibid.   [56] Percy and Ridley 1985: 209.

[57] Built to commemorate the fallen British soldiers of the Rand Regiments in the Anglo-Boer War, the memorial was renamed the 'National Anglo-Boer War Memorial' in 1999 in the interests of promoting national unity.

[58] Ibid., 190.

[59] Lutyens's attitude to local craftsmen is made clear in one account of his experiences with Indian workers engaged on the Viceroy's Palace in New Delhi: 'The Indian craftsmen gradually grew in excellence and accuracy, as time went on. One mason, in the earlier days, cut a stone so inaccurately that he was discovered altering the template to fit his ill-cut stone. This man was discharged, but was reinstated, in that he was the first of the masons who showed any sign of a dawning intelligence': Lutyens, 'Notes regarding the building of New Delhi and Viceroy's House', speech made by Sir Edwin Lutyens at a meeting of the India Society on 2 February 1933, Royal Institute of British Architects Archives, London, LuE/32/4/2 (1933), 4.

classical tradition. This explains the sober restraint of the Art Gallery, with its austere Tuscan Doric portico, undecorated pediment, and windowless, ashlar walls relieved only by symmetrically placed pedimented niches (Fig. 2.6).

The Rand Regiments Memorial is the first of a number of memorial arches that Lutyens was to design after World War I.[60] The memorial is essentially a pavilion in the form of a triumphal arch with four intersecting vaults (Fig. 2.4) – as Roderick Gradidge points out, Lutyens believed that the arch was 'more suitable for the memorial to the dead than for displays of victory'.[61] The pavilion is surmounted by a low dome on which is perched an almost disproportionately large bronze sculpture entitled the *Angel of Peace* – the gift of Lionel Phillips to the good citizens of Johannesburg – by the Russian-born sculptor Naoum Aronson (1872–1943). The two high arched openings on the east–west axis break through the cornice pediments in a typical Lutyens mannerism,[62] lending the memorial an air of Baroque flamboyance that is entirely lacking in both the Johannesburg Art Gallery and his subsequent memorial arches. Lutyens originally intended the memorial to be set amongst balustraded terraces with minor groups of allegorical sculptures and four reflecting basins of water.[63] This was never realised, and today the memorial stands all but engulfed by its suburban setting,[64] its grandiloquent statement of imperial triumph 'fenced off and rendered innocuous', as Clive Chipkin puts it, 'like the caged animals in the adjacent Zoo'.[65]

At the same time that Lutyens was working on his Johannesburg commissions, his contemporary Herbert Baker had already established his reputation as the pre-eminent South African architect, and was working on one of the most significant commissions of his career, the Union Buildings. Baker had accomplished much since his arrival as a young man at the Cape in 1892. Rapidly assimilated into Cape Town society, he soon became one of Cecil Rhodes's protégés, and was given the task of restoring Rhodes's home Groote Schuur. This was Baker's first engagement with the Cape colonial idiom, for which Rhodes had a particular affinity, and which was to have a far-reaching effect on Baker's *oeuvre*. Indeed, in

[60] Gradidge (1981: 78) notes that, 'In all [Lutyens] designed almost as many war memorials as he had designed houses in the early part of his career.' See Amery 1982 for a comprehensive list of all Lutyens's war memorials.
[61] Gradidge 1981: 77.   [62] Greig 1978: 2.   [63] Greig 1978: 1.
[64] Lutyens was not happy with the site from the outset. After being taken to see it for the first time, he wrote to his wife that 'the site where the Duke of "Cannot" [i.e. the Duke of Connaught] laid a foundation stone is an impossible place'. Miller 2002: 161, 225.
[65] Chipkin 1993: 41.

Baker, Rhodes found 'a sympathetic architect who had the mental outlook and ability to give form to [his] aspirations and Imperial ambitions'[66] (Artefacts, n.d. A), and Rhodes in turn was instrumental in shaping Baker's world view,[67] particularly with regard to notions of service to the British Empire. Under the sway of Rhodes, Baker came to believe implicitly in the project of imperialism, and the place of architecture 'to provide a framework of architectural order analogous to the law and order provided by colonial rule'.[68] In 1900 Rhodes had paid for Baker to make a tour of classical sites in the Mediterranean, such that the young architect could acquire first-hand knowledge of the classical temples and Italian villas.[69] This of course had a profound effect on Baker's development as an architect. Not only did he profit significantly from it in the Italianate villas that he built for his well-heeled clients, but more significantly his ability to use the classical orders 'with style and knowledge'[70] leant his work an inimitable gravitas that in time cemented his reputation, with Lutyens, as the pre-eminent architect of British imperialism.[71]

Baker, in partnership with Francis Masey (1861–1912), had designed a number of domestic, sacred and commercial buildings in Cape Town before coming to Johannesburg in 1902 at the conclusion of the Anglo-Boer War to assist with post-war reconstruction. It was in the Transvaal, as Michael Keath notes, that Baker 'through the auspices of Lord Alfred Milner . . . was given his greatest opportunities and achieved his most notable successes'.[72] In addition to a number of Randlords' mansions in Parktown (including Villa Arcadia, the home of the Phillipses), these included *inter alia* the South African Institute for Medical Research; Roedean School; St Andrew's School for Girls and St John's College in Johannesburg; the Pretoria Railway Station; and of course the Union

---

[66] Artefacts, *Baker, Sir Herbert John*, www.artefacts.co.za/main/Buildings/archframes.php?archid=60&countadd=0.

[67] Baker's undisguised admiration for Rhodes is evident in his published biography (Baker 1934).

[68] Ridley 1998: 77. To the extent that Baker is not only considered, with Lutyens, to be one of the most distinguished architects in the service of empire, but is also considered a peripheral members of Milner's Kindergarten.

[69] Gradidge (1981: 64) notes that 'Baker had been led to Classicism by Rhodes, and it is . . . likely that it was Baker who led Lutyens to Classicism. Certainly he was designing completely Classical buildings well before Lutyens'.

[70] Ibid.

[71] In addition to his work in South Africa and India, Baker designed government buildings in Kenya and Rhodesia, dominion war memorials at Delville Wood, and four important 'empire' buildings in London, viz. South Africa House, India House, the Royal Empire Society and London House, a hostel for dominion students.

[72] Keath 1998: 79.

Figure 2.17 Herbert Baker, Union Buildings, Pretoria, 1909–13. Detail of one of the inner courtyards, revealing Baker's interest in the Italianate villa as an appropriate reference point for a South African imperial style.

Buildings. Baker's influence on generations of South African architects cannot be underestimated – as Keath shows, Baker's 'school' certainly dominated South African architecture for the first decades of the twentieth century. A significant divergence from the principles that he established first appeared only with Transvaal Group in the 1930s and the Pretoria Regionalists in the 1940s, while the architecture of the Public Works Department continued to be generally informed by his principles well into the 1950s.

Informed on the one hand by his interest in the craft-based, vernacular traditions of the Cape colonial style, and on the other by what he termed 'the eternal principles of the ordered beauty of classical architecture',[73] Baker developed what has become known as the 'Union Classical Style'. Inspired by the open courtyards, loggias, porticoes and Cordova-tiled roofs of Mediterranean architecture (Fig. 2.17), this was essentially an attempt to create a classically inspired style that was seen to be appropriate both to climate and cultural context. As the South African Builder put it in 1923,

---

[73] Baker 1944: 71.

In arriving at a happy solution to the problem of developing a South African style we could not do better than to turn to Italy and the Renaissance movement [*sic*] for inspiration. The open cortile, the heavy cornices and the piazzas and belvederes were all the type of thing, which naturally developed in a land where there were blue skies, and an abundance of sunshine.[74]

With hindsight, we can see that this is in fact an integral aspect of the imperialist imaginary exemplified by Cecil Rhodes' Cape-to-Cairo fantasy. Peter Merrington describes this as a 'cultural matrix' which

generated a particular founding myth for the colonial state of the Union of South Africa in 1910 and which also lent to foreign visitors, tourists, and immigrants a readily understood interpretation of South Africa and the Cape as 'Mediterranean' rather than as 'African'.[75]

This notion is surprisingly persistent, manifest, as it is in the ongoing fashion for Italianate, 'Tuscan' villas in South African suburban homes and speculative housing developments. In a bewildering fantasy of pseudo-regionalism, this style claims to be appropriate to climate and context.

The synthesis of the Cape colonial with Mediterranean references had a further ideological resonance in the context of the Union Buildings, the seat of the imperial government, and a prominent symbol of the union of the 'two [white] races of South Africa'.[76] The inclusion of Cape colonial elements (shuttered windows, carved fanlights and characteristic door frames and brass work) imbues the building with a politically expedient sense of regionalism that ostensibly speaks as much to the values of the Afrikaner component of the Union's constituency, as to those of its British Imperial masters. In effect, the stylistic tensions that result from the references to what are essentially domestic architectural traditions conflated with the grand gesture of imperialist classicism makes a clear statement about the subordination of the local and the specific to the generalised and authoritarian, complacently packaged in the unassailable rhetoric of 'home'. For Baker it was quintessentially representative of 'a better and more permanent order of architecture ... [an] architecture which establishes a nation'.[77]

Similar principles were applied in Baker's next important commission, to design – with Lutyens – the imperial capital of New Delhi. The desired

---

[74] 25 November 1923   [75] Merrington 2001: 323.   [76] Baker 1944: 61.

[77] Baker 1944: 48. Baker is extrapolating here from one of his favourite quotations, to which he often returns, from Christopher Wren: 'Architecture has its political Use: publick Buildings being the Ornament of a Country; it establishes a Nation, draws People and Commerce; makes the people love their native Country': Baker 1944: 58.

Figure 2.18 Leith & Moerdijk, Park Station, Johannesburg, 1930, consistent with Baker's blend of classicism and regionalism. Below the loggia, with its paired and fluted Tuscan Doric columns, is a frieze by Anton van Wouw depicting the history of transport, and below that stylised African elephant heads.

effect – pioneered in the Union Buildings – was one of monumentality in the Western classical tradition, tempered with just enough regional flavour to naturalise it in the eyes of the local subjects.[78] The resultant style – succinctly characterised by Edwin Lutyens as 'an Englishman dressed for the climate'[79] – thus affirmed cultural links with the metropole, whilst simultaneously appropriating, manipulating, or inventing 'native' traditions in order to validate colonial authority. In New Delhi, this meant the selective appropriation of Mughal forms, grafted onto 'the eternal principles of the ordered beauty of classical architecture'.[80] This would ostensibly result, as Baker put it in a letter to Lutyens outlining his vision for the new capital, in an architecture that would 'not be Indian, nor English, nor Roman, but ... Imperial. In two thousand years there must be an Imperial Lutyens tradition in Indian architecture ... Hurrah for despotism!'[81] In effect, as Mark Crinson notes, the Indian references – as with the 'Cape Dutch' references in the Union Buildings – are pushed to the insignificant margins of the composition where they are in no danger of

[78] Foster 2004: 270.   [79] Irving 1982: 7.   [80] Baker 1944: 71.
[81] Quoted in Hussey 1950: 247.

destabilising the grand narrative of imperial classicism, but rather, participate calmly within it.[82] In effect, it served to create the illusion of calm dignity and grandeur on the surface of an increasingly querulous and unwieldy colonial administration struggling with the conflicting demands of modernity, tradition and nationalism.

In the South African context, this blend of classicism and regionalism set a trend for public architecture well into the 1930s, with classical facades (or stripped classical facades, in the case of more 'modernistic' buildings) being adorned with an extended repertoire of 'regional' motifs: Particularly favoured were stylised representations of indigenous fauna and flora along with images of 'tribal' black people. Through these devices, architects could engage discourses of 'belonging' by claiming a direct link with the land.[83] In effect, the use of indigenous materials and imagery implies, in much the same way as the classical orders did for the British establishment, a sense of permanence and inevitability, but with the added advantage of being located in a temporal and geographical present. Notable examples of this style in Johannesburg include Leith and Moerdyk's Park Station (Fig. 2.18) and Burnett, Tait and Lorne's Headquarters of the Anglo American Corporation, 44 Main Street (Fig. 2.19).

In Johannesburg classicism thus played an important role in articulating white middle-class identity, appealing as much to the self-aggrandisement of the Randlords, as to imperialist sentiment: in both cases it was used to invent a sense of history and thus impose legitimacy for the new town. Nonetheless, although much was invested in the construction of worthy monuments to the newfound wealth of the Randlords and their descendents, the bulk of Johannesburg's buildings – then as now – were speculative. This accounts not only for the lack of cohesion in terms of style and scale that characterises the city, but also for the interest in both novelty on the one hand and the implied 'permanence' of the classical on the other, as a sure way to maximise immediate return on investment. This, what Clive Chipkin describes as the city's 'rentier architecture and dustbin of discarded styles',[84] rather than Boyer's 'architecture of ceremonial power' and notions historic civic identity in turn shaped – and indeed continues to shape – Johannesburg's architecture and public spaces.

[82] Crinson 2003: 12. For his part, Lutyens had little patience with indigenous Indian architecture, particularly as regarded the pointed arch. 'One cannot tinker with the rounded arch,' he wrote. 'God did not make the Eastern rainbow pointed to show His wide sympathies.' Stamp 1981: 37.

[83] For a discussion of the political implications of these kinds of decorative programmes in the context of the 'fusion' politics of the 1930s, see Freschi 2004, 2005, 2009.

[84] Chipkin 1993: vii.

Figure 2.19 Burnet, Tait & Lorne, 44 Main Street, Johannesburg, 1938. The low-relief frieze surrounding 44 Main Street was designed by the British artist Donald Gilbert (son of Walter Gilbert, who designed the bronze work), and features stylised representations of indigenous South African fauna and flora.

Writing on this problematic aspect of Johannesburg's architectural identity, John Fassler argued in 1952 that

it is clear that considered from the point of view of emotional responses to an atmosphere deriving from an historical past, [Johannesburg] has nothing to offer. It is still too newly born. It has so recently emerged from the chrysalis of the mining camp. It lacks, and during our time will continue to lack, that rich leavening of architecture and association, which . . . are so much part of London and Bath, and which endear them to residents and visitors alike. Johannesburg cannot be blamed for its lack of history. Its administrators can be criticised however for neglecting to make the most of the public buildings which have been erected, and for not developing open spaces in relation thereto, to provide proper settings for them.[85]

In many respects, this assessment still rings true. Something of the 'mining camp' mentality still seems to prevail. Driven by decentralisation and the concomitant inner-city decay, there is, on the one hand, a gross indifference to architectural heritage that leads to what one might term the 'demolition by neglect' of many notable buildings. On the other, rampant

[85] Fassler 1952: 7.

commercialism fuelled by Johannesburg's status as the regional economic powerhouse means that the pursuit of novelty for its own sake – designed to attract attention and thus maximise return on investment – triumphs over any sense of a sustained and historically invested urban identity. Johannesburg, true to its nature as a mining town, continues to be reshaped, rezoned and reimagined according to the demands of market forces, with little regard for urban aesthetics or markers of civic identity. Indeed, decentralisation means increasingly that public spaces are artificially constructed; less and less is invested in grand gestures of civic space with signature buildings at their centre, and more and more in the empty gestures of global capitalism, where 'public' space is entirely in thrall to commercial interests.

4. Conclusion: The Imagined Refuge of History

If, as Heathcote argues, our homes – and by extensions cities – are indeed built 'on the memories and souls of the dead', then the continued existence of classicism, with all its complex layering of history, power and memory in Johannesburg raises some urgent troubling questions: Whose memories are at stake? Whose identity? The souls of whose dead? Mbembe speaks of metropolitan built forms as being the 'projective extension of the society's archaic or primal fantasies, the ghost dances and the slave spectacles at is foundation'.[86] The foundation of Johannesburg's architecture, as I have noted above, has always been speculative: driven largely by motives of profit, it seems that the single abiding element of Johannesburg's architectural identity has been an indifference to notions of heritage and identity, yet the persistence of classicism is an ongoing reminder of the 'slave spectacle' at its foundation. 'More than ever before in its history,' Mbembe continues, 'Johannesburg's city space is a product that is marked, measured, marketed, and transacted. It is a commodity. As such, its representational form has become ever more stylized.'[87]

As one of the most culturally loaded of representational forms, classicism in Johannesburg is also a plangent reminder of the extent to which architecture, as Paul Jones argues, expresses 'the tension and fluidity inherent in how identities are constructed'.[88] Which brings us back to where we started, trying to make sense of the 'frantically baroque' excesses

---

[86] Mbembe 2008: 38.   [87] Mbembe 2008: 54.   [88] Jones 2006: 562.

of Number 90, First Road: Despite its egregiousness – or perhaps because of it – there is a certain poignancy in its attempt to claim the grandeur and grace of classicism. This 'poetry in a pidgin language' – ill-informed and misguided as it may be – seems ultimately to be about a desire to belong, to claim out of the ever-fraught geopolitical space of this complex and contradictory city a sense of place, identity and legitimacy, and the imagined refuge of history.

3 | Cecil John Rhodes, the Classics and Imperialism

JOHN HILTON

It is well known that Cecil John Rhodes (hereafter 'Rhodes') found the time, while consolidating his control of the diamond field at Kimberley, to take a 'pass degree' in Classics at Oriel College, Oxford,[1] that he had earlier won a Classics scholarship at his grammar school at Bishop's Stortford,[2] and that his library at Groote Schuur testifies to an abiding interest in the subject.[3] However, this enthusiasm often appears ironic and even trivial at times, as can be seen in the humorous 'No Smoking' inscription carved in worn uppercase Classical Greek characters in the vestibule of Rhodes House in Oxford (ΜΗΔΕΙΣ ΚΑΠΝΟΦΟΡΟΣ ΕΙΣΙΤΩ).[4] Nevertheless, this chapter argues that Rhodes' Classical education and his continuing interest in Ancient History did play a significant part in shaping his imperialist ideas and that the Classically inspired commemorations of his life by his followers shaped the very terrain and cultural outlook of South Africa.

The key issue is imperialism. Rhodes fervently advocated the expansion of the British Empire over the entire world and beyond, if that were

---

[1] The importance of this degree for Rhodes is apparent from one of the bronze plaques around the base of the equestrian statue of Rhodes at Kimberley, which depicts Rhodes being capped at his graduation ceremony (Fig. 3.1). See also Rotberg 1988: 84–107.

[2] Michell 1910: 1.17. However, Michell notes that his best subjects at school were history and geography. There are many biographies of Rhodes written in many languages. The best recent treatment is Maylam 2005: 175–76, which lists 33 studies. There are also novels and films. Favourable views of Rhodes are given by, for example, Michell 1910, Jourdan 1910, le Sueur 1913. For a more critical recent assessment see Thomas 1996.

[3] For the classical books in Rhodes' library see Wardle (this volume). The sculptural legacy of Rhodes and his followers is investigated by Tietze (also in this volume); Claassen 2009. For Rhodes and classics in South Africa see Lambert 2011, chapter 2; Hilton 2007: 17–22.

[4] A play, of course, on the inscription at the entrance of Plato's Academy: 'Let no one without geometry enter': ΑΓΕΩΜΕΤΡΗΤΟΣ ΜΗΔΕΙΣ ΕΙΣΙΤΩ. See also the inscription around Rhodes House in Oxford: 'This house has honoured the name and example of Cecil John Rhodes and commends it forever' DOMUS HAEC NOMEN ET EXEMPLUM CAECILII JOHANIS RHODES OXONIAE DILEXIT IN PERPETUUM COMMENDAT and the quotation Horace *Odes* 3.30.6 *non omnis moriar* above the lintel leading to the rotunda vestibule. These inscriptions were erected by Rhodes' memorialists, principally his architect, Herbert Baker, but probably reflect his own ideas, since Rhodes often discussed his legacy with his friends. For this reason, no attempt is made in this chapter to distinguish between the views of Rhodes and his followers.

possible.[5] In this he may have been influenced by the example set by Rome's control of much of the known world in the first four centuries of our era.[6] Rhodes lived at a time, before the traumatic devastation of the Boer War and World War I, when anything seemed possible for British adventurism, and when a route from the Cape to Cairo seemed entirely feasible and worthwhile.[7] As yet the intellectual and ethical debate associated with the names of Bernard Holland, Francis Haverfield, Edward Baring (Lord Cromer), Charles Lucas, James Bryce, J. A. Cramb and others, on British imperialism and its relationship with its Roman predecessor, had not taken place within Victorian society.[8] Indeed, it may be true to say that this furore in British politics was precipitated in large measure by Rhodes and his unscrupulous acquisition of much of the available territory in Southern Africa on behalf of the British South Africa Chartered Company.[9]

The Victorians were, of course, highly aware of the rapid expansion of British interests throughout the world in the eighteenth and early nineteenth centuries as a result of what may be termed 'fi-power' – 'a combination of financial power and fire-power'.[10] When Rhodes returned to England to undertake his studies at Oxford, one of the key intellectual figures of the day was the eccentric Slade Professor of Fine Art at Oxford, John Ruskin, whose call to the young men of Britain to 'found colonies as fast and as far as she (i.e. Britain) is able' in his 1870 Oxford inaugural was widely discussed among educated Britons.[11] Rhodes cannot have avoided the patriotic fervour for imperialism aroused by this speech, and there is no doubt that he later owned a copy of Ruskin's collected works.[12] In 1872 Winwood Reade published his massively successful anti-Christian paean to social Darwinism, *The Martyrdom of Man* – a book that Rhodes claimed

---

[5] Stead 1902: 190.

[6] For the notion of the Roman Empire as a 'world' empire and a model for European unity today, see Boris Johnson 2006: 31; Alföldy 1999.

[7] Ferguson 2003a: xviii, discusses whether the whole imperial enterprise was worth the cost for anyone. On this point, see also Baumgart 1982: 31. Baumgart (145) asks whether Britain had any choice in the matter, in view of the social problems consequent on the Industrial Revolution.

[8] Holland 1901; Haverfield 1905, 1915; Cromer 1910; Lucas 1912; Bryce 1914; Cramb 1915. See Hingley 2000, 2001, 2005.

[9] At least one, the Liberal parliamentarian James Bryce, had visited South Africa: Bryce 1897.

[10] Ferguson 2003a: 222. See also Judd 2001.

[11] This passage from Ruskin's lecture is widely quoted, among others by Clark 1947: 9–10.

[12] Rhodes did not attend the inaugural lecture, as is sometimes implied, since he arrived in Oxford only in 1873. On this point, see Marks and Trapido 2004: 594. However, his library at Groote Schuur contains nine volumes of Ruskin's writings. For the strong influence of Ruskin on Rhodes, see Clark 1947: 10.

made him who he was.[13] Reade believed that, just as the early Christians had proved the value of their faith through martyrdom, so progressive people who believed in science and its possibilities would need to demonstrate the force of their convictions in overcoming a religion that no longer conformed to the ideas of the age.[14] Just as Ruskin rejected Classicism in favour of Gothic principles of art,[15] Reade viewed the Roman Empire as an even more inferior dispensation than Victorian England:

[t]he civilised world has outgrown that [Christian] religion, and is now in the condition of the Roman Empire in the pagan days—a cold-hearted infidelity above, a sordid superstition below; a school of Plutarchs who endeavour to reconcile the fables of a barbarous people with the facts of science and the lofty conceptions of philosophy; a multitude of augurs who sometime smile when they meet, but who more often feel inclined to sigh, for they are mostly serious and worthy men.[16]

Thus the model of Roman imperialism was not necessarily viewed positively by energetic nineteenth-century Englishmen such as Reade and Rhodes, who were convinced of the overwhelming importance of British science and technological progress.[17] One of the most substantial of the many biographies of Rhodes argues that he also 'imbibed a heady, mystical brew justifying and extolling the fervor of imperialism which was already turning British heads' from his reading of Gibbon's *Decline and Fall of the Roman Empire* during his years at Oxford.[18] But Gibbon's historical analysis revealed the chronic political instability and, to the Victorian mind, the moral decadence and political autocracy of the Later Roman Empire that made it a distinct failure in their eyes by comparison with its Anglo-Saxon avatar. The Romans were likened to the cruel and luxury-loving Ottoman Turks, basking in sensual sloth and self-indulgence.[19] Such at least was the view of J. R. Seeley, whose *Lectures*

[13] Reade 1934; Thomas 1996: 111; Baumgart 1982: 88–89; Marlowe 1972: 58–59; Lockhart and Woodhouse 1963: 65. Consider the following statement by Reade 1934: 407 – instantly recognisable in Rhodes's well-known paternalism towards Blacks and his detestation of 'shirking': '. . . a European government ought perhaps to introduce compulsory labour among the barbarous races that acknowledge its sovereignty and occupy its land. Children are ruled and schooled by force, and it is not an empty metaphor to say that savages are children.' Reade's book is written in a powerful rhetorical style. It went through numerous editions and was still being reprinted in 1934, shortly before the outbreak of World War II.

[14] Reade 1934: 434–35.   [15] Clark 1947: 6.   [16] Reade 1934: 434.

[17] Rhodes owned a number of books that reveal a lasting interest in such social Darwinism: Ritchie 1891; Romanes 1888; Laing 1892; Drummond 1894. Ritchie opposed Emil Reich (1890).

[18] Rotberg 1988: 95. On Rhodes' interest in Gibbon, see Wardle (this volume).

[19] For the theoretical context of Seeley's comments, see Said 1993.

and Essays, first published in 1870, is listed in the 'Literature' section of the Groote Schuur catalogue. Seeley tackled the topic of Roman imperialism in three lectures. In the first, 'The Great Roman Revolution' (1–31), he traces the process whereby Caesar wrested political control of the Republic away from his competitors, noting in passing Caesar's utter indifference to the plight of the 'provincials' (7–8, 29).[20] Caesar's success, Seeley observes, came at the expense of political freedom, which was crushed in a way that Englishmen would find difficult to understand, given their success in reconciling standing armies with freedom (12), unlike France and Russia, who had experience of Napoleon and the Czar (21). In the second, 'The Proximate Cause of the Fall of the Roman Empire' (32–58), he shows how destructive the impact of Roman imperialism on the subject people of the Empire had been,[21] and points out the resultant 'perpetual and irrepressible stream of barbaric immigration' (50). Unlike the Anglo-Saxon version, he suggests (53), Roman civilisation was 'not of this creative kind. It was military, that is, destructive'. In the third lecture, 'The Later Roman Empire' (59–88), Seeley inveighs against the increased despotism and Oriental way of life in the Roman Empire (66).[22] Rhodes must, of course, have read these lectures. What he took out of them, it seems, was that it was best to be born English and that his life's mission was to 'to make the world English'.[23]

---

[20] Seeley 1870. 7–8: '. . . there is nothing in his (i.e. Cicero's) letters to show that, in the hot discussions which must have been everywhere going on, any general principles were appealed to by the Caesarians; that it had occurred to any Caesarian to suggest, what occurs so naturally to us who know the sequel, that it was a monstrous injustice that the world should be governed in the interest of a single city; that the Senate were the authors and supporters of this system; that Caesar was the man to put it down, and had undertaken to do so. The Caesarians were a party without ideas.' On Seeley, see Hingley 2000: 23–25.

[21] Seeley 1870: 52: 'We know how dangerous is the sudden introduction of civilised habits and manners among barbarians. We know how fatally the contact of Anglo-Saxons has worked upon Indians, Australians, and New Zealanders. The effect of Roman civilisation upon Gauls and Britons was similar, if we may take the evidence of Tacitus. They exchanged too suddenly a life of rude and violent adventure for the Roman baths and schools of rhetoric.'

[22] Seeley 1870: 66: 'They (i.e. the despotic emperors) destroyed what we may call the classical view of life, which asserts human free will, and regards government merely as a useful and respectable machinery for economizing power, and introducing order, beauty, and virtue into human affairs. In place of it they introduced the Asiatic view, which rests upon unalterable necessity, and elevates government into a divinity, teaching the subject to endure whatever it may inflict, not only without resistance, but without even an inward murmur; and, in short, to say to government what religion commands us to say to Providence, "Thy will be done."'

[23] Thomas 1996: 114, quoting from Rhodes 'Confession of faith', for which see Flint 1974: 248–52. See also Sheppard 1861: 131 – a book not in the Groote Schuur library, but which Rhodes may conceivably have read in Oxford.

Rhodes' view of the benefits to the world of Anglo-Saxon rule would also have been strengthened by his reading of another book in his collection – Charles Kingsley's *Roman and Teuton*.[24] These exuberant lectures read much like sermons. Only two are relevant to the present purpose. The first, 'The Forest Children' (1–17), is a playful evocation, along the lines of a Grimm folktale, of the theme that nations, like individuals, pass through a cycle of growth, maturity and decline, applied specifically to the Teutonic race, which in Roman times was in its childhood. According to Kingsley, the Roman Empire escaped destruction and survived long enough to produce a universal religion, Christianity, only because the Teutons, with whom Seeley associated the Anglo-Saxons, were still in their infancy.[25] In the second, 'The Dying Empire' (18–51), Kingsley takes sides against those who argued that 'Roman Imperialism was the type of all good government, and a desirable precedent for ourselves'.[26] Instead, he argues, the Roman Empire was a cruel slave society (20), in which men lived only for pleasure 'like the Turkish and Chinese empires in our own days' (18). In a speech anticipating Enoch Powell's 'Rivers of Blood' oration of 1968, Kingsley vividly evokes a Britain overrun by barbarous tribes, a place where (28–29) erstwhile slaves are drafted into the British Army and later into British society. These men, he envisages, would be:

Beggars on horseback, only too literally; married, most of them, to Englishwomen of the highest rank; but looking on England merely as a prey; without patriotism, without principle; they would destroy the old aristocracy by legal murders, grind the people, fight against their yet barbarian cousins outside, as long as they were in luck; but the moment luck turned against them, would call in those barbarian cousins to help them, and invade England every ten years with heathen hordes, armed no more with tulwar and match-lock, but the Enfield rifle and Whitworth cannon.

[24] Kingsley 1864.

[25] Kingsley 1864: 13: [if the Germans had destroyed Rome earlier] 'Christianity would have been stifled in its very cradle; and with Christianity all chance – be sure of it – of their progress. Roman law, order, and discipline, the very things which they needed to acquire by a contact of five hundred years, would have been swept away. All classic literature and classic art, which they learnt to admire with an almost superstitious awe, would have perished likewise. Greek philosophy, the germs of physical science, and all that we owe to the ancients, would have perished; and we should have truly had an invasion of the barbarians, follow by truly dark ages, in which Europe would have had to begin all anew, without the help of the generations which had gone before.'

[26] Kingsley 1864: 22–23 citing the support of Professor G. Smith's *Oxford Essays* of 1856 against Richard Congreve. Congreve had made a study of the Roman empire: *The Roman Empire of the West: four lectures delivered at the philosophical institution, Edinburgh, February 1855* (1855), but opposed British rule in India in *India: Denying England's right to retain her Indian possessions* (1857), and later protested against the annexation of the Transvaal in *The Transvaal: a protest against the annexation of the Transvaal, dated 7 January 1881 and signed: Richard Congreve* (1881).

Kingsley's powerfully imaginative dramatisation of what life would be like in a Britain that followed the precedent of the Roman Empire is a brilliant and extended rant that must have made an indelible impression on Rhodes when he first read it. However, while reading Kingsley confirmed Rhodes' belief that Britons needed to bring other qualities to the imperial enterprise than the Romans had done, the theoretical problem of the expansion and decline of Roman power in the Mediterranean would also have exercised his mind during his undergraduate years. It is worth asking what histories of Rome he was likely to have read at Oxford. In the nineteenth century, the study of Roman history in Britain was strongly influenced by Niebuhr and Mommsen.[27] Rhodes owned, and presumably had read, works by both of these German historians in their English translations and they are now listed in the catalogue of the Groote Schuur library.[28] Also present are the Roman histories of Thomas Arnold, Oliver Goldsmith, Charles Merivale and Montesquieu's *Considerations on the causes of the greatness of the Romans and their decline* (1734).[29] It is difficult to say what Rhodes made of these histories. Certainly, he would have taken from Arnold the idea that the study of the past teaches students in the present moral lessons and depicts memorable human characters (such as Hannibal, to whom Arnold devoted considerable attention in his study of the Second Punic War);[30] from Goldsmith the reasons for the growth and decline of empires; and from Montesquieu a critique of sclerotic religion and the disunity of the Empire.[31]

It is abundantly clear from the events of Rhodes' life, however, that he preferred actions to ideas and that he thought of himself as living out history rather than reading about it. The comparison between Rhodes and Caesar has repeatedly been drawn.[32] The question is which one? Julius Caesar, Augustus,

[27] Dowling 1985; Gooch 1913: 14–24 and 454–74.

[28] According to the Groote Schuur library catalogue, Rhodes owned M. Isler's edition of Niebuhr's *Lectures on Roman History* (translated by H. M. Chepmell and F. Demmler, 1875) rather than his *History of Rome* (translated by J. C. Hare and C. Thirlwall, 1855). He also possessed Mommsen's *History of Rome* (translated by Dero A. Saunders and John H. Collins, 1875). The catalogue does not provide the dates of these editions.

[29] Arnold 1848; Arnold and Arnold 1886; Goldsmith 1860; Merivale 1865; Montesquieu 1965.

[30] Rhodes also owned a copy of John Pentland Mahaffy's study of Alexander (1887).

[31] Arnold 1848: vi–viii; Goldsmith 1860: iv; 'The attentive reader will no doubt come to the conclusion, that integrity at home, strict unbending justice abroad, with a love of country superior to every consideration, carried the power of Rome over every nation on the globe; and that insatiable ambition, over-refined luxury, and the abandonment of every virtue that adorns and elevates the human character, have made the Romans the pity and the scorn of every feeling mind.' Montesquieu 1965: 91–96.

[32] Hilton 2007b: 17–22.

Titus or Marcus Aurelius?[33] Like Julius Caesar, Rhodes was involved in
military action during the conquest of the kingdom of Lobengula and the
siege of Kimberley.[34] Like the Roman dictator Rhodes had diplomatic skills in
dealing with the rebellious Matabele.[35] Rhodes owned and may have studied
Warde Fowler's study of Julius Caesar as the founder of the Roman Imperial
system.[36] On the other hand, like Augustus, Rhodes had a certain inscrut-
ability, and it is perhaps no accident that John Buchan, who wrote a study of
Augustus, later visited South Africa and endorsed Rhodes' policies.[37] Rhodes
also had a physical resemblance to the Roman emperor Titus and this likeness
is accentuated in the bust of the mining magnate in the rotunda in Rhodes
House in Oxford (Fig. 3.4). Finally, Rhodes is said to have marked one
passage in the *Meditations* of Marcus Aurelius that would surely have been
significant for him in view of his allegedly precarious health. This was the
final paragraph of the work (12.36) in which Marcus Aurelius consoles his
reader for the shortness of life. This book was under his pillow in his
Muizenberg cottage when he died.[38]

[33] Rhodes also owned biographies of Hadrian and Julian: Neander 1850 and Gregorovius 1898.

[34] Rhodes himself compared his invasion of Matabele territory to the conquests of Pizarro and
Cortez: Rotberg 1988: 446. Rotberg (1988: 624) describes Rhodes' actions during the siege of
Kimberley in terms of the reckless behaviour of an Alexander during the attack on the
fortified town of the Malli in the Punjab (Arrian, *Anabasis* 6.10–11; Curtius Rufus, *History
of Alexander* 9.5) or a Caesar in the struggle against the Nervii in Gaul (*Gallic War* 2.4), both
of whom would heedlessly commit himself to the area of a battlefield where the fighting was
most intense in the knowledge that his soldiers would fight with increased valour in the
defence of their leader.

[35] As recorded on a bronze plaque on the equestrian statue of Rhodes in Kimberley. Rhodes is
seated prominently in the foreground with the Matabele indunas squatting around him in
council (Figs 3.2–3). The statue has an original Latin inscription on the dedicatory plaque,
possibly put up by the patron of the project, Alfred Beit: EHEU QUANTO MINUS EST CUM
ALIIS VERSARI QUAM TUI MEMINISSE ('Alas how much less it is to have others for
company than to remember you'). The intimate personal tone on a public monument is
remarkable.

[36] Fowler 1892: 380: 'Whether we study the government of the Empire, or its law, its religion, its
society, its army, we feel that a great change has taken place, and that even if it be a change
which in some ways, as for example in art and literature, has lowered the level of human effort,
it is yet one which has raised the mass of mankind in material well-being, and has made them
the constituent body of a great protective political union. And more than this, it has even
brought within their reach a simple and universal doctrine of right and wrong; a rule of conduct
based on beliefs and hopes, for which the older world, which knew no such union, could not, so
far as we can guess, have ever found a place. Under the Empire art and literature slowly decay,
with the decay of that civic or national life in which they seem best to flourish; but in the
imperial unity room is found for other influences more suited to the needs of the age and of
more universal efficacy.'

[37] Buchan 1937, 1903. Buchan endorsed Rhodes' labour legislation (the Glen Grey Act), 307, and
the colonisation of South Africa in general, 393.

[38] Burke et al. 1953: 24; Stead 1902: 184.

Figure 3.1 C. J. Rhodes graduating at Oxford University: bronze relief panel on the base of Rhodes' equestrian statue, Kimberley. Photograph by John Filmalter. See also Rotberg 1988: 84–107.

Friend, you have been a citizen in this great city; and what does it matter whether for five years or three? The law is the same for us all. Where is the hardship, then, if it be no tyrant's stroke, no unjust judge, that send you into exile, but the same Nature that brought you here, even as the master of the show dismisses the actor that he put on the stage?

Stead quotes, apparently verbatim, Rhodes' own expression of his Stoical and consolatory view of life, which clearly owes much to the *Meditations* of Aurelius, but also reveals Rhodes' strong identification with the Caesars of the Roman Empire:

When I was inclined to take too tragic a view of the consequences of apparently imminent disaster, I used to reflect what the old Roman emperors must have felt when (as often happened) their legions were scattered, and they fled from a

Figure 3.2 Equestrian statue of Cecil John Rhodes, Kimberley. Historical photograph ca. 1930s. See footnote 35.

Figure 3.3 Rhodes addressing the Indunas of Matabeleland: bronze relief panel on the base of Rhodes' equestrian statue, Kimberley. Photograph by John Filmalter. See footnote 35.

Figure 3.4 Bust of C. J. Rhodes, Rhodes House, Oxford.

stricken field, knowing that they had lost the empire of the world. To such men at such times it must have seemed as if their world was going to pieces around them. But after all [. . .] the sun rose the next day, the river flowed between its banks, and the world went on very much the same despite it all, and thinking of this, I used to go to bed and sleep like a child.[39]

Rhodes no doubt owed to his Classical education the strong dichotomy between civilisation and barbarism.[40] This was, of course, one of the stereotypes of ancient imperialism – for English and Blacks read Greeks/ Romans and Others – and one articulated best by Aristotle (*Pol.* 1255a26).[41] In a speech delivered on the second reading of the Glen Grey Act in the Cape parliament on 30 July 1894, Rhodes stated:[42]

What we may expect after a hundred years of civilisation I do not know. If I may venture a comparison, I would compare the natives generally, with regard to European civilisation to fellow-tribesmen of the Druids, and just suppose that they were come to life after two thousand years which have elapsed since their

---

[39] Stead 1902: 180.   [40] See, for example, Vindex 1900: 159.   [41] See Isaac 2004: 177–78.
[42] Vindex 1900: 379.

existence. That is the position. The honourable member for Fort Beaufort simply wants to get rid of the two thousand years that lie between us and the natives.[43]

When pressed on charges of atrocities committed in Matabeleland, Rhodes responded with an argument drawn from his reading of Gibbon's *Decline and Fall of the Roman Empire*:[44]

If you will wander with me into the classics, into the history of the Roman empire two thousand years ago, you will find that the conduct of a certain section was to make money by vilifying any one who got above the crowd.

The reference is cryptic but it would appear that he had in mind charges brought by informers (*delatores*) under the Roman Empire. If so, this comment reveals a lot about Rhodes' psychology: he seems to view himself as a Roman patrician general such as Tacitus' father-in-law Agricola, straining to extend the boundaries of the Empire, but ever watchful of possible charges of treason against the emperor, or, in his case, the empress, Queen Victoria. Ironically, Rhodes was implicated in the Jameson Raid, in which 63 of his followers were accused of treason and put on trial under the *Lex Julia de Maiestate* in terms of which the penalty was death.[45]

The worst side of Rhodes' character is apparent in his utterance on the education of Blacks. In his capacity as Minister for Native Affairs he toured the Eastern Cape and came to learn of the educational efforts of the Lovedale Mission – especially their education of native ministers of religion. He comments:[46]

I have travelled through the Transkei, and have found some excellent establishments where the natives are taught Latin and Greek. They are turning out Kaffir parsons, most excellent individuals, but the thing is overdone. I find that these people cannot find congregations for them. There are Kaffir parsons everywhere – these institutions are turning them out by the dozen. They are turning into a dangerous class.[47]

---

[43] Vindex 1900: 369 comments: 'Mr. Rhodes' comparison of the natives to British tribesmen of the time of the Druids conveys a deep truth in reminding us that the British Empire has to do for the native African exactly what the Roman Empire did for the native Briton, and that the duty of passing on the civilisation we have received and developed will pay us well, makes the performance of the duty a business arrangement. Our profit is the price of their schooling.' Evidence of the classical education of Vindex is apparent from his allusion to Sophocles' *Oedipus the King*, line 67.

[44] Speech delivered at a mayoral banquet, 6 January 1894, edited by Vindex 1900: 351.

[45] Van der Poel 1951: 167.   [46] Vindex 1900: 382.

[47] See also Vindex 1900: 386: 'My idea is that the natives should be kept in these native reserves and not be mixed with the white men at all.'

It should also be pointed out, however, that these attitudes were shared by some of Rhodes' contemporaries also.[48]

Rhodes' classical outlook is most evident by proxy in the architectural creations of Herbert Baker that were to form Rhodes' legacy and it is in the aesthetic domain that the Classical outlook of Rhodes and his followers is most apparent.[49] According to Greig, 'he [sc. Rhodes] wanted Baker to visit classical countries, because in classical architecture he could see a means of expressing imperialism and, by imprinting it on the minds of men, make it a permanent part of their thinking'.[50] That Baker came to share this vision is clear from his article in *The Times* (3 October 1912) in which he quotes approvingly an article in the *Round Table* in which the role of England in governing India is judged greatly superior to Rome's genius for law and order and administration. Just as the Romans celebrated in poetry their world dominion, so England had a right to claim even greater accolades.[51]

The Kimberley war memorial, for example (Fig. 3.5), owes something to Rhodes' liking for the so-called 'Tomb of Romulus' monument in the Alban Hills outside Rome. This was not the tomb of the founder of the city of Rome, although excavations in the forum had in 1899 revealed a tomb of black stone, inscribed with gold letters, which was supposed to be the tomb of Romulus, the founder.[52] It may have been that Rhodes was under the impression that the monument he had seen during his own tour of Italy was the tomb of the founder of the Roman state and that he was exploring the connection between himself as founder of the South African nation and the first Roman king. The title of Rotberg's biography is *The Founder*. However that may be, the 'tomb of Romulus' was in fact a mausoleum of the son of a Roman emperor who died in 309, located two miles outside Rome on the Via Appia leading to the Alban hills. This mausoleum consisted of a rotunda with a cupola roof, preceded by a *pronaos* similar to the Pantheon, which recalls Rhodes House in Oxford. This latter Roman monument seen by Baker in Italy consisted of 'on a high podium four tall cones, which, no doubt, represented the *metae*, or goal, of the Roman circus; and in the monument were symbols

---

[48] See, for example, Buchan 1903: 307. [49] See especially Jenkyns 1980, 1991; Vance 1997.

[50] Greig 1970: 100.

[51] Baker 1944: 219. Neoclassicism can be seen conspicuously also in Baker's design of the Bank of England in London.

[52] Smith 1899; Ashby 1904. Baker's original design featured two phallic cones resembling the *metae* of the Roman Circus Maximus. It was this design that Kipling commented on (Baker 1934: 52–53, 38). It is worth noting that Rhodes owned a copy of J. Henry Middleton (1892) and other archaeological and antiquarian works.

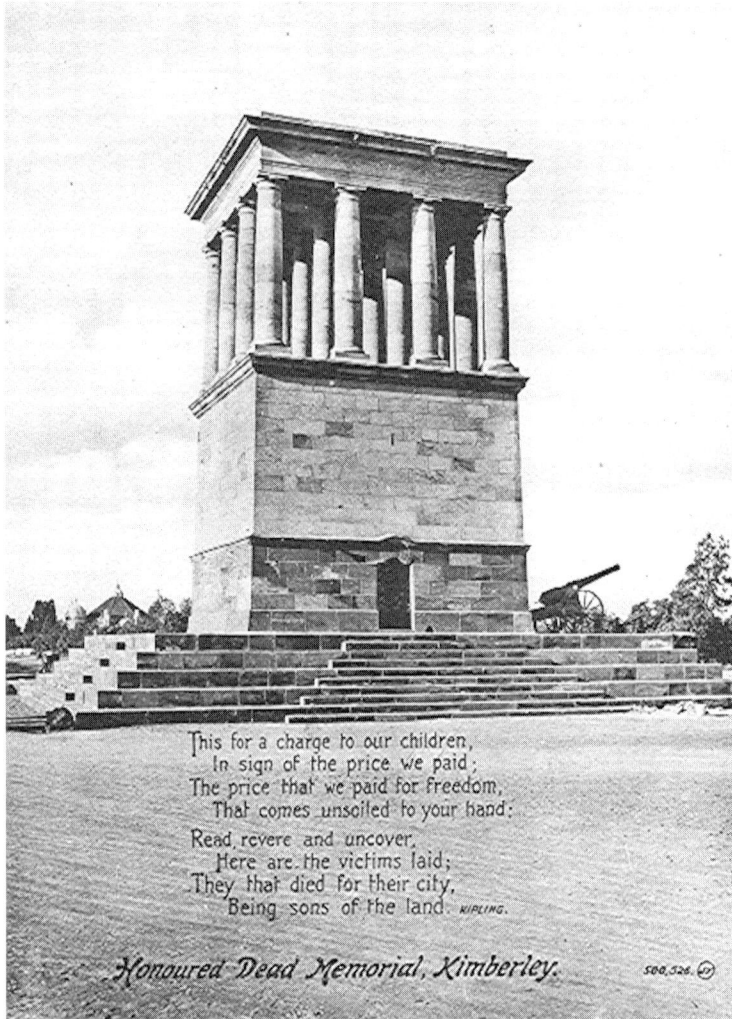

This for a charge to our children,
  In sign of the price we paid;
The price that we paid for freedom,
  That comes unsoiled to your hand;
Read, revere and uncover,
  Here are the victims laid;
They that died for their city,
  Being sons of the land. *KIPLING*

Honoured Dead Memorial, Kimberley.

Figure 3.5 Sir Herbert Baker and Francis Edward Masey, Honoured Dead Memorial, Kimberley, 1904.

of victory'.[53] Baker produced a design in which the four cones were reduced to two, representing the alliance of the two races in South Africa. Rhodes liked the design because the cones reminded him of the conical tower in the circular temple of the Zimbabwe Ruins.[54] Kipling also approved of the drawing on the grounds that they represented a number

[53] Baker 1934: 39.
[54] For Rhodes interest in African archaeology and the Zimbabwe Ruins, see Buchan 1903: 97–98. Rhodes and Buchan believed that the Zimbabwe Ruins were a Phoenician settlement.

of things allegorically including the 'two pillars of Strength and Beauty – Jorchin and Boaz – of the masonic ritual'.[55] However, such a monument was ultimately judged inappropriate for a site in the crossroads of Kimberley and instead Baker based his plan on the Tomb of Theron in Agrigentum in Sicily, which he had sketched on his tour of Classical sites.

The architecture of Rhodes House in Oxford reveals much about the ideas of its patron. Rhodes appears to have thought of himself in the Oxford manner as a philosophical rather than as a military man. His early ambitions, it has been said, were fuelled by Aristotle's emphasis on the importance of having a career sufficiently lofty to justify spending one's life to attain it, or, to put it another way, he was mindful of the same philosopher's definition of virtue as the highest activity of the soul living for the highest object in a perfect and complete life (*Nicomachean Ethics* 1098a16–18). This text is inscribed in gold uppercase Greek characters around the dome of Rhodes house in Oxford.

Goodness in Man occurs when the energy of the soul is directed towards virtue. If there are many virtues then it occurs when directed towards the best and most perfect virtue, but only in a complete life.

ΤΟ ΑΝΘΡΩΠΙΝΟΝ ΑΓΑΘΟΝ ΨΥΧΗΣ ΕΝΕΡΓΕΙΑ ΓΙΝΕΤΑΙ ΚΑΤ ΑΡΕΤΗΝ ΕΙ ΔΕ ΠΛΕΙΟΥΣ ΑΙ ΑΡΕΤΑΙ ΚΑΤΑ ΤΗΝ ΑΡΙΣΤΗΝ ΚΑΙ ΤΕΛΕΙΟΤΑΤΗΝ ΕΤΙ Δ ΕΝ ΒΙΩΙ ΤΕΛΕΙΩΙ.

To the hagiographers of Cecil John Rhodes, the mining magnate was not an imperial philosopher but a far more energetic figure – Prometheus. Rhodes is portrayed as the benevolent Greek Titan benevolently driving out Adamastor, 'the wrecker of ships' from Table Mountain, and standing on guard against 'evil'.[56] The epigram is composed in Classical Greek iambic pentameters by an acolyte, Dougal Malcolm, one of 'Milner's Kindergarten' – the ardent imperialists of the late nineteenth and early twentieth centuries.

> Τὸν ῥαιστῆρα νεῶν Ἀδαμάστορα τῆσδε Προμηθεὺς
> ἐξελάσας σκοπιᾶς ἧμαι ἀλεξίκακος.
> πόλλ' ὑπὲρ ἀνθρώπων κατ' ἐμὴν φρένα μερμηρίζων
> πόλλ' ἐπόνουν ψυχαῖς σπέρμα βαλὼν ἀρετῆς.

> I, Prometheus, having driven out Adamastor, the wrecker of ships,
>   from this mountain watch-tower, sit here a warder-off of evil;
>   pondering many things in my mind on behalf of mankind. I laboured
>   much, sowing in their souls the seeds of active virtue.

---

[55] Baker 1934: 28. Rhodes was himself a freemason: Cooper 1986: 68–69.   [56] Baker 1934: 159.

The name Adamastor comes from Luis Vaz de Camões *Lusiads*. In Canto V, stanza 51 of this poem, Adamastor, the spirit of the Cape rises from the ocean to confront the Portuguese explorers and to condemn them for daring to sail into the southern seas. When challenged, he explains that he was one of the Titans who rebelled against Jupiter after the sea nymph Thetis, who had been promised to him in marriage by her mother, rejected his love. In the war against the Olympian gods he was defeated and his body became the Cape peninsula. This justly famous episode has had an enormous influence on South African and world literature.[57] In South African writing, many poets and playwrights have made use of the name, but it is particularly associated with Roy Campbell's prophetic poem, 'Rounding the Cape', first published in 1930 in an eponymous anthology. There Adamastor 'threatens' the Portuguese, but the threat is not made specific. The poem ends with the 'murmurs' of 'Night, the Negro' in his sleep. Campbell here links Adamastor with the black people of Africa, especially as his source, Camões, explicitly describes the Titan as black. For supporters of Rhodes, the mining magnate was a figure of enlightenment who would bring civilisation to Africa and its savage people. The reference to 'seeds of active virtue' in the epigram clearly recalls the lines from Aristotle's *Nicomachean Ethics* that Rhodes admired so much and which are inscribed on the rotunda of Rhodes House in Oxford (see above).

Immediately below the Greek epigram to Rhodes as Adamastor, Baker quotes the concluding lines of Shelley's *Prometheus Unbound* (1820) 4.573–78:

> To love, and bear; to hope till Hope creates
> From its own wreck the thing it contemplates:
> Neither to change, nor falter, nor repent;
> This, like thy glory, Titan! is to be
> Good, great, and joyous, beautiful and free
> This alone Life, Joy, Empire, and Victory!

Prometheus figures on two fireplace designs in Rhodes House, Oxford (Figs 3.6–7). In the first, Prometheus takes up a burning brand from the earth. He looks over his shoulder at the arm of Zeus, which appears from a cloud. The arm wields a lightning-bolt and is accompanied by an eagle. The inscription reads in continuous uppercase classical Greek characters in four columns:

[57] For the Adamastor myth, see Hilton 2006, 2009.

Figure 3.6 Fireplace, Rhodes House, Oxford.

Figure 3.7 Fireplace, Rhodes House, Oxford.

ΔΕΞΑΙ ΡΡΟΜΗΘΕΥΝΑΜΑ
ΡΑΝΔΩΡΟΥΠΥΡΟΣ
ΚΑΙ ΤΟΙ ΦΥΛΑΞΑΙ
ΣΥΝΚΑΛΩΙΤΟΡΑΜΦΑΓΟΝ

Prometheus, take the torch
of fire that gives everything,
and guard together
with beauty the all-eating thing.

In the second a small figure is shown pinioned to Table Mountain. Over this figure an eagle circles, directing its beak towards the man. In the foreground a male figure, presumably Prometheus, lifts up the burning brand. The inscription reads:

ΦΕΥΦΦΕΥΖΕΥΣΟΡΘΕΧΡΗΣΕΦΛΟΞ
ΕΙΟΙΚΕΠΑΜΦΑΓΟΣ
ΠΑΝΩΛΕΘΡΟΝΓΗΝ
DENDRAΣUNKARΠΟΙΣΟLEIN

Alas, alas, Zeus prophesied rightly.
The all-devouring flame appears
to be all-destroying and
wastes the trees together with the fruit.

The small figure pinned to Table Mountain suggests a distinction between Rhodes and Prometheus. This would be in keeping with the pessimism of the lines. However, this fireplace design recalls a more optimistic sketch on the frontispiece to Baker's biography of Rhodes, in which a male human figure is portrayed (Fig. 3.8) seated on the mountain overlooking Table Bay with the bright light of dawn bursting over Devil's Peak (actually dawn breaks over the Hottentots Hollands Mountains to the right of the picture).

The architecture of the memorial to Rhodes on the slopes of Table Mountain is in keeping the association between Rhodes and Prometheus as it culminates in a violently energetic image of a human personification of energy leading a powerful horse (Fig. 3.9). This sculpture was donated to Rhodes by the sculptor, George Watts. It is delicately poised on a raised plinth which bears the inscription 'ENERGY: THE WORK OF G. F. WATTS R. A. AND BY HIM GIVEN TO THE GENIUS OF CECIL RHODES'. The monument itself is designed to flow down the slope of the mountain and to culminate in the equestrian sculpture. At present vegetation obscures this effect which can be seen more clearly in the photograph

Figure 3.8 Frontispiece of Herbert Baker, *Cecil John Rhodes by his Architect* (1938).

taken on completion of the monument in the Cape Archives. This famous memorial was also designed by Baker and is clearly Classical in inspiration. Rhodes is said to have had in mind the temple of Poseidon at Paestum in which lions would move through the great columns.[58] The memorial was intended to gain architectural immortality for Rhodes, as the monuments of the Caesars had done for them.[59] Clearly, however, the final monument bears little relationship to the Paestum temple.

Baker thought that the Temple of Concord at Agrigentum would suit Rhodes' idea better but the final monument clearly owes more to the Great Altar of Zeus at Pergamum (now in the Berlin Museum) or the Propylaea of the Acropolis at Athens. The possibility is mentioned by

[58] Greig 1970: 101.   [59] For a discussion of the memorial to Rhodes, see Maylam 2005: 48–54.

Figure 3.9 Memorial to Cecil John Rhodes, dedicated on 5 July 1912. Cape Town, Cape. 20 November 1993. Photograph by David Goldblatt.

Lord Curzon in his report on the memorial. Lord Curzon criticised the monument for the lack of prominence given to its main subject – Rhodes himself. He writes:

If the Athenians had erected a Memorial to Pericles, on the Acropolis at Athens, if this Memorial had taken the form of the great stairway and pillared porticoes of the Propylaea (from which the Cape Town Memorial is to a large extent adapted) and if Phideas had further undertaken to depict the patriotism or the character of Pericles by some imaginary conception at the foot of the steps – is it not certain that in visiting the site, we of a later age, would have gazed at and admired the handiwork of Pheidias, in its relation to the art of Pheidias; but when we had mounted to the summit would not our first observation have been – But where is Pericles?[60]

---

[60] Quoted from the report of Lord Curzon on the memorial held among the Early Grey papers in the Cape Archives.

The result was an imposing structure featuring a portico with six Doric columns containing four empty niches and an alcove housing the bust of Rhodes sculpted by J. W. Swan. The bust is surrounded by two inscriptions: one composed by Rudyard Kipling ('The immense and brooding spirit still shall quicken and control / Living he was the land and dead his soul shall be her soul') and another by the monument commission ('To the spirit and life work of Cecil John Rhodes who loved and served South Africa 1853 – 1902'). The bust and its inscriptions are recessive and difficult to view even from the portico itself. Full sunlight only enters the portico at dawn and does not fall on the bust itself except at the winter solstice (*experto crede*). The portico containing the bust of Rhodes is flanked by two outriding square groups of 32 Doric columns flanking at the top of the monument a cascade of broad stairs. These square groups of columns recall the Kimberley monument.

The perspective of the memorial has been described as one of 'class privilege' in the tradition of the English landscape tradition in which the viewer looks out over a picturesque scene.[61] A more natural explanation would be that this was the vantage point that Rhodes habitually used. The memorial was constructed on his favourite meditation spot on the mountain. It has also been suggested that the memorial has solved the contradiction between monument and site by splitting the focal point in two – one concentrating on the meditative bust of Rhodes and the other on Watts's equestrian statue of 'Physical Energy', one representing paternal authority or care, the other the force required to administer it. But this is to misread the monument perversely. The bust of Rhodes is linked to the physical energy statue by the flanking lions, so that a unitary flow of thought and action, intelligence and power, is represented.[62] There is no subordination of imperialist and subject, since there is no representation of the colonised people of Africa in the memorial.

The architect has enhanced the Mediterranean feel of the monument by planting Corsican pines at the rear of the monument and oleander bushes around the sides. These plants were a popular subject in the neoclassical art of Lawrence Alma-Tadema, who was a contemporary of Rhodes (Fig. 3.10). The reshaping of the landscape to suit the aesthetic preferences of the colonisers has been noted by Wittenberg:[63]

This process of effacing what is there and replacing it with the culture of the coloniser, in this case classical ideals, is also clearly evident in the site of Rhodes memorial. The landscape itself is appropriate, domesticated. Around Rhodes

[61] Bunn 1998: 99.   [62] Ibid.   [63] Wittenberg 1993.

Figure 3.10 Lawrence Alma-Tadema, 'The Voice of Spring' (1910): detail with Corsican pines. Oil on canvas, 48.6 × 114.9 cm.

Memorial this was done by replacing the indigenous fynbos vegetation by exotic species: Mediterranean stone pines, firs, oaks and green pastures where visitors, in Grey's words, could come in reverent homage and revive their flagging spirits by 'feasting their eyes on the rich green carpet beneath the pines' (*CT* 6 July 1912).

However, due consideration has to be made for the instinctively European viewpoint of the English settlers in the Cape. The inverse relationship between the task of Europeans to civilise North Africa and the task of Europeans to bring enlightenment to South Africa was noted already by John Herschel, one of the leading exponents of the English Enlightenment, during his famous philanthropic and educational visit to the Cape in 1834, although he was pessimistic about the outcome.[64] The 'white man's burden' of civilising the African continent, is a ubiquitous theme in the literature of the day. Mr Lawley, a contemporary of Rhodes, stated at Bulawayo in a speech on 17 September 1898 that 'what was attempted by Alexander, Cambyses, and Napoleon, we practical people are going to finish'.[65] This was a sentiment shared by Rhodes, according to the editor

[64] See Hilton 2006b.   [65] Vindex 1900: 609.

of his speeches.[66] Somewhat later Sir Lionel and Lady Florence Phillips donated money to excavations in Egypt and Rome and had Herbert Baker design a Mediterranean villa for them in Johannesburg. The descriptions of the Cape by Dorothea Fairbridge give a good idea of this neo-Classical vision of the Cape.[67] For her, the Helderberg was Soracte, Pan piped on Table Mountain; the raging south-east wind was a combination of the Furies Alecto, Megaera and Tisiphone; the Hottentots were the mysterious Hyksos of Egypt; a coloured labourer treading grapes becomes Bacchus; allegorical female figures appear as the Winged Victory of Samothrace; and the heroic forebears of patriotic South Africans were Judaeo-Christian heroines: 'the mothers in Israel, the women of Sparta, the matrons of Rome, from Deborah to Antigone, from the daughter of Jephtha to Iphigeneia, a procession of noble shadows came down the ages and kissed her on the forehead'.[68]

However, to some extent the memorial is, in fact, indigenous. It is constructed using South African rough-hewn stone. However, Bunn sees in the squaring and dressing of the stone an 'imperialist vision' that recalls the use on stone in classical and medieval ruins. He writes: 'the idea of bringing territories under control of the metropolitan paternal authority is closely associated with the idea of following older precedents, such as the Roman, Babylonian or Phoenician empires, with whom there is sympathetic identification'.[69] He notes that the expedition into the hinterland in Rider Haggard's *She* is inspired by the 'discovery of ancient stone masonry'.[70] The connection is reinforced by the gesture made by the rider in Watts's equestrian statue. The rider shades his eyes to look northwards towards Africa as if surveying further lands to conquer. Bunn notes that, by the use of dressed stone, which is reminiscent of Roman architecture, 'Imperial power is dramatized in an almost erotic desire to carve a place for the white body out of the very rock of Africa'.[71]

The stairs are lined on each side by four bronze lions cast by J. W. Swan (Fig. 3.9) which call to mind Lawrence Alma-Tadema's famous painting

---

[66] Vindex 1900: 13: 'The magnetism of the Dark Continent, with its vast unknown interior, which had touched even world-worn warriors like Cambyses and Napoleon, was brought to bear on him when young enough to feel its full influence.'

[67] For the Cape as 'Mediterranean' in culture, see Merrington 2001 and this volume.

[68] Fairbridge 1928: 188–89. See Merrington 1995: esp. 648–50.   [69] Bunn 1998: 96.

[70] The 'problematic relationship' between monument and site is also noted by Bunn 1998: 95, who notes the use of indigenous stone as a reference to classical imperialistic monuments in Baker's work.

[71] Bunn 1998: 99.

Figure 3.11 Lawrence Alma-Tadema, 'A Coign of Vantage' (1895). Oil on canvas, 64 × 44.5 cm.

'Coign of Vantage' (Fig. 3.11).[72] The lions also add an Egyptian touch in keeping with Rhodes' own fascination with that country, and hinting at the imperialist goal of constructing a chain of British colonies from the Cape to Cairo. Rather than being inspired by the series of ram-headed lions of Pharaonic Karnak, however, these were more probably influenced by the

---

[72] For this see Jenkyns 1991: 192–250, esp. 235.

sphinx-headed lions that flank Cleopatra's Needle on the Thames Embankment near Waterloo Bridge, which had been brought to this location amid great publicity and with help from Egyptomanes with Cape connections in 1878.[73]

Rhodes was not a wholehearted enthusiast for the Classics, as is clear from the criteria for selection of Rhodes scholars laid down in his will.[74] He appears to have viewed his studies as more of a pastime or as one of the standard accomplishments of an English gentleman.[75] It is true that he took his Liddell and Scott with him to Africa and that this lexicon was in his baggage at the diamond fields of Kimberley,[76] but he probably needed it only to improve his Greek to gain admission to an Oxford college, where proficiency in Greek was a requirement until 1920.[77] He certainly preferred to read the Classics in translation and commissioned his own versions at great expense.[78] Much of the neoclassical character of the Rhodes memorial can be attributed to Baker, rather than to Rhodes. Other buildings designed by him show strong Classical influences.[79]

Perhaps the last word should be left to the Afrikaans poet, Peter Blum. In an Italian sonnet consisting of two quatrains and two tercets, and entitled 'Oor monnements gepraat', he writes a dramatic monologue in the local dialect of the local 'coloured' population:[80]

Wat spog jul so met julle monnement?
Hy's groot ma' lielak, en hy staan so kaal
da' op sy koppie. Wie't vir hom betaal –
al daai graniet en marmer en sement?

O ja, hy's groter as 'n sirkustent –
ma' waa's die pêd, die mooi nooi innie saal?
die lekka *clowns*, die leeus in hul kraal?
Nei, daa's g'n spôts nie vir jou Kaapse kjend!

Hier het ons stetjoes, elkeen soos 'n mens:
ou Afduim-Murray, Hofmeyr met sy pens;
hier's Jan van Riebeeck, bakgat aangetrek

[73] On Cape involvement in the transportation of Cleopatra's Needle, see Hilton 2006b: 117–34.
[74] See Stead 1902: 36–44, quoting Rhodes himself (39): 'You know I am all against letting the scholarships [go?] merely to people who swot over books, who have spent all their time over Latin and Greek.'
[75] See Burke et al. 1953: 25; Michell 1910: I.81.   [76] Burke et al. 1953: 25.
[77] According to Rotberg (1988: 86), social rather than linguistic factors blocked his entry to University College, Oxford.
[78] His library at Groote Schuur contains six bound volumes of typescript translation of Greek and Latin Classics. See Wardle below.
[79] For these see Baker 1944.   [80] Blum 1955: 46.

in sy *plus-fours*; Cecil Rhodes wat jou wys
wa' die reisiesbaan lê; en vorie Paalmint-hys
ou Mies Victôria met ha' klein spanspek.

(Why do you brag so about your monument?
It's big, but ugly, and he stands so naked
On his hill there. Who paid for it?
All that granite, marble and cement?

Oh yes, it is bigger than a circus tent,
But where's the pony, the pretty girl in the saddle?
The jolly clowns, the lions in their cage?
No, there are no sports there for your child of the Cape!

We have statues here, every one just like a person:
Old Murray with his missing thumb, Hofmeyr with his paunch;
Here's Van Riebeeck jauntily attired

In his plus-fours; Cecil Rhodes who shows you
Where the race course is, and in front of the Parliament
Old Miss Victoria with her little melon.)

This poem deliberately undercuts the grandeur of historical monuments and statues and emphasises the distance between the lofty imperialist ideals of the artists and architects who made them and the way they are perceived by the local Coloured population. According to the speaker in the poem, the statue of Rhodes in the Gardens is pointing to the racecourse rather than to the unexplored and underdeveloped north. Not only does the poem question the expense of the elaborate granite, marble and cement that went into the construction of the Rhodes memorial, but he (or she) describes the nude equestrian rider as ugly, and pities his exposure to the cold winds. For the speaker in the poem horses mean only a pretty girl on a pony and clowns doing tricks in the circus. The lions of the monument recall circus lions in their cages. The Dutch Reformed missionary Andrew Murray, whose statue stands in Wellington (1923), is referred to as 'old Murray with his missing thumb'; attention is drawn to Jan Hofmeyr's large belly in another statue; the monument to Jan van Riebeeck on the foreshore is described as 'nattily togged out in his plus-fours'; and Queen Victoria's imperial orb becomes a small melon. Altogether, a different world from the grandiose vision of statesmen.[81]

---

[81] A similar critical approach to memorials to Rhodes can be seen in the works of Denise Penfold and other artists on the website Artthrob as part of a Heritage Day 1999 exhibition, Denise

Rhodes, like most of his contemporaries, often thought about the world in terms of the ancient classical authors. His moral and aesthetic ideas were shaped by the ancient Mediterranean view of man. In particular, he promoted Aristotle's definition of energetic virtue to be the first principle of his ethical life. While we have enough of Rhodes' own speeches to be able to say that he thought his task resembled in some way that of the Caesars – to bring Western civilisation to the barbarians – it is also true that his memory has been shaped by his Classicising architect and Classically educated contemporaries. His friends viewed him as a Romantic demigod, a Prometheus, whose task it was to bring the blessings of civilisation to the world. They saw the Cape as the counterpart of the Mediterranean and tried to construct a neoclassical fantasy on the slopes of Table Mountain. Rhodes and his associates saw no traces of culture in the Cape, so they set about trying to realise their own vision of what it should be, drawing from the ancient Mediterranean civilisations to do so. The aesthetic of Rhodes, Baker, Grey and Curzon was neoclassical and as such inevitably imperial. However, Rhodes himself was actuated by far larger and more pragmatic and quasi-Darwinian ideas – to corner the wealth of the new land and to control its domains – and these ideas are probably universal and in no way unique to Rome or Greece. It may even be said that, although Rhodes and his contemporaries attempted to recreate the Mediterranean cultures in southern Africa, they missed some of the more lasting and fundamental ideas produced by Rome, such as universal humanism and the Hellenistic brotherhood of man.[82]

Penfold, *P. T. O. – Public monuments reconsidered* www.artthrob.co.za/99oct/reviews.html. In these the statue of Rhodes in the Cape Town Gardens was weighed down with bricks on string (John Nankin), lions on the Rhodes memorial were enclosed in a cage (Brendan Dickerson) and the Rhodes Memorial bust was given a heavy pink heart inscribed with the names of African possessions (Penfold).

[82] This chapter was written before the 2015 'Rhodes Must Fall' campaign in South Africa, which was later taken up at the University of Oxford. These demonstrations against Rhodes' imperial ideals and his exploitation of the natural resources of South Africa to finance them underline how controversial he was and still is in the debate surrounding the economic development and political transformation of the country.

4 | The 'Mediterranean' Cape: Reconstructing an Ethos

PETER MERRINGTON

> Haply 'twas here the Titans hurled their last;
> The rocks remain.
> Here crag-drifts at the ensuing gods they cast –
> Not all in vain.
> Here, at this world-end, space to sleep they found –
> To fold their goats, and reap their furrowed ground.[1]

In his memoirs, the Cape-born mural artist Jan Juta recalls a family Shakespeare performance on the mountain slopes behind Cecil Rhodes's great villa of Groote Schuur.[2] It took place at some point in the late 1890s, when Rhodes was Premier of the Cape Colony and Juta's father was Cape Attorney General. The scene he refers to was from *A Midsummer Night's Dream*. Rhodes and Rudyard Kipling were present (Kipling, a near neighbour, 'loved the play and directed the whole idea, acting the role of Bottom himself'), and the Juta and Kipling children took part. The setting was spectacular, with the Table Mountain chain looming directly above, the lower slopes planted with stone pines as if it were an Italian landscape, and the view below looking out over the wooded Peninsula and white lime-washed farmhouses, across to the unspoilt 'water meadows' (the then-current phrase for 'wetlands') of the Cape Flats, with sea on either side and the far mountains of the escarpment in the distance. The *Dream* presented a fantasy world of Greek Arcadian antiquity interpreted and blended with English folklore by the 'English Bard' as Shakespeare was patriotically termed. Kipling worked on his English national histories during his sojourns in Cape Town. *Puck of Pook's Hill* opens, in fact, with three children informally staging, outdoors, the identical scenes from the *Dream*. Rhodes ('fascinated by Kipling', as Juta says) would have approved – his life mission, as his hagiographers avowed, was spurred by the words of John Ruskin, urging young Englishmen to emulate ancient

---

[1] From A. S. Cripps, 'Saturnia Regna', cited by Fairbridge 1928: 185 (as epigraph to her final chapter, 'The spell of the Cape'). Cripps was a graduate of Trinity College, Oxford, and then-Rhodesian missionary and poet.

[2] Juta 1972: 52.

Rome and build colonies as fast as they could for the greater good of Britain – in the Elizabethan spirit of Raleigh, Drake and Frobisher.[3] The caste and audience, the script, context and setting, spoke of deep cultural fantasies with which to adorn and to reinforce a British loyalist colonial presence in South Africa.

The imported stone pines are still there, behind Groote Schuur estate. The extensive mountainside woods and forests remain. Rhodes bequeathed a swathe of mountain and his vast estate to the South African nation. Parts of the Cape Peninsula retain an Arcadian and 'Mediterranean' atmosphere. The symmetrical, baroque and on occasion Palladian, white, gabled and thatched Cape Dutch farmsteads (including Groote Schuur) were adopted as the type for a national architectural idiom.[4] The genteel loyalist vision, with its emphasis on cultivated natural landscapes, gardens, arboreta and domestic architecture, high literature and the classics as mainstay of a liberal education, became – for a transitionary but formative period in the making of the new nation state of the Union of South Africa – the leading vision. It set the tone, the agenda and a cumulative prospectus for the cultural identity of the nation at large, between more or less the years 1895 and 1915 – years that bracket the establishment in 1910 of the Union of South Africa. It was an elitist vision, originating in the Cape Peninsula and sponsored by the wealth of politically sympathetic or familiarly related mining magnates on the Witwatersrand and in Kimberley.[5] It was a class act, in a world where all social relations including race relations were dominated by protocols of social class in the later nineteenth-century English sense of the term.

Foremost among this elite caste of imaginers was the Cape author and acknowledged 'nation builder' Dorothea Fairbridge, who picked up on Shakespeare's and Kipling's theme when writing about Kirstenbosch Botanical Gardens. Kirstenbosch was laid out in 1913 on the same Rhodes estate, a kilometre or two from the Groote Schuur site, at the instigation of Fairbridge and her friends. She speaks of the precinct as follows:

Come higher up the hill-side to where, from a great rock, you may see your goodly heritage, from Cape Point even to Table Bay. The forest primeval still remains in

---

[3] Ruskin's inaugural lecture as Slade Professor of Fine Art at Oxford, 8 February 1870, reproduced in Boehmer 1998: 16–20.

[4] See Baker 1909. Here he explicitly compares Cape Dutch building styles with Mediterranean styles, and compares climates and the quality of sunlight.

[5] A comprehensive reconstruction of the ethos and the main protagonists, their cultural vision and links to the mining houses, is given by Gutsche 1966.

places, such as Kirstenbosch, though fast falling elsewhere. There is a mighty clump of silver-trees, gnarled and twisted, but crowned with radiance, where once I heard a little boy say in hushed tones – 'This is the wood of fairies and enchantments.' And so it is. Did we not know, on good authority, that Puck has never left England, we should look for him here. But sit still – very still – and the silver-tree wood will soon be full of voices which will charm you with no mortal spell.[6]

Fairbridge extends her gesture to the world of Arcady:

On that night of nights, when the awed whisper ran through the world – 'Pan – Pan is dead' – did the gods of Greece and Rome in very truth droop and die? Or were they drawn into the service of the new faith, and bent to its use, until the altars which had been raised to Venus Anadyomene became the altars of the Blessed Virgin, and the garlands which had been twined for the brows of Apollo rested upon the head of St John?

. . . .

And if this be so, and Pan and the fauns and dryads not dead, but only in their own places, we in the Cape Peninsula know where they are to be found. Mark Phoebus Apollo as he rises in his strength from behind the Drakenstein Mountains.[7]

This essay is not about the classics as a discipline, but rather the classical (and generic 'Mediterranean') world as ethos in South Africa. Interpreting Cape landscape and history from their Western European frames of reference, Juta, Fairbridge and their social caste developed a vision that was intended, through various forms of narrative and by means of material and textual images and symbols, to explain and valorise the new country at large, and identify and espouse a related sense of 'heritage' for the land and its people. Fairbridge took the phrase 'goodly heritage' from Psalm 16. This phrase was frequently quoted at the time – a shibboleth of national (and global) English identity that brought into the folkloric equation a sense of Judaeo-Christian destiny (vide Kipling's 'Recessional'). 'A goodly heritage' stood as mnemonic for an entire heritage paradigm that emerged in the English-speaking world from the 1890s onwards, embracing legal, political, public cultural, ethnic and spiritual dimensions of the concept.[8] Graeco-Roman and English folkloric antiquity were intimately part of this densely subscribed vision.

Timing, place and space are key components in the vision. Much has been written over the past decade on both time and place (and space) in relation to identity at all levels, from the personal to the national and beyond. It is a commonplace among commentators on these matters that

---

[6] Fairbridge 1928: 188.   [7] Ibid., 185.
[8] The idea of a period 'heritage paradigm' was proposed by the present author: Merrington 2006.

the period in question, the cusp between the liberal humanist world of the nineteenth century and the cosmopolitan platform of the twentieth, casts up momentous new understandings of both time and place.[9] In the arts, Modernism is the name for this broad shift towards a new modernity where time, place and space are the governing topoi; and a reconstruction of the nation-building ethos in South Africa at the time needs to allow a modernist context.

The spirit of the times encouraged such a context and there is plenty of evidence of a desire in South Africa to embrace aspects of modernism; but the facts of social and cultural life in this country at the turn of the century were abundantly contrary. The land was in a state of near-abjection and fundamental reconstruction after the South African War of 1899–1902. Tough sectarian politics engaged peoples' energies. The defeated Afrikaner-Dutch were in dire need of social upliftment. Black South Africa was largely still a rural peasantry – soon to be further challenged by the 1913 SA Natives' Land Act. Modernity, in South Africa, meant two things – a new political dispensation under the auspices of a cosmopolitan British imperial regime and the concomitant emphasis on imported 'progressive' cultural and economic activity. Modernism is a self-conscious awareness of period modernity, and by this definition a kind of modernism drove the visioning of the new nation – though, just as in the modernist experience in England (distinct from the continental European experience), South African modernism was at times elite and reactive, dominated by senses of the land, ruralism and ancient title (as in Forster's *Howard's End*, or in the Sackville-West mould).

In South Africa the modernising/sentimental-modernist vision was interpreted by the dominant ethos in various overlapping ways. The first is that the Cape has a generalised and composite 'Mediterranean' climate and geographical character.[10] A second, related to this, was the Cape as Arcadian. A third, of particular importance, is evident from the quest for a local 'vernacular'. This quest stemmed directly from national cultural debates in England and Europe, with a move away from the nineteenth-century Gothic public imagination to national or nationalist vernacular idiom in language, the performing arts, architecture, gardening and the folklorist movement in Western Europe with its ethnic sentiment. In England the trend towards vernacular idiom was seen initially in the

---

[9] See e.g. Thacker 2003, for a good survey of literature on the topic of modernity, modernism and theories of space and place. The locus classicus for these topics in relation to the Mediterranean is Fussell's *Abroad* (1980).

[10] Dallman 1998: 119–42.

Arts and Crafts Movement and, partially, among the pre-Raphaelite Brotherhood and their successors, and thereafter in the mid-nineties with the foundation of the National Trust, *Country Life* magazine and Ebenezer Howard's Garden Cities movement, as well as developments at Stratford-upon-Avon, the vernacular architectural and gardening revival, and the rise in popularity of the historical performance genre of 'new pageantry' or historical pageantry.[11]

Most of these events and trends had some bearing on initiatives in the Cape at the time when South African Union within the British Empire was debated and established. Implicated in the Mediterranean and Arcadian views of the Cape was a newly energised sense of 'Englishness', which expressed itself in a nostalgia for all things 'Elizabethan'. In sum, a new emphasis on vernacular (local and national) was held in conjunction with a renewed adaptation of classical antiquity – a combination that served British dominion politics of identity by shaping 'folk' sentiment within the universalising global ethos of empire.

The main lobby behind the Anglicisation of the 'new South Africa' was Alfred Milner's group of young Oxford graduates whom he recruited to manage the region after the South African War. Milner was educated at Balliol under Benjamin Jowett's neo-Hegelian philosophical regime and its promotion of ideals of citizenship, duty and the state. Most of his 'Kindergarten' received similar tuition. Dominant among the neo-Hegelians was F. H. Bradley, philosopher and classical scholar, brother to A. C. Bradley the pioneer tutor in English literary studies (and Shakespeare – the 'national bard' – in particular). Thus, in the formative education of this echelon of political control in the years leading to Union, the twin paradigms of classicism and Shakespearean Englishness were implicit. They can be traced in the subsequent work of such Kindergarten fellows as John Buchan, Phillip Kerr – Marquess of Lothian – and Lionel Curtis, the advocate of Commonwealth 'closer union'. This Kindergarten think tank with lifelong ties to Balliol, New College and All Souls, and an academicism fused with an overriding sense of political and civic duty, brought – with their political mission – a lively sense of 'heroic' comradeship in exile, expressed here in jocular tone by Leo Amery:

'[A]n All Souls' Gaudy, celebrated in Johannesburg *super flumina Babylonis*, by Robinson, Peter Perry, Brand, and myself [all 'kindergarten' colleagues], ending in

---

[11] Tillyard has convincingly demonstrated how the late nineteenth-century aesthetic movements such as those referred to here were at the root of English modernism (1988). The same pattern is discernible in South Africa.

a drive by a glorious full moon, Peter and myself standing on the seat of the Cape cart and chanting Homer.[12]

Their values, vision and mission were given experiential shape in South Africa and thereafter extended to the broader Commonwealth platform up until at least the mid-1930s.[13] Quaint yet hegemonic Englishness (in the vein of Rudyard Kipling's *Puck of Pook's Hill* and *Rewards and Fairies*) became modulated into a ubiquitous global cultural discourse epitomised at popular and domestic level in the widely circulated children's educational material of Arthur Mee – a world of intrepid navigators (vide the Oxford think tank that superseded the Kindergarten, the 'Raleigh Club' and its toast to the 'Empire of the Bretaygnes'), Cavaliers and Roundheads, explorers and nation-builders, Arthurian romance, chivalry, English ruralism and 'faerie', and behind these national figures the eternal shaping 'universality' of Greece and Rome. In this context, it might be concluded that South Africa circa 1910 was inducted into a pro-tempore globalised ethos that was dominated by a loose model of classical sentiment.[14]

The period material that reveals the twin emphases of Englishness and Mediterranean antiquity in the Cape speaks, variously, of 'progressive' British modernity alongside the deep *ur*-precedents of the ancient world; or as the universally 'modern' or relevant ethos of the classical world alongside prized Anglo-Saxon/Celtic and Norman English cultural legacies. Set up against these colonial models was an interpretation of local Cape Afrikaner culture as rebarbative, ill-educated, superstitious and myopic, mired in an uninspiring and un-self-reflective culture that discounted its own finer legacy. This finer legacy was, to the colonising mind, landscape and architecture. Thus, since the 1890s and the importation to the Cape of ideas of vernacular revival, Cape English commentators evolved a high-minded discourse around the provenance, history, legacy and conservation of 'Cape Dutch' baroque farmsteads and Palladian architecture. The narrative removed this topic from Dutch/Afrikaner ownership and clad it in self-appointed interpretations of French Huguenot grace and refinement.

A particular challenge to local Afrikaner nationalism was the importation, via the Milnerite graduates and by the appointment of R. F. L. Hoernlé

---

[12] Amery 1953: I, 321.

[13] For detailed background to Oxford and the idea of the British Empire and Commonwealth, see Madden and Fieldhouse 1982. Nimmocks 1968 is authoritative on the Oxford background of this group, as is O'Brien 1979 on their leading figure.

[14] The Kindergarten member Lionel Curtis's three-volume magnum opus, *Civitas Dei*, is testament to the 'high seriousness' of this globalising project 1938.

as first Professor of Philosophy at the new University of Cape Town, of a globalising neo-Hegelian philosophy of history, which in effect eclipsed local attempts at historiography.[15] More immediately, for the purpose of this essay, Hegel's *Philosophy of History* brought with it a powerful but disabling metaphor concerning civilisation, the sun and enlightenment. This text notoriously speaks of the passage (meaning evolutionary history) of civilisation across the globe from east to west with the perceived path of the sun along the latitudinal belt of China, India, Persia, Greece, Rome and Western Europe. Africa is left out by the logic of Hegel's analogy, standing only on the 'threshold of history', save for Egypt and Carthage on its Mediterranean coastline.[16]

The task for these neo-Hegelian emissaries was to visualise a modern Western-modelled nation state at the southern tip of Africa, brought into the global narrative of Hegel's view of history, and yoked by strategic and cultural geography, as well as by British imperial sentiment, with a 'family of nations' and with Europe.[17] Dawning, sunrise, torchbearers, the helio-tropic imagery of the European Enlightenment and Hegel in particular, spoke of an assumed awakening of consciousness that, in context, was exclusively a colonialist European cultural archetype. Dorothea Fairbridge, born in Cape Town in 1862 and regarded in her day as a South African loyalist nation builder, celebrated the full gamut of neo-Hegelian, Milnerite and British imperial sentiment in her 13 books on South Africa. With her own experience of the socially requisite travel abroad, she replicates the iconography:

Once, at five of an April morning, I saw the day-spring in Spain. . . .. It flushed the distant mountains with wine-colour. All Spain seemed bathed in glory – the glory of her past.

But, to those who watch the sun break from behind the South African moun-tains, it is a sign set in the sky, a beacon-light of hope for the future of this young country.[18]

One more prefatory point must be made: the period material set out in this essay, at the Cape as no doubt elsewhere in fin de siècle British colonial society, is a thick discourse of identity and heritage-invention, evident in

---

[15] See Nash 1985.   [16] Hegel 1872: 93, 105.

[17] Lionel Curtis and Philip Kerr of the Kindergarten began and edited a monthly journal, *The State*, in South Africa from 1908 to 1912 for the express purpose of propagandising such a model of a new nation state.

[18] Fairbridge 1928: 186–87. Paul Fussell suggested that nineteenth-century English culture was dominated by lunar imagery while the twentieth century exhibited a rampant 'heliophily'. Fussell 1980: 137–40.

journalism, documentary and history writing, travel narratives, fiction, conservation agendas, new architectural initiatives, the institutions of civil society (libraries, elite schools, universities, the Established Church, philosophical and scientific bodies) and their interaction with the colonial and imperial state. This interaction, official or unofficial, might best be conceived as performance. At every level or reach of the elite discourse there is evidence of platform, cast(e) and audience, script and scene-setting, gesture, costume, personae, rehearsal and the careful calibrating of voice.

1.   The Cape as 'Mediterranean'

It is common ground among geographers that the Western Cape has a 'Mediterranean' climate and ecology. Modern climate categories were first established, based on observations of flora, by the Russian scientist Wladimir Koppen between 1884 and 1900, and these included the extension of the idea of 'Mediterranean' locales to ecologies far from the Midland Sea, in parts of Australia, California, Chile and South Africa.[19] The history of adoption and use of this category by climatologists in South Africa is beyond the scope of the present paper but would contribute to a cultural history of colonial science and its continuing paradigms. Flora became a theme in the emergence, at that very time between the 1880s and 1900, of the concept of Africana.[20] Victorian habits of observation, specimen gathering, book and art collecting, gardens and arboreta, and villa-construction for the genteel, underpin the rise of 'Africana'; and the rapid development of interest in this new field of activity and knowledge indicates a sense among the post-Victorian colonial elite that the new country was worth 'owning' in the sense of avowal or serious acknowledgement. Africana became the term for a local and national vernacular that was deemed worthy of assessment, possession and demonstration.

   Abroad, the same social caste already espoused its affinity with the Mediterranean – for extended vacations, study tours, diplomatic romance and intrigue, liberated sexuality, adventure, identification with the antique world, valetudinarian concerns and affordability for the genteel poor. Much has been written on the subject of English society in Rome and Naples. Travel scholarship over the past decade has explored the itineraries

---

[19]   The concept of a 'Mediterranean' climate category was introduced in 1884 by the Russian-born geographer Wladimir Köppen, with his world system of climate categories. See McKnight and Hess 2000: 200–1.

[20]   See Van Sittert 2004.

and practices of characters such as Amelia Edwards on the Nile, or the turbaned John Lane and his *The Manners and Customs of the Modern Egyptians*. Most of English society with any pretension to interest in their colonial world spent a season or so in Egypt or passed through Suez on the way to India. While elite English social mobility was global it was centrally defined by Graeco-Roman and Levantine or Middle Eastern affiliations. Thomas Cook, who opened up the Mediterranean for a new caste of English travellers or group tourists, was merely tracing well-established social patterns; and it is no surprise that when Cook and Sons began their first packaged tours in South Africa (sightseeing of the battlefields of the South African War) their promotional material was modelled on their Middle Eastern programmes.[21]

Several of the dominant figures in South Africa during that war had also gained, or advanced, their colonial experience in Egypt – Kitchener and Milner in particular. Milner's *England in Egypt* was a high-handed memorandum for modern British colonial administration that clearly determined his views on how to manage South Africa. With Milner and his latter-day colonialism came a host of privileged visitors, also primed by their Mediterranean experience and ready to draw comparisons. The *Egyptian Gazette* of the period gives detailed notice of famous travellers and their movements between the Cape, Suez, Cairo and England, and the events of the Egyptian social season. Cairo appears to have been treated as a stage setting by these visitors, both as a strategic political platform and as mise en scène of a costume drama in the spirit of the *Ballets Russes* and their popular Orientalism. Further, commentators in Cairo speculated on the northward movement of South African settlers.

The 'Cape-to-Cairo' continental fantasy, mostly associated with Cecil Rhodes and his vision of a north–south railway and telegraph, was held before the public eye for several decades, circa 1890 to 1930, in a variety of contexts (Figs 4.1–2).[22] This fantasy is a strategic geographical vision but it also served ideological purposes, further reinforcing the idea that the Cape was somehow yoked to the northern or Mediterranean seaboard of Africa, over and against the main extent of the continent – in consonance with the Hegelian view of Africa and of civilisation. John Buchan cited Roman expansionary initiative in his own comment on the Cape-to-Cairo axis:

[21] Bickford-Smith 2009.

[22] The main vehicle for this concept was the *Africa News and Cape-to-Cairo Gazette*, edited for several decades in London by an expatriate South African journalist, Leo Weinthal, who also published a five-volume opus, *The Story of the Cape to Cairo Railway and River Route, 1887–1922* (1922), as well as guidebooks to Egypt.

Figure 4.1 Ex libris logo of Sidney Mendelssohn (1860–1917), depicting a map of the Cape-to-Cairo route and listing the names of famous modern travellers. A diamond merchant turned book collector and amateur scholar, he compiled *Mendelssohn's South Africa Bibliography* (1910) as well as books on Jewish history.

The romance which is inseparable from all roads belongs especially to those great arteries of the world which traverse countries and continents, and unite different zones and climates, and pass through extreme variations of humankind. . . . And it is a peculiarity of the world's roads that this breath of romance blows most strongly on the paths which point to the Pole-star. The Aemilian Way, up which the Roman legions clanked to the battlefields of Gaul and Britain, or that great track which leads through India to the mountains of the north and thence to the steppes of Turkestan, captures the fancy more completely than any lateral traverse of the globe. . . . Of all north roads I suppose the greatest to be that which runs from the Cape to Egypt, greatest both for its political meaning, the strangeness of the countries to which it penetrates, the difficulties and terrors of the journey, and, above all, for the fact that it is a traverse of the extreme length of a vast and mysterious continent.

   With a profound respect for the road, I am constrained to admit that it makes bad going, . . . and that it is apt to cease suddenly and leave the traveller to his own

Figure 4.2 'Cape to Cairo': the Rhodes Colossus, caricature by Edward Linley Sambourne, *Punch* 10 December 1892.

devices. But for the eye of Faith, that wonderful possession of raw youth and wise old age, it is as broad and solid as the Appian Way; the wheels of empire and commerce pass over it, and cities, fairer than a mirage, seem to rise along its shadowy course.[23]

From the world of highly mobile tourists, administrators and military and their voyaging between, in particular, the Mediterranean and India, there is a large archive of commentary from the period in which the Cape is compared with the antique world. A variety of extended quotations are given here in order to replicate the ethos of the comparisons. The topic is

---

[23] Buchan 1903: 146–48.

'discursively bound', all the more so in terms of period rhetoric and textual ornament.

In his memoirs, the architect Sir Herbert Baker (Cecil Rhodes's protégé, designer of the Union Buildings in Pretoria and the Tuscan-styled Rhodes Memorial, among much else) recollects his sense of Cape landscape from some forty years prior:

> The view from the Grotto, as it was called [a cottage on the Groote Schuur estate on the slopes of Table Mountain], was of great beauty; it was a narrow vignette of that seen from the garden above Groote Schuur, the firwoods of the Flats and the distant blue-grey mountains being framed and thrown back in perspective by the dark velvet-green stone-pines, as was Turner's use of the pine tree in the foregrounds of his Italian landscapes.[24]

In the same text Baker speaks of 'the air on the top of [Table Mountain], as pellucid as that on Hymettus', and 'The calm sea [of False Bay], like a Venetian lagoon, [that] reflected the mountain peaks coloured by the low morning sun'. The tourist authorities in Edwardian Cape Town advertised their city as the 'Venice of the South Atlantic' and the 'Naples of the South'. John Buchan wrote in his memoirs as follows: 'In the Cape Peninsula you have the classic graces of Italy, stony, sun-baked hills rising from orchards and vineyards and water-meadows'; and 'If you seek the true classical landscape outside Italy and Greece you will find it rather in the Cape Peninsula, in places like the Paarl and Stellenbosch'.[25] Lord Randolph Churchill is quoted as saying how 'the lofty granite mass of Table Mountain, the distant ranges of hills stretching over half the horizon and the calm waters of Table Bay brought into the mind successively Gibraltar, the Riviera, and the Bay of Palermo'.[26]

Here again is a description of Cape weather by Dorothea Fairbridge:

> It is not always calm in the Cape Peninsula. If Pan still pipes among the flowers and reeds of Table Mountain, rude Boreas still rides the storm.
>
> Stand on the beach at Camp's Bay when the south-easter is blowing. How the wind shouts and exults as it sweeps down the valley and flings itself out to sea. Over the heads of the Twelve Apostles it soars, over the great mountain behind Cape Town, wrapped in its mantle of vapour. It hurls itself against the Lion's Head and is deflected out to sea, singing a wild paean of triumph as it beats down the poplars and tears the wild geraniums from their stems.
>
> Rude Boreas, did I say?

---

[24] Baker 1944: 32.   [25] Buchan 1940: 35, 117.
[26] Lord Randolph Churchill, cited in *The Cape of Good Hope* 1911: 2.

Nay, here are Alecto, Megaera, and Tisiphone, shrieking down the blast, churning the green waves to foam, tearing the white sand from the beaches to fling it in your face, stinging and blinding you. Black Auster rides abroad to-night, with Eurus on his right hand. For the spirits of the Winds and the Furies are holding Saturnalia on the Camp's Bay beach.[27]

These are memes and mythemes, commonplace tropes of late Victorian and Edwardian landscape writing, deriving from the example of Ruskin, from the ubiquitous influence of travel guides such as Murray or Baedeker, or (in the last quotation) the thespian spirit of art nouveau. The first tourist handbook to be published by the Corporation of Cape Town in 1911 adjures the traveller to 'bring your volumes of Ruskin when starting 'Southward Ho!' The editor of the guidebook quotes at length from *The Stones of Venice* to indicate how apposite this text is to the Cape.

The following quotation from the account of a journey to South Africa in 1894 illustrates this use of Mediterranean allusions as a frame of reference in English travel-writing in the late Victorian and the Edwardian age:

CARE AMICE, – When I sent you word that I was going to South Africa in search of health, you first tried to dissuade me from my purpose; . . . You urged me to come eastward; the Golden Horn alone was worth all the beauties of South Africa put together; . . . In South Africa these charms would be conspicuous by their absence. The country had nothing in common with one's love of antiquity and beauty; no ancient towns, no architectural monuments; none of the refined atmosphere always surrounding places 'with a history' as with a halo. . . . You referred to our old Egyptian days; to Cairo, its tombs and mosques; the desert and its wonderful freedom: to our delightful evenings, when you instructed me in the art of coffee-making, and conversation never flagged, and magic surrounded us, and the sands of life were gilded by the charms of a new-found friendship.[28]

Despite this dissuasive start, the author then applies the same frame of reference to his new-found pleasure in the Cape coastal landscape:

Point after point stretching out into a succession of lovely bays, and the sea today rolled over the white sand with a soothing, sleepy murmur: the most wonderfully green, transparent water imaginable. Not more lovely the waters of the Mediterranean which you have watched beating against the classic shores of Alexandria: not more lovely the waters which flow upwards to the mouth of your beloved Golden Horn.[29]

Finding a blue lotus flower in a pool on the road to Stellenbosch, this traveller waxes nostalgic for the orient:

---

[27] Fairbridge 1928: 188–89.   [28] Wood 1894: 48–50.   [29] Wood 1894: 144.

Visions of a flashing sunlit Nile; of moonlit Pyramids steeped in the solemn silence of midnight, the solitude of endless plains; of wonderful mosques; of the tombs of the Caliphs, where we spent those magic hours under the moonbeams... We would have plucked and carried away this wonderful solitary lotus flower, but it was out of reach, and we had to leave it to blossom in its earthly paradise.[30]

Finally, by a rather more violent effort of the imagination, he compares the new urban growth on the Rand to the phenomenon of the city of Memphis among the desert sands of Egypt:

Here in the midst of a desert rose this wonderful hive. All building material had to be brought from an immense distance, reminding one a little of the Egyptians of old, building the Pyramids. And verily we might call Johannesburg a modern Cairo or Memphis, stripped of all beauty and romance.

[and . . .]

[In ten years' time, it will] be important and imposing, more nearly approaching the modern Memphis we have compared it to: and its temples will be underground, and its obelisks will be factory chimneys. These are the features of the 19th century; and in the year 4000 these will be its 'buried treasures'.[31]

Valetudinarian travel by Northern Europeans habitually turned towards the Mediterranean. A report, in the *Egyptian Gazette* of 5 July 1898, of a *conversazione* given by the British Balneological and Climatological Society, commended the health facilities in Egypt and South Africa as superior to those to be found on the continent:

Continental health resorts are often unsuited – stressful, costly, unhygienic, and bad. . . . This must of necessity lead to the opening up of the unrivalled health resorts of the British colonies. Egypt and South Africa have already begun to reap the benefits, and Australia, New Zealand and Canada will no doubt soon do so.

Perhaps the most celebrated Victorian consumptive at the Cape was Lucie Duff Gordon, who after twelve months there went on to Egypt for her health. 'This climate', she wrote about the Cape, 'is evidently a styptic of great power. I shall write a few lines to the *Lancet* about Caledon and its hot baths'.[32] Her *Letters from the Cape* (1861) were followed by the publication of *Letters from Egypt* (1865).

Her condition demanded the drier climate of Egypt and she became a celebrity on the banks of the Nile, living in a house built on top of the temple of Philae at Luxor. Lucie Duff Gordon was a leading figure in London literary society, a friend of George Meredith and of Kinglake, the author of the orientalist classic *Eothen*. Her writings about the 'Malays' and

[30] Wood 1894: 230.   [31] Wood 1894: 310, 316.   [32] Duff Gordon 1927: 191.

'Mohammedans' are the mainstay of an orientalist tradition in the Cape, which we trace first from Lady Anne Barnard, through Duff Gordon, via Dorothea Fairbridge (who edited both Barnard's and Duff Gordon's diaries and letters), to I. D. du Plessis, the Afrikaans poet and self-appointed patron of the 'Cape Malays'.

After the Victorians, the emphasis shifts to Mediterranean fauvism, sexual fantasy and modernist yearnings for an archaic or mythical world outside of mechanised and mercantile Northern Europe.[33]

D. H. Lawrence, in Italy, sported with the Pan cult that was so prevalent at the turn of the century in writings set in Italy and Greece, and which persisted into the 1920s – observable in short stories by E. M. Forster, and, for instance, in John Buchan's novel *The Dancing Floor* (1926), which deals with the return of archaic ritual in a modern-day Greek island. This Pan cult, alternatively a Dionysian cult, emerges in modernist literary discourses of the same period set in the Cape. The following scene from Fairbridge's *The Torchbearer* is a fair though tame example. The setting is a cellar on a Cape wine farm. A worker is crushing grapes with his feet:

A mist hung before Katherine's eyes after a time, and the cellar seemed to have widened out until it was the width of the whole world. The little dancing figure had grown taller and more graceful. His hair was hair now – not pepper-corns – and it clustered over his ears and concealed them. Vine-leaves were wreathed round his head, a leopard-skin hung from his shoulders. And still he sang and danced – and as he sang the meaning of the song was revealed to her. He sang of the life-giving sun and of the joy of existence, of the sparkle on the waves, of the song of the birds, the scent of flowers, the cool softness of the breeze, the ecstasy that is youth. And then he clashed together the cymbals which he held in his hands, and in a low voice that vibrated through every chord of Katherine's being, he sang of love. Of love of man for woman, of woman for man. Of love triumphant and rejoicing – and his voice rang out in rapture as he sang of the love that is the greatest thing in this world. And then the beautiful voice fell to deep, vibrant tones as he sang of the love that is sacrifice, of the love that knows no earthly fruition, of the love that is greater than death itself.[34]

Perhaps the most striking and typical of contemporary Cape interest in the Mediterranean was, however, architectural. Herbert Baker recognised the value of the grand style, of classical simplicity, for the design of public

---

[33] See Pemble 1987 for a good introduction to 'Mediterranean' sexuality; though this aspect is absent (or certainly tamed) in the discourses on the Cape.

[34] Fairbridge 1915: 256.

spaces and buildings in South Africa, a country (says Baker in an early essay) that 'the Arch-Architect has designed so essentially in the "grand manner"'.[35] 'It would be easy to imagine', he continues, 'a Pergamos or Halicarnassus growing out of any semi-circle of the cliffs that stretch from Muizenberg to Simon's Town, or rising from any of the encircling hills of Pretoria or Bloemfontein'. In the same essay Baker clearly states the link between climate and architectural style:

It is the South African architect's privilege, and one much envied by his fellow craftsmen in northern Europe, to have always at hand the most valuable of all materials for his craft (which the Greeks and Romans also had), warm sun bathed wall surfaces contrasted with deep, cool shadows.[36]

In 1900 Cecil Rhodes sent Baker 'to visit the old countries of the Mediterranean'. Says Baker in his autobiography: 'He wished me particularly to see "Rome, Paestum, Agrigentum, Thebes, and Athens", and to study other such great masterpieces of architecture and sculpture'.[37] Baker subsequently travelled in Egypt, Greece, Italy and Sicily, and established an architectural scholarship at the British School at Rome for South African students, in order to give them 'the opportunity of studying the great architectural and artistic traditions of classical art in the Mediterranean countries which have a similar range of climatic conditions to those which prevail in South Africa'.[38] As is well known, his own career saw him designing public buildings (other than in England) in Salisbury (Harare), Nairobi, Cairo, Khartoum and – together with Sir Edwin Lutyens – the vast 'Capitoline' project of New Delhi in India.[39]

Landscape, architecture and literary mythemes were not the only vehicles for popular comparison between South Africa and the Mediterranean. Predictably, 'race' became a topic for romantic speculation too. If the landscape and built environment are the stage setting, ethnographics determined the hierarchy and typology of dramatis personae and their roles.

The Cape-born mural artist Jan Juta's sister, Réné, emigrated to the south of France where (after travelling in Sicily with D. H. and Frieda Lawrence) she wrote two travel books in the Lawrencean dithyrambic style, illustrated by her brother. In her book *Cannes and the Hills* (dedicated to Rudyard Kipling), she makes the following statement which is typical of this romantic primitivism:

---

[35] Baker 1909: 517.   [36] Baker 1909: 522.   [37] Baker 1944: 35.   [38] Baker 1909: 36.
[39] On the subject of 'Egyptian' architecture in South Africa, see Cornelius 2001 and Claassen 2009. The authoritative study of Baker and Lutyens in New Delhi is Irving 1981.

But gone are the old songs and dances, the dances of Provence wherein lay a literature of the people. In the late seventeenth century, the dance called 'Rigaudin' was forbidden on pain of a beating, and later, on pain of death; it being regarded as a public disgrace, so curious were the gestures and figures of the dance. I suspect the Rigaudin of being the remains of a pagan, sacrificial, ritualistic dance, less bacchanalian, more like the curious obscene dances of the Hottentots of Africa, who so oddly resemble the small mountain race which lived in the caves above Nice.[40]

There are numerous other such speculations from the period, reaching back, in fact, to the mid-nineteenth century and the rise of ethno-philological speculation. This latter, with its dominant Indo-Aryan model, rooted in classical scholarship via Liddell and Scott, arrived in Cape Town in the person of the philologist Wilhelm Bleek with his theory that Cape 'San' languages might be linked to Egyptian Hyksos peoples. The theory was smartly abandoned by the scholar Bleek, but sustained in popular sentiment. Musing on the portrait of a Cape 'coloured' boy, the narrator in a novel by Dorothea Fairbridge speculates as follows:

Leaving out the revelation of the boy's soul, we could have traced the proportion of European influence as compared with that of the aboriginal Hottentot, together with the considerations of surroundings and their influence on the mother, as distinguished from heredity. Then, taking the Hottentot as a starting point, we would have pursued our investigations into the history of that curious race, debating whether the theory which links them (through the Bushmen) to the Cave Dwellers of ancient Spain, is tenable, and whether there is anything to be said in favour of those who assert that the Hyksos Kings of Egypt were in reality Hottentots, and that the so-called Egyptian type may be traced throughout Africa from north to south.[41]

There is a broad narrative desire behind this speculation. Dorothea Fairbridge exemplifies this colonial desire in her *History of South Africa*:

It is possible that [the early travellers] made their way farther south than Punt, and eyes which looked on Moses may also have gazed on Table Mountain, but of this there is no record. What we do know is that Pharaoh Necho, who ruled in Egypt six hundred years before the birth of Christ, sent an expedition from the Red Sea, manned by Phoenician sailors, which sailed round Africa. Three years, the journey took, for the sailors landed at different places on the coast, dug the ground and sowed it with corn. When the crop had ripened it was gathered and sail was made for the next halting-place. Southward and southward they went, says the old chronicler, until, as they declared, the sun was on their right hand as they sailed.

---

[40] Juta 1924: 94.   [41] Fairbridge 1926: 128.

In the third year they doubled the Pillars of Hercules and came safe home. Think of the courage of it. Perhaps they put in at Table Bay or Durban or elsewhere on the coast, and made their temporary gardens in the kindly soil of South Africa. It is curious to think that the slender Egyptian explorers may have stood at the foot of Table Mountain and worshipped the Sun God as he rose over the Drakenstein. We may picture to ourselves their return after that three years' journey – how they sailed up the west coast and through the Pillars of Hercules and down the blue Mediterranean, until they came to the Rosetta mouth of the Nile and to the noble city of Sais, then the capital of Egypt.

And after this the curtain falls for nearly two thousand years, to rise again in A.D. 1434, in which year that 'dreamer devout' Prince Henry the Navigator sent an expedition from Portugal which succeeded in rounding Cape Bojador and paved the way for the discovery of the sea-route to India.[42]

Fairbridge packs a great deal of geographical doctrine and colonial iconography into this passage. The idea of a connection between the southernmost and northernmost seaboards of Africa (the latter falling within European cultural reach) was held for several decades as the 'Cape-to-Cairo' fantasy, notably by Cecil Rhodes. The connection was a geographical metaphor for a constellation of strategic intentions. The ripening corn, solar navigation and sun worship indicate once again the neo-Hegelian heliocentric tropology. Dayspring, New Dawn, was the dominant trope of new South African nationhood for Fairbridge and her friends from the Oxford Kindergarten lobby.

'And after this', adds Fairbridge, 'the curtain falls'. The next act in the performance is Portuguese, and with this the Portuguese national epic, Camoens's Lusiads, and the framing of the continent of Africa in terms of Homeric/Vergilian episode and yet another neoclassical root metaphor for the Cape in the hirsute person of the local Titan Adamastor.

2. Performance of Identity

> If it is not 'Assouan' it is 'Durbar'! Mostly you take your choice – a great many people take both. Among these are Mr and Mrs Rochefort Maguire; but then the Durbar, in their case, is only one incident in a comprehensive tour of India. Sir George and Lady Farrar are also 'Durbar-ing'.[43]

The article adds that the Duke and Duchess of Connaught are to leave London for Egypt to attend the opening of the Assouan Dam, then

---

[42] Fairbridge 1918: 16.   [43] *The African World and Cape-to-Cairo Express*, 15 November 1902.

afterwards on HMS *Renown* to India for the Delhi Durbar; that the Royal Academician and painter of Odalisques and harem scenes Sir Lawrence Alma-Tadema arrives in Cairo; and that Joe Chamberlain sails for the Cape on HMS *Good Hope*, via Suez. The Duke laid the foundation stone of the dam with Masonic ritual; as the *Good Hope* bearing the Colonial Secretary neared Table Bay she was welcomed by a mass performance on the flanks of the Twelve Apostles by thousands of schoolchildren manipulating tiny mirrors against the sun. In Edwardian public culture travel, tourism, performance, ritual and fantasy are of a piece. Thomas Cook's *Traveller's Gazette, Excursionist and Tourist Advertiser* for September 1910, a decade later and once again 'durbar' time (as Edward VII is replaced with the new King Emperor George V), recommended the following event at the Cape:

Visitors to the Cape during the early part of November will be able to add an extra item of exceptional interest to the usual programme of sightseeing, viz., the Pageant at Cape Town, arranged in order to celebrate the opening of the Union Parliament, at which the Duke of Connaught will be present. The various scenes in this great spectacle will be presented at the foot of Table Mountain, on a scale closely resembling that held on the Plains of Abraham in Canada last year. The mastership of the Pageant has been entrusted to Mr Frank Lascelles, who is organising the Festival of Empire and Pageant of London to be held at the Crystal Palace next year.

The same Frank Lascelles (graduate of Keble College, Oxford) produced the Quebec Tercentenary pageant referred to here, and (in the busy coronation year of 1911) staged both the Festival of Empire and a coronation durbar in Calcutta.

In the planning of the 1910 South African Union pageant the public were invited to submit ideas. Réné Juta, at whose parents' home Kipling and Lascelles met to plan the pageant, wrote and published her own contribution titled 'The Masque of the Silver Trees'. It is in the nature of a Jacobean neoclassical masque, blending English and antique frames of reference in a performance fantasy for South African national celebration. It was not used, but motifs from her masque were taken up by Lascelles in his final script or 'book of words' for the SA Pageant.

The personae in Juta's short masque are as follows: The Ancient Keeper of the Forests; The Spirit of Table Mountain; The Spirit of the Silver Trees; The Fir Tree Spirit; The Oak Tree Spirit; The Spirit of the Weeds; The Spirit of the Veldt; The South East Wind; The North West Wind; and the Elf of the Prologue.

The occasion is the nuptials of Orpheus and Eurydice on Table Mountain. For the event all the trees of the mountain were to exchange their green for virgin silver. Because of conflict between the South East and North West winds, the message failed to reach the silver trees (*leucadendron argenteum*, of the protea family). The masque is a drama of metamorphosis in which the silver trees are brought into compliance and chastised. Their penance in perpetuity is to wear silver leaves instead of green.

The Spirit of the Veldt wanders in, and is challenged by the Ancient Keeper. Veldt responds thus:

A message from your gods! The gods of Greece, of founts and vales and groves and lawns! – the gods who grant ye sheltered corners of the earth where ye may sit and brood in shade!

Before Olympus rose by hot volcano driven from the sea, before the birth of Pan and all the gods, before great Nature moved in chains, as slave before the rule of gods, I lived, and craved no gods but Liberty and Sun. Ah! give us sun – no cool dark woods to chill the fire of my soul, but always space and sun, vast plains and mountains, bush and stones – of colouring unknown to ye. Give me the crunch of hot dry earth, the burning red of aloe and of pear – in turn, the scent of the rhenoster bush just after rain. The soft and heavy clouds seem loathe to leave the plains, and then the roar of river rising for the flood. Comes chaos with the flood: the gaping kloofs and unused river beds receive the rain and burst their banks and crash and thunder out the seething mass. And in the purple hour of the night, when rest and peace return, we wait impatiently until the morn to see the traces of the flood. A trace of flowers all unknown to ye – flowers of colours of the sun, – small, bright, quick things – which spring and cover all the harm that's done: and miles and miles of such. Ah, Spirits in this Veldtland, grand and free, would ye then have us listen to the gods!

[And the Ancient Keeper retorts:]

Go on your way, O Spirit of the Veldt, and trouble not our world with rebel fears; we know that ye are severed from our rule and owe no tribute to our gods. Begone and come not here again.[44]

This is a curious moment where Western European Arcadian pastoral faces up to the South African landscape proper. Réné Juta's text is ambivalent: the Veldt is sympathetically described in natural terms but treated as an Afrikaner/Dutch 'Cape Rebel' would have been, seeking 'Liberty', disloyal to the pantheon of transcendental signifiers of Crown and Empire, or the 'loyalist' gods and spirits of the Cape Peninsula whose habitat is so unlike the tough semi-desert flora of the Hantam or Karroo. Arcadian

---

[44] Juta 1909.

virtue is guarded by the 'Ancient Keeper', a symbol of both *ur*-antiquity and vigilant English loyalism. The symbolism of the Union Pageant focused on 'unity' and 'reconciliation' whereas Réné Juta's masque deals with rebellion and compliance. The silver trees are unique to Table Mountain and thence essentially local, but their broader allegiance is duly enforced. The Juta family of attorneys and advocates themselves lived out these ambivalences. Réné Juta's father was Cape Attorney General under the premiership of Cecil Rhodes while an uncle held a similar post in Paul Kruger's Transvaal Republic.

Frank Lascelles's great Union Pageant of 1910 concluded with an 'Allegorical tableau emblematic of the Union of South Africa'. This finale was entitled 'The Progress of Prosperity: A Masque of Consummation and Consecration', and it draws on Réné Juta's imagery. The Masque began with 'a vast, silent veldt', 'the eternal sea', 'immutable mountains'. Then, says the script,

Suddenly on all sides [. . .] a host of dark forms fleeing in disordered motion, and uttering half-articulate cries of woe [. . .] the hordes of ignorance, cruelty, savagery, unbelief, war, pestilence, famine and their ilk, the pitiless progenitors of all the misery of man, the inwohners of black night.

In an instant the music changes and silver-clad children appear with branches of the silver tree in their hands [. . .] The forms of darkness are driven back and put to rout.[45]

The silver children sing an Orphic ode, 'Hence, ye dreary, night-nursed crew', which becomes an invocation to Nature's bounty, and while they work their way through this, successive dumb shows pass by (a 'pageant of resources' with 'gold-washers, vineyarders, harvesters, shepherds' and so forth, a 'band of nymphs' and then a 'vast concourse of the heroes of South Africa: Portuguese, Dutch, Huguenot, English and men from many other lands'). The symbolism in this masque not only rehearses the fantasy of imperial-evolutionary racial progression or the 'March of Man', but also the commonplace of enlightenment in the 'dark continent'.

The climax is heralded by peals of silver trumpets and the entry of the 'Procession of United South Africa' in which very local references are elevated into a semblance of Athenian sacrament or Roman victory:

First, twenty maidens in white, with silver horns of plenty; next ten horsemen in silver, mounted on white horses led by pages in gold, bearing banners and trophies; then Rhodesia, a youth in saffron and gold, attended by boys in saffron; then the

---

[45] *Souvenir* 1910: 93.

Cape Colony, Transvaal, Orange River Colony and Natal, walking side by side, but at a certain distance, and attended each by bands of maidens in white with scarves of silver; and finally, upon a car drawn by ten span of oxen and attended by maidens in gold and pages in silver, United South Africa.

Advancing slowly to the throne they sing a hymn, to the air of 'God Save the King'. Then shall the whole multitude join in singing the Te Deum ('Holy! Holy! Holy! Lord God of Sabaoth').[46]

And after this, everybody joins in with a 'Volkslied' which was awarded the First Prize in the *South African News* National Anthem Competition, composed (in English) by the loyal Afrikaner C. E. Viljoen, BA.

The conclusion is self-evident. Public rhetoric and performance of identity in loyalist South Africa circa 1910 reflected the idealist symbolism of art nouveau. This idealising ethos was driven by patriotic sentiment (and the sentiment of often contrary lobbies such as craft unions) not only in England and the British Empire but in other polities around the world, including emergent Afrikaner nationalism in South Africa. To the local and national was added the universalising ethos of latter-day neoclassicism, as evinced in the new era of the Olympic Games and in the imperial-monumental scale of work by Baker and Lutyens, in Johannesburg, Pretoria, New Delhi, London and Oxford, as well as on the dramatic platform of the Imperial War Graves Commission after World War I (which, incidentally, also had its origins in the South African War and an initiative by Dorothea Fairbridge and her Guild of Loyal Women).[47]

Performance of identity entailed learning the script (the exemplary pageant of the 'March of Man') and having at least a sense of the weight of classical culture that served as a caste shibboleth; dressing the part; negotiating one's role between 'universal' ideals and local contingency; landscaping the stage and its sets; exhorting an audience with cogent rhetoric as to the desirability of the illusion; door-keeping at the box office (social class, gender and race were carefully marshalled); building the great amphitheatres, temples and monuments, the forum and agora, in granite and golden sandstone; laying out the schola, academe, gymnasium, the national universities for youthful minds and bodies; imagining with due ritual an imperium of custom, law, faith and value, creed, precedent, power and constitutionalism,

---

[46] *Souvenir* 1910: 96.
[47] See Harris and Stamp 1977 on the topic of the War Graves Commission, the neoclassical motifs in the Commission's work and the involvement here of Baker and Kipling.

Figure 4.3 Constance Penstone, watercolour depicting Malay bride. Dust jacket of Dorothea Fairbridge's novel, *Piet of Italy* (1913). (A black and white version of this figure will appear in some formats. For the colour version, please refer to the plate section.)

within what was, at the time, and up until the 1920s, deemed to be a universal global ethos.

One final quote suggests, with a touch of gauche pathos, the challenge that local individuals, socially and culturally excluded from the grand script, might feel about this ethos. The eponymous hero of Dorothea Fairbridge's novel *Piet of Italy* grows up in the 'Malay' community of Cape Town, attending the mosque and speaking the 'taal' or informal Afrikaans, until, later, a startling revelation changes everything (Fig. 4.3 and Plate 4). He is talented at art and here, in a trysting place on the mountain above the city, he presents his 'Malay' or Cape Indonesian girlfriend, Nissa, with a clay statuette that symbolises, for him, the new country:

From the shoulders to the bare feet her drapery fell in rigid folds, crudely but powerfully suggestive of the archaic period of Greek art. Restraint showed in every line, the hands hung straight down at her side – not loosely, but with strong tenacity of purpose. But the chin was uplifted, the eyes fixed on some far distant horizon, and the poise of the lovely head was instinct with vitality, and tense with nobility of purpose.

A light that Nissa had never seen before shone in Piet's eyes, as he looked at the rough figure in his hands.

'She is South Africa,' he said softly. 'She sees what is yet to come.'

Dead silence fell for the space of some minutes. Then Nissa sprang up with a choking cry.

'Take me away – I want to go home. You frighten me when you look so. I dono what for you bring me here to show that silly, ugly thing.'[48]

Piet is granted by Fairbridge an instinct for antiquity and its 'timeless' aesthetic; he shapes and reads the symbolism that binds this to the ethic of modernity and the time to come. Nissa is frightened by his reach of vision. She is excluded. Piet (in due course reconfigured as Pietro) enters into a lost legacy that propels him onto the stage of history; Nissa retreats below the threshold to a marginal place among the helots of the Cape. The talisman vouches for Piet's belonging, calling and allegiance. To Fairbridge's discredit the talisman also closes doors. Just as the new vernacular, and the universal idealism, admitted some into the club, so they firmly shut the door on others who were considered at best mere auxiliaries in the ranks of the new Rome.

---

[48] Fairbridge 1913: 85–86.

PART III

Conceiving the Nation

The ascendancy of Afrikaner nationalism in the early twentieth century coincides with a period of heightened South African engagement with Graeco-Roman antiquity – at least in an institutional sense, and at least for those who benefitted from its privileges of race and class. It is all the more significant that the essays in this section show a peculiarly ambivalent relation of Afrikanerdom to antiquity. Gerard Moerdyk publicly downplayed classical influence in his design of the Voortrekker Monument; but in reality, Greek and Roman architecture deeply imbued his training, with inevitable impact. Moerdyk's classicism was thus a matter of training (*paideia*) rather than ideology (**Rankin and Schneider**). On the other hand, the compilers of the Afrikaner Kinderensiklopedie (children's encyclopædia) reveal considerable interest in ancient Greece and Rome, a feature that earned criticism from hard-line Afrikaner nationalists at the time (**Bosman**). In both cases, classical antiquity seemed, for some, to contain the potential of a challenge to Calvinism and the Christian-nationalist state. By contrast, we have already glimpsed outright critique of Afrikaner nationalism, articulated by means of antiquity, in André Brink and other dissident figures (Parker, above).

5	'Copy Nothing': Classical Ideals and Afrikaner Ideologies at the Voortrekker Monument

ELIZABETH RANKIN AND ROLF MICHAEL SCHNEIDER

The idea to erect a memorial to the Voortrekkers emerged in the later nineteenth century. An early advocate was Paul Kruger, President of the Zuid-Afrikaansche Republiek (1882–1902), who addressed it in the aftermath of the First Boer War, when he visited the site of the Battle of Blood River on its fiftieth anniversary, on 16 December 1888.[1] Yet it was not until its upcoming centenary that the Voortrekker Monument was seriously conceived. In 1931 the Sentrale Volksmonument Komitee (SVK) was formed – a veritable 'Who's Who' of contemporary Afrikaners – to oversee the creation of a monument to commemorate the centenary of the 'Great Trek'.[2] Norman Etherington, among others, has unpicked the complexity and misreading of the 'Great Trek', a construct consolidated in hindsight from a series of treks, in themselves part of many migrations in the hinterland of southern Africa in the nineteenth century.[3] For the purposes of this essay with its focus on classical heritage in the Voortrekker Monument, it has not been possible to give full weight to these subtleties: our concern has rather been to unfold the narrative of the 'Great Trek' from the point of view of those who designed the Monument and developed its historical frieze.

   From 1835 discontented Dutch-speaking farmers had started to leave the then British Cape, undertaking 'treks' into the interior, and by 1845 'some 2,308 families, or fifteen thousand burghers and their families, accompanied by an estimated five thousand servants', had left (Fig. 5.1).[4] But the independent republics – the Zuid-Afrikaansche Republiek and the

---

[1] Steytler 1958: 6.

[2] The SVK (Central National Monuments Committee) was formed by the Federasie van Afrikaanse Kultuurvereniginge (FAK, Federation of Afrikaans Culture Organisations), today sited at the Voortrekker Monument; the FAK was founded in 1929 by the Broederbond, a highly influential secret organisation promoting Afrikaner nationalism. SVK members are listed in *The Voortrekker Monument Pretoria, official guide* (hereafter *Official Guide*) (1955), 24. All quotations are from the 1970 edition, which is by and large consistent in substance with the first edition (1955).

[3] Etherington 2001: esp. 243–72.

[4] Giliomee 2003: 161. Giliomee is an excellent source on the 'treks', esp. 144–57 and 161–75.

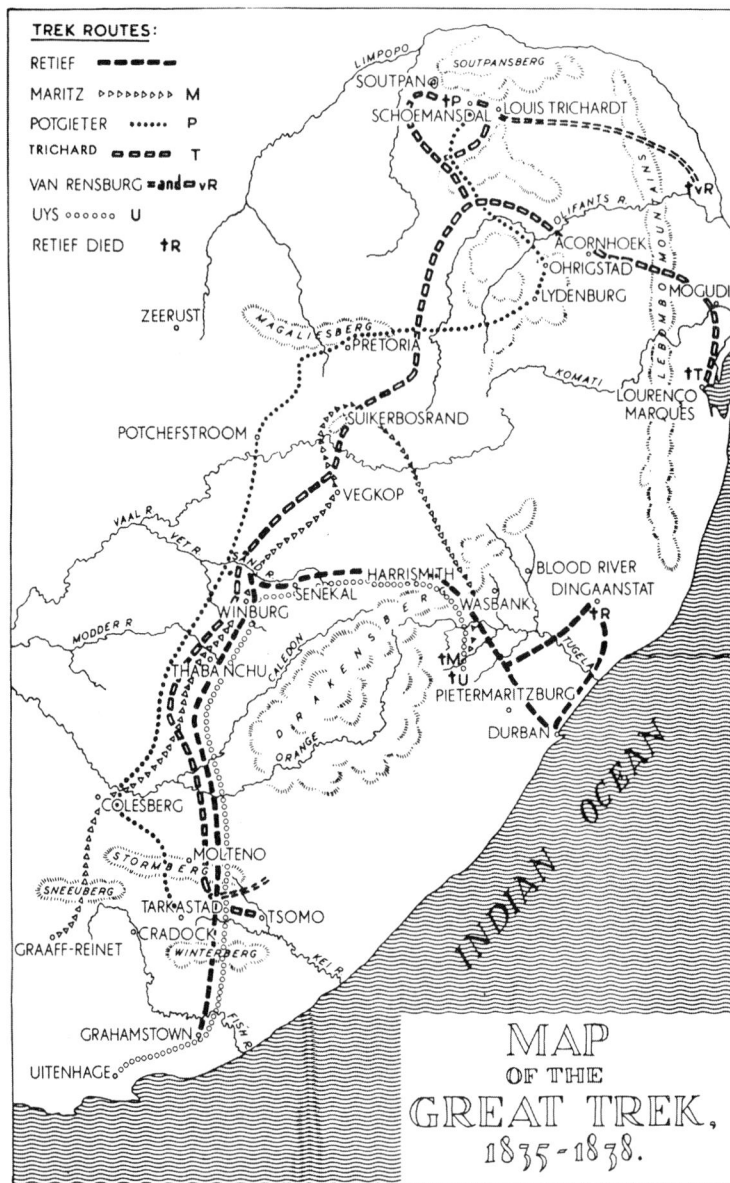

Figure 5.1 Map of the trek routes, 1835–38. From *The Voortrekker Monument Pretoria, Official Guide* (1970).

Republiek van die Oranje-Vrijstaat – that they set up beyond the colonial control of Great Britain were forfeit after their defeat in the Anglo-Boer War in 1902. Despite their republics becoming provinces with equivalent status to the former British colonies of the Cape and Natal under the Union of 1910, and the growing number of Afrikaans speakers active in parliament, Afrikaners felt disempowered in the land they considered their birthright.[5] Moreover, in the wake of the Depression, the number of impoverished Afrikaans-speaking 'poor whites' had been rising rapidly in the old Boer republics. The centenary celebrations of the treks were intended to commemorate the achievements of their forebears and to give Afrikaners a greater sense of self-worth and unity. In keeping with the heritage they sought to recognise and conserve, the festivities were planned to culminate in Pretoria, the capital of the former Zuid-Afrikaansche Republiek, on 16 December 1938. This was the Day of the Vow, known as Dingaan's Day, initiated by the Calvinist Voortrekkers in thanks for divine help in their victory over the Zulu at Blood River on that date in 1838.[6]

The Voortrekker Monument was to prove a lengthy project. Although the architect Gerard Leendert Pieter Moerdyk (1890–1958) had been appointed as architect in 1936,[7] and the elevated site outside Pretoria had been selected later that year,[8] building was only far enough advanced for the foundation stone to be laid on 16 December 1938.[9] This was nonetheless the climactic moment of the re-enactment of the

---

[5] Marx 1998: 19–267, provides a comprehensive analysis of growing Afrikaner nationalism at the time.

[6] Preller 1928, Kluppels 2009.

[7] The SVK received the recommendation of the 'Vorm' (Form) subcommittee to appoint Moerdyk at their meeting of 7 April 1936, and he was invited to that meeting to discuss his design, recorded in the SVK Notule (Minutes), 7 April 1936, (Pretoria, National Archives Repository (NAR), Archives of the Department of the Interior of South Africa, Source reference: BNS, vol. 298, file no. 146/73, vol. 1). Duffey 2005: 5 suggests that the SVK may have had him in mind as architect from the outset. Indeed, Moerdyk had already attended an early SVK meeting in 1932 when plans for the monument were being discussed (SVK Minutes, 14 April 1932, NAR, Engelenburg, file no. 140/3, Sub-File 14). The architect's name can be spelt Moerdijk or Moerdyk (the Afrikaans version of the original Dutch), which we have preferred, as this is the spelling used in the official documents of the Voortrekker Monument. For Moerdyk, see Vermeulen 1999; Fisher 2003: 28–37; Fisher and Clarke 2010: 151–60; see also Chipkin 1993: 132–33, 280–81.

[8] Notule van die Konferensie wat besluit het oor die plek waar die Voortrekkermonument geplaas sal word (Minutes of the Conference that decided on the site where the Voortrekker Monument would be placed), 6 October 1936 (NAR Pretoria, Engelenburg, 140/3, Sub-File 14).

[9] Although the designs for the Voortrekker Monument were chosen in open competition, it seems clear that the intention was to have an Afrikaner architect in order to best represent Afrikaner ideals, just as it was intended (at least from 1940) to use only white builders. This was ostensibly to provide work for Afrikaners during the economic recession, but no doubt also to maintain the Monument's 'purity' – although labour shortages during the war ultimately led to the employment of 12 black workers after 1942, their input was limited to menial jobs such as mixing concrete and cleaning the site. See Pretorius 2003; Steenkamp 2008a: 133; Kruger and Pretorius 2009.

nineteenth-century migrations into the interior which formed the focus of the commemorative festivities: latter-day Voortrekkers travelled in traditional dress in replicas of the historical ox wagons across South Africa to much popular acclaim; and a sacred flame that would later be installed in the Monument was carried from Cape Town to Pretoria.[10] The second 'Great Trek' was a thoroughly orchestrated ritual which marked Afrikaner nationalism as a vital social and political movement.[11] The term 'Voortrekker' (pioneer) was first applied to those who settled in Natal around 1840. It only came into popular use for the participants of the 'Great Trek' later in the nineteenth century,[12] in anticipation of the growing importance of an Afrikaner ideology in shaping white South African identity. In this vein, Moerdyk claimed in the *Official Guide* of the Voortrekker Monument that the design of the architecture and its sculptural narrative 'was to serve as a tangible tribute to a group of people who through their stupendous efforts had laid the foundation of a white civilisation to be built in the interior of Southern Africa'.[13] He then, rather surprisingly, substantiates the alleged uniqueness of the Voortrekkers' conquest by a comparison with ancient Mediterranean cultures:

The Voortrekkers were the first white people to succeed in taming the interior of Africa. There were others who preceded them. Six centuries before Christ, during the time of Pharaoh Necho, the Phoenicians sailed around Africa. The Romans, who conquered the whole of the then known world, could not get farther south than the Mountains of the Moon ... It was left to the Voortrekkers ... to force, at a great price, an entry into the interior and establish a white civilisation.[14]

A similar connection to ancient world history had already been construed only two days after the laying of the Monument's foundation stone in 1938. At a requiem service for the Voortrekkers held in the Hellenic Church of Pretoria, Dr A. N. Nicolopoulos declared in his address:

The history of the Greek nation is a history of hundreds and thousands of years. From it we have inherited experiences and feelings which help us to enter whole heartedly into the Voortrekker commemoration at this time: ... from the defensive

---

[10] See Mostert 1940; Duvenage 1988.   [11] Marx 1998: esp. 247–60.   [12] Muller 1987: 19–20.

[13] *Official Guide*, 29.

[14] *Official Guide*, 30–31. Much earlier, Moerdyk himself drew a direct analogy with Greece at the unveiling of his Women's Monument in Klerksdorp in 1921, comparing Afrikaners with Greeks in the service of Rome. He also equated Afrikaners with Periclean Greeks and stated that 'the art of the memorial in the Greek tradition persist [sic] in the face of the demise of the great Roman Empire, in drawing a parallel with its fall he hints at a celebration of the demise of the British Empire.' Fisher and Clarke 2010: 153.

Figure 5.2 North façade, Voortrekker Monument, December 1949. (A black and white version of this figure will appear in some formats. For the colour version, please refer to the plate section.)

warfare against the Persians and the Turks of Asia, the Romans and the Venetians of Europe, we have inherited a sympathetic understanding of the bitterness and struggle of a nation striving to preserve its national existence.[15]

The delayed timing of the building's completion until 1949 was ultimately opportune, for by then Afrikaners were in full ascendancy. The inauguration of the Monument,[16] attended by an estimated 250,000 (Figs 5.2–3),[17] was presided over by Afrikaner Prime Minister Daniel François Malan. His National Party was voted into power for the first time in 1948, initiating a form of government based on the pernicious premise of apartheid that was to endure for over forty years.[18] It might be

---

[15] Translation of address delivered by Dr A. N. Nicolopoulos at the Voortrekker requiem service held at the Hellenic Church, Pretoria, 18 December 1938 (Moerdyk files, Africana section, Merensky Library, University of Pretoria).

[16] *Amptelike program* (1949).

[17] Evans 2007: 145 cites an even larger number, 400,000. However, *The London Illustrated News* (31 December 1949) talks of 'the vast crowd of 250,000 people, a tenth of the white population of South Africa', and this number is given by Crampton 2001: 237, and Steenkamp 2008a: 92–94, who further notes that some 30,000 camped in the *feesstad* or festival city that was set up at the Monument for the celebrations.

[18] Ross et al. 2011: 319–491; Enwezor and Bester 2013.

Figure 5.3 Inauguration, Voortrekker Monument from South-West,
16 December 1949.

suggested that the Voortrekker Monument itself played some part in this
ascendancy as a material signifier of Afrikanerdom. The Foreword to the
Official Guide describes the Monument as a focus of pride, patriotism and
faith in God, intended to induce visitors 'to devote their lives to the duty and
the privilege of building a nation'.[19] Conversely, it was regarded by opponents of the National Party as an authoritarian icon of Afrikaner power and
a detested symbol of apartheid. Hence it is of more than art historical interest
to analyse the visual forms of the Monument and how it came to stand for
a new sense of Afrikaner nationhood.

The *Official Guide*, published by the Board of Control of the
Voortrekker Monument in 1955, and reprinted continuously for almost
twenty years, is vital for our study.[20] It kept alive the intended Afrikaner
reading of the Monument, 'built to last a thousand years and more so that it

[19] S. G. J. van Niekerk (chairman of the Board of Control), *Official Guide*, 12.
[20] The contents of the *Official Guide* were outlined by the Beheerraad van die Voortrekkermonument
(Board of Control of the Voortrekker Monument), as noted by the Honorary
Secretary, M. C. Botha, on 18 November 1952 (ARCA Bloemfontein, PV94 1/75/2/1).

may interpret to coming generations the history and significance of the
Great Trek'.[21] As chief author, it is Moerdyk, the architect, who expounds
the design and symbolism of the sculpture and architecture of the
Monument.[22] Moerdyk had responsibility for the entire project (not unlike
Phidias charged with supervising the Parthenon), and it was he who
definitively explained its meaning: the builders and the sculptors who
created the fabric of the Monument were given no voice.[23] Focusing on
Moerdyk's interpretation means that we discuss primarily Afrikaner thinking authorised by the SVK. This does not, however, mean that we forget the
Monument's propensity for different readings from viewers with different
frameworks. On the contrary, we wish to underline that, the moment
a monument is released to the public, it is open to almost any reading –
even including the refusal to read it at all. This should not be forgotten in
what is to follow. Indeed, it is fundamental to an understanding of our own
reading.

1.   Designing Afrikaner Architecture: Bypassing
the Classical?

The symmetrical cube of the Monument, 62 metres high, dominates
a hill site overlooking the south entrance to central Pretoria (Fig. 5.2 and
Plate 5).[24] Built of steel and concrete with granite facing, the building is
set on a large square podium, around 40 by 40 metres, and some 7 metres
high (Figs 5.4–5). The only access is from the north, where several flights of
stairs that traverse the steep slope are ordered in calculated symmetry,
forcing the visitor to a respectful slow motion, and heightening the
awareness of the monument. Additionally, at the entrance a compelling

---

[21] *Official Guide*, 29.

[22] *Official Guide*, 38–51. That the sculptors were considered secondary to the architect's overall
role (in contrast to their esteem in ancient Greece and Rome) is also suggested by the fact that
initially the panels were not signed, and the sculptors were not to be given recognition in the
inauguration ceremonies at the Monument; see Potgieter 1987: 43–44. The undervaluing of the
role of the sculptors still rankled with Potgieter forty years later when he was interviewed by
Elizabeth Rankin in 1989: to set the record straight was an important motivation in writing his
manuscript. Only later did Potgieter obtain permission to carve signatures for the four artists
onto the panels (the date is uncertain, but must have been between 1976 and 1987).

[23] *Official Guide*, 10, conveniently claims that 'Dr G. Moerdijk was the architect and the designer
of the Monument and of the historical frieze in the Hall of Heroes.'

[24] The Monument's architecture deserves a thorough study. For the main data see *Official Guide*;
Heymans and Theart-Peddle 2009; for the Monument's height, ibid. 4; and Steenkamp 2008a
and her four articles listed in the bibliography. For a 360-degree view of the site: www.360cities
.net/image/voortrekker-monument-north-roof.

Figure 5.4 Voortrekker Monument, section drawing from North-West by Gerard Moerdyk, c. 1937.

message is conveyed by a huge 4.1 metre bronze. Instead of a more likely male protagonist, it shows a resolute Voortrekker mother protecting a girl and a boy, the first sculpture to attract the visitor's eye (Fig. 5.2 and Plate 5). Standing guard on the podium's corners, positioned at 45 degrees to look out across the surrounding veld, four colossal granite figures, 5.5 metres high, represent Voortrekker leaders:[25] Piet Retief and Andries Pretorius flank the north front side, while Hendrik Potgieter and the 'Unknown

[25] These figures may owe something to Coert Steynberg's initial proposal for the Monument – a 45-foot Voortrekker figure of granite on a 30-foot pedestal – although Steynberg dissociated himself from the project and declined invitations to work on these figures, instead taking up a commission to carve an altar-like ox wagon in granite for the Blood River site. See Steynberg 1982: 31–35; Hagg 1989: 12–19; Vermeulen 1999: 128.

Figure 5.5 Aerial view from North, Voortrekker Monument, December 1949.

Voortrekker' are on the south. As though in support of these sentinel figures, there are tower-like recessed blocks above them on each corner. The façade that looms above those climbing the steps is dominated by a single arched window, repeated on all four elevations, each window with five vertical sections densely filled with a filigree of ordered granite diagonals. This design is echoed in two lines of zigzag chevrons that run around the upper walls. The rough *rustica* surface, its insistent pattern created by narrow horizontal elements of warm-tinted granite from the Zoutpansberg, softens the hard surface of the facade, catching the sunlight at different angles. Crowning the building, the substantial attic is set back and framed by small support walls that curve away from the facade, creating deeply shadowed recesses. The roof terrace at this level, reached by spiral staircases in the towers, offers panoramic views of the surrounding landscape, reinforcing a sense of the commanding position of the Monument (Fig. 5.5).

   Despite the textured surface created by the distinctively cut granite and the Art Deco decorative elements, the overall effect of the building is hieratic and monolithic. Its sole purpose is to house the Hall of Heroes, an expansive uninterrupted space into which the single entrance door leads, and the subterranean Lower Hall located in the podium. Together they present two solitary artefacts: a historical marble frieze around the

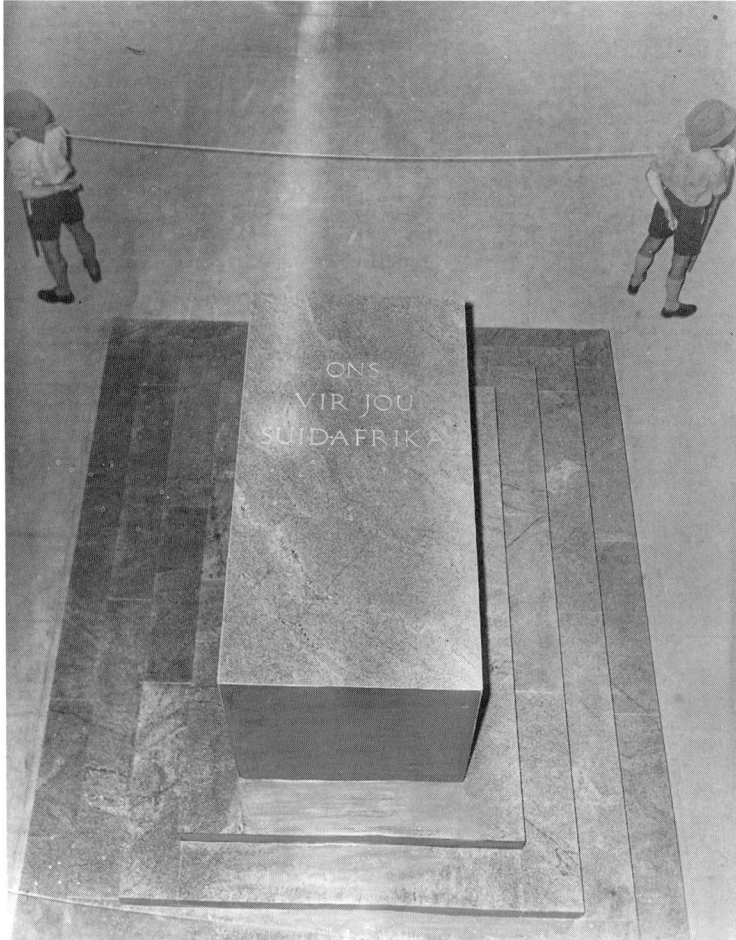

Figure 5.6 Cenotaph, Lower Hall, Voortrekker Monument, 16 December 1949.

four walls of the upper hall, and a cenotaph below, visible through a central opening in the floor (Fig. 5.6–7).[26] The building is roofed by a vast double dome, the higher one just visible above the oculus piercing the lower dome that spans the Hall of Heroes (Fig. 5.4). Moerdyk's daughter Irma Vermeulen identifies the walkway around the dome as a third level in the monument, the triple structure in 'stille erkening' (silent recognition) of the Holy Trinity. She also speaks of the steep spiral staircase that leads up to the walkway as a symbolic indication of the amount of

---

[26] The galleries around the lower hall today provide space for a museum, presenting documents and objects related to the history of the Voortrekkers and the construction of their Monument. For a nuanced history of the collection, see Grobler 2005: 77–103.

Figure 5.7 Hall of Heroes, Voortrekker Monument, after 1950.

work and 'steil opdraandes' (steep ascents) that still lay ahead before the end of the struggle would be reached.[27]

Built to enshrine the achievements of the Afrikaner people, the Voortrekker Monument was designed to embody an enduring monumentality that can be associated with revered memorials of the past. While the Monument does not directly mimic historical styles, it evokes classical traditions in a variety of ways. It is constituted of materials favoured since antiquity – granite, marble and bronze. The elevated location recalls the acropolis sites of Greece, even incorporating a theatre excavated from its slopes, a concurrence well known from classical Athens. And the Monument's scale and domed concrete structure parallels monumental vaulted architecture in ancient Rome. Yet to seek evidence of the influence of antiquity at the Monument seems at first glance a project doomed to failure. In an interview for *Die Vaderland* newspaper of 10 December 1936, Moerdyk stressed that the Monument 'did not employ a single European style motif'.[28] When writing for the *Official Guide*, he for the most part

---

[27] Vermeulen 1999: 129.

[28] Steenkamp 2008a: 111. She offers a succinct discussion of negative Afrikaans responses to any foreign style in the design of the Monument, and Moerdyk's persuasive case for its Afrikaner qualities, in 2008b: 63–65.

avoided mention of any debt to classical heritage, making only a passing reference to the Mausoleum of Halicarnassus as a monument 'which became the forerunner of this type of structure'.[29]

It might be expected that an architect engaged in designing an important monument would have been eager to claim ancient forebears, which would endow the project with a venerable heritage. But this is to forget the Afrikaner context within which the Monument was built. There was strong public resistance to the idea of a Greek model for the Voortrekker Monument. E. G. Jansen as chairman and J. J. Scheepers as secretary of the SVK responded quickly, issuing a statement to reassure those who wanted no hint of foreign sources in a monument intended to affirm their unique identity:

Die Monument sal van eg Suid-Afrikaanse aard wees, en om to se, soos in sommige ongemagtigde koerantberigte gedoen is, dat dit 'n Griekse of enige ander sort monument sal wees, is heeltemal verkeerd.[30]

The Monument will be of a true South African nature, and to say, as has been done in some unauthorised newspaper articles, that it will be Greek or another sort of monument, is entirely incorrect.

So it is hardly surprising that Moerdyk generally avoided citing classical prototypes when discussing the origins of his design. Such forerunners would have been particularly abhorrent to an Afrikaner audience because they conjured up British imperial connections – not least the Union Buildings to which the Voortrekker Monument was to provide a considered counterpoint, as the two edifices faced each other across the city of Pretoria. The British chose the classical style, with 'its "eternal principles" and "ordered beauty" . . . to embody in stone the spirit of the empire', and 'to enhance the moral worth . . . of their political handiwork'.[31] But the Monument emphatically eschewed the colonnaded

---

[29] *Official Guide*, 35. The essays in the guide seem to have been modelled closely on Moerdyk's writing for the inauguration booklet in 1949, analysed by Grundlingh 2009: 157–77. Perhaps it flattered Moerdyk's Afrikaner reading that the Mausoleum was not ordered by a famous Greek but a native Carian, the Persian satrap Maussollos, who ruled in the fourth century BC. For reconstructions of the almost lost Mausoleum, see Jeppesen 2002.

[30] To emphasise this point, the quoted paragraph is printed in bold typeface: *Die Vaderland*, 14 April 1936, 'Massiewe bouwerk van granite binne ringmuur met waens. Komitee-besluit oor vorm van Voortrek-monument. Plek nog nie beslis nie.' (Massive construction of granite within a ring wall of wagons. Committee decides on the form of the Voortrekker Monument. Place not yet decided.), Moerdyk files, Special Collections, Merensky Library, University of Pretoria.

[31] Metcalf 1980: 12.

elegance of the European tradition.[32] Yet, even as Moerdyk rejected any British, and along with it any obviously classical connections, for his architectural design, he was seeking to achieve exactly such a sense of eternity, order and morality to embody the qualities of the Afrikaner nation. Instead of citing any prior tradition, however, he proposed an innovative form that would be the first in a new architectural line.

In the *Official Guide*, Moerdyk – perhaps mendaciously and certainly misleadingly – speaks of 'The Book' (the Bible) as a sole source of inspiration for himself as it had been for the devout Voortrekkers.[33] Afrikaners had developed no monumental architectural tradition for him to draw upon, he reminds his reader. In 'The Book' he discovers an analogy in Abraham of the Old Testament who built altars to the Lord while travelling from Ur to the new land promised him by God.[34] There was no knowledge of what such edifices might have looked like to guide – or constrain – Moerdyk, but the biblical association lent authority to the idea that the Voortrekker would have 'made his monument a religious one' and, like Abraham, built an altar.[35] As would be portrayed in the frieze, the Voortrekkers were regarded as 'chosen' people travelling to a 'promised' land.

The focal point of the Monument is indeed an altar-like structure: a cenotaph made of highly polished South African granite, the symbolic resting place of Piet Retief and other Voortrekkers who lost their lives in

---

[32] Moerdyk 1919: 7, stated dogmatically that works such as Sir Herbert Baker's Union Buildings – in the dead albeit lovely Italian Renaissance style – could never be part of 'die wese van ons volk' (the being of our people). Nevertheless, there are relationships between Moerdyk's designs and the seemingly inimical work of Baker. Both promote local materials, and Bunn 1998 points out that Baker's vernacular style is dependent on 'roughly dressed stone'. This is similar to the treatment of the granite at the Voortrekker Monument. Both men were also interested in Cape Dutch architecture, which Moerdyk documented with support from a Carnegie grant, awarded in 1920: Vermeulen 1999: 46.

[33] *Official Guide*, 32.

[34] Abraham, whose journeys are described in Genesis 12, was an appropriate precursor for the Voortrekkers, both as a devoutly religious man, and because he too left his place of birth to found a new nation. A further analogy for the Afrikaner was drawn with God's injunction to Abraham to 'be fruitful and multiply' (*Official Guide*, 36), 'waaruit die gedagte voortvloei om Suid-Afrika 'n witmansland te maak en te hou' (which gave rise to the idea to make and keep South Africa a white man's land), as Moerdyk wrote in the inauguration programme, quoted in Vermeulen 1999: 133. Moerdyk's ubiquitous metaphor of fertility in the chevron symbol of water also relates to this idea.

[35] *Official Guide*, 32. That Moerdyk thought of the Monument as the equivalent of a church is confirmed in his daughter Irma's marriage to Tinus Vermeulen there in 1946, before the building's completion. She writes that he wanted her to marry 'in die grootste kerk wat hy gebou het, die heiligdom van die Afrikanervolk' (in the biggest church that he built, the sanctuary of the Afrikaner people), see Vermeulen 1999: x.

the course of the 'Great Trek' (Fig. 5.6).[36] The cenotaph stands in solitary solemnity in the Lower Hall, framed by the circular opening in the Hall of Heroes above. A glowing, almost spiritual light permeates the Hall through the yellow Belgian glass of the huge windows, picked up in the optical flicker of the patterned marble floor. The floor's radiating lines of golden chevrons against a tawny background converge on the central opening, a design read by sculptor Hennie Potgieter as circular ripples, with the central cenotaph symbolising the stone of civilisation thrown into a pool of barbarism (Fig. 5.7).[37] The importance of the cenotaph is also emphasised by the architectural staging which requires that everyone who wants to look at it from the Hall 'involuntarily has to bow down his head' and pay respect to the legendary Voortrekkers.[38] The circular opening has a further function: it allows the rays of the sun, directed through a small aperture in the upper dome and the wider oculus below, to shine onto the cenotaph at midday on the Day of the Vow (Figs 5.4, 6) – specifically onto the inscription of the last line of the Afrikaans national anthem 'Ons vir jou Suid Afrika' (We for thee South Africa). The Day of the Vow has become part of the cosmic circle.[39]

All the elements of the architecture collude to highlight the only three-dimensional artefact within the Monument: the cenotaph at its heart. And, as the domed building encircles the cenotaph, it is in turn enclosed by a ring of wagons (Fig. 5.5). This defensive laager symbolically protects the Afrikaner ideals embodied in the Monument, just as it protected the Voortrekkers at the Battle of Blood River, to which the 64 wagons pay homage.[40] Depicted in coloured synthetic granite reliefs on both sides of the encircling wall, the wagons, each 4.6 metres long and 2.7 metres high, replicate the design and scale of those used by the original Voortrekkers and their 1938 successors. Although it never eventuated, their routes were

[36] Moerdyk's original intention to inter the remains of Piet Retief and others killed by the Zulu in 1838 in the Lower Hall was rejected (Steenkamp 2008a: 101–2). The concept of a symbolic empty tomb has a clear precedent in Lutyens' Whitehall Cenotaph erected in London at the end of World War I, a memorial form emulated in many British colonies.

[37] Potgieter 1987: 40.   [38] *Official Guide*, 33.

[39] As Elizabeth Delmont expresses it, 'conflating the spiritual symbol of the altar with the symbolic grave of a war hero and the closing words of the national anthem, and the sunlight with divine blessing, the connection between God and Country is overtly made': 1993: 88.

[40] The proposal for the laager came from Professors E. C. Pienaar and A. C. Bouman. Moerdyk's suggestions for combining the two forms were recorded in SVK Minutes, 7 April 1936, Item 5 (Voortrekker Monument Heritage Site Archive and Research Centre). The wagons were made under the guidance of one of the sculptors of the frieze, Frikkie Kruger, by the Italian firm Lupini in Johannesburg. Kruger also undertook the creation of the four Voortrekker figures for the corners of the Monument: a local stone mason from Johannesburg was employed to carve the works in granite, enlarged from Kruger's life-size plasters (Potgieter 1987: 50).

to be memorialised on the dome which for Moerdyk represented 'the globe with South Africa on top': 'It is planned at a later stage to map out South Africa in bas-relief on the dome. On this map a silver thread will indicate the routes of the Great Trek.'[41]

It was no doubt an attractive notion to an architect to claim that he was working with a *tabula rasa* uninfluenced by any other architecture, and it matches ideas of developing a unique South African style that Moerdyk had expressed as early as 1919 in a self-published book on church design:

Alleen dan kan ons 'n styl van waarde kry wanneer dit 'n groeie is uit ons eie tydperk en uit ons eie land. *Kopier niks nie*. Soos ek alreeds gese het as ons ernstig en sonder bedrog werk, as ons die beste en geskikste materiale logies gebruik en as ons geinspireer word deur kunstenaars wat genoeë in hulle skeppinge neem sal ons ook 'n styl kry waar ons met reg trots op kan wees.[42]

We can only have a style of value when it grows out of our own time and our own land. *Copy nothing*. As I have already said, if we are earnest and work without guile, if we make rational use of the best and most suitable materials, and if we are inspired by artists who take satisfaction in their creations, then we will also achieve a style of which we can justly be proud.

These aesthetic principles of earnest integrity and self-reliance complemented the intensifying sense of an independent Afrikaner heritage with which Moerdyk closely aligned himself, and which would shape the foundations on which Afrikaner nationalist policies were built.[43]

2. The Architect: Classical Education Versus the Afrikaner Cause

Moerdyk's personal history is pertinent in reaching an understanding both of his commitment to the Afrikaner cause and of the pronounced classical associations that we will argue are central to the Voortrekker Monument, notwithstanding protestations to the contrary. Although Moerdyk's parents were immigrants from the Netherlands, his father fought on the Afrikaner side in the Anglo-Boer War against the British 'kakies' (so named for their khaki uniforms), and his mother and the rest

---

[41] *Official Guide*, 34.   [42] Moerdyk 1919: 5–7 (our italics).

[43] The contemporary South African architects Gordon Leith and Gerard Moerdyk, as well as artist Hendrik Pierneef, were at the forefront in proclaiming that the country needed to develop a new national style (Chipkin 1993: 132–33).

of the family suffered considerable hardship during his absence when they were interned in a British concentration camp. Memories of these horrific experiences as a boy must have engendered strong anti-British sentiments for Moerdyk, leading him to reject military service in World War I. They would equally have fostered his intense sense of identification with the Afrikaner people,[44] and his later involvement in memorialising their early history, although his own forebears had not been a part of it.

Yet despite this, Moerdyk had strong affiliations with Britain that were important in shaping his architectural career and his aesthetic sense. Surprisingly, he chose to go to England to study (the Netherlands might have seemed a more obvious choice) and was to become an Associate of the Royal Institute of British Architects. Some of his experiences during his studies at the London School of Architecture from 1910 to 1912 suggest their importance for his later development. In an early letter home on 6 October 1910, Moerdyk enthused about the evening lectures, and one recently heard on Greek architecture, where the lantern slides made it possible to 'travel' through all of Athens, seeing buildings that were still recognisable, and others reduced to ruins, which were the subject of lectures. He wrote:

Dit is wonderlik om to sien hoe hulle die ouwe verblyf selfs weer oplap, en 'n gebou vertoon 'as it was' 500 v.Ch.[45]

It is wonderful to see how they reconstruct the remains, and show a building 'as it was' 500 BC.

And just over a year later, on 24 November 1911, he wrote with pride that he had passed the gruelling Intermediate examinations, and passed them well:

Ek is 17de uit Engeland, en in Klassieke Argitektuur [dit is sy hoofvak] is ek nommer 1 van die hele spul. (24 November 1911).[46]

---

[44] Moerdyk's marriage in 1917 to Sylva Pirow was another factor in his identification with Afrikanerdom: his German-born father-in-law was pro-Afrikaner, and his brother-in-law, Oswald Pirow, was active in Afrikaner law and politics, as was Sylva herself. Vermeulen (1999: 49) notes that Moerdyk was asked to join the nationalistic Broederbond in 1920, an indication of his acceptance by a select inner circle of Afrikaners, and records his considered decision to work for Afrikaner clients, although it was not to his economic advantage (44, 48–9, and passim).

[45] Ibid., 23. Moerdyk's original letters in 'Hollands' (Dutch) were translated into Afrikaans by Sylva Moerdyk and Naka Pillman (ibid., 21). The translation to English is our own. Moerdyk's enthusiasm for classical architecture was to endure. At one point he calls it the greatest inheritance of civilised man (1919: 4).

[46] Vermeulen 1999: 29. She notes that Classical Architecture would be known today as the History of Architecture (ibid., 35) and acknowledges Moerdyk's longstanding interest in antiquity, first

> I am 17th in England, and in Classical Architecture [this is his major], I am
> number 1 of the whole bunch.

It was an achievement that he would repeat in his final examinations in
1912, when he was placed first in Classical Architecture in the British
Commonwealth.[47] However much Moerdyk may have set aside such
interests when describing the Voortrekker Monument, it is clear that
historical architecture was not only a part of his curriculum, but
a relished subject in which he excelled. Reinforcing this, he went on
a 'Grand Tour' of Europe after passing his Intermediate examinations,
travels which continued later in his life. His historical interests are
further confirmed by his publication in English of a number of articles
on architectural history,[48] and a short history of architecture, *Die
Geskiedenis van Boukuns*, was published for Afrikaans readers in 1935.
In it he acknowledges that no architectural style can be uninfluenced by
what went before, so it would be foolish to think that South African
architecture could come 'into full flower' without the guidance of old
building styles.[49] And he claims classical edifices to be so beautiful in
concept and embodying such high aspirations that architectural students
of all countries and all times look to the buildings of ancient Greece as
the best that have been made by human hands. Moerdyk's engagement
with historical buildings is everywhere apparent in his architectural
practice: his Art Deco modernism incorporated ideas gleaned from his
studies, from the Cape Dutch in South Africa to the Byzantine,
Romanesque and Renaissance styles that informed his church
designs.[50] Nor did he deny his indebtedness to a range of precedents:
as in the classical tradition, there was no disgrace in making use of

---

prompted by studies at the British School of Archaeology (*sic*) at Rome, but suggests that his
later focus was on African antiquities (ibid., 50).

[47] Ibid., 35.

[48] Fisher 2003: 30, 36; he cites one entitled 'Greek history and Greek temples' (Moerdijk 1917).

[49] Moerdyk 1935: 44. Moerdyk's history does make a case for a nationalist architecture, but
without addressing style specifically, claiming that to be good, art and architecture must be
national. He writes that architecture must grow out of the soil, reflecting the character of the
people who build it and realising their ideals in concrete form (ibid., 16). His most doctrinaire
application of this, in the notion of an independent Afrikaner style free of alien influences,
seems to come into play when writing about projects with an overtly Afrikaner agenda, such as
Reformed churches and the Voortrekker Monument.

[50] Moerdyk's Reformed church designs, while drawing on multiple forms of European
architecture, created a distinctive style for the Afrikaner congregations he served, notably in
curved seating plans focused on the pulpit, not unlike the arrangement of Greek theatres,
and placing emphasis on preaching rather than the processional ritual of longitudinal
churches.

multiple styles which were customary for many architects at the time, and in his case more broadly based than for most.[51]

Yet when Moerdyk wrote about the Voortrekker Monument for the *Official Guide*, he avoided such acknowledgements.[52] That this focus on an unsullied Afrikaner style was politically motivated is suggested by the fact that his daughter, writing *Man en monument* in the very different context of the 1990s, does not avoid reference to many influences, such as Biblical, Aztec, Assyrian and German inspiration. Although she does not mention classical antiquity, she continues, 'Die klassieke invloed van die Renaissance kom in die simmetrie van die ontwerp voor met sy delikaat gerproporsioneerde vensters en onderdele' (The classical influence of the Renaissance comes in the symmetry of the design with its delicately proportioned windows and elements).[53] In writing about the Monument, however, Moerdyk focused not on elements of the building's planning and design that might have revealed specific historical links with Europe, but on the scale of the edifice and its materials, sufficiently generalised aspects for him to be able to conjure up sweeping analogies. He compared the grand dimensions with the vastness of Africa as a continent and the monumental stone structures of Egypt and Great Zimbabwe. The granite, he claimed, 'is of the same quality as that found in the Egyptian quarries at Aswan. Buildings and structures in Egypt are still standing to-day after the lapse of 4,000 years . . . As far as can be seen, the monument will stand forever'.[54] However, no specific formal comparison was made, only the principles of vastness and imperishability were mooted.

Moerdyk deployed various devices to stress the monumentality of the building, such as the diminishing height of the granite courses on the exterior, and the enormous scale of the higher dome, which represented 'the magnitude of the "heroic deed"' of the Trek.[55] Yet he was quick to point out (with seeming modesty) that the Monument was not extravagant in its dimensions despite its impression of magnitude,[56] remarking that it was of similar size to the Mausoleum of Halicarnassus and considerably

[51] Nonetheless, this approach was considered problematic by some, as Moerdyk's style was 'at odds with his contemporaries at the Wits School who, at the time, were vigorous disciples of the Modern Movement as an international style' (Fisher quoted in Vermeulen 1999: 142).

[52] *Official Guide*, esp. 35.   [53] Vermeulen 1999: 136.   [54] *Official Guide*, 55.   [55] Ibid., 34.

[56] One wonders whether this may have been a response to Calvinist parsimony (Moerdyk was well known for his economical designs). But little expense was spared on the Monument. The total cost was R719,200: despite not yet being Nationalist, the government contributed R676,000, the balance having been raised by Afrikaner supporters (ibid., 58). As Delmont comments, it was ironic that the Monument was 'largely funded by the government in power, which was supporting a cause that was eventually to lead to its downfall in 1948' (1993: 79).

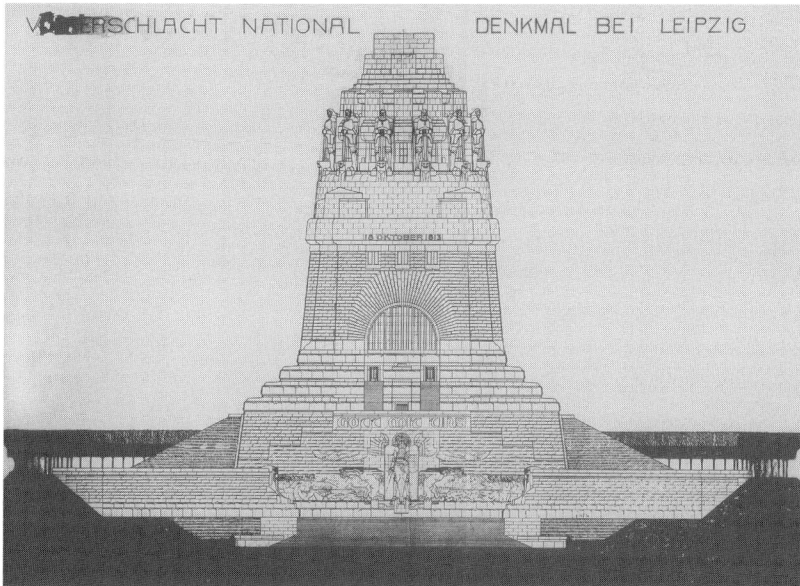

Figure 5.8 Völkerschlachtdenkmal, Leipzig; elevation drawing by Bruno Schmitz, 1913. After Volker Rodekamp (ed.) *Völkerschlachtdenkmal* (2009).

smaller in scale than other comparable buildings. This afforded him the opportunity to refer to an inventory of international monuments of larger dimensions – the Hotel des Invalides in Paris housing the tomb of Napoleon; India's Taj Mahal; the Völkerschlachtdenkmal in Leipzig (Figs 5.8–9); the Great Pyramids of Egypt; even the Great Wall of China – a list so diverse that besides size and fame no clear lineage is suggested.[57] It was a clever strategy that not only demonstrated Moerdyk's own wide knowledge, but also placed the Monument in the company of some of the world's greatest architecture. Even while he was at pains to deny foreign influences, Moerdyk was implying that the Voortrekker Monument was part of a history of celebrated civilisations with noble architectural traditions. Yet he stressed in an interview of 1936 that, while similar in function to sanctuaries, these buildings were inappropriate models in that they did not 'reflect the Voortrekker or our country or ourselves'.[58] He continued, 'The Voortrekker brought civilisation. Civilisation in architecture means order and geometry'. Moerdyk claimed

---

[57] *Official Guide*, 35. In his unpublished papers, Moerdyk adds the Pantheon and St Peter's in Rome to this list (Steenkamp 2008a: 105).

[58] Monument Moet Verlede Sowel As Volkskarakter Weerspieel: Mnr. Moerdyk Verduidelik Idee Van Sy Ontwerp' (Monument must reflect the past as well as the [Afrikaans] national character: Mr Moerdyk explains the idea of his design), *Die Vaderland*, 10 December 1936.

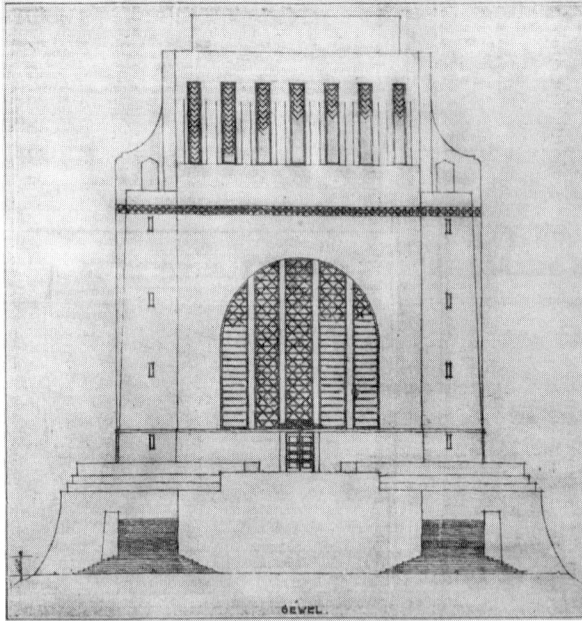

Figure 5.9 North façade, Voortrekker Monument; elevation drawing by Gerard Moerdyk. After *Die Volkstem*, 11 September 1936.

this differentiated the Monument from the work of 'the savage [who] had an architecture, but without geometry. The largest old building in South Africa, namely at Zimbabwe, was without any geometry.'[59] The Monument's uniqueness lay in 'a logical geometric application of Afrikaans building material',[60] not following any pre-existing architectural forms.

The Völkerschlachtdenkmal (1897–1913), according to Moerdyk 11 times the size of the Voortrekker Monument, and possibly the least-known edifice in his comparisons of scale, no doubt found its way onto his list because it was on his mind.[61] It is in many ways the closest prototype for the Voortrekker Monument – certainly far more than any Greek or Roman forerunner, although it too referenced ancient monuments in general terms in its size and symmetry, and its rich sculptural ensemble. The Leipzig memorial offers a close even if inconsistent point of

[59] Ibid. This view is also found in *Die Geskiedenis van Boukuns* where Moerdyk comments on the total absence of geometric knowledge at Great Zimbabwe (1935: 27).
[60] Steenkamp 2008a: 111.
[61] Neumeister and Haeberle 1897; Hutter 1990; Rodekamp 2009. Although overwhelming in scale, the Völkerschlachtdenkmal is considerably smaller than Moerdyk posits: it is 91 metres high on a plinth of 70 by 80 metres; the domed hall is 68 metres high.

reference for the Voortrekker Monument, and makes a more detailed comparison seem mandatory. That the resemblance is no mere coincidence also seems confirmed when one learns that three volumes, *Drei Kaiserdenkmäler: Ausgeführte Architekturwerke*, depicting works by Bruno Schmitz, credited with the design of the Leipzig memorial,[62] were available to Moerdyk. These and other records were dispatched to South Africa in response to requests for sketches or photographs of monuments, sent at the beginning of 1936 by the Secretary of Foreign Affairs on behalf of the SVK to Paris, Rome, Berlin, New York and London.[63] However, these publications would have arrived too late to have influenced Moerdyk's first plans, and the Völkerschlachtdenkmal itself was not part of the three volumes, and indeed never published by Schmitz. Yet the similarities suggest that Moerdyk was familiar with the Leipzig monument. It is even reported that Moerdyk visited Leipzig in 1936,[64] and saw the Völkerschlachtdenkmal for himself, which would suggest his interest in the monument.

Built a hundred years later to commemorate the 1813 victory over Napoleon at the Battle of Nations at Leipzig, the Völkerschlachtdenkmal looked back at a key moment in the emergence of a sense of a unified German identity, not dissimilar to the nationalist concepts embodied for Afrikaners in the Voortrekker Monument. They share a number of architectural features. Like its South African counterpart, the Leipzig building on its high podium is unadorned with classical columns and presents a formidable granite exterior, elevated above imposing flights of steps. The buildings share a centralised plan: vast interiors roofed with a dome; a large arched window on each façade, ordered by vertical sections

---

[62] The roles of the Patriotenbund and Leipzig architect Clement Thieme were of considerable significance in the design and execution of the monument, as were the two sculptors Christian Behrens and Franz Metzner (see Topfstedt 2009). In contrast, although overseen by the SVK, Moerdyk seems to have had a much freer hand in the shaping of the Voortrekker Monument.

[63] The three volumes of Schmitz 1900 are in the Voortrekker Monument Heritage Site Archive and Research Centre, as are photographs of other monuments, such as the Monument International de la Reformation, Geneva, and the Scottish American War Memorial, Edinburgh, as well as various German examples including the classical Walhalla near Regensburg, that must have been sent in response to requests for international models. See the Minutes of the SVK Vorm Komitee of 26 January 1936: Item 1 recorded that Senator Malan would approach the Secretary of Foreign Affairs to request from the South African embassies in Rome, Paris, Berlin, New York and London images of relevant historical monuments in those countries. Item 4 required Mr Jordaan to assemble from publications other examples such as the Shrine of Remembrance in Melbourne and the statue of Abraham Lincoln in Washington (Voortrekker Monument Heritage Site, Archive and Research Centre, Pretoria).

[64] Perhaps while visiting Germany for the Olympic Games that year, as recounted by Werner Kirchhoff, December 2013.

and filled with coloured glass; a circular opening allowing a view from the upper to the lower hall, at Leipzig known as the Hall of Fame and the Crypt respectively.[65] Forms of construction too share similar aspects; both are built of concrete with granite facing, which, unlike costly polished surfaces of classical granite, is left artificially rough, with elongated granite blocks laid in courses.[66] Like Moerdyk, the architect of the Völkerschlachtdenkmal had excluded established historical forms from its design to invent a national (in this case Germanic) style, here articulated in contemporary Art Nouveau forms, yet pressing these qualities to aesthetic extremes.[67]

But when you experience the Völkerschlachtdenkmal itself, in its verticality and sheer monumentality it far outstrips the Voortrekker Monument (Figs 5.8–9). The elevation of the Leipzig edifice with its huge granite blocks, some as heavy as 18 tons, over its substructure of 120,000 cubic metres of concrete, is overpowering. So too is the multitude of symbolic granite figures, within and without, that both mourn the historical dead and defend the national future, including 8 pairs of warriors, 6 metres high in the Crypt, and another 12 of 13 metres on the crown of the building. Compared with these gargantuan effigies, the 5.5 metre corner figures of Voortrekker leaders on the Pretoria monument seem isolated and somehow modest, and the distinctive use of the marble frieze offers a narrative on human scale, conveying its refinement and link to classical heritage. The Voortrekker Monument's interior spaces have the effect overall of a greater simplicity and coherence than the radical plasticity of the Völkerschlachtdenkmal, with its complex relationship of rectilinear, multi-layered exterior and curved, convoluted interior plans. In both design and general impact the Voortrekker Monument's dependence on the intensely anti-classical Völkerschlachtdenkmal, important as it is, may well have been overemphasised.[68]

There are also comparisons to be made with other monuments, such as two war memorials that had recently been completed in Australia, both dedicated in 1934.[69] The Anzac War Memorial in Sydney shares a similar

---

[65]   The likely debt to the distinctive circular opening in the grandiose presentation of Napoleon's tomb beneath the dome of Les Invalides, Paris, suggests that this might be a common source for both the German and South African monuments.

[66]   The courses at the Voortrekker Monument are considerably narrower, a characteristic related by Moerdyk to the small units of stone used in building Great Zimbabwe: Vermeulen 1999: 133.

[67]   Hutter 1990: 132–34.   [68]   *Inter alia*, Steenkamp 2009: 150–60.

[69]   Inglis 2005: 303–13 (Sydney, Anzac War Memorial) and 315–29 (Melbourne, Shrine of Remembrance). It contextualises the Art Deco aspect of the Voortrekker Monument, that Inglis notes of the Sydney memorial that 'any detail was welcome on a basically plain design so long as it was not from the classical tradition' (306).

Figure 5.10 ANZAC War Memorial, Sydney, 1929–34.

silhouette with the Voortrekker Monument, as well as Art Deco detailing (Fig. 5.10).[70] Comparable arched windows of tinted glass on each façade bathe the interior in a golden light, and a balustraded circular opening in the interior allows viewers to gaze down on a symbolic sculpture of *Sacrifice*.[71] The Memorial in Sydney also has large-scale sculptured figures on each corner, though at the crown, not the base of the building, and it recounts achievements of Australian troops in relief friezes, in this case in

[70] While we had noted similarities, it was useful to learn that it was likely that Moerdyk would have seen the building illustrated in the *Architect, Builder & Engineer* (March 1935, 9), as pointed out in the Moerdyk article on the Artefacts website devoted to the South African Built Environment, kindly brought to our attention by Professor Roger Fisher and Nicholas Clarke, www.artefacts.co.za./main/Buildings/archframes.php?archid=1102&orig_form=archlistframes .php%20bldgorder=%60tblbldg%60.%60name%60&%20orderby=Surname&initial=M&source= 0&backbutton=1.

[71] Albeit more modest in scale, this feature, like the circular openings at the Völkerschlachtdenkmal and the Voortrekker Monument, is probably indebted to Napoleon's tomb in Les Invalides.

bronze and installed over the east and west doorways. The Shrine of Remembrance in Melbourne, which is strongly indebted to (reconstructions of) the Mausoleum of Halicarnassus, also employs a frieze to recount episodes of the war. Here it is inside the building, as at the Voortrekker Monument, although the Melbourne frieze is elevated above the entablature of the sanctuary's Ionic peristyle, and divided into panels by flat pilasters. Another feature at Melbourne that relates closely to the Monument is the incorporation of an aperture in the roof to direct a ray of light onto the inscription 'Greater love hath no man' on a Stone of Remembrance beneath the floor of the sanctuary. The illumination in this case occurs at the time that marked the end of World War I in 1918, the eleventh hour of the eleventh day of the eleventh month: a different war and a different motto, but a similar concept to that at the Monument. The inscription underscored the ties to the British Empire in the Australian monuments: ties which would have been inimical to Moerdyk, and which no doubt discouraged him from acknowledging any ideas he might have gleaned from these sources.

There were thus a number of recent precedents for the Voortrekker Monument, yet these and others of more historical origin were suppressed by Moerdyk in favour of the ideology of a new architecture for a new nation. He preferred to pick out elements which seem to link the design to Africa. Curiously, Moerdyk makes no reference to a natural African source near Nylstroom where he spent his earliest childhood, the silhouette of Kranskop, which Vermeulen cites as the originating idea for the form of the Monument.[72] The distinctive flat-topped South African outcrops or 'koppies', indeed reminiscent of the Monument, are clearly depicted in some of the scenes in the Monument frieze (e.g. Figs 5.22, 32). Vermeulen further relates the building's narrowing silhouette to African rock formations, claiming that this, as well as its use of local granite, makes the Monument a true part of the enduring land.[73] Moerdyk's emphasis was rather on the analogies of scale and endurance already discussed. And he mentioned that, flanking Van Wouw's bronze of a Voortrekker mother

---

[72] Vermeulen 1999: 8. For the idiosyncratic Voortrekkermonumentkoppie, see Duffey 2005: figure 3.

[73] Ibid., 36. Alta Steenkamp notes Moerdyk's claim that 'the geometry of the design was further related to a category close to the Afrikaner's heart: the squares, cubes, circles and planes used, he stated, put the monument in perfect harmony with 'our tabular landscape' ('Architecture rethought in relation to space, power and the body', 65). Analogies could also be drawn with the cubistic landscapes of Jacobus Hendrik Pierneef, who would create an iconic painting of the Monument in 1949, today housed in the Lower Hall. For Pierneef see Coetzee 1992.

protecting a girl and a boy at the entrance,[74] (black) wildebeest panels represented the Voortrekker's routed Zulu opponents; a carved buffalo head over the central doorway was an African symbol of defence;[75] and the superstructure's decorative band of zigzag chevrons, echoing those of Great Zimbabwe, denoted water and fertility in Africa.[76] But these are mere details. No hint is given of the many possible prototypes that he could – and undoubtedly did – draw upon for the concept of the building as a whole, including ideas closely related to antiquity.

In 1936, at the time Moerdyk was preparing his designs, he had also journeyed to Egypt.[77] Even before this, his earliest proposal, submitted together with sculptor Anton van Wouw, had apparently been a pair of enormous truncated obelisks, perhaps not unlike the pylon gateway of an Egyptian temple façade.[78] In the end, however, he achieved an analogy with Egypt through monumental scale and enduring materials rather than any particular form. While specific links may seem minimal, though, it seems worth mentioning Egypt here as it is the only ancient culture that Moerdyk singles out.[79] He is fulsome in his admiration for the scale and lasting qualities of Egyptian architecture, praise that then reflects on the similar qualities he describes in the Monument, supporting his claim for its Africanness. But it might be well to remember that Egypt is a part of the

---

[74] Memories of one 'volk' tragedy can incite others: particularly as Van Wouw also created the *Vrouemonument* in Bloemfontein, Afrikaner viewers confronting his colossal Voortrekker mother protecting her children might be reminded of British atrocities during the Anglo-Boer War, when 4,177 women and 22,074 children incarcerated in British concentration camps died wretchedly: Giliomee 2003: 253–56.

[75] As recorded in *Official Guide*, 53, the buffalo head was designed by Hennie Potgieter and the wildebeest by Ernest Ullmann, a German-born sculptor working in Johannesburg.

[76] Marschall 2001: 141 points out that similar details – a chevron frieze and carvings of African animals – were used by Moerdyk in his 1937 designs for the Merensky Library, University of Pretoria, an institution that also 'played a leading role in propagating Afrikaner culture'. Similarities in building design too have led to speculation that the library was a prototype for the Monument, but Nicholas Clarke points out that the two buildings were conceived at much the same time, even though the library was completed some years before the Monument (interview, Pretoria, December 2013).

[77] Vermeulen asserts the importance of this Egyptian trip for Moerdyk's architectural career, but provides little detail (1999: 105–6).

[78] The relationship between Moerdyk and Van Wouw and the form of their 'Egyptian' design, dating back to 1933, are discussed by Duffey (2005). He quotes the description of 'twee massiewe naalde, kortgekap en sê 85 voet hoog' (two massive needles, cut short and, say, 85 feet tall) from *Die Vaderland* of 26 August 1933 (3). Moerdyk also produced a drawing of a monumental Egyptianising building structure, published by Fisher and Clarke 2010: 155–56, Fig. 8.

[79] *Official Guide*, 35 and 55. Moerdyk (implicitly?) follows some of the nineteenth-century visions of ancient Egypt invented by the British elite in (and for) South Africa, see Peter Merrington's rich essay in this book.

continent that has never quite been subsumed into the African story, but retains strong links to the Mediterranean. It was a qualified sense of Africa that Moerdyk was acknowledging.

The lower dome with its oculus paid homage architecturally to a culture that was also a part of the civilising crucible of the Mediterranean, and one more directly a part of the classical tradition: the configuration clearly referenced one of Rome's great buildings, the Pantheon.[80] In accord with the Monument, structurally the Pantheon had needed to be built of concrete, the *opus caementicium* that had revolutionised architecture since the second century BC.[81] And the interiors of both constructions are faced with coloured marble. Even more than in the similar construction, however, significant correspondences lie in the proportions of the buildings, a symbolic geometry which Moerdyk had identified as a characteristic of what he called civilised architecture. As at the Pantheon, there is a careful correlation of the various dimensions of the Voortrekker Monument: Moerdyk states that 'the Hall of Heroes is 100 feet by 100 feet by 100 feet high',[82] thus forming a cube that would precisely contain the virtual sphere described by the hemisphere of the lower dome were it completed (Fig. 5.4).[83] There is a clear intention to create a thoroughly ordered harmony, a principle that had its origins in the sacred architecture of ancient Greece and Rome, however different in appearance this building may be.

3.   The Frieze: Turning History into Marble

Far more than the architecture, however, the element that most closely bears a relationship to ancient prototypes is the marble frieze that surrounds the walls of the Hall of Heroes: 27 panels, 2.3 metres high and 92 metres long overall (Figs 5.22–48), weighing 180 metric tons in their finished state – daunting dimensions when one considers that they

---

[80] Jones 2000: 177–213; Graßhoff et al. 2009. Moerdyk refers to the Pantheon as the 'most perfect' of circular temples 1935: 54.

[81] Lechtman and Hobbs 1986.

[82] *Official Guide*, 58. Vermeulen claims that these were symbolic numbers commemorating the centenary (1999: 133).

[83] The proportional relationships of the Pantheon were available in a number of publications, such as Fletcher (1897), a standard text for architectural students. Steenkamp 2008a: 105 points out that Moerdyk used Fletcher for the measurements of the different buildings he cites in comparison with the Monument.

Figure 5.11 Hall of Heroes, south and west walls, Voortrekker Monument, 2012. (A black and white version of this figure will appear in some formats. For the colour version, please refer to the plate section.)

had to be transported from Italy where they were carved. To the visitor entering this almost anti-classical building, the classical marble frieze is its biggest surprise (Fig. 5.11 and Plate 6).[84] The stylistic discrepancy of architecture and frieze carries even more weight as the carved reliefs were no decorative afterthought but a key element in the Monument,[85] giving permanent form to the history of the treks and thus making explicit the purpose of the building as a whole. So much of the *Official Guide* is devoted to the frieze that it reads almost as though the building had been erected primarily to present it. Moerdyk did not relate the Voortrekker frieze to the friezes of antiquity, other than to dwell yet again on an issue of scale, claiming proudly that it was the largest sculptural frieze in history, with the exception of that of the Altar of Zeus at Pergamon, had it survived intact.[86] Yet it is immediately apparent that the chief precedents for the Voortrekker frieze are to be found in

[84] For a 360-degree view of the frieze see: 360 South Africa Virtual Tour Photography, 'Voortrekker Monument Hall of Heroes', www.360cities.net/image/voortrekker-monument-hall-of-heroes#-54.08,-6.23,70.0.

[85] The central importance of the frieze is confirmed by the extent of the discussion allocated to it in publications on the Monument, such as the longest chapter in *Official Guide*, 38–51. Evans' phrase, 'a monument to house a monument', although directed at the panel on the Church of the Vow, seems entirely apposite (2007: 148).

[86] *Official Guide*, 39.

Greek and Roman architectural sculpture, with close parallels provided by the war-related narratives of imperial Rome (see Figs 5.18–19), namely the columns of Trajan and Marcus Aurelius.[87]

As an architectural student, Moerdyk's awareness of classical antiquity would have been fostered not only through his studies already discussed, but by the museums of London. The two Architectural Courts of the Victoria and Albert Museum in South Kensington were a rich resource with their multitude of life-size replicas of architectural sculpture, as well as architectural drawings and models included in the early exhibits. In particular, it offered a unique opportunity to examine the narrative relief ribbon of Trajan's column, 'the only [full-scale] reconstruction of the entire monument in existence'.[88] Because it was too tall to fit into the court (now gallery 46A), it was exhibited in two parts, thus affording the advantage of being considerably more visible than the monument itself in Rome. Of equal importance was the range of original examples of Greek art and architecture in the British Museum. A number of friezes dominated the collection: that of the Parthenon is no doubt the best known, but those of Apollo at Bassae, the Nereid Monument from Xanthos and the Mausoleum of Halicarnassus too were prominently displayed.[89] These works demonstrated the role of relief sculpture as an ennobling element of classical monuments. It seems it was a principle that Moerdyk did not easily forget.[90]

It could be argued that friezes were typically applied to the exterior of classical architecture. However, temple friezes were not always on outer walls: that of the Parthenon was within the peristyle, of Bassae inside the naos itself. Both were originally in elevated positions as part of the entablatures of classical orders. But, significantly, Moerdyk's first-hand knowledge of the friezes would have been in modern interiors, installed around the walls of the British Museum at eye-level, a position more compelling to the viewer.[91] These installations provide a direct parallel to the design of the Voortrekker Monument frieze, whose scale, design and purpose were defined by Moerdyk as architect.

---

[87] Coarelli 2000, 2008; Griebel 2013. These books refer to earlier publications that Moerdyk might well have consulted.

[88] Bilbey and Trusted 2010: 473. Commissioned in 1864 to be made from moulds at the Louvre that had been created on the orders of Napoleon III, the casts of Trajan's column have dominated the Architectural Courts since they opened in 1873.

[89] Ian Jenkins traces the exhibition history of these sculptures, which confirms that the works were on display when Moerdyk was studying in London; see Jenkins 1992: esp. 75–101 and 211–30.

[90] Moerdyk picks out Greek architectural sculpture for special mention in his history of architecture, writing that the Greeks' sculptural mastery is attested in the friezes and bas reliefs of their temples (1935: 47).

[91] Exemplary on this point: Beard and Henderson 1995: 1–5.

An expert Historiese Komitee (Historical Committee) was appointed by the SVK to oversee the all-important task of selecting, unifying and dramatising the oral, written and material evidence still available from the different treks, turning 17 years of history into 92 metres of marble.[92] This was an extremely challenging task: separate treks had to be fused into one idealised 'Great Trek'; different readings of the same incident had to be harmonised; historical deeds had to be changed into symbolic representations; individual actions had to be converted into collective models. In other words, historical diversity had to be refashioned into a coherent visual sequence, 'a story with a beginning, a climax and a conclusion', as Moerdyk has it.[93] In 1937 making sketches for the envisaged narrative was entrusted to Willem Hermanus Coetzer (1900–83), a painter who had like Moerdyk trained in London, and like him too was committed to the Afrikaner cause.[94] Coetzer, who was considered very knowledgeable about Voortrekker history, presented 22 pencil sketches to the SVK (e.g. Fig. 5.16). The Historical Committee met on 4 September 1937 to discuss the sketches in detail, proposing amendments to enhance the appropriateness and authenticity of the scenes.[95] Item 4 of the Minutes lists the thematic order of the sketches (translation and figure number for the related scene of the marble frieze are added in brackets; for final layout, see Fig. 5.19):

[a] *Die uittog uit die kolonie* (The departure from the colony; Fig. 5.22); [b] *Uys ontvang die Bybel* (Uys receives the Bible; Fig. 5.23); [c] *Trichardt in Soutpansberg* (Trichardt in Soutpansberg; Fig. 5.24); [d] *Trichardt in Delagoabaai* (Trichardt in Delagoa Bay; Fig. 5.25); [e] *Vegkop* (Vegkop; Fig. 5.26); [f] *Boere onderhandel met Maroko* (Boers negotiate with Maroko; Fig. 5.29); [g] *Inswering van Retief* (Swearing in of Retief; Fig. 5.27); [h] *Blyde Vooruitzicht* ('Beautiful Prospect', the

---

[92] For negotiating the topics of the frieze see *Official Guide*, esp. 31, 34, 38–51 (ibid., 38, naming the members of its expert committee), which can be found in detail in the SVK minutes.

[93] Ibid., 38.

[94] Coetzer also designed the commemorative Great Trek stamps in 1938 and 1949, as well as the later tapestries of the Trek, made by Afrikaner women, for many years considered unsuitable for the Monument, but today installed in the Lower Hall. For the artist, see Coetzer 1947, 1980; De Beer 1969; Coetzee 1988; Schoonraad 1988.

[95] Notule van die eerste vergadering van die SVK Historiese Komitee (Minutes of the first meeting of the SVK Historical Committee), held in Moerdyk's office, 4 September 1937. The set referred to here is in ARCA, University of Bloemfontein, PV94 1/75/5/1, but a second variant set of 21 sketches, evidently responding to modifications suggested by the committee, is in the image collection of Museum Africa, Johannesburg; see Kennedy 1971: 152–56, numbers C1084–C1104.

first Natal site, merged with [i]; Fig. 5.30); [i] *Aftog van de Drakensberge* (Descent from the Drakensberg; Fig. 5.32); [j] *Tekening van traktaat* (Signing of treaty; Fig. 5.33); [k] *Moord op Retief* (Murder of Retief; Fig. 5.34); [l] Die Groot Moord (The great murder; Fig. 5.35); [m] *Dood van Dirkie Uys* (Death of Dirkie Uys; Fig. 5.37); [n] *Die vroue eis vergelding* (The women demand retribution; Fig. 5.39); [o] *Aankoms van Gen. Pretorius* (Arrival of General Pretorius; Fig. 5.40); [p] *Daanskraal* (Daanskraal, the place of the vow; Fig. 5.41); [q] *Bloedrivier* (Blood River; Fig. 5.42); [r] *Die Geloftekerkie* (Church of the Vow; Fig. 5.43); [s] *Kroning van Panda* (Crowning of Panda; Fig. 5.45); [t] *Terug oor die Drakensberge* (Back over the Drakensberg; Fig. 5.47); [u] *Ondertekening van traktate* (Signing of treaties; Fig. 5.33, 48); [v] *Allegoriese voorstelling* (Symbolic representation; rejected).

Moerdyk recounts that it was decided to appoint Afrikaans sculptors to convert the sketches into reliefs, but it was not until 1942 that four were selected from the 21 professional sculptors identified in South Africa at that time.[96] As well as selection being guided by their appropriate heritage for the sacred task,[97] it seems that their diverse but chiefly Reformed church affiliations may have been taken into account:[98] Frikkie Kruger (1907–66) was a member of the Nederduitse Hervormde Kerk; Laurika Postma (1903–87) of the Gerformeerde Kerk; and Hennie Potgieter (1917–92) of the Nederduitse Gereformeerde Kerk. But the fourth sculptor, Peter Kirchhoff (1893–1976), the only non-Afrikaner, was German and an atheist. His long experience as a sculptor, particularly on architectural projects, meant that he was appointed *primus inter pares*.[99] He had also already been involved in work for the Monument when he was appointed as Van Wouw's assistant to complete the sculpture of the Voortrekker woman for the entrance.[100]

---

[96] *Official Guide*, 38. Potgieter records that he received a letter of appointment on 13 March 1942, with suggested starting dates of 16 March (taken up by the others) or 1 April (when he elected to begin). He mentions that the sculptors had not previously met, although he believed that one reason for their selection was that their styles were considered compatible (1987: 40).

[97] See also Rankin 1991.

[98] Ibid., 1; Duffey 2005: 9, notes that his source for this explanation was information from Postma and Potgieter.

[99] SVK Minutes, 15–16 January 1942, Item 11 (NAR, Die Sentrale Volksmonument Komitee, vol 1, file no. A141. For the sculptors, on Postma see Duffey (1993) and Pillman (1984); on Potgieter see Van der Westhuysen (1984); on Kirchhoff see Duffey (2008).

[100] Information supplied by the sculptor's son, Werner Kirchhoff, interview, Johannesburg, December 2013. The appointment of an assistant for Van Wouw is mentioned a number of times in SVK minutes of 1937 and 1938, but Kirchhoff is not named.

Figure 5.12 Sculptors working on the full-scale clay model (subsequently destroyed) for 'Voortrekkers leave Cape Colony' (Fig. 5.22), Harmoniesaal, Pretoria, 1943.

Hennie Potgieter provides important insights concerning some of the debates around making the models for the marble frieze. According to him, the four artists considered Coetzer's sketches inappropriate because the conventions of pictorial images were not suited to sculpture, and the '... sculptors decided to use only Coetzer's knowledge, as undoubtedly the greatest specialist of Africana, and not his designs'.[101] In the end two of Coetzer's sketches were rejected,[102] all of them altered and six new scenes added (Figs 5.28, 31, 36, 38, 44, 46).

To provide a sculpture workshop, the SVK rented Harmoniesaal (Harmony Hall) in central Pretoria from Moerdyk (Fig. 5.12).[103] The completion of this stage of the work was to take almost half a decade

---

[101]　Potgieter 1987: 41: '... beeldhouers het toe besluit om slegs van Coetzer se kennis, as seker die grootste kenner van Africana, gebruik te maak en nie sy ontwerpe nie.'

[102]　Potgieter 1987: 43 refers to the rejection of two scenes. The first is a symbolic image (one of the sketches at ARCA, University of the Free State, Bloemfontein, PV94 1/75/5/1, number x; interestingly a scene similar to this was included in Coetzer's designs for stamps and the later Groot Trek tapestries). The second that he describes as Voortrekkers selling possessions is probably the left-hand section of Departure (Fig. 5.22) and must be ARCA PV94 1/75/5/1, number a.

[103]　Ibid., 41; now the Breytenbach Theatre, 137 Gerard Moerdyk Street.

Figure 5.13 Studio Romanelli, Florence, 1948: (L–R) Romano Romanelli, Gerard Moerdyk, Laurika Postma, Hennie Potgieter; two Italian sculptors are in the background, next to the marble panel 'British present Bible to Jacobus Uys' (Fig. 5.23).

(1942–46). The long collaboration reflects some of the great difficulties faced in shaping a coherent narrative for a frieze of this scale, an unprecedented undertaking in South African art history. The sculptors produced at least three different prototypes for each of the 27 scenes: first, they made their own drawings based on but by no means identical to Coetzer's sketches, which they had found unsuitable; second, small clay panels then plaster replicas measuring roughly one-third of the marble frieze (Figs 5.14–15); and, third, full scale clay models for the final plaster panels for use by the Italian masons (Figs 5.12–13).

During the lengthy preparatory phase of the frieze, Potgieter reports substantial modifications of its thematic and visual layout.[104] Through Moerdyk, Potgieter convinced the SVK to abandon two of Coetzer's designs, which he describes as a scene of Voortrekkers selling their possessions, and a symbolic representation of wagon-wheels, rising sun, powder-horn and 'other things' that he deemed unsuitable for a sculpture;[105] the two were to be replaced by one large representation of the dramatic Battle of Kapain (Fig. 5.28). Another debate revolved

---

[104] For the critique of some of the models, see Schwenke 2009.

[105] Potgieter 1987: 43; see also footnote 102.

Figure 5.14 Study for 'Retief is sworn in', plaster cast of a destroyed small clay panel by Hennie Potgieter, 1942–43.

around a scene selected to portray the heroism of fifteen-year-old Dirkie Uys (Fig. 5.37), where members of the SVK took opposing views.[106] It was generally believed that Dirkie Uys had killed three Zulu in a desperate attempt to defend his fallen father. Yet some said it was with a rifle, others a rifle butt, some from the saddle, others from the ground. The Uys family and other eyewitnesses, however, insisted that the boy had been killed by Zulu while fleeing. Predictably, the heroic account was the one chosen for the frieze. To resolve the details, the artists concluded amongst themselves that a boy of his age was unlikely to have killed three Zulu, and certainly not with a rifle butt, and Laurika Postma portrayed him in a valorous pose kneeling next to his father while shooting at attacking Zulu.

[106] Potgieter 1987: 46.

Figure 5.15 'Retief is sworn in'; copied into marble c. 1947–49, after plaster casts of the destroyed full-scale clay panel by Hennie Potgieter, 1943–46.

Perhaps the most significant change was initiated in 1945, when Prime Minister Jan Smuts and Treasury Secretary Jan Hofmeyr raised objections to a savage portrayal of a Zulu swinging a baby by its feet to smash it against the wheel of a wagon in the Bloukrans panel (based on the drawing in Fig. 5.16).[107] An early protest against this representation had surfaced in the *Rand Daily Mail* of 14 February 1945 under the headline 'Gruesome Friezes in the Voortrekker Monument'.[108] In response to objections, the chairman of the SVK, E. G. Jansen, wrote to the Secretary of Interior on 21 March 1945, urging the government not 'to

[107] Potgieter 1987: 50; Schwenke 2009: 17. The debate about the critique and required change of the Bloukrans panel is recorded in various SVK Minutes, esp. 22 February 1946, Item 4 (NAR, BNS vol. 299, file no. 146/73, vol. 4); 26 June 1946, Item 4, and 5 August 1947, Item 4 (NAR, Die Sentrale Volksmonumente-Komitee, vol. 2, file no. A141). The obnoxious motif which depicts extreme violence is, no doubt inadvertently, similar to some rare red-figured Attic pots, *circa* 500 BC, depicting the Greek hero Neoptolemos clubbing Priam to death with the dead body of Hector's son, Astyanax; see Anderson 1997: 194–99.

[108] NAR, BNS vol. 298, file no. 146/73, vol. 3 contains additional clippings and correspondence on this controversy. We are grateful to Astrid Schwenke for bringing to our attention an undated newspaper illustration of the panel.

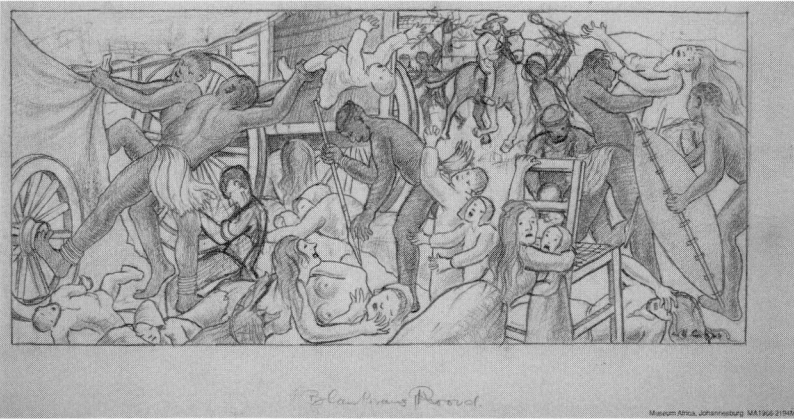

Figure 5.16 Study for 'Massacre at Bloukrans', pencil drawing by Willem Hermanus Coetzer, 1937.

Figure 5.17 'Massacre at Bloukrans'; copied into marble 1949–50, after plaster casts of the destroyed full-scale clay panel by Laurika Postma, c. 1943–48.

prevent the truthful portrayal of Voortrekker history'.[109] For the final depiction, however, the controversial figure was entirely replaced, now represented with an oddly extended right arm stretching out to set fire to the cover of the same wagon (Fig. 5.17). Despite his awareness of the less vicious interpretation, Moerdyk still reads the scene in a particularly racist way: 'It is said that natives in their primitive state grow drunk

---

[109] NAR Pretoria, 298, BNS 146/73, vol. 3, '. . . te verhinder dat die Voortrekkergeskiedenis getrou uitgebeeld word . . .'.

75 Trajan in port with sanctuary	76 Aftermath of war	77 Trajan addresses army	78 Roman Victory	*79-155 Continuing scenes, upper half*	
71 Attacking Dacian fortifications / Subjugation of Dacians		72 Battle	73 Trajan addresses army	74 Subjugation of Dacians	
65 Building fortifications	66-67 Battle / Subjugation of Dacians		68-69 Presenting Dacian prisoner / Fortification, forest works		70-71 Battle
57-59 Advance over mountains	60 Building a camp	61 Messenger and Trajan	62 Camp in mountains	63-64 Advance / Dacians attack Roman cavalry of Moors	
48-50 Army departs	51 Army unites	52 Forest works / Dacian legation	53 Sacrifice	54 Trajan addresses army	55-56 Road, bridge works
41 Battle at Adamklissi	42 Trajan addresses army	43 Dacian prisoners	44 Distribution of rewards	45 Torture	46-47 Return of Trajan
36 Advance of Roman army	37 Pursuit of Sarmatians	38 Attacking Dacian laager	39 Moesians beg protection	40-41 Battle at Adamklissi	
29-30 Aftermath of war	31 Dacians crossing Danube	32 Dacians attack Roman fortification	33 Trajan departs by ship	34 Trajan on Danube	35 Arrival of Trajan
23 Road works	24 Battle at Tapae	25 Trajan at Dacian ramparts	26 Crossing a river	27-28 Trajan addresses army / Dacian delegation	
13-14 Building fortifications	15 Clearing forest	16-17 Building fortifications	18 Dacian prisoner	19-20 Building works	21-22 Army departs
6-7 Army departs / Council	8 Trajan makes sacrifice	9 Messenger and Trajan	10 Trajan addresses army	11-12 Building fortifications	
			1-2 Bank of Danube		3-5 Roman army departs
S	E	N	W		S

Figure 5.18 Trajan's Column, Rome: order and topics of scenes 1–78, AD 106–13.

when they smell or drink blood . . . the scene depicted gives an impression of a drunken orgy.'[110]

Alongside imaginative invention and political constraint in creating the historical story, a great deal of trouble was taken to achieve verism in the antiquarian details. As Potgieter stated, 'considerable research was required for historical accuracy, verifiable myths, period clothing, indigenous animal types, and so on'.[111] The SVK asked Kotie Roodt-Coetzee, an Afrikaans cultural historian and member of the Historical Committee, to organise an exhibition of Afrikaner antiquities: held in the sculptors' workshop from 22 to 25 May 1943, it was the first of its kind in the country.[112] Potgieter was at pains to point out not only the use of authentic

[110] *Official Guide*, 48.
[111] Potgieter 1987: 46; 'Daar was vir ons beeldhouers baie navorsingwerk oor historiese juisthede, aanneemlike mites, kleredrag, diere en so meer.'
[112] Grobler 2005: 79–80.

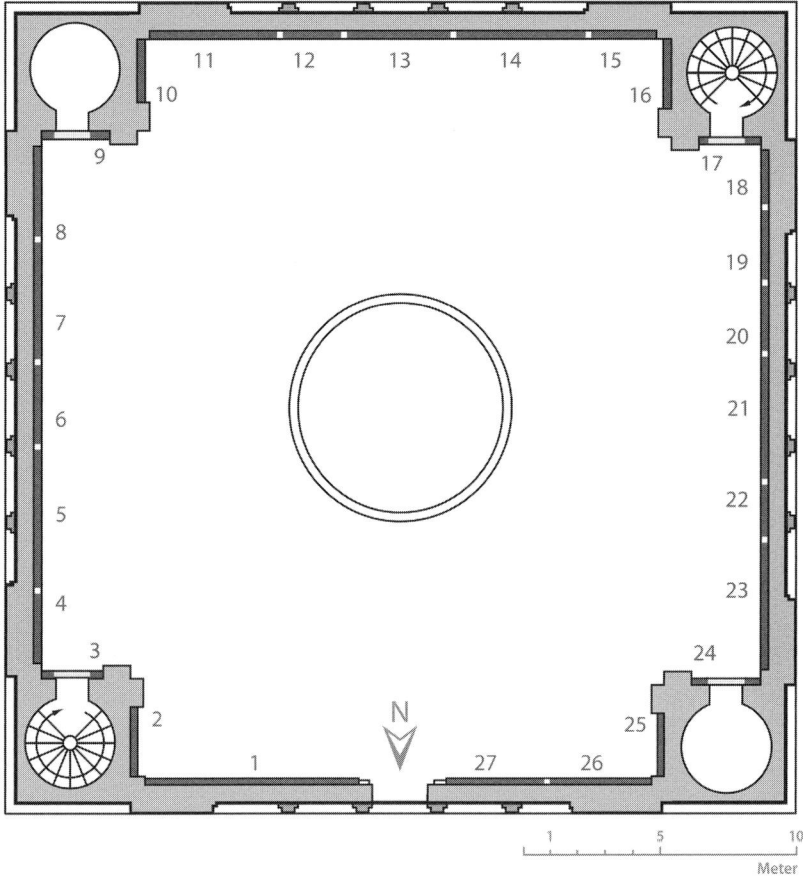

Figure 5.19 Ground plan with scenes of frieze, Hall of Heroes, Voortrekker Monument, 2014.

1 Voortrekkers leave Cape colony (1835-37)
2 British present Bible to Jacobus Uys (Apr 1837)
3 Trichardt in Soutpansberg (1836-37)
4 Trichardt in Delagoa Bay (Apr 1838)
5 Battle of Vegkop (Oct 1836)
6 Retief is sworn in (Jun 1837)
7 Battle of Kapain (Nov 1837)
8 Negotiations with Moroka (late 1836)
9 Report on Dingane (Nov 1837)
10 Retief's daughter paints his name (12 Nov 1837)
11 Crossing the Drakensberg (late 1837)
12 Retief and Dingane sign treaty (Feb 1838)
13 Murder of Retief and his men (Feb 1838)
14 Massacre at Bloukrans (Feb 1838)
15 Warning against Zulu (Feb 1838)
16 Dirkie Uys protects father (Apr 1838)

17 Oosthuizen aids besieged laager (Feb 1838)
18 Women spur men on (1838/43)
19 Arrival of Pretorius (Nov 1838)
20 Making the Vow (Dec 1838)
21 Battle of Blood River (16 Dec 1838)
22 Church of the Vow (1839-41)
23 Women sow, till and defend (c. 1838)
24 Mpande becomes King (Feb 1840)
25 Dingane is killed by Swazi (Feb 1840)
26 Voortrekkers retreat from Natal (1843)
27 Sand River Convention (17 Jan 1852)

Peter Kirchhoff (1893-1978): 1, 21-23, 27
Hennie Potgieter (1916-92): 2-7, 9
Frikkie Kruger (1907-66): 8, 11-13, 15, 24, 26
Laurika Postma (1903-87): 10, 14, 16-20, 25

Figure 5.20 Negotiations with Maroko, detail of marble panel (Fig. 5.29), late 1836.

weapons such as the muzzle-loader rifles borrowed from the Historical Museum, but also Voortrekker clothing examined in museums and in meticulously stitched copies,[113] and such minutiae as the choice of

---

[113] Such replicas were likewise carefully sewn for wearing at the 1938 centenary celebrations and the 1949 inauguration of the Monument, when many participants wore what had come to be considered 'national' dress.

Figure 5.21 Minister of Arts and Culture, Paul Mashatile, in front of the Blood River marble panel (Fig. 5.42), inaugurating the Voortrekker Monument as a National Heritage Site, 16 March 2012.

Figure 5.22 North wall, Voortrekkers leave Cape Colony, 1835–37. Peter Kirchhoff.

Merino sheep as models because the breed had been introduced before the treks and, similarly, the inclusion of musical instruments like the concertina and the guitar known to the Voortrekkers (Fig. 5.22).[114] The painstaking antiquarianism underpins the symbolic readings of the narrative. In contrast to historical reality, but in accord with visual rhetoric, every item depicted on the frieze is portrayed in a pristine state, without any trace of actual use.

---

[114] Potgieter 1987: 10 and passim.

Figure 5.23 North-east projection, British present Bible to Jacobus Uys, April 1837. Hennie Potgieter.

In the case of the selection of models for the figures on the frieze, not only did the artists, backed up by the SVK, attempt to find contemporary visual records or seek out descendants of well-known Voortrekkers to pose for them,[115] they even took into consideration the nationality of their sitters. Potgieter listed many of the models: the wife of the Portuguese ambassador in Pretoria, Maria Eunia Da Fonsecca, posed for the wife of the Portuguese governor (Fig. 5.25),[116] for example, and an Italian woman, Lea Spanno, for the brave Teresa Viglione (Fig. 5.36).[117] So anxious were the artists to invoke accuracy that three Zulu men – named by Potgieter as

---

[115] See, for example, 'Die onbekende Voortrekker. Die skilder GERT VAN DER WALT vertel hoe hy model geword het vir F. J. Kruger se beeld' (The unknown Voortrekker. The painter Gert van der Walt recounts how he became a model for F. J. Kruger's image), in *Die Huisgenoot*, 6 December 1974, 80–82.

[116] Potgieter 1987: 42. In notes on the scenes, 10–39, the names of models for the figures are listed for the sketch diagrams, an important source for identification.

[117] Ibid., 27, 42. The *Official Guide*, 48, has the spelling Theresa Viglione.

Figure 5.24 North-east projection, Trichardt in Soutpansberg, 1836–37. Hennie Potgieter.

'Ngubeni, Umtetwa en Ntuli'[118] – were brought from Natal especially to model for the African figures in indigenous dress. Potgieter explains that, because the Matabele had been part of the Zulu nation just prior to this period, these men could be used to represent both these groups; the studio's Basuto servant Piet Malotho posed for Baralong figures (Fig. 5.29), however, as they were related to the Sotho.[119] It speaks for itself that so few models were considered sufficient for the many Africans portrayed, as opposed to the careful differentiation of the European figures. Family members and Afrikaner friends, and the sculptors themselves, deemed ethnically appropriate, stood in for each of the Voortrekker figures, each treated like an individual portrait. Liberties were occasionally taken as when Pieter Kirchhoff was shown as the first Voortrekker of the entire frieze, his work on the Monument presumably entitling him

---

[118] Potgieter 1987: 48.   [119] Potgieter 1987: 42.

Figure 5.25 East wall, Trichardt in Delagoa Bay, April 1838. Hennie Potgieter.

Figure 5.26 East wall, Battle of Vegkop, October 1836. Hennie Potgieter.

to honorary Afrikaner status (Fig. 5.22, first on the left).[120] But such exceptions were rare. Moerdyk's fervently Nationalist wife, Sylva Pirow,

[120] Kirchhoff's wife and daughter accompany him in this scene, and his son Werner was the model for Dirkie Uys (Fig. 5.37); communication from Werner Kirchhoff, December 2013.

Figure 5.27 East wall, Retief is sworn in, June 1837. Hennie Potgieter.

Figure 5.28 East wall, Battle of Kapain, November 1837. Hennie Potgieter.

Figure 5.29 East wall, Negotiations with Maroko, November 1836. Frikkie Kruger.

modelled for Susanna Smit (Fig. 5.39), the Afrikaner heroine who proclaimed after the British had annexed Natal in 1843, 'We are prepared to return barefoot over the Drakensberg, to meet our independence or our death, sooner than bow down before a government which has treated us as the British Government has done'.[121] Moerdyk had an even more appropriate role, and one that underlined his commitment to the Afrikaner cause – the builder of the Church of the Vow (Fig. 5.43, first on the left). The quality originally admired in Coetzer's frieze designs was a historicising concept of accuracy and this was maintained in the final reliefs. Like Potgieter, Moerdyk took time in the *Official Guide* to discuss some of these particularities. It was as though being able to verify the reconstructed authenticity of each detail in the frieze confirmed the overall validity of the historical narrative.

Perhaps this was also a response to the need to merge the different episodes of the treks under different leaders into a continuous visual

---

[121] *Official Guide*, 49. Placed earlier in the frieze, this panel captures the vital role of the women throughout the treks, and conflates their determination to stay in Natal after their sufferings at the hands of the Zulu with their equal determination to leave once the British had taken over.

Figure 5.30 South-east projection, Report on Dingane, November 1837. Hennie Potgieter.

story with a sense of unfolding drama.[122] Such visual reinvention was a well-established pictorial strategy, but one which challenged the veracity of the narrative. Paralleling this, although models were used for almost all the figures, and their life-size scale means that individual features are clearly visible in the frieze, the way they are presented tends to blend detail and create a unified effect that upholds the construed continuity. The frieze had to serve a higher purpose, in the words of Moerdyk, 'as a symbolic document showing the Afrikaner's proprietary right to South Africa ... the price the Afrikaner paid to call South Africa his fatherland'.[123] He clearly believed that the task surpassed any

---

[122] Nico Coetzee raises issues related to the merging of the different treks into a single chronology, stressing that the choice of key episodes was not a factual matter but the result of interpretation and ideology: 1988: especially 184.

[123] *Official Guide*, 34

Figure 5.31 South-east projection, Retief's daughter paints her father's name, 12 November 1837. Laurika Postma.

personal ambitions of the artists, writing, 'By following examples of the work of those masters [Renaissance sculptors Verrocchio and Donatello] and constantly consulting one another, the four sculptors succeeded wonderfully well in submerging their own individuality and achieving a harmonious whole.'[124] There are also practical explanations for the sense of stylistic coherence. First, although the initial one-third-scale models for the panels were assigned to the four different artists independently, the sculptors assisted each other in the ultimate full-scale models, which is likely to have countered most specificities of style and representation. This is clearly seen if one compares the final scenes with the initial smaller maquettes, which tend to be more vigorous in the modelled clay surfaces than the final panels in marble (compare, for example, Figs 5.14–15). Moreover, the carving of the Italian marble cutters who

[124] *Official Guide*, 38–39.

Figure 5.32 South wall, Crossing the Drakensberg, late 1837. Frikkie Kruger.

Figure 5.33 South wall, Retief and Dingane sign treaty, February 1838. Frikkie Kruger.

Figure 5.34 South wall, Murder of Retief and his men, February 1838. Frikkie Kruger.

Figure 5.35 South wall, Massacre at Bloukrans, February 1838. Laurika Postma.

executed the final marble frieze would have further diluted individual idiosyncrasies.

The completed full-scale models in plaster were set up inside the monument, and put to test for 'light and rhythm',[125] before being shipped to

---

[125] SVK Minutes, 22 February 1946, Item 4 (NAR, BNS vol. 299, 146/73, vol. 4).

Figure 5.36 South wall, Warning against Zulu, February 1838. Frikkie Kruger.

Professor Romano Romanelli's workshop in Florence (Fig. 5.13),[126] with the last plaster completed in later 1946.[127] There they were hewn in Querceta, a hard, white and uniform type of Carrara marble, quarried about 9 miles south of the eponymous city. Found in the Apuan Alps around the top of Monte Altissimo near Seravezza,[128] this was 'the quarry

---

[126] Pretorius (2003) notes that Romanelli was interested in the history of South Africa and made a thorough study of the Great Trek. For his studio, see Campana 1998: esp. 245–53.

[127] The plaster panels were sent to Italy in batches as they were ready. Moerdyk first reported that eight panels had been dispatched in August 1947 (SVK Dagbestuur Komitee Notule, 5 August 1947, Item 10, see NAR, Die Sentrale Volksmonumente-Komitee, vol. 2, file no. A141).

[128] Moerdyk referred to the frieze being of Carrara marble, whereas Potgieter (1987: 9, 50 [quote]) declares that 'dit in werklikheid Quercetta-marmer was' (it was actually Quercetta marble). Querceta, to spell the name correctly, is a town situated below Seravezza, nearer Forte dei

Figure 5.37 South-west projection, Dirkie Uys protects father, April 1838. Laurika Postma.

from which Michael Angelo obtained the marble he used for his master-pieces', as Moerdyk boasts.[129] Working in the classical tradition, Romanelli's studio provided the technical expertise and up to 50 sculptors to undertake the carving with maximum efficiency.[130] Apart from the advantages of utilising such sculptural proficiency, unavailable in South Africa, it was cheaper to ship the finished marbles from Italy instead of

Marmi, the harbour from which this marble used to be shipped. Raffaello Romanelli, sculptor and great-grandson of Romano Romanelli, who with his sister Rubina continues the Romanelli studio today, considers marble from Seravezza to be the finest and hardest to carve (interview, Florence, 4 September 2013). For Querceta see www.fondazionehenraux.it/uk/he nraux/the-quarries.asp.

[129] *Official Guide*, 39. In this publication, Moerdyk locates the source of the marble as 'Forti di Marmi in the Apennines' (ibid.).

[130] Potgieter claims there were 50 sculptors (1987: 49) but an undated document (c. 1958) from the Romanelli studio, *Studio laboratorio di sculptura in marmo: Borgo san Frediano 70/7 di proprietà: Raffaello Romanelli* (1926–2003), talks of 25 being employed for three years.

Figure 5.38 South-west projection, Oosthuizen aids besieged laager, February 1838. Laurika Postma.

transporting double the weight of quarry blocks (180 instead of 360 metric tons) for carving.[131] However, despite all efforts, a number of the panels were not in place when the Monument was inaugurated, among them, ironically, the controversial Bloukrans panel showing Zulu massacring Voortrekker women and children (Fig. 5.17), and the crucial scene with the Battle of Blood River (Fig. 5.42).

For close supervision of the Florentine sculptors, in December 1947 two of the South African sculptors, Postma and Potgieter (Fig. 5.13), 'were sent to Italy to guard against any un-Afrikaans elements stealing into the work'.[132] Both stayed in Europe for about a year. While the studio sculptors used a pointing system which guaranteed a close relationship to the general composition, they inevitably brought their

[131] Pretorius, 'The Italians and the Voortrekker Monument', unpaginated ('Historical Frieze').
[132] *Official Guide*, 39.

Figure 5.39 West wall, Women spur men on, 1838 or 1843. Laurika Postma.

knowledge of the classical tradition to bear in the way they carved and in their interpretation of the detail. This is backed up by an anecdote recounted by Potgieter. He found that the plaster blobs that signified the tightly curled hair of the Zulu figures in the plaster models – hair he described as 'peperkorrels' or peppercorns – had been interpreted by the Italians as Roman curls. He had to spend some time training a studio sculptor to produce forms that represented distinctive African hair,[133] so that the sculptor could go from studio to studio carving this detail on each of the relevant panels.

Sculptural conventions familiar to the studio sculptors undoubtedly influenced their work and resulted in a strong sense of stylistic coherence. In this the work echoed the general consistency of Greek and Roman friezes where multiple hands had been involved in the carving

---

[133] Potgieter 1987: 49–50.

Figure 5.40 West wall, Arrival of Pretorius, November 1838. Laurika Postma.

also. Further, the marble in which they worked endows the forms with a quality surpassing mere representation through the homogenising aura of its whiteness, and the associations with the classical tradition that this invokes.[134] Such classical treatment has a profound effect on the reading of the frieze. A narrative carved in marble generates a more potent reality than a written text, because its sheer physicality both brings history alive and petrifies it for posterity. Any narrative in marble is particularly powerful for the very reason that it is in essence almost irreversible: its fabric cannot simply be rewritten. Should one want to remove any part of a narrative in stone, the force required would leave traces of the erasure forever. Hence it seems safe to assume that, at least for the general public, the Monument's marble frieze became the

---

[134] There was clearly no thought of colouring the frieze as had been the practice in antiquity, although rarely visible on extant friezes: see Brinkmann et al. (2010).

Figure 5.41 West wall, Making the Vow, December 1838. Laurika Postma.

authoritative (visual) account of the 'Great Trek', the foundational narrative of Afrikaner history.

4.   The Panels: A Reading in Context

Apart from the significance of turning history into marble, a close iconographic examination of the panel sequence, we argue, shows that it is the characteristic formation of the narrative which links the frieze to the classical tradition, rather than adaptations of specific ancient motifs as others have suggested (Figs 5.18–19).[135] The basic story is effortlessly readable. In the first scene, white families, well-equipped

---

[135] See especially Evans 2007: 147–53.

Figure 5.42 West wall, Battle of Blood River, 16 December 1838 . Peter Kirchhoff.

Figure 5.43 West wall, Church of the Vow, 1839–41. Peter Kirchhoff.

Figure 5.44 West wall, Women sow, till and defend, c. 1838. Peter Kirchhoff.

Figure 5.45 North-west projection, Mpande becomes king, February 1840. Frikkie
Kruger.

Figure 5.46 North-west projection, Dingane is killed by Swazi, February 1840. Laurika Postma.

Figure 5.47 North wall, Voortrekkers retreat from Natal, 1843. Frikkie Kruger.

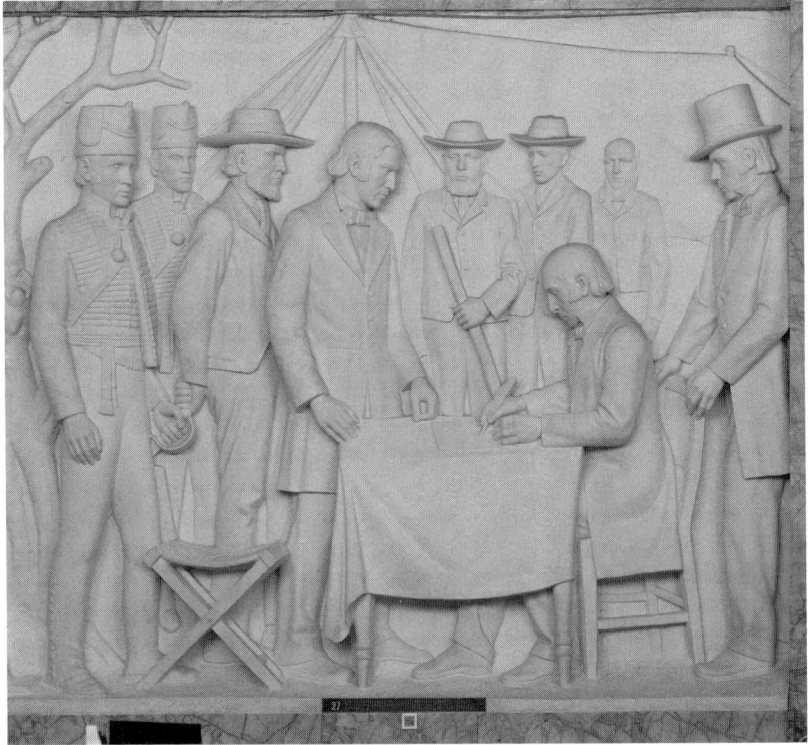

Figure 5.48 North wall, Sand River Convention, 17 January 1852 . Peter Kirchhoff.

and neatly dressed, set out on a journey (Fig. 5.22). Their habitus is calm and controlled, and they set the scene for the driving force of the narrative: white civilisation carried to the black hinterland. In a variety of symbolic scenes, Voortrekkers pay respect to Afrikaner law, Christian faith and well-ordered family life. White women and children of model behaviour play a crucial part, including their participation in war. The whites negotiate with and fight against the blacks; they are ultimately victors, but they also experience dreadful sufferings. While blacks, too, take part in negotiations, in the majority of panels they attack and kill whites, or are killed by them, and in one case kill one of their own (Zulu King Dingane; Fig. 5.46). In the concluding scene it is whites alone who sign the document that provides a fitting finale (Fig. 5.48). With additional knowledge a more nuanced reading is possible. We will briefly analyse the narrative of each scene, grouped in three blocks: scenes 1 to 11, 12 to 25, 26 and 27. In the absence of set titles, our captions for the scenes aim to provide a specific designation for each and its place in the intended narrative, drawing on the *Official*

Guide and other sources, such as SVK Minutes and Hennie Potgieter's *Voortrekker Monument Pretoria*. It is our purpose here to explore the way they have been structured into a narrative, not to question the historical validity of the events.

Scenes 1 to 11: Setting the Stage

As already noted, the first scene (Fig. 5.22), the largest of all, is a telling initiation of the subsequent narrative. Against the backdrop of flat-topped mountains in a recognisable eastern Cape landscape, we find a visual précis of the material core of Voortrekker civilisation: men, women and children; wagons; weapons; livestock; agricultural implements; domestic goods; musical instruments; personal belongings.

The following ten scenes address the ethical values of Voortrekker civilisation and the scope of their territorial outreach. Scene 2 (Fig. 5.23) introduces religious and political statements: British settlers show sympathy with the trekkers' decision to leave the colony by presenting a Bible to the Voortrekker patriarch, Jacobus Uys. The very formal attire of all the participants demonstrates the importance of such symbolic acts from the outset. References to Christian faith become a rationale for Afrikaner appropriation of the 'promised' land that the 'chosen people' set out to colonise.[136] In the next scene (Fig. 5.24), Louis Trichardt and his men arrive in the far north at Soutpansberg, where they establish 'proper' education, marked by several books in the foreground and a school building in the background, the first built in the Transvaal. Scene 4 (Fig. 5.25) depicts a group of Voortrekkers arriving at the port of Delagoa Bay, indicated by a fortified building and a sailing ship beyond. As a token of peace Trichardt hands over his rifle to the Portuguese governor, while Trichardt's wife, prostrate with malaria, is supported by the governor's wife. Both scenes testify to the Voortrekker's ability to endure extreme hardship and their pioneering work, backed up by education and civilised conduct.

Further scenes refer to the Voortrekkers' belief in law and authority based on Christian ethics and constitutional principles, particularly highlighted in the solemn swearing in of Piet Retief as governor of the

---

[136] Etherington points out that an understanding of the Voortrekkers as 'a divinely inspired vanguard of a nation . . . only developed later in connection with the rise of Afrikaner nationalism': 2001: 343.

Voortrekkers (Fig. 5.27); their investment in formal (albeit ultimately unsuccessful) negotiation with blacks (Figs 5.20, 29); the picture-book life of children who, even without adults, portray the essence of Voortrekker civilisation (Fig. 5.31); and the well-organised move of immaculate trekker families into Natal (Fig. 5.32). Scene 9 (Fig. 5.30) contextualises the seemingly good news of Piet Retief's negotiation with the Zulu. It is delivered by a Voortrekker on horseback, amidst a scene of white industry and craftsmanship, such as making shoes, needlework, hunting and, in the background, the arduous task of tanning and braiding skin into leather thongs. The latter is done by a black servant, shown from the back, one of only two portrayed in the entire frieze (see also Fig. 5.40).[137] One of the grievances that contributed to the Voortrekkers' decision to leave the Cape was Britain's abolition of slavery and new legislation upholding the rights of employees, and, though so few are depicted, they took an estimated five thousand servants with them.[138] In contrast to the portrayal of the Voortrekkers, the servant does his work half-naked, wearing only trousers, symbolically locating him in a liminal zone between the well-dressed Voortrekkers and their unclothed African adversaries.

In calculated juxtaposition between these civic representations of Voortrekker virtues, their superior military conduct is shown in two scenes depicting victories over the Matabele. In the 1836 Battle of Vegkop, Voortrekker men, women and children are shown inside their wagon laager in coordinated action that will put thousands of black attackers to flight, their thronged presence indicated in tiny scale outside the laager (Fig. 5.26). Paul Kruger, later President of the Zuid-Afrikaansche Republiek, who took part in this battle at the age of 11, is prominently staged in the middle of the scene, as the boy with the powder-horn; for his portrait, one of Kruger's great-grandsons posed![139] In the 1837 Battle of Kapain, Voortrekkers move in easy efficiency on horseback against the advancing Matabele, some of whom ride on ungainly oxen, while others are dead and dying, dramatically collapsing on the ground (Fig. 5.28). The chaos of the Matabele is set against the discipline of the Barolong allies in the next scene, a compact group with whom the more spaciously arranged Voortrekkers negotiate (Fig. 5.29).

---

[137] Delmont 1993: 93.   [138] Venter 1991; Giliomee 2003: 146–47 and 161.

[139] *Official Guide*, 45. Potgieter 1987: 47, and *Die Huisgenoot*, 6 December 1974, 80, which names him as Louis Jacobs.

Scenes 12 to 25: Winning the Imperative Victory

While the first 11 scenes show different treks and are arranged in only a loose sequential order, the next 13 all focus on stories leading up to or following the Battle of Blood River on 16 December 1838 (see Fig. 5.19). These panels mark the narrative climax of the frieze, designed around concepts merging chronological order with drama and ideology.

In front of the native capital of uMgungundlovu (Fig. 5.33), the Zulu king Dingane and the Voortrekker leader Piet Retief, both seated, sign a (contested) treaty in early February 1838, sanctioning Voortrekker settlement in Natal.[140] The ceremony is witnessed by kneeling Zulu, their heads not allowed to be higher than the king's, whereas attendant Voortrekkers are portrayed upright in superior stance. The next scene (Fig. 5.34) portrays the subsequent massacre of Piet Retief and his men by Zulu using clubs and rocks. Piet Retief is forced to witness this slaughtering of his people, before he is killed himself. The bound but erect and defiant Retief, his satchel with the (disputed) treaty at his feet, is a fulcrum in the south frieze, presented unbowed, according to Moerdyk, 'to symbolise the victory of European civilisation over barbarism'.[141] Yet the background shows a second, aerial view of uMgungundlovu, whose vastness and strict symmetry represents Dingane's power.

Later in February, Voortrekker women and children are brutally slain in surprise Zulu attacks at Bloukrans and Weenen (Fig. 5.35). If scenes 12 to 14 reveal the extent of the atrocities perpetrated by the Zulu, scenes 15 to 18 further stress their barbarism by contrasting civilised valour, as women and children rally in support of Voortrekker men. Teresa Viglione, from a nearby band of Italian pedlars, risks her life riding on her own to warn the laager of Gerrit Maritz of the impending Zulu attack (Fig. 5.36). In opposition to Dingane's treachery, this narrative underlines unconditional help among civilised whites. The same courage is found among the Voortrekker children. Fifteen-year-old Dirkie Uys (Fig. 5.37) defends his fallen father against a group of attacking Zulu, and young Marthinus Oosthuizen (Fig. 5.38) gallops through Zulu lines to take gunpowder to Van Rensburg's men who had run out of ammunition, which 'saved the Van Rensburg trek from extermination'.[142]

---

[140] There is disagreement about the authenticity of this document and its date, particularly as missionary Owen's account of the event placed it on 6 February; see Preller 1928; Jay Naidoo 1985; Etherington 2001: 281–82; Grobler 2011.

[141] *Official Guide*, 48.   [142] Ibid., 49.

In the scene that follows (Fig. 5.39), resolute Voortrekker women spur
on their menfolk, who are disheartened and dejected, forming a
transition to the next two scenes that are a final prelude to the battle of
Blood River. In November 1838, Andries Pretorius arrives as newly
appointed commander to replace Retief, tall, urbanely dressed with
a top hat, and the sole person armed with a pistol (Fig. 5.40). He is
also the only Voortrekker associated with a black servant, who stands
obediently in the background holding the reins of his master's horse.
In December, Sarel Cilliers, a Voortrekker leader and preacher, has
mounted the canon 'Old Grietjie' to vow to God that the Voortrekkers
would forever celebrate that day as 'a day of thanksgiving like the
Sabbath' if granted victory over the Zulu (Fig. 5.41).[143] With the arrival
of a new leader and their steadfast faith, the Voortrekkers are ready for
the decisive battle of Blood River.

On 16 December, against the backdrop of the laager where the Zulu
attack had been repulsed, the Voortrekkers ride out to attack the
overwhelming force of twelve to fifteen thousand Zulu on foot
(Fig. 5.42). Faced by the staged offensive of high-mounted riders, the
Zulu collapse. On the next scene (Fig. 5.43), given a prominent place
immediately after their victory over the Zulu at Blood River,
Voortrekkers build the Church of the Vow at Pietermaritzburg.
Moerdyk, shown here as the Voortrekker architect, proclaims of this
scene in the *Official Guide*, 'wherever the Afrikaner settles and builds
a town, the church is the largest and one of the first of the public
buildings he erects'.[144] That most of Moerdyk's buildings were
churches speaks for itself.[145]

In the following scene (Fig. 5.44), men depart on commando, while
gracefully portrayed Voortrekker women run the laager. Sowing wheat
and tilling the soil, and firing rifles to repel distant attacking Zulu, the
women demonstrate impeccable style. In February 1840 (Fig. 5.45),
Mpande (Panda) is inaugurated as the new Zulu king, saluted by male
Zulu and Voortrekkers alike. Both parties are standing, seemingly on
equal terms (unlike Fig. 5.33), yet, unmistakeably, top-hatted Pretorius
is taller than the adjacent Zulu king. In March 1840 (Fig. 5.46), the fate
of the former Zulu king Dingane is sealed: Swazi warriors force him to
the ground before they kill him. Next to their humiliated king stand four
of his young wives, wearing traditional aprons and carrying containers
on their heads. A reminder of Dingane's polygamy, they oppose

---

[143] Ibid., 5.   [144] Ibid., 50.   [145] See Vermeulen 1999: 150–51.

Christian principles, a moral contrast also suggested by the erotic flair of their near nudity against the chastely clothed Voortrekker women in the other scenes. It stresses the strong ideological tenor of the frieze that the killing of one black by another is the sole panel which focuses exclusively on blacks, and also the only one which portrays African females.

The four scenes following the victory at Blood River (Figs 5.43–46) thus focus on a variety of symbolic actions in its aftermath: the building of the Church of the Vow; the achievements of Voortrekker women in peace and war; the inauguration of a new Zulu king witnessed by a group of Voortrekkers; and, in contrast, the inevitable death of Dingane portrayed as an affair for blacks only.

Scenes 26 and 27: Finalising the Conquest

The remaining two scenes bring the story to an end by making a clear statement about the Voortrekkers' victory over the land and its African occupants – who are now no longer a part of the narrative – but also their continuing efforts to win their freedom from British imperial rule. The large scene (Fig. 5.47) shows the dramatic departure of Voortrekkers who felt forced to leave Natal after the British occupation of 1843. Against the impressive Drakensberg mountains, the combined force of men and oxen drag a wagon up a precipitous slope, emphasising once again the physical challenge of the trek, while a wounded but upright Voortrekker man and his family stand by in loyal support. The last scene (Fig. 5.48) portrays the Convention of Sand River on 17 January 1852, seventeen years after the Voortrekkers had left the Cape Colony, when Britain at last recognised the independence of the Transvaal, paving the way for the Zuid-Afrikaansche Republiek. Set against the backdrop of a tent, nine people gather, the five hardy Voortrekkers outnumbering the four British representatives, two commissioners accompanied by two soldiers. Voortrekker dominance is underlined as Pretorius, if it is he, distinguished by the tall hat, watches over the seated British commissioner who signs the convention, placing his hands on the back of the chair in a gesture of control. The ceremonial grouping around the table echoes earlier scenes that also depict solemn rituals among white people – the presentation of a Bible to Uys by British settlers (Fig. 5.23) and the inauguration of Retief as Voortrekker governor (Figs 5.15, 27). All three scenes are centred on a cloth-covered table reminiscent of an altar, reinforcing the religious underpinning of the Voortrekkers' endeavours. The similar presence of a table – in this case tellingly uncovered – for the signing of the treaty between Dingane and Retief serves to stress the treachery of the Zulu king, and his unfitness to participate in the activities of civilised men. Again and again the frieze reinforces a superior character for the Voortrekkers and justifies their actions.

5.   The Visual Narrative: Locus Classicus of Afrikanerdom

The narrative of the frieze which has shaped the authoritative imagery of the 'Great Trek' interlocks selected incidents of Voortrekker history such as victories over strangers, official communications, domestic duties and individual deeds with acts that have symbolic purpose. All scenes refer in one way or another to principles such as religious commitment, cultural superiority, manliness, female virtues, family values and the gallantry of children who share the adults' principles and reinforce the Voortrekkers' collective innocence. Underplaying the fact that, as Norman Etherington points out, by 'mid-1837 they counted some 1600 armed and mounted men in their ranks – a fighting force of unprecedented destructive power',[146] acts of war on the part of the Voortrekkers are presented as a necessary response to African aggression or treachery.[147]

   Yet blending historical data with ideological claims was not enough to create a comprehensible narrative that would be both compelling and enduring. For this the artists deployed antiquarian accuracy, ceremonial staging, pointed drama, stylistic consistency and material uniformity – characteristics that belong to a longstanding classical tradition of visual narrative. No-one educated in European arts and challenged to design a narrative in marble like the Voortrekker frieze would be able to ignore one of the world's most famous friezes, the relief ribbon of Trajan's column in Rome.[148] About 220 metres in length, it is a unique manifestation of the overweening self-esteem of Rome and her emperor Trajan, portraying the city's superior religious, cultural and military achievements in the course of Trajan's victorious

[146] Etherington 2001: 243.
[147] Moerdyk stressed that 'the Voortrekkers wished to partition the country and to live in peace. . . . But the Bantu were not amenable to reason. He respected one thing only and that was force.' (*Official Guide*, 31).
[148] As previously discussed, Moerdyk would have been familiar with the reliefs from the Architectural Court at the Victoria and Albert Museum, and may well have recommended them to the sculptors.

campaigns against the Dacians. The structural similarities of portraying the two stories in marble are obvious, whether the Voortrekker
frieze was following the Roman narrative intentionally or accidentally
(see Figs 5.18–19).[149] Both portray a coherent narrative, with
a remarkable concurrence of topics, such as the departure from
home (Fig. 5.22), the annexation of new territory (Figs 5.32–33, 43–
44, 48), the commitment to religion (Figs 5.23, 27, 41, 43), negotiations with foreign people (Fig. 5.29, 33, 45) as well as the victory over
them (Figs 5.26, 28, 42), and the superiority of the patron's culture
including discipline, tactics, armoury and building activities (Figs 5.22,
24, 26, 30, 43–44). In both narratives, Roman and Voortrekker men hardly
ever die when fighting a battle.[150] Both compose their stories with a deftly
designed balance between scenes of dramatic activity and scenes of ceremonial solemnity, grounded in a selection of symbolic acts and gestures as
an intrinsic part of their fabric. Both are striking justifications of the right
to conquer. Above all, these narratives provide a definitive self-affirmation
calculated to last forever.

In contrast to the structural similarities of the two narratives, individual motifs and their arrangement in the Voortrekker Monument frieze
differ substantially from the classical tradition, Trajan's column
included.[151] One of the most striking features of the frieze is its modern
concept of perspective as we know it from European painting. Despite
Potgieter's complaint of the unsuitability of these features in Coetzer's
original designs, the sculptors developed them for their own purposes.
They utilised pictorial devices such as changes in scale of people, objects
and natural features; occasionally linear perspective to show recession;[152]
and an effect of aerial perspective with a deeper cutting for foreground
figures against shallower distant motifs. Yet, in another non-classical
idiosyncrasy, these figures are never cut free from the panel, despite the
depth of carving (about 21 cm); all the elements remain solidly connected
to the marble fabric.

When we turn to the iconography, we find other disparities. Unknown to
the classical is the enormous density of detail with which landscape and

---

[149] For structural analogies in Trajan's column, see Baumer et al. 1991.

[150] The wounded Voortrekker lying in the foreground of the Battle of Vegkop (Fig. 5.26) is shown
not to emphasise weakness but to demonstrate the proper endurance of hardship and the
exemplary care for the injured in the midst of battle. Similarly, Dirkie Uys is portrayed
protecting his dying father (Fig. 5.37). The Voortrekker deaths (Fig. 5.34–35) are not the result
of battles but of what were understood as treacherous and unprovoked attacks.

[151] For classical narratives of war, see Hölscher 2003.

[152] This leads to visual oddities, such as the disproportionate shift of scale in Fig. 5.44.

settlements are depicted in the frieze, even if only in the background.[153] Again, this interest in the environment can be seen to have its roots in modern landscape painting and its valorisation of the natural world. But this trope also has a symbolic role as it is invested with the Voortrekker's close relationship to the land. Other differences from the classical are also indicative of different cultural values, such as the systematic profusion of Boer family life within a narrative related to hardship and war. Women and children are portrayed in the majority of the panels and are actively involved in both civic and military scenes, where women fight like men (Fig. 5.26, 44), and boys step into adult roles (Fig. 5.26, 37–38). Such elements show the value of the family unit. So too does another non-classical feature within the genre of war-related narrative – the continuous interest in depicting the age of both sexes, from infants to the elderly, which captures the close social bond between young and old.[154] As with the inclusive treatment of women, it further demonstrates the entire gamut of human resources as the key to the Voortrekkers' future, and the enduring establishment of white civilisation in the hinterland. The vulnerability of women, youths and the aged also adds to the range of emotion and drama. Moreover, the detailed staging of severe suffering and brutal killing of the ancestors of the people who commissioned the frieze, including Afrikaners of both sexes and all ages (Fig. 5.26, 34, 35, 37),[155] is alien to the visual tradition of ancient Rome, which invariably glorified and immortalised Roman achievements.

Yet, even when such differences are acknowledged, a sense of a strong debt to the classical remains. Apart from the evocation of ancient traditions in the white marble, the reason is as simple as it is surprising: it is the concept of the naked body, and it rests in the portrayal of the African adversaries in the frieze.[156] They are shown as well-built, athletic men with naked limbs and torsos and smooth muscled flesh. African facial features

---

[153] These features include mountains Figs 5.22, 24, 29, 32–42, 44, 47), trees (Figs 5.30, 35, 44, 47, 48), plants (Figs 5.22, 36, 47), a field (Fig. 5.44), livestock (Figs 5.22, 29), a sailing ship (Fig. 5.25), wagons (Figs 5.22–24, 26, 27, 32, 35, 36, 40–42, 44), settlements (Figs 5.25, 33, 34), a school (Fig. 5.24), a church (Fig. 5.43) and a tent (Fig. 5.48).

[154] African family life or children are never portrayed, and only occasionally are blacks distinguished in age, mainly to underline social status and hierarchy (Figs 5.29, 33, 46)

[155] For a specific Voortrekker 'rhetoric of suffering' see Van der Watt 1997.

[156] In the representation of the Voortrekkers as being civilised, particularly being Christian and civilised, was equated with being clothed. It is noteworthy that dressing converts in western clothing to show their newly Christian status was a recurrent theme at mission stations in Africa. A sense of impropriety regarding nudity was not limited to whites, however: the model who posed for the African females (Fig. 5.46) for Laurika Postma insisted that she do so behind a screen, and the male models too had problems with some poses being too revealing when they wore no underwear beneath Matabele 'riempie' skirts: Potgieter 1987: 47–48.

and sometimes slightly awkward poses aside, the artists shaped most black bodies in keeping with the classical tradition of masculine beauty and strength – a sole exception being the more bloated form of the Zulu King Dingane, the Voortrekkers' arch enemy. Moerdyk considered it important to stress in the *Official Guide* 'that throughout the frieze natives are never depicted as inferior beings – they are always represented as worthy opponents, very well developed as far as their physical characteristics are concerned'.[157] Given the requirement for semi-nude figures, the artists had hardly any other choice but to conceive them with forms and proportions that echoed those pre-modelled in classical bodies, familiar precedents in the mind of any sculptor trained in a western tradition. However, only one figure is portrayed in a purely classical stance: the Barolong standing on the far left (Fig. 5.20) is in a contrapposto pose, his weight on his left leg, his right arm a little bent, his head slightly turned to the left. Some Zulu warriors with raised assegais also come close to classicising poses, but the collapsing and supine poses of the defeated are more in line with Hellenistic pathos and Roman drama, visual concepts widely dispersed in the aftermath of Alexander the Great.

Throughout the frieze most standing figures, particularly the many Voortrekker men, have their weight sturdily distributed across both feet. This erect stance may be read as a metonym of their upright character, and its firmness their bond to the land. The distinctively utilitarian trousers and jackets that they wear lend them a sense of European formality and Christian decorum, leaving the field open for the African figures to commandeer classical concepts of male beauty and naked heroism. Likewise, the all-concealing dresses of the Voortrekker women, which mask any sense of limbs beneath their garments, stress their propriety and, like their bonnets, generally conceal the qualities we associate with feminine attractiveness. Rather it is an upright bourgeois respectability that is portrayed for both sexes. The only hint of nudity among the modestly clad female Voortrekkers is found when savage drama is addressed: in the foreground of the Bloukrans panel (Fig. 5.35) a supine woman, close to death, whose dress slips from her shoulders. Her hair too has come loose from any constraining bands, and her curiously extended limbs are revealed through the clinging fabric of her skirt. Within the classical tradition these features are well-known motifs for beautiful females: the half-exposed breast and half-revealed legs suggest an erotic desirability, while the loosely falling hair characterises women in extreme

---

[157] *Official Guide*, 51.

circumstances, such as Proserpina when abducted by Hades.[158] The semi-nudity of the fallen Voortrekker woman is echoed nearby in the sensitively carved dying man with bared shoulder and torso behind the figure of Piet Retief as he stands before his murderers (Fig. 5.34). In their exceptional treatment, the dying man and woman seem to take up the convention of figures in Greek and Roman art where nudity may portray not only beauty and sensuality, but also vulnerability and disorder, often associated with the liminal state between life and death.

But these figures are rarities. Among the Voortrekkers portrayed on the frieze, emotion is present but generally understated to suggest an admirable *habitus* in the face of extreme hardship. Similarly, action is represented but frozen in time to maintain a sense of dignity. The restraint of the Voortrekkers' behaviour is as much a sign of their Christian culture as is their western garb. When compared to the dramatic activity of their adversaries, their demeanour suggests control and civilisation as opposed to inferior status and often savage barbarism – however classical the bodies of the African figures may be. Yet to mark the white Voortrekker as superior and exemplary, it needed the African black to act as a counter model.

One could say that the relationship with classicism that underpins the Monument's sculptured frieze is based on conflicting conceptions creating a fundamental ambivalence that in itself seems anti-classical. It is an ambivalence provoked not only by the clash between architectural design and the frieze, but also by conflicting conceptions of classicism and the use of marble within the frieze itself. There is a paradoxical interplay between Voortrekker figures that are characterised by the well-ordered calm that we associate with images of ancient Greek and Roman heroes but lack their formal beauty, and the opposing African figures that adopt the conventions of beautiful classical bodies but lack the restraint of their classical forerunners. Similarly, if the purity of the white marble conjured up the prevailing concept of the purity of the Afrikaner people – perhaps even of the white race that they sought to promote and preserve – then representing the Zulu in the same medium indicates an unintended irony as narratives of colour are transformed into the whiteness of marble. These contradictions form an apt if uncon-scious metaphor of the unresolvable contradictions of the messages of the frieze: the inevitable conflation of multiple treks into a single plot to support a grand nationalist narrative; the emphasis on non-violent

[158] Zanker 2004: 91, Fig. 73.

negotiation and restraint juxtaposed with aggressive confrontation;[159] an admiration for Zulu valour yet a demonisation of African people as a basis for racist beliefs of white superiority.

The association with such racism of a monument dedicated to the founding narrative of Afrikaner political mythology underlined its links to apartheid, which made it seem inevitable that the Monument would be overthrown together with such bigotry when a democratic South Africa was established. Yet against all expectations it has survived. The Voortrekker Monument is living proof of the debate weighing the obligation to forget, and forgive, against the irrefutable need to remember. It is a profoundly classical debate in which political powers since the fifth century BC have, in the cause of peace, generally opted for non-remembrance (ancient Greek: *amnestía*) in order to suppress the recollection of 'bad' history.[160] But classical *amnestía* is no option when confronted with extreme inhumanity, such as the unprecedented horrors of the Holocaust. The aberrations of apartheid too could not be forgotten: yet an exceptional pathway to appeasement was initiated when South Africa established the Truth and Reconciliation Commission in 1995 to reveal and relive its unspeakable past as an act of healing.

6.   Reframing the Afrikaner Locus

Only a short distance away from the Voortrekker Monument, on a third elevated site in Pretoria, a new memorial, Freedom Park, has been built to enshrine the Struggle.[161] Encompassing all battles for human rights in South Africa, its message trumps British imperialism at the Union Buildings and Afrikaner power at the Monument. While the Union Buildings have retained a purpose, housing the new post-apartheid government, the Voortrekker Monument does not lend itself easily to this kind of salvage.[162] Reinvented instead as heritage, packaged more for

---

[159] Crampton describes how 'atrocities committed by the trekkers are justified as necessary evils on the road to a law-abiding society' (2001: 231).

[160] This is debated in Meier's thought-provoking book, in which he also reviews post-apartheid South Africa (2010: 85–87).

[161] Rankin 2013.

[162] On the eve of the first democratic elections of 1994, the Monument was kept 'out of the hands of a future government [by] a consortium of Afrikaner cultural organizations, which managed to draw in culturalists of varied political hues, formed a Section-21 company, legally constituting a privatized non-profit organization' (Grundlingh 2009: 164); see also Heymans and Theart-Peddle 2009: 4.

tourists, foreign or local, than national patriots, the Monument site has since 1994 gradually been de-politicised, suggesting indifference on the part of the new regime which has chosen not to tear down this bastion of Afrikaner nationalism. As Marc Ross points out, 'locating Freedom Park in the vicinity of the Voortrekker Monument will offer an alternative narrative of South African history without a direct confrontation'.[163] On 10 September 2013, a presidential address to Parliament marking Heritage Month expressed an even more reconciliatory approach. Having stressed that 'the building of a new cultural and heritage landscape' has developed new monuments and museums that 'define the new, free, non-racial and democratic South Africa', the controversial Jacob Zuma said,

The uniqueness of South Africa also emerges in some of the [existing] monuments. For example, in Pretoria, Gauteng, a road has been built linking Voortrekker Monument and Freedom Park as part of our on-going commitment to reconciliation, social cohesion and nation building.[164]

Thus, over time, the Monument has also been re-politicised, its original Afrikaner passion and political potency counterbalanced by new messages. Although it was initially a rallying ground for far-right opposition to the end of apartheid rule, the Monument was nonetheless allowed to survive. It seems that a diversity of influential political and ethnic groups have conceded that, unavoidably, it represents part of South Africa's history and national heritage.[165] One might also imagine a reluctant admiration for the monumental fabric of the building and its historical frieze that seemed too impressive and too impervious to simply be obliterated. In a new context the symbolism of the Monument could also be thought of as inverted, the old message celebrating Afrikaner victory over savage Africa overtaken by a new: the Monument as 'a signifier of what blacks had to overcome'.[166] Visiting the site in 1996, Tokyo Sexwale, then premier of Gauteng province where the Monument stands, skilfully appropriated its symbols to match fresh ideology. He argued, for example, that the assegais on the Monument's gates, ubiquitous too in the interior frieze, invoked the military wing of the ANC,

---

[163] Ross 2007: 250.
[164] 'Address by President Jacob Zuma to the Joint Sitting of Parliament on the occasion marking Heritage Month, National Assembly, Cape Town' (Zuma 2013). Zuma made a similar claim for 'the construction of a bridge linking Ncome Museum and the Blood River Monument [which] has also been completed, symbolising reconciliation and a new beginning amongst communities that sought to destroy each other in the past.'
[165] Herwitz 2012: 80–134.   [166] Grundlingh 2009: 169.

Umkhonto we Sizwe (Spear of the Nation), which 'opened up the path of civilisation' for a new dispensation.[167] His interpretation neatly overturned the Voortrekker perception that African warriors hindered the process of civilising the interior.

From a more inclusive position came Nelson Mandela's statement when he visited Fort Schanskop on 6 March 2002, now part of the Voortrekker Monument Heritage Site. Mandela was there to unveil a statue of Danie Theron, hero of the Second Anglo-Boer War (1899–1902), at the invitation of Gerrit Opperman, then chief executive officer of the Site, in an astute bid to increase interest in the Voortrekker Monument complex. Always ready to promote reconciliation, Mandela spoke (for the most part) Afrikaans, something he rarely did in public, and claimed, '"that shared experience of fighting for one's freedom binds us in a manner that is most profound." He noted that Blacks and Afrikaners shared a common experience in struggling against British colonial rule.'[168] Despite grave differences with some political Afrikaner leaders in the past, Mandela said, blacks do appreciate the role of Afrikaners 'in building our common land'.[169] In a further unexpected gesture of reconciliation, the Minister of Arts and Culture, Paul Mashatile, standing in front of the Blood River panel at a ceremony on 16 March 2012 (Fig. 5.21), made an announcement of a new status for the Voortrekker Monument, saying:

> The declaration of the Voortrekker Monument as the first Afrikaans national heritage site since the advance of democracy is a significant milestone to building a united and diverse South Africa.[170]

As the Voortrekker Monument Heritage Site has become more and more loosened – even if never detached – from its Afrikaner past, it has become increasingly open to emancipated and nuanced readings. It is within this widening and challenging debate that the Monument provides a fascinating example of the ongoing reception of the classical. At the Monument's inception, however accidentally, it proved impossible for Moerdyk, the artists and the members of the SVK to entirely efface and override classical models – despite the Afrikaner rhetoric with which they presented the Monument as so expressly not indebted to Greek and Roman antiquity. Especially for people with European roots, the archetypes of

---

[167] Coombes 2003: 37. For a wider backdrop of responses see her thorough analysis, 19–53.
[168] Ross 2007: 246.   [169] 'Madiba praises Afrikaner hero', *Herald*, 7 March 2002.
[170] 'Voortrekker monument now a national heritage site', *South African Government News Agency*, 16 March 2012 (www.sanews.gov.za/south-africa/voortrekker-monument-now-national-heritage-site).

antiquity have been difficult to avoid, so deeply have they penetrated the fabric of western thought and art. The continuing transformation of classical models into national icons of western power has corrupted them profoundly, and ultimately rendered them open to almost any ideological claim. The Voortrekker Monument is a telling example of how such forms, first appropriated in this case for Afrikaner nationalism, lend themselves to further reinvention in a new cause.

6 | Greeks, Romans and Volks-Education in the *Afrikaanse Kinderensiklopedie*

PHILIP R. BOSMAN

South Africa's cultural diversity provides depth and texture to its apparently empty physical expanses. Classical antiquity arrived on the scene with the early European settlements, and ever since infiltrated the South African landscape both literally and figuratively, as the contributions in this volume intend to remind us. Figurative infiltration is no doubt the more difficult to demonstrate, but nonetheless undeniably present in various forms. One such infiltration, this article would like to argue, happened by way of the abundant presence of the ancient world in the *Afrikaanse Kinderensiklopedie*, a much-hailed and much-loved publication which opened a world of knowledge to generations of Afrikaans-speaking children (and their teachers and parents) since the end of World War II.

This article presents an exploration of the references to Graeco-Roman antiquity in the *Afrikaanse Kinderensiklopedie* (henceforth AKE), for mainly two reasons. First, the encyclopædia constituted a landmark in South African publishing: it was at the time of publication the largest publishing enterprise in the country's history. Still, it has never before been the object of investigation. With referencing works increasingly moving to electronic mode, the AKE is sinking into oblivion together with similar dinosaurs of twentieth-century printing, thus acquiring antiquarian rather than utilitarian value. For this reason, documenting the use of the Classics in the AKE should be a worthwhile exercise, if only to provide an indication of the role it played in educational ideals of the era.

Secondly, the time of its publication makes it a noteworthy historical document. It hails from the decade 1943–53, the only publication of its kind from the era notorious for the formation and implementation of apartheid. As such, it is a product of Afrikaner nationalism from a crucial period in the country's history. References to the Classics in the AKE should consequently illuminate the manner in which Graeco-Roman antiquity played a part in the nationalist cause of the era, contributing to the debate on the ideological uses and abuses of the Classics.

In the following, I shall briefly outline the history of the AKE, before giving a survey of typical trends in how the various contributors made use of the classical world. In a final section, I will present brief comments on

213

how the classical references related to and stood in service of Afrikaner nationalism during the 1940s and 1950s. For the purposes of this study, I relied mainly on three sources: the second edition/reprint of the AKE (1953), the collection of documents on the AKE that its editor C. F. Albertyn bequeathed to the Special Collections and Documents Centre of the J. S. Gericke Library in Stellenbosch, and Hermann Giliomee's monumental *The Afrikaners* (2003) for the complexities of Afrikaner nationalism during the first half of the previous century.[1]

1.   The Making of the AKE

A children's encyclopædia in Afrikaans first came up in May 1938, when J. S. du Preez Scholtz, later professor at the University of Cape Town and close friend of the poet-intellectual N. P. van Wyk Louw, raised the idea to a small 'group of friends', as C. F. Albertyn referred to the meeting which turned out – in private conversation – to have been a general meeting of the Afrikaner-Broederbond.[2] Albertyn, then editor of the successful Afrikaans youth magazine *Die Jongspan*, mulled over the idea for another two years before starting to study existing encyclopædiæ, children's encyclopædiæ, educational series and school curricula. Having drawn up a scheme for his intended publication in June 1941, Albertyn approached five people to form a small committee, among them N. P. van Wyk Louw, eminent intellectual of the nationalist movement and generally considered the greatest Afrikaans poet of the twentieth century.[3] On 13 September 1941, four members of the committee accepted his proposed scheme and started working even before getting the go-ahead from the Nasionale Pers. Seven days after the meeting van Wyk Louw writes to his brother Gladstone that he expects much of this 'kultuurwerk':

Even in Dutch nothing similar exists, and if you know what Arthur Mee's *Encyclopedia* and others mean for the English child (also in South Africa), you will realize the kind of bulwark for our cause such an Afrikaans undertaking can

---

[1]   Giliomee's observations are integrated into his history of the Afrikaner people; on the rise and nature of Afrikaner nationalism during the nineteenth century, cf. van Jaarsveld 1961.

[2]   Steyn 1998: I, 334. On the early history of the Broederbond, cf. Pelzer 1979; Giliomee 2003: 400–1, 420–22. On the basis of unpublished research by E. L. P. Stals, Giliomee notes that the Bond had little political influence during the 30s and 40s and concentrated on culture and education for the purpose of raising self-consciousness among Afrikaners.

[3]   The other members of the initial committee were J. C. Pauw and G. O. Neser, both Paarl school teachers at the time, Anna Rothman and L. D. Boonstra of the South African Museum in Cape Town.

be . . . This kind of work is today more important to the continued existence of our people than all the theatrical gestures of the politicians.[4]

The mere fact of the AKE's publication is testimony to the idealism and determination of its editor. When Afrikaans became an official language of the Union less than two decades earlier, even ardent supporters of the language, like poet C. Louis Leipoldt, expressed reservations regarding its suitability for an official role independent from Dutch.[5] At the time, its literary accomplishments were still few and far between, its speakers still staggering from impoverishment caused by the Anglo-Boer War (1899–1902) and the Great Depression of the thirties, followed by World War II.[6] Fortunately, his idealism was from the start backed up by sound financial planning and a selfless conviction of the need for the work. He could also count on the enthusiasm of his small team of competent collaborators. The project kicked off in earnest in 1942 with 26 contributors, which grew to 99 over the next decade (excluding artists and others working on the project).

Albertyn modeled his idea mainly on the *Children's Encyclopedia* of Arthur Mee (1908–1910). It was not to be the usual alphabetic entry type of encyclopædia, but structured around a number of themes that were to run through all of the initial eight volumes (another two volumes were envisaged, should the need arise).[7] Unlike Mee's encyclopædia, the AKE held all entries belonging to the theme together under that heading. Above all, it aimed at 'bringing to the child the knowledge he [sic] needs in a simple, fantasy-filled and visual manner'. Especially the 'fantasy-filled' aspect Albertyn certainly stated under the spell of Mee, for little of that materialised in the final product.[8] But great care was taken to collect an abundance of visual material, which was not only obtained from local repositories and even photographs

---

[4] *N. P. van Wyk Louw Collection*, Documents Centre, J. S. Gericke Library, University of Stellenbosch, 158.K.Lo 29 (27). Translations into English from Afrikaans originals in this article are my own.

[5] Giliomee 2003: 377–78.

[6] In the 20s and 30s, the percentage of Afrikaners considered 'poor whites' was established as between 17 per cent and 25 per cent, and when 'poor' and 'very poor' were added together, it amounted to 56 per cent: Giliomee 2003: 347.

[7] Mee said of an 'Alphabet of Facts' the following: 'Admirable as that is for a busy man, it is useless torture for a child. Nothing can be more forbidding to a young mind than a collection of subjects arranged in the order in which the accident of the alphabet brings them.' Mee 1925: 3.

[8] Mee states the objective of the work as follows: 'It seeks to stir the mind and to awake a sense of wonder. Its purpose is to fascinate and educate', ibid. One running section of the *Children's Encyclopedia* was called 'Wonder'; cf. also Hammerton 1946.

taken by individuals during overseas holidays, but also from institutions across the world.[9]

From the start, the scale of the project caused considerable anxiety, with fear often 'clamping around the heart', as Albertyn reflected in later years.[10] Each volume was to have roughly 500 pages, approximately half of which were allotted to illustrations. The complete set of ten volumes comprised 2.5 million words, more than 10,000 photographs and illustrations, and involving a total of 200 collaborators. The publishers invested £130,000 in the project as a whole and envisaged – like the editor and the contributors – little material profit from it.[11] But the risk paid dividends: the first volume, published in September 1943, was sold out within four weeks and the publisher had to scramble for sufficient supply of paper for an immediate reprint of another 5000 copies.[12] Raving reviews soon started appearing in the Afrikaans press, with terms like 'kultuurgebeurtenis' (cultural happening), 'ryke erfenis' (rich legacy) and 'fulfilling a dire need for the Afrikaner youth' featuring prominently. *Die Burger* (Cape-based Afrikaans newspaper) of 7 September 1943 expressed its gratitude for the 'dryfkrag en deursettingsvermoë' (drive and endurance) of the editor and publisher: 'The Afrikaans child is indeed privileged above many others in that he so early in the development of our people is enabled by this book to see life not in bits and pieces, but as a whole, as Afrikaner'.[13] On 24 September 1943, *Die Huisgenoot* (back then known as the 'university of the people') calls it 'one of the most important publications ever undertaken by an Afrikaans firm and a most important event in the cultural life of the Afrikaner, the full significance of which will only be realized in years to come'.

Reviews remained positive for the remaining volumes, often expressing the wish that every school and household in the country should own a complete set. *Die Unie* (mouthpiece of the South African Teachers Union) of 1 April 1949 makes it the third most important book in Afrikaans: 'Here is the order [of precedence]: first the Bible, second the Hymn Book ... third the Children's Encyclopædia for the Afrikaner

---

[9]   The editor selected most of these himself from a collection comprising 30,000 pictures: *C. F. Albertyn Collection*, Documents Centre, J. S. Gericke Library, University of Stellenbosch, 234/1.29.

[10] *C. F. Albertyn Collection* 234/4.48.

[11] The contract with Nasionale Pers stated that Albertyn was to be paid R40 per month to produce one part per year or £100 per part, to be paid back should the project fail; *C. F. Albertyn Collection* 234/1.2. The profit per book, based on an issue of 3000, was 5 shillings and 6 pence.

[12] The scarcity of paper during the war limited the first impression to 3000 copies.

[13] *C. F. Albertyn Collection* 234/4.52.

child'.[14] Particularly lyrical was an SABC insert, published in the public broadcaster's mouthpiece *Die Soeklig* of 17 March 1953:

We are led through the treasure chambers of the world's literature, music, painting and sculpture, we drink in its beauty and refresh ourselves with the most beautiful thoughts of the world's greatest authors, poets and thinkers . . . [The complete set] is a precious cultural possession of the Afrikaans people, a living monument to our language, a source of knowledge and joy to children, parents and teachers. It is a publishing enterprise that brilliantly holds its own in comparison with the best in the world.[15]

When the final Volume X appeared in 1953, the impression stood at 17,000, of which 15,000 were subscriptions. A second edition was printed in 1953, a third in 1963 and a restructured version as the *Nuwe Afrikaanse Kinderensiklopedie* in 1983. At that time the publication already had an old-fashioned look to it and was overtaken in the market by more attractive but – unfortunately – less substantial publications in this particular niche.[16]

2. AKE References to the Classical World

Albertyn kept closely to his initial conception of the work accepted by the editorial committee in September 1941. Editorial guidelines to subeditors and collaborators were restricted to the minimum: they should aim at twelve-year-olds, but the material should be presented in such a way as to be of benefit for readers between 8 and 80; the tone should be conversational; illustrations should not explain but continue the conversation. Albertyn was happy to leave the decision of how sections should be subdivided to the subeditors themselves. United by the common cause of general education, the team became something of a family, affectionately referring to the series as 'ons Groot Kinderboek' (our Great Children's Book).

Since Albertyn was not prescriptive about the content of the various subsections, we may assume that the regular references to the ancient world probably came from the contributors themselves. The material, though resistant to neat organisation, can be grouped under the headings of those viewing products of the ancient world as of enduring value in themselves, and those fitting them into a broadly conceived cultural and

---

[14] *C. F. Albertyn Collection* 234/4.28. [15] *C. F. Albertyn Collection* 234/4.42.
[16] E.g. Hauman 1978; *Wêreldspektrum* (1983–94); and recently van Lill 2010.

intellectual history. The classical references mentioned in the paragraphs below are not exhaustive, but aim to represent typical features and trends.

3.   The Roots of Almost Everything

'Cradle of civilisation' Entries

A number of treatments of the Graeco-Roman world can be found in the context of antiquity as the 'bakermat' (cradle) of civilisation. These occur under the running subsections of 'Man's life with other people' and 'The story of the peoples of the world'.[17]

D. J. J. de Villiers (introduced simply as 'inspector of schools') was responsible for two entries on antiquity in the former subsection. Vol. I, 60–76 deals with the 'Roots of our civilisation in antiquity' and includes the civilisations of Egypt, Assyria and Babylonia, the Jews and the Phoenicians, the Greeks and the Romans (see section below).[18] The second part of the little series goes under the heading 'How the oldest peoples lived', but this time includes only the Egyptians and Mesopotamians (Vol. II, 476–89). The series 'The story of the peoples of the world' treat Graeco-Roman antiquity in Vols. II, 585–614 and III, 1025–40.[19] The two entries (by Dr P. S. du Toit, then teacher at the Hoërskool Jan van Riebeeck in Cape Town)[20] consist of a fair number of pages on the civilisations of antiquity – the same ones as mentioned by De Villiers, with the addition of Crete, 'the real cradle of European civilisation' (pp. 598–600). Greek and Roman history is slightly expanded, with paragraphs on cultural highlights of both. Du Toits claims that Greek culture is 'more relevant to our own civilisation than the three old civilizations' (Egypt, Mesopotamia and Crete and the Aegean, p. 600) and is rightly regarded as 'the greatest civilization of all time' (p. 608). He mentions specifically in this regard their architecture, sculpture, literature, philosophy and science (pp. 608–10). The Romans, on the other hand, left a twofold legacy: apart from their own contributions to Western culture (family; religion; literature;

---

[17] Subsections under the heading 'Die mens' (Man); the other four headings are 'The earth we inhabit and the wonderful universe', 'The animal kingdom', 'Plants' and 'Man draws from nature's treasures'.

[18] Page references in this article are to the second edition of the AKE: Albertyn 1953.

[19] The entry in Vol. I under this subsection, dealing with human evolution and written by J. C. Pauw, proved to be controversial; see Section 6 below.

[20] Du Toit later became professor in Education at the University of Stellenbosch; cf. Du Toit 1966: 121.

language; calendar; law and architecture, pp. 1030–33), they were instrumental in conserving the legacies of the other ancient cultures (p. 1033).

'Origins' Entries

Some of the most interesting references to the classical world occur in
treatments of topics of which the origins are to be found in antiquity.
In general, the discussions in the AKE over a broad spectrum (i.e. not
restricted to the humanities) have a remarkably diachronic approach:
topics are consistently treated by tracing their history from where they
presumably first appeared.[21] Very often, natural sciences topics are interspersed with fascinating titbits of information stemming from the classical
world.

   A prominent emphasis on origins is to be found in etymological explanations of unfamiliar words. These occur throughout the set, such as the
astronomical terms perihelion (*peri* = close to + *helios* = sun) and aphelion
(apo = away from + helios = sun) right at the start of Vol. I (p. 20), clastic
and metamorphic rocks (Vol. II, 419), and the humble member of the lily
family eriospernum, from 'two Greek words meaning "hairy" and "seed"'
(Vol. IV, 1690). The addition of scientific names in especially the sections
on vertebrates, invertebrates and plants was probably a contentious issue,
as it is probably not compatible with the needs and abilities of the average
twelve-year-old; the decision to retain them compelled Albertyn to mention in the short preface (repeated in all volumes) that readers need not
read or learn these words as they are meant for adults who wish to learn
more.

   Related to etymological explanations are the discussions on the history
of languages, dealt with in exemplary fashion by J. S. du P. Scholtz, the
same man who fathered the idea of such an encyclopædia. In Volume I,
Scholtz briefly tells the history of grammatical investigations, starting with
Herodotus's story of Psammeticus' quest for the oldest language. He also
mentions the earliest language theory we know of, namely the Greek idea
of a natural link between an object and its name. However, Aristotle, 'the
wisest Greek of them all', disagreed with this theory and rather devoted his
attention to grammatical analysis, thereby identifying the various parts of
speech we still use today (p. 35). The Romans were also interested in the
origins of words and came up with peculiar answers: *lucus* from *lucere,*

---

[21] This applies also to topics where we would not expect it, from wheat, maize and tobacco to
      vitamins, flags and glass.

lepus from *levis* + *pes*, etc. (p. 35–36). In Vol. II, 439–45 Scholtz surveys the world's language families and in Vol. V he presents a concise but informative discussion of the influence of Latin on Afrikaans through Germanic (Vol. V, 1791–93).

Treatments of topics such as astronomy and architecture run through a number of volumes, so that references to the classical origins of these mostly occur in the first two to three volumes of the set. Astronomy is a good case in point. The very first section of Volume I, written by G. G. Cillié jnr. (professor in mathematics at University of Stellenbosch),[22] discusses the earth's composition, dimension and history. Cillié distinguishes deftly between the 'old Greeks' who thought the earth was a flat disk, and philosophers like Pythagoras and Aristotle, who deduced its spherical form from lunar eclipses (pp. 12–14). Also mentioned are Eratosthenes' remarkable attempt at calculating the circumference of the earth (p. 14), and Julius Caesar's calendar reform based on the advice of the peripatetic astronomer Sosigenes (p. 23–24). In Volume IV, Cillié devotes a whole section to ancient astronomy, including the contributions of the Chinese, the Babylonians, Chaldaeans and Egyptians (pp. 1307–16). The Greeks, however, must get the credit for putting the previously disconnected observations on a scientific basis. The Greeks are, however, not above reproach, since they regrettably neglected the fact that conclusions should be supported by observation, and they foolhardily – on the authority of Aristotle – clung to the belief that the earth forms a fixed point in the universe (pp. 1316–17).[23] The title of greatest astronomer before Newton should go to Hipparchus of Rhodes (fl. 150 BC), whose calculating the distances to the sun and the moon were 'brave attempts' and whose star catalogue remained in use for almost 2000 years (p. 1318).[24] Cillié concludes his astronomical history with a discussion of the Arabian astronomers, the true heirs of the Greeks through Ptolemy's *Almagest* (pp. 1319–21). The key to the success of Cillié's historical survey is that he manages in an entertaining and informative way to present the accomplishments in antiquity as fundamental to understanding the current state of the science, not simply as an attempt to resuscitate expired knowledge.

---

[22] Du Toit 1966: 98; Booyens 1966.

[23] Also mentioned are Thales' prediction of a solar eclipse on 28 May 585 BC, showing that he knew the Chaldaean discovery of the Saros cycle; Pythagoras's secret knowledge (only divulged to his pupils) that the earth circles around the sun was slightly adapted by Philolaus; Meton's discovery of his lunisolar cycle in the mid-fifth century was greeted with jubilation at the Olympic Games and the 'golden number' was brought on to an Athenian temple; Plato's theory of circular movements led to the system of Ptolemaios five and a half centuries later.

[24] Cf. also Vol. VI, 2237.

Cillié is not alone in voicing criticism against the Greek accomplishments. A tongue-in-cheek critical tone is found regarding Aristotle's faulty hypothesis of a king-bee, held to be true until Jan Swemmerdam in 1673 proved 'him' to be a 'her' (Vol. II, 375). Regarding Galen's view of blood circulation, R. S. Verster observes: 'This old Greek made everybody believe that blood wells up in the liver like a fountain and flows away through the veins in the body like fountain water in the tall grass . . . But where it ends up, Galen forgot to tell us!' (Vol. VIII, 3187).[25]

Some origin entries are wonderfully idealising. In Volume I, Cape Town architect Magda Sauer expresses severe judgment over Egyptian and Roman architecture as opposed to that of the Greeks: Egyptian architecture has something 'depressing' about it: 'the temples are gloomy and overwhelming, and it seems as if they were meant to instill fear into the people' (p. 117). Greek temples, on the other hand, have nothing somber about them: they made use of the most beautiful building material on earth and adorned their temples with statues never surpassed in their beauty. They reflect a 'free and happy people with an extraordinary sense of beauty': 'Even today, with the temples old and severely damaged, they stand sparkling and splendid against the deep-blue sky of the landscape along the Mediterranean – the sky that looks so much like our own South African sky' (pp. 117–18).[26] Roman architecture resembles that of the Greeks to some extent, but it is more ungainly and coarse, intended to create the impression of wealth and power (119). The same judgment applies to places of entertainment, although the Romans come off a little better regarding their amphitheatres, circuses and *thermae* (Vol. V, 1890–95). But whereas the precise marble blocks of the Greeks were the work of skilful artisans, the Romans made use of slave labour for their rough brickwork, only requiring skilled labour for their marble panelling. The Romans are at least laudable for inventing the strong cement that made their buildings last for centuries (Vol. VIII).

Hellenophilic sentiments appear to have dominated art and architectural schools at the time, as they are also reflected in May Hillhouse's contribution on folk art (Vol. IX, 3841–43). Greek art – in her Winckelmannean view cultivated from Greek philosophy, religion and the ideals of perfect proportion – was formative for Greek taste. The subordinate arts, even the most humble objects of daily life, reflect

---

[25] Cf. also Vol. VII, 2733. Similarly, Pliny misled us by naming the Phoenicians the inventors of glass, while we now know that the Egyptians already knew the art four millennia earlier, Vol. I, 382–83.

[26] Cf. also Vol. VI, 2355; Vol. VII, 2843–45 on houses.

their lofty sense of 'fraai verhoudinge en ingetoë skoonheid' (fine proportions and restrained beauty). The Egyptians, again, tried to instill awe, and
the practical Romans, sadly, could only imitate: 'The mixture in taste
noticeable in the Roman art form displays an undigested concoction that
through the ages devolved into the blend of Greek and Eastern influences
we today know under the designation of Byzantine art' (Vol. IX, 3843).

To what extent the AKE contributors consulted Mee's encyclopædia
would be difficult to gauge. Direct borrowing is not conspicuous, and
the similarities in sentiment they reflect should probably be ascribed to
what was common for the learned world at the time. Regarding the
Greek aesthetic sense, the *Children's Encyclopædia* comments: 'Never
had the world seen any such beauty as Athens gave it, and all future
efforts to express our human sense of divine loveliness will be inspired
by the Greeks' idea of restraint, repose and simplicity' (Vol. II, 1290).
And regarding the origins of the modern (Western) world, even more
bluntly: 'To the Hebrews we owe our idea of God. To the Romans we
owe our idea of sanitary science. To the Greeks we owe nearly everything else' (Vol. V, 3119).

The AKE treats a good number of 'everything else', even though it does
give the Romans credit for at least proper roads (Vol. I, 124), bridges
(Vol. II, 550) and postal services (Vol. VII, 2859). Mostly, both cultures
get mentioned in a form of cultural evolution, the Romans functioning as
bridge between the Greeks and later Western Europe. For example, after
treating the family among the Andamanese, Bushmen (Khoisan) and
black tribes of Africa, A. J. Böeseken finds the origins of the Afrikaner
family with the Greeks and the Romans, through the Germanic tribes
(Vol. IV, 1379–89). And while they did not invent them, the Greeks and
Romans have honorary positions in the history of armory (Vol. III, 906),
ceramic art (Vol. III, 983), money and coinage (Vol. V, 1926–28), commerce (Vol. III, 1012–15) and law (Vol. VI, 2297–98). As would fit
a children's encyclopædia, a good amount of space gets devoted to
sport, entertainment and games among the Greeks and the Romans.
The games played by Greek and Roman children show much greater
similarity to those played by modern children than the kinds of entertainment of ancient and modern grown-ups (Vol. VII, 2765–71). Both Greeks
and Romans played a form of football (Vol. VIII, 3227) and of course the
Greeks also originated the Olympic Games, which were ruined by greed
and profit to such an extent that Theodosius in AD 394 finally put an end
to them (Vol. IX, 3747–48).

4.   Cultural Products of Lasting Value

Literature, Philosophy and Exempla

Some entries may be grouped together on the basis that they do not place emphasis on Graeco-Roman culture as the origin of cultural phenomena or as a stage in an evolutionary history. Rather, they stress accomplishments that by themselves are still worthy of attention today. The literature and philosophy of the Greeks and Romans, and the stories of their greatest figures may be considered in this category.

The entries probably of most interest to students of literature are those by van Wyk Louw himself. The poet and intellectual was assigned responsibility for the running section entitled 'Kunsskatte van die wêreld' (art treasures of the world). Louw did a splendid job of the section, treating an astounding breadth of topics on literature, visual art, music and architecture (the section grew to 111 pages in Vol. IX). The literary entries alone cover many national literatures: much attention is naturally devoted to Afrikaans literature, but many others get their turn: from the Icelandic *Eddas* (Vol. IX, 3823) to Sotho and Zulu stories (Vol. IX, 3829–3841), from medieval Latin (Vol. III, 931–38) to modern Indian (Vol. IX, 3809–10), from Middle Dutch (Vol. II, 494–97) to women's poetry (Sappho gets an innings at the start of this entry; Vol. VI, 2330–35). For the purpose he made use of a great number of specialists, but wrote the classical entries himself: on Homer's *Iliad* (Vol. I, 76–79), the philosophers and Aesop (Vol. II, 497–99; 510–513); Greek drama (Vol. IV, 1401–13) and Vergil's *Aeneid* (Vol. V, 1840–45; 'the golden age of Latin literature'). These consist mainly of paraphrases: Louw obviously used the opportunity to simply introduce his readers to the narratives, relying on the strength of the stories themselves in their retelling – a wise decision as prior knowledge could not be assumed and the stories would be what children would remember best. The retellings are accompanied by brief contextual observations, e.g. on Homer, Greek drama and the age of Augustus.

More ordinary is Louw's mention of the 'triad' Socrates, Plato and Aristotle, which does not at all attempt to convey the essence of their philosophies apart from 'deep thoughts' about man, life and death, truth and beauty (Vol. II, 497–99). Covering approximately the same terrain (the Stoics and Augustine are added), A. H. Murray is more successful in conveying what their 'deep thoughts' were actually about (Vol. V, 1090–97).

To the same category would belong a lengthy entry on 'Famous men and women of the world, from the days of Athens and Rome', by J. C. Pauw (Vol. VI, 2486–2501). The section treats a (necessarily highly selective) group of individuals, probably on the basis of superlatives to be added to their names: Solon – one of the best known wise men, poet and statesman of antiquity; Pericles – 'the great Greek statesman'; Demosthenes – 'greatest orator of all time'; Alexander the Great; Horatius – 'one of the bravest men of the world'; Hannibal – 'one of the most brilliant generals of the world and Rome's most formidable enemy'; Julius Caesar – 'greatest of all Romans'; Constantine the Great. The stories are broad historical outlines sprinkled with typical material that would interest a child: Solon's madness; Pericles, 'from one of the most brilliant and democratic families in Greece' who not only encouraged and inspired Herodotus and Thucydides, Pheidias and Sophocles to produce their masterpieces, but also gave the most lowly citizen the opportunity to enjoy them; Demosthenes's various methods to improve his performance; Alexander and Bucephalus; Hannibal's oath and elephants; Caesar among the pirates (Fig. 6.1) and his spectacular death. Pauw, a good friend of Albertyn, probably got the 'superlative' approach from Mee, who typically called the Bible 'the most beautiful book in the world', gave Plato the title 'king of thought' and Handel that of 'king of music'.

Myths, Legends and Anecdotes

One kind of reference to the classical world fits uncomfortably into any of the typical categories above, because their purpose seems to be little else than to provide amusing diversion and enrichment of the topic under discussion. These references are among the most delightful, enlivening the topic under discussion and luring the reader to further investigation (while also showing the erudition of the contributors and the extent in which the classics were considered part of general education). Examples include the myth of Icarus (Leonard Gill on birds and why wings would be of no use to humans, Vol. I, 281), red mullets on Roman elite dinner tables (C. van Bonde on why fish change their colour, Vol. I, 312), Xenarchus' reference to the luck of cicadas for having mute spouses (A. J. Hesse on the senses of insects; Vol. I, 342), Petronius' story of Nero beheading the brilliant glass-blower (G. O. Neser on the malleability of glass, Vol. I, 388). In a section entitled 'Gold, our biggest source of revenue' (Vol. II, 567), W. and C. G. W. Schumann tell no fewer than four stories to show that the ancients already admired the yellow metal: Midas, Atalanta

Figure 6.1 Caesar among the pirates, illustration from *Afrikaanse Kinderensiklopedie.*

and the golden apples, the golden fleece of Jason and the Argonauts, and the golden calf of the Israelites.

A very successful contributor to the AKE in terms of information imparted at the level of children in vivacious style, is C. S. Grobbelaar, beloved lecturer in zoology at the University of Stellenbosch.[27] In his delightful pieces on mammals, Grobbelaar makes frequent reference to all sorts of side issues, among them stories from Greek mythology: Amalthea and her copious horn (Vol. II, 691), the Ceryneian hind of Heracles' labours and the stag that Apollo's friend Cyparissus accidentally killed (Vol. III, 1127). Even the section on the common sheep Grobbelaar enlivens with the ancient fable of the sheep who came to complain with Zeus, 'at that moment sitting under one of his lovely oak trees at the foot of Mount Olympus' of his lack of bravery and fighting skills (Vol. V, 2071). Later on he mentions the reports of Herodotus, Diodorus and Leo Africanus on fat-tailed sheep (Vol. V, 2077). The section on cattle includes a discussion on how *monokeros* and *unicornis* can be related to the Assyrian 'oeros' (primeval ox, Vol. IV, 1602).[28] Reading the entries of Grobbelaar and his fellow contributors, one has to wonder how many zoologists of today can boast such a broad frame of reference, and only lament the present trend of erecting walls between disciplines and particularly between the Humanities and the Natural Sciences.

5. The AKE and the Nationalist Cause

If the survey above can be summarised, two features stand out: the use of classical antiquity as educational enrichment, and as providing an authoritative point of orientation in the evolution of humankind. Both knowledge about the ancient world and the pervasive diachronic approach to knowledge is simply taken for granted as important to, as Albertyn states in the preface of Volume I, 'answering the questions that every child so often asks himself about the universe, the earth, nature, humankind and his neighbours'. Undoubtedly the model of Mee's encyclopædia, in which the ancient world also has a pervasive presence, played its part, but the practice first and foremost reflects the general educational methods of the times: things could only be properly understood if their 'story' was known, and that story more often than not started in antiquity.

It should be borne in mind that the AKE project stems from the general purpose of Afrikaner nationalist movement at the time, namely to uplift

---

[27] De Kock 1987: V, 307.
[28] Grobbelaar even mentions, albeit erroneously, Ctesias as the source of this tradition.

the Afrikaner people by means of education in their own language.[29] This educational ideal, by no means narrowly conceived, was expressed in an influential speech by Tobie Muller in 1914, which argued the case for a legitimate nationalism with a 'moral purpose and universal value' to counter 'jingo-imperialism' in South Africa. It was not enough, in Muller's view, to rally against the English and other nations from a sense of inferiority and marginality; rather, Afrikaners had to cultivate an identity rooted in the soil but with a universal perspective.[30] Education along the lines of 'universally' accepted practice was considered a key factor to the success of the cause.[31]

Looking closer at how the content was sometimes interpreted, it emerges that the diachronic approach nonetheless facilitated the more political aim of uniting the Afrikaner people in a common identity, namely that of European stock implanted into the soil of uncivilised Africa. Graeco-Roman civilisation presented the opportunity to anchor Afrikaner culture and language in the long and honorable cultural history of the great civilisations of Greece and Rome. While this is common to other Western nations, in the South African context this stress had the further consequence of differentiating the Afrikaners, and whites in general, from the barbarous indigenous peoples of the land.

The entry by D. J. J. de Villiers in Vol. I, 60–76 might serve to illustrate how this cultural *cum* racial superiority operates, and is indicative of the growing prominence of the 'Naturellevraagstuk' (native problem) among intellectuals at the time. Before treating the ancient civilisations, De Villiers gives a brief lesson on the social evolution of humankind, to be applied to the indigenous peoples of South Africa. It starts with the statement that all people have the common goal of happiness, but that each separate people have their own rules and customs in order to achieve that goal (embryonic apartheid). De Villiers briefly describes the social evolution of humankind over thousands of years from hunters and gatherers to herdsmen and farmers and finally to civilisation. At the time when the first Europeans (the 'white people') settled in the Cape, they encountered peoples in all three earlier stadia of evolution. It should be remembered, though, that the ancestors of these very Europeans also went through the same difficult

---

[29] Cf. Giliomee 2003: 355–446, for a description of the era under the revealing headings 'To stop being agterryers' (i.e. lagging behind the English-speaking section of the populace) and 'Fusion and war'.

[30] Muller 1990: 128–53, in Giliomee 2003: 371.

[31] Van Wyk Louw in 1935 refers to the real challenge for those concerned with the Afrikaner cause 'to articulate universal values in Afrikaans from an Afrikaans viewpoint': Giliomee 2003: 402.

stages of evolution over a very long period, so that it is unfair to judge people from an earlier stage of evolution. The message is clear: while other cultures are to be respected even when lagging behind the Europeans, the Afrikaners should align themselves with the advanced 'kultuurvolkere' of Greece and Rome, as did their forefathers in far-off Europe. The great European tradition offered a means of consolidating Afrikaner identity which easily slipped into racial solidarity, albeit tempered by a liberal sense of respect for all cultures and races.[32]

Classical antiquity furthermore offered material which could be utilised to educate the Afrikaner youth in their duty to preserve their culture and identity in the country. In the light of the need for solidarity in own ranks, the Peloponnesian war is described with a tone of regret as a civil war, while the fourth-century struggle for Greek hegemony is depicted as inner discord which made Greece prey to the 'rough and uncivilised hunters and farmers' of Macedon (P. S. du Toit, Vol. II, 606). But Afrikaners also had a God-given duty of spreading the light of civilisation into Africa, hence is the greatness of Alexander (à la Plutarch and Tarn) due to his devotion to the same task over such vast tracts of the ancient world (pp. 606–7). Greek and Roman religion is also employed as warning against the dangers of apostasy, moral decline and – ultimately – national disintegration. 'Sunday School Secretary of the Cape' P. K. Albertyn strikes an ambiguous tone of romantic idealisation and disappointment and reproach in his treatment of Graeco-Roman religion (Vol. V, 1829–32). The Greek sense of divinity was integrated with nature: 'The murmur of every stream was to them the voice of a water nymph. The rustle of leaves in a forest announced the passage of the gods …' (p. 1830). But the author continues with a somewhat confusing *praeparatio evangelica* approach. The Greeks' worship of Zeus was promising (quoting Aratus) but their religion degenerated into polytheism and anthropomorphism, which caused all respect for the gods to vanish. Their wise men warned that the demise of their religion would lead to 'the muddy pool of moral ruin', but '[d]eeper and deeper the people sank, and by the time of Christ the Greek religion was obsolete … [t]he people were ripe for a new religion' (pp. 1830–31). The Romans followed suit, but the author slips in a warning against divine disrespect and moral laxity, clearly directed at his contemporaries: Seneca, Cicero and Tacitus warned the Romans in vain, and 'when all

---

[32] The latter attitude of course occurred widely in colonial powers of the time and was also shared by Arthur Mee, as observed by a recent biographer: Tracy 2008.

respect for the gods disappeared, the Roman people fell prey to immorality' and were consequently conquered by nations they themselves previously despised as barbarians (p. 1832).

Two root causes for the formulation of the system of apartheid have been identified as the 'fear complex' and the 'superiority complex' among Afrikaners.[33] To this may be added the 'inferiority complex' of Afrikaners towards the British imperialists mentioned by Tobie Muller, especially after the humiliation of and destitution following the Anglo-Boer War. These psychological driving forces are all mirrored in the use of classical antiquity within the AKE project: inferiority taken care of by means of education, and fear for survival by means of group solidarity expressed as cultural and racial superiority. Religion was co-opted as bulwark against that moral degeneration which would surely lead to defeat in the struggle for Afrikaner survival.

6. The AKE and Afrikaner Emancipation

It would be unfair to condemn all collaborators to the AKE as contributing towards the later aberrations of the Afrikaner nationalist project. Despite the occasional heavily tendentious entry, the AKE emerges as a manifestation of liberal nationalism, as envisioned by the likes of Tobie Muller and of which N. P. van Wyk Louw became the foremost exponent. The philosophical basis from which entries proceeded would require in-depth scrutiny of the contributors' education, although it is safe to assume that modernism and positivism would have made their impact felt. A remarkable aspect of the AKE is that the Bible played a diminished role in the diachronic approach of the contributors, much less prominent than in Mee's work which has a whole separate running section devoted to the Bible. This fact is surprising in view of the dominant position of the Bible in the ideology of the Afrikaner people, who are generally brought up with Eve rather than Pandora, with Samson rather than Heracles, and with David rather than Achilles. Even though Albertyn gave the assurance that the 'religion of the fathers' will not in any way be neglected, the overall impression is that content was dictated by non-religious and non-theological considerations. Even more surprising, the approach was welcomed by all but a small fringe in the Afrikaner community.

---

[33] Cf. the Rev. Z. R. Mahabane's observation, as quoted by Giliomee 2003: 471. Mahabane can be forgiven for underestimating the impact on the Afrikaner psyche of deeply entrenched feelings of inferiority towards the English-speaking population.

Some backlash erupted at the publication of Volume I in 1943, providing hints at how the Classics may be contextualised within the AKE's educational programme. Volume I elicited a lengthy response from Dr F. J. M. Potgieter in two issues of *Die Kerkbode* (mouthpiece of the Dutch Reformed Church), 12 and 19 February 1944. Potgieter's criticism was aimed at the endorsement of evolutionism in the AKE and the general tenor of positivism: he feared that 'positivism had not only neutralised the message of the Church, but had already taken its place in these eventful ('veelbewoë') days of the coming of age of our people'.[34] Concern was consequently expressed at some synods of the Dutch Reformed Church that entries in the AKE breathed the 'evolutionistic hypothesis' and entered the soul of the child ('kindersiel') by means of the luring package of choice Afrikaans, attractive narrative style and rich illustrations.

Seldom going so far as to the reject the whole enterprise (some in fact did return their copies and cancelled their subscriptions), Potgieter and other voices from the Afrikaans churches requested that the theoretical nature of evolutionism should be explicitly stated. Albertyn, not wishing the issue to detract from his proud accomplishment, refused to get involved in polemics, diplomatically responding to objections that the AKE entries included nothing not already taught at the country's universities, but that the matter would be properly considered when reviewing the work for its second edition. However, in a personal letter to J. C. Pauw, one of those responsible for evolutionist ideas, he reassuringly wrote not to be concerned about the issue, and in a letter to H. F. Verwoerd – later apartheid architect but then editor-in-chief of the northern daily newspaper *Die Transvaler*, who requested a copy for review – Albertyn wryly observes that the controversy seems to have enhanced sales, as they could not meet the demand.[35]

Probably the most acute observations on the position of the AKE in Afrikaner history came from an article in *The Forum* of 8 November 1947, which Albertyn significantly filed among his documents.[36] The anonymous author (calling him/herself 'L. R.') pairs the AKE with new directions in Afrikaans literature (by name, D. J. Opperman's *Heilige Beeste*, for which the poet was recently awarded the coveted Hertzog prize) as signals of Afrikaner emancipation from the Dutch Reformed Church: like his peers around the globe, the educated Afrikaner developed a thirst for reading and rejects prescription in his tastes whether for commercial literature

---

[34] *Die Kerkbode*, 19 January 1944; similar in *Die Kerkblad*, 3 March 1944.
[35] *C. F. Albertyn Collection* 234/4.14.   [36] *C. F. Albertyn Collection* 234/4.22.

devoid of values (e.g. romance and crime literature) or for educational and serious literature. The tone of all of these literatures is secular, the sentiment humanistic. L. R., writing on the occasion of the Dutch Reformed Church requesting the Censor Board to protect society against the erosion of Christian values, comments that the 'Church, in short, is no longer the arbiter to whom publishers and readers look for advice and approval', and that by turning to the Censor Board it tries to 'divert the stream of Afrikaans literature from what it considers the muddy waters of secularism'.[37]

As the authors in *Die Kerkbode* and *The Forum* both noted, the *Afrikaanse Kinderensiklopedie* came at a pivotal time in the history of the Afrikaner people. While the classical world played no explicit role in the evolutionist controversy, it formed an integral part of the overall educational strategy among Afrikaner intelligentsia during the 1940s and 1950s. The emphasis on the high cultures of antiquity served to tie Afrikaner identity to Europe and Western tradition, but it also served to introduce a universal and humanist perspective into the educational programme. One can only speculate about the impact of the programme on generations of AKE readers during the years of the rise and fall of apartheid, but perhaps the 'ideals of Solon of law and justice and democracy' (J. C. Pauw, Vol. VI, 2487) did enable some to overcome the ever-present fear for national extinction.

---

[37] Ibid., p. 28

PART IV

____

Law, Virtue and Truth-Telling

Ancient Greece and Rome have intersected with abstract thought in several respects. **Allen** focuses on three intellectuals of the earlier twentieth century to show how antiquity served as a template for commentary on imperialism and nationalism, and to a lesser extent on race. Two of the three, J. H. Hofmeyr (later deputy prime minister) and T. J. Haarhoff, engaged with the widely prevalent analogy drawn between British and Roman imperialism, whereas the third, Martin Versfeld, took a more inward-looking approach in which the figure of Socrates was a model of social critique. For all of them, antiquity provided a source of political principles. Taken together, they exhibit what may be called a 'competing discourse' on imperialism. All three were of Afrikaner origin but studied at the English-speaking University of Cape Town.

A more institutionalised kind of classical presence has been visible in the South African legal system since colonial times. The European common law tradition owes much to Dutch humanism, and ultimately to Roman law. On the one hand, the link is an indirect one, in that it is merely one part, and a chronologically most distant one, of contemporary law, in what has been described as a mixed legal system par excellence. On the other hand, the ancient texts themselves can be consulted directly and are sometimes still cited in judgments. Cicero is a key figure in the link between antiquity and contemporary South Africa, both because of his connection with the Greek philosophical tradition of Plato and Aristotle and because of his special status among the humanists of early modern Europe. In particular, the core virtues of justice, equity and reasonableness are a link between antiquity and the present day. These very values are what **Van Zyl** finds in the preamble to the New Constitution (1996), so that the constitution itself might be considered the presence of Cicero in South Africa. Certainly, Cicero has been a source of wisdom and inspiration for a scholar-jurist such as Van Zyl. It emerges that the (literary) concept of reception is problematic in a juristic context.

7 | A Competing Discourse on Empire

JONATHAN ALLEN

Historically, there have been three main cultural and social sources of support for the study of classics in South Africa. It has been related, first, to the desire for a marker of 'civilisation' and a form of legitimising the rule of colonial and 'European' racial elites over subordinate groups.[1] Second, it has served as a means of social advancement within the racial elite – as part of the training of candidates for the ministry in the Dutch Reformed Church from the first half of the nineteenth century to the present, and as an official requirement for those wishing to enter the legal profession, at least until 1994.[2] The third stimulus for engagement with the classics intersected with the first two, but originated outside South Africa, in the official justificatory discourse of British Imperialism. It is this third influence – manifested chiefly in the comparisons drawn between the Roman and British Empires – that gave the classics a significant focal role in the history of political thought in twentieth-century South Africa, along with more obvious and self-standing candidates such as neo-Calvinism, Afrikaner Nationalism, British Idealism, Black Consciousness and Marxism.

The focus of this chapter will be on the reflections on empire, nation and race produced by three classically trained and rather atypical Afrikaner intellectuals: J. H. Hofmeyr, T. J. Haarhoff and Martin Versfeld. The background of these three men in the thought and history of the Greeks and Romans allowed them to formulate distinctive outlooks concerning empire, nationalism, and, to a lesser extent, race. I shall refer to their work as a 'competing discourse' on imperialism.[3]

The perspectives of Hofmeyr and Haarhoff were made possible and given significance by the prominence of attempts to legitimise and

---

[1] See Lambert 2011: 22–35. Lambert discusses the habit of giving 'classical names' (especially martial ones) to slaves at the Cape from 1656 to 1762.

[2] Lambert 2011: 33–35, 56–57.

[3] Andrew Nash has recently – and a little controversially – identified a 'rival tradition' among South African intellectuals, critical of apartheid and committed to freedom of speech and open dialogue as a way of life. See Nash 2009: 14. The 'competing discourse' I refer to here is far less coherent and less influential, and it is ambiguous in its political significance.

reshape the purposes of British Imperialism through explicit comparisons with Imperial Rome. Hofmeyr and Haarhoff envisaged a form of
empire that would tolerate and encourage a variety of national identities,
and that would decentralise power and reconcile *imperium* and *libertas*.
Both also imagined a society in which racial identities would become less
salient and people of all races could be incorporated into the imperial
framework, though their visions were seriously flawed in this respect.
While Hofmeyr and Haarhoff had personal reasons to be critical of the
British Empire, and while their views seek to harness and redirect its
project, both also accepted that framework as the indispensable vehicle of
their political ideas. Martin Versfeld, on the other hand, turned away
from the idea of secular empire as an agent of moral universalism
altogether. Unusually for an Afrikaans intellectual, he became a Roman
Catholic, substituting the City of God for the City of Man, over whose
values Hofmeyr and Haarhoff contended. Versfeld's Augustine is very
much a Platonist, and Versfeld's Socratic conception of philosophy is
focused on the personal – in some ways an anticipation of contemporary
interest in the late antique tradition of practical philosophy and care of
the self.[4]

What broader lessons may we learn from studying these three unusual,
sometimes downright eccentric, Afrikaners? In what follows, I will suggest
that examining them allows us in the first place to reconsider the significance of imperialism as a carrier of Western modernisation, and of reactions against imperialism and its legitimising strategies. Hofmeyr
and Haarhoff saw themselves as defenders of universal values, and sought
to accommodate and constrain nationalist aspirations within those
values. Second, and closely connected to this, they took up the British
debate concerning the possibility of reconciling *imperium* and *libertas*.
In an era when neoconservative enthusiasts for American Empire affect
to see no tensions between empire and liberty, it is instructive to be
reminded of this debate.[5] Third, we may identify both the potential and
limits of knowledge of the classics as a critical resource for questioning the
goals and uses of political power. Finally, these discourses force us to
reconsider, or supplement, the claims made recently by Ian Buruma and
Avishai Margalit in their provocative study of critiques of Western

[4] See Hadot 1995: 47–71, 206–15, 264–76.
[5] Though there is strikingly little attention to this particular debate, the general relevance of the
British experience has not been lost on American neoconservatives and their fellow travellers.
See Boot 2001; Derbyshire 2003; Ferguson 2003, 2006; Hanson 2007.

modernity, *Occidentalism*.[6] The competing discourse of classics in South Africa was not anti-urban, anti-bourgeois, anti-secular or anti-rationalist; none of the themes Buruma and Margalit see as typical of the anti-modernist outlook figure prominently in it – at least, not in an extreme form. The competing discourse did, however, pose deeply important questions about the moral character and record of British imperialism as an agent of political and cultural modernisation.

I am of course interested here in retrieving a specific aspect of South Africa's complex and conflicted intellectual history – an element that can easily be missed from the vantage point of South Africa's new politics. But it is obvious that the South African context is not isolated. Rather, it is best seen as part of the global thrust of Western modernity and modernisation. Contemporary political theorists, who sometimes seem curiously innocent of the ways in which modern values are bound up with imperial projects and other forms of political power, have something to learn from the concerns of Hofmeyr, Haarhoff and Versfeld.

1.   The Imperial Imagination: Rome and Britain

The connection between British Imperialism and a classical education began in the early nineteenth century, as part of the training of candidates for the Indian Civil Service (ICS). As in the case of classics at the Cape, the reason for including a classical education in the curriculum was the need to produce a class that would be perceived as the bearer of authority. The education of a class of ruling 'gentlemen' in the classics was initially based at Haileybury College; a key motivation was to ensure the civility, cultivation and acceptable class background of the 'Men invested in Public Trusts'.[7] In the 1850s, as a result of the energetic support of Thomas Babington Macaulay and Benjamin Jowett, entry into the ICS was opened to competitive examination, and the centre of training moved to Oxford and Cambridge. While a range of subjects was taught, and none was compulsory, heavy weight was given in the examination papers to knowledge of Greek and Latin.[8] The role of classics in the

---

[6] Buruma and Margalit 2004. See also the critical review by Gray 2004. For a view that – rather puzzlingly – accuses critics of British Imperialism of being influenced by Hegel, himself an influence on British Imperialism through the medium of British Idealism, see Windschuttle 1998.

[7] This phrase, taken from an 1804 report proposing changes to the training of candidates for the Indian Civil Service, is quoted in Vasunia 2008: 64.

[8] Vasunia 2008: 70.

preparation of colonial civil servants continued well into the twentieth century. In South Africa, the first High Commissioner appointed after the Anglo-Boer War was Alfred Milner, who had received a first-class degree in classics in 1877 under Jowett, and many of the staff of young members of the South African Civil Service known as 'Milner's Kindergarten' were drawn from Jowett's old college, Balliol.[9]

The emphasis placed on classics in the training of imperial civil servants regulated their social status and helped to ensure a monopoly of native-born Britons over civil service positions. Even more important, in the last quarter of the nineteenth century comparisons between the British and the Roman Empires became widespread. Particularly after the publication of the historical work of Theodor Mommsen, the earlier view of Rome as essentially brutal and barbaric was succeeded by an emphasis on the order and civilisation of the Roman Empire. Mommsen's work presented a vision of the Roman Empire that appealed to supporters of Britain's new imperialism. These supporters came in two basic variants. There were the acolytes of Benjamin Disraeli, who saw empire primarily in terms of territorial expansion and control, and who viewed the advent of an empire so vast that the sun never set on it as the age of a greater successor of Rome. This attitude was later ably satirised as 'kilometritis' by J. A. Hobson.[10] Rudyard Kipling's stories *Puck of Pook's Hill* and *Regulus* popularised the idea that Britain had become Rome's far-flung heir.[11] In South Africa, Cecil John Rhodes, who manoeuvred to extend British territorial control from Cape Town to Cairo, and who had studied classics at school and at Oriel College, Oxford, imagined himself as a modern Roman. He carried a copy of Marcus Aurelius' *Meditations* on his person, and he had a team of classicists translate the ancient sources of Edward Gibbon's *Decline and Fall of the Roman Empire* for his personal library.[12] Rhodes was reportedly flattered by his facial resemblance to busts of the Emperor Titus, and his favourite saying was, 'Remember always that you are a Roman'.[13] Yet, while the Disraeli version of empire was brashly unembarrassed by the exercise of imperial power and coercion that troubled its liberal

---

[9] New College was another source of members of the Kindergarten. See Marks and Trapido 1979: 54. On Lionel Curtis and his New College associates, see Dubow 1997: 60–61.

[10] Quoted in Pitts 2010: 21. See also Arendt 1946: 604–8 Arendt 1973: 124–27.

[11] For a nuanced view of Kipling, see Varley 1953; cf. Plotz 1993.

[12] See Lambert 2011: 62–64. Rhodes also had biographies of 18 Roman emperors shipped to his library at *Groote Schuur*.

[13] Betts 1971: 151. For another excellent discussion of the nature and function of the comparison between Britain and Rome, see Vasunia 2005: 38–61.

competitors, its supporters too asserted a sense of responsibility for subject peoples, most famously in Kipling's *Recessional*.

A second group of Liberal imperialists formed in reaction to the first around William Ewart Gladstone. Such figures, including Lord Rosebery, Lord James Bryce, Sir Charles Dilke and Sir John Seeley, stressed a conception of empire as a civilising responsibility, aimed eventually at the encouragement of self-government in Britain's colonies. For them, it was important that both Rome and Britain had stumbled into the acquisition of an empire, with misgivings.[14] In their view, the significance of the Roman Empire lay in the *Pax Romana*, the Roman administrative genius, experiments in decentralisation of power and the creation of a stable network for trade. Liberal imperialists tended also to emphasise contrasts between the Roman and British Empires: where Rome had been tyrannical and exploitative, Britain was humanitarian and commercial; where Rome had not been able to combine the power of empire and liberty, Britain would somehow succeed in reconciling the two. For some, the most important difference was that Rome had been a unitary and territorially contiguous empire, while the British Empire was separated by oceans and divided into a commonwealth of dominions populated by English-speakers and a politically subordinate tropical empire, ruled unilaterally by force.[15] Commenting on British rule in India, Sir John Seeley tried to argue that this had not been initiated by the state, but had been founded by 'certain Englishmen who rose to the head of affairs in times of anarchy',[16] Seeley claimed that the rule of force over India was necessitated by disorder. He insisted that Britain had in fact benefited India by replacing a medieval world with modernity, but admitted – a little shamefacedly – that Indians might perhaps not find this very attractive and might not after all be especially grateful for it.[17]

Both the Disraeli camp and the Liberal imperialists in Britain were thus faced with a problem not encountered by other nations engaged in imperial ventures: the challenge of showing that the empire was indeed aimed at the promotion of liberty and that the modes of imperial rule were compatible with the pursuit of liberty, rather than a source of the corruption of domestic liberties.[18] This quandary was exacerbated as forms of national resistance to British imperialism multiplied and grew in strength. The war

---

[14] Seeley was responsible for the famous claim that Britain's empire was won 'in a fit of absence of mind'. The phrase is quoted in Ward 2006: 265.

[15] Betts 1971: 154–156. There were, however, multiple ways of classifying 'civilized' and 'barbarian' societies. On this issue, see Bell 2006: 283–84, 287–89.

[16] Quoted in Betts 1971: 156.   [17] Ibid.   [18] See Pagden 2006: 42–43.

against the Boer Republics in South Africa posed the challenge especially acutely because the economic interests that were evidently involved made it hard to sustain the pristine picture of a mission of cultural upliftment, and because the Boers themselves could not simply be dismissed as non-European 'savages'.[19] Accusations that the British were committing 'crimes against humanity' and using 'methods of barbarism' in South Africa – the burning of farms and the internment of Boer women and children in 'concentration camps', where 26,000 died – caused soul-searching among Liberal imperialists and jolted their hitherto untroubled reliance on high-flown humanitarian rhetoric.

Moreover, as Anthony Pagden observes, 'Roman proprietor' views of imperial sovereignty stimulated belief in national self-determination and raised the inevitable issue of whether the Empire would someday become obsolete, replaced perhaps by a federation of equal and fully autonomous states. While British officials energetically attempted to delay the fateful moment of emancipation from imperial tutelage, belief among subject peoples that 'national self-determination' required full state independence grew. Pagden writes, 'No longer content merely to share sovereignty with their conquerors and usurpers, the peoples of the imperial territories came increasingly to demand undivided sovereignty for themselves ... The ancient illusion of autochthony had returned, in another guise'.[20] Imperialism – even Liberal imperialism – increasingly stimulated intransigent forms of nationalism.

2. The Competing Discourse in South Africa: Classics, Empire, Nation and Race

The three Afrikaner intellectuals I have identified as authors of a competing discourse concerning imperialism thus found themselves in a position that was extremely challenging to negotiate. Very soon after the end of the Boer War, local pressure and the new Liberal government of Sir Henry Campbell-Bannerman in Britain had produced 'responsible self-government' in the former Boer republics. In 1910, this resulted in the creation of the Union of South Africa, under the premiership of Louis Botha, closely assisted and later succeeded by Jan Christiaan Smuts. Both had been Boer generals during the war. Both now collaborated in the creation of a political party and policies aimed at promoting unity

[19] See Pitts 2010: 8–9 and Varley 1953: 124.   [20] Pagden 2005: 46.

among white South Africans and conciliation with Britain. Their Afrikaans supporters were under pressure to demonstrate their backing for imperial ideals of modernisation, industrial development and political unification on the one hand, but felt the pull of national identity on the other. J. H. Hofmeyr and T. J. Haarhoff were two of the most accomplished Afrikaans intellectuals to perform this precarious balancing act, and both relied on their classical education in order to do so.

J. H. Hofmeyr: Ancient Imperialism and Liberal Imperialism

Jan Hendrik Hofmeyr was born in Cape Town, in 1894, to a politically prominent Cape Dutch Afrikaner family. His uncle, '*Onze* Jan' Hofmeyr, had been a leading member of the Afrikaner Bond, a political party that advanced the interests of Cape Dutch Afrikaners in the Cape Parliament. Yet although '*Onze* Jan' participated in some early manifestations of Afrikaner nationalism, he was moderate and politically pragmatic, able to cooperate with the arch-imperialist Rhodes until Rhodes's involvement in the Jameson Raid became clear.[21] J. H. Hofmeyr was educated in prominent English-language institutions – at the South African College Schools and at the South African College (later the University of Cape Town), where he studied classics.[22] In 1911 he was asked to write a biography of his uncle, which he did, in English, subsequently translating it into Dutch.

Hofmeyr was brilliant and academically precocious. He began his studies at the University of Cape Town at the age of 13 and received his BA with first-class Honours three years later. He was awarded a Rhodes Scholarship in 1909 and accepted it – a potentially controversial move for someone with an Afrikaans background – though he delayed taking it up until 1913, when he attended Balliol College at Oxford and came first in Classical 'Mods' and 'Greats'.[23] Before doing so, he had completed a BSc and an MA in Classics at the University of Cape Town. In 1916 he returned to South Africa and took up an academic career, first teaching classics at the South African College and then at the South African School of Mines (later to become the University of the Witwatersrand). After a brief move back to the University of Cape Town, he returned to the South African School of Mines as its Principal, at the age of 24. Though initially reluctant

---

[21] For a brief biography of Hofmeyr, see Lambert 2011: 64–66.
[22] To avoid confusion, I will simply refer to the University of Cape Town in the future.
[23] By contrast, Tobie Muller, who briefly became a leading figure in philosophy at Stellenbosch, refused the Rhodes Scholarship in 1903, in protest of its connection to imperialism. See Nash 2009: 72.

to enter partisan politics, Hofmeyr accepted a non-partisan position as Administrator of the Transvaal from J. C. Smuts, then Prime Minister. In 1928 he became a candidate for Smuts's party, running against the National Party. During the 1930s, Hofmeyr developed a reputation for being a leading liberal on the so-called 'native question'. He played a role in bringing Smuts's party together with the National Party, but he later resigned from the cabinet and from his party caucus over Nationalist moves against the 'coloured' (mixed race) and black franchise. During World War II, under Smuts's premiership, Hofmeyr became Minister of Education and acted as Prime Minister while Smuts was occupied with wartime duties. He was expected to succeed Smuts as Prime Minister after the war. However, in 1948 Smuts was defeated by the National Party, which was to control politics and preside over the institution and maintenance of apartheid for the next forty years. Hofmeyr died six months after the election defeat, at the age of 52.

Thirty years earlier, in 1918, Hofmeyr delivered a public lecture on 'Imperialism and Liberty in Ancient History' to the South African School of Mines. Despite claiming to approach the topic 'purely from the academic point of view', the lecture explicitly draws parallels between ancient forms of imperialism and the South African experience of British Imperialism.[24] There is no trace in Hofmeyr's lecture of the far more radical criticisms of Liberal Empire articulated by J. A. Hobson as early as 1902, which homed in on the economic motivations underpinning imperialism. By contrast, Hofmeyr largely accepts the normative framework of Liberal imperialism. Yet in several areas, his views diverge from the earlier optimism of liberal defences of empire, and muted criticisms of British policy appear. It would indeed be astonishing to find no strains in Hofmeyr's relation to British imperialism, considering his own mother's internment by the British in a concentration camp during the Boer War.[25]

The lecture begins by posing the problem of the 'relation between Imperialism and Liberty', which Hofmeyr immediately restates as the problem of the relation 'between the Empire and the nation'.[26] Hofmeyr's colonial perspective is instantly apparent; he is not at all concerned with the implications of imperialism for traditions of liberty and constitutional government in Britain, but with the status of Dominions or 'nations' within the Empire. He immediately sounds a note of warning.

---

[24] Hofmeyr 1920: 3.   [25] See Parker 2009: 232.

[26] Hofmeyr 1920: 5–6. In this passage, he also describes the struggle between empire and liberty as a 'struggle between the dominion of the all-embracing Empire and freedom of the self-determining nationality'.

World War I has precipitated a crisis concerning the relation between nation and empire, and it has made it impossible to regard the autonomy of Dominions as a settled question. Hofmeyr turns to ancient history to gain perspective on the kinds of relations between Empire and nation that could be hoped for in the future. The options seem to boil down to three: a relation of subordination between a centralised imperial power and its subject peoples; a 'federation between a mother country and daughter-states'; some sort of 'alliance between free sister-states'.[27]

   The first third of Hofmeyr's lecture surveys the Assyrian, Persian, Athenian and Macedonian empires at high speed. He concedes that imperialism 'originated in predatory instincts', and sees the cruelty of the Assyrians as illustrative of this 'stark brutality'.[28] Persia, by contrast, distanced itself from these origins and provided peace, good government, organisation and toleration in religious matters, albeit a toleration motivated by instrumental considerations of power. Athens, according to Hofmeyr, turned a free defensive league into a tyranny, motivated by a 'narrow patriotism'. Interestingly, he claims that this 'Jingo Imperialism' lies behind and distorts the 'lofty idealism' of Pericles' Funeral Oration.[29] As Hofmeyr describes it, Pericles sounds like a Disraeli-imperialist, who thinks that subject peoples are automatically benefited by coming within the circle of imperial influence and that dependence on empire simply is liberty as far as they are concerned.[30] Hofmeyr brings this part of his discussion to a close by considering Alexander the Great and the Macedonian Empire. Alexander, he claims, went far beyond the Athenians in developing the organisation and toleration of empire and in promoting the idea of local autonomy. As Hofmeyr puts it, he 'conceived the notion of an Empire, at once European and Asiatic, in which no national element should be dominated by any other . . .'[31]

   The remainder of the lecture is dedicated to the questions of how Rome acquired and maintained its empire. Hofmeyr begins by getting in a dig at Disraeli-imperialism's obsession with territorial expansion; he notes that judging an empire by the 'number of subject square miles' makes about as much sense as ranking statesmen by the size of their hats.[32] He then repeats the liberal imperialist claim that Rome entered into imperial relations reluctantly and haphazardly, as an unintended consequence of its defensive alliances. While there were 'expansionists' such as Pompey and Julius

---

[27] The second two options are expressed clearly in Hofmeyr 1920: 5. Tactfully, Hofmeyr does not state the first explicitly, but he begins by showing that ancient empires that relied on force and subordination were inferior and weaker, and ultimately left a diminished legacy to posterity.
[28] Hofmeyr 1920: 7–8.   [29] Ibid., 11.   [30] Ibid., 11–12.   [31] Ibid., 13.   [32] Ibid.

Caesar, their projects were redirected and controlled by Augustus. As far as the maintenance of Rome's empire was concerned, Hofmeyr sees the influence of aristocrats in the republican Senate as damaging; they sought to govern the provinces as their personal possessions. The principate, or 'empire properly so-called', performed better. Hofmeyr follows Mommsen in arguing that despite the bad press given to the emperors by historians such as Tacitus, who was nostalgic for republican civic virtues, 'the Empire was well-governed even under bad emperors, that though Nero may have been a tyrannical prince, he ruled a happy world'.[33] It is interesting to contrast this judgment with that of contemporary advocates of 'civic republicanism', who reverse Hofmeyr's judgment in the name of republican ideals of liberty and active citizenship.

For Hofmeyr, the Roman contribution to political thought does not rest in republican conceptions of liberty or free citizenship, but rather in its prioritisation of peace and its promotion of civilisation, prosperity and a world-state in which member nations were equal and the difference between citizens and provincials ultimately disappeared. Here he goes further than most liberal imperialists, pointing out that eventually Rome itself was decentered as capital, hinting perhaps towards a future in which London would lose its status as the imperial metropole and Britain itself would simply form one of the alliance of 'free sister-states'.[34] Thus, Rome serves as the inspiration for the third imperial option, best adapted to accommodate national autonomy. To the objection that all this was purchased at the price of despotism – an objection one can easily imagine in the mouths of contemporary civic republicans or of Hofmeyr's own nationalist critics – Hofmeyr answers that liberty was indeed taken from the aristocratic Senate, but it was then given to the world. Far from crushing national feeling, the Empire supposedly encouraged it in the cases of Greeks, Jews and Western Europeans, refraining from interfering in local languages or religious beliefs. He concludes that 'Equality, self-government and sympathy with national feelings were . . . the three guiding principles of Roman imperial organization'.[35]

Hofmeyr's radicalisation of the discourse of liberal imperialism is thus concentrated on the issue of national identity and political autonomy. This is the source of the distinctive strength of his competing discourse, but also of its weaknesses, for Hofmeyr accords no central value to the freedoms of individual citizens or classes of citizens; he seems untroubled by the fact that civic freedoms did not prove compatible with empire. Nor does he

[33] Ibid., 25.   [34] Ibid., 22.   [35] Ibid., 28.

have much to say about the Roman Empire as the source of a vision of a multicultural, multiethnic and multiracial form of political association. For a more explicit, though ultimately unsatisfactory account of this, we have to turn to his friend and associate, T. J. Haarhoff.

Before doing so, however, it is important to note Hofmeyr's somewhat confused and decidedly limited views on race. In fairness, Hofmeyr probably does deserve his reputation for holding views on race that were in advance of his time and milieu. At the time of the National Party's electoral victory in 1929, he expressed regret at the rise in racial prejudice and fear that it signalled.[36] By 1937, he was willing to express the belief that the task of avoiding racial conflict was the true drama of South African history.[37] He was also clear that the territorial segregation proposed by the National Party (a forerunner of apartheid) was impractical because it failed to take into account the ways in which black South African's cultures and living conditions had already been irremediably altered by modernity and because it was based on fear and force. Even a 'constructive segregation' was impossible – because of whites' unwillingness to provide the amount of land needed to make that viable and fair.[38] All of these views place Hofmeyr well ahead of most whites, and certainly ahead of his political mentor, Smuts. What is more, while two decades earlier, in his lecture on ancient imperialism, Hofmeyr gave no serious attention to racial conflict, he was now able to see its centrality, presenting it as 'an aspect of a general and ancient problem – how the different races may live together in peace and harmony'.[39] He notes critically the tendency of white South Africans to see 'racial harmony' as a matter of reconciling differences among whites only – a tendency shared by the British Liberal imperialism of the Edwardian era.

What is consistently absent in Hofmeyr's thought, however, is a genuinely liberal appreciation for individual freedoms, or for the moral equality of individuals. In his 1937 reflections on the 'native problem', he expresses disgust at the idea of racial mixing or 'ultimate social equality' and argues, as he does concerning liberty in his lecture on imperialism, that equality is valuable only insofar as it is compatible with the common good.[40] Just as twenty years previously he had seen the reconciliation of imperialism and liberty as a matter of accommodating national autonomy, he now sees racial reconciliation as a 'problem of living together in a single community', but he gives no special moral priority to ensuring that the

---

[36] Hofmeyr 1929b: 133–34.   [37] Hofmeyr 1937: 274.   [38] Ibid., 291–92.   [39] Ibid., 273.
[40] Ibid., 283, citing J. H. Oldham as an authority.

terms of communal cooperation distribute burdens justly or respect rights.[41] Hofmeyr's classics-inspired modification of British liberal imperialism redirects imperial aspirations and covertly transforms them into a framework for accommodating national aspirations. But his call to adopt a 'restrained liberalism' in matters of race for reasons of pragmatism, rather than take a stand on principle, indicates the limits of what he took from the classics.

T. J. Haarhoff: Roman Provincials and the Unity of Mankind

A friend and associate of Hofmeyr and of his mentor, Jan Smuts, Theo Haarhoff was born in 1892, in Paarl, about 40 miles inland from Cape Town, and died in 1971, after a long and prolific academic career, spent mostly at the University of the Witwatersrand (formerly the School of Mines presided over by Hofmeyr), preceded by brief stints at Victoria College (later Stellenbosch University) and the University of Cape Town. His background was interestingly similar to Hofmeyr's: born into an Afrikaans family, he nevertheless attended the English-speaking South African College Schools and the University of Cape Town, from which he obtained a BA with Honours. Haarhoff studied briefly in Berlin, then won a Rhodes scholarship to Worcester College at Oxford. Here, he worked under Gilbert Murray, the Australian-born authority on the classical world, who was also known for his public support for the Liberal Party and for his anti-imperialism. Haarhoff received the degree of BLitt from Oxford in 1915 and the degree of DLitt from the University of Amsterdam in 1931, though he probably did not spend much time there.

His academic work was written in English, but he was also an active poet, writing his creative work in Afrikaans, and supportive of the status of the Afrikaans language as distinct from Dutch.[42] Haarhoff was unable for personal reasons to take up the chair of Nederlands and Afrikaans at the University of Cape Town in 1930, and Nationalist opposition blocked his appointment as Rector of the University College of the Orange Free State in 1944. Thus, rather like Hofmeyr, Haarhoff participated in institutions indebted to the British imperial presence in South Africa, while at the

[41] Ibid., 295. He explicitly rejects talk about rights in this passage.

[42] For his enthusiastic support of Afrikaans, see T. J. Haarhoff's, 'Afrikaans in the national life', and 'The difficulties of a Johannesburger' in Haarhoff and van den Heever 1934: 1–39, 87–97. Haarhoff's first contribution was originally delivered as a lecture in Oxford in 1936, but in the 'Author's note' at the beginning of the book, he and van den Heever state that proceeds from the sales of the volume will go towards the construction of the Voortrekker Monument. Haarhoff's balancing act is very much in evidence here. On this point, see also Lambert 2011: 47–49.

same time asserting a moderate but enthusiastic sense of Afrikaner national identity – moderate enough to set him permanently at odds with more hard-line nationalists. Like Hofmeyr, Haarhoff's classical training allowed him to inflect and compete with the Romanised discourse of British Liberal imperialism. To show this, I mean to concentrate on two publications – 'Principles and Practice of the Roman Empire', published in 1920 along with Hofmeyr's 'Imperialism and Liberty in Ancient History', and *The Stranger at the Gate*, first published in 1938 and then reissued in a second edition in 1948 in the later stages of Haarhoff's career.

Some of the same themes evident in Hofmeyr's piece on imperialism are also present in the companion piece by Haarhoff. Like Hofmeyr, Haarhoff sees the Roman Empire as a higher form of political development than the Greek city-state, which he finds guilty of narrow patriotism and prejudice towards outsiders. He praises Roman imperialism for conquering other peoples without 'living off them'.[43] Despite occasional and apparently uncharacteristic lapses into 'jingoism', Roman imperialism created the principle of federation and developed a 'flexible federalism', which was adapted to the customs and circumstances of different tribes, city-states, regions, etc., and which reflected the Romans' relative lack of prejudice towards outsiders. He stresses that as early as 89 BC, all Italians had Roman citizenship, and by AD 212, the whole empire was enfranchised.[44] The empire also conferred peace and material benefits on its provinces, despite the regrettably rapacious behaviour of corrupt individual governors.

There are interesting differences between Haarhoff and Hofmeyr, however. For example, Haarhoff exhibits a greater overt scepticism towards the rhetoric of empire than Hofmeyr. In his later work, he notes that claims about waging war for the good of the conquered are usually pretexts.[45] Perhaps influenced by Hobson via Gilbert Murray, he states that economic motives often underlie imperial wars.[46]

Moreover, while Hofmeyr blames the Senate for Roman 'jingoism', Haarhoff sees the people as the culprits and attributes enthusiasm for expansion and war to the element of 'hardness' in the Roman character, which required the control of Augustus to restore a sense of balance and moderation. In his later work, he sees the 'spiritual' influence of Vergil as a key factor in balancing 'hardness', again differing from Hofmeyr's much more negative judgment of Vergil. We can perhaps make sense of Haarhoff's views here by considering his complex relationship to

[43] See Haarhoff 1920: 34.   [44] Ibid., 35.   [45] Haarhoff 1948: 67.   [46] Ibid., 61

Afrikaner nationalism and by noting the function of references to Vergil in the work of British Imperialists. Writers such as Seeley, Bryce and Cromer identified Vergil as a 'national poet of Empire' and 'an enthusiastic imperialist', and they read the *Aeneid* as the definitive statement of the Roman imperial mission.[47] By contrast, for Haarhoff, it is Vergil's provincial origins and praise of rural virtues that demands attention.

Both in this text and in *Vergil, the Universal*, Haarhoff draws an explicit comparison between Afrikaners (he uses the word 'Boers', also meaning 'farmers') and Romans, and Vergil is presented as a humane and generous spirit, the possessor of bucolic virtues, a 'larger humour' and a 'unifying imagination'.[48] Haarhoff comments: 'Vergil binds up the fragments of his world'.[49] The message seems to be that the rustic virtues that Afrikaners share with Vergil can contribute to the enlargement of a sense of humanity, but only if they are drawn into a larger association that allows them to serve the cause of integration, not nationalist self-assertion and disintegration. This introduces a new element into Haarhoff's competing discourse. While Hofmeyr accepts the Liberal imperialist picture of Britons as Romans, Haarhoff promotes the idea that the Afrikaans provincials are in some respects more Roman than the British.

However incongruous it may seem, his linkage of Romans and Afrikaners accomplishes two objectives. It allows for the possibility that previously subjugated nations could rise to positions of prominence in an imperial framework.[50] It also presents Afrikaners as bearers of the republican virtues often associated with farmers. This view is distinct from the nationalist evocation of the mystical connection of blood and soil; instead, it appeals to the virtues of a simple, unpretentious, yeoman lifestyle, themes often invoked against urban corruption and luxury by republican pamphleteers and later by critics of the inequality and coldness of relations under capitalism.[51] Yet it is not characterised by the absolute antipathy for

---

[47] See Vasunia 2005: 58.

[48] Haarhoff 1948: 270–72. See also Haarhoff 1949: 1–2, 19–29, 51–71. In a later text on Jan Smuts, Haarhoff compares Smuts's attempt to reconcile English- and Afrikaans-speaking white South Africans to Vergil's project of 'harmonisation', and once again makes the connection between simple Boer virtues and Vergil's Italian farmers. See Haarhoff 1970: 25–26, 28–32.

[49] Haarhoff 1948: 270.   [50] This is especially clear in Haarhoff (1970).

[51] For a recent version of this view, see MacIntyre (1998). References to country virtues, opposed to the corruption of court and town, were central to the Opposition literature of the Radical Whigs of the earlier eighteenth century in England, which in turn drew inspiration from seventeenth-century classical republicans such as John Harrington, John Milton and Algernon Sidney. See Wood 1969: 15–16. For this reason, I disagree with Grant Parker's judgment that Haarhoff's vision of Afrikaners brings him close to nationalist 'gods' of 'blood and earth'. See Parker 2009: 224.

urbanism identified as a hallmark of anti-modern attitudes by Buruma and Margalit. The point is to reinfuse urbane imperialism with the vigour and directness of a colonial yeomanry.[52]

There are two further promising but unsustained developments in Haarhoff's thought. Unlike Hofmeyr, he signals his awareness that Roman imperialism had a negative impact on individual or private liberties. He notes that 'the Roman disposition to worship discipline led him to disregard the rights of personality'.[53] This concession is largely suppressed in the rest of his work, however. He recognises that the individual enterprise of 'provincials' may have been impaired and that they may have lost individual civic freedoms as a result of the 'hardness' of the Roman character, but he denies that this is due to Roman political ideas and arrangements, which somehow seem to be infused with more humanitarian *pietas* than harsh *gravitas*. Moreover, Haarhoff quickly claims that 'political liberty', understood as membership in the empire, and the benefits of peace and material prosperity outweighed whatever losses in republican civic liberty may have been incurred. There are elements in his view that suggest that the greater opportunities conferred by membership in an empire, provided that empire is 'universal' in the sense that it confers a roughly equal status on individual members, are more than adequate compensation for the loss of rights of participatory citizenship. This could be read as a version of Benjamin Constant's conception of the displacement of ancient liberties of participation by modern liberties of private self-development.[54] But perhaps because of the influence of Smuts's theory of holism – essentially a rather abstract account of processes of growth and integration in both nature and culture – and perhaps because he shares a Herderian conception of cultures as discrete and coherent wholes, Haarhoff's promise of greater sensitivity to individual liberties is overtaken by his tendency to see freedom as a matter of national opportunities for growth and development.[55]

The same abstraction and tendency to discount concerns of individual justice are evident in Haarhoff's views on race. At first, in his 1920 publication, his appreciation for the 'universality' of the Roman Empire – its contribution to the 'unity of mankind' – leads him to make the exciting

---

[52] See Comaroff 1989: 667–68 on the theme of the fallen British yeomanry and the need to reconstruct this in the colonial context.

[53] Haarhoff 1920: 32.   [54] See Constant 1988: 309–28.

[55] The influence of Herder is contestable, for while Herder played an important role in seeing cultures as coherent, authentic wholes, he was also a powerful critic of the modern state and an even more impassioned critic of the promotion of uniformity by Western imperialism. If Haarhoff was at all influenced by Herder, this affects his conception of culture, not his politics.

claim that Julius Caesar's '... object was to include in an Empire in which there should be no race domination, all men irrespective of race and colour'.[56] He praises the Romans for seeing citizenship as a far more important tie than racial identity. Yet Haarhoff fails to draw what might seem to be the obvious lesson for South Africa. Instead, in *The Stranger at the Gate*, we find him intrigued but apparently also repelled by Alexander the Great's decision to order his officers to marry Persian women. Alexander's decision promoted 'artificial' unity, according to Haarhoff – it did not truly maintain the integrity of the different cultures and it provoked a backlash among the Macedonians, who were afraid of losing their distinctive customs. Haarhoff judges that Alexander '... went too far. A sudden fusion of different racial elements is hardly ever a success; it is safer to let them grow together, in such a way that what deserves to survive on either side preserves its identity'.[57] Earlier in the same text, in the context of a discussion of Plato's *Laws*, Haarhoff comments, 'With Plato's objection to an indiscriminate mixture resulting in rootless cosmopolitanism, we may certainly sympathise ...'[58] He refers to the 'racial admixture' of Alexandria, but then immediately notes that 'it was precisely in Alexandria that racial strife was most violent'.[59] Part of what Haarhoff seems to see as the distinctively Roman contribution to 'the unity of humankind' was that while they extended citizenship broadly, they also maintained the distinctiveness of different peoples and created a variety of administrative relationships with them, rather than a single standardised system. Yet he seems not to have learned his own lesson concerning empires – that their members 'if they are not all equal at the outset, must not feel that their status is defined rigidly and for ever, but must be able to look forward to adjustments and an increase of privileges'.[60] One is tempted to ask: if there is to be no adjustment of status now for Black South Africans, when will the time be right for it?

Haarhoff's position is complex and subject to serious tensions. On the one hand, he claims to be committed to a 'universality' that integrates the virtues of different peoples, rather than subjecting all to a single standard. This may be read as a critique of the ways in which forces of modernisation and Western cultural arrogance promote negative uniformity and suppress cultural difference. On the other hand, his belief that cultures are authentic wholes lends support to a revulsion for hybridity and 'racial mixing', which leads him to resist what appears to be the clear example of ancient empires'

---

[56] Haarhoff 1920: 39–40.   [57] Haarhoff 1948: 72.   [58] Ibid., 66.   [59] Ibid., 86
[60] Ibid., 115.

relative indifference towards race. This reaches a low point in his observation on the 'rigid exclusiveness' of early Afrikaners: 'Had it [i.e. their exclusiveness] not been rigid, the descendants of the Voortrekkers would today quite certainly have been coffee-coloured; and Mr Shaw may think that desirable, but South Africans do not.'[61] It is clear at this juncture that for all the initial promise of his competing discourse, Haarhoff's theoretical commitments as well his personal prejudices render him unable to use his classical sources as a fully effective criticism of racism and cultural imperialism in South Africa.

Martin Versfeld: Socrates and Augustine in the Kitchen

To conclude this account of the competing discourse on imperialism, I turn to the philosopher, Martin Versfeld. Versfeld was born in 1909 and, like Hofmeyr and Haarhoff, studied at the English-speaking University of Cape Town despite his Afrikaans background. Versfeld, however, chose philosophy rather than classics as his field, and he won a Queen Victoria Scholarship to the University of Glasgow, where he received his doctorate in 1934.[62] While at Glasgow, he worked under Archibald Bowman, the author of several important books on the philosophy of religion. He identifies Bowman – not by name, but the reference is clear – as the source of his dawning conviction that one could be 'a singularly honest thinker, and . . . [one] who believed sincerely in God'.[63]

What led him beyond this to Roman Catholicism seems to have been the example of another Catholic Afrikaner intellectual, Monsignor F. C. Kolbe, who began teaching at the University of Cape Town (then the South African College) in the 1880s and died shortly after Versfeld's return to Cape Town from Glasgow in 1936.[64] Among Kolbe's numerous accomplishments was a lecture on Socrates, delivered in 1884 in Cape Town, in which he depicts Socrates as a representative of the Ancient Greek

---

[61] Ibid., 299. Haarhoff is here referring to George Bernard Shaw's *The Adventures of the Black Girl in her Search for God* (1932), whose portrayal of mixed-race children caused controversy.

[62] For much of this information, I am grateful to the on-duty archivists at the University of Glasgow, as well as to a personal communication from Professor David Benatar, Chair of the University of Cape Town Department of Philosophy, who was kind enough to forward information from Professor Howard Phillips of the Historical Studies Department at UCT concerning Versfeld's life and career. I have also benefited enormously from communications with Andrew Nash, Ernst Wolff and Johan Snyman.

[63] Versfeld 1960: 17.

[64] I owe this insight to Andrew Nash, in a personal communication, as well as from Nash (2009).

commitment to wisdom, as opposed to the 'Oriental' drive for power, and stresses Socrates' belief that 'morality is an art' rather than a doctrine.[65] Kolbe lists the Buddha, Confucius, Pythagoras, Augustine and Aquinas, along with Socrates as 'the real authorities in morals'. As Andrew Nash observes, these emphases have the intriguing effect of stressing the importance of authority in moral matters, while at the same time 'removing that authority from any specific doctrinal basis, or even any basis in a specifically Western tradition'.[66] These tendencies are clearly visible in Versfeld's thought too. Kolbe was also politically independent, publicly criticising martial law and British aggression at the time of the Boer War.[67] Versfeld seems to have followed Kolbe's example in this respect; he was an outspoken pacifist during World War II, and he took the position that modern wars between countries also always involved wars against minorities within those countries. In his view, the idea of a war for civilisation is absurd.[68]

On issues of racial justice, Kolbe was well ahead of his time. In a piece commemorating Kolbe's life, Versfeld approvingly cites the following statement:

I have a strong affection for the Bantu race, and I believe in their future. They are only beginning to have their chance in the world's story. They will go far ... There are men who talk furiously about this being a white man's country ... Anybody who has read the book of history and can turn over a page or two of the future should know that this must be a country where white and black can live in concord, liberty and justice with equal happiness for both. Either that, or black and white pandemonium.[69]

In 1937, Versfeld began teaching at the University of Cape Town, eventually becoming a full professor at the same institution in 1970. He was awarded honorary doctorates by UCT and the Rand Afrikaans University in 1987, and he died in 1995. His academic output was prolific and displays a fascinating diversity. He published internationally recognised work in English on Augustine, Catholic philosophy and Socrates, as well as reflections on English literature and a translation of some of the work of Laozi into Afrikaans. He also wrote a series of books in Afrikaans and English that combine cookery and philosophy, blending the two to reflect on the

---

[65] Quoted in Nash 2009: 58. Nash notes that Kolbe was not the first intellectual figure at the Cape to discuss the example of Socrates. Predecessors included representatives of theological liberalism within the Dutch Reformed Church such as P. N. Ham and J. W. G. van Oordt in the 1860s. See Nash 2009: 55–58.
[66] Nash 2009: 59.   [67] Ibid.   [68] See the interesting discussion in Wolff 2010.
[69] Cited in Versfeld 1960: 41–42, 'Commemoration of Mgr. F. C. Kolbe'.

basic human experience. Like Hofmeyr and Haarhoff, Versfeld was at home in an English academic environment but also comfortable with his Afrikaner identity. Like them, he kept his distance from all forms of Afrikaner nationalism, and he was possibly even more comfortable about using English as well as Afrikaans to express his most basic convictions.[70]

The inclusion of Versfeld as the third contributor to a competing discourse on imperialism informed by knowledge of the classics may seem forced. Unlike Hofmeyr and Haarhoff, he produced no explicit work on imperialism, and next to none on South African politics. A number of his students and associates, however, in different ways, engaged in intense public criticism of apartheid: specifically, the Marxist-existentialist philosopher Rick Turner, the Afrikaans poet Breyten Breytenbach and the dramatist Athol Fugard. Despite the paucity of Versfeld's work on politics, it is instructive to read his affiliation with Roman Catholicism and his work on Socrates, and on Catholic thought in general and Augustine in particular, as a rejection of secular empire and politics as well as Western cultural imperialism in the name of individual humanity and *parrhesia*, the ancient Greek practice of frank speech, or truth-telling.[71]

In his stimulating study of the 'dialectical tradition' in South Africa, Andrew Nash describes Versfeld as the least actively politically engaged member of a group of Afrikaans intellectuals in the 1960s and 1970s, mostly based at the University of Stellenbosch, who were committed to the Socratic ideal of freedom of speech and critical dialogue 'as a precondition for a good society'.[72] Yet he also notes that Versfeld was more sympathetic to Marxism, seeing the Marxist critique of alienation as a central part of the 'moral tradition of humanity', anticipated by Jesus Christ, the Buddha and Socrates.[73] To understand this rather idiosyncratic view of Marx, and to show its relation to our current concern with the competing discourse on imperialism, we should begin by considering the Augustinian element in Versfeld's Catholicism.

---

[70] Ernst Wolff notes that a radio review of Versfeld's first book written in Afrikaans, *Oor Gode en Afgode* ('Concerning gods and idols', published in 1948), took him to task for 'satisfactory' but 'not quite idiomatic Afrikaans'. He also points to archival evidence that Versfeld seems often to have written his philosophical pieces first in English, speculates that he 'thought literarily in English' (my paraphrase and translation) and discusses Versfeld's explicit defence of the English influence in South African philosophy. See Wolff 2010: 270–71. In my judgment, Versfeld's command of English prose style is total, mischievous and extremely impressive.

[71] On *parrhesia*, see Foucault 2001: 9–23. This is the published version of his lecture series, 'Discourse and truth', delivered at the University of California, Berkeley in 1983.

[72] Nash 2009: 1, 161. Other members of this group included James Oglethorpe, Johan Degenaar, Daantjie Oosthuizen, etc. See also Du Toit 2005: 42.

[73] Quoted in Nash 2009: 161.

Versfeld's Augustinianism was first given sustained expression in *A Guide to the City of God*, which appeared in 1958. Among other issues, he discusses Augustine's complex attitude towards secular authority in general and Rome in particular. Versfeld describes – and clearly endorses – Augustine's rejection of the idea of a secular cosmopolis. He notes that Augustine refers to Rome as 'the great Western Babylon', and he states that in doing so Augustine is not talking about an ideal or spiritual entity, but about 'an actual imperialism'.[74] In words whose significance for the South African experience of British imperialism and its early language policies would not have been lost on his local readers, Versfeld evokes Augustine's emphasis on the naturalness of different languages:

Philosophers may dream of a cosmopolis, but common reason requires common speech. The nearest we have got to that is the Roman attempt to impose Latin everywhere, and whatever good that may have done, this imperialism has meant war and massacres. He who can look on these without compassion 'has lost the natural feeling of a man.'[75]

This is a much more forthright condemnation of secular empire than it is possible to find in the work of either Hofmeyr or Haarhoff. It is not quite a total rejection, for, like Augustine, Versfeld recognises that all human forms of political and communal organisation embody some desire for peace, however distorted that may be. Even empire may have its uses, though a commitment to a spiritual, Christian universalism will prevent any emotional investment in secular imperial projects; the Christian will exist on the back of empire, like a parasite, or within it, like a miserable but dutiful subject whose true allegiances lie elsewhere.[76] While Hofmeyr and Haarhoff seek to redirect British imperialism's modernising undertakings, Versfeld's Augustinianism prevents even their type of conditional and critical commitment to such projects.

Versfeld continues by considering whether an Augustinian must always view 'activity from within an organization to combat the evils within it', as more compatible with commitment to the spiritual universalism of the City of God than an attempt to 'set up an organization which endeavours to obviate those evils'.[77] He is reluctant to accept what he takes to be Augustine's position – that '. . . I shall be unable to carry out my project without importing, if not the world's sin willingly, then the world's misery unwillingly, into my organization. It would still be part of the *civitas terrena*, though one more easily used for eternal life'.[78] Versfeld complains

---

[74] Versfeld 1958: 75.   [75] Ibid.   [76] See ibid., 83–84.   [77] Ibid., 84.   [78] Ibid.

that the distinction between *uti*, or illegitimate use, and *frui*, or proper enjoyment of goods given by God, which underlies Augustine's sharp distinction between earthly and spiritual forms of association, is in fact blurred; true enjoyment of a good implies that an actual institutional apparatus of use already exists. Moreover, an institution that is primarily evil in its goals is importantly different from one aimed at combating those evils; while both may be earthly institutions, the second is not part of the *civitas terrena* in the same sense.[79] We should not interpret Versfeld's reservations, however, as an endorsement – even a tepid endorsement – of any secular political projects. A few pages later, he claims that it is consistent for Augustine to see the Roman Empire as belonging to the *civitas terrena*, while seeing the Emperor as a citizen of the *Civitas Dei*.[80] His criticisms of Augustine make more sense as defences of the relatively privileged moral status of the institution of the Roman Catholic Church, with its 'supranational character'.[81] He is endorsing the spiritual universalism of the community of true believers, supported by the partly earthly institutional universalism of the Church. The rejection of secular political enterprises and their legitimising claims to be promoting universal civilisation is total.

However, other elements of Versfeld's Augustinianism lead him to formulate an unusually original and sympathetic interpretation of Marx's account of alienation. Social and political orders, with all the legal and moral rules that accompany them, ultimately derive from the inner division of the sinful self, torn from its anchoring point in God by the lust for ambition and control over others. These frameworks always constitute restrictions on human freedom, which individuals place over themselves as a result of their inner division, which also divides them from their fellow humans.[82] This is experienced as pain, and to suppress this suffering, individuals create the opiate of a false religion – which provides support for the admiration of material success and status, and produces people who worship rules, roles and respectability, losing their shared humanity in the process. As Versfeld puts it, 'The true self is ... hidden and covered over. Our behaviour also becomes mechanical. What is repressed then becomes a psychic danger. We may perhaps become predictable, but not reliable. We always become the teacher, the doctor, the minister, whether or not this is appropriate'.[83] He notes that only the true self is genuinely creative, while the self that is governed by images, especially communal idols such as

[79] Ibid., 83–85. 　[80] Ibid., 87. 　[81] Ibid., 90. 　[82] See Versfeld 1969: 69–71.
[83] Versfeld 1969: 75, my translation.

Afrikaner nationalism or other political ideologies, can create nothing. Augustine and Marx (Plato, Nietzsche and Freud too, as well as Buddhism in the East) turn out to be defenders of an authentic sense of shared humanity, which cannot be encapsulated by any set of rules or doctrines, and threatens to burst the bonds of all such artificial chains.

If anything, Versfeld's sense of the true community of individuals marked by an authentic commitment to a world view and set of values seems more pronounced in his later work. Once again, this is developed with reference to ancient thinkers, possibly inspired by Kolbe's lecture on 'moral authorities'. Thus, at his inauguration as professor at UCT in 1970, Versfeld delivered a typically idiosyncratic lecture, later published as 'The Socratic Spirit'. In it, he presents a picture of Socrates that in some ways anticipates contemporary interest in the ancient idea that philosophy consists in a rigorous training for the critical moment when it becomes necessary, as a matter of integrity of character, to tell the truth. Versfeld's picture has an illustrious and more directly political predecessor in South Africa – Mohandas K. Gandhi's Gujerati translation and English summary of the *Apology* and the *Crito*, written while he was in prison in 1908, jailed for protesting racial policies concerning Indians in South Africa. In his tantalisingly brief summary, Gandhi emphasises Socrates' commitment to the pursuit of truth and to the willingness to suffer rather than be guilty of injustice towards others. He makes a pointed application of the example of Socrates to the South African case, writing that 'We must learn to live and die like Socrates ... We ... saw in the words of Socrates the qualities of an elixir. We wanted our readers, therefore, to imbibe a deep draught of it, so that they might be able to fight – and help others fight – the disease'.[84]

Versfeld displays no awareness of Gandhi's political appropriation of Socrates. Yet he shares with Gandhi a keen sense of the nature of philosophy as a form of care of the self with practical consequences for life. As Versfeld puts it, there is a union of philosophy and life in the person of Socrates, and this 'personalism' is his founding legacy to Western thought. The Socratic spirit is the attempt to confront the paradox of knowing yourself and knowing that you know nothing. Versfeld asks: 'Taken together, do they mean that when you know yourself, you know that you know nothing?'[85] Truth is not a matter of logic or fidelity to observed facts, but rather 'lies in a certain fidelity to ourselves'.[86] In each case, that is unique because each full individual person is unique.

---

[84] Gandhi 1958–, 8, 247–248.   [85] Versfeld 1972: 239.   [86] Ibid.

The Socrates described by Versfeld is thus an ancient existentialist mystic who deliberately refuses to produce written doctrines, preferring instead to inscribe his truths on persons.[87] Yet despite appearances to the contrary, Versfeld's Socrates is not a radical individualist; he recognises that 'our being is a being-with-others'.[88] His relentless questioning is 'political' and 'patriotic', perhaps in the sense that hostility to dogmatism contributes to the moral health of the polity; Versfeld redefines patriotism as an inner dialogue, which recognises that far from defending your country, 'riches and power' in fact 'sell it down the river'.[89] In the name of this tolerant and sceptical inner dialogue, he rejects a dominant conception of modernisation – what he calls the dogmatic confidence arising from the Cartesian cogito, which produces the motive of power over nature, reflected in one way in the attitudes of Western science and in another in religious fundamentalism.[90]

Versfeld's perspective is clearly able to generate a critique of Western modernity.[91] Yet is there any stronger sense in which his conception of 'inner dialogue' could be political? Nash points to the degree to which Versfeld's Socrates is 'defined by his distance from the Athenian Assembly'.[92] Why is this so? One reason may be that participation in any kind of public life leads one to believe abstractions – the kinds of simplifications encouraged by ideologies, and the half-truths that allegiance to a political movement or figure requires of us.[93] Here, Versfeld's views are similar to the suspicion of politics evident in Montaigne's or Thoreau's version of 'care of the self' – public life and its priorities threaten individual integrity and humane scepticism. Versfeld clearly aligns himself with this view in his laconic comment, 'Personalities are unique . . . This is why race classification is so repugnant'.[94]

A second reason, emphasised in the interpretations of Socratic *parrhesia* presented by George Kateb and Dana Villa, is that integrity sometimes requires a refusal of action – as in Socrates' refusal to condemn the Athenian admirals accused of treason, or his refusal to assist the Thirty Tyrants in the capture of Leon of Salamis.[95] Kateb and Villa emphasise that

---

[87] Ibid., 238.   [88] Ibid.   [89] Ibid., 243.

[90] Ibid. Versfeld explicitly alludes to 'Puritan fundamentalism', obviously thinking of the religious sources of inspiration for extreme Afrikaner nationalism.

[91] Versfeld's Augustinianism forms the basis of a critique of Western civilisation in 1979: 38–51 and in 1992: 199–209.

[92] Nash 2009: 163.   [93] See Michel de Montaigne, 'Of vanity', in 1965: 758–59.

[94] Versfeld 1972: 239.

[95] George Kateb draws on Socrates' discussion of these incidents in the *Apology* to suggest that 'everything in Socrates' intellectual life is devoted to the moral end of reducing injustice in the

this aspect of Socratic integrity can sustain a kind of 'negative citizenship'. Something like this may lie behind Versfeld's domestication of philosophical dialogue; he advises, 'Build your house, cook your food, make your clothes, catch your fish. There is no other understanding of God and the world.'[96] To live outside the simple conditions of ordinary life, and to give allegiance to any ideology and its priorities, is to lend oneself not merely to inauthenticity but to wrongdoing. Keeping one's feet on the ground can prevent the ideological flight into abstraction that so easily justifies harming others in the name of a spurious good.[97]

What is genuinely valuable about Versfeld's attempt to pull the Western philosophical legacy down to earth, and to locate it in the earthy experiences of dialogue among ordinary people, engaged in everyday activities, is its deflation of all high-flown ideological talk about 'civilising missions'. If what is most significant about human beings is our shared, authentic experience of everyday life and its needs, then ideologies and modernising projects of all sorts cannot constitute a truly civilising legacy, and no culture or race has the right to claim to be the tutor or guardian of another. We have thus moved very far indeed from the Liberal imperialism and justification of racial tutelage still accepted by Hofmeyr and Haarhoff.

But unlike contemporary advocates of Socratic integrity, Versfeld does not call for a dramatic gesture of withdrawal or refusal of public evil. His withdrawal is for the most part quiet and ambiguous. In the South African context, it lends itself almost as easily to the toleration of public racial injustice as does the abstract and nervous humanism of Hofmeyr and Haarhoff. There is one partial exception to this general characterisation. In a magazine article written late in life, Versfeld makes a fleeting political application of his concern for domestic life. Reflecting on the three hundredth anniversary of the arrival of Huguenots in South Africa, Versfeld writes,

When I think about the Huguenots, the question occurs to me: 'how does it feel to be uprooted, to have to flee your fatherland, to have to measure your conscience against the injustice in your country, to be forcibly moved, to exist as an exile, to see your local "here" violated by a bulldozer?'[98]

world'. (Kateb 2006: 231). Dana Villa argues that this form of integrity can form the basis of a type of 'negative citizenship', sceptical of claims to know what virtue or justice requires and determined not to participate in injustice (2001: 56–58).
[96] Quoted in Nash 2009: 162.   [97] For similar views, see Villa 2001: 302–5.
[98] Versfeld 1988: 41, my translation.

Later, in the same text, Versfeld sharpens the political point of this remark:

There are many martyrs among us. Forced removal, either within our own country or to another, is also martyrdom – because your home is the expression of your body and your soul. Don't look for our Protestants in the churches. Look for them in the jails or the trade unions – or in the airliners . . .[99]

Yet this kind of comment is rare in Versfeld's *oeuvre*, and it is never sustained. Nash is not mistaken to complain that

In South Africa at that time, Versfeld's distinction between the real world of domesticity, outdoor recreation and the like, on the one hand, and the abstract realm of politics, on the other, was itself thoroughly abstract . . . It took no account of the countless ways in which the politics of apartheid invaded the real lives of South Africans.[100]

While Versfeld's use of Augustine and Socrates to reject imperialism and modernisation is far more complete than the competing discourse of Hofmeyr and Haarhoff, for different reasons, he also remains unable to address racism and racial injustice satisfactorily at the public level.

3.   Conclusion

The significance of the use of classics in the thought of J. H. Hofmeyr, T. J. Haarhoff and Martin Versfeld emerges clearly in relation to the ways in which a classical education figured as a source of legitimation for British Imperialism, both in its cruder form as territorial expansion and in its liberal form as a 'civilising mission'. By virtue of their liminal provinciality, half in and half out of the world of imperialism, these three figures were able to turn aspects of their knowledge of the ancient world against the ideologies of imperialism. Their work licenses us to speak of a competing discourse on imperialism, one that we can draw from in our own confrontation with contemporary justifications of imperialism.

The competing discourse is not straightforwardly anti-modern. It belies the assertion that critiques of modernisation, and of imperialism as the carrier of Western claims to represent universal moral values, inevitably

[99]   Versfeld 1988: 42, my translation. The closing phrase is odd. Does Versfeld suppose that exiles typically left the country in airliners? If so, he is strikingly ignorant of the experience of most black South African exiles.

[100]   Nash 2009: 163.

become anti-urban, anti-secular and anti-rationalist, degenerating into an unwholesome fascist soup. On the contrary, Hofmeyr and Haarhoff explicitly admire the rational balance of Roman civilisation and its intellectual, material and technological achievements. They champion the cause of suppressed nationalities without becoming nationalists. Haarhoff defends the vigour and simplicity of rural cultures against the over-sophistication of urban civilisations without rejecting the latter. Versfeld's own turn to domesticity is a kind of simple urbanity; if Jürgen Habermas could once with justice refer to Hans-Georg Gadamer's thought as 'urbanised Heidegger', it is equally appropriate to think of Versfeld's work as urban, but earthy.[101]

This ability of the authors of the competing discourse to criticise modernity and its carrier, imperialism, without rejecting all modern values or the idea of moral universalism out of hand, is important. For while those who have indeed attempted to reject these values completely have often been guilty of sanctioning great atrocities, it should not be denied that modernising imperialism has caused enormous suffering. The 26,000 dead Boer women and children are a real, though ultimately small, part of that complex reckoning. So are the victims of apartheid, that creation of imperial policies and the chauvinistic nationalism that reacted against them. So, perhaps, are those who are dying in Iraq and Afghanistan today: deaths that have repeatedly been justified as the necessary collateral damage of the defence of Western civilisation against the irrational forces of Islamic Fundamentalism. Martin Versfeld's warning against the abstractions of ideologies and political dogmatism is indeed timely here. For too long, defenders of Western modernity have failed to take into account the costs of their abstractions – or indeed, to ask whether those abstractions make any sense in the first place.

The competing discourse also has the virtue of at least raising the question of the compatibility of liberty and imperialism, even if it answers this question unsatisfactorily. While Hofmeyr and Haarhoff fail to assess adequately the cost of imperial power to individual freedoms, either ignoring this altogether or seeing it as outweighed by opportunities for national

---

[101] I am thinking here of an anecdote for whose veracity I am sadly unable to vouch. Versfeld was reportedly an avid gardener – so enthusiastic that he would garden on the campus of UCT when the mood took him. On one occasion, he went straight to class after digging in the flower-beds, forgetting to wash the earth from his hands before his lecture. To add another layer to my invocation of 'earthiness', Versfeld also defends the place of bawdiness in human experience and wisdom. See Versfeld 1962: 137–38. For Habermas's comment, see the observation that Gadamer 'urbanizes the Heideggerian province' in Habermas 1985: 190.

development or by materials gains, they do at least see that effective political domination by a single power (as opposed to alliances of equals) cannot be compatible with liberty, however that is understood. That is already an advance over defenders of American imperialism, who sometimes like to describe all as winners in the wake of an America whose allies or beneficiaries could never be publicly permitted to question or redirect its foreign policy. Versfeld's defence of individual integrity goes still further in reminding us of the costs of imperialism's ideological abstractions.

It is on the matter of racism that the competing discourse reveals its limitations. The reasons for this are complex, however. In the case of Hofmeyr and Haarhoff, the example of Rome, which they inherit from the discourse of imperialism, leads them to undervalue equal political freedoms in favour of national accommodation, progress in the arts and sciences, and security. But it is not necessarily the examples provided by classics that are at fault here. One might equally well criticise the assumption that cultures must be authentic wholes, or the authors' lack of imagination and resolve in recognising and applying the lessons of ancient experiments in fostering cultural and racial hybridity.

Versfeld's turn to Augustine and Socrates is more radical in rejecting core assumptions of imperial discourse. His conception of the true Western – or human – legacy as scepticism and ordinary, everyday dialogue puts him in a position to resist claims to cultural superiority based on intellectual sophistication or technological accomplishments. He explicitly counsels against active support for organised racism. That he fails to consider seriously the need for public engagement, or the possibility of injecting the world of politics with the kind of individual integrity and scepticism that he champions in the domestic context, is perhaps his error, but also the error of an intractable ideological politics.

In sum, the legacy of classics on twentieth-century political thought in South Africa is a complex one. It is right to complain, as Grant Parker does, that it has functioned as a 'place marker of colonial silence'. But it has also provided invaluable resources to a competing discourse that has attempted – with partial success – to criticise Western imperialism and racism. Perhaps nothing less should be expected of knowledge of the antique world – itself a world of great complexity and contradictions, neither fully supportive of modernity nor entirely at odds with it.

8 | After Cicero: Legal Thought from Antiquity to the New Constitution

DEON H. VAN ZYL

> In a codified form I have every hope that the Roman Dutch law will survive in South Africa, in the same way that much of the old French law and a great deal of the Civil Law have survived in France. Without a code my fears for the Roman Dutch law are great, mainly because dreary and pedantic schoolmasters and professors have conspired to rob Latin of its vitality as a language and converted it into an examination engine for torturing growing boys and girls. How many boys of eighteen today have read half a dozen books of Virgil, the odes of Horace or a hundred consecutive pages of any Roman prose-writer? The schoolboys of today who are learning Latin snippets to get through their examinations are not going to read Cujacius or Voet when they become qualified barristers. They are going to put their trust in Halsbury's *Laws of England* and Mew's *Digest of English Case Law* – with a hurried look at Maasdorp's *Institutes* and Kotzé's van Leeuwen – just to give their law a little local colouring. To save the Roman Dutch law we must take its essential principles out of the Latin folios and arrange them methodically in a well thought out, compact, but efficient code.[1]

The relevance of my early and subsequent exposure to the classics must, for purposes of the present contribution, be understood against the background of my simultaneous study of law, for which at least a first-year course in Latin was, at the time, a statutory requirement.[2] Even after that requirement had fallen away, classical Latin and Greek, together with at least modern Dutch, French, German and Italian, were essential tools for researching and understanding Roman law in its various phases of development, including its reception in Europe and elsewhere. Its reception in

---

[1] Wessels 1920: 284.

[2] When the editor approached me to contribute to the current volume, I was unable to avoid a nostalgic recollection of my first Latin lesson at Springs Boys' High School in January 1957. As the small class of boys, who had opted for Latin rather than bookkeeping, took their seats, they were welcomed in impeccable Latin by Mrs Jean Smart – sternly, but with a twinkle in the eye. Her *salvete pueri* ('be greeted boys') ignited an interest that has remained with me to the present day. This interest inspired me to major in Latin and Greek at the University of Pretoria. I continued these studies with a BA (Hons) (1967) and MA (1968) in Latin before eventually completing a DLitt in Latin at the University of the Free State in 1989, with a thesis entitled *Justice and Equity in Cicero: a critical evaluation in contextual perspective.*

the Netherlands gave rise to the creation and growth of Roman-Dutch law – the common law of South Africa and much of southern Africa. Roman-Dutch law in turn was basic to the history and development of South African law.[3]

Legal history went hand in hand with comparative law in a South African context, in that it related not only to the development of Roman-Dutch law as common law, but also to the introduction and development of English law when South Africa was a British colony. Virtually all South Africa's law of procedure and evidence, both civil and criminal, and its various aspects of commercial law, including company law, insolvency, intellectual property (patents, trademarks and copyright) and the like, are based on English law and jurisprudence. This has made it a mixed legal system *par excellence*, along with other southern African legal systems, and the similarly mixed legal systems of Scotland and Sri Lanka.[4]

These mixed legal systems are distinguished from, but still comparable with, the legal systems based on the French *Code Civil* of 1804, such as those of Quebec in Canada, New Orleans in Louisiana, USA and the Francophone countries of Africa. Just as the Roman-Dutch common law was the product of the reception of Roman law in the Netherlands, and more particularly the province of Holland, so the French *Code Civil* was the product of the reception of Roman law in France and surrounding areas. For this reason I prefer to use the general concept of 'Roman-European' rather than 'Roman-Dutch' or 'Roman-French' law, which could be confusing.

1. Classical Greek and Roman Origins

The Roman law received in Europe prior to the *Code Civil* was based on classical Roman law as developed by great teachers and practitioners, starting in the first century AD and culminating in the Emperor Justinian's *Corpus Iuris Civilis* during the sixth century AD. Cicero expounded classical law in impeccable classical Latin, revealing the deep influence of the Greek tradition of Plato and Aristotle and, beyond them, Plato's teacher, Socrates. To the degree Socrates' teachings can be reconstructed, they seem to have emphasised that true happiness and well-being

---

[3] On the historical development of South African common law see Wessels 1908; Van Zyl 1979.

[4] For a comparison between aspects of Scottish and South African law as mixed legal systems see Zimmermann et al. 2004.

(*eudaimonia*) were premised on two principles: never to do wrong and to acquire knowledge of what is right, just and good.[5]

Plato expanded on Socrates' teaching in developing his own philosophy in his various works, particularly *The Republic* and *Laws*. In *The Republic* he deals with the concept of justice and the ideal state in which laws should not simply be of general application, whereas in *Laws* he adopts a more pragmatic approach, arguing that rulers should not be endowed with absolute powers but should adhere to the laws, even if they are not perfect.[6]

Aristotle, in his *Politics* and *Nicomachean Ethics*, rejected Plato's theory of ideas by teaching that the world of sense-perception was a material and concrete reality. All changes in this reality stemmed from an eternal, immovable force in terms of which 'good' was equated with 'God' or divinity. To a large extent, Aristotle's thought revolved around his perception of justice (*dikaiosyne*), which he described as the most perfect of all virtues and the foundation of a stable, peaceful and harmonious community. Its counterpart was injustice (*adikia*), which he regarded as intentionally wrongful conduct in conflict with the law (*para ton nomon*).[7]

The philosophy of Plato and Aristotle featured strongly in the legal and other writings of Cicero. As an eclectic, Cicero borrowed widely, adapting and modifying Greek philosophical concepts to Roman thought.[8] His main works on the state and laws, *De re publica* and *De legibus*, are mindful of Plato's *The Republic* and *Laws* in that they deal with similar topics against the background of the cardinal virtues and like concepts. Nonetheless, he saw justice as a virtue underlying all human relationships on the basis of shared interests and the need 'to accord to each his own' (*suum cuique tribuere*). As a pragmatist he focused on 'practical wisdom' or 'common sense' rather than on wisdom in its theoretical sense.

Cicero's view on the concept of equity or fairness (*aequitas*) was inextricably linked with his concepts of justice and good faith underlying civil law (*ius civile*). He in fact defined civil law as 'the equity constituted for members of the same state so that each may receive his own'.[9] This

---

[5] On Socrates as a man and philosopher see in general Vlastos 1971 and Morrison 2011. See also the observations in Van Zyl 1991b: 19–20.

[6] See Van Zyl 1991b: 21–25, and now more generally Benson 2009.

[7] On Aristotle see Van Zyl 1991b: 25–30; for a range of aspects, Anagnostopoulos 2009.

[8] Cicero's development as a lawyer and philosopher is dealt with comprehensively in Van Zyl 1991a: 1–33. As an eclectic he was an adherent of the Stoic doctrines of Diodotus and Zeno, the Epicurean school of Epicurus and Zeno of Sidon and Platonism tempered by Scepticism (21–27).

[9] *Topica* 2.9: 'Ius civile est aequitas constituta eis qui eiusdem civitatis sunt ad res suas obtinendas . . .'

definition was followed by Ulpian, who was citing with approval a passage from Celsus when he stated that 'law is the art of the good and the fair'.[10]

For Cicero and later Roman lawyers and philosophers justice went hand in hand with the concepts of equity, reasonableness, good faith and a spectrum of other virtues – values and moral considerations required for sustaining a positive interpersonal relationship among community members.[11] Although, as an eclectic, he has justifiably been regarded as a translator and interpreter of classical Greek terminology, he played an immensely important role in laying the foundations of post-classical and later law.

It is small wonder then that later generations of lawyers – including Gaius, Papinian, Paul, Ulpian and Modestinus – frequently relied on Cicero in their own works. Such works, for the most part, constituted the substance of the jurisprudence contained in the Digest (*Digesta*) which, along with the Institutes (*Institutiones*), Code (*Codex*) and Novels (*Novellae Constitutiones*), made up the collective body of law later to be known as the *Corpus Iuris Civilis* of the emperor Justinian.[12]

2.   The Later Development of Roman Law as a European *Ius Commune*

In the five centuries after Justinian, Roman law as contained in the *Corpus Iuris Civilis* continued to exist in the eastern Roman Empire through the activities of the ecclesiastical courts and a new genre of legal literature contained in a variety of commentaries on Justinianic law. Although the Church was said to live in accordance with Roman law (*ecclesia vivit secundum legem Romanam*), the rules of the church developed into canon law (*ius canonicum*), codified in the ninth century as the *Lex Romana canonice compta*. At the same time, notarial practice outside the church kept Roman law alive by recording rules, precedents and *formulae* in procedural and evidentiary law. In addition, later generations of intellectuals continued to marvel at the achievements of the Roman Empire, both western and eastern, and to study Roman literary, legal and other sources.[13]

---

[10] *Digest* 1.1.1 pr: '. . . ut eleganter Celsus definit, ius est ars boni et aequi'.

[11] See the discussion of Cicero's moral philosophy in Van Zyl 1991a: 34–56 and 96–100.

[12] On the legislation of Justinian (r. 527–65) see Van Zyl 1983: 61–75.

[13] See in general, on the factors underlying the continuation of Roman law after Justinian, the discussion in Van Zyl 1979: 71–80. Canon law is dealt with in more detail at 160–84 with reference to a large number of sources.

The revival of Roman law during the twelfth and thirteenth centuries in Bologna, Italy constituted a veritable renaissance of law. The school of glossators (*glossatores*), such as Azo, Accursius, Odofredus and the 'four doctors' (*quattuor doctores*), namely Bulgarus, Martinus, Jacobus and Hugo, undertook detailed research of the surviving Roman law of Justinian by appending 'notes' (*glossae*) to specific texts, particularly from the *Digest* (*Digesta*) and other parts of the *Corpus Iuris Civilis*. They also consolidated their notes (*apparatus* and *summae*) and debated case studies, distinctions and issues in lectures (*lecturae*) and opinions (*consilia*). So important was their work that it was said that a person who did not acknowledge the *glossa* did not recognise the power of the court (*qui non agnoscit glossa non agnoscit forum*). Accursius was closely linked with an authoritative compilation of the *glossae* known as the *Glossa Ordinaria*, which became the basis of much further research and learning in medieval legal science.[14]

This methodology spread to other Italian cities like Pavia, Pisa, Florence and Ravenna and later, during the thirteenth and fourteenth centuries, gave rise to the development of an important law school at the University of Orléans in France, where legal researchers like Jacques de Révigny and Pierre de Belleperche studied Roman and canon law with a view to becoming 'doctors of both laws' (*doctores utriusque iuris*). The School of Orléans also wrote *glossae* and similar studies based on the Roman sources. Their influential learning subsequently spread to other parts of France, such as Montpellier and Toulouse.[15]

Roman law underwent a significant development in Italy during the fourteenth and fifteenth centuries, when the successors to the glossators formed a new school known as the 'post-glossators' or 'commentators'. Rather than simply appending notes, they wrote full commentaries (*commenta* or *lecturae*) on titles of the *Corpus Iuris Civilis* and select passages from canon law. They also wrote about the customary law and practice of their time, thus becoming known as *consiliatores*. In the process, they introduced a new genre of legal science appropriately termed 'Italian custom' (*mos italicus*). The most famous representatives of this school were Bartolus de Saxoferrato and Baldus de Ubaldis, whose followers were respectively known as *Bartolistae* and *Baldistae* and whose monumental works formed the basis of the *ius commune* of Europe and even

---

[14] On the school of glossators see the full discussion in Van Zyl 1979: 83–110.

[15] It also played an important role in the later development of legal science in Italy. On the school of Orléans and its burgeoning influence see Van Zyl 1979: 110–24.

played an important role in the development of law in England and Scotland.[16]

A reaction to the glossators and commentators occurred during the fifteenth to seventeenth centuries, when the French humanists of Bourges and elsewhere in France countered the *mos italicus* of Italy with their 'French custom' (*mos gallicus*). The latter focused on the humanities in historical context, as developed from the classical culture of ancient Greece and Rome, and rejected the exaggerated scholasticism and dialectics of the glossators and commentators. They likewise rejected what they regarded as the barbaric Latin and poor style of these schools and sought 'to seek the sources' (*petere fontes*) of classical Roman law as perpetuated by Cicero in his elegant classical Latin.[17]

Although the humanist movement took root in Bourges, under the leadership of the Italian Andrea Alciato, it soon extended to Paris, where Guillaume Budé taught humanistic doctrine, and subsequently spread to other parts of Europe such as Germany and the Netherlands, where Ulrich Zasius and Nicolaus Everardus respectively gained humanistic prominence. The most famous humanists by far were Jacques Cujas and Hugues Doneau, both of whom studied and taught in Toulouse and Bourges. Although they and their followers were regarded as academic rather than practical, they played an extremely important role in developing a European *ius commune* in the pre-codification era.[18]

In the development of this *ius commune* the norms and doctrines emanating from natural law (*ius naturalis*) or the law of nature (*ius naturae*) played a significant role.[19] In a general sense natural law may be described as the law that was common to all peoples and nations and was based on natural reason and equitable principles. Throughout its development and application in law and legal systems, natural law was strongly influenced by the rules and principles of ethics, morality, law and philosophy. Natural law was likewise influenced by the 'theological' norms of canon law, such as justice (*iustitia*), equity (*aequitas*), good faith (*bona fides*) and good morals (*boni mores*) contained in values such as conscience (*conscientia*), integrity (*honestas*) and compassion (*misericordia*), thus

---

[16] On the Commentators and their wide-ranging influence see Van Zyl 1979: 124–40.

[17] They similarly rejected outright the refusal of the glossators to research and consult original Greek sources on the basis that such sources should not be read (*graeca non leguntur*).

[18] See in general on the humanists and humanism Van Zyl 1979: 140–60.

[19] This links up with Cicero's view, in *De re publica* 3.22.33, that 'true law is right reason in conformity with nature' ('vera lex recta ratio naturae congruens').

becoming a natural ingredient of the *ius commune* in Europe and elsewhere.[20]

3.   The Pre-Codification Development of European Law

The reception and development of Roman law in Europe was particularly prominent in the north and south of France, which experienced significant changes from medieval times to the pre-codification period and thereafter. Customary law was strongly influenced by Roman and canon law as taught in law and theological schools and applied in legal practice. The reception process reached its culmination during the growth of the humanistic movement in Bourges and elsewhere, and subsequently paved the way for the development of French common law (*droit commun*) as national law and as a precursor to the codification movement. Charles Dumoulin (Carolus Molinaeus), Jean Domat and Robert-Josèphe Pothier played an important role in creating the French Civil Code (*Code Civil*) of 1804.[21]

A similar process of legal development in medieval Europe soon became prominent in countries like Germany, attributable to the gradual reception of Roman law resulting from the increase of mercantile, notarial and cultural relations between Germanic and other European states. In addition, German students studied in French and Italian universities before returning to teach in German universities or to practise in German courts. In the process, they played an important role in the reception of Roman law in Germany and in the preparation of the German Civil Code (*Bürgerliches Gesetzbuch – BGB*) of 1896, which has been operational since 1 January 1900. This was preceded in the seventeenth and eighteenth centuries by the German legal development known as the 'modern application (use) of the pandects' (*usus modernus pandectarum*), which was directed at the academic and practical study of the Digest (*Digesta*) or Pandects (*Pandectae*) of Justinian. It also became known as contemporary customs (*mores hodiernae*) or 'new practice' (*nova practica*).[22]

---

[20] See in general the discussion in Van Zyl 1979: 185–204, where reference is made to the development of natural law during the medieval period as illustrated in the thirteenth-century works of theologians and philosophers like Thomas Aquinas.

[21] On this development see Van Zyl 1979: 207–27.

[22] See Van Zyl 1979: 227–89, with reference, among others, to writers of the *usus modernus pandectarum* such as Carpzovius (1595–1666), Brunnemann (1608–72), Mevius (1609–70), Struvius (1619–92), Stryk (1640–1710), Böhmer (1674–1749), Leyser (1683–1752) and Heineccius (1681–1741). This was followed by the historical school of lawyers like Savigny

Undoubtedly the most important area of reception of Roman law as 'Roman-Dutch' law was the Netherlands or the 'Lower Countries' (*Pays Bas*). Particularly prominent was the province of Holland, although substantial reception also took place in other provinces, such as Utrecht, Groningen and Friesland, as well as in Flanders and Brabant (modern-day Belgium) to the south. It is generally accepted that 'Roman-Dutch' law subsequently underwent a reception in South Africa, but it must be noted that this is a wider-ranging term than 'the law of Roman-Holland' ('Romeins-Hollandse reg'), which appears in Afrikaans, Dutch or Flemish works and is apparently limited to Roman law as received in the province of Holland.[23] Even 'Roman-Dutch' is too limited, since the Roman law as received in other European countries such as France, Spain and Germany is also regarded as *ius commune* or *droit commun*, hence justifying its description as 'Roman-European law' or 'European common law'.[24]

For present purposes, the most important phase of legal development in the Netherlands, when Roman-Dutch law was said to have blossomed, took place during the seventeenth and eighteenth centuries. This development was particularly important for South Africa since it was during that period, on 6 April 1652, that Jan van Riebeeck, an official of the Dutch East India Company, set foot on South African soil to establish a refreshment station in what later became known as Cape Town and the Western Cape. He brought with him the Roman-Dutch law or 'European common law', which was to become the common law of South Africa. This included various written and unwritten sources of law such as customary law (*oude hercomen*), urban law (*stadrecht*) and regional law (*landrecht*). The Roman-Dutch law also included statutes, known as *placaeten, ordonnantiën* and *keuren*, court decisions (*decisiones* or *gewijsde saecken*) and legal opinions. When these sources of law were published as collections, such as the *Ewige Edik* (1540), the *Politieke Ordonnantie* (1580) and the *Groot Placaet-Boek* (1658–1797), they became all the more authoritative.[25]

By far the most important source of Roman-Dutch law was the vast number of commentaries and dissertations on various aspects of law. Their authors were, for the most part, academic jurists and practising lawyers

---

(1779–1861) and pandectists such as Windscheid (1872–92). It was subsequently extended to countries like Italy, Spain, Portugal, Austria, Switzerland, England and Scotland.

[23] The concept 'Roman-Dutch law' was first used by the jurist Simon van Leeuwen (1626–82) in his famous work entitled *Roomsch-Hollandsch Recht* (1664). On the reception of Roman law in the Netherlands see Wessels 1908: 95–111 and 123–29; Van Zyl 1979: 303–15.

[24] See Van Zyl 1979: 7–9, 265–66, 290–91.

[25] On these and other sources and collections of sources see Van Zyl 1979: 316–28.

whose contributions were in many instances directed at elucidating and applying Roman law sources, in accordance with the needs and circumstances prevailing in the province or region to which the contribution related.[26]

Chief among the seventeenth-century jurists was Hugo Grotius, author of an introduction to Dutch law (*Inleidinge tot de Hollandsche Rechtsgeleertheyt*) and a famous dissertation on the law of war and peace (*De jure belli ac pacis*). Other prominent authors were Arnoldus Vinnius, Antonius Matthaeus II, Simon van Groenewegen, Simon van Leeuwen (author of *Het Roomsch-Hollandsch Recht*), Ulrich Huber and Johannes Voet, author of the *Commentarius ad Pandectas*.[27]

During the eighteenth century, the best-known jurists were D. G. van der Keessel and Johannes van der Linden. Van der Keessel was the author of lectures (*Dictata* or *Praelectiones*) on De Groot's *Inleidinge tot de Hollandsche Rechtsgeleertheyt* and select theses on the law of Holland and Zeeland (*Theses selectae juris Hollandici et Zelandici*).[28] Van der Linden, a practising advocate for more than fifty years, produced the well-known *Koopmans Handboek* and a number of other practical contributions.

4.   The 'Reception' of Roman-Dutch Law in South Africa

The introduction of Roman-Dutch law into the Cape and later throughout South Africa was influenced by a number of factors, not least of which was the British colonisation of the country and the introduction of English law in many spheres of law, such as those of procedure, evidence, commercial law, intellectual property law and the like. This made the South African legal system a mixed legal system *par excellence*. On the other hand, the classical element of Roman-Dutch law, with its Roman legal origins, was boosted by the creation of law faculties at the Universities of Stellenbosch

---

[26] Van Zyl 1979: 329–415, presents the most prominent jurists and lawyers as successive schools of thought culminating in the seventeenth and eighteenth centuries. Much of their work emanated from universities such as those of Leiden (Leyden), Franeker, Groningen and Utrecht.

[27] This *magnum opus* was translated by a South African judge, Percival Gane, as *The Selective Voet, being the Commentary on the Pandects by Johannes Voet* (Durban: Butterworths, 1955–58). Reference may also be made to Gerhard Noodt (1647–1725) and Cornelis van Bijnkershoek (1673–1743) as prominent representatives of seventeenth-century jurisprudence.

[28] This was published in 1939 by Professor E. M. Meijers of the University of Leiden under the title *Praelectiones juris hodierni ad Hugonis Grotii Introductionem ad jurisprudentiam Hollandicam*. It was later (1961–1975) translated into Afrikaans by Professor H. L. Gonin, sometime Professor of Latin at the University of Pretoria, among others.

(1920) and Pretoria (1927), where strong emphasis was placed on Latin, Roman law and Roman-Dutch law as compulsory subjects for the study of law.[29]

After the right of appeal to the Privy Council of the House of Lords in England was abolished in 1950, Roman-Dutch law, as reflected in its Latin and Dutch sources, was revitalised and, indeed, underwent what has been described as 'the second life of Roman-Dutch law'.[30] This was not so much a 'reception' of Roman-Dutch law in South Africa as a transfer or transplantation of the entire legal system as it applied in Holland during the mid-seventeenth century. If there was any form of reception it related rather to the piecemeal reception of English law into the South African legal system at the time of the British colonisation of South Africa during the nineteenth and early twentieth centuries. It may be more accurate, however, to speak of English legal influence on South African law rather than the reception of English law into South Africa at the time in question.[31]

In order better to understand the concepts of transplantation, reception and influence it must be remembered that the history of South African law falls comfortably into four main periods: (a) the period from 1652 to 1795, when the Cape was under the control and authority of the Dutch East India Company (VOC); (b) the period from 1795 to 1910, when the Cape and the rest of South Africa was under British rule;[32] (c) the period between 1910 and 1994, when South Africa was initially a Union (from 1910 to 1961) and then a Republic (from 1961 to 1994); and (d) the period from 1994 to the present, when South Africa became a constitutional state ruled by a democratically elected government in accordance with the provisions of the Constitution of the Republic of South Africa (Act 108 of 1996).

For present purposes, I will deal in particular with the last two periods, encompassing South African legal development from 1910 to the present time, when classicism, in the form of what may be called Graeco-Roman law and legal philosophy was, and still is, particularly prevalent. This does not mean that the earlier periods were not relevant in this regard. During the seventeenth and eighteenth centuries, the courts in the Cape applied

---

[29] For more on the role of Latin in legal training see Dircksen 2010.

[30] Hahlo and Kahn 1968: 566.

[31] The idea of a transfer rather than a reception is clarified in an article by Professor D. Pont 1971–72. See the discussion and authorities referred to in Van Zyl 1979: 420–23.

[32] Except for the short period between 1803 and 1806, when the Cape was under the interim rule of the Batavian Republic.

Roman-Dutch law as the common law of the Cape.[33] The same applied to the period between 1795 and 1910, when the Roman-Dutch law, as developed in the Cape, became the law of other parts of South Africa, particularly after the Great Trek of 1836 and later. The courts of the Transvaal, the Orange Free State and Natal frequently referred in their judgments to jurists like De Groot, Van Leeuwen, Voet, Groenewegen and Van der Linden, but also cited English authorities.[34]

The incorporation of the Cape, the Transvaal, the Orange Free State and Natal in the Union of South Africa on 31 May 1910 brought with it the significant growth of the Roman-Dutch common law hitherto applied in these provinces and now applicable to the whole country. The most significant factor in this process was the creation of the Supreme Court of South Africa, with divisions in all major cities and with its Appellate Division in Bloemfontein.[35]

A large number of judgments emanating from these courts, in particular the Appellate Division, contained numerous references to and developments of the relevant Roman law and Roman-Dutch common law. Such references were usually in the original language (Latin, Greek or Dutch) of the source referred to and were frequently aligned to or compared with sources from other European countries where 'Roman-European' law applied. These were sources originating in France, Germany, Italy and Spain, where the original classical sources occurred in books and commentaries published in the native languages of such countries.

From its very inception, the Appellate Division applied Roman-Dutch law as the common law of South Africa, adopting a flexible approach and adapting the law in accordance with the changing needs and circumstances of the time.[36] This did not, however, mean that English law ceased to play

[33] See Visagie 1969: 69–76; Van Zyl 1979: 423–42.

[34] Van Zyl 1979: 444–76. At 453–58 the author deals with the reception of English law in the Cape between 1806 and 1910. Roman-Dutch law remained in force but lawyers were frequently tempted to refer to English law.

[35] A further right of appeal to the Privy Council of the House of Lords in England was abrogated by Act 16 of 1950. In terms of sections 166 and 167 of the present Constitution (Act 108 of 1996) the Supreme Court is now known as the High Court and the Appellate Division as the Supreme Court of Appeal, which functions as a court of appeal in non-constitutional matters. Constitutional matters are dealt with by the Constitutional Court, which is *de facto* and *de iure* the highest court in the land.

[36] This was in line with the approach enunciated in early cases such as *Henderson and Another v Hanekom* 20 SC (1903) 513 at 519 (*per* Lord Henry de Villiers): 'However anxious the Court may be to maintain the Roman-Dutch law in all its integrity, there must, in the ordinary course, be a progressive development of the law, keeping pace with modern requirements.' See also *Blower v Van Noorden* 1909 TS 890 at 905: 'There come times in the growth of every living system of law when old practice and ancient formulae must be modified in order to keep in

a prominent role. In a number of cases it was followed as an alternative source of law where the common law did not appear to provide an answer to the question under consideration, or where it had been applied in practice over a long period of time, or where there was 'no difference in principle' between the Roman-Dutch and English law and guidance could be obtained from English court decisions.[37] In other cases, however, there was resistance to this approach and courts were prepared to reassert fundamental principles of common law even if it meant reversing long-standing judgments.[38]

This approach was not generally acceptable to legal academics, one of whom saw it as the reversal of legal development by an attempted 'purification' of the law, directed at 'purging' the law of institutions and doctrines of English origin.[39] Some academics felt that English law was 'part of the very warp and woof of South African law'.[40] This gave rise to what Mulligan referred to as a 'juristic war' (*bellum juridicum*) between 'purists', 'pollutionists' and 'pragmatists'. The first were those who wanted to root out all that was English, the second were those who were content with retaining English doctrine, and the third were those who sought a practical middle course or *via media*.[41]

Between 1951 and 1992, shortly before the new constitutional dispensation commenced in 1994, judgments of the Appellate Division indicated an increasing interest in Roman-Dutch legal sources and a decreased interest in Roman law as such.[42] This stimulated my own interest in encouraging our courts to apply the legal historical method rather than simply to rely on the Roman-Dutch sources of the seventeenth and eighteenth centuries. In this way, the logical development of law from Roman times through the Middle Ages to the pre-codification period in Europe could be traced.[43]

---

touch with the expansion of legal ideas, and to keep pace with the requirements of changing conditions.' This approach was likewise followed by Lord Tomlinson in *Pearl Assurance Co v Union Government* 1934 AD 560 at 563: 'That law is a virile, living system of law, ever seeking, as every such system must, to adapt itself consistently with its inherent basic principles to deal effectively with the increasing complexities of modern organised society.'

[37] See *Rolfes, Nebel & Co v Zweigenhaft* 1903 TS 185 at 206; *Webster v Ellison* 1910 AD 299 at 300; *Mancho v South African Railways and Harbours* 1928 AD 89 at 100; *Feldman (Pty) Ltd v Mall* 1945 AD 733 at 776; *Linton v Corser* 1952 (3) SA 685 (A) at 695–696; *R v Sibiya* 1955 (4) SA 247 (A) at 256E-F.

[38] See *Dukes v Marthinusen* 1937 AD 12 at 22–23; *Baines Motors v Piek* 1955 (1) SA 534 (A) at 543B-C; *Preller and Others v Jordaan* 1956 (1) SA 483 (A) at 504E; *Trust Bank van Afrika Bpk v Eksteen* 1964 (3) SA 402 (A) at 410–411.

[39] Proculus Redevivus 1965: 23.   [40] Hahlo and Kahn 1960: 47.   [41] Mulligan 1952.

[42] See the reference to J. J. Henning's research in this regard: Van Zyl 1979: 486–88.

[43] See Van Zyl 1972. This is the text of my inaugural lecture as professor of Roman law and legal history at the University of the Orange Free State, now the University of the Free State.

Our courts have not distinguished between writers from Holland and other provinces of the Netherlands, but have indeed referred to writers from these provinces and also to those of the southern Netherlands (present-day Belgium) and other European countries. It is therefore clear that the concept 'Roman-Dutch law' is far too limited. The 'Roman-Dutch' common law of South Africa was, and is, in fact, no less than the European *ius commune* referred to above. The only problem is that, from 1910 to the present, our courts have frequently made general reference to such authorities in a disordered or inharmonious manner, without attempting to deal with them in any particular legal historical order or even chronologically. Therefore, it may be more accurate simply to describe the common law of South Africa as 'South African' rather than as 'Roman-Dutch' or even 'Roman-European'.[44]

Even a change of nomenclature may not be sufficient to save the wealth of the legal historical sources making up the South African common law. As Chief Justice Sir Johannes Wessels had already stated in 1920, in the epigraph with which this chapter begins, the old sources needed codification if they were to be preserved for later generations. In practice, no code was forthcoming, but the establishing of law faculties at the Universities of Stellenbosch and Pretoria in the 1920s, as well as the founding of the *Tydskrif vir Hedendaagse Romeins-Hollandse Reg* ('Journal for Contemporary Roman-Dutch Law') in 1937 did much to maintain and preserve the old authorities for South African law. Similarly, the translation from Latin or Dutch of a number of such authorities served to make these available to the legal profession for purposes of both academic research and their application in legal practice.[45]

---

[44] On the development of common law in South Africa after 1910 see generally the discussion in Van Zyl, *Geskiedenis*, 1979: 476–94 with observations on the role of academics and legal journals at 495–98 and concluding remarks on the future of Roman-Dutch law at 498–503. In *R v Goseb* 1956 (2) SA 696 (SWA) at 698, J. P. Claassen described the term 'Roman-Dutch law' as confusing, because our common law is in fact 'South African common law'.

[45] John Gilbert Kotzé translated Simon van Leeuwen's *Het Roomsch-Hollandsch Recht* as *Commentaries on Roman-Dutch Law* (1881–86), while Percival Gane was responsible for the translation of Ulrich Huber's *Heedendaegse Rechtsgeleertheyt* as *The Jurisprudence of my Time* (5th edn., Durban: Butterworth, 1939) and Voet's monumental *Commentarius ad Pandectas* as *The Selective Voet, Being the Commentary on the Pandects by Johannes Voet (1647–1713) and the Supplement to that Work by Johannes van der Linden (1756–1835)* (Durban: Butterworth, 1955–58). Since that time a number of further translations have seen the light – see Van Zyl 1979: 497–98; more recently those of Antonius Matthaeus's *De Criminibus* as *On Crimes*, tr. M. L. Hewett (1987–94), and Gerard Noodt's *Foenus et Usurae* as *The Three Books on Interest-bearing Loans and Interest*, tr. David M. Kriel (Pretoria: Pretoria University Law Press, 2009).

5.   The New Constitutional Dispensation

The new constitutional dispensation in South Africa officially commenced on 27 April 1994 and was confirmed on 10 May 1994, when Nelson Mandela was inaugurated as the first democratically elected President of South Africa. The new dispensation brought with it a new Constitution, containing an exemplary Bill of Rights and a flurry of new legislation in line with and supplementing the Constitution. However, the common law, as developed over the years, did not fall by the wayside. It was, and still is, valid, binding and generally applicable, despite some debate on its relevance.[46] In the period since 1994 our courts have continued frequently to refer to Roman and Roman-Dutch (Roman-European) legal sources. They have likewise fully acknowledged the important role of English law, with its wealth of precedent, in developing the common law and creating South Africa's mixed legal system. The courts have done this by relying on what may be regarded as the best aspects of two legal worlds to lay the foundations of a well-nigh unique legal system with its own special character.

Legal development of this nature has frequently been associated with public policy or policy considerations, which may be roughly equated with the 'good morals' (*boni mores*) of Roman law. This prompted former Chief Justice Michael Corbett to express the following view:[47]

[T]he policy decisions of our courts which shape and, at times, refashion the common law must also reflect the wishes, often unspoken, and the perceptions, often but dimly discerned, of the people. A community has certain common values and norms. These are in part a heritage from the past. To some extent too they are the product of the influence of other communities; of the interaction that takes place between peoples in all spheres of human activity; of the sayings and writings of the philosophers, the thinkers, the leaders, which have universal human appeal; of the living example which other societies provide. It is these values and norms that the judge must apply in making his decision. And in doing so he must become 'the living voice of the people'; he must 'know us better than we know ourselves'; he must interpret society to itself.

In my own somewhat idealistic approach to law and justice I have, in my judgments as a High Court judge, relied on the ancient principles of justice, equity, reasonableness, good faith and public policy or good morals in

---

[46]   See Scott 1993; Van der Merwe 1994; Fagan 1996; Van Reenen 1996; Church 1996: 317–18; Van Zyl 2000.

[47]   Corbett 1987: 67–68.

order to achieve what the community expects of a judge, which is to do justice in such a way that it can clearly be seen to be done.[48]

The question which immediately came to the fore when the new Constitution was introduced was whether or not it would usher in improvements to the existing system.[49] The pessimists assumed that the Constitution would mean the end of the common law, while the optimists (and idealists) saw it as an exciting opportunity to develop the common law further. Graeco-Roman values, as developed through the classical and post-classical Roman era and the medieval revival and development of Roman law prior to the codification process in Europe, remained strongly prevalent in the new constitutional dispensation. This will be observed when the Constitution is considered in order to assess the values set forth therein.

In the preamble to the Constitution the concepts of justice, honour, freedom and respect come to the fore immediately: recognition is given to 'the injustices of our past', honour is bestowed on 'those who suffered for justice and freedom in our land', respect is shown to 'those who have worked to build and develop our country' and the belief is expressed that 'South Africa belongs to all who live in it, united in our diversity'.

The aim of the Constitution is hence, firstly, to 'heal the divisions of the past and establish a society based on democratic values, social justice and fundamental human rights'; secondly, to 'lay the foundations for a democratic and open society in which government is based on the will of the people and every citizen is equally protected law'; thirdly, to 'improve the quality of life of all citizens and free the potential of each person'; and, fourthly, to 'build a united and democratic South Africa able to take its rightful place as a sovereign state in the family of nations'.

The ancient Greek and Roman philosophers and lawyers were not a direct source of this preamble. Nonetheless, the virtues and values expressed in it might have come from any number of passages in

[48] See for example *Van Erk v Holmer* 1992 (2) SA 636 (W) at 649; *Aucamp v The University of Stellenbosch* 2002 CLR 97 (C) par [68]; *Anglo-Dutch Meats (Exports) Ltd v Blaauwberg Meat Wholesalers CC* 2002 CLR 292 (C) par [34]; *Di Giulio v First National Bank of South Africa Ltd* 2002 (6) SA 281 (C) par [38]; *Eisenberg and Associates v Minister of Home Affairs and Others* 2003 (5) BCLR 514 (C) par [23]; *Victoria & Alfred Waterfront (Pty) Ltd v Platinum Holdings (Pty) Ltd* 2003 CLR 331 (C) par [146]; *Heyneman v Waterfront Marine CC* 2004 CLR 398 (C) par [67]; *Society of Lloyd's v Romahn and Two Other Cases* 2006 (4) SA 23 (C) par [86]; *D'Ambrosi v Bane and Others* [2007] 1 All SA 570 (C) par [39].
[49] Initially there was an interim Constitution (Act 200 of 1993), chapter 3 of which constituted a Bill of Rights. It was replaced by the final Constitution (Act 108 of 1996), with chapter 2 constituting the Bill of Rights.

Cicero's *De officiis, De re publica* or *De legibus*. The same applies to the founding provisions contained in section 1*(a)* of the Constitution, where we are told that South Africa is a 'sovereign, democratic state' founded on the values of 'human dignity, the achievement of equality and the advancement of human rights and freedoms'. This is even more prevalent in the Bill of Rights, where section 7(1) provides that such Bill of Rights is 'a cornerstone of democracy in South Africa' that 'enshrines the rights of all people in our country and affirms the democratic values of human dignity, equality and freedom'.

The application of the Bill of Rights is set out in section 8, which provides that the Bill is applicable to 'all law' and is binding on the legislature, executive, judiciary and 'all organs of state'. Section 8(2) provides that the Bill also binds natural and juristic persons subject to the nature of the right and 'any duty imposed by the right'. There is specific reference to the common law in section 8(3), which provides that, when applying a provision of the Bill of Rights to a natural or juristic person, a court: (a) in order to give effect to a right in the Bill, must apply, or if necessary develop, the common law to the extent that legislation does not give effect to that right; and (b) may develop rules of the common law to limit the right, provided that the limitation is in accordance with section 36(1), to which reference is made below.

The right to equality is addressed in section 9, which provides, in section 9(1), that 'everyone is equal before the law and has the right to equal protection and benefit of the law'. Section 9(2) provides that 'equality includes the full and equal enjoyment of all rights and freedoms', in which regard legislation and other measures are envisaged for the achievement of equality and the protection or advancement of persons 'disadvantaged by unfair discrimination', as set forth in section 9(3), (4) and (5).

The democratic value of human dignity is dealt with in section 10, which states that all persons have 'inherent dignity' and the right to have such dignity 'respected and protected'.

The right to life contained in section 11 simply stipulates that 'everyone has the right to life'. This right is closely linked to the right to freedom and security of the person described in section 12(1) as including the right: (a) not to be deprived of freedom arbitrarily or without just cause; (b) not to be detained without trial; (c) to be free from all forms of violence from either public or private sources; (d) not to be tortured in any way; and (e) not to be treated or punished in a cruel, inhuman or degrading way.

Also, closely linked is the right that everyone has to privacy (section 14), which is extended to not having: (a) their person or home searched; (b) their property searched; (c) their possessions seized; or (d) the privacy of their communications infringed.

The rights of children (persons under the age of eighteen years), which are particularly important, appear in section 28. Section 28(1)(g) provides that a child has the right 'not to be detained except as a measure of last resort' and 'for the shortest appropriate period of time'. A child must be 'kept separately from detained persons over the age of 18 years' and must be 'treated in a manner, and kept in conditions that take account of the child's age'. The overriding provision in this regard, contained in section 28(2), is that 'a child's best interests are of paramount importance in every matter concerning the child'.

A good example of the link between justice, fairness and reasonableness appears from section 33(1), which provides that all persons have 'the right to administrative action that is lawful, reasonable and procedurally fair'. This goes hand in hand with the right of access to courts in section 34, which provides that 'everyone has the right to have any dispute that can be resolved by the application of law decided in a fair public hearing before a court or, where appropriate, another independent and impartial tribunal or forum'.

The rights of arrested, detained and accused persons appear in section 35. Section 35(1)(f) provides that detained persons have the right 'to be released from detention if the interests of justice permit, subject to reasonable conditions'. If they remain in detention for whatever reason, however, they have the right, in terms of section 35(2)(e), 'to conditions of detention that are consistent with human dignity, including at least exercise and the provision, at state expense, of adequate accommodation, nutrition, reading material and medical treatment'.

Persons who stand accused in a court of law have the right, in terms of section 35(3), to a 'fair trial', which includes the right, in terms of section 35(3)(d), 'to have their trial begin and conclude without unreasonable delay'. The aspect of fairness is revisited in section 35(5), which provides that 'evidence obtained in a manner that violates any right in the Bill of Rights must be excluded if the admission of that evidence would render the trial unfair or otherwise be detrimental to the administration of justice'.

These rights may be limited in terms of section 36, but 'only in terms of law of general application to the extent that the limitation is reasonable and justifiable in an open and democratic society based on human dignity, equality and freedom'. It must also take account of 'all relevant factors' including: (a) the nature of the right; (b) the importance of the purpose of the limitation; (c) the nature and extent of the limitation; (d) the relation between the limitation and its purpose; and (e) less restrictive means to achieve the purpose.

The limitation of a right often involves a question of interpretation of the Bill of Rights in terms of section 39. Section 39(1)(a) provides that a court, tribunal or other forum engaged in interpreting the Bill of Rights 'must promote the values that underlie an open and democratic society based on human dignity, equality and freedom'. In doing so it *must*, in terms of section 39(1)(a), consider international law and *may*, in terms of section 39(1)(b), consider foreign law. Section 39(2), again, provides that a court, tribunal or forum, 'when interpreting any legislation, and when developing the common law or customary law' is required to 'promote the spirit, purport and objects of the Bill of Rights'. Section 39(3), in turn, provides that the Bill of Rights 'does not deny the existence of any other rights or freedoms that are recognised or conferred by common law, customary law or legislation, to the extent that they are consistent with the Bill'.

These provisions link up with section 1(a) of the founding provisions and section 7(1) of the Bill of Rights as discussed above. The provisions also link up with section 172(1)(b) regarding the power of a court in constitutional matters to 'make any order that is just and equitable'. This power is consonant with the 'inherent power' of superior courts, in terms of section 173, 'to develop the common law, taking into account the interests of justice'. Section 6 of Schedule 2 of the Constitution therefore requires all judicial officers to swear an oath or solemnly affirm that they 'will be faithful to the Republic of South Africa, will uphold and protect the Constitution and the human rights entrenched in it, and will administer justice to all persons alike without fear, favour or prejudice, in accordance with the Constitution and the law'.

6.   Concluding Observations

Graeco-Roman virtues and values, which originated in Greek philosophy and were transferred to Roman and later law and philosophy by Cicero and other Roman writers, have undoubtedly withstood the test of time and become an enduring part of European and South African common law. As we have seen, our courts and academic writers have acknowledged the importance of these ancient sources and they have become part and parcel of our new constitutional dispensation. Justice, equity or fairness, reasonableness, good faith and good morals or public policy occur in numerous sources of law – from their Graeco-Roman origins, through their lengthy development in Europe and elsewhere, to their application in the new constitutional dispensation in South Africa. The historical basis of the new Constitution and the Graeco-Roman character of many of its provisions should, I believe, be a source of pride for South Africans and, indeed, for the international community that has become linked to ours by those very Graeco-Roman eternal values. Such values continue to have a role in creating an exemplary legal dispensation.

PART V

Cultures of Collecting

Collections tell much about the individuals and societies involved, particularly when the focus moves from the collection itself to the processes of collecting. A wide-ranging survey offers the first overview yet made of South African collections of Graeco-Roman antiquities (**Masters**). Especially interesting is the relation between private and public practices of collecting, as reflected both in national collections (notably those that are now part of the Iziko Museums of South Africa consortium) and in educational ones (notably the Museum of Classical Antiquities at the University of KwaZulu-Natal in Durban). It emerges that both kinds of museum closely reflect private beneficence. The connection between collecting and imperial histories is a familiar theme, with regard to both ancient and modern empires. Cecil John Rhodes is no exception. The translations of classical texts commissioned by Rhodes are a unique collection, which over the decades has been sequestered in imposing red leather binding at Groote Schuur estate – formerly Rhodes' own dwelling and then from 1910 to 1984 the residence of the head of state (**Wardle**). The gift of plaster casts to the city of Cape Town on behalf of another Randlord, Alfred Beit, failed to find a good home and has almost completely gone missing. The story is as strange as it is telling (**Tietze**).

Museum Space and Displacement: Collecting Classical Antiquities in South Africa

SAMANTHA MASTERS[*]

Several South African museums have classical antiquities collections of various sizes and composition; a provisional survey reveals the total number of such collections to be approximately 16.[1] It could be conjectured that the proliferation of such iconically 'European' material in South African museums may have coincided with the arrival of the institution of the museum itself, which formally made an appearance on southern African shores during the era of British colonisation.[2] However, the history of the South African antiquities collections and their reception is not a simple story of a former colony inheriting these dusty tokens of an Empire's wealth and glory. Nor is there a straightforward or trouble-free account of their current meaning in a post-colonial, post-apartheid context.

A neat, cohesive account of these antiquities collections is rendered impossible by several factors, not least of all the complex political and social history of South Africa itself. Adding to the complexity of the story are difficulties around accessing or retrieving information,

---

[*] I would like to acknowledge the generous assistance, in particular, of Esther Esmyol (of Iziko Museums of Cape Town), Anlen Boshoff (previously of Iziko), Anne Mackay of the University of Auckland, New Zealand (previously of the University of Natal) and Adrian Ryan (of the University of KwaZulu-Natal). Other individuals who have helped me to put together the pieces of this puzzle are: John Atkinson, Emile Badenhorst, Johan Binneman, Izak (Sakkie) Cornelius, Sandy de Kock, Alex Duffey, Nkosinathi Gumede, Jessie Maritz, Lalou Meltzer, Alex Nice, David Pike, Mike Lambert, Denis Saddington, David Scourfield, Suzanne Sharland, Warren Snowball, Elke Steinmeyer, Jenny Stretton, John Hilton and Charmaine Wynne.

[1] It is possible that there are other artefacts or small collections belonging to museums that I have not managed to track down. However, the key collections in the country have been covered here and are listed in Tables A and B.

[2] Though there were, in fact, Dutch museum-like forerunners at the Cape. Some 'non-zoological' material was originally part of the collections of a German mercenary soldier Joachim Nickolaus von Dessin (1704–61) from Mecklenburg, who collected 'books, pictures, coins, medals and "curiosities" which he bequeathed to the church'. See Mackenzie 2009: 79. Known as the Dessinian Collection, these items became part of the South African Museum collection in 1861: Summers 1975: 43.

since all of these artefacts or collections were acquired before the expediency of digital record-keeping and the existing article records have not yet been converted to digital databases. Finding the original records and gaining access to them has, in many cases, proved something of a challenge. In many instances the institutional knowledge or oral histories related to collections or artefacts have disappeared along with key curators and scholars. The result is that information is often lacking, anecdotal, haphazard or, in some cases, simply lost.

Amidst and despite such challenges this article represents an important first step in the mapping out of classical antiquities collections in South Africa. This groundwork will be elaborated further and the information will be consolidated as part of an in-depth project on these rich collections which form part of the diverse heritage of this country. Until then, the current article has two, more modest objectives. The first goal is to conduct a survey: to establish which collections exist where, the approximate extent of the collections, where possible to pinpoint some dates and means of acquisition, and finally to describe briefly the current physical status of the artefacts in the collections.

The second goal is to investigate two collections more closely; the Iziko Collection in the city of Cape Town, which previously belonged to the South African Museum (SAM) and then the South African Cultural History Museum (SACHM); and the collection belonging to the Museum of Classical Archaeology, at the University of KwaZulu-Natal (UKZN), Durban. I will explore the unique histories and reception of these two very different collections, briefly tracing how and for what purpose these collections were established. In both case studies, the collections underwent threats of displacement from their museum spaces in the late 1990s and the early 2000s. After the fall of apartheid in 1994, museums as well as other custodians of knowledge, heritage and culture became part of a new national agenda of transformation. The aim of the ANC-led government was to create heritage institutions that could serve all sectors of the South African public.[3] This article will briefly address the question of how policy changes after the fall of apartheid may or may not have affected the South African antiquities collections.

---

[3] Several works examine these issues of heritage practice and memory, e.g. Nuttall and Coetzee 2000 and Yoashida and Mack 2008.

1.   A Survey of Antiquities Collections

Some Boundaries and Definitions

The scope of the material considered in this survey can be defined with reference to three key terms. Firstly, as is commonplace, *classical* antiquities are loosely defined here as items from the Greek or Roman 'worlds' rather than strictly from Greece or Rome.[4] Other antiquities collections do exist in South Africa, including a rich crop of ancient Egyptian and Near Eastern material. These artefacts have largely been omitted from the current study due to practical considerations. However, some objects that have found their way into the classical collections, such as clay lamps, are of unknown provenance and therefore difficult to categorise with certainty.

Secondly, *antiquities* implies original ancient artefacts, which means that while most collections do contain casts and replicas of various kinds, these have not been considered here.[5] Finally, for the purposes of this study *collections* means groups of classical artefacts that are part of public or publicly accessible museum collections. Private collections have not been studied *per se*, though many of the museum collections have been built up around significant pieces or groups of pieces donated or bequeathed by generous private collectors. These private collectors will be seen to have played a pivotal role in the nature and make-up of the museum collections; this is certainly evident in both case studies to varying degrees.

The South African Collections

Tables 9.1 and 9.2 list the 16 collections of classical antiquities of which I am aware. An overview of the collections quickly reveals that there are two distinct types – those belonging to public or state museums on the one hand, and the university or tertiary institutional collections on the other. The tables have been structured to reflect this distinction.

---

[4] Defining boundaries and strict categorisation of material is often a problematic process, as a conversation with Anlen Boshoff (Egyptologist and previously a curator of Iziko) made clearer to me. Since cultural boundaries are often artificial in any case (as Boshoff posed: 'Are artefacts made by Greeks but found in Egypt and made of local material Egyptian or Greek?'), classical antiquities are usually defined a little more broadly as ancient artefacts from the wider Greek or Roman 'worlds'.

[5] See Anne Tietze's paper on the Beit bequest of casts in this volume.

Table 9.1: *South African State Museum Collections*

Museum/collection	Approximate no and type of artefacts	Dates and methods of acquisition	Current status
Iziko Museums of South Africa (previously belonging to the SAM and the SACHM)[6]	Total number unknown, approx. 500–800? A variety of material including fine Attic pottery, Roman glass, 'every day' items such as surgical instruments. Originally included the large Mann Collection of Hispano-Roman coins, recalled from permanent loan in 1991, in view of concerns over political stability.[7]	c. 1825–2000 Bequests, purchases and donations, including that of Mr J. Offord in 1897–99 and especially Mr A. De Pass in 1929/1931	In storage at The Iziko Social History Centre (ISHC), the Old National Mutual Building on Church Square, Cape Town
Albany Museum, Grahamstown[8]	Number unavailable, two small boxes, 'including metal and pottery items'	Information unavailable	All objects in storage at the Albany Museum
Durban Art Gallery[9]	Eight small stone sculptures, including a marble head of Aphrodite (the likely provenance is Egypt)	Dates unavailable, perhaps bequeathed by R. H. Whitwell	On loan to and on display at UKZN Museum of Classical Archaeology
Durban Local History Museum[10]	Approx. 150 items, the majority are small terracotta heads and figurines.	Some donations mentioned include a miniature squat *lekythos* 'from Athens, Greece, presented by Mrs A. (BM) McKinnon in 1953'; 1947 Mrs Baskin	On loan to and on display at UKZN Museum of Classical Archaeology

[6] Sources: SAM catalogue cards; Annual Reports of the South African Museum; numerous conversations with Iziko curators A. Boshoff and E. Esmyol in 2010–11.

[7] Collected by Mann, mainly from Cortigo del Rocadillo, in the bay Algeciras, the site of the ancient town of Carteia. Mann was stationed at Gibraltar in the early nineteenth century. His son 'served at the observatory in Cape Town, leaving his coins to his descendants, who have placed them on loan in the museum': Saddington 1987: 94.

[8] Email correspondence with Dr J. Binneman (28 September 2010) and Ms C. Booth (20 June 2011), Archaeology Department, Grahamstown University.

[9] Email correspondence with Ms J. Stretton, Durban Art Gallery (20 June 2011); University of KwaZulu-Natal, Museum of Classical Archaeology *Loans Register*, 189.

[10] Ibid., 191–92.

Table 9.1: (*Cont.*)

Museum/collection	Approximate no and type of artefacts	Dates and methods of acquisition	Current status
Durban, Natural History Museum[11]	68 objects, including material from Malta and a 'Collection made at Petra, Jordan, in c.1932, by Mr and Mrs Willoughby'[12]	Donations made in 1934, 1947 and 1953	On loan to and on display at UKZN Museum of Classical Archaeology
Bayworld, Port Elizabeth (formerly The Port Elizabeth Museum)[13]	22 objects, including 12 Roman coins; a Roman lamp; a fragment of a Roman sculpture; bronze nails and surgical instruments	1920s–1940s FW Fitzsimons, the first Director of the Museum, collected items on travels as part of 'world histories, curiosities'	On display in the Bayworld Museum as 'Curiosity Corner'
Museum Africa, Johannesburg (formerly The Africana Museum)[14]	20 objects, including Roman and Etruscan lamps, potsherds from Hadrian's Wall, Samian ware fragments and two Greek (?) bronze jugs	Gardner Collection (1923); Smuts Collection (1927)	In storage at Museum Africa
The South African Mint Museum, Johannesburg[15]	Four Roman coins	Unavailable	On display in the South African Mint Museum

Table 9.2: *South African University Collections*

Museum/collection	Approximate no and type of artefacts	Dates and methods of acquisition	Current status
Classics Museum, Rhodes University, Grahamstown[16]	Number unavailable. A variety of objects, including coins, Greek painted	1940s–1990s purchases, donations and bequests. Purchases: 1940s Professor K. D. White collected	On display in the Classics Museum, Classics Section,

[11] Ibid., 188 and 190.   [12] Ibid., 188.

[13] Email correspondence with Mr E. Badenhorst, Bayworld (11 March 2010 and 26 August 2010).

[14] Email correspondence with Dr A. Nice, formerly of University of the Witwatersrand (1 October 2010 and 8 November 2010; *Museum Africa: Artefacts* (list of artefacts, n.d.).

[15] Email correspondence with Ms S. de Kock, South African Mint Museum (25 August 2010).

[16] Email and telephonic correspondence with Mr W. Snowball, Rhodes University, Grahamstown (11 March 2010 and 15 September 2010); Dietrich and Dietrich 1966; three papers by B. C. Dietrich (1971, 1972, 1975); Snowball and Snowball 2005.

Table 9.2: (*Cont.*)

Museum/collection	Approximate no and type of artefacts	Dates and methods of acquisition	Current status
	pottery, writing and surgical instruments	coins; 1970s Professor B. C. Dietrich collected pottery; Professor D. B. Gain (1978–1997) collected everyday items Whitworth and Bower bequests	New Arts Building, Rhodes University
Department of Ancient Studies, University of Stellenbosch, Stellenbosch[17]	170 coins; approx. 20 objects including a Roman jar; (Greek?) *aryballos*; lamps from Palestine; statuette of a Greek goddess from Selinos, Sicily	Donations, bequests? Beginning in the early 1960s	On display in the Department of Ancient Studies, University of Stellenbosch. Coins are viewed by appointment.
Museum of Classical Archaeology, Department of Classics, University of KwaZulu-Natal (UKZN, formerly the University of Natal), Durban[18]	45 coins; +/−54 objects including painted Attic pottery, writing implements, coins, etc.	1976–present Purchases, donations and bequests. Particularly the donations of Mrs Joan Law (1988–current)	On display in the UKZN Museum of Classical Archaeology, Memorial Tower Building
Durban University of Technology (formerly Natal Technikon)[19]	About 40 objects, mainly terracotta figurines, lamps, flasks and a few items of Roman glass	Unavailable	On display at the Durban University of Technology Library

[17] Informal departmental records; Van Stekelenburg 1978; Schneider 2005; University of Stellenbosch, Department of Ancient Studies, *Inventory: coins.*

[18] UKZN, *Museum of Classical Archaeology Accessions Register*; email and telephonic conversations with Dr A. Ryan, UKZN Classics Programme (12 March 2010, 18 August 2010, 17 June 2011); email correspondence with Professor E. A. Mackay, formerly of UKZN Classics Department, now at the University of Auckland (14 March 2010).

[19] UKZN *Loans* 95; email correspondence with Ms N. Gumede, curator, Durban University of Technology (16 September 2010; 18 and 25 January 2011).

Table 9.2: (*Cont.*)

Museum/collection	Approximate no and type of artefacts	Dates and methods of acquisition	Current status
University of KwaZulu-Natal, Pietermaritzburg[20]	Coins	Unavailable	Housed in the Department of Classics
Department of Classics (formerly), University of the Witwatersrand, Johannesburg[21]	60 coins	September/October 1932 Donated by J. Reckie?[22]	Housed in the School of Literature and Language Studies, University of the Witwatersrand
Department of Archaeology (formerly) University of the Witwatersrand[23]	12 objects, including 'antiquarian relics from Roman excavations at Dorchester, England, posted to Johannesburg city librarian in +/− 1937'[24]	No purchases, all donations, dating from 1945 to 1979	Department of Geography, Archaeology and Environmental Studies?
J. A. van Tilburg Museum, University of Pretoria, Van Tilburg Collection[25]	Three objects: a bronze lamp, a marble bust of a young man from Cyrenaika, a glass bottle c. AD 200	November 1976 Bequeathed by Jacob Abraham van Tilburg	On display in the J. A. van Tilburg Museum, Old Arts Building, University of Pretoria

[20] Email correspondence with Professor M. Lambert, University of KwaZulu-Natal, Pietermaritzburg campus (15 September 2010); Gosling 1989.

[21] Email correspondence with Dr A. Nice, formerly of University of the Witwatersrand (1 October 2010 and 8 November 2010); and A. Nice, *Some unpublished Roman Imperial coins in the Department of Classics, University of the Witwatersrand* (unpublished research, n. d.); email correspondence with Professor D. Saddington (23 September 2010).

[22] An inscription on the original display case bears this name and date (Nice, *Imperial coins*, 1).

[23] Dr A. Nice, *Wits Museum of Archaeology* (list of artefacts, n. d.); email correspondence with Professor D. Saddington (23 September 2010).

[24] Nice, *Wits Museum*.

[25] Email correspondence with Professor A. Duffey, curator of the J. A. van Tilburg Collection, University of Pretoria (10 March 2010).

2. Two Case Studies

2.1a The Iziko Collection in Cape Town

The antiquities owned by Iziko Museums of South Africa amount to the most voluminous collection in South Africa.[26] Having first belonged to South Africa's oldest museum, the SAM, this collection of antiquities may also be the oldest in the country. The idea of 'the museum' itself goes back to early modern continental Europe, particularly the *Kunst-* and *Wunderkammer* (cabinets of curiosities) of the late sixteenth century.[27] But, as Mackenzie shows in *Museums and Empire*, Britain exported its own distinctive version thereof to its various colonies. In Australia, New Zealand, Canada, Ceylon (Sri Lanka), Singapore and India museums in the British mould were established under British colonial administration.[28] In the South African context, while there were Dutch settlers prior to the British occupation of the Cape who practised collecting and the display of items, such as trophies of the hunt,[29] the oldest enduring museums were also established during the heyday of British colonial rule, not long after the British officially took control of the Cape in 1806.[30]

The SAM was established in 1825 when the British Governor, Lord Charles Somerset, advertised regarding the need for a museum and appointed Dr Andrew Smith, a medical doctor in the civil service, as its founder curator/director.[31] It was housed in the Old Supreme Court Building, formerly the Slave Lodge of the Dutch East India Company. Other 'colonial' museums followed; the Albany Museum was inaugurated in Grahamstown in 1855, the Port Elizabeth Museum in 1857 and the Durban Natural History Museum in 1887.[32] These museums all acquired classical items over time, though their antiquities collections were never as large as Cape Town's.

---

[26] The volume is difficult to assess accurately for various reasons, some of which were discussed in footnote 3. In addition, since the records are not yet digitised and during the writing of this article the records were in transit from one site to another, it was not possible to study each catalogue card and count the relevant items. Since the catalogue cards are organised not according to collection but by acquisition dates, it would be a laborious task to pull out the catalogue cards of only classical items and count them. However, with no possibility for digital searches, it is currently the only feasible way to gain a more accurate number. Boshoff's estimation is that there are more than 500, but fewer than 1,000, classical items (email correspondence 14 September 2010).

[27] Kaufmann 1997: 166–83.   [28] Mackenzie 2009: 2.   [29] See note 3.

[30] Mackenzie 2009: 79–80.

[31] Andrew Smith was curator/director from 1825–37: Summers 1975: 12.

[32] Mackenzie 2009: 79.

The nineteenth-century arrival of the institution of the museum in South Africa does not necessarily mean that the majority of the classical artefacts were acquired in these early days of collecting. Nor does it mean that antiquities were particularly sought-after, prestige items in the same way that they were in British or European museums. In the decades before the founding of the SAM, Lord Elgin was dismantling and dispatching his famous hoard from the Acropolis of Athens to Britain, where it was acquired amid controversy and has subsequently been displayed by the British Museum. Other British museums were also actively collecting classical antiquities during the 1800s.[33] Though the colonial museums were emulating much of what was happening in the 'metropole', and partly thereby asserting their 'Britishness', they also had their own distinct colonial identities and roles to play.[34]

2.1b Classical Antiquities and the SAM

Assessing the presence and number of classical items in the early SAM collection is difficult since records from this time are incomplete; a catalogue produced by Smith in 1826 is lost, and early registers have also disappeared.[35] The notice in the *Cape Town Gazette and African Advertiser* (1825) nevertheless clearly presents the Museum's original intention to be a museum of natural history, and indigenous natural history at that. Its purpose is stated as 'to showcase the endless diversity and novelty of the *natural products* of the *colony ...*' and stipulates that the museum is 'designed for the reception and classification of the various objects of the *Animal, Vegetable and Mineral Kingdoms*, so that the colonists might become acquainted with the general and local resources *of the Colony*'.[36] This clearly outlines a uniquely colonial and local agenda. It also points to a concept of antiquarianism which is distinctly European; and which has become a powerful scheme of ordering objects and, in turn, of implementing ideas of empire.

Despite this emphatic statement of priority, an impossibly small start-up budget of 2,000 rix-dollars (about £154 at the time, equivalent to about £6,500 in modern currency)[37] led the museum to publically advertise for

---

[33] For example, the Liverpool Museum (now the World Museum), the Ashmolean, the Fitzwilliam, to name a few.

[34] This is one of the general conclusions of Mackenzie 2009.   [35] Summers 1975: 29.

[36] Quoted in Mackenzie 2009: 80–81.

[37] Compare this meagre figure to the 16,000 rix-dollars or £1,230 (equivalent to about £52,000 in modern currency) allocated to the setting up of the South African Library: Summers 1975: 6.

donations to its collections – and to accept virtually anything that it was offered. This practice of almost indiscriminate acceptance of items remained a significant influence on the museum's collecting habits thereafter, strongly affecting the content of its various collections. *The Annual Report* by the South African Institute for 1830 describes the museum's current holdings according to nine categories of natural history and one entitled 'Works of Art';[38] however, no classical items are specifically listed here.

The museum suffered a setback when Smith returned to London in 1837, taking his sizeable private collection with him. From 1837–55 the museum was effectively defunct, and the remaining collection, perhaps containing antiquities, was loaned to the South African College (forerunner of the University of Cape Town) as a teaching collection.[39] However, instigated again by the resolve of a British Governor, the SAM was revived and 'refounded' in 1855 after Sir George Grey (Governor of the Cape Colony from 1854–61) advertised his intention to set up a 'properly appointed museum'.[40]

Two reports to the Trustees of the SAM issued in 1855 by the new curator, Edgar Leopold Layard (curator of the SAM 1855–72), now explicitly mention the donation of classical items. The first report records the donation of 'One Silver Greek Coin; one Gold Persian Coin' by a J. C. Overbeek,[41] while the second mentions still more coins, including two of Alexander the Great,[42] donated by Mr Williams, and 'an excellent Bactrian, or Tudo-Greek [*sic*] coin, found in tope in Sindh presented by Mr. Gibb'.[43] In the same year Mr Gibb also donated tesserae from Pompeii. It is likely that there were other such items already in the collection since Layard's Report to the Trustees the following year mentions both coins and 'Grecian relics' as part of an account[44] of the layout and contents of the museum (by this stage located above Brittain's Bookshop in

[38] Summers 1975: 14.   [39] Summers 1975: 18.

[40] Colonial Office of the Cape of Good Hope, 'Government Notice (No. 25 of 1855)' dated 25 June 1855. Grey (1812–98), at different times governor of South Australia, New Zealand (twice) and the Cape Colony, was a particularly complex figure. A benefactor of cultural enterprises, including a major gift of books and manuscripts to the Cape Town Public Library in 1861, he also had a ruthless side, seen for example in his handling of the aftermath of the Xhosa 'Cattle-killing' of 1856–58. See Belich 2004.

[41] South African Museum, *Report to the Trustees of The South African Museum*, 1855 (1), published as Government Notice no. 185.

[42] 'Two very ancient and curious Coins, bearing the name of Alexander' (South African Museum, *Report to the Trustees of The South African Museum*, 1855 (2).

[43] Ibid. The meaning of 'Tudo-Greek' is mysterious, possibly a misreading of 'Indo-Greek', or 'Pseudo-Greek'.

[44] Ibid.

St George's Street[45]). Though the Greek antiquities in the case are not specifically named, their context of display deserves noting:

In the centre of the room stand the eight figures presented by Mr. Van Reenen, of Constantia,[46] which will ere long be appropriately clothed, as before stated; a case of coins, some of which are rare and valuable, and of great beauty of workmanship; a huge Boa, from the forests of South America; and a case containing a mixed assortment of birds' eggs, Egyptian and Grecian relics, casts of celebrated men, and lastly, an embroidered Greek jacket worn by the Poet Byron, an interesting relic, preserved by an old and faithful domestic, now, like his master, where the weary have rest.[47]

This fascinating description by Layard is invaluable both as an indicator of the nature of the collection in the mid-nineteenth century and of the young museum's approach to its material and collecting. The case in which the antiquities are idiosyncratically displayed alongside birds' eggs and busts of famous men evokes the 'cabinet of curiosities' that was typical of British private collections.[48] The same aura seems characteristic of the entire museum. Other contents include the juxtaposition of animal horns; 'implements of war and the chase'; an aquarium with a (live!) Burmese alligator; a geological collection 'of Colonial Ores' and specimens; shells (more than 1100 species); mounted birds; an African rhinoceros head; skulls; insects, including Lepidoptera (butterflies); models of a suspension bridge; 'Anatomical and Pathological subjects in spirits'; wax models of the human ear and eye; and various bottles containing preserved specimens such as 'fish, annelids, frogs, lizards and snakes'.[49] The museum's policy of mingling classical artefacts with zoological and geological specimens is different from the public museums in Europe, which displayed objects of natural and cultural history in separate rooms.

Under Layard's curatorship, then, and parallel with the collection of indigenous natural material, the acceptance of 'curiosities' or 'exotica' and 'works of art' clearly continued, and it was surely in this category that the

---

[45] According to Summers, this was either at 42 or 44 St George's Street. The museum first occupied one level and then took over two levels: Summers 1975: 33.

[46] Life-size figures of members of local tribes, elaborated below.

[47] South African Museum. *Report to the Trustees of the South African Museum*, 1856, published as Government Notice no. 24; Summers 1975: 33.

[48] British public museums, on the other hand, had long since become more specialised. Thus, the British Museum (Natural History) in Kensington, now the Natural History Museum, was established in 1877 as a branch of the older British Museum. The private collections of the physician, Sir Hans Sloane (1660–1753), which in part reflected his own Caribbean travels, formed the core of the British Museum collection when it was established in 1753.

[49] SAM, *Report to the Trustees* 1856.

ancient 'relics' were classified. Summers asserts that Layard indeed had a genuine interest in curiosities, and that '[i]f he had had his way, the South African Museum would have become a nineteenth-century "Cabinet of Curiosities" as well as a natural history museum'.[50] The nature of the growing collection was surely also related to acquisition methods. Layard's special parliamentary grant 'in aid of formation of the Collection' was a mere £300:[51] almost double that of Smith's, but still grossly inadequate.[52] This was supplemented by what appears to be a grant for expenses (including his own salary of £100)[53] and annual subscriptions of a guinea each. The total income for 1855/56 amounted to £676.[54] Yet only £30 was spent on acquisitions,[55] while more substantial amounts were spent on repairs to the premises, materials and the construction of furniture (cases). The museum's collecting, therefore, was still largely dependent on what its typical donors – affluent, white, colonial gentlemen – were privately collecting and donating. A key factor in this was surely the need to show due deference and gratitude to donors and patrons (including the one guinea subscribers). Rather than risking offence by refusing their gifts the museum may well have accepted all manner of items that it would not have done otherwise.

Either way, during the latter 1800s the museum, which had now moved to an impressive new building in the Botanical Gardens,[56] was better equipped to accommodate its growing collections, and it was also acquiring more 'ethnographic material'. Layard had a broad interest in human cultures and his *Catalogue* (published in 1862) also describes an array of ethnographic items, fairly haphazardly interspersed with the natural history collections (Fig. 9.1).[57]

---

[50] Summers 1975: 28.   [51] Close to £18,000 in modern currency.

[52] Statement of the receipts and disbursements of the Trustees of the South African Museum, SAM *Report to the Trustees*, 1856; Summers 1975: 25.

[53] About £6,000 in modern currency.   [54] About £40,000 in modern currency.

[55] Equivalent to approximately £1,800 in modern currency. The acquisitions are listed as 'Purchase of Specimens', therefore implying items of natural history rather than artefacts.

[56] The South African Museum shared the premises with the South African Library. The design of the new building in the Botanical Gardens, now still the South African Library, was based on the neoclassical Fitzwilliam Museum in Cambridge, and opened to the public by HRH Prince Alfred in 1860 in the presence of Sir George Grey: Summers 1975: 40–41.

[57] 'At the door, is a collection of manufactured articles, ancient as well as modern, pottery, glass and Kafir ornaments, &c.: and on one side of the long case containing the Mammalia is the Entomological collection ... On the Mammalian case are specimens of native vessels in wood and basket work, and Hindoo and Buddistical Deities, a trophy of New Zealand weapons and a suit of Sikh mail. On the walls above the cases are, on the right (or north wall) a series of weapons from Australia and Polynesia. In front of the visitor (still supposing him standing in the entrance) a group composed of the assegais used by various tribes in this colony; to the left, trophies of arms from Madagascar, the East Coast of Africa, China, &c.; while dispersed about

Figure 9.1 Interior of the South African Museum, in the building it shared with the South African Library, ca. 1880.

His earlier description of the museum collections however also reveals an implicit ideological prejudice typical of the age. The descriptions of ethnographic material imply a division into the products of 'civilised' and 'uncivilised' races; the museum minutes of the 1880s use this exact terminology.[58] It is telling that the terminology was changed in 1890 from 'uncivilised' races to 'native' races,[59] clearly revealing the implicit prejudice rather than disguising it. This ideological division persisted well beyond the colonial era in South Africa into the eras of Union (post 1910) and the National Party government (post 1948).

are lesser groups of bows and arrows, used respectively by the Bushmen of South Africa, the Tartar and the Esquimaux of the Frozen North.' (quoted in Summers 1975: 40–41)

[58] Layard uses descriptions such as 'these weapons all exhibit *a great superiority* in manufacture over those of the Bushmen and of the Kafirs, of which the next [case] is constructed, being Assegais of different descriptions, for stabbing, throwing, &c. The next, on the wall facing the visitor is of a very different class to those already described; here are gathered together a few articles manufactured *by ancient and more civilised nations* – the Matchlock of the Chinese . . . the gold inlaid Battle-axes of India, which have probably borne a part in the gorgeous pageantry of her native princes . . .'. SAM, *Report to the Trustees*, 1856. The minutes of the 1880s explicitly differentiate the products of 'civilised races' and the products of 'uncivilised races': Mackenzie 2009: 92.

[59] Mackenzie 2009: 102; South African Museum, *Annual Report to the Trustees* 1890.

Figure 9.2 South African Museum in the Company's Garden, ca. 1917. Postcard by The Valentine & Sons Publishing Co. Ltd, Cape Town.

By 1896 the SAM had commissioned, built and moved to a yet more impressive building in the upper part of the Company's Gardens, its current location (Fig. 9.2). The new building cost a massive £28,000,[60] and the budget was now approaching £2,000;[61] Mackenzie attributes the museum's enhanced fortunes to the diamond trade at Kimberly.[62] No longer sharing space with the South African Library, the SAM was now well established as an important colonial natural history museum. The *Annals of the South African Museum* of 1898 describe its reorganisation into six departments: Vertebrates, Land Invertebrates, Marine Invertebrates, Entomology, Geology and Minerology, and Anthropology.

Under the directorships of Louis Albert Péringuey (1906–24) and Edwin Leonard Gill (1925–42), the first half of the twentieth century brought an ever-increasing interest in ethnography and cultures at the SAM, in particular South African prehistory involving the San people ('Bushmen') and their rock art. Two significant appointments in the 1930s signalled the importance of this area of interest: that of A. J. H. Goodwin as Honorary Keeper of Prehistoric Archaeology in 1930 and Margaret Shaw in 1933, the first permanent appointment in Ethnography.[63] However, it was not only the products of local peoples that were avidly collected, namely pots, beaded

[60] Equivalent to approximately £1,675,000 in modern currency.
[61] Equivalent to approximately £120,000 in modern currency.   [62] Mackenzie 2009: 89; 101.
[63] Summers 1975: 138–9.

Figure 9.3 The so-called 'Bushman diorama' in the South African Museum.

items, snuff boxes and the like, but the peoples themselves.[64] They were studied, cast, dressed 'authentically' and later displayed 'in their natural habitats' – as part of a diorama. In retrospect, such a mode of display is unnervingly similar to the way in which mounted animal specimens were curated.[65]

This now controversial ethnographic project of casting indigenous races and mounting them in the museum space was extremely popular in the early 1900s. The 'Bushman' figures created by Drury between circa 1906 and 1927 would become one of the museum's key attractions for much of the century. In the 1950s the figures were repositioned in an 'idealised diorama, depicting a nineteenth-century hunter-gatherer encampment in the Karoo' (Fig. 9.3).[66] The practice of human casting was revived under the directorship of Thomas Henry Barry (1964–84) and in May 1973 a new display of the Cape Nguni tribes was opened to the public.[67] This kind of objectification and display of the indigenous people of Southern Africa remains a sensitive discussion point in the

[64] Layard was the first curator to receive full-scale manufactured 'figures' of local tribespeople into the museum (eight figures donated by van Reenen in SAM *Report to the Trustees*, 1856). In this regard, he certainly was not the last, since this practice continued until as late as the 1970s.

[65] Summers, writing in 1975, notes that the casts 'are so lifelike that it is sometimes difficult to convince visitors that the Museum does not go in for human taxidermy!' (Summers 1975: 104).

[66] Davison 2000: 144.   [67] Summers 1975: 206.

reconciliation process that is still unfolding in post-apartheid South Africa. The history of these figures attests to the stereotyped 'othering' of indigenous peoples by the colonial regime, and it also reflects the rising scientific racism that, while not unique to South Africa, certainly validated the political ideologies of the apartheid regime in the twentieth century.[68]

In the first decades of the twentieth century there was also clearly a developing interest in antiquity, archaeology and social history. The *Annual Report* of 1906 explicitly states a desire to develop the 'ethnological *and antiquarian* side of the collection'.[69] The SAM contributed to the Egypt Exploration Fund (EEF), whereby excavations in Egypt were funded in exchange for ancient artefacts from these sites.[70] Artefacts were also received from the British School of Archaeology in Egypt (BSAE)'s excavations in Tarkhan (Flinders Petrie's excavations), though, as Boshoff asserts, there is no mention of any financial contribution from the SAM and so these ought to be regarded as donations.[71]

There was apparently no such arrangement with Greek or Roman excavations. The biggest influx of classical material into the collection of the SAM occurred in the form of the Alfred Aaron de Pass donations, during the directorship of Gill (1925–42).[72] De Pass' grandfather arrived in the Cape Colony from Britain in1846 during the frontier wars. From humble beginnings – his grandfather first opened a boot and shoe shop in Cape Town – the family prospered, with interests in guano, diamonds, and sugar in Natal, and at one point even owning the strip of coast from Lüderitz to Baker's Cove in South West Africa (subsequently lost by the German encroachment).[73] Alfred's great nephew writes that 'Alfred, although astute and competent [at business] decided in 1888 to retire and devote himself to collecting and connoisseurship. His father's gain from evil-smelling yet valuable guano was devoted by Alfred to beauty'.[74]

---

[68] The so-called 'Bushman' diorama was updated in 1989 in an attempt to contextualise the real people behind the casts. An exhibition curated by Pippa Skotnes at the South African National Gallery entitled 'Miscast: negotiating KhoiSan history and material culture' (14 April–14 September 1996), that set out to interrogate this process of human casting and objectification of race was met with heated controversy from the KhoiSan community. The diorama exhibit is currently closed and the cast figures remain in a(nother) state of limbo, as the SAM deliberates over what to do with these controversial 'artefacts'.

[69] South African Museum, *Annual Report to the Trustees of the South African Museum*, 1906.

[70] South African Museum, Minutes of the South African Museum 1911; and 1929. Mackenzie 2009: 92; Summers 1975: 144; Boshoff 1995: 105.

[71] Boshoff 1995: 105.   [72] Gill, 'Foreward' (1934).   [73] Philips 1981: 5.   [74] Ibid.

Plate 1 (= **Figure 1.6**) Cyril Coetzee, *T'kama-Adamastor* (1999): oil on canvas, 8.64 m × 3.26 m, William Cullen Library, University of the Witwatersrand, Johannesburg. Photograph by Russell Scott.

Plate 2 (= **Figure 1.20**) Luciana Acquisto, President Zuma as Cupid: cartoon in the style of Zapiro, painted on a flower pot. Original artwork, University of Stellenbosch, 2010. Courtesy of Samantha Masters.

Plate 3 (= **Figure 2.1**) Architect unknown, Number 90, First Road, Hyde Park, Johannesburg, 2011. A newly built house in the upmarket Johannesburg suburb of Hyde Park, this project reveals the contemporary suburban taste for 'Tuscan' styling. Courtesy of Federico Freschi.

Plate 4 (= **Figure 4.3**) Constance Penstone, watercolour depicting Malay bride. Dust jacket of Dorothea Fairbridge's novel, *Piet of Italy* (1913).

Plate 5 (= **Figure 5.2**) North façade, Voortrekker Monument. Photograph by Russell Scott.

Plate 6 (= **Figure 5.11**) Hall of Heroes, south and west walls, Voortrekker Monument, 2012. Photograph by Russell Scott.

Plate 7 (= **Figure 9.4**) Attic red-figure *stamnos* by the Chicago Painter, ca. 450 BC, one of the most important pieces donated by De Pass.

Plate 8 (= **Figure 11.4**) The Rhodes Collection, Groote Schuur Estate. Photograph by Paul Weinberg.

Plate 9 (= **Figure 15.3**) 'A map of the Cape of Good Hope with its true situation'. Johannes Nieuhof, London, 1703. 27 × 35 cm. From the Dr Oscar I. Norwich Collection of maps of Africa and its islands, 1486 – ca. 1865 (NOR 0209), Stanford University Libraries. Courtesy of Stanford University Libraries.

Plate 10 Scene from Monteverdi's *Il ritorno d'Ulisse*, Venice 2008: Telemachus and Penelope with Ulisse 1 and Ulisse 2. Courtesy of Handspring Puppet Company.

Plate 11 Scene from Monteverdi's *Il ritorno d'Ulisse*, Venice 2008: Ulisse 1 and Ulisse 2. Courtesy of Handspring Puppet Company.

Plate 12 (= **Figure 18.5**) Peter Clarke, *Annunciation* (1987). Courtesy of the late Peter Clarke.

Retiring at the early age of 27, De Pass dedicated his time to the informal study and appreciation of art.[75] He donated munificently. Museums and galleries in Britain (where he had a house at Falmouth, Cornwall) also benefitted from his generosity.[76] His greatest local act of benefaction was the complete refurbishment of the Groot Constantia Manor House, which had been laid waste by the fire of 1925. He also donated paintings to the South African National Gallery.[77] From 1929–31 he donated to the SAM; some objects were bought specifically for the museum and others came from his private collection of *objets d'art* which he kept at Falmouth.[78] The latter included Greek pieces, 'early Chinese productions in pottery and jade', 'beautiful examples of Persian work in porcelain and earthenware', 'Babylonian cylinder seals, examples of Roman glass, and [...] four Moorish copper bowls'.[79]

This rich and valuable donation of over 100 objects in total was gratefully and enthusiastically received by Gill. They were set up in the museum (with the help of De Pass himself, apparently) in a room which became known as the De Pass Room.[80] The fine classical material included several high-quality black- and red-figure Greek vases; of particular value is the exquisite stamnos by the Chicago Painter of the mid-fifth century BC, a column krater showing Hephaistos' return to Olympus, and a late red-figure *hydria* with Dionysos, maenads, Eros and satyrs (Fig. 9.4 and Plate 7). Other smaller cups, *lekythoi*, an *askos, kyathos, kothon* and *oinochoe* make the collection representative of several vessel shapes in both the red- and black-figure techniques.[81] Two Etruscan bucchero *kantharoi* and a few Tanagra figurines were also included in the gift, and the Roman glass collection contains three vessels from Pompeii, one of which is described in the catalogue as 'encrusted with lava'.[82]

Though appreciated, the Greek and Roman artefacts were, however, unsolicited. While preparing an exhibition of artefacts from the ruins at Great Zimbabwe which included fragments of Chinese and Persian pottery, Gill had in fact asked De Pass if he had any Chinese or Persian ware to show what such pieces may have looked like intact.[83] But he had not, it

---

[75] Ibid.

[76] He donated to the National Portrait Gallery, the Tate, the National Gallery, the Royal Institution of Cornwall, the Bristol Museum, the Plymouth City Museum and the Fitzwilliam Museum in Cambridge, ibid., 5–6).

[77] Tietze 1995.   [78] Gill 1934: 3.   [79] Ibid.   [80] Summers 1975: 145.

[81] In addition to Gill's initial catalogue of the collection produced in 1934, John Boardman and Maurice Pope produced a specialist catalogue for the museum entitled *Greek Vases in Cape Town* (1961).

[82] Gill 1934: 20, artefact no. 137, Fig. 12.   [83] Gill 1934: 3.

Figure 9.4 Attic red-figure *stamnos* by the Chicago Painter, ca. 450 BC, one of the most important pieces donated by De Pass. (A black and white version of this figure will appear in some formats. For the colour version, please refer to the plate section.)

seems, specifically requested Greek or Roman material. It was De Pass himself who noticed the museum had what he perceived to be a dearth of Greek and Egyptian objects; according to Gill, De Pass 'felt that [the existing collection was] by no means adequate as samples of the art of these two great civilisations'.[84] It seems that before the influx of these items there was no deliberate and explicit policy on the museum's part to collect classical antiquities. They were certainly very 'nice to have', though, and this particularly generous donation from the man who was described as the 'fairy godfather of South African galleries'[85] may have

[84] Ibid. The existing collection by this point included some Greek painted pottery items, donated by J. Offord. The Offord collection arrived in South Africa between 1897 and 1899; the acquisition cards show that at least 20 classical items were donated in 1899, including *lekythoi, aryballoi* and similar smaller pottery items (these include the SACHM accession nos 1365–1410).

[85] *Cape Argus*, 2 July 1948.

sparked a later interest in collecting antiquities to add to the now decent core collection.

In the 1930s and 40s other such 'fairy godfathers' made similar donations or bequests from their own private collections (though not of classical antiquities), and the De Pass gift therefore sits within a broader pattern of such benefaction. In 1948 Judge Reginald Percy Basil Davis bequeathed a collection of about 100 exquisite and valuable Chinese ceramics, which were exhibited in the De Pass Room.[86] Humphrey John Talbot's bequest of various items of furniture and *objets d'art* amounting to 534 pieces was given so that 'South Africans could appreciate the appearance of the interior of an English 'stately home'.[87] Surprisingly, Talbot had never ventured to South Africa, and his gesture remains a curious act of benefaction. Harry Robinson of Cape Town owned a collection of Malayan silver from Singapore, which was given to the museum by his widow on his death.[88] Mackenzie adds that the 1930s and 40s was an era 'when wealthy businessmen and professionals, who had collected in earlier years, were dying and sought to commemorate themselves by placing their passions in the public domain'.[89]

It had been thought as early as the 1930s that there was a need for a separate museum to house the growing 'Cultural History' collections, making them distinct from 'Natural History' collections and in the 1960s this long-held plan came to fruition. The 'Historical collections' (various artefacts from Dutch and English colonial history as well as ancient civilisations) were moved from the SAM in 1963 to the new SACHM in the Old Supreme Court Building, the former Slave Lodge. In 1969 the SACHM became its own legal entity.[90] The most peculiar aspect of this split between Natural and Cultural History was the fact that the ethnographic collections, i.e. the history of the pre-Colonial and indigenous cultures of Southern Africa, remained part of Natural History. This division of material has been seen to mirror the deliberate polarisation between, on the one hand, the 'natives' as perpetual children of nature, wild and uncultivated, belonging to the landscape, and at the other end of the spectrum, the (white) colonial historical past (aligned with ancient civilisations), imagined to be civilised or 'cultured'.[91] Even unconsciously, such thinking clearly reflected and supported the prevailing apartheid ideology.

After Dr van der Meulen, the first Director of the SACHM, left to take up an international appointment, the post was filled by Dr W. Schneewind (Director 1966–81). These were politically torrid times in South Africa, and

[86] Mackenzie 2009: 97–98; Summers 1975: 171; Grobbelaar 1988. [87] Olivier 1992.
[88] Summers 1975: 171. [89] Mackenzie 2009: 98. [90] Summers 1975: 178.
[91] Mackenzie 2009: 91.

Figure 9.5 Vitrines from the antiquities galleries, South African Cultural History Museum, 1980s, now Slave Lodge, Iziko Museums of South Africa.

the effect on the SACHM cannot be fully described or assessed here. Regarding antiquities however, the museum continued to acquire material of classical provenance (Figs 9.5–6); donations and bequests continued to arrive, though never again on the scale of the De Pass gift. In the 1970s and 80s in particular the acquisition cards show that the museum made several purchases of mainly small – and therefore not extremely costly – items that would supplement the museum's already decent range of 'everyday life' items, and flesh out certain classes of artefacts.[92] For example, a number of Roman glass vessels were purchased in the 1970s from Folio Fine Art and in the same decade several other small items such as a fish plate, a Roman incense shovel, an athlete's strigil and some pottery items were purchased from Charles Ede in London.[93] The Bulletins of the SACHM from 1980–93 include details of selected recent acquisitions; several purchases are mentioned in these years, including a terracotta bust of Isis-Selene of the first century AD from Alexandria (Fig. 9.7).[94]

Large-scale political and social changes in the early 1990s impacted also the SACHM. The fall of apartheid and the arrival of democracy, officially

[92] The earliest purchase of a classical item that I have managed to track down is a Roman strainer, purchased from Folio Fine Art, London on 26 May 1970, accession number 70/116.
[93] SAM/SACHM accession cards.
[94] These are only a sample of the acquisitions, so these figures are not representative of all purchases made, nor is it possible to calculate a percentage of items of classical provenance to compare with other areas of cultural history.

Figure 9.6 Remembering Slavery: part of the permanent exhibit at the Slave Lodge.

Figure 9.7 Isis-Selene, terracotta figurine, ca. first century AD. Social History Collections, Iziko Museums of South Africa.

ushered in with the historic first democratic election in 1994, heralded transformation in many areas of society including heritage institutions. The new ANC-led government set out to redefine and 're-imagine' the cultural heritage of the country, replacing the 'Eurocentric' vision held by the previous governments with one that embraces the diverse heritage of all the peoples of the country.[95] The new vision is epitomised in the then Deputy President, Thabo Mbeki's landmark statement, 'I am an African';[96] the focus is on an Afrocentric and non-racial understanding of heritage and culture. This emphasis is further reflected in the new Constitution of the Republic of South Africa, in the country's motto *!ke e: /xarra //ke* ('people who are diverse unite')[97] and Coat of Arms, both launched in 2000, and various other new national policies and laws that were drafted, discussed and promulgated in the 1990s and 2000s.[98]

Libraries, archives, art galleries and museums were all affected by this scrutiny and rewriting of heritage policies. In 1993, the cover of the SACHM *Bulletin* (no. 14) featured a recent acquisition (Fig. 9.8); the complex and vividly colourful painted earthenware 'Tea Party' by KwaZulu-Natal ceramic artist, Bonnie Ntshalintshali.[99] Inside, however, the editorial emphatically states that 'during the last decade the Museum has moved away from the policy of only concentrating on the decorative arts. This shift in emphasis does not, however, in any way mean a disregard for collections such as the early Chinese ceramics . . . this collection is still nationally and internationally recognised as one of our most important holdings'. Only some of the Chinese ware is still on display in the building which was previously the SACHM, but which reverted to being named the Slave Lodge in 1998 to memorialise its prior identity as the slave quarters and prison of the Dutch East India Company.

---

[95] A useful summary of this is found in Bredekamp 2001. Professor Bredekamp was the CEO of Iziko until his retirement in 2010.
[96] Mbeki 1996.
[97] A saying in the language of the /Xam Khoisan people: Bredekamp 2001: 1–3.
[98] Much policy was written and several laws were passed in the 1990s and 2000s after the birth of the new democracy. For example, the White Paper on Arts, Culture and Heritage, Department of Arts, Culture, Science And Technology (1996); Amareswar Galla's discussion document (1996); National Archives of South Africa Act (1996), amended in 2001 as the National Archives and Records Service of South Africa (NARS) Act; National Arts Council Act, (Act 56 of 1997); Cultural Institutions Act (1998); National Heritage Resources Act, (Act 25 of 1999) which replaced the National Monuments Act; National Heritage Council Act (Act 11 of 1999); and the Heritage Transformation Charter (drafted in 2008).
[99] SACHM *Bulletin* No. 93. Bonnie Ntshalintshali was born on the Ardmore Farm, near Winterton, KwaZulu-Natal in 1967. She was a prizewinning ceramicist whose career and life was cut short when she succumbed to an HIV-related illness in 1999, Artthrob (1999).

Figure 9.8 Bonnie Ntshalintshali, 'Tea Party', painted earthenware, 1993. Iziko South African National Gallery, Cape Town.

Legislation passed in 1998 reorganised the heritage institutions of South Africa in various ways; certain institutions in Cape Town were merged to create the Southern Flagship Institution, matched by a similar process in Gauteng that produced the Northern Flagship Institution.[100] In 2001 the Southern Flagship Institution was renamed Iziko Museums

[100] These institutions were the Michaelis Collection; the South African Cultural History Museum; the South African Museum; the South African National Gallery; and the William Fehr Collection. The Northern Flagship Institution amalgamated the National Cultural History Museum; the South African National Museum for Military History; and the Transvaal Museum. Cultural Institutions Act, 1998, Act No. 119, 1998 (6) 2.

Figure 9.9 The Slave Lodge, formerly the South African Cultural History Museum, Cape Town.

of Cape Town, then broadened in 2012 to Iziko Museums of South Africa. *Iziko* is the *isiXhosa* word for 'hearth' and the name was chosen to represent the institution as '... both a hub of cultural activity, and a central place for gathering together South Africa's diverse heritage'.[101] After the emergence of Iziko the exhibits in the Slave Lodge were completely reorganised between 2003 and 2006. The lower floors (that had previously housed the classical and Egyptian antiquities galleries) became 'a slave memory centre', the aim of which is to render the neglected history of slavery at the Cape for the first time (Figs 9.9–10, cf. 1.2).[102] The new temporary exhibitions bring to life – and back into South African memory – a prior era of colonial exploitation; that of the Dutch East India Company's activities at the Cape. Many of the social history collections previously housed in the SACHM space were redistributed to other sites around Cape Town or put into storage. The classical Greek and Roman galleries were necessary casualties of

---

[101] www.iziko.org.za/static/landing/about-us.

[102] Iziko Museums of Cape Town (2006). Between 1679 and 1811 the building was a prison that housed around 9,000 inmates, consisting of slaves, convicts and the mentally ill.

Figure 9.10 Remembering Slavery, poster in the foyer of the Slave Lodge.

this new recentered approach; as the current Director of the Social History Collections, Lalou Meltzer, explains:

The decision to tell the story of slavery which had not been done in the old SA Cultural History Museum, despite the building being the most significant building associated with slavery in South Africa, was the motivation behind dismantling the older displays, including the 'the ancient world'. As a part solution to removing these important collections from display a significant proportion was later lent to Stellenbosch University and a small part of ancient Egypt redisplayed upstairs where the educators in the museum continue to use the collection. Thematic identities for our museum are being reassessed and the next few years will see reevaluations of our various twelve sites. However, meanwhile, we aim to incorporate objects in our collections, as relevant, in changing temporary displays.[103]

As Ms Meltzer describes above, Iziko was unable to keep the ancient collections on permanent exhibition owing to the need to render a more topical and previously neglected history: that of slavery.[104] They are effectively displaced by the slavery exhibit; part of a general plan to represent the history of the country anew. That goal is laudable enough, but it might also be true that the antiquities were simply in the wrong place at the wrong time. The lower level of the building was transformed into the slavery exhibit; the upper levels remain a semi-remnant of the old SACHM, with an Egyptian gallery, a selection of colonial toys, weapons, English, Dutch, Russian and Malaysian silver, clocks and a ceramics gallery containing ancient Chinese pieces alongside Linn ware and contemporary South African ceramics. Bonnie Ntshalintshali's 'Tea Party' has spent some time here as well.

As Ms Meltzer also points out, a selection of the classical antiquities, including the important Greek *stamnos*, were given new life as part of a successful loan agreement to the University of Stellenbosch's Sasol Art Museum. After being in storage for two years at Iziko's Old National Mutual Building on Church Square (Fig. 9.11), some pieces were selected for the exhibition 'Living Antiquity' (2005–07), followed by the smaller 'Containing Antiquity' (2007–11, Fig. 9.12).[105] Such loan exhibitions are, of course, temporary by nature and the space was recalled in September 2011. The antiquities were packed up once more and returned to the facility where they were stored between 2003 and 2005.

In their six-year absence, the Old National Mutual Building had been renovated to properly accommodate the over 250,000 Iziko social history artefacts that are not currently on display (Fig. 9.11). The building now houses the Iziko Social History Centre (ISHC), with library, record room, archives, offices and storage space, where a new project is finally unfolding:

---

[103] Email correspondence with L. Meltzer (15 September 2010).

[104] Slavery became particularly popular in the 2000s, especially approaching the bicentenary of the abolition of the transatlantic slave trade. Some examples of slavery exhibits or museums are: The International Slavery Museum (Liverpool, UK) opened in August 2007; London, Sugar and Slavery at the Museum of London (Docklands, London) 10 November 2007 to 28 February 2009; 'Breaking the chains, the fight to end slavery' 2007; Brown University, Providence, RI curated four exhibitions on slavery in 2007, including 'Venus in Chains: representations of sex and slavery in the Caribbean Basin'.

[105] Masters 2008.

Figure 9.11 Iziko Social History Centre, Church Square, Cape Town, with Anton van Wouw's statue of Jan Hendrik ('Onze Jan') Hofmeyr, grandfather of later deputy prime minister, in the foreground. Figs 1.2 and 1.13 depict the same location from different points.

Figure 9.12 *Containing Antiquity* exhibition, Sasol Art Museum, Dr Samantha Masters with students of the Department of Ancient Studies, University of Stellenbosch.

the merging of the collections of 'indigenous' ethnographic objects previously in the holdings of the SAM and those previously held by the
SACHM as items of 'cultural history'. All items of social history and
ethnography will now be kept in this facility. Almost fifty years after
Cultural History and Natural History were separated, and seventeen
years after the fall of apartheid, the pottery of ancient Greece, figurines
from Egypt, ceramics from China, English silver and snuff boxes, head rests
and pottery of local indigenous African peoples will finally be allowed to
cohabit once more.

2.2   A University Teaching Collection: The University of KwaZulu-Natal, Durban

The antiquities collection belonging to the Museum of Classical
Archaeology, University of KwaZulu-Natal (UKZN) – previously the
University of Natal, Durban (UND) – was established in a vastly different
era from the 'colonial' museums. It is in fact the youngest museum to begin
collecting classical antiquities; the museum's first purchase was an
Athenian wine-cup, bought in 1975 or 1976 by Professor B. X. de Wet,
then Head of the Department of Classics, from the Swiss antiquities
dealership, Münzen und Medaillen in Basel.[106] Since that first acquisition,
the museum has continued to receive material through all three normal
avenues: donations, bequests and acquisitions. This collection is, as far as
I am aware, the only one that is growing; the Museum, currently under the
curatorship of Ms Szerdi Nagy, is the only South African museum still
making acquisitions of classical antiquities.

From the outset, the Museum of Classical Antiquities had a well-
defined goal, focus and target market. Its goals were educational (and
ideological), its focus was the ancient world – initially primarily the
'classical world' – and the target audience was mainly students.
The museum aimed to bring the world of antiquity to life for students
enrolled in departmental courses (Ancient Greek, Latin and Classical
Civilisations) and to provide a tangible link between their contemporary
world and antiquity.[107] Professor E. A. Mackay, the curator of the
museum (1988–2001) and Head of Department (1990–2000) elucidates
this goal, describing how '[a] modern thumb can be placed over a thumb-
print left accidentally by a potter twenty-five or more centuries ago, and
antiquity acquires a historical reality'.[108] This primary goal of course

---

[106] UKZN, *Accessions*, 1; Accession no 1976.1; Mackay 1992.   [107] Ibid.   [108] Ibid.

never excluded the availability of the museum as a resource for the larger academic and local community. Tours of schoolchildren and interested parties were – and still are – conducted by staff and senior students of the department on arrangement.

In the 1970s, the UND Classics Department was housed on the second floor of the Memorial Tower Building, King George V Avenue. It was here in 1976 that this first purchase was displayed alongside replicas of ancient artefacts, in a glass cabinet in the open corridor of the department.[109] When Dr Mackay arrived at the university in 1978, this drinking cup was still the only genuine antiquity in the collection. In 1980–83 several acquisitions were made to complement this piece, many of which were from the antiquities dealer, Charles Ede in Brook Street, London. These years saw the purchase of a *hydria* from Campania, a Roman glass jug and a Corinthian *kotile* in 1980, a black-figured *lekythos* in 1981,[110] and in 1983 a high-quality fragment of an Athenian black-figure lip cup, attributed to the Centaur Painter.[111]

The growing collection – not yet actually called a museum – was moved to the ground level of the Memorial Tower Building when the Classics Department took over the space previously occupied by the university's Law Library.[112] The department was designed, by the architecturally adept Professor de Wet, around a large central foyer through which all students and visitors to the department would necessarily pass to reach the lecturers' offices and other rooms. This generous foyer became the site of the new Museum of Classical Archaeology, officially named thus after the acquisition of the first large amphora in 1988 (an Attic black-figure neck amphora) rendered the collection 'sufficiently big and impressive to be called a Museum'.[113]

At about the same time Dr Mackay officially became the Museum's curator and the acquisitions of the decade 1980–90 reflect her particular specialisation and interest in painted Attic pottery. A splendid though fragmentary Attic black-figure amphora by the Princeton Painter, acquired in 1990 during her curatorship, remains a cornerstone of the collection.[114] This vase also demonstrates her prudent approach to acquisitions, specifically tailored to a teaching collection with budgetary constraints. Under Mackay's curatorship the museum purchased items according to the

[109] E. A. Mackay email communication (14 March 2010).   [110] UKZN *Accessions* 1980.2–4.
[111] UKZN *Accessions* 1983.9; Mackay 1993a: 149.
[112] The Law Library moved next door to the Howard College Building.
[113] UKZN *Accessions* 1987.17; Mackay 1992: 140.
[114] UKZN *Accessions* 1990.30; Mackay 1993b: 104–14.

philosophy that 'for the money it is better to exhibit a substantial or typical fragment of a work by a significant artist rather than a virtually intact piece which is of poor quality in the potting and/or painting'.[115]

The inauguration of the Museum in 1988 brought three significant loan exhibitions from other Durban museums; the Durban Art Museum offered on loan eight small scale stone sculptures;[116] and various assortments of material were loaned by the Natal Technikon;[117] the Durban Natural History Museum;[118] and the Durban Local History Museum.[119] Several display cases were also supplied on long-term loan by the Natural History Museum. It was, says Mackay, 'as though every other week there would be another offer of antiquities on loan'.[120] These enthusiastic loans may well have signalled a corresponding decline of enthusiasm for these collections in the city museums. The museum's goal of building up 'a small, but representative collection of original ancient art works and artefacts'[121] was greatly bolstered by the loans, which resulted in the influx of items from a broader geographical and chronological range. This included objects from the Mediterranean, North Africa and Egypt, and the Roman Empire, and most of this material is still present in the collection on extended long-term agreements.

Another significant gift was a donation of three full-size plaster casts of three famous Greek sculptures by the Government of Greece in 1995 (Fig. 9.13).[122] The core collection was also boosted by fairly regular donations from private individuals such as the stalwart benefactor, Ms Joan Law, who also first donated objects around the time of the inauguration of the Museum.[123] Ms Law is still a regular benefactor: in 1996–97 her donations of funds allowed the museum to purchase a papyrus fragment and a metal stylus, a new area of interest that lead to a special exhibition of paraphernalia related to ancient writing from the sixth century BC onwards.[124]

The late 1990s brought a crisis to the museum. As the teaching collection belonging to a department of classics, the museum owed its

[115] Mackay 1993a: 152.   [116] UKZN *Loans* 1988.0.1–8.
[117] UKZN *Loans* 1989.J.1–39, the material was collected in 1990.
[118] UKZN *Loans* 1989.L.148–167.   [119] UKZN *Loans* 1989.M.1–147.   [120] Mackay 1992: 140.
[121] Ibid.
[122] This donation was facilitated by the then Greek Consul in Durban, Ilias Fotopoulos. The specific pieces were the Peplos kore, Ball players' relief and Victory untying her sandal. See Mackay 1995. These casts complemented the gift of three other casts of ancient Greek heads, donated to the department by a tour group that was led around Crete, Sicily and Greece by Professor de Wet and Dr Mackay in 1984. E. A. Mackay, email communication 4 August 2011.
[123] UKZN *Accessions* 1989, 19–21.   [124] Mackay 1998.

Figure 9.13 The University of KwaZulu-Natal Museum of Classical Archaeology, Durban, 2014.

existence to the existence of that department. After the fall of apartheid, South African universities, like museums, were also subject to intense ideological debate and there was a general call for higher education institutions to re-centre their vision. The need to transform affected various universities and classics departments in South Africa in vastly different ways, and again the topic stretches well beyond the ambit of the current article.[125] This was, however, an era of 'rationalisation' at the University of Natal and the Classics Department, which by this stage had become the Classics Programme, narrowly survived an ideologically-driven attempt to close it down. The Museum of Classical Archaeology survived, and it also managed to retain its space. Attempts to relocate the entire department followed; a proposal to move the department to much smaller premises upstairs in the building, unsuitable for the conservation or display of artefacts, was unsuccessful.[126] Had that come about, the artefacts owned by the department would have had to be stored or sold,

---

[125] For example, the Classics Department of the University of the Witwatersrand was closed in 2001. Another result of this era of rationalisation was the large-scale mergers of various higher education institutions across the country.

[126] There might have been space to display part of the collection, but the greatest concern was the serious problem (in the hot and humid Durban climate) of climate control. The space proposed was in the top level of the MTB building, right up under the roof in the north wing, with no insulation from the heat.

but the bulk would have been returned to the owners or donors of the pieces.[127] The department remained *in situ* but subsequently lost sections of its office and seminar room space. The museum remained intact. Given this complex situation, it could be argued that the very existence of the museum influenced the decision to allow the department to remain both in existence and *in situ*.

With Professor Mackay's departure in 2001, Dr Adrian Ryan became the new curator of the antiquities, though no acquisitions were made again until 2004. In that year five Roman coins[128] were purchased – again through funds donated by Ms Law – and other purchases have been made since. The museum, led since 2015 by Szerdi Nagy, is still housed in the original foyer space designed for this purpose in 1988, and the collection is still growing, though at a slower pace than before. This is currently, as far as I know, the only museum in South Africa that continues to make acquisitions of items of classical provenance, and it continues to operate according to its original mandate, namely to serve as a university teaching collection.

3. Preliminary Conclusions: Museum Space and Displacement

A museum constitutes a prized and even sanctified space: it gives authority or ideological preference to particular objects, or intangible items of memory, which signals their importance – at that time and place and for a particular audience. For the SAM and SACHM, the collecting of antiquities was seldom a matter of deliberate policy. Items that resulted mainly from acts of benefaction were subject to severe limits in their prominence and prestige value, seldom, if ever, becoming more than a sideshow to any museum. What makes the story of classical collecting in the SAM and SACHM interesting is its relation to natural history and ethnographic displays. There can be no doubt that natural history and ethnography, including the controversial diorama figures, have been far more important to the SAM's curators and visitors.

At UKZN, on the other hand, the deliberate collection of classical pieces was the goal from the outset, and the museum received the status of a main attraction in and for the department. The collections successfully engaged a captive audience of students who were there with the explicit purpose to

---

[127] E. A. Mackay email communication (14 March 2010).   [128] Ryan and Gosling 2003.

interact with the ancient world. It brought (and still brings) aspects of that world to life in concrete form, particularly for students enrolled in Classics or Classical Civilisations courses, where the museum's contents provide ideal original material for close academic study.

The displacement of the antiquities collections from the Slave Lodge and the threat to the space experienced by the UKZN Museum of Classical Archaeology occurred in the same era: it seems likely that both will continue to be subject to debates concerning the post-apartheid processes of transformation and redress. What is clear is that the collection of classical antiquities, by state and by university museums in South Africa, is a practice of a bygone era, and its demise goes beyond the increased constraints on the international trade of antiquities.[129] However, to draw specific correlations with local governmental policies and laws would be to offer too neat an explanation for processes that may be more complex or actually even mundane. More in-depth research will serve to elucidate these connections between the country's troubled past and the present status of classical antiquities collections in South Africa.

---

[129] Since the early 1970s, UNESCO legislation has increasingly regulated the terms of international antiquities trading.

ANNA TIETZE

In June 1908, the first of a large consignment of statuary arrived in Cape Town from London, bound for the Cape Town Art Gallery. It was a gift of plaster casts of famous antique statuary, made by D. Brucciani and Co., *formatori* and modellers.[1] It included the over-life-size *Illissos* and *Venus Genetrix*, the *Belvedere Torso, Dancing Faun, Venus de Milo, Victory of Samothrace* and many others. In November of the same year a second shipment followed. This one included the *Borghese Gladiator*, a bust of Pericles, the *Boy Extracting a Thorn*, the *Apollo Sauroctonus* and three sections from the Parthenon frieze, all again of considerable weight and size. When complete, the total gift amounted to 46 pieces, a number of them over life-size. It was purchased under the terms of the will of Sir Alfred Beit, who had made a fortune in South African mining, and was presented with a view to furthering the educational needs of the Cape. But it has now, over 100 years later, largely disappeared. In what follows, the odd story of this bequest will be explored with a view to explaining why such a gift was deemed valuable, why it might have been particularly significant given its time, place and purchasers, and how it fared once it arrived in South Africa.

The predilection for antique statuary is one of the more interesting examples of the fickleness of aesthetic taste, revealing how impermanent our sense of what is artistically important can be. For an extended period of history, from the fifteenth century until the late nineteenth or even early twentieth, the belief in the importance and beauty of antique statuary was widespread and considerable. This art was believed to be a natural and obvious good, and so it was enthusiastically collected and copied. But it has suffered a dramatic decline, and though antique sculpture is by no means now dismissed, this body of art holds nothing like the status it once held for collectors, museumgoers and art students. It has been a victim of both the

---

[1] For more on the taste for plaster casts of celebrated statuary, see Frederiksen and Marchand 2010; Connor 1989; and Haskell and Penny 1982: 79–91. For details of Brucciani and Co., see Jenkins 1990: 108–10.

general decline of interest in the classical tradition and, in the field of visual art, the more specific decline of interest in sculpture as a didactic medium.

From the fifteenth century, collections such as those of the Vatican and the Capitoline Museum in Rome, as well as those of the Farnese, Borghese and Medici families, helped establish a Europe-wide sense of the importance of this kind of art and were instrumental in creating a canon of the works it was deemed necessary to own in order to count as a serious connoisseur in the field. In the following centuries, the collecting fashion spread to the European courts and, in the palaces of Francis I, Charles I and Philip IV, sumptuous collections of antique statuary were arranged in special galleries or as outdoor decoration in gardens and entranceways. They were among the chief artistic treasures to be visited by the *cognoscenti* of the eighteenth-century Grand Tours. For these eager spectators, the assumption was that prolonged exposure to these sculptural works would not only vividly bring to life the great texts that they illustrated, but also encourage internalisation of their poses and gestures, conferring on latter-day admirers some of the ancient sculptures' dignity and beauty, as well as a pronounced therapeutic calm. The effect was still being felt in the late nineteenth century when Henry James visited the Capitoline collection. In a state of rapture he reported back to his sister Alice that the antique statues were,

all unspeakably simple and noble and eloquent of the breadth of human genius. There's little to say or do about them, save to sit and enjoy them and let them act upon your nerves and confirm your esteem for completeness, purity and perfection.[2]

Meanwhile a less passive – though no less committed – use of antique statuary was that offered by art schools, and specifically by art academies. These, from their inception in the mid-seventeenth century, prioritised the study of antique and later classical statuary, with the aim of providing trainee artists with a repertoire of noble poses and gestures that they might reproduce in their paintings. One kind of painting in particular – History Painting – was the culmination of the academy's training. This was the painting of heroic and mythical deeds as recounted by the classical writers. Binding visual art tightly to high literature – and separating it from the old workshop tradition, with its associated 'low' themes – the art academies gave visual art practice a new status as one of the liberal arts and a career worthy of a gentleman.

---

[2] Letter of 7 November 1969, quoted in untitled review of *Taste and the Antique*: Lloyd 1985.

Consequently, by the nineteenth century, two rather different uses for antique statuary had been established: the use of it by the spectator – either art collector, or later, museum visitor – and the more engaged use of it by the art student, keen to copy and internalise the successful techniques employed by the ancient Greek or Roman sculptors. For both museumgoer and art student, however, the esteem for antique statuary was based upon the same core idea: that the human figure was central to artistic expression. This was of course no normal human figure, but a figure refined and improved so that it had none of the faults of proportion or blemish possessed by people in real life. It was an ideal human figure – a figure to aspire to – and, the theory went, from either the practical study of this figure or the passive spectatorship of it, one could be expected to imbibe something of this bodily perfection. In this perfection lay Beauty. It is worth spelling this out in order to contextualise the discussion that follows with regard to the gift of antique statuary to Cape Town, for it will be argued that while the aesthetic idealism inherent in the taste for antique statuary very much underlay the decision to *present* the Beit statuary, this same kind of idealism was absent from the art world of turn-of-the-century Cape Town. The city's art world was marked by a strong propensity for what might be called Northern European rather than Mediterranean artistic tastes: a taste for landscape over the human figure, for realism over idealism, contemporaneity over the ancient past. When Taine visited England in the mid-nineteenth century, he noted scornfully of its art that 'heroic painting is rare and poor, as likewise figure painting … Noble classical painting, the feeling for a beautiful body … has never taken root here'.[3] Quite absent in England was what he called a 'learned paganism'.[4] But if England was averse to such things in the field of visual art, late nineteenth-century and early twentieth-century South Africa was even more so.[5] As a result, the Beit gift was never hugely appreciated, and at worst was regarded as something of a burden.

Given the ambivalent response to the Beit gift, once it reached South Africa, it is worth considering who precisely was responsible for the choice of such a gift and why they thought it appropriate. It was bought under the terms of Beit's will, a will that set aside £50,000 to be spent for educational purposes in the various provinces of South Africa. But it is highly unlikely that it was suggested by Beit before his death as an appropriate purchase for the country. Indeed, given the kind of art that Beit bought for his own

[3] From Hippolyte Taine's 1885 *Notes on England*. Quoted in Jenkyns 1980: 298.   [4] Ibid.
[5] As Stephen Dyson notes, the taste for landscape painting was a feature of late nineteenth-century American visual culture also: Dyson 2010: 559.

considerable private art collection during his life, antique statuary might have been far from his thoughts. As Michael Stevenson has shown in his detailed study of Beit's collecting habits,[6] Beit had a pronounced taste for Northern European schools of painting, favouring and buying Dutch and Flemish genre painting and English eighteenth-century portraiture. These purchases conflicted with the taste of his advisors, Wilhelm von Bode and Rodolphe Kann, for Italian painting. Beit did amass an outstanding collection of Renaissance bronzes and majolica, but it is significant that his main painting purchases were the rather meticulous studies of ordinary Dutch life that went under the name of 'genre painting'.[7] This was a long way, artistically, from the tradition to which antique statuary belonged.

If the idea for this bequest did not come from Beit, then did it perhaps originate with the executors of his will, Dr Jameson and Lewis Michell? Jameson, a close friend of Cecil Rhodes, headed the Unionist party and was prime minister of the Cape 1904–08. Michell, a one-time general manager of South Africa's Standard Bank and another of Rhodes's circle of associates, took over Rhodes's position as chairman of De Beers mining corporation after 1902, and in 1904 he became a minister without portfolio in Jameson's government. These men, who, along with Beit, had been instrumental in forming the British South Africa Company in 1889, were all closely involved in the notorious Jameson Raid and were instrumental in events that led to the Boer War. Very clearly, they were key players in the imperial endeavour in South Africa and further north, and all were magnetised by the imperial vision that Rhodes had for South Africa.

As is well known, the classics were central to Rhodes's imperial vision for South Africa, offering inspiration not only for the political system but also for the cultural and artistic future of the country. In the latter, the collaboration between Rhodes and British architect Herbert Baker was hugely important and shot through with classicising aims. Meeting Rhodes soon after his arrival in South Africa in 1882, Baker quickly joined Rhodes's favoured circle and began to receive architectural commissions from him. Some of these, such as the late 1890s renovation of the Cape Dutch homestead, Groote Schuur, involved working in the architectural vernacular of Cape Dutch style. Impressed by Baker's work, Rhodes soon began to encourage him in a very different direction, towards classical rather than

---

[6] Stevenson 1997: 81–138.
[7] And it is noteworthy that Beit particularly avoided the so-called 'Italianate' Dutch genre scenes. See Stevenson 1997: 118–19.

vernacular forms. Rhodes felt that while the latter had their place in promoting local pride, it was classical architecture that symbolised the big ideas and the concept of Empire. In South Africa, with its hot climate and sublime scenery, the grandeur of classical forms would find an appropriate backdrop and rouse the people to higher ideals. Cape Town was to be the centre of this great South Africa. As Baker recalled, 'it was [Rhodes's] ambition to make it a capital worthy of the future greatness of united South Africa. "Civic pride built Rome," he told the citizens of Cape Town. "They must work together to make it a city worthy of the beauty with which it has been endowed by nature."'[8]

In order to advance his plans, Rhodes sent Baker on a fact-finding trip to Egypt, Greece and Rome in 1900. He had visited the countries himself the previous year, in the company of Jameson, to imbibe the spirit of each place. With a brief to visit the same sites, Baker was sent off to gather ideas for classical architecture in South Africa. Out of this four-month trip of Baker's came some ideas that remained on the drawing board: Roman-style baths for Kimberley and a lion house in the style of a Paestum temple on the slopes of Table Mountain.[9] Others, such as the Monument to the Dead in Kimberley, came to fruition. With these classically inspired structures, Rhodes hoped to signify imperial grandeur and inspire South Africans to high ideals.

The marriage between imperialism and classical forms was, therefore, central to the thinking of Rhodes – and given that Jameson accompanied him on his 1899 trip to the southern Mediterranean, we can assume that Jameson also felt passionately about the ideological symbolism of classical forms. For all this, however, it seems likely that the main motivation for the idea of a gift of classical statuary came not from Rhodes or Jameson, but from another of their circle, Rudyard Kipling. When Lewis Michell first contacted the Cape Town art gallery with news of the proposed gift, he began: 'this is simply to tell you that Kipling's happy thought is taking effect. I hope shortly to present the art gallery with a large collection of plaster casts of celebrated statues, torsos and friezes.'[10] No further written record seems to remain of this 'happy thought', but it is an intriguing reference and one we can take as decisive. Kipling was apparently the

---

[8] Herbert Baker in Baker and Stead 1977: 54.

[9] Baker recalled of the latter project: 'a Paestum temple was in his mind where the king of beasts would be admired in his natural strength and dignity. The old Roman in him pictured the beauty of the lions moving through great columns.' Baker and Stead 1977: 46.

[10] Letter of 6 December 1907 from Michell to Muir, in *Acquisitions, 1870–1947*, South African National Gallery (SANG) archives.

instigator of a large gift of underappreciated classical statuary to Cape Town.

Rudyard Kipling had first come out to South Africa in 1898, just before Rhodes's trip to the Mediterranean. He was already established as a major literary figure by this time, and he quickly became friendly with Rhodes and his circle. For the next ten years, excepting the year of 1899, the Kipling family travelled over to South Africa to spend the European winter in Cape Town. The house they stayed in was the Woolsack, a Baker retreat on the Rhodes estate, built to fulfil its owner's dream of a 'cottage in the woods for poets and artists'.[11] Here Kipling, Rhodes and others of the inner circle spent much time talking about the political future of the Cape and South Africa, with Kipling an enthusiastic champion of the imperial project. But apart from discussing the narrowly political issues of the country, Rhodes and Kipling must have often discussed creative projects and aims for South Africa, and with his verbal fluency and ease in expressing ideas, Kipling would have struck Rhodes as a valuable intellectual cipher. 'The inarticulate Rhodes', one biographer notes, 'would call on Rudyard for words to clothe his ideas.'[12] So possibly the 'happy thought' of Kipling's arose out of one such conversation, in the early days before Rhodes's premature death in 1902.

Although Kipling was a writer, he had plenty of secondary experience of the contemporary art world and of art-training institutions. Two of his mother's sisters were married to the celebrated figures of the English art world, Edward Burne-Jones and Edwin Poynter, while his father, Lockwood Kipling, spent the majority of his career in art schools in India, first as a teacher at the Bombay School of Art (1865–74) and then as Director of the Mayo School of Art in Lahore (1875–93) and curator of the city's museum. Rudyard was close to his father and admired him professionally as an 'expert fellow-craftsman',[13] but the writer would not have imbibed ideas about the superiority of classical art from his father. As Tarapor shows,[14] a good deal of Lockwood Kipling's career was devoted to *overcoming* attempts to import Western artistic models into Indian art training. What he favoured instead, and actively supported, was the resurgence of indigenous artistic traditions and skills. With inspiration from William Morris, the elder Kipling sought to assert the importance of crafts and to keep alive the threatened local tastes in materials, colours and decoration.

---

[11] Baker and Stead 1977: 44.   [12] Laski 1987: 139.   [13] Tarapor 1980: 53.
[14] Tarapor 1980: 62–68.

If Rudyard Kipling absorbed ideas about the importance of the classical tradition from his family background, it was more likely to have been from his famous uncles. He spent much time with the Burne-Jones family, but his relationship with Poynter might have been the more artistically influential. In the final decades of the nineteenth century, Poynter enjoyed a meteoric passage through most of the top positions in the London art world: he was appointed the first Slade Professor of Fine Art at University College, London in 1871, became the Director of the South Kensington National School of Art in 1875, Director of the National Gallery in 1894 (from which followed control of what became the Tate Gallery), and the President of the Royal Academy in 1896. The art lectures he gave while Slade Professor were published in 1879 as *Ten Lectures on Art*. They advised on pedagogical theory and made plentiful reference to classical art as inspiration for the modern painter. Meanwhile, throughout this late-century period, Poynter was finding time to produce grand historical paintings that aimed to recreate antiquity in both content and style and that earned him a place among the 'Victorian Olympians'. Kipling's attitude to his uncle was sometimes wry, but there is evidence that he genuinely respected him also.[15] He may well have helped to establish in Kipling a respect for high art, as represented by the grand classical tradition – the very tradition that his father, Lockwood Kipling, had struggled to keep out of his schools in India. Certainly, it seems that by the early twentieth century, Rudyard Kipling had decided that classical art was pre-eminently suited to the needs of Cape Town.

When the classical statuary presented to Cape Town arrived in the city, it would have fallen under the supervision of Thomas Muir, the Cape Superintendent-General of Education. Muir had studied classics, his first love, while at the University of Glasgow, but had been persuaded to change to mathematics. After graduating, he went on to teach this subject at the university and then at a Glasgow high school before meeting Rhodes on one of the latter's visits back to Britain. Muir was at this time considering a post at Stanford University, but he was persuaded by Rhodes to come out to the Cape to take on the task of running the education system: a post he held from 1892–1915.[16] As Superintendent-General, Muir's task was to rationalise the management of education in the Cape. All tiers of education – from elementary

---

[15] Flanders 2002: 255, 268.

[16] Muir said of Rhodes, 'I fell under the glamour of his personality. It was his influence that decided me to go to the Cape.' Quoted in Borman 1989: 123.

teaching up to tertiary training – were brought under his control and were run with a new efficiency. Three years after he took up his post, the Cape Town School of Art, which had previously been administered by the South African Fine Arts Association (SAFAA), was subsumed into the Education Department. Meanwhile, Muir also served as Chairman of the Board of Trustees for the Cape Town Art Gallery and it was for this gallery that the casts were intended. So here was another figure central to the story of the Beit bequest. Like all the others considered – Rhodes, Michell, Jameson and Kipling – Muir had no first-hand experience as a practising artist or as an art collector or curator. What he had, however, was a wide knowledge of and respect for the classical tradition.

A final factor in this choice of casts for Cape Town is the example set by those other far-flung British colonies, Australia and New Zealand. In Australia, the Australian Museum in Sydney had received a gift of antique casts in 1854 and the National Gallery of Victoria in Melbourne purchased a collection between 1859 and 1862, while in New Zealand the Canterbury Museum in Christchurch was presented with a gift of such casts in 1873, and a similar donation was announced to the Auckland Museum in 1878.[17] It is almost certain that those responsible for Cape Town's gift would have been aware of these acquisitions and keen to emulate them.

When Lewis Michell first contacted the Cape Town art gallery from London to announce the imminent arrival of the plaster casts, it was to Thomas Muir as Chairman of the Board that he wrote. Noting his awareness that Muir was 'much taken with the idea' of the gift, Michell asked if Muir would 'make the presentation on our behalf'.[18] Thomas Muir, then, seemed to have been consulted beforehand about the wisdom of this gift and to have approved it, but it is unclear how many other interested parties were involved in the negotiations. When Michell announced the gift's imminent arrival he added breezily, 'I assume that there is adequate room to show off the statuary properly. Its weight is 45 tons and the packing, freight and insurance are proving very expensive.'[19] His optimism could not have been more misplaced. The gift was destined for a tiny art gallery crammed into the annexe of the South African Museum. The government had for some time promised funds to build a proper gallery, but other financial commitments always seemed to take

---

[17] See Cooke 2010 and Galbally 1988.

[18] Letter from Michell (of British South Africa Company) to Muir, 6 December 1907, *Acquisitions 1870–1947*, SANG archives.

[19] Ibid.

precedence. While the gallery's collection was a modest one of mostly small paintings the problem was not acute, but the imminent arrival of 46 pieces of statuary was a very different matter. However, by mid-1908, Rhodes was long dead, and Kipling had left Cape Town, never to return, so the chief architects of the statuary scheme did not witness just how poorly the gift was received.

Early in 1908, the gallery trustees met the Colonial Secretary to remind him that the Government had promised, ten years earlier, to build an art gallery as soon as funds permitted. They noted that now 'in view of the Beit Bequest the matter might be dealt with as urgently as possible', and in the meantime they asked for temporary accommodation for the statuary somewhere in the city.[20] The Colonial Secretary made reassuring noises in response to both requests and promised to see whether a temporary structure 'could be erected upon the Museum grounds', hoping the trustees could take care of the casts satisfactorily on their own.[21] A further appeal, this time to the Public Works Department, was similarly frustrating. The trustees asked for 'the loan of a wood and iron building' for the statuary,[22] and the matter was referred to Prime Minister John X. Merriman. In a meeting between him and the trustees in April 1908,[23] it was made clear that he objected to the erection of a temporary structure near the museum on both financial and aesthetic grounds, fearing the 'disfigurement' of the surrounding area; the Board minutes noted that all he could do was offer 'something more or less of the nature of a promise to ascertain whether the Railway or other Department had any wood-and-iron structures available'.[24] But by June 1908, the press was reporting an interview with the Prime Minister in which he 'stated that though he was in full sympathy with the trustees in their dilemma, the state of the finances of the country were such that he could not assist them in any way whatever'.[25]

So the trustees found themselves solely responsible for the unwieldy Beit gift, which was, by July, beginning to arrive in Cape Town, and for which there was no proper accommodation, nor any demonstrable concern outside their own. Late in the day, it seems to have occurred to the presenters

---

[20] SANG *Board Minutes 1, 1896–1908*, SANG archives.   [21] Ibid.

[22] Letter of 12 March 1908, from J. Fairbairn, Parliamentary Secretary to trustees, to Public Works Department, *Acquisitions 1870–1947*, SANG archives.

[23] Documented for trustees' meeting of 15 April 1908, *Board Minutes 1, 1896–1908*, SANG archives.

[24] Ibid. The contrast with the Auckland Museum's reception of their cast collection could not be greater. Here, in the early days, the classical casts were proudly displayed in the same rooms as natural history exhibits. See Cooke 2010: 581–83.

[25] Press report of 15 June 1908, fn 1, *Acquisitions 1870–1947*, SANG archives.

of the gift that it might be causing some practical problems. A memorandum from Muir to the trustees, of May 1908, noted that 'Sir Lewis Michell called and . . . informed me that Mr Kipling had told him by letter that difficulties might arise in reference to the housing of the statuary.' Muir must have heartily agreed. He notes that, in response to this, Michell then 'suggested that the offer of the gift to some other Colonial town, like Port Elizabeth or Grahamstown, might *cause the people of Cape Town to bestir themselves*; but I naturally pointed out the great objections to such a course. He finally left the matter in the hands of the trustees'[26] (emphasis added).

However, while the problems of housing the Beit gift were acute, the most telling long-term problem was the South African view of such art. Here, whether one considers local art production in the Cape or its conception of art training, what emerges is a taste for significantly anti-classical artistic modes. For the first, one needs to look at the work that was exhibited at the Cape Town art exhibitions that began in the second half of the nineteenth century. Four of these were held in Cape Town before 1870 and were called, simply, the 'Fine Arts Exhibitions'. On the basis of these, the South African Fine Arts Association (SAFAA) was formed in 1871, to promote and improve local art production. It took over the responsibility for these art exhibitions, sought to encourage entries by offering prizes, and laid the groundwork for a permanent Cape art collection by buying some of the exhibited works and donating them to the Cape Town art gallery, which was established under SAFAA custody shortly after.

There were a large number of entries to the early Cape Town art exhibitions, but many of these were of (artistically modest) works bought abroad. Others were copies of old masters, done by local talents. But if one examines the original work done by the Cape-based artists in these shows, the so-called 'colonial productions', it is clear that the overwhelming preference is for landscape scenes, with portraiture and still life following.

Notable too is that the scenes are often of a topographical nature and executed by artist-travellers like Thomas Bowler, who were recording remote and exotic places. In this connection it is interesting to note how important a part was played in the early Cape Town art world by employees of the Surveyor-General's office. Two of the artists who featured heavily in the early art exhibitions were Charles Bell, Surveyor-General at the Cape from 1848 to 1872, and Abraham de Smidt, Surveyor-General from 1872 to

---

[26] Muir to trustees, 20 May 1908, *Acquisitions 1870–1947*, SANG archives.

1889. When not busy with their government posts, these men painted; their paintings recorded the landscape and, in the case of Bell particularly, the peoples of South Africa. It was an art of outdoors which, while it might sometimes borrow pose and gesture from the classical repertoire, was centrally dedicated to documenting an alien 'other' world, remote from the concerns of classical imagery and narrative.

Abraham de Smidt was perhaps the most vocal and intense champion of a Cape Town art gallery, in the days before one came into existence. In 1871 he wrote on the subject in an article in the *Cape Monthly Magazine*,[27] arguing for an art gallery along lines familiar from many British nineteenth-century reformers and philanthropists: art elevates the mind from practical tasks, it distracts us from the coarser pleasures of drink and gambling, it increases our awareness of and pleasure in our visual environment, and it offers a refined entertainment to the illiterate. These were all the prescriptions of a man in the colonies, concerned about the very raw tendencies of life around him; for de Smidt, an art gallery was a vital alternative to 'haunts of debasement and debauch'.[28] But de Smidt's essay revealed some conflict in the man between theory and practice, for when he came to outline the ideal acquisitions of this new gallery, his first thought was for classical statuary: 'sculptures are of course too costly to be thought of for a long time, but casts may be cheaply procured from respectable London dealers'.[29] He went on to offer a lengthy discussion of 16 recommended antique sculptures. To this he added references to more recent statuary, and then only a brief reference to 'oil-paintings, water-colour drawings, chromo-lithographs, engravings, and photographs'.[30]

But if in theory de Smidt offered very traditional, 'high art' suggestions for a future art gallery, in practice he was an empiricist, with an interest in the land. This was a taste that was shared by so many others in the Cape Town art world, and when the Cape Town art gallery opened in 1875, a large part of its core collection was the landscapes, topographical studies and still lifes that had been acquired by the SAFAA from its occasional exhibitions. By the 1890s, de Smidt was living in England, where he was asked by the Cape Town art gallery to act as one of their overseas buyers. As such, he was advised by the gallery to avoid inappropriate subjects and, in particular, 'pronounced nudes'. De Smidt agreed, adding that 'what you have to do is to hit the popular taste, as far as you can, without sacrifices of

[27] De Smidt 1871.   [28] De Smidt 1871: 246.   [29] De Smidt 1871: 241.
[30] De Smidt 1871: 242.

Art principles and the requirements of a training School for Artists'.[31] A little later, he is recorded as having sent back to South Africa, as new acquisitions, some 'true transcripts of Nature', which would assist 'students in the fascinating study of landscape painting'.[32] It was only one case of many of the gallery prioritising the non-classical.

By 1908, when the Beit casts began to arrive, the gallery's collection of art had grown and the gallery itself had moved (in 1900) from its first premises in Queen Victoria Street to an annexe of the South African Museum. Space here was extremely limited so there was a call for an alternative temporary home for the casts. When this was not forth-coming, the casts were fitted into a lower room of the gallery, on their own. In their end-of-year report, the trustees of the gallery recorded their 'deep appreciation of the thoughtful and generous gift' of the statuary, noted that it had 'given the greatest satisfaction to the public', and anticipated the long-term 'good likely to be conferred on the Cape Colony by the generous gift'.[33] But in practice, the casts seemed to have caused all kinds of embarrassment. Not only were they hastily put into a lower room, but they were treated as exhibits that many visitors would not be advised to look at. The trustee tasked with finding space for the casts explained to Chairman Thomas Muir: 'a screen has been erected with a door for access to any person interested in the bequest. This was done as it was not considered advisable to admit the general public.'[34] The problem was that many of these sculptures were studies of 'pronounced nudes'. It was of course the core motif of the Greek visual tradition, for which the ideal nude body was the epitome of Beauty. For the Cape Town art-gallery visitor, however, the human body, if seen at all, was generally seen in portraiture or in genre scenes of contemporary life, and in both art forms, of course, it would be generally a well-clothed human body. A commentator, reminiscing some years later about the early Cape Town art gallery, recalled that 'in those Victorian days [of the early century] the nude gladiators, athletes, gods and goddesses were kept behind baize doors, of which the curator held the key. He, poor man, had to use his discretion in allowing young persons to view the nudities or not.'[35]

---

[31] Bull 1975: 131.   [32] Bull 1975: 133.

[33] Annual Report of the Trustees, Dec. 1908, *Board Minutes 1, 1896–1908*, SANG archives.

[34] Note from trustee Westhofen to Muir, 8 July 1908, *Acquisitions 1870–1947*, SANG archives.

[35] Anon, *The Monitor*, November 1946 in *Newscutting Book*, SANG library. This had been an absorbing concern in early nineteenth-century American museums, but was likely not such a problem by the twentieth century. See McNutt 1990: 163–64.

Problems of space and the alien nature of the antique cast collection meant that it never occupied prime position at the gallery. Indeed, from the moment it arrived, it was regarded as burdensome, and moves were made to find alternative accommodation for it. The obvious alternative to the art gallery was an art school, where the casts would not be passively gazed on by the spectator, but used by art students as models for their own work. In 1915, there is the first record of the Cape Town Art School receiving some of the casts on loan, but the account of the loan makes it clear that the casts were being grudgingly taken by the art school in order to help out the gallery. Minutes of a trustees' meeting note that they had 'decided to *relieve* the lower room of the Gallery of a few of the Beit statues', adding that,

> ... it was first discussed whether a sufficient number could be removed so as to enable the screen to be taken away and the room made a whole once more. Eventually it was found that this was not possible, and it only remained to ascertain how many pieces of statuary the Art School could *absorb*. Messrs Groves and Thatcher thought that they could take four of the ordinary-sized pieces and possibly a relief-slab or two.[36] (emphasis added)

In 1919, an addendum to the gallery's annual report notes that further loans of casts were made to the art school, where they would be 'accessible only to the students and not to the general public'.[37]

The general tone of these memos strongly suggests that the art school felt it was doing the gallery a favour by taking over some of the Beit casts. This is explained by the fact that the art school was absolutely not in the Academy mould discussed at the outset. It had opened in 1880, in response to the perceived paucity of local exhibits – and attendance – at the Cape Town art exhibitions, but the man who was brought out from England to head the new school – James Ford – was a product of the South Kensington art training system. This system, established in the mid-nineteenth century by Henry Cole, was expressly designed to offer an alternative to Academic art training and its curriculum. It aimed to be more socially inclusive in its student intake and fostered graduates who might go on to work in industrial design rather than 'pure' painting. To further the latter aim, it radically de-emphasised the academic stress upon study of the human figure and focused far more upon study of ornament and pattern-making. To this end, drawing was a central part of the curriculum, but it was drawing of stylised plant forms, basic organic and geometric shapes, and the like.

[36] Minutes of Board meeting, 26 May 1915, *Acquisitions 1870–1947*, SANG archives.
[37] SANG, Annual Report of the Trustees, Dec. 1919, SANG archives.

It was not surprising that Cape Town, with its 'informal' aesthetic in painting practice, should have tapped into such a system, but it was certainly not going to be an art-training system that made heavy use of antique statuary. While drawing 'from the antique' features in the curriculum of the art school in the early years of the twentieth century, it seems, from the evidence of Examiners' reports, that it was little taught in practice, or rarely chosen by students.[38]

When the Cape Town Art School merged into the University of Cape Town's newly formed school of art – the Michaelis School – in the 1920s, the Beit casts received a little more serious attention. John Wheatley, who arrived in 1925, was appointed the first Chair of Fine Art at the university. He had been trained at the Slade School of Fine Art in London, which methodologically trod a line between the Academic and the South Kensington systems and took inspiration from modern French art-training practice. Under this system, strong emphasis was placed upon careful drawing, but drawing of the human figure as well as of natural forms. Soon after he took up his new post, John Wheatley requested – actively requested – some of the Beit casts from the art gallery. A memo of January 1926 notes that 'permission [was] given to Wheatley to have 2 figures for use at Mich. school in add to the 4 on loan at the present'.[39] In fact, in making this request of the art gallery, Wheatley was asking for the casts to be taken from one of his domains to the other, since with the establishment of the new art school the decision had been taken to make the Professor of Fine Art double as Honorary Director of the art gallery. Wheatley's tenure of the latter post brought a new stability to the desperately underfunded gallery, but as he took over, it became clear how chaotic the earlier years had been for the acquisition and storage of works. The Beit casts were among the victims of this. By the late 1920s, 11 of them were recorded as being 'missing from the stocks of the gallery'.[40] A stock-take seems to have confirmed that six of them were the ones given on loan to the art school in 1926 and some years earlier, but others of these earlier loans had simply gone missing, since five of the missing 11 were recorded as

[38] See for example *Cape Education Gazette* 8.18, 4 February 1909, 390. Classical casts had served a useful purpose in nineteenth-century American art schools, where live nude models were shunned. See Dyson 2010: 558 and McNutt 1990: 165. Early twentieth-century South Africa seemed to be having problems adjusting even to the plaster cast nudes, although the objection was as much to the traditionalism of the exercise as to the nudity of the bodies.
[39] Undated handwritten note, added at later date to 1908 Trustees' Report, *Board Minutes 1, 1896–1908*, SANG archives.
[40] Ibid.

completely untraceable. Just twenty years after its arrival in Cape Town, then, part of the bequest was lost.

In late 1930, after many years of waiting, the art gallery was finally able to move into specially built premises on Government Avenue, near the South African Museum. As was the norm for such buildings, the architecture of the new gallery borrowed some of the features of a Greek temple, with its colonnaded and raised entrance and atrium inside. In this atrium the Beit casts now found a 'permanent' home. They had been 'stuffed away behind the museum for so many years',[41] but now they were 'suitably arranged in the Roman-like central court'.[42] A few years later they received 'five new wooden thrones', presumably supports for some of them,[43] and a photograph of the atrium taken for a 1940 news article shows them still in place.[44] But it is significant that earlier plans for a gallery building that showcased the statuary more prominently, in conjunction with Old Master paintings, had never come to fruition. When the Michaelis collection of Dutch and Flemish Old Master paintings was presented to the nation in 1913, the gallery trustees had envisaged that these Old Masters would occupy one wing, contemporary art another, and between them would be 'a Hall of Statuary containing reproductions of the finest examples of Greek and Roman Art', clearly the Beit bequest.[45] The plan never materialised; it was in fact quickly quashed by Max Michaelis's associate Lionel Phillips, who had been asked by Michaelis to resolve the question of where his Dutch and Flemish art collection should be housed. Phillips was clear: the Michaelis collection should be housed quite separately from the existing gallery. His explanation was that it was 'entirely improper to place pictures of this age in the same building with modern pictures'.[46] The Michaelis collection was housed in the Old Town House in central Cape Town, where it remains to this day. But the underlying reasoning was familiar: the main art gallery was a repository of largely recent works,

---

[41] Press report, '"Hanging" at new art gallery', 3 November 1930, *SANG, Newscutting Book E1*, SANG library.

[42] Press report, n.d., *Newscutting Book E1*, SANG library.

[43] Keeper's Report, May–June 1935, Minutes Book 3, SANG archives.

[44] Press report, *Naweek*, 17 October 1940, 'Items other than Catalogues' box file, SANG library.

[45] From the Report of the Trustees of the South African Art Gallery and the South African Fine Arts Association for the year ending 31 December 1913, 6. Quoted in Stevenson 2002: 96.

[46] Memo from Lionel Phillips to the Mayor of Cape Town, 7 May 1913. Quoted in Stevenson 2002: 99.

of informal subjects and style, and any art of great age or connection with Tradition was out of character with the growing collection.

In the post-World War I era, a sense of the importance of ancient art was being questioned wherever in the world such collections were to be found. In Cape Town it was a matter of a hardening of resistance to something that had never quite fitted the local culture. Sometime in the late 1930s, influential local artist and teacher Ruth Prowse told a meeting of the South African Museums Association that visitors to the art gallery 'go into a courtyard that gives the impression of a Campo Sancto with its dead white casts of classical statuary known in every art school as The Antique'.[47] It was a criticism that was bound to be voiced at some stage. This was a period of increasing debate on the issue of what was an appropriate acquisitions policy for a 'National' gallery in South Africa – and while deep divisions were growing between British and Afrikaner interest groups, common ground was found in the assumption that the art that was acquired would be contemporary or recent and thematically relevant to South Africa. Encouragement of a South African school of art was paramount in the minds of gallery trustees – and time and again this emerging school produced studies of local peoples and places, of the great outdoors and those who lived in it. It was hardly an artistic project that required study of antique poses and narratives.

However, the Beit casts remained in their atrium, untouched, it would seem, for a number of years. But a decisive change at the art gallery came in 1949 with the new professionalisation of the post of Director. From now on, the gallery's Director was a full-time appointee, and the headship of the nearby art school was quite separate. John Paris, brought out from Liverpool's Walker Art Gallery to fill this first full-time post, was charged with putting the gallery's organisation on a new professional footing and with modernising its acquisitions policy, including a brief to strengthen holdings of South African art. Formerly 'South African' had meant, in practice, either British or Dutch/German-inspired art, by White artists, but coming from outside South Africa, and with rather more enlightened views than many who had grown up there, Paris was in the forefront of moves to enlarge the notion of 'South African' to include Black art production. One of his first moves on taking up the post was to clear the atrium of the Beit casts 'in order to show indigenous arts'.[48] It was decisively the end of an era. John Paris did not

---

[47] Undated press report, Ruth Prowse papers MSB 632 box 1, file no. 15, National Library of South Africa.

[48] University of Cape Town, *Annual Report of the Trustees, 1949/50*, University of Cape Town Library.

remain in the post for many years; he seems to have been driven out partly by narrow sectarian jealousies and left abruptly in the early sixties. But in a sense the Beit casts never recovered; they belonged to the pre-professional era of the gallery and had been removed with the ending of that era.

Where the Beit casts were taken and when they were removed from the gallery atrium is unclear. No records are available of their storage arrangements. Presumably most were stored at the gallery itself, but possibly some were moved to the art school, to join the others that had been 'loaned' in 1915, 1919 and 1926. The Director of the art school in the 1980s, Neville Dubow, remembered some bedraggled casts, damaged by the elements, on display in the courtyard when he first joined the staff in the 1960s. Others were apparently in the sculpture studios at this time.[49] The 1970s in South Africa saw a growth of artistic iconoclasm, and the Beit casts seemed to symbolise the old order. Dubow produced a photographic series in the early 1970s that was based playfully, mockingly, around the Beit cast of *Venus de Milo* (cf. Fig. 15.1), and he recalled that this and other of the casts were regularly daubed with paint and otherwise defaced by students in that decade. Now they are gone from the school's sculpture studios and from its courtyard, and only two pieces appear to remain here (Fig. 10.1). These are casts of two fragments of the Parthenon frieze, hanging high on the entrance wall to the art school's library, Hiddingh Hall, dusty but safe. Few visitors notice or inquire about them.

Apart from these remnants, the whereabouts of most of the Beit gift is a mystery, though presumably much has been destroyed. It is a sad and odd ending to the story of this bequest, though one that is familiar from other centres where large antique cast collections were once held.[50] Nevertheless, there is an interesting twist to the story. Art students at Rhodes University in Grahamstown in the 1970s were given rigorous drawing instruction, along Academic lines, long after such teaching had disappeared from Cape Town's art school. Their models included a plaster cast of an antique sculpture, and one that was much studied and copied was the head of a horse.[51] Almost certainly, this was the 'antique horse's head', lot number 303.0, that appears on the Brucciani list of works dispatched to Cape Town in 1908. Others from the Beit collection seem to have found their way to the

---

[49] Conversation between author and N. Dubow.

[50] Although some of these early cast collections have fared much better. See Ian Cooke on the current care of the Auckland collection (2010: 593–94); also, Dyson on the rehabilitation of some of the American collections (2010: 574–75).

[51] Conversation between author and M. van Blommestein, student of Rhodes University art school in the 1970s.

Figure 10.1 Two friezes from the Beit Collection: Art Library, Hiddingh Hall, University of Cape Town, 2012.

Rhodes Classics department, presumably after the art school there had finally grown tired of them. Three are known to survive, namely a Head of Apollo (lot number 1615), the Bust of Young Augustus (lot number 458) and the Torso of Eros (lot number 2700). When they were dispatched to Grahamstown is unclear, but almost certainly it was prior to John Wheatley's arrival at Cape Town's art school in 1925. Possibly it happened not long after Lewis Michell controversially proposed this plan in 1908.[52] By an odd stroke of fate, however, one of these 'Grahamstown Beit casts' has now returned to Cape Town, along with the move of a Classics staff member from Rhodes to the University of Cape Town some years ago (Fig. 10.2). The Torso of Eros bears the manufacturer's name of Brucciani and the number 2700, revealing that it is indeed a remnant of the 1908 bequest. Having spent some time in the University of Cape Town Classics department, it is now displayed in the office of the Dean of Humanities, a dignified ending to a long life.

   In conclusion, what emerges from this study is the massive decline in status of a once-revered art form. As the twentieth century progressed, original works of antiquity were no longer regarded as vital to an aesthetic

---

[52] See note 26.

Figure 10.2 Statue of youth from the Beit Collection: Beattie Building, University of Cape Town, 2014.

education by art lovers or art students. Meanwhile plaster copies of them suffered an even more precipitous drop in perceived value. They were being terminally affected from the late nineteenth century by technological developments such as photography, which made for simpler reproduction of originals, and they were being rendered near-obsolete, too, by the growth of a new wealthy elite art audience, keen to show its discrimination by the purchase of expensive original artworks rather than by the provision of cheaper, useful copies. This was a significant change. As Dyson has said of the American art world at the end of the nineteenth century,

The Jeffersonian ideal of an 'educated demos' whose tastes were to be elevated by the cast-laden museum was yielding to notions of the museum as a 'temple of culture' whose treasures could only be appreciated by a new elite, which was distinguished as much by its money as by its education. This money could ... buy original works of art on the European market which made their way in increasing numbers to America.[53]

In the case of South Africa, there was no hope of securing the originals of classical casts, or of virtually any other valuable art of the past, for that matter. But as has been argued, this was in any case a centre whose art world felt uncomfortable with art of a distant past, and that always defined itself in terms of a relatively recent history and with landscape above all else. So the Beit bequest to Cape Town was *never* properly appreciated in its South African home. It was the brainchild of a group of Imperialists, Kipling and Rhodes most centrally, whose classicising cultural plans for the Cape did not take into account the local tastes of the public. With the death or departure from the Cape of this Rhodes group, a local aesthetic asserted itself in the art gallery sphere, which was markedly Northern European rather than Mediterranean in nature, and which had little use for a body of classical statuary. With perennially poor governmental support and minimal public involvement in the visual arts, the Cape Town art world was never able to counter popular tastes and sustain an 'alternative' culture of the classical tradition in the way that richer art institutions in Australia and New Zealand could do. And in time, the rise of interest in 'indigenous' African art only further diminished the relevance of the Beit bequest. Meanwhile, art-training methods in Cape Town were also antithetical to the classical tradition, and while the casts were occasionally used for serious study, more often they seemed to have served as material for artistic satire. No art form or artist is completely guaranteed a life of unbroken veneration, and few enjoy it. Classical statuary has suffered a quite spectacular decline in status worldwide, as art training methods and the tastes of museumgoers have changed. But this is nothing by comparison with the decline of interest in the plaster cast of the antique, one of the greatest victims of the inconstancy of taste and aesthetic value, and an art form particularly ill-suited to South Africa.

---

[53] Dyson 2010: 572.

11 | Cecil Rhodes as a Reader of the Classics:
The Groote Schuur Collection[*]

DAVID WARDLE

In the flourishing discipline of book history fascinating studies are emerging on the personal libraries collected by prominent figures that illustrate the intellectual influences to which they exposed themselves and their interaction with these texts.[1] For example, Hitler's extensive annotations over more than a hundred pages of the 1934 edition of Paul Lagarde's *German Letters*, a collection of nineteenth-century essays in favour of the physical removal of the Jewish population of western Europe, illuminate well particular notions that attracted Hitler's attention and how he would read to bolster his already firmly held opinions. Whereas many of the 16,000 books that are known to have been in Hitler's libraries were gifts by authors eager to curry favour and not an indication of Hitler's interests, Cecil Rhodes's library is essentially different. For his primary residence in Cape Town, Groote Schuur, Rhodes ordered a sizeable library to be gathered together. Apollon Davidson calls this wide-ranging collection of books 'probably one of the best libraries in Africa' at the time and points out that in addition to areas that might naturally be thought of interest to Rhodes the library had copies of Friedrich Engels's *Socialism, Utopian and Scientific* and Edward Aveling's *The Students' Marx: An Introduction to the Study of Karl Marx's Capital*.[2] In general, however, the catalogue demonstrates that Rhodes's library was carefully selected around areas that were of specific interest to him: Africa, exploration and above all Classics. The subject of this chapter is one part of Rhodes's Classics library that could in other circumstances and places have had a greater prominence in the discipline of Classics both in South Africa and in the wider world.

---

[*] A much shorter, earlier version of this chapter appeared as Wardle 1993. The current version has benefitted from further visits to Groote Schuur to work in the library and smoking room.

    As an Orielensis who benefitted directly from Rhodes's generosity by having a room in the Rhodes building for two years, and a staff-member of UCT working on a site bequeathed by Rhodes, I may look more favourably on the man than is the norm today. Contrast Mdudumane 2005.

[1] For the very different figures of Oscar Wilde and Adolf Hitler, see Wright 2008 and Ryback 2009.

[2] Davidson 2003: 238. In 1910 Rhodes's trustees had a catalogue of his books drawn up. I consulted the copy of this held at Groote Schuur.

Virtually all of the biographies that discuss Cecil Rhodes's private life, as opposed to his political and business career, record that his favourite reading was Marcus Aurelius' *Meditations* and Edward Gibbon's *Decline and Fall of the Roman Empire*: his copy of the former accompanied him even during his final days at Muizenberg.[3] Although Rhodes's own copy of the *Meditations*, the translation by George Long, has not survived, it is possible to reconstruct the scale and focus of Rhodes's fascination from the fact that he underlined 101 passages, as we learn from Cecelia Sauer's fortunate copying of Rhodes's underlinings into her own copy, passages arranged around four themes: death, the need for intellect to take precedence over emotion, the need to do what was important and right rather than what was trivial or popular, and, lastly, the importance of being able to change one's mind if one's friends offered convincing arguments, as life required working with others.[4] A striking confirmation of Rhodes's interest in Marcus Aurelius is found in volume five of the collected scholarship on Marcus Aurelius that Rhodes had prepared for himself: a translation of E. de Suckau's *Marcus Aurelius: His Life and Teachings*, a work originally published in French in 1857, has several passages underlined and marked in the margin by Rhodes himself, which illustrate Rhodes's engagement with the text (Fig. 11.1–3). For example (page 1698) he underlines 'he was always most considerate when he corrected anyone', presumably as a course of action to be followed; elsewhere (page 1710) he underlines a quotation from Cicero: 'to speak fluently, but at the same time discreetly, is better than the keenest thought without eloquence: because thought is self-contained, while eloquence embraces those with whom we meet', and further (page 1733) he both underlines and marks in both margins Suckau's summation of the emperor's learning from the peripatetic philosopher Severus, 'the conception of a free state in which the natural equality of all the citizens and of their rights is the ruling power, and the idea of a royalty, which sets before all duties respect for the liberty of the subject'.

It is his fascination with Gibbon's *Decline and Fall*, however, that led to a project that could have been a considerable contribution to Classical

---

[3] Fuller 1910: 134, 245; Williams 1921: 223; Plomer 1933: 133; Lockhart and Woodhouse 1963: 22, 30, 64, 66, 67, 208; Rotberg 1988: 384–85. One may surmise that Rhodes's most private annotations and underlinings were felt too private to survive him, even into the relatively secure library bequeathed to his successors as Prime Minister of the Cape. Brooke Simons erroneously describes the work as 'an English translation of the writings of Marcus Aurelius' (1996: 58–59).

[4] Rotberg 1988: 384–85.

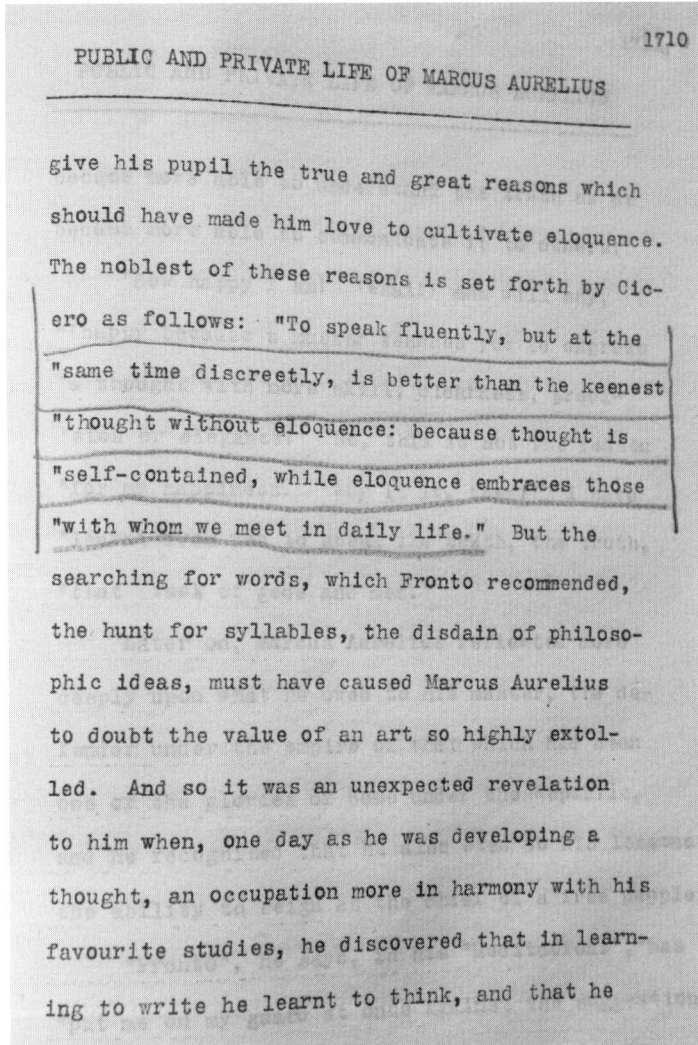

Figure 11.1 Rhodes' underlinings in his translation of E. de Suckau's *Marcus Aurelius: his life and teachings*. Photograph by Paul Weinberg.

scholarship. The scheme was some time in its formulation, as the original idea was conceived on his lengthy visit to England in 1888 (before his return in August 1889), when he was chiefly occupied with securing a Royal charter for the British South Africa Company.[5] It was not until around 1893 that the plan was put into action, when Rhodes had been

---

[5] See the memoir by Mr A. Humphreys in Fuller, *The Right Honourable* 1910: 133–34 – quoted below *in extenso*.

ius learnt particularly from the peripatetic Severus, and which he has handed down to us in these
terms: "To Severus I owe my knowledge of Thrasea,
"Helvidius, Cato, Dion, Brutus, the conception
"of a free state in which the natural equality
"of all the citizens and of their rights is the
"ruling power, and the idea of a royalty, which
"sets before all duties respect for the liberty
"of the subject."
    Marcus Aurelius did not confine this severe

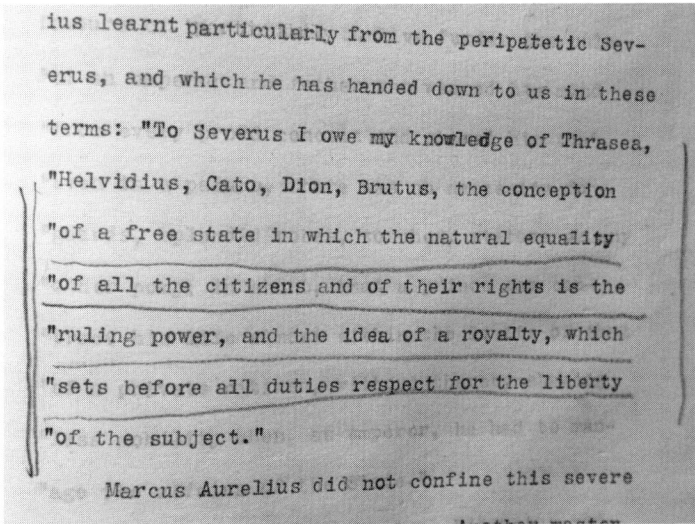

Figure 11.2 Rhodes' underlinings in his translation of E. de Suckau's *Marcus Aurelius: his life and teachings*. Photograph by Paul Weinberg.

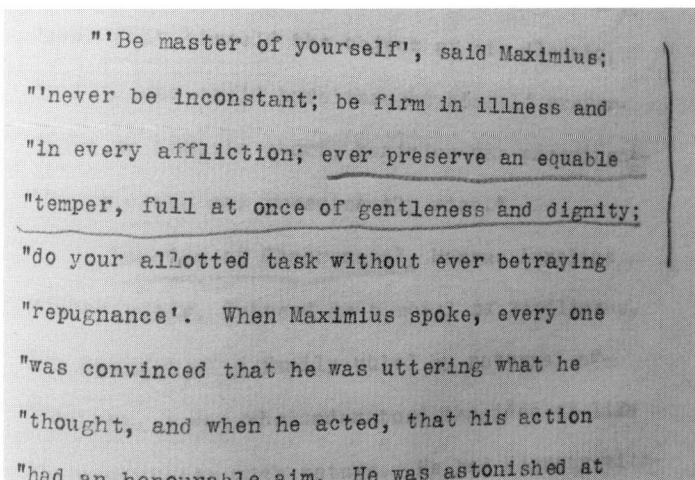

"'Be master of yourself', said Maximius;
"'never be inconstant; be firm in illness and
"in every affliction; ever preserve an equable
"temper, full at once of gentleness and dignity;
"do your allotted task without ever betraying
"repugnance'. When Maximius spoke, every one
"was convinced that he was uttering what he
"thought, and when he acted, that his action
"had an honourable aim. He was astonished at

Figure 11.3 Rhodes' underlinings in his translation of E. de Suckau's *Marcus Aurelius: his life and teachings*. Photograph by Paul Weinberg.

renting Groote Schuur since January 1891 and had decided to purchase the house.[6] In discussing Gibbon 'during a country house visit',[7] Rhodes

---

[6] Mr Humphreys' account requires that Rhodes was in England to initiate the project – further visits took place in the winters of 1890–91 and 1894–95. For Rhodes's residency and purchase of Groote Schuur in September 1893, see Brooke Simons 1996: 14–16.

[7] Williams 1921: 223.

regretted that he could not read in the original Greek and Latin the ancient authorities quoted by Gibbon and that there were no good translations readily available; he was advised to consult Mr Arthur Lee Humphreys of Hatchards. The following is Mr Humphreys' account of what happened:

One afternoon about the year 1893, Mr. Rhodes, accompanied by Mr. Rochfort Maguire called on me. Mr. Rhodes stated his business at once which was, that on his last trip over from South Africa he had re-read Gibbon's *Decline and Fall of the Roman Empire*, and he had been so much impressed by the book that he thought of forming a library, which was to consist of all the original authorities used by Gibbon in writing his history. I talked the matter over with him for some considerable time that afternoon, and broad lines were roughly laid down upon which the work should proceed. Mr. Rhodes, I remember, emphasised two things from the start. These were: first, that whatever I sent him should be in English, and whatever authors required translation, they should be sent completely unabridged. And secondly, he stated that he realised the magnitude of the undertaking, and that he hoped I should get a body of men together who would be glad to cooperate in such a work, and whoever was employed, he said he wished to be well paid. This was the first interview I ever had with Mr. Rhodes. He took out his chequebook before he went, and left me a cheque for a handsome sum towards the work.

I soon got together a body of scholars, and appointed one who was to be a general editor of the whole series of volumes. The work proceeded, and a large number of volumes were sent out, Mr. Rhodes writing to me from time to time general directions how to proceed, and very clearly stating his special interest in various aspects of the matter . . ..

At one time I had as many as twenty scholars[8] engaged to do the work, in addition to indexers, typists, binders . . .

Mr Humphreys also writes that 'some hundreds of volumes were sent out', but this figure includes more than the classical translations.[9] Indeed a sizeable proportion of the books represent an extension of the original plan, to include translations of relatively modern biographies of the emperors and recent works on Classical history. For example, on Julius Caesar there are translations of French works by Ramée (1870) and Dubois-

---

[8] Brooke Simons 1996: 121 alleges that 'several learned ladies' from Oxford and Cambridge were recruited to join the team of translators and that 'their modest Victorian cheeks must have blushed when they encountered some decidedly erotic passages in the texts'. The source of these surmises remains unclear, but the tabloid characterisation is clear, and suspect.

[9] There are, in fact, 208 volumes of typed translations of ancient Latin and Greek authors. Only when the other kinds of typed volumes (see below) are included does Mr Humphreys' figure become justifiable. Brooke Simons 1996: 121 makes the overall total of some 440.

Guchon (1880); on Domitian translations of French biographies by Crevier (1814)[10] and the Count de Champagny (1863)[11] and, of particular interest, of the magisterial work of S. Gsell published only in 1894; and among other recent works of French classical scholarship is René Cagnat's *L'armée romaine d'Afrique et l'occupation militaire de l'Afrique sous les empereurs* (1913).[12]

According to Williams, the collection was originally planned to be even larger and include the works of the Church Fathers quoted by Gibbon, 'but when it came to the apparently endless series of the complete works of the Fathers of the Church, from whom Gibbon had quarried, he (Rhodes) had to cry halt, and issued an order that the Fathers must cease'.[13] This rather rhetorical description must be inaccurate: no work of any of the Fathers survives in the collection today and Mr Humphreys mentions no intention of translating the Christian works.[14] Perhaps there was a suggestion that they should be included in the plan, which never went any further, but the works of the Fathers were never part of Rhodes's interests – he drew his philosophical comfort rather from the *Meditations* of Marcus Aurelius – and it seems very unlikely that he seriously contemplated including them in the collection.[15]

For Williams, the cost of the (expanded?) project led Rhodes to cancel it – but only after some £8,000 had been spent; in modern terms this would represent an investment of several million Rands.

An intriguing feature of the project is that the names of the scholars engaged to do the translations remain unknown: none of the volumes contains any name or indication of their identity. In the odd volume there are pencilled notes, for example 'corrected by J. H. F.', but this is no guide to

---

[10] Rhodes's translation was done from a reprint of M. Crevier, *Histoire des Empereurs Romains, depuis Auguste jusqu'à Constantin. Tome 7*, which first appeared in 1766.

[11] Franz Joseph, Comte de Champagny, whose *Les Césars* appeared first in 1841.

[12] This section of the project includes much older biographies – several with notable engravings and illustrations – translated from Hulsius' Latin works on the wives of Julius Caesar and Caligula (Levinus Hulsius (Lievin Hulst), *XII Primorum Caesarum et ipsorum uxorum et parentum ex antiquis numismatibus* (Frankfurt, 1597). Again, numerous antiquarian works from the earlier period: for example, Johannes Meursius's treatise on the luxury of the Romans: *Roma luxurians, sive de luxu Romanorum* (Copenhagen, 1605).

[13] Williams 1921: 223.

[14] The translation of Juvencus' *Evangeliorum Libri IV*, a version of the gospels in Latin hexameters, hardly belongs among the Fathers, despite its Christian theme. The major fire at Groote Schuur on 29 December 1896 which, according to Williams 1921: 224, destroyed some books, should not be adduced to explain the non-appearance of the Fathers. It would be an extraordinary coincidence if all the Fathers had been destroyed without trace of damage to the pagan authors. I have seen no trace of damage in any of the Rhodes translations.

[15] For Rhodes's exceptionally lukewarm attitude to Christianity see Rotberg 1988: 282, 415.

Figure 11.4 The Rhodes Collection, Groote Schuur Estate. Photograph by Paul Weinberg. (A black and white version of this figure will appear in some formats. For the colour version, please refer to the plate section.)

the translator. Indeed, the kind of correction seen in the translations suggests that the correctors were little more than proof-readers; improvements to the substance of the translation are not made. If any record of the identity of the translators and editors survived among Hatchards' archives, that was lost during the Blitz. The books themselves present an impressive sight in the Library at Groote Schuur with their bright red Morocco bindings and titles engraved in gilt on the spine (Fig. 11.4 and Plate 8). Their internal appearance, however, is far less impressive: the translations are typed in double-spacing, often with errors corrected in manuscript.

Some of Rhodes's biographers are dismissive of the whole project: according to Williams, 'the collection is a freak hardly worthy of Rhodes', and Lockhart and Woodhouse decry it as 'an extravagant and unrewarding experiment'.[16] Plomer's thorough and unscholarly traduction of Rhodes adds the following scurrilous details: 'the collection naturally included works "of a decidedly erotic nature", all suitably illustrated – much to the delight of some dependent, who cut the pictures out privily and carried them off.'[17] In fact, from a personal examination of those volumes most likely to have contained obscene illustrations – for example, the pederastic and erotic epigrams from the

---

[16] 1963: 204.   [17] Cf. the slur also in Flint's parenthetical remarks: 1974: 172.

Greek Anthology – I can attest that there is no evidence of any illustrations having been removed.

Here I propose to look at one aspect of Rhodes's classical project. Mr Humphrey's record of the project emphasises Rhodes's concern that the translations be unabridged. Any attempt to explain why Rhodes made this stipulation will founder on the absence of first-hand testimony by Rhodes. As we have seen, biographers hostile to Rhodes fastened on the idea that the collection contained 'obscene' material, implying that Rhodes's desire to read such material explains his commission and that by 'unabridged' we should understand 'unexpurgated'. Those who place great store by psychologising explanations of character and personality will be tempted to connect Rhodes's putative homosexuality.[18] A fair amount has been written in recent years about Victorian attitudes to homosexuality and the important role that classical texts played in the thinking of those who set themselves against prevailing Victorian attitudes.[19] If Rhodes was interested in classical texts on this subject and did not trust his own abilities to translate them, in the context of the 1890s he would have struggled to find translations readily available to assist him, as the legacy of Dr Bowdler's sanitisation of Shakespeare was widespread.[20] If, however, wider concerns than these are to be considered, we could attribute to Rhodes a certain level of intellectual curiosity without in any way elevating this to the academic – when a subject interested him, Rhodes read widely and voraciously. A genuine concern to be presented with all the information offered by the ancient sources is not impossible.

If we cannot pin down exactly Rhodes's motivation in requesting unabridged or unexpurgated translations, we can assess what the Hatchards' translators did with material that was subject to expurgation. Given Rhodes's fascination with the early Roman emperors, it is certain that one text he consulted and wanted unexpurgated was Suetonius' *De vita Caesarum*. Although his library contained the seventeenth-century translation by Philemon Holland, the Hatchards' translators produced a new

---

[18] Many of his biographers feel obliged to include something on the subject; see esp. Rotberg 1988: 396–408. Certainly, there is nothing to link Rhodes in attitudes or lifestyle with the likes of John Addington Symonds or Walter Pater, let alone with the contemporary aesthetes such as Oscar Wilde.

[19] Of particular relevance to Rhodes, given his education, see Dowling 1994. Most recently, Blanshard 2010 esp. 143–63, and of older material Jenkyns 1980 esp. 280–97.

[20] For a general study, see Perrin 1970. Pre-Victorian translations did not exhibit the later prudishness. For some authors Hatchards were able to source earlier translations (see footnotes in the appendix).

three-volume typescript. Two notorious passages, the former of which John Rolfe's famous Loeb translation left in Latin, illustrate what Rhodes received for his money:[21]

(i) Maiore adhuc ac turpiore infamia flagrauit, uix ut referri audiriue, nedum credi fas sit, quasi pueros primae teneritudinis, quos pisciculos uocabat, institueret, ut natanti sibi inter femina uersarentur ac luderent lingua morsuque sensim adpetentes; atque etiam quasi infantes firmiores, necdum tamen lacte depulsos, inguini ceu papillae admoueret, pronior sane ad id genus libidinis et natura et aetate. (*Tiberius* 44)

He incurred yet the infamie of greater and more shameful filthinesse, such as may not well be named or heard, and much lesse believed: to wit, that hee should traine up and teach fine boyes the tenderest and daintiest that might be had (whom he called his little fishes) to converse and play between his thighes as he was swimming, and pretily with tongue and teeth seeme to make unto his secret parts, and there to nibble: whom likewise, as babes of good grouth and strength, howbeit as yet not weaned, he should set unto his privie member as unto the nipple of a breast, to sucke. And verily, both by nature and for his yeares, more prone he was and given to lust in this kind (*irrumatio*). Holland

He suffered from a worse and more disgraceful ill-repute that is scarcely right to be told or heard, still less to be believed; that boys of quite tender years, whom he called his little fish, were trained to play and sport between his thighs as he swam, gently assailing him with tongue and lips; and that he put stronger infants, but not yet weaned, to his thigh as to a breast, being in fact more prone to that kind of licentiousness both by nature and by age.

Holland's translation is in fact excellent and clear as to the depravities in which Tiberius indulged, but adds material not in the original, namely 'his secret parts, and there to nibble', explicating what Suetonius intended his reader to understand. The Hatchards' translator by contrast sticks far closer to the Latin in this instance, rendering *adpetentes* by 'assailing him', but then completely misrepresents the *irrumatio* that Tiberius expected of his *infantes firmiores*: s/he mistranslates *inguini* as 'thigh'.

(ii) M. Lepidum, Mnesterem pantomimum, quosdam obsides dilexisse fertur commercio mutui stupri. Valerius Catullus, consulari familia iuuenis, stupratum a se ac latera sibi contubernio eius defessa etiam uociferatus est. (*Caligula* 36.1)

M. Lepidus Mnester the pantomime, yea and certain hostages he kept and loved, as the speech went, by way of reciprocall commerce in mutuall impurity, doing and suffering against kind. Valerius Catullus, a yong gentleman decended from

---

[21] The translation of Alexander Thomson, MD, first published in 1796, prints asterisks and the Latin text in a footnote.

a familie of consuls degree, complained and openly cried out, that hee was unnaturally by him abused and that his verie sides were weried, and tyred out with his filthie companie. (Holland)

He is said to have had the most abominable connections with Marcus Lepidus, Mnester the clown and several hostages. Valerius Catullus declared loudly that he had fallen exhausted from the emperor's vile embrace.

Holland's translation represents well the pejorative sense of *stuprum* and the range of sexual activity to be inferred from *commercium mutuum*; likewise, his interpretation of Caligula's sexual relationship with Valerius Catullus rightly brings out the emperor's passive role. The Hatchards' translator fails to bring out the mutual aspect of the relationship with Lepidus and completely omits Caligula's being sodomised by Catullus.

Further test cases can be taken from Catullus and Martial, both obvious authors to consult for sexual language.[22]

(iii) pedicabo ego vos et irrumabo,
   Aureli pathice et cinaede Furi (Catullus 16.1–2)
   I will defile you and I will lick you both, Aurelius and Furius, who lie under men.[23]

While the translation 'lie under men' captures the essence of *pathicus*, 'defile' is a euphemistic translation of *pedicare*, utterly ignoring the appropriate register.

(iv) te miserum malique fati
   Quem attractis pedibus patente porta
   Percurrent raphanique mugilesque (Cat 15.17–19)
   You ill-starred wretch, radishes and mullets shall pierce you while your feet are bound and your fundament is wide open!

The translator has produced an accurate and suitably explicit rendering, by comparison with the standard translation that appeared in the Loeb twenty years later.[24]

---

[22] An odd phenomenon is that the library contains a duplicate copy of the three volumes of Martial translation; one set differs from the other in having a header which enables the reader to know in which Book he is on any page. To me the duplication suggests that the copy without a header was found unsatisfactory, whether by Rhodes or Hatchards is unclear, and that a version that made use easier was requested. Another explanation may be connected to the fire, but there are no signs of fire damage on either copy.

[23] Postgate's Loeb translation, published first in 1913, omits the first two lines completely.

[24] Postgate translates *patente porta* by 'before the city's gaze', an example of what a bowdleriser could do with Catullus' vulgarity, and paraphrases 'radishes and mullets' with 'as cruelly as an adulterer'.

(v) Non dixi, Coracine, te cinaedum:

  Non sum tam temerarius nec audax . . .

  Dixi te, Coracine, cunnilingum (Mart. 4.43, 1–2, 11)

  No, Coracinus, I never said you were a sodomite. I am not so rash . . . What
I said, Coracinus, was that you were a lick-spittle.

While the translator deals adequately with *cinaedus*, his/her courage fails
at *cunnilingus*: 'lick-spittle', a nineteenth-century creation according to the
Oxford English Dictionary connotes primarily toadying, and so delivers
the idea of humiliation that Martial's insult requires, but not the sexual
element that is key to the Latin term.[25]

So, from this brief sample I would conclude that Rhodes was not ill-
served by the Hatchards' translators given the temper of the times, but
that they were not a marked improvement on, for example, Holland's
Suetonius in relation to the translation of the obscene.[26] More broadly,
the translations that I examined back in the early 1990s are of a high
standard when judged against other translations produced in the
Victorian period.[27]

At the time of its creation the Rhodes Collection was a unique scholarly enterprise in terms of scope and concept: many of the works had no
English translations. However, because they were a private commission
destined for a private library and the books were largely unknown to the
international Classics community, they have languished unused and
unappreciated. Although the passing of time, even since the early
1990s, has diminished the potential value of the Rhodes collection as
far as publication is concerned – for example, there is now an English

---

[25] Soldevilla 2006: 319–16 correctly locates the terms *cinaedus* and *cunnilingus* in their semantic
field, the latter being specifically degrading and unmanly.

[26] A useful study might be to compare the Hatchards translations of the poems in *Musa puerilis*
and other pederastic material with what was being produced by 'the Uranians'. Cf. Blanshard
2010: 146.

[27] This is my impression from a perusal of a selection of the volumes. I have studied with
greater attention the translation of the *Ephemeris Belli Troiani by* Dictys of Crete, which is of
serviceable quality. The translator has captured the spirit of Dictys, whilst treating his
syntax freely. (S)he, for example, has the annoying habit of ignoring temporal expressions
such as *interea*, and *inter haec*. There has been an inevitable dating of some aspects of
language since the late nineteenth century, but on the whole the work is pleasantly readable.
Before her untimely death in 2000 Dr M. R. Mezzabotta was working on an updating of the
Rhodes translation of Servius' Commentary on *Aeneid* I. Based on the standard text of Thilo
and Hagen this is the only English translation known to me of even a part of Servius'
commentary and deserves exposure to a wider audience. Perhaps one day it can form the
basis of a new translation, once the text of Servius's work has a scholarly edition that has
won wide acceptance.

translation of Censorinus' *De die natali*[28] – some of the works have still not been translated into English, although the texts are important to students of ancient and Byzantine history and literature. In this last category, and most likely to be of interest, are L. Ampelius' *Liber memorialis*,[29] Aethicus Ister's *Cosmographia*, Julius Valerius' *Res gestae Alexandri Magni* and the complete *Nova Historia* of Zonaras.

Professor J. E. Atkinson fought a long battle with successive Ministers and officials for the possibility of using the collection, culminating in access being granted during the presidency of F. W. de Klerk. A larger scale, scholarly evaluation remains a desideratum, and publication of those volumes that would serve a scholarly purpose should be considered.

Appendix: Classical translations in the Rhodes Collection

Author	Title of Work	Volume No.
Aelian	*Varia Historia*	9[30]
	Epistulae	8
Aelius Aristides	*Opera omnia*	30–36
Aeschylus	*Tragoediae*	10
Aethicus Ister	*Cosmographia*	11
Agathias	*Historia*	12–13
Alciphron	*Epistulae*	14
Ampelius	*Liber memorialis*	16
Anacreon	*Poemata*	17
Anna Comnena	*Alexiad*	18–20
Antiphon	*Orationes*	21
Antonius Diogenes	*Mirabilia utra Thulem*	238
Apicius	*De re coquinaria*	22
Apuleius	*Opera omnia*	25–28
Aristaenetus	*Epistulae*	29
Aristophanes	*Comoediae*	37–38
[Arrian]	*Periplus maris Erythraei*	239

---

[28] Parker 2007. Further examples illustrate the obscurity in which the Rhodes Collection has lain: neither the most recent editor of the critical text of Agathias, Rudolf Keydell, nor its English translator, Joseph D. Frendo, who claims the honour of having made 'the first complete English translation of the *Histories* ever to appear', had any idea of Rhodes's Agathias: see Frendo 1975: xi. Likewise, Murphy 1977 was unaware of any complete translation of Avienus. Thomas Banchich did not know of any English translation of Zonaras since the seventeenth century: Banchich and Lane 2009: 11.

[29] Lashbrook 1960.   [30] A retyping of the translation printed for Thomas Dringin (1665).

(*cont.*)

Author	Title of Work	Volume No.
Attaliata, Michael	*Historia*	9–40
Ausonius	*Opera omnia*	41–42
Avienus	*Aratea phaenomena et prognostica*	43
Bassus, Saleius	*Panegyricus ad Calpurnium Pisonem*	16
Berosus	*Babyloniaca*	59
Boethius	*De consolation philosophiae*	60
Caelius Symphosius	*Enigmata*	16
Calpurnius Siculus	*Eclogae*	65
Cameniata, Johannes	*De captura Thessalonicae*	66
Catullus	*Poemata*	72
Censorinus	*De die natali*	73
Cicero	*Rhetorica ad Herennium*	76
Cinnamus	*Historiae*	78–79
Claudian	*Opera omnia*	80–81
Constantine Porphyrogenitus	*De Ceremoniis*	250–54
Cornutus	*Compendium theologiae Graecae*	43
Cosmas Indicopleustes	*Christiana topographia*	83
Curtius Rufus	*De rebus gestis Alexandri Magni*	261–62
Dares	*De excidio Troiae historia*	113
Dexippus	*Scythica*	16
Dictys Cretensis	*Encheiridion De bello Troiano*	113
Dio Cassius	*Historiae*	114–23
Dio Chrysostom	*Orations, discourses, Treatises*	124–29
Etruscus, Maximianus	*Elegiae*	139
Euripides	*Dramata* (not complete)	140–41
Exuperantius	*Bella Civilia*	16
Frontinus	*De aquis*	65
Fronto	*Epistulae*	144
Greek Anthology	Selection	82
	Pederastic epigrams (*Musa puerilis*)	217
	Erotic epigrams	138
Herodas	*Mimae*	151
Herodes Atticus	*De re publica* (and minor works)	16
Hesychius	*De Sophistis*	152
Horace	*Saturae*	153
Hyginus	*Fabulae*	155
	De munitionibus castrorum	152
	Astronomiae	156
Jordanes	*Getica*	166–67
	Romana	168

(*cont.*)

Author	Title of Work	Volume No.
Julian	*Opera omnia*	167–73[31]
Justin	*Historiae Philippicae*	174–76
Juvencus	*Evangeliorum libri IV*	73
Laonicus Chalcocondyles	*History of the Turks*	74–75
Latin Anthology	*various items*[32]	184–85
Lucian	*Amores*	188
Lycurgus	*Adversus Leocratem*	189
Macrobius	*Opera omnia*	190–93
Malchus	*De legationibus*	194
Marcellinus	*Chronicon*	152
Martial	*Epigrammata*	195–99
Menander the Guardsman	*De legationibus*	214
Musonius Rufus	*De luxuria*	218
Namatianus	*De reditu*	16
Nemesianus	*Cynegetica*	65
Nicetas	*Historia*	219–21
Nicolaus Damascenus	*Historiae*	92
Obsequens	*Liber prodigiorum*	11
Olympiodorus	*Chronicles* (excerpts)	222
Ovid	*Opera Omnia*	226–33
Panegyrici veteres	*Panegyricae*	236–37
Parthenius	*Erotica*	238
Phaedrus	*Fabulae*	240
Philostratus	*Vita Apollonii*	241–42
	Apologia and Letters	243
	Vita sophistorum	244–45
Plautus	*Comoediae*	246–49
Polemon	*Declamationes*	11
Priscus of Panium	*Historia*	255
Procopius	*Secret History*	260[33]
	Historia bellorum Justiniani	256–59[34]
Scriptores Historiae Augustae	*Historia Augusta*	265–68
Scylitzes, John	*History*	268–70
Seneca	*Epistulae, Dialogi*	271–79[35]

[31] *Orationes* iv and v translated by Thomas Taylor

[32] Contents include Seneca's epigrams, Vergiliana, Octavian, Dido's epistle to Aeneas, Achilles' speech at Scyros.

[33] Retyping of translation printed for John Barkisdale of London (1674).

[34] Retyping of translation by Henry Holcroft (1653).

[35] Retyping of edition printed by W. Stansby of London (1620).

(*cont.*)

Author	Title of Work	Volume No.
	Naturales Quaestiones	142
Servius	*Comm. in Aeneidem* I	282–83
Sextus Empiricus	*Adversus mathematicos*	284–86
	Adversus Pyrrhonem	287
Silius Italicus	*Punica*	288–90
Solinus	*Collectanea rerum memorabilium*	291
Statius	*Silvae*	292
Suetonius	*De vita Caesarum*	410–12
Symmachus	*Epistulae*	293–95
Terence	*Comoediae*	296–97
Theognis	*Elegiae*	298
Theophylactus Simocatta	*Historiae*	299–300
Valerius, Julius	*De rebus gestis Alexandri Magni*	301
Valerius Flaccus	*Argonauticon*	142
Vegetius	*Epitoma rei militaris*	302[36]
Vibius Sequester	*Geographical glossary*	16
Victor, Sex. Aurelius	*Epitome de Caesaribus*	303
Zonaras	*Epitome historiarum*	304–13
Zosimus	*Historia Nova*	314–15

[36] Retyping of translation by Lieutenant John Clarke (1767).

PART VI

Boundary Crossers

In *The Classics and South African Identities*, Michael Lambert demonstrates how antiquity has played a role in the self-fashioning of South Africans. Access to antiquity has been extremely unequal, with few blacks given the opportunity to learn Latin or Greek. It comes as no surprise that the four individuals covered in this section show four very different kinds of engagement with antiquity. Only one of them, D. D. T. Jabavu, was born in South Africa, though each spent a significant part or his or her career in the country. At least three may be considered public intellectuals, in that they spoke out on issues of the day. Jabavu is an historically important figure, in that he was the first black professor of Classics at Fort Hare University at a time when the Mandela generation of Southern African political leaders studied there. (A century later, he remains the only black person to have held a chair of Classics in the country.) Jabavu's classics and moderate politics went hand in hand. He diverged from the more radical black politicians who went on to form the ANC and also from white liberals who, to his surprise and dismay, at a crucial juncture supported the dispossession of black landowners (**Claassen**). Benjamin Farrington was perhaps the most flamboyant of the public intellectuals, espousing several different causes, national and international, partly inspired by ancient Epicureanism; on occasion, he drastically changed course (**Atkinson**). Though Mary Renault is well known as a historical novelist writing on classical themes, her lengthy South African sojourn is less familiar, though Cape Town was the base of many of her greatest literary successes. Keenly involved in an anti-apartheid organisation, the Black Sash, she nonetheless avoided contemporary politics in her writings (**Endres**). The lyric poet Douglas Livingstone, who developed an interest in classical literature only in later life, made varied and nuanced use of antiquity (**Coleman**). In all, it appears that in each case classicism articulated some kind of critical distance from the immediate community: Jabavu's was part of, and perhaps inspired by, the liberal humanist tradition; for Farrington in the 1920s, atomic theory was linked to Marxian thought; for Renault, classical antiquity and the 'Mediterranean' Cape afforded welcome personal freedoms; in the case of Livingstone, most subtly, classical antiquity offered pointed ways in which to question social and political orthodoxies of the time and to focus anew on the artistic sphere.

1 2 | 'You Are People Like These Romans Were!': D. D. T. Jabavu of Fort Hare

JO-MARIE CLAASSEN

Davidson Don Tengu Jabavu of the 'South African Native[1] College' (established 1916), later Fort Hare University, at Alice in the Eastern Cape, was the first Black African teacher of Classics at a South African institution of higher learning. First and foremost, he was an educator whose classical training imbued his thoughts and informed his conversation to such an extent that he would as readily use an example from Roman history to illustrate a point about local agriculture to an uneducated farmer, as he would employ the term 'Spartan' to designate before an international audience the rural mothers of the Xhosa children about whose educational future he was passionately concerned. He was also intensely involved in the early struggle history in South Africa against the increasingly restrictive political and economic repression that in his lifetime virtually tied South African Black people hand and foot.

1. Inextricability of Being a Black Academic and a Proponent of Liberation

No South African Black academic has ever been able – or has wanted – to withdraw to an ivory tower and stand outside the politics of his day. This was as true of Professor Jabavu as of any of those of his students who would eventually feature as the struggle heroes who oversaw the dawn of our democracy. Nelson Mandela was one of Jabavu's students, but after early student unrest, he left the Eastern Cape and continued his studies at the University of South Africa, a renowned 'distance learning' institution. The late Chris Hani studied Latin for three years under Jabavu. One of Jabavu's most brilliant products was Professor Z. K. Matthews, one of the original 'treason trialists' of the early 1960s.

---

[1] 'Native' was the term for South African Blacks in common use at the time. The term was freely used by Jabavu himself in his various writings, but, to suit the sensibilities of the present day, this article will place the term in quotation marks, or substitute for it the more common currency of today: 'Black' using upper case, as also for 'White'.

Politics and religion served very much to shape the course of
D. D. T. Jabavu's life. He was a Xhosa speaker, but from the Mfengu
group that early in the nineteenth century had fled the Natal Colony to
avoid the bellicose attentions of King Shaka. The British had settled them
in the Eastern Cape under the care of the Wesleyan (Methodist) missionary
Ayliff and induced them to swear allegiance to both the Crown and the
Cross.[2] His religious convictions coloured every aspect of Jabavu's life as
educator, political activist and family man.

When young Davidson Don was of the age to enter high school, his father,
John Tengu Jabavu, the editor and publisher of a Xhosa-language newspaper, himself exceptionally well-educated (given the circumstances of most
Xhosa speakers of the second half of the nineteenth century) and deeply
involved in the affairs of the church and of colonial politics, sought, as a tax-
paying citizen, to enrol his son at Dale College in King William's Town in the
Eastern Cape Province. The school's board of governors turned them down
on the pretext that 'it would set a dangerous precedent' for the breakdown of
South African segregationist customs of the time.[3] This resulted in the young
man in 1903 being sent to study in England, where he remained for a full ten
years, returning in 1913 with a degree from London University and
a teacher's diploma from Birmingham (Fig. 12.1). By 1916 Davidson Don
Jabavu was appointed the first lecturer in languages at the fledgling 'Native
College' which had just been established, largely thanks to the efforts of his
father. Soon after, he was married to Florence Makiwane, an accomplished
pianist who had also studied in Birmingham. The families had arranged the
marriage, with both Western and traditional trappings.

Politics continued to haunt the lives of the Jabavus, father and son.
Before the third generation male Jabavu, D. D. T.'s son Tengu, could
continue their tradition of liberal political activism, he was killed in
a bizarre mishap while studying medicine at the University of the
Witwatersrand in Johannesburg.[4] The first two Jabavus both found that
their essentially 'gradualist', conciliatory stance toward those whom they
considered the 'best and most just' of Afrikaner politicians of their respec-
tive times, would in the end let them down. Both men, at the end of a life of

---

[2] Brownlee 1970: 2 gives an overview of this history.

[3] This is narrated dispassionately in the third person by D. D. T. Jabavu himself in his biography, *John Tengu Jabavu, a great Bantu patriot* (1922: 69–75). This refusal elicited a great deal of correspondence in the Cape newspapers, and the *Cape Times* reported Rev. W. B. Shaw's denouncing it as 'directly opposed to the Gospel of Paul'.

[4] Noni Jabavu tells about her brother's death (1960: 15–17). People in Johannesburg needed 'protection' from a gangster against other gangsters; Tengu's 'protectioner' shot him. Professor Jabavu's biographer refers merely to a 'shooting accident': Higgs 1997: 154.

Arrival in South Africa.
October 1914.

Figure 12.1 D. D. T. Jabavu upon his return to South Africa, October 1914.

activism, had to deal with the disappointment of having lost some of the respect of their more militant colleagues and friends in the South African struggle for equality.[5] Both father and son had in the end to be content with a placid retirement outside the heat of the continued political fray, when each in turn had been voted out of the positions of political leadership he

[5] John Tengu Jabavu could not believe that his friend J. W. Sauer would do other than turn the proposed 'Land Act' of 1913 in favour of Black Africans and hence he initially supported it, to his later extreme discomfiture. D. D. T. Jabavu 1922: 47–48. Between 1927 and 1937, when the increase of political segregation and the diminution of long-held Black rights were in constant dispute between hardliners and liberals, the son was actively engaged in negotiations. Initially he favoured the mooted idea of a separate voters' roll on the principle of half a loaf being better than no bread. He hence continued in friendship with some White politicians, thereby losing the trust of his more fiery Black colleagues and, in the end, gained no positive concessions for his people, not even from liberal politicians such as Smuts and Hofmeyr. Cf. Higgs 1997: 121–43.

had enjoyed. Each, however, continued to exert moral leadership, virtually until the comparatively early demise of each.

2. Sources

As with any hero from literature, the character of Davidson Don Jabavu can be read from what he did, what he said (or, in our era, what he wrote) and what others said (or wrote) about him. The most complete description of Jabavu's life and work is to be found in a comprehensive biography by Catherine Higgs.[6] Jabavu was an indefatigable pamphleteer and very many of his writings are available, mostly published in compendia by the Missionary Press of the Lovedale Institution (about which more below),[7] but also in an excellent collection of political source material by Karis and Carter.[8] Very few of Jabavu's writings may be classed as 'Classical' or even 'scholarly' in the modern 'publish-or-perish' tradition, but that fact does not detract from his accomplishments as the first Black South African Classics lecturer, a great educator of African youth and a fashioner of Black African thought in his time.[9]

His own biography of his late father, published soon after the death of the latter, in its adulatory and largely uncritical tone 'borders', in the words of Higgs, 'on hagiography'.[10] From it one gains a picture not only of Jabavu

[6] In spite of the second part of her title for the biography of Jabavu, 'The public lives of D. D. T. Jabavu', Higgs admits: '[with Jabavu there was] no mask: no public face for the white world and private face for the black' (1997: 2).

[7] For this chapter, I have consulted only a representative few of Jabavu's works: *The Black Problem: Papers and Addresses on Various Native Problems* (1920), a compilation of mostly public addresses from 1918–29 with an abbreviation of a report written in 1913, arranged into a comprehensive whole; *The Influence of English on Bantu Literature* (n.d.).; *John Tengu Jabavu* (1922); *The Segregation Fallacy and other papers* (1928); 'Higher education and the professional training of Bantu' (1929); 'The Child as he comes to school', Part 1 of Chap. XVII 'The African child and what the school makes of him' in Malherbe 1937: 432–35.

[8] Karis and Carter 1973.

[9] Here Jabavu was like, or even ahead of, several of his White contemporaries at South African institutions of higher learning. Helen A. Sargent of the first women's college, Huguenot College at Wellington in the Western Cape, came to South Africa in about 1905 with a BA degree from Oberlin College in the USA. This was later ratified as an MA by the University of Cape Town, but she never published any learned articles, remaining content to get her students to read, parse and translate reams of Latin texts, without any attempt at placing these into a wider literary or cultural context. She was a dedicated Latin teacher, who could also teach Greek but did not contribute to scholarship in any way. My sources are two of her students from the 1920s and a collection of her letters to her family found in her house when she moved to a frail-care home, which was later returned to Oberlin.

[10] Higgs 1997: 2. The work in question is Jabavu's *John Tengu Jabavu*.

senior but also of the son who sought to live up to his father's ideals for him as academic leader of his people, while at the same time reflecting and continuing with the older man's sedate, yet impassioned, enthusiasm for education as the means toward the upliftment of all Black South Africans.

From the writings of others we gain a picture of the centrally important role D. D. T. Jabavu played as virtually the sole academic representative of the early strivings of the dispossessed and marginalised in South Africa. No conference on the so-called 'Bantu problem' held between 1920 and 1945 (and there were many) was held without him, and his name appears in the indices (and his opinions are cited in the pages) of every learned tome from that era that even remotely touches on the contemporary political position of South African Black people.[11]

Finally, from the pages of the autobiography of one of his students, Z. K. Matthews,[12] and from two books written by D. D. T. Jabavu's older daughter Noni,[13] the learned professor and inspired political activist emerges as an ebullient and benevolent teacher and parent, whose enthusiasm for languages in general and for the Classics in particular was matched by his love for music, for his church and for the social life common to third-generation, conservatively Westernised Xhosa speakers. At the same time it is clear that he remained true to the best in his own indigenous culture.[14] From those closest to him we can also see the great man's little foibles, chief of which was his personal vanity (he was particularly proud of his voice and of his skill as a pianist).

3. The Lovedale Institute, Fort Hare 'Native College' and What They Stood For

The institution that later became the University of Fort Hare was in a large way the brainchild and fruit of the fundraising skills of the elder Jabavu

---

[11] For example, Brookes 1924 has 14 references to D. D. T. Jabavu. This work largely formed the basis of the segregationist policies of the then emerging Afrikaner Nationalists. Brookes himself later told how, by 1930, he had repudiated this approach (1977: 45–46). After fifty years Brookes republished the historical component of his earlier book, stripped of its segregationist recommendations (1974). It, too, quotes from Jabavu's *Black Problem* (1974: 95, n. 22 and 186, n. 26).

[12] Matthews 1981. Matthews also composed an obituary (1959).

[13] Helen Nontando Jabavu (lived 1919–2008): 1960 and 1963.

[14] Here I largely differ with Lambert 2011: 119–21, who discerns a discomfort in Jabavu about his dual role as product of a European education and African patriot. Jabavu seemed to bestride two worlds with consummate ease, without either pandering to or being intimidated by either.

Figure 12.2 South African Native College, Fort Hare, Cape Province, South Africa, 1930.

(Fig. 12.2).[15] It was erected within the borders of the area traditionally inhabited by Xhosa speakers, but from the beginning it was intended as an institution for higher learning for Black students from all the different tribal and linguistic groupings of Southern Africa, with a reach up to and including the borders of what was then Rhodesia (Robert Mugabe is a notable alumnus), Botswana (then 'Bechuanaland') and even Mozambique.[16] The college was erected at Fort Hare, close to the

[15] In 1901 Isaiah Bud-Mbelle (leader of the Mfengu people living at Kimberley) proposed a 'Queen Victoria memorial' fundraising campaign to establish a university college for Black students. The third chapter of Jabavu's *John Tengu Jabavu* (1922: 69–104) gives a complete overview of this process and Jabavu senior's role in it. Fort Hare's 'Native College' was opened in 1916 by General Louis Botha. Until 1923 it functioned as a secondary school preparing candidates for matriculation, when it was at last incorporated as a declared institute for higher education, producing its first candidate for a BA degree from the University of South Africa in 1924. In 1951 when the constituent colleges of UNISA gained autonomy under the 'Rhodes University (Private) Act' the 'University College of Fort Hare' was affiliated to Rhodes University and from 1955–59, under the combined 'Universities Act' and 'Fort Hare Transfer Act' it gained so-called 'independence', but by 1960 its Black Senate was no longer autonomous and was relegated to becoming an 'advisory body'. Jabavu delivered the address at its first graduation ceremony in 1956.

[16] Later students came from as far as Uganda. Jabavu's younger daughter, Noni's sister, was briefly (and disastrously) married to a Ugandan whom she met at Fort Hare, but who reverted to the

Figure 12.3 National conference of Black and White students, South African Native College, Fort Hare, Cape Province, South Africa, 1930. See Claassen 1997.

Presbyterian missionary college known as the Lovedale Institute. Both institutions were situated in the town of Alice in the Eastern Cape.

The so-called 'South African Native College' was fiercely independent from any missionary intervention. From the beginning it housed an inter-denominational faculty of theology and a faculty of agriculture. The only concession to parochialism was that each of certain mainstream Christian denominations was allowed to erect and run a students' residence. Its first principal was a Scot, Alexander Kirk, who, together with the young Jabavu and one other, comprised the whole of the faculty in the early years.[17] From the beginning, women were also admitted. The first class had two. In the first few years the 'Native College' merely prepared students for matricula-tion under the South African Matriculation Board; that is, they were brought to the point where they were able to sit for the type of examination that would allow them entrance to tertiary education. In time its University courses prepared those students to sit for examinations of the University

customary patriarchism of his own culture, a culture very much at odds with the liberal attitude to women of her own father. The marriage did not survive. Cf. Noni Jabavu 1960: 106–87.

[17] Higgs 1997: 35, lists as Jabavu's assignment in the early years Xhosa, Zulu, Sesotho, South African and European history and Latin. She ascribes his 'extraordinary dedication' to an awareness that 'his own reputation would rise and fall with the success or failure of the College'.

of South Africa, of which it was a constituent college. The first of the Fort Hare matriculants to graduate with a BA, Z. K. Matthews, a native of Botswana and a Tswana-speaker who had grown up Kimberley, later became Professor of Anthropology at Fort Hare and briefly acted as Principal after the retirement of Professor Kirk.[18]

4. D. D. T. Jabavu's Father, John Tengu Jabavu

From the son's book a picture emerges of one of the two people who most influenced him. This was his father. John Tengu Jabavu had, at age 17, started as a teacher with a 'Government Certificate of Competency' at Somerset East, while also serving as preacher at the local Wesleyan church and working as an apprentice at a local printer's workshop. After school hours he had studied privately under Professor Kyd of Gill College, where he excelled at his favourite subjects, Greek and Latin. He had subsequently briefly worked at Lovedale College as editor of its college journal and taught some classes in elementary Latin and Xhosa. In 1883 he became the second Black South African to matriculate.[19]

John Tengu Jabavu was an impassioned activist for the advancement and political liberation of his people, and when it became clear that his political enthusiasm would not sit well within the sedate walls of a missionary institution, he resigned, and, with the financial support of White friends, started the Xhosa-language newspaper, *Imvu Zabantsundu* [Black People's Opinion]. J. T. Jabavu wrote for and published the paper for virtually the rest of his life, while also engaging in political activism, and writing fervently in support of many causes affecting the wellbeing of Black Africans. He was on occasion asked by the Dutch and Xhosa speakers of the Peddie district, where he had bought a farm, to stand for Parliament – this was then still possible for a Black man in the Cape Colony – but he argued that his White friend, the liberal James Rose-Innes, would be able to exert more power on their behalf and he canvassed for Rose-Innes 'without remuneration', according to the younger Jabavu.[20] By this time he was already married, and Davidson Don (named after a liberal Scottish missionary) was born in 1885.

Jabavu Senior's liberal attitude and fiery nature brought him the friendship – and on occasion the enmity – of many, including White liberal

---

[18] Two papers by Z. K. Matthews, published while Professor Jabavu was still alive, give a good picture of the status that university education for Black South Africans had achieved in his time: 1946: 138–41 and 1950: 164–65.

[19] The first was Simon P. Sihlali, in 1880: Davis 1979: 16.   [20] Jabavu 1922: 17.

politicians of his era. He was very sceptical of the South Africa Act of 1909 that would lead to the Union of 1910. He predicted (correctly) that amalgamation of the Cape Province (where a more liberal attitude to Black people prevailed and where they had enjoyed a qualified franchise since 1854) with the more illiberal northern provinces would lead to attrition of the rights of Black people, also in the Cape Province. When the notorious 1913 Land Act was first mooted, he opposed the idea vigorously, but was persuaded by his friend, the liberal politician Sauer, that the 'Native Reserves' it proposed would bring benefit to his people. In this J. T. Jabavu was bitterly disappointed when the opposite proved true, and, by his earlier qualified support of the Act, he also forfeited much of the respect of Black South Africans he had formerly enjoyed and lost his pre-eminence in matters political. However, he still believed passionately in the need for a 'Native College' and was the prime mover and chief fundraiser for the accomplishment of his ideal, for which he seems to have groomed his son from an early age. He continued with these activities until the college was established, after which he served on its board until his death in 1922. His editorship of *Imvu* was in time taken over by another of his sons.

5. School and University

While the political and spatial noose was gradually being drawn tighter around the Cape 'Native's' neck, J. T. Jabavu maintained the lavish but conservative domestic establishment of a typical Victorian newspaperman. After the death of his first wife, the well-educated Edna Sakuba, he married Gertrude Joninga, also the product of a missionary upbringing, who proved a kind and loving stepmother. Young Davidson Don grew up in comparative urban luxury, but also enjoyed at weekends the freedom of a typical rural boy, when the whole Jabavu household moved from their town house in an affluent part of King William's Town to his father's farm near Peddie. The young boy never outgrew his familiarity with cattle-keeping and his love for horses. Even when he was later established as lecturer at Fort Hare, he would prefer travelling on horseback to any other means of conveyance. Even his later courtship of Florence Madikane was conducted on horseback.[21]

---

[21] Noni Jabavu relates that her father had, soon after his return from England, submitted to having his family arrange a marriage for him (1963: 252). Florence was an accomplished horsewoman. The young couple got to know each other well, and fell in love, while going riding together in the countryside around Fort Hare. Noni earlier writes lovingly of her father's 'blind devotion to horses and trains' that led him to be the last in his family to acquire a motor car (1963: 22).

After his initial schooling in the town, his father decided that Davidson Don, then about 14, should learn another African language, and sent him off to school at Morija in today's Lesotho (then Basotholand Protectorate), where he remained for several years. The boy survived the upheaval, even thrived on being plunged into 'immersion schooling' in a tongue as foreign to him as the related Germanic language Dutch would be to a boy used to speaking only English. On his return by train through the Free State at vacation time, Davidson Don saw at first hand the ravages wrought by the Anglo-Boer War on the land of poverty-stricken farmers, both Black and White. In the end, when the war made train travel impossible and after a journey that had entailed an arduous two-week-long 'lift' by ox-wagon to the Aliwal-North railhead, the boy had to stay in Lesotho for a full year, even during vacations.[22] After the next vacation at home, he did not go back, but instead entered Lovedale College, where Latin was added to his now almost formidable array of languages.[23]

It was after Davidson's completion of the so-called 'Junior Certificate' that the elder Jabavu sought to enter his son at Dale College, and, when they were rebuffed, it was decided that he should go to England. By 1903 the young man, then already 18, left by ship for Colwyn Bay Missionary School in Wales, where he at last achieved a matriculation certificate in the kind of academic subjects that would allow his entrance to London University, where he studied French, logic, Latin and English for his BA. Young Jabavu's subsequent excursion into postgraduate work included Gothic and Middle English, but he landed among the unsuccessful forty per cent of the English Honours class of 1912.

For ten years almost the only contact the young man had with his family was by letter. When on occasion Jabavu Senior went on a deputation to the British Parliament to protest the then imminent passing of the Land Act, he could visit his son. Life in London was for the rest made happier by the young man's connection with the Society of Friends ('Quakers') with whom his father had ties. His biographer Higgs notes that Davidson Don Jabavu managed to scrape by with only a 'third-class' pass in English and Classics, but that, when he started teacher

---

[22] Noni Jabavu, sensitively describes his first train journey 'as an unhappy small boy' to Lesotho (1963: 247–51). Her father must often have regaled his family on his reminiscences.

[23] Noni Jabavu ascribes familiarity with seven modern languages plus Latin to her father (1963: 253).

training at Birmingham University, the gifted aspiring teacher came into his own, at the end of the course achieving his teacher's certificate with distinction. His teaching practice had been conducted at Queen Mary's Grammar School in Walsall, where he earned the praise of the Classics master as 'a keen and quick-witted man of culture' with 'distinct charm and a cheerful and inspiring influence'.[24] Teaching, not only formally in the classroom, but the habit of informally passing on to others his wide knowledge of men and matters, remained D. D. T. Jabavu's lifelong, abiding passion.

Before his return Jabavu Junior travelled to the United States of America, where he enjoyed visits to various cities, but, in particular, spent time at Tuskegee Institute, the training college for American Black artisans started and run by the gifted African-American reformer, Booker T. Washington. Washington was the second person to have an abiding formative influence on Davidson Don,[25] and the practical management of the Institute profoundly affected the young teacher's management of students at Fort Hare, as well as giving him material with which to instigate and inspire the training of Black farmers in his home country. When it became known that he was to visit Tuskegee, the young Jabavu was asked by the South African government to write a report on the Institute, which he did, completing a detailed, copious document in record time.[26] On his return to South Africa, however, the report was no longer required, political wheels having once again turned. It was, however, later published in abbreviated form in one of his compendia of articles, and it continued to inform his whole approach to teaching.[27]

[24] Higgs 1997: 29.

[25] Higgs (1997: 24–25) asserts that Jabavu was disappointed in Washington's taciturnity, but that he paradoxically admired both Washington's conciliatory attitude to Whites, which accorded well with his and his father's views, and the trenchant confrontationism of the Harvard-educated W. E. B. Du Bois.

[26] Epitomised and incorporated as 'Section 1' of 'Part II': Jabavu 1920: 27–98.

[27] Students at Tuskegee would alternate between theoretical classes, including mathematics, chemistry and physics, and practical application in workshops and in the fields of the Institute. All were obliged to alternate mental and physical labour. Many paid off their total study debt through putting in extra hours of labour. The scientific farming methods introduced at Tuskegee under an inspired Carver were also avidly noted by the young Jabavu and subsequently broadcast to agricultural associations and clubs in the Eastern Cape, where Jabavu became indirectly instrumental in the training of many indigenous farmers. The Tuskegee ideas were also carried over to the training of the elite youth studying at Fort Hare. Matthews describes how he and his classmates were expected to help with the construction of many of the minor buildings on the Fort Hare campus, and were worked hard at clearing the gardens of weeds, planting and constructing pathways. He ascribes this regimen to the austerity of Alexander Kirk, but its format smacks of Tuskegee (1981: 52).

6. Appointment at Fort Hare

On his return Davidson Don Jabavu walked into the appointment as
lecturer in Classical and African languages at Fort Hare for which his
father had groomed him. He was accorded the courtesy title of
'Professor' from the beginning, but the position was conferred upon
him only much later (in 1942, two years before his retirement). As one of
only three faculty members, he had a full teaching load, and to all
accounts he was an inspired teacher, imbuing, in the words of
Matthews, even the 'dead languages' with the brilliant fire of his enthusiasm. His one vanity was his awareness of the attractiveness of his
striking baritone, which was equally impressive in either oratory or
music. He would hold forth to his students, allowing Ciceronian periods
or Virgilian hexameters to roll mellifluously off his tongue, accompanying his verbal pyrotechnics with suitable gestures. Generations of future
African leaders sat under his tutelage, which was not limited to his
academic role as teacher of languages. Weekends were filled with clubs
and other activities in which he joined with his students: Students'
Christian Association meetings on Friday nights, tennis and cricket on
Saturdays, with, in the evening, concerts or musical soirees. On Sundays
he would often deliver the sermon in the College chapel.

For many years, until his workload proved too heavy, 'Jili',[28] as he was
affectionately known at the College, also conducted the College choir and
even led them on a successful tour of the Province. Their recital in the Cape
Town City Hall was very well received.

Many students came from far and were too indigent to afford residence
fees, so that the Jabavu household, which rapidly grew with a succession of
babies (of whom one, a little girl, died in infancy) usually had a number of
non-paying guests, most often cousins, but even more distant relatives.
Florence herself taught music and also tried to raise awareness of basic
household hygiene, childcare and the need for a balanced diet by running
a mothers' club for local women.

Throughout Jabavu remained an enthusiastic teacher. A contribution of
his on 'the Bantu child' before a countrywide educational conference held
in 1934 displays an awareness not only of the kind of academic training
such children should enjoy, but of those strengths and weaknesses which

[28] It is Xhosa practice to use a person's clan name (something wider than a 'surname') as a term of
endearment. So, both D. D. T. Jabavu and his father, and later his daughter, were familiarly
addressed as 'Jili', just as the South African elder statesman Nelson Mandela was affectionately
known the world over as 'Madiba'.

should, respectively, be built upon or allowed to languish. Revealing are the statistics he cites: only one in three ever sees the inside of a school; of these, fewer than two per cent proceed to higher education. The 'strengths' cited are equally revealing of the culture to which he, as an educated Xhosa speaker, but also as international academic, still stood close: awareness of numbers (because young herders were expected to keep tally of the cattle in their care); linguistic sophistication in their ability to memorise an endless array of terms for differently coloured cattle (especially among Sotho children); their natural aptitude for music; their familiarity with fables; the training in deference to elders and respect for authority instilled in them by tribal custom; their powers of observation, living, as they did, so close to nature; their hardiness (inculcated through the obligation to cover long distances to school and their helping at home with arduous domestic and agricultural chores); and, not least, their sense of responsibility: children as young as four being sent on errands and, at five, being entrusted with the care of a younger sibling. The educator, ever aware of the physical as well as mental needs of any potential charges, also lists the advantages of a rural diet above the food to which urban Black children of his time were mostly exposed.

7. Political Interests

This was not the only conference at which D. D. T. Jabavu spoke. During the twenties and thirties there was a whole series of so-called 'Bantu-European' conferences that debated matters of common interest,[29] as well as a great surge and counter-surge of various political movements among Black and so-called 'Coloured' South Africans. These all lie within the interesting and complicated history of the South African struggle for freedom (and hence outside the parameters of my topic).[30]

---

[29] Interestingly, in 1928, at an 'All-Student Conference' of the National Union of South African Students, deploring their 'absolute ignorance' of one another, Jabavu revived an earlier suggestion by Edgar Brookes that such a conference of Black and White students be held under the auspices of the Students' Christian Association (Jabavu 1928: 25–28). A series of such Christian conferences, with religion rather than politics as the main topic, followed. My parents met at one of these, held at Fort Hare in 1929. See Claassen 1997 and cf. Fig. 12.3.

[30] A brief history of the important 'All-African Convention' (AAC) which was constituted in 1935 under chairmanship of Professor Jabavu and which for a time served as the 'cultural arm' of struggle politics (and sometimes seemed in prominence to rival the more overtly political African National Congress, ANC) is to be found at South African History Online, All Africa Convention, www.sahistory.org.za/world-and-african-history/all-africa-convention. Jabavu's

To a great number of these Jabavu was a valued contributor, not least in his indignant battle against the encroaching Nationalist movement among White Afrikaners, whose ideals were far from those of the liberals whose friendship he enjoyed. He often served as level-headed chair at heated debates.

Whereas his father (and he, as a teenager) had espoused the cause of the White Afrikaner during the Anglo-Boer War, Jabavu now became increasingly aware of the dangers to the qualified African franchise of the movement under Herzog to curtail the rights of Black Africans, under the guise of giving them 'autonomy' in so-called 'Reserves', a slightly larger area than had been allowed them in the 1913 dispensation. By 1943 he still felt reluctantly obliged to oppose the call by the 'Non-European Unity Movement' to boycott the proposed new 'Natives' Representative Council'. In the words of Higgs: 'He saw no sense in boycotting what was left of the 1854 law that had allowed some rights to Black people.'[31] Jabavu could not believe that his liberal friends, among whom he counted General Smuts, could mean ill by their Black countrymen, and he acquiesced in the end to the legislation that would enlarge the Reserves, not fully realising that it would spell the end of the 'Native' franchise, also in the Cape Province. For this he earned the ire of less 'gradualist' political activists of his time, and after this his political influence waned.[32]

8. Teaching: Curricular and Extracurricular

Jili's teaching career until his retirement in 1944 was marked throughout with signal success, imbuing young African students with an enthusiasm for African and Classical languages and literature, in particular for what could be taken from literature to enrich their lives and open their minds. To the delight of his whole family and clan and of the town and countryside around Fort Hare, ten years after his retirement Rhodes University awarded D. D. T. Jabavu a doctorate *honoris causa*, two years after it had

relationship with its functionaries and its political direction often seemed fraught with ambivalence. By 1948 he was largely sidelined when Wycliff Totsi replaced him as its president.

[31] Higgs 1997: 142. He was essentially an academic thinker, with a Cicero-like impartiality.

[32] Higgs 1997: 121–47, titles the chapter that traces this process, 'The fall of an African politician'. Jabavu's gradualism was misunderstood as a potential for selling out, but: 'His tragedy was . . . [to be] thought too radical by some of his white liberal allies and too conservative by many of his African colleagues' (129). The AAC, which he had continued espousing, failed to unite with the ANC, and both it and Jabavu were spent forces by the time of the Nationalist takeover under D. F. Malan in 1948.

first been proposed by Professor Kirk. If ever a man needed to be rewarded for being the breathing embodiment of the education he had taken from the Classics, Professor Jabavu was this man. Like Cicero, he had the 'lawyer's ability to see both sides of a question' and a burning desire to see justice done, albeit gradually and without rancour. At the same time he retained a boyish enthusiasm for life. Z. K. Matthews writes with enthusiasm of how a 'work session' in the College gardens would magically become a public *recitatio* by their beloved professor, who would entertain the young men with tales from his 'rich fund of experience'.[33]

Stories about his travels abroad would be graphically told, 'complete with sounds and gestures': concerts of Paderewski or Caruso, Parliamentary exchanges between David Lloyd George and Herbert Asquith. 'Jili', as his students called him fondly,[34] would come prepared for their questions, bringing 'programmes of a well-remembered performance, a copy of the play or the texts of speeches'. His student recalls: 'He loved language ... [and] would read with full effect ... [and] loved the songs which he sang for us in a voice that, to his own inner ear, was also a voice that might have rung out in Covent Garden'. In this way, the much-travelled educator was opening up the world for young people, who, in many instances, had not even travelled as far as Cape Town.[35] Matthews gives a brief run-down of the major facets of 'Jili's' educational career, noting that he 'became a scholar and leader in his own right during a long, distinguished career', but his 'true love was always music'. Matthews tells of meeting a doctor who had been with Professor Jabavu at Tuskegee: 'Does he still have that little notebook in which he jotted down words of songs he liked, and does he still pull it out as he sits down at the piano to play and sing song after song?'

Also within lecture halls Jabavu imbued whatever he touched with some of his own ebullience. Matthews recalls:

He brought to the classroom the same vital and unquenchable enthusiasm he gave to his music. He taught us Latin, which can be a very dull subject indeed. But Latin with Jabavu was interesting because Jabavu was interesting and was, moreover, a true classical scholar. His love of language was such that in his classes we discovered both the richness of the ancient tongue and the power of the English

---

[33] 1981: 52.

[34] Another nickname was '*Mhleli*' or 'Editor'. At this stage he still worked on his father's newspaper *Imvu* at weekends.

[35] Matthews recounts that his own participation in the Fort Hare choir, which Jabavu took on a tour of the Cape Province, offered him a first opportunity to see 'other parts of the Cape', adding: 'Jabavu as conductor was quite a show in himself': 1981: 53.

into which it might be translated. By his own peculiar alchemy, Jabavu brought the dead to life. Latin became one of the most popular subjects.[36]

Generations of students[37] carried away from Fort Hare an impression of the importance of learning for its own sake, of the Classics as of formative value to all that could study it under the guidance of their gifted teacher. They cherished their memory of a student life enriched by contact with a kind father figure and a man with an endless sense of fun. Extracurricular cultural activities at the College had also been enriched by his participation. Z. K. Matthews remembers students listening 'with pleasure and laughter to the witty, learned and instructive remarks of Jabavu, Murdock and others at the weekly College meeting ... one of the richest traditions of the college', a regular extracurricular cultural event, which was designated by Alexander Kirk as 'not a waste of time, but time for both students and faculty to get away from the narrow limits of their required study courses'.[38]

Matthews tells of Students' Christian Association meetings and Debating Society challenges at weekends. Monica Wilson, editor of Z. K. Matthews' memoir, writes of Jabavu's 'delighting students by "interpreting" speeches, picking up a halting English speech, refashioning it and delivering it in Xhosa with many embellishments'. She adds that he was 'an orator in the flowery court tradition of the Xhosa people'. She remembers him as a 'superb entertainer' and relates her wish, as small girl in 1915, when he came to lunch at her parents' house, that 'other lunch guests were half as interesting'. Referring to the love that both Jabavu and Matthews bore for 'Latin and the classical Latin metres' she speculates 'whether this were not partly on account of a similarity between the Roman preoccupation with the law, and that of the Tswana and Xhosa, and a similar sense of obligation to the shades'.[39]

9. Publications

Professor Jabavu remained throughout an indefatigable author. One of his earliest published works was the adulatory biography of his father, cited above. At the same time he wrote pamphlets espousing the cause of

---

[36] 1981: 53.
[37] Jabavu's biographer Higgs lists interviews with about twenty of his former students during her research for the book. Many were able, after thirty years, still to quote snippets of Latin learned from their teacher.
[38] 1981: 65–67.   [39] 1981: 226–27, 231.

the retention in the Cape Province of the qualified franchise, but also its extension to the northern provinces. His contribution on the 'Segregation fallacy' (1928) is an exemplary, well-considered document. His first 'international' publication had appeared in the *Kent Messenger* while he was still in London. Titled 'Christmas in South Africa and other topics', it contrasted the brutality of oppressive Whites with African 'savagery', and a display of erudite references to English authors, scientists and politicians seemed aimed at showing off the abilities of an educated, Westernised African, while simultaneously appealing for funds for the future 'Native College'.[40]

As a third-generation Westernised Xhosa speaker straddling two cultures with ease, Jabavu appears to have had the ability to distance himself intellectually from his people, while at the same time remaining emotionally committed to their welfare. It was no hardship for him to write dispassionately about 'the Native', his wants, needs and aspirations, while at the same time, often equally dispassionately, relating the hardships that he as an educated 'Native' had frequently to endure at the hands of insensitive clerks wielding irksomely petty civic rules and state laws.

However, Jabavu did not hesitate also to criticise his own people where he deemed it necessary. His list in a later publication of 14 bad practices that 'the Natives' should learn to eschew, is revealing.[41] For each he has a remedy to hand. This catch-all list comprises: *'religious laxity'* (abandonment of moral scruples by both pagans and Christians); '[xenophobic] *racialism'*; *'ignorance'*, bringing with it *'the Petty Spirit of Narrowness'* (that is, prejudice against learning good agricultural or domestic practices from White people); *'the bad training of the young of our days'*; *'educational needs'* (especially the lack of training in 'Hygiene, Cookery and Agriculture'[42]; *'disease'* (although as layman he will 'not propose to expatiate on these diseases', limiting his comments to the need for practical hygiene and acceptance of modern medical treatment and a call for the training of many more than the handful of British-educated Black doctors then in practice); *'alcoholism'* (he was a lifelong abstainer); *'improvidence'* (with a short homily on banking and saving); leading to *'indebtedness'*; then, surprisingly, *'low wages'* (shown to lie within the Black person's own control if trade unions were to be organised and if people would 'act as one man

[40] Higgs 1997: 21.
[41] Jabavu 1920: 157–75 reprises an address on 'Social reform' given in 1920 before a 'Native' audience in King William's Town.
[42] His abbreviated report on Tuskegee in this volume (27–70) enthusiastically endorses their curriculum, which included these subjects. See n. 26 above.

when asking for an increase in wages'; *'wrong foods'* (to be avoided by returning to a diet of maize porridge, curdled milk and green vegetables, freely to be culled 'in the fields'); *'bad farming'* (the lifelong object of Jabavu's most vigorous educational campaigning); *'poverty'* (with a call to diligent activism and service so that Black people's 'combined ... forces [would]... drive away this wolf from our doors').

The book ends with an impassioned rhetorical flourish. After describing the heights of culture and wealth reached by African Americans that he had observed in Georgia, he writes (p. 175):

> – all this fired my soul to believe that there were no altitudes in civilisation outside the compass of a black-skinned man if he only have the inspiration and determina-tion to attain thereunto. Let us therefore strive to accomplish what is expected of this generation, so that in that beautiful future when the Bantu race is weighed in the balance it shall, thanks to our efforts, not be found wanting.

Jabavu's style was comparable to that of any of the learned essayists of his time, with measured periodic sentences and an easy assumption of his readers' familiarity with Latin phraseology and Roman historical refer-ences. The foreword of his biography of his father begins with Emerson's 'A man Caesar is born, and for ages after we have a Roman empire'.[43] In an article on 'The Bantu and the Gospel' he explains that Black people are no longer a *tabula rasa*, but are affected, perhaps 'contaminated', by European society. He goes on: 'They are not going to take as long as two thousand years to overtake modern European culture because they have immeasur-ably greater advantages than the ancient Britons had during the wars of Julius Caesar.'[44] Later in the same volume he terms the denial of equal treatment before the law of Black people the *'fons et origo mali'*, the source of all other hardship and the 'biggest racial stumbling block'.[45] Writing home from the USA, where he had travelled (after visiting in England) to put the case of Black South Africans against the Herzog government's increasing oppressiveness, he portrays himself as another Caesar: *'Veni, vidi, vici!'* reads the succinct description of his reception in Boston.[46]

D. D. T. Jabavu wrote with equal facility in English and Xhosa. For the purposes of this paper I examined a number of his English-language

---

[43] Jabavu 1922: 128. His assessment of his father's English style was that it was 'concise ... partial to Latin derivatives and polysyllables'. He also admires the older man's facility in coining political terminology in Xhosa, as in *'u-Tung'amlomo'*, 'the Mouth-Stitcher' for Sprigg's 'Native Registration Bill' that became generally known as 'The Native Disenfranchisement Bill'.

[44] In Jabavu 1928: 106–15, especially 111–13.

[45] In 'Christian missions and the Bantu', in Jabavu 1928: 116–37; the Latin phrase is on page 128.

[46] Higgs 1997: 71.

publications, but can only report on what others say about his Xhosa effusions. From the titles of the latter breathes the same spirit of enthusiasm for the education and upliftment of his people as in his polemical writings in English. A tour of the United States produced a travelogue, which would serve to open the eyes of at least his literate fellows to a wider world.[47] The same may be said of his Xhosa-language description of a visit to Jerusalem.[48] His interest in language produced a privately published compilation of Xhosa clan names and genealogies, of which the Xhosa title, *Imbumba yamaNyama* ('unity of Black people') is vaguely reminiscent of the then South African national slogan, *Ex unitate vires*. The closest he came to publishing an autobiography was his (again private) publication of praise poems about himself, titled *Izithuko*. These would not have been originally composed by him but by the *imbongi* (praise singer) that regularly performed at Fort Hare's annual graduation ceremonies. We may assume that 'Jili' had a hand in transcribing and editing this product of an essentially oral literary medium.

The papers collected by Karis and Carter are useful not only for their political contents but also for the opportunity they present to examine the literary and argumentative style of various activist authors.[49] The testimony of Jabavu before the Parliamentary Select Committee on 'Native Bills' (1932), in his capacity as representative of nine different councils and associations, gives a good idea of his lucidity in argument.[50] It was offered in the form of a pamphlet that he requested be 'taken up' in his evidence.[51] A short historical overview of the Black franchise in the Cape is followed by a tripartite analysis of the proposals of the 'Franchise Bill', each of which is rebutted. An acceptable alternative to each is proposed. The author then moves to a list of eight arguments raised in 1925 against the Cape 'Native' franchise by the then Prime Minister. Each of these is suitably refuted. The final argument, 'that such voting power will increase bitterness against Blacks in White men', is rejected on the grounds

---

[47] 'My Tuskegee Pilgrimage' (1913), the title of which Higgs (1997: 24) considers to have been derived from Bunyan's *Pilgrim's Progress*, perhaps via Tiya Soga's 1866 translation, *Uhambo LomHambi*.

[48] The flyleaf of Jabavu's *Black Problem* (1922) announces three works 'awaiting publication'. Beside *The Tuskegee Institute Report*, which was shelved in its original format, two more travel books feature, in English and Xhosa respectively, *Atlantic Voyage Notes (to America and Cape Town)* and *i-Hambo* ('The journey'). Of these, the latter was later published.

[49] Karis and Carter 1973.

[50] Again, an easy assumption of common familiarity with history or the classics underlies references to King Canute or 'Cassandra policies' and his use of phrases such as *imperium in imperio, ipso facto* and *status quo*.

[51] Ibid., 202–9.

that it is based on two false assumptions: that Whites 'hold an incorrigible hatred' for Blacks and that the two groups are hence 'irreconcilable enemies'. Jabavu bases this rejection on the fact that 'the Natives have always divided along ordinary Parliamentary lines'.[52] Historically, some favoured Onze Jan Hofmeyr's (Afrikaner) politics, others the Progressives and Dr Jameson. The evidence ends on an impassioned plea for the retention of the qualified Cape 'Native' franchise, which saved them from the worst excesses of the 'pass laws' and the stripping away of their land under the 1913 Land Act, as was the case in the northern Provinces. This plea is based on an assumption in his hearers of Christian values. Jabavu ends with an offer of assistance to the Government in devising a viable, acceptable 'Native policy'.

The most overtly 'academic' of Jabavu's publications is a small (23 pages in total) hardcover booklet from the Lovedale Press, entitled *The Influence of English on Bantu Literature*. It consists largely of lists of available books (history, novels, collections of short stories or of proverbs) in half a dozen South African Bantu languages, with short discussions of their probable intertextual connection with English works of literature, and short exemplary excerpts translated from the most notable books in each language. Perhaps the most remarkable aspect of this brief monograph is the author's clearly intimate familiarity with all these languages, a familiarity sufficient to enable him to judge of the influence on each of a vast array of English literary works in which he seemed equally at home.

An article on African higher education is sharply insightful about the disadvantages stemming from educating Bantu youth in a second language, an issue that has still not been adequately resolved today, more than eighty years later. Differences in environment are 'heavy handicaps in subjects like English literature and physics (depending on the standard of culture in one's own home) ... [while] in Law, ethics and Latin the disadvantage is due to the *medium* of the English language not being the mother tongue'. At the same time he warns against the dangers inherent in 'only development along our "own lines" ... [that would lead to] a land of colour-bars'.[53] The article goes on to criticise the 'virtual colour-bar', which he sees as stemming from White's awareness of the '5 – 1' disparity between Black and White in the population. This gives rise to their ostracism of even well-educated Black people from 'a fear of degradation by contact'. This was a problem that had haunted and would continue to haunt the family for three generations. Jabavu here pleads for a 'practical

---

[52] Ibid., 207.   [53] Jabavu 1929: 935.

modus vivendi' that would give an equal chance to Black professionals. His daughter Noni in the mid-1950s tells of her exclusion from a Kenyan 'European' swimming pool when she visited her sister, the wife of a barrister, and her urge to cry out '*Civis Britannicus sum!*' (*sic*) and claim equal treatment.[54]

10.   Personal Life

All who write of D. D. T. Jabavu refer to his ebullient, expansive personality, his ready wit and measured judgment – and of his small vanities. His daughter (herself born in 1919) writes with great affection of her father in his comparative old age. The first of her books, *Drawn in Colour*, published in 1960 (soon after his death), tells of the fraught time (some five years previously) when she had to travel to Africa post-haste from London for the funeral of her younger brother, and her subsequent protracted visit to Uganda, to bring her sister into the picture in the customary way. Noni Jabavu had her father's facility of standing as it were outside of the culture in which she had grown up, an insider explaining it to outsiders. She appears to have inherited her father's sensitivity to the nuances of language, and takes time to explain the subtle fluctuations of meaning that lie in the careful manipulation by native speakers of periphrastic tenses and moods within the Xhosa language.[55]

Noni explains the Xhosa custom that obliges all relatives, no matter how distant, to attend a family funeral, when the immediately bereaved are expected to retire into a graded seclusion, where others must join them in their mourning. She tells of some distant cousins arriving on the same train on which her brother's body had been sent from Johannesburg, and of one of these young men falling foul of an officious railway policeman on King William's Town station.[56] He was arrested and thrown into a cell. Her father, although the most closely secluded in the house of mourning, on hearing the news of his relative's arrest, went to the telephone and spoke to the chief of police at King William's Town to plead for the release of the young man, who was accused of no more than being 'uppity'. The highly-educated Xhosa-speaking professor's innate tact and his knowledge of men

---

[54] Noni Jabavu 1960: 178. By that time the 'virtual colour bar' about which her father had expostulated had become a very real one in South Africa.

[55] Noni Jabavu explains how 'language can skirt around a problem, referring without referring', in particular because the Bantu languages have 'a system of inflexion—as in Latin' (1963: 93–94).

[56] Noni Jabavu, 1960: 9–12.

is illustrated by the fact that he spoke in Afrikaans, was suitably subservient to the policeman, and humbly thanked him with *'Dankie, Baas!'* ['Thanks, Boss!'] when the petty official relented. Jabavu himself went to town to fetch the young man on his release early the next morning, the day of the funeral.[57]

Shortly before his son's death, Florence, too, had passed away, and after the son's funeral a family conclave decided that dear Jili could not be left alone like that and a suitable wife, a widow, was once again found for him. In this he willingly acquiesced, and soon after, with his daughter and the magistrate's clerk as witnesses, he and Betty Marambana were quietly married, but not before an appropriate ante-nuptial contract had been drawn up in record time by his friend the White lawyer Burl. Noni Jabavu's second book, *The Ochre People* (1963) tells of her problem, on a subsequent visit, in becoming used to her father's being married to a domesticated and rather simple housewife, so different from her highly educated, social activist mother. Again, Noni's appreciation for the nuances of language and of custom in the close-knit family's intimate and delicate approach to her problem reveals the fascinating combination of tradition and Westernisation which informed the social lives of her father and his relatives.

11.   Conclusion

In her second book Noni describes an idyllically pastoral vignette: her then seventy-year-old father and an (uneducated) friend of his youth were sitting together on their porch overlooking the rolling landscape, comparing notes on matters agricultural.[58] Says 'Jili' to his old friend: 'If you had been taught *isiLatini* ... I would recite passages in that golden tongue ... Roman warriors ... conquering the whole ... world ... chewed grains of boiled maize (*sic*). When I taught our young men and women Latin at Fort Hare ... construe, translate ... this food ... *zinkobe* ... [they would say,] "So these Romans were people like us?" [and I would reply,] "You are people like these Romans were!"' Replies his amazed companion:

---

[57]   Noni Jabavu writes in 1960: 60 of her own antagonism to Afrikaans as the language of the oppressor, whereas her father had run a column in an African children's magazine, 'teaching Afrikaans for beginners'; his rationale: 'to know someone truly, study his language'.

[58]   Noni Jabavu 1963: 109. Elsewhere she records her father's ability to 'keep the common touch' even with 'pagans', who called him 'Lover-of-the-people' (1963: 61).

'The Romans of the Holy Bible? *AmaRoma?'* Both venerable men then lapsed into a ruminative silence.

Davidson Don Jabavu towers in the history of South African political life as the voice of reason, an impassioned enthusiast for the twin necessities for the upliftment of Black people: education and political freedom. The deaths, in 2008, of Noni Jabavu and subsequently, in August 2010, of the retired politician Joe Matthews (son of Z. K. and, with his father, co-accused with Nelson Mandela in the infamous Treason Trial of the 1960s), have broken two of the last links between the present era and the time when D. D. T. Jabavu wielded influence on the South African educational and political stage, but his legacy deserves a place in any history of either education or political activism. Edgar Brookes in 1977 wrote: 'I would give much to have Jabavu back on earth again', recalling his 'delightful personality' and the fact that 'he never ceased to be an African'.[59]

The measured judgment of Z. K. Matthews serves as a suitable epitaph: '[D. D. T. Jabavu] remained until his death in 1959 one of the most influential and respected of all African leaders'.[60] The obituary by the same author epitomises him as an 'African educationist, patriot and statesman'.[61] He had been awarded a DPhil *honoris causa* by Rhodes University, a Coronation Medal by Queen Elizabeth and a Bronze Medal of the Royal Empire Society of London for 'outstanding service to Africa' and had been elected 'Professor Emeritus' of the University College of Fort Hare. A scholarship fund was established in his honour by some former students,[62] but above all, 'hundreds of students had spent many happy hours in his stimulating lectures, interspersed with amusing anecdotes'. The lives of several generations had been enriched by this man for all seasons and *'isiLatini'* had been thoroughly Africanised.

---

[59] Brookes 1977: 40–41.   [60] Matthews 1981: 53.   [61] Matthews 1959: 83–85.

[62] In similar vein, in the mid-1990s, when I was involved in running the so-called Latin Olympiad for South African schools of the Classical Association of South Africa, we instituted a 'Jabavu Prize' for the highest-scoring participant with an African home language background.

13 | Benjamin Farrington and the Science
     of the Swerve

JOHN ATKINSON

Benjamin Farrington (1891–1974) arrived in Cape Town in March 1920 to
take up a lectureship in Greek. He was promoted to Senior Lecturer in
Classics in 1922, and then to the Chair of Latin in 1930. He left Cape Town
in 1934, and after a brief spell in Bristol, he assumed the professorship of
Classics at University College, Swansea, which he held from 1936 to 1956,
during which period he was also a member of the British Communist
Party.[1] He was born in Cork, the family being middle-class, Protestant and
more precisely Congregationalist. He studied at University College Cork
and then at Trinity College, Dublin, where he combined with Classics the
study of Old and Middle English, graduating in 1915. Then, while lecturing
in Classics at Queen's University, Belfast (from 1916), he gained his
Master's degree in English from University College, Cork, in 1917, with
a thesis entitled *Shelley's Translations from the Greek*.

   The choice of subject for the thesis seems to be self-explanatory, but the
number of parallels in their ideas and values suggest that Farrington's
interest in Shelley went beyond the practice of translation. Of immediate
relevance is the point that Shelley (b. 1792) had made it his mission to
campaign for the repeal of the Legislative Union Act and the emancipation
of the Catholics. He argued his case in his *An Address to the Irish People*,
which he published in 1812 and promoted by visiting Dublin
in February 1812 to distribute copies and to speak in public. In this
Address he repeatedly urged the Irish to disavow violence: 'Have nothing
to do with force or violence, and things will safely and surely make their
way to the right point.'[2] 'Let . . . the Irish votaries of Freedom . . . resist
oppression, not by force of arms, but by power of mind and reliance on
truth and justice.'[3] His call for Protestants to tolerate Catholicism was not

---

[1] Hence the comment of E. R. Dodds, a fellow Anglo-Irishman and contemporary at Trinity
College, that he was 'a gifted and charming man whose career was even more bedevilled by
politics than my own': Dodds 1977: 68. Dodds's comment emerges from his own participation in
the students' Labour Party in Oxford. I have dealt more fully with the political context of
Farrington's stay in Cape Town and his political activities in Atkinson 2010.

[2] 'An Address to the Irish People', privately published, February 1812; text in Clark 1954: 39–59;
quotation from 48.

[3] Clark 1954: 47.

based on any religious argument – indeed he claimed neutrality, as he was neither Protestant nor Catholic[4] – but as an issue affecting the rational ordering of society. At the more immediate level he argued that sectarianism was inimical to the cause of the liberation of the Irish: 'The Catholic Emancipation, I consider, is certain. I do not see that anything but violence and intolerance among yourselves can leave an excuse for your enemies for continuing your slavery.'[5] Of course, Shelley was writing in the context of the campaign by the Protestants for the independence of Ireland under continued Protestant dominance, and indeed when he spoke in Dublin on 28 February 1812, with as much presence as a twenty-year-old could command, he was hissed when he introduced the subject of Catholic emancipation. The printed text includes a lengthy section (41–44) on the history of intolerance on both the Catholic and the Protestant sides to show its wrong-headedness, destructiveness and ultimate futility.[6]

Shelley went to Dublin as an outsider to hearten those looking for Irish independence; Farrington went to Cape Town, ten years older and wiser, as a supporter of Sinn Fein, and with, if not because of, a strong sense of sympathy with the Boers in their struggle for independence. Thus, within six months of his arrival, he wrote a series of articles in September 1920, published in Afrikaans, for the Cape Town Afrikaner newspaper, *De Burger*. In these columns he set out to win Afrikaner support for the newly proclaimed Irish Republic. Like Shelley he had to confront the religious divide when, writing for a Calvinist readership, he presented the Sinn Fein case; and, like Shelley, he could claim neutrality, as, in the Sinn Fein context, he was counted in the tiny minority of Protestant supporters (and as a Congregationalist by birth, if not by conviction, he belonged to a minority group within the Protestant fold). Like Shelley he was not an advocate of violence, and made the explicit point that 'religious and racial differences' should not be 'settled by the sword'.[7]

Farrington soon received some form of warning that the University of Cape Town did not take kindly to his writing political pieces for *De Burger*.[8] The series he had published had probably already reached its natural end, but he did not repeat the exercise. Nevertheless, like Shelley,

---

[4] Clark 1954: 41. He was in fact by now a deist, and in texts of 1813 he was rejecting creationism.
[5] Clark 1954: 50.　　[6] Clark 1954: 41–44.
[7] Hirson 2001: 127, referring to the second article, of 17 September 1920.
[8] Hirson 2001: 128, citing a published letter of 12 October 1920 by R. I. C. Scott Hayward of the IRASA. Much later another UCT Classicist, H. C. Baldry, ran a similar risk by writing anti-establishment columns under the pen name Vigilator for *The Guardian* from its launch in 1937 to 1948. The paper became the mouthpiece for the South African Communist Party. I have dealt with Baldry and *The Unity of Mankind* in Atkinson 2014.

he was opposed to censorship, and he found a fresh avenue for political journalism within the Irish community. He was seen as the leading light in the formation of the Irish Republican Association of South Africa (IRASA),[9] and was the founding, and sole, editor of its organ, *The Republic*, which ran to some 41 issues from November 1920 to June 1922. The tone was set with the first issue, which featured on the front cover a portrait of Terence McSwiney, the Lord Mayor of Cork, who had recently died while on a hunger strike in prison. Farrington's editorial on the following page spelled out to the new Governor General, HRH Prince Arthur, Duke of Connaught, why the Irish community could not welcome him, nor wish him well.

The issues of *The Republic* were fairly substantial, typically running to 16 pages, and included, apart from news items from IRASA branches and overseas, articles on political historical and cultural matters. The epic *Táin bó Cúailnge (The Iliad of Ireland)* was serialised in nine parts. The life span of *The Republic* roughly coincided with that of Farrington's Big Idea for a *Magna Hibernia*.

The Big Idea might have owed something to the tract which Shelley wrote as a follow-up to his *Address to the Irish People*, which was entitled *Proposals for an Association of Philanthropists* (March 1812). This suggested the establishment of an international association 'which shall have for its immediate objects Catholic Emancipation and the Repeal of the Act of Union between Great Britain and Ireland'.[10] *Proposals* included attacks on his usual targets of religious intolerance, aristocracy and the ecclesiastical hierarchy, along with their consequences, the pauperisation of the majority, and the suppression of freedom and reason. Shelley had his dream of where his vision of philanthropy would lead: 'I hear the teeth of the palsied beldame Superstition chatter, and I see her descending to the gravel.'[11]

Farrington's Big Idea was more down to earth, though still ambitious, as he proposed the foundation of an Irish World Organisation (IWO). He raised this first in IRASA circles in early 1921, and the idea was picked up in Dublin and led to the convening of the Irish Race Conference held in Paris in January 1922. We can reasonably credit Farrington with originating this proposal, since at the time he was so credited by MacNeill, de Valera,[12] and others, though cynics might add, 'because it failed'.

---

[9] On the history of the IRASA see McCracken 1996: 46–66.

[10] Text in Clark 1954: 60–69, quotation from 60.   [11] Clark 1954: 61.

[12] Hirson 2001: 136; cf. Foster 2003: 206–7 and 705; and Keown 2001, who suggests that Farrington was moved by naïvety, but also some political ambition.

The plan included a proposal that expatriate communities around the globe should separately raise funds for developmental projects such as the building of libraries in the capital of every county in Ireland.[13] Unfortunately, the Paris conference was mired in controversy even before it began because the acceptance of the British offer of a treaty in December 1921 caused an instant and bitter division between pragmatists willing to work with the Treaty and extremists led by de Valera, who wanted nothing short of a fully independent Irish Republic, without Dominion status. Even more unfortunately for Farrington, both sides in this battle were at least agreed in seeing that the central committee of the proposed IWO, the Fine Ghaedal or Fine Gael, would dictate policy to the expatriate Irish communities. He did not want to be dictated to by a committee any more than he wished to submit to the discipline of the Comintern when he first turned to Marxism. Thus, ironically, Farrington in Paris shifted from being the promoter of the great idea, to joining other delegates from the southern hemisphere in a move to ensure that the IWO was stillborn.[14] Shelley would have approved.

Back in Cape Town, humiliated and disillusioned by the turn of events in Paris, Farrington made his feelings known, and in the issue of *The Republic* of 22 April 1922 he defied the IRASA policy of neutrality and openly attacked de Valera for his encouragement of a personality cult and for his intransigence, which admitted little alternative to violence and was indeed to lead to the civil war that began in June 1922. *The Republic* did not appear again after the first issue in June, and the IRASA seems to have perished with it.

As it happened, events of early 1922 gave Farrington cause to distance himself further from Afrikaner nationalists. The Rand Revolt escalated in February that year when white workers in the Johannesburg area went on strike, and this led to violent clashes with police and military units deployed by the Smuts government, as well as random attacks on Blacks by strikers and their sympathisers. At the time many thought that the industrial action initiated by Communists had been hijacked by Afrikaner 'commandos', as Roux puts it, and the revolt became a rallying cry for Afrikaner nationalists.[15] Racist elements were not confined to Afrikaner

---

[13] Daniel 1991: 169–70, quoting from a report in *The Republic*.

[14] Daniel 1991: 172; cf. the record of the Dáil Éireann session of 2 March 1922 Dáil Éireann Debate Vol. S2 No. 3. p. 25 Fine Gaedheal. Thursday, 2 March 1922 debates.oireachtas.ie/dail/1922/03/02/00025.asp.

[15] Roux 1964: 148. Krikler 2005: 104–9 challenges this old orthodoxy and argues that the role of Afrikaner nationalism in the revolt has been greatly exaggerated.

nationalists, however, as can be seen from the press photograph of white women proudly displaying the banner with the slogan 'WORKERS OF THE WORLD, FIGHT AND UNITE FOR A WHITE SOUTH AFRICA'.[16] Another reality was that the militant strikers were joined by a group styling themselves the Irish Brigade. The mix of racism, nationalism, and gratuitous violence would not have gelled with Farrington's values and there is no further evidence of sympathy on his part for the Afrikaner cause.

Thus, by mid-1922, Farrington had shed his naïve hopes for Afrikaner nationalism, had no stomach for the feuding within the IRASA and felt alienated from the cause of Irish republicanism. He became more concerned about class issues, later invoking the influence of James Connolly (1868–1916), who had shown him how one could provide intellectual leadership while remaining true to one's working class background and in touch with ordinary people. But in the period between the rather parasitic Shelley and the son-of toil, James Connolly, there were two other major sources of influence on Farrington: first the circle of Ruth Schechter, and secondly Karl Marx's thesis on Epicurean atomism – or so it might seem. The influence of Ruth Schechter's circle was real enough. He met her shortly after his arrival in Cape Town, and she 'had the only salon which attracted the Cape Town intelligentsia', according to Lancelot Hogben (at UCT 1927–1930 as Professor of Zoology).[17] Ruth, the daughter of Solomon Schechter, famous for his work on the documents of the Cairo Genizah, was married to Morris Alexander, an eminent civil rights lawyer who served in Parliament from 1921 to 1929 as the sole representative of the Constitutional Democratic Party and was returned to Parliament again in 1931. Her relationship with Farrington became very close, and she left her husband and South Africa in December 1933, and, following a divorce, married Farrington in August 1935.[18] Ruth's main philanthropic venture was creating a play centre for children of indigent Coloureds in District Six: she was also an intellectual in her own right as a regular contributor of

[16] Krikler 2005: 110 with plate 8.   [17] Hogben 1998: 99.
[18] Ruth and Morris had drifted apart, but the breaking point came in 1930, when he supported the bill to extend the franchise to women, while Ruth was horrified that it only benefited white women: cf. Enid Alexander 1953: 172. Benjamin's position at UCT had no doubt become a little problematic as Morris Alexander became a member of the University Council in 1930, and remained so till 1936. The affair might have seemed scandalous to those who did not share Shelley's liberal views on the institution of marriage, reflected, for example, in his comment that 'an enlightened philosophy . . . must condemn the laws by which an indulgence in the sexual instinct is usually regulated', Percy Bysshe Shelley, 'Discourse on the manners of the antient Greeks relative to the subject of love', in Notopoulos 1949.

literary and political articles and reviews to periodicals and Cape Town newspapers, as well as the author of an unpublished novel, *The Exiles*.

The character of Ruth's circle is indicated by Hogben's comment on the artist Herbert Meyerowitz: 'his political outlook was intelligently, not dogmatically, Marxist. Like all members of the circle of friends we had in Cape Town, he was anti-segregationist.'[19] Hogben found his professorial colleagues at UCT not stimulating, writing:

but several of the junior academic staff were companionable, among them Benjamin Farrington, then a lecturer who taught Greek, and Frederick Bodmer, senior lecturer in the Department of German . . . Farrington awakened my interest in early Greek science and the Greek atomists sufficiently to make me read everything accessible about them – including the doctoral thesis of Karl Marx.[20]

This might imply that Farrington had himself read the thesis by 1930, but he was later to claim that he only did so much later, in 1942. Nevertheless, he was in a circle of young intellectuals in Cape Town who were liberal on racial issues and at least sympathetic to Marxism.

For those on the political left the 1920s were an exciting time in Cape Town. The Communist Party of South Africa (CPSA) was established in 1921, with its inaugural conference in Cape Town. Farrington was not interested in signing up, especially after the Rand Revolt when David Ivon Jones informed his masters in Moscow that 'the Comintern will henceforth have to take over direct responsibility for the native masses'.[21] Farrington did not wish to have the Comintern in his life, any more than he wanted to take orders from an Irish World Organisation, or indeed the Vatican. He gravitated to the Trotskyist groups, and there were plenty of them as well as anti-Trotskyist clubs. For communism spawned splinter groups in the same way as Christianity spawned separatist churches in the townships in the dark days of apartheid. The International Socialist Club absorbed members rejected by the CPSA. Trotskyists then left it to establish the Marxist Educational League, while others left the Cape Town Labour Party to join the Independent Labour Party. Communists set up the October Club to counter Trotskyism.[22] The Gezelschaft far Erd, made up largely of Yiddish-speaking Jews, was likewise dedicated to opposing Trotskyism.

[19] Hogben 1998: 99.
[20] Hogben 1998: 105. This would have been about the time that Cyril Bailey published his note 'Karl Marx on atomism' (1928), emphasising the significance of Marx's appreciation of Epicurus' divergence from Democritean atomism with his introduction of the notion of swerve. Marx's thesis bore the title *Über die Differenz der demokritischen und epicureischen Naturphilosophie* (Jena 1841, reprinted Berlin: Dietz, 1983).
[21] Drew 2002: 63.   [22] But the Comintern had it entered as a Trotskyist club: Drew 2002: 186.

The Gezelschaft weeded out closet Trotskyists, and they went on to found the Lenin Club in July 1933. Thus the core of the Lenin Club was Yiddish-speaking, and it attracted radical intellectuals from UCT, including Benjamin Farrington, who lectured to the group on dialectics.[23]

But it is time to turn to Farrington's 'day job' as a lecturer in Classics at UCT. The old South African College had achieved university status in 1918, and when Farrington arrived the institution was still grappling with the problems presented by returning servicemen, with the need for admissions and course concessions, financial aid and the integration of these seniors into a student body that was predominantly younger, more immature and more accepting of academic discipline. The transitional arrangements shifted the balance from Afrikaans to English as the first language of the majority of students. There was no matching programme to attract Coloured or Black students.

The Department of Classics was similarly conservative. The Latinist William Ritchie, Professor from 1882 to 1929, was the senior citizen at institutional level, able to stand in as Acting Principal when required. There was also Theo le Roux, Professor of Greek,[24] who gave his spare time to student administration and supporting sporting societies, and William Rollo, who joined the department in 1926 and brought strength to it as a researcher in mainstream classical studies. Farrington's publication record shows that he was certainly no slouch, but his range of research topics was more exotic. For example, he risked raising eyebrows when he published *Samuel Butler and the Odyssey* (1929)[25] – an oddity that may suggest the lingering influence of J. P. Mahaffy, to whom we shall return.

As for his major research interests, his record in Cape Town points to the guiding principles of materialism and humanism, though his most significant publications in that period were translations, while his major publications on science and politics appeared after he left Cape Town. Of course his interest in translation had already been declared in his Master's thesis on Shelley's translations from the Greek; and Shelley had preached the primacy of Greek science, philosophy and literature, and the need to make translations available to the Greek-less without 'prudish' pre-

---

[23] Drew 2002: 139–42. By the time Farrington left UCT the Lenin Club had split into the Workers' Party and what became the Fourth International, and the Workers' Party produced an offshoot in the Spartacist Club: Roux 1964: 312.

[24] From 1919 until his death in 1948.

[25] The book takes a maverick (but not original) line on the gender of the composer of the Odyssey, picking up on the idea of Samuel Butler (1922) and on the identification of Homer's Scheria and Ithaca. Butler's idea has been revived more recently by Nagy (1996) and Dalby (2006: esp. 150–53), but with few takers.

selection or proscription, so that the enquiring individual might acquire 'an exact and comprehensive conception of the history of man'.[26] In the university context in Farrington's day, Classicists tended to be strongly opposed to offering courses based on texts in translation as this might threaten the survival of the language courses. The Classics Department at UCT was more progressive, but Farrington still covered his back when recording this departure from tradition in a letter written to Professor Smuts as late as 1960:

The chief innovation that came in my time was the introduction of a course in Classical Culture through the medium of English. Although I had misgivings about the wisdom of permitting such a course, since I hold that the job of a university Department of Classics is to teach Greek and Latin, I consented to give the course myself.[27]

But it was not so necessary to be defensive about offering translation as a research interest: Professor Ritchie, whom Farrington described as 'a scholar of distinction', made his name by translating comedies of Plautus and Terence; and in Britain, for example, Farrington's contemporary and fellow Anglo-Irishman, E. R. Dodds, was busy in the early 1920s translating Plotinus.

Something of Farrington's ambition for translation in another regard may be detected in his *Primum Graius Homo: An Anthology of Latin Translations from the Greek* (1927), where he comments that 'The Roman translators for the most part were not translators in our modern sense. That is to say they were not engaged in supplying for a curious and instructed public, for such a public did not exist, Latin versions of Greek masterpieces faithfully reproducing the style and contents of the originals.'[28] Thus the literature of the recipient language could be enriched by the creative process of translation, and the culture could benefit from the appropriation of ideas from outside. I think that it is not without significance that Farrington produced this book in a society where

---

[26] Shelley, *Discourse on the Manners of the Ancient Greeks*, 407.

[27] Letter of 30 May 1960, cited by Smuts 1960: 19. Prof. Smuts was relatively progressive, but Farrington knew him as a senior classicist at the conservative Afrikaans University of Stellenbosch. Furthermore, Farrington's formulation reflects the fact that he was not the innovator, as Theo le Roux began offering courses in English at UCT on classical culture in 1920: Robertson 1984: chap. 6, 750. Because of the demand for Greek courses for theology students and Latin courses for lawyers, the Afrikaans institutions were generally more inclined to keep the two language sections separate and to avoid offering classical courses that depended on translations. For a general introduction on all this see Lambert 2011.

[28] Farrington 1927: 3.

a community was seeking to establish recognition and a literary identity for its language, and here I refer to Afrikaans, which, as noted above, he engaged with in his first year at UCT.[29] It may be added that one of his first contacts in Cape Town was G. P. Lestrade, who had studied African languages and Classics, and was later (in 1935) to return to UCT as Professor of Bantu Languages.

This may help to explain why Farrington went his own way in the choice of texts to translate. He did not follow Shelley's precept and concentrate on major Greek texts, but jumped a track and chose to work on Africana texts, thus engaging with the society in which he had settled and opening up new material for those willing to study the African past. He made two significant contributions with his translations of Wilhelm ten Rhyne's *Schediasma de Promontorio Bonae Spei ejusve tractus incolis Hottentotis* (Schaffhausen, 1686) and J. G. Grevenbroek's *Elegans et accurata gentis Africanae circa Promontorium Capitis Bonae Spei, vulgo Hottentotten nuncupatae, descriptio* (from a letter written in 1695).[30] In the critical notes he does draw on his classical knowledge, and in places he indicates that his own special interest in Greek science and philosophy attracted him to these texts. Thus, for example, in his introduction to the translation of ten Rhyne he notes that the author 'had imbibed his hostility to the *a priori* method of interpreting natural philosophy from an early work of Greek science that has attracted much attention in modern times. In 1669 and again in 1672 Ten Rhyne published discussions on the Hippocratic tract *On Ancient Medicine*.'[31] Then Farrington's political attitude to his material may be reflected in his comment that Grevenbroek 'attracts by his honest indignation at the abuses of the time and by his charming, if absurdly expressed, enthusiasm for the Cape and its native inhabitants'.[32]

Of direct relevance to Farrington's materialist interest in science and medicine was his work on Vesalius as well as his translation of the preface of *De fabrica corporis humani*.[33] Vesalius was important because he engaged directly in dissection, vivisection and surgery; Farrington, in his own work on ancient science and medicine, emphasised the prime

---

[29] Ironically the earliest texts in Afrikaans were written in the Arabic script by Cape Muslims. One might add that UCT at this time had also been challenged to give recognition to the indigenous languages.

[30] Benjamin Farrington (tr.) W. ten Rhyne, *Schediasma de Promontorio Bonae Spei ejusve tractus incolis Hottentotis* and J. G. (de) Grevenbroek, *Elegans et accurata gentis Africanae circa Promontorium Capitis Bonae Spei, vulgo Hottentotten nuncupatae, descriptio*, in Schapera 1933: 82–299. Grevenbroek generally signed himself de Grevenbroek. The VRS text was the first printed version of his *Descriptio*.

[31] Schapera 1933: 83.   [32] Schapera 1933: 170.   [33] Farrington 1932.

importance of direct observation and experiment, and he presented its absence as a major reason why Greek science regressed after the ground-breaking work of the Ionians.[34]

This prompts another reference to Shelley, who, while stressing the pre-eminence of Greek thought, was not blind to the failures and limitations of the Greeks and their systems:

> Whilst many institutions and opinions, which in ancient Greece were obstacles to the improvement of the human race, have been abolished among modern nations, how many pernicious superstitions and new contrivances of misrule, and unheard of complications of public mischief, have not been invented by the ever-watchful spirit of avarice and tyranny.[35]

Farrington was to make his name by writing on the way in which Athenian democracy and the 'superstition' promoted by Platonism blocked the progress of Ionian speculative and experimental science.

He left Cape Town with a wealth of diverse experiences, as an Anglo-Irishman among Gaelic republicans, then Afrikaner nationalists, Yiddish-speaking Marxists, and conservative colonialists. He joined the British Communist Party, and this must have been at about the same time as did George Thomson, who, apart from being a fellow Marxist and though born in London, had a passionate interest in Gaelic and Irish politics, and published in the same year *Tosnu na Feallsúnachta* (Dublin, 1935), on the history of early Greek philosophy.[36] After a year in Bristol, Farrington moved to the University College of Swansea in 1936.[37]

For his inaugural lecture he chose to speak on Diodorus Siculus. He readily conceded that 'as an original thinker Diodorus does not count',[38] but he noted that Diodorus' very mediocrity had value in that he was the more likely to 'mirror some aspects of his time'. He also followed Wesseling in commending him for providing 'instruction with regard to the history, laws and manners of the Egyptians, Ethiopians, Scythians, Assyrians, Persians, Greeks, Romans, Carthaginians, and many other peoples'.[39] But Farrington was particularly attracted to Diodorus by his humanism,

---

[34] Farrington 1965: 57.   [35] Shelley, *Discourse on the Manners of the Ancient Greeks*, 406.

[36] Farrington seems to have been sparing in his references to Thomson's work, but contributed to his Festschrift: Farrington 1963. Thomson 1941 includes Farrington's inaugural lecture in his bibliography, and appears to reflect it at 160–62; cf. 453 on Farrington 1939. In his chapter on the *Prometheus Bound*, Farrington begins by accepting the key conclusions of Thomson 1932 on the dating of the play and on Aeschylus' political stance: Farrington 1965: 69.

[37] Thus, a year before Thomson took the Chair of Greek in Birmingham, in succession to E. R. Dodds.

[38] Farrington 1937: 8.   [39] Ibid., 9.

reflected in the passage in his preface where he says 'to write universal history is to be a servant of divine providence; for a universal history unites in one composition all mankind, who though separated in space are all brothers in blood' (Diodorus Siculus 1.1.3).[40] The preface is not exactly programmatic, as by the time Diodorus came to write it he had been working on the project for thirty years and had completed his history at least down to 59 BC (Diodorus Siculus 1.4.1, 7); but the preface shows that by the time he composed it he had become quite a good historian, as it marks 'the high-water mark of [his] intellectual achievement'.[41] I guess that Farrington felt some affinity for this Sicilian Greek with the determination to write universal history, an intellectual on the periphery of whoever's empire.

Farrington sets out to explain how the early Stoics' acceptance of Chaldaean astrology[42] freed Diodorus to be critical of the Greek model of education (Diodorus Siculus 2. 29–31),[43] though Diodorus saw that it had the power to liberate the mind from superstition (Diodorus Siculus 3.6).[44] Then the Stoic notion of the 'unity of the universe' encompassed both the cosmic universe and the human race,[45] which meant that Diodorus could believe in the brotherhood of man.

Farrington commends Diodorus particularly for his sentiment of 'pity', but adds that the lack of irony detracts from the quality of Diodorus' work. This failure is later illustrated by reference to Diodorus' 'stupidity' in apparently accepting as historical the geographical and anthropological account of the Islands of the Sun attributed to Iambulus (Diodorus Siculus 2.55–60), though it was only a fictional Stoic utopia.[46] Diodorus' humanism comes out most strongly in what he says about the brutal treatment of

---

[40] As translated by Farrington 1937: 10. Atkinson 2000: 307–25 deals with the significance of Diodorus in the context of historiography of the late Republic and Augustan age.

[41] Farrington 1937: 10. Felix Jacoby suggested that the preface was based on Ephorus' model *Die Fragmente der griechischen Historiker*, vol. IIA (Berlin: Weidmann, 1926), no. 70, F7–9, with his commentary thereon at p. 43), while some think that his Stoic line on divine providence and the brotherhood of man was drawn from Posidonius. But Burton (1972: 36–37) finds no linguistic evidence of dependence on Posidonius, yet considers it highly likely that Diodorus was influenced by Posidonius.

[42] On Stoicism and the accommodation of astrology see Wardle 2006: esp. 92–5 and 111–31.

[43] Farrington 1937: 13.   [44] Ibid., 36.

[45] Ibid., 12. Spoerri 1959 argues against the diverse attempts by Reinhardt, Dahlmann and Vlastos to link elements of Diodorus' references to cosmogony and the genesis of culture to the atomist Democritus or the Epicureans. Thus Spoerri indirectly strengthened Farrington's interpretation.

[46] Farrington 1937: 25–32. For another example of Diodorus' credulity see 5.39.2 on Ligurian farmers having to 'quarry' rather than plough their land. Here he took as gospel truth what Posidonius offered as a joke: Edelstein and Kidd 1972: F268 = Strabo, *Geography* 5.2.1 C218.

slaves and the succession of slave revolts in the late Republic.[47] He also commended the Indians for the perception that equality before the law could not cohere with differentials in wealth (Diodorus Siculus 2.39.5).

The lines of thought followed in the inaugural lecture led into Farrington's later work on Greek science and politics, and into his study of Epicurus. But his treatment of the unity of mankind invites comment first on the linkage between that idea and the Alexander myth. In the field of Alexander studies he can be placed somewhere on the matrix between Mahaffy and W. W. Tarn. He commended the way Macedon came to promote the noble 'ideal ... of the well-being of the inhabited world as a whole',[48] with which he contrasted the 'religious and political particularism' of the citizens of the Greek city-state, and their acceptance of the distinction between freeman and slave as 'a law of nature'.[49] This might seem to echo Mahaffy's observation about Alexander that 'his campaigns ... must have ... forced this upon his mind, that the deep separation which had hitherto existed between East and West would make a homogeneous empire impossible, if pains were not taken to fuse the races by some large and peaceful process'.[50] In the concluding section of his earlier treatment of Alexander (1887) Mahaffy similarly praised Alexander as being 'the father and protector [of the Orientals] against the insolence and tyranny of Macedonians and Greeks'.[51]

Unsurprisingly, Farrington did not like John Pentland Mahaffy (1839–1919), an *Anglo*-Irishman, the first Professor of Ancient History at Trinity College, Dublin, and towards the end of his life its Provost, and in that role as controversial as ever. In reviewing the Stanford and McDowell biography of Mahaffy, Farrington says,

When Balfour was deciding against Mahaffy for Provost of T.C.D. he noted ... that he aroused in people 'not merely antagonism, but something near contempt'. I shared this feeling, and I measure the success of this book ... by the fact that it made me look with so much more sympathy on its subject.'[52]

---

[47] Farrington 1937: 17–24.   [48] Farrington 1965: 121.   [49] Farrington 1937: 14–15.
[50] Mahaffy 1892: 160.
[51] Mahaffy 1887: 42. I take this to be a coded attack on British jingoist imperialism, and I suggest that Farrington may have been a little like Mahaffy in thinking of the narrow-minded Athenians, whom he often criticises, as a substitute for the little-Englanders who characterised London. Mahaffy elsewhere uses 'England' for the modern *comparandum*.
[52] Farrington 1971: 217. As links between Farrington and George Thomson are suggested elsewhere in this chapter, it may be noted that Thomson 1941: 321–22 pours scorn on Mahaffy's presentation of Zeus in Aeschylus' *Prometheus Bound* as conforming to his anti-democratic 'ideal of the Anglo-Irish aristocracy'. Thomson goes on to praise Shelley (the subject of Farrington's thesis) as 'a revolutionary poet'.

Despite Farrington's profession of something near contempt, I suspect
that Mahaffy may have provided the siren call that lured Farrington into
writing *Samuel Butler and the Odyssey* (1929), with its maverick (but not
original) line on the gender of the composer of the Odyssey and on the
identification of Homer's Scheria and Ithaca.[53] The influence of Mahaffy
seems to be obvious in Farrington's references to Alexander's promotion of
the unity of mankind. Mahaffy's odd commendation of Alexander's protection of the Orientals against 'the insolence and tyranny of Macedonians
and Greeks' seems to be echoed in Farrington's condemnation of the
particularism of the Greek city-states. One may suggest that for these two
Irishmen 'the Greeks' and 'the Greek city-states' meant Athens, and that
Athens could be a coded reference to London.

Between Mahaffy's formulation and Farrington's judgment came Tarn's
Raleigh Lecture, 'Alexander the Great and the unity of mankind' (1933), to
which Farrington makes numerous allusions.[54] The key phrase in the
discussion comes at the end of Arrian's account of the banquet at Opis in
324 BC, when Alexander prayed for 'harmony (*homonoia*) and partnership
in rule between Macedonians and Persians' (Arrian *Anabasis* 7.11.9). Tarn
took the first limb to indicate a broader mission 'to promote Homonoia
among his subjects – all his subjects without distinction of race'.[55] He later
clarified his interpretation of the second limb by emending the translation
to read 'partnership in the realm'.[56] Had Alexander lived he would have
presided over an empire made up of various national groups, all living in
'fellowship and concord'.[57] Farrington seems to echo Tarn in his description of the Hellenistic kingdoms that emerged after Alexander's death:
'monarchies with cosmopolitan tendencies, in which petty distinctions of
race, religion, and city were to some extent effaced by the one great contrast

[53] Butler, *Authoress*: see note 25 above. Farrington might have been influenced just by Mahaffy's
extraordinary range of interests and love of controversy, but of more immediate relevance is
Mahaffy's claim that he had broken new ground by his identification of the psychological
treatment of Penelope as 'the most modern of the many modern features of the *Odyssey*':
Mahaffy 1897: 63.
[54] Apart from the direct references to W. W. Tarn one notes that Farrington's lengthy coverage of
the Iambulus story was anticipated by Tarn's treatment in his *Alexander the Great and the Unity
of Mankind* (1933: 9–10).
[55] Tarn 1933: 27.   [56] Tarn 1948: 400.
[57] Tarn 1933: 26–27. The Hon. J. H. Hofmeyr, addressing the conference of CASA in 1928,
similarly invoked the image of the British Commonwealth, 'a partnership of sister nations', as
matching the achievement of the Romans in creating 'a world state on a basis of equality, with
no suggestion of superiority of a dominant state': Hofmeyr 1929a: 13. Tarn (1948: 422) clarified
his position further by stating that 'no trace of cosmopolitan ideas can be found in Alexander',
and that he was not about 'abolishing race and treating all mankind as one people, as
a cosmopolitan state'.

between monarch and subject', for which Zeno and the Stoics offered a new morality.[58] Unfortunately, in revising *Science and Politics* for the new edition, he failed to take account of Badian's demolition of the Raleigh Lecture in his 'Alexander the Great and the unity of mankind', which included his observation that Alexander 'certainly did not intend to become the figure-head of a free Commonwealth of Nations'.[59]

Farrington reprinted his inaugural lecture as chapter three of his *Head and Hand in Ancient Greece* (1947). The most important section of this brief book was the second chapter, 'The hand in healing: a study in Greek medicine from Hippocrates to Ramazzini', which dealt with medicine within the field of 'the social relations of science'. He argued that the science of medicine went into decline because of the antipathy of status-seeking Greeks to manual labour and mechanical trades, and because of the gap that developed between medical care for the free and medicine for slaves. Gentlemen doctors, at least after the time of Galen,[60] were content to leave surgery and hands-on engagement with anatomy to technicians, generally slaves, as later it was left to barbers to handle physical medicine. As for the different categories of patient, Farrington argues that the slave required first aid or other forms of direct medical assistance – essentially pit-stop attention, while the wealthy free man was more likely to be suffering from hypochondria and requiring what is now termed lifestyle prescription. In this context, empiricism suffered by 'the invasion of medical science by a priori philosophical concepts'.[61]

The chapter on medicine in *Head and Hand* is something of a conversation piece when set beside Farrington's *Science in Antiquity* and *Science and Politics in the Ancient World*. In *Science in Antiquity* he recognises the priority of Cos in medicine as 'the first scientific institution from which complete treatises have come down to us',[62] although the development of scientific medicine was fostered by the less scientific sacerdotal medicine, and 'the physiological speculations of the philosophers', and the need of the habitués of the gymnasiums for orthopaedic procedures and what might now be called sports science.

Ironically, Farrington was criticised for failing to give sufficient weight to the socio-political and economic factors that would account for the

---

[58] Farrington 1965: 194–95.   [59] Badian 1958: 432.   [60] Farrington 1947a: 34.
[61] Farrington 1947a: 30. A reference to Gordon Childe on the same page prompts the comment that in about 1923 the selection committee for a lectureship in Classics at UCT ranked him as their second choice, and of even less relevance is the fact that the selection committee for a lectureship in English at the same time ranked Tolkien as number two in their list of preferences.
[62] Farrington 1947b: 88.

decay of Greek science in the period after the early Ionian discoveries. Thus, in his review of the first edition of *Science and Politics* in 1939, G. E. Kirk complains that Farrington does not make clear whether he considers class-antagonism 'the sole or only the principal factor in the stagnation of ancient thought'. He concedes that 'it has become fashionable to disavow Marxism', but goes on to affirm that 'it is hard to find a reason for the decay of ancient science that does not inevitably lead us back to the social structure of ancient society'.[63] He then deals with the issue of slavery, whereas Farrington was more concerned with the lower class, that is the citizen majority (shades of 1922). A Trotskyist view was that Farrington concentrated on the linkage between the technical means of production and the development of science in Greece, but failed to consider the socio-economic forces at work.[64]

By 1949 these three books on science and medicine had all appeared in print in their original incarnation, together with his *Francis Bacon: Philosopher of Industrial Science*.[65] He was attracted to Bacon, as he was to Diodorus Siculus, by his compassion and pity for mankind.[66] Bacon too was to be respected for his attacks on science that rested on *a priori* assumptions and received wisdom rather than objective observation and experiment,[67] as well as for his concern that science should make positive contributions to society.

As noted above, Farrington joined the British Communist Party, and the strength of his commitment to the cause is evidenced by the eulogy that he delivered for Ruth at her funeral in March 1942. He was at pains to show that her conversion to communism had been a personal choice and had not been precipitate: she had reached the point of decision after she had studied 'the Stalin constitution' of 1936.[68] He read out extracts of the

---

[63] Kirk 1939.

[64] Jack Meltzer offered a review of Farrington's *Greek Science* at a meeting of the Forum Club, Cape Town, which appeared in its duplicated proceedings, vol. 1.2 (n.d.). Meltzer was taught by Ben Farrington at UCT, became the Head of Trafalgar High School, and after retirement returned to UCT where he was for a time a colleague of mine. I had the greatest admiration for him and he sparked my initial interest in Farrington.

[65] Farrington 1949 followed by 1953a.   [66] Farrington 1949: 70.

[67] Lulat (2005: 454–55) refers to Bacon as 'a fervent proselytiser of the experimental method, the knowledge of which he had acquired from the Muslims through their translated works while studying at Oxford University'.

[68] The Constitution, actually drafted by Bukharin, guaranteed civil liberty, freedom of speech and universal franchise. Stalin was greeted with nauseating rapture when he presented it at the Extraordinary Eighth Congress of the Soviets: Edvard Radzinsky, *Stalin*, translated by H. T. Willetts (London: Doubleday, 1996), 351–53. Bukharin hailed the Constitution and Stalin in a signed article in *Izvestiya* on 6 July 1936, but included an attack on fascist dictatorship with its apotheosis of the hero, and its 'complicated network of decorative deceit in words and

document, and provided a catalogue of the groups she had addressed as a member of the Party.[69] After her death he remained a Communist, but these were testing times.

In May 1942, thus not long after Ruth's death, he attended a meeting of the Classical Association in Cambridge and heard Francis Cornford deliver a paper entitled 'The Marxist view of ancient philosophy'.[70] This turned out to be a blistering attack on Farrington's *Science and Politics* and elements of George Thomson's *Aeschylus and Athens*. Farrington deferred a rebuttal until March 1953, when he delivered 'Second thoughts on Epicurus' at a meeting held in Cambridge to honour the memory of (Rupert) John Cornford, Francis' son, who had been killed in Spain in 1936. John had joined the International Brigades to fight against Franco; he was a full member of the British Communist Party, and Farrington had a deep respect for him, for he 'understood, I believe, a truth about the world which his father did not understand at all',[71] and Farrington claimed that he had written *Science and Politics* 'with a heat engendered by the Spanish civil war'.[72] There were reasons why Farrington might have held back in 1942. Francis Cornford was already a sick man (and died in January 1943), and Farrington had recently defended Ruth's commitment to the Communist Party in his eulogy at her funeral: that was not the time to be scrapping with Cornford Senior about his Marxist ideas.

In his lecture in Cambridge Cornford had attacked Farrington along three lines: he had misrepresented Ionian rationalisation and speculation as scientific investigation and experiment; he had claimed that Ionian philosophy was 'useful to humanity' as though it were applied science; and he had presented the Ionian renaissance as 'a *popular* movement'.[73] In 1952 Farrington answered back that it was sheer shoddy scholarship to apply the label 'Marxist' to an individual or a work without producing any evidence to justify what was intended as a slur; and in the immediate case he asserted that when he wrote *Science and Politics* (1939) he had not yet read the crucial text, Marx's thesis on Epicurus, and had not even read Shackleton Bailey's article on it in *Classical Quarterly* (1928). He nowhere referred to Marx or Marxism in the book 'because I did not venture to include ... what I so imperfectly understood'.[74] Now this seems to be at

---

action'. The article was a thinly veiled denunciation of Stalin's conversion of the Soviet Union into a fascist regime. Katkov 1969: 94–96.

[69] Hirson 2001: 226, summarising a record of the Memorial Service.
[70] Cornford 1967: 117–37.   [71] Farrington 1953b: 328.   [72] Farrington 1953b: 327.
[73] Cornford's attack followed the lines of Momigliano's review (Momigliano 1941).
[74] Farrington 1953b: 328.

variance with what is said about Farrington's engagement with Marxism in
Cape Town, including Hogben's reference to Farrington as having encouraged him to read Marx's thesis and the record of his speaking to Marxist
groups; and it seems to be improbable that he had not seen Bailey's article
in *Classical Quarterly*, a copy of which was definitely in the UCT library not
long after its publication. But Farrington's disclaimer has to be seen in its
political, rhetorical and chronological contexts, and one realises that the
Marxist label can be resisted with the same spirit as, for example, mon-
etarists have been known to resist the label Friedmanite or Thatcherite. He
rather deflects attention from Cornford's attack with a series of devices.
He generally avoids tags such as 'class struggles', which Cornford used to
characterise Marxist discourse, but says, for example, that when he
wrote he 'had no clear idea of the Marxist doctrine of the origin of
consciousness'.[75] He had approached his subject more 'as a rationalist
than as a Marxist', and he had been influenced more by thinkers like
J. M. Robertson (presumably the chemical crystallographer, 1900–1989)
and A. W. Benn (1843–1915).[76] If he wrote in 'a mood of righteous
indignation' (to borrow Cornford's phrase), it was because he wrote
'with a heat engendered by the Spanish civil war'.[77] All this suggests that
the paper of 1952 should be seen in its context, and should not be taken
as subverting the picture we have of him in his Cape Town days. At the
same time, as we have noted, Cape Town's Marxists were rather like the
Epicurean atoms, all going in the same direction, but with significant
switching of tracks as each true believer sought to put distance between
himself, or herself, and the heretics. Furthermore, he was criticised by those
on the left for failing in *Science and Politics* to apply the standard line on
class conflict.

Certainly, from 1952 he had mounting reason to worry about his
affiliation to the Communist Party, and he finally quit after the Russian
invasion of Hungary in 1956. Thereafter he was content to reissue *Science
and Politics*, without any substantive alteration. His attack on the imposi-
tion of superstition, or what Francis Wheen calls Mumbo-Jumbo,[78]
remained his message: the reader is left to guess that the meta-textual
references had shifted.

What was new after his break from the Communist Party was his book
on Epicurus (1967), which also covered those who came under the

---

[75] Farrington 1953b: 326.
[76] The author of *The Greek Philosophers* (London: Paul, Trench and Co., 1882).
[77] 1953b: 326–27.   [78] Wheen 2004.

influence of Epicurus and Epicureanism, from Lucretius to Lorenzo Valla and Erasmus, and on to Keble and Marx. Farrington's switch to Epicurus was not a random swerve, nor an abandonment of engagement with the political issues of the day for quietism, but rather the bringing together of a number of issues that he had been exploring along the way. On the history of science he held to his line that Plato was the enemy of the Ionian scientific tradition by his insistence on the primacy of disembodied arithmetic and geometry, and by substituting for rational astronomy astral theology: 'Greek religion did shift from a human to an astral conception of the divine. Those who approve these changes may stay to worship at Plato's shrine.'[79] But Farrington did now back off from his earlier blunt insistence on experimentalism as the *sine qua non* of the scientific method, and was more ready to accept the value of experiential evidence, what was collected from the senses,[80] and indeed credited 'Epicurus' stout championship of the experiential test in physics' with playing a role in the emergence of modern science'.[81]

Farrington still ends up in the paradoxical situation of arguing that science, ideally experimental science, has the power to liberate the masses from superstition. Epicurus took from Democritus the atomic theory, and thus rescued science from the doctrinaire obscurantism and superstition of his age, though atomism was as yet beyond experimental proof. However, to counter Democritean determinism, Epicurus introduced a different concept of the swerve in the trajectory of the moving atoms.[82] The meaning of the swerve has been much debated, and I incline to the view of another former Professor of Classics at UCT, Maurice Pope, that it referred to 'downward-falling atoms' moving with 'an instantaneous side-step' and not 'a change of direction'.[83] To this, as Farrington presents it,

---

[79] Farrington 1967: 87. Since Farrington lauds Hippocratic medicine but is derogatory towards Chaldaean astrology, it might be noted that one would now place more emphasis on the linkage between Babylonian astronomy and medicine and the influence it may have had on Egyptian and then Greek medicine. In very simple terms, Hippocratic medicine was about systematically collecting data to facilitate prognosis.

[80] 1967: 45–47. Momigliano's review of *Science and Politics* soundly attacked him for dismissing Plato as the key player in choking science, and for insisting on experiment as the quintessential element of science. He also noted that, despite the prominence that Farrington gave to Hippocrates and Democritus in the development of Greek science, neither could be said to have exemplified experimental science.

[81] 1967: 94

[82] As noted by Karl Marx: Bailey 1928. Epicurus' idea on the swerve is alluded to in Diogenes of Oinoanda, frag. 54 in the edition of Smith 1993; cf. Bailey 1947, esp. II 837–42 on Lucretius 2.216–93.

[83] Pope 1986: 77–97, esp. 77 and 84–86. Englert 1987, publishing just after Pope but apparently unaware of his paper, comes to roughly the same conclusion.

Epicurus added the notion that atoms could diverge from their track as a conscious act of volition. This was a necessary adjustment of atomic theory to accommodate the notion of free will in humans. Thus 'dubious physics'[84] was introduced to serve a political or ethical purpose.

Farrington opens the book with the line that Epicurus 'forbade his followers to take part in public life',[85] but that certainly did not mean that the Epicureans stood aside from the real world. In the chapter headed 'The revolt of Epicurus' he describes him as 'a reformer whose every thought was directed to the practical problems of his age'.[86] 'He was founding a movement that aimed at taking in adherents at every level of culture.'[87] Cicero gives the impression that by his day Epicureanism had become a mass movement in Italy (*Tusculanae Disputationes* 4.7; *de finibus* 2.44), but, as Momigliano irreverently puts it, we cannot imagine that Cicero seriously had in mind 'a red army of Epicureans',[88] and Farrington duly acknowledges the problems of mounting a successful programme to educate adults.[89] He invokes the image of missionary training as the core business of the Garden.[90] He might have referred to these missionaries as the intellectual vanguard of Epicurus' movement, but chose an image that is now equally archaic. In a telling observation, Farrington says of Epicurus that 'he never doubted the extent of the influence that can be exerted by one man who shuns the path of ambition, if he has something to say to his age. From the beginning Epicurus was a public figure.'[91] Substitute the phrase 'public intellectual' for 'public figure' and I am sure that is how Benjamin Farrington would have liked to be remembered, and a public intellectual rather like the Epicurean atom, quite capable of the odd swerve.

---

[84] Farrington 1967: 114.   [85] Ibid., 1.   [86] Ibid., 76.   [87] Ibid., 122.
[88] Momigliano 1941: 150.   [89] Farrington 1967: 107–8.   [90] Ibid., 122–25.   [91] Ibid., 78.

14 | Athens and Apartheid: Mary Renault and Classics in South Africa

NIKOLAI ENDRES

> We'll make a new thing; two good wines blended to make a better, in a great loving-cup.
>
> Alexander the Great in *The Persian Boy*

> The perpetual stream of human nature is formed into ever-changing shallows, eddies, falls and pools by the land over which it passes. Perhaps the only real value of history lies in considering this endlessly varied play between the essence and the accidents.
>
> Author's Note in *The Mask of Apollo*

Mary Renault's historical novels paint a vivid picture of a world long past yet still alive: from Ariadne to Alexander, from Demosthenes to Darius, from Phaedra to Phaedo, from Xerxes to Xenophon. Her accomplishments as a writer are beyond dispute, but her political engagement (or failure thereof) has created controversy. Of course, she was a lifelong fighter against apartheid in South Africa, but her democratic involvement remained lukewarm at best. Only in her fiction does she sing democracy's praise. In what follows, I will give short biographical background, briefly introduce her literature, and discuss her notion of democracy, focusing on Socrates, Alcibiades, political (in)stability, Demosthenes and Alexander the Great.

1. Classical Learning

Mary Renault, née Eileen Mary Challans, was born in London in 1905. Her formal education began at Romford House School, where she soon discovered the allures of literature. After World War I, she continued her schooling at Clifton Girls' School in Bristol, where she learned, among other subjects, Latin. In 1925, Renault went to St Hugh's College in Oxford, where she studied classical languages (independently adding a little Greek to her linguistic repertoire), mythology, philosophy, history and ancient literatures. Her favourite professors were the medievalist J. R. R. Tolkien, author of *Lord of the Rings* and editor of the *Oxford English Dictionary*, and the classicist Gilbert Murray, a renegade scholar who investigated 'the barbaric and tribal elements underlying Hellenic civilisation, a revolutionary view at a time when the ancient world was most often depicted as classically Aryan'.[1] In 1928, Renault graduated with a degree in English. The obvious professional path was teaching, but Renault decided to train as a nurse at Radcliffe Infirmary, not having enough money to study medicine. In 1933, she met a fellow student, Julie Mullard, who became her partner for the rest of her life. In 1947, Renault won an MGM prize for one of her novels, which secured her financial independence. That same year, the British royal family undertook a highly publicised trip to South Africa, which put the former colony on the map. A year later, Renault and her partner followed suit. They lived in Durban for a while and eventually settled at the Cape.

Soon, Renault reached a momentous decision: '[O]ne of the greatest fascinations of historical writing is to compare the dilemmas of the present with those of the past, to try to sort out the universal, basic stuff of human nature from the emphemeridae, sometimes overwhelming in their momentary impact, of the particular society and environment.'[2] In 1954, travelling as tourists and scholars alike, she and Mullard sailed to Greece, where they investigated archaeological excavations, admired ancient art, marvelled at the rugged geography and ate traditional Greek food. The itinerary included locations of the greatest significance: Piraeus, Athens, Crete, Delos (also the name of their first house in Cape Town), Knossos and Marathon. Two years later, after diligent research on how Plato, Xenophon, Herodotus, Thucydides, Plutarch, Diogenes Laertius, Macrobius, Atenaeus and others recollect or reconstruct the world of Socrates (her 'patron saint'), Renault's first historical novel was published. Huge chests of books, ordered from Blackwell's in the United Kingdom, continued to arrive in Camps Bay, where Renault established 'the best private classical library in sub-Saharan Africa'.[3] In 1962, Renault and Mullard returned to a more commercial Greece and added Delphi, Corinth, Sounion and Epidaurus to their repertoire. Unfortunately, travelling put a physical strain on Renault, which made this trip their last journey to the centre of her imagination as a writer, indeed her last voyage ever. Renault died in 1983. Mullard scattered her ashes over Ceres in the Cape mountains, a final tribute to the fruitfulness of the past.

---

[1] Sweetman 1993: 36.   [2] Zilboorg 2001: 139.   [3] Sweetman 1993: 244.

2. South African Life

Incidentally, Renault and her partner arrived in South Africa on the day of the momentous election of 26 May 1948, when the National Party began its grip on power and inaugurated apartheid as the country's government ideology. Renault soon joined the opposition: the Women's Defence of the Constitution League or Black Sash and the Progressive Party. Throughout her life, she opposed apartheid, a courageous trait for a white woman, but the extent of her resistance remains controversial. In 1960, for example, she was at the height of her career when British Prime Minister Harold Macmillan spread his message of 'wind of change' throughout the former colonies, followed by the Sharpeville Massacre, when the police opened fire on a peaceful crowd, killing 69 and wounding many more. That year also saw the attack on Prime Minister Hendrik Verwoerd's life, which he survived and interpreted as a messianic call to action, and the country's departure from the Commonwealth. In 1966, Senator Robert Kennedy spoke to enthusiastic crowds in South Africa. In the Seventies, Angola, Mozambique and Rhodesia/Zimbabwe became independent. In 1976, matters came to a head with the Soweto riots and death of Black Consciousness Movement leader Steve Biko. Yet none of this appears explicitly in Renault's oeuvre. Her refusal – failure, to others – to address the volatile political situation of her time at the expense of 'escapist' classical fiction thus became a bone of contention. Similarly, when Renault was elected a Fellow of the Royal Society of Literature and served as the president of the South African chapter of the writers' association PEN (1964), she came in conflict with Nadine Gordimer in Johannesburg over whether standards for admitting black members should be lowered. (Apartheid publishing made the requirement of two books a virtual impossibility for black writers.) Renault believed in a meritocracy, just as she has Alexander the Great famously bequeath his kingdom *hoti to kratisto*, to the best man.[4]

3. Fact and Fiction

Renault wrote 14 novels, eight of which deal with classical antiquity. Her first five, mostly out of print now, are 'nurse romances'. *The Charioteer* (1953), her sixth and last contemporary work (and first text composed in

---

[4] 1981: 9.

South Africa), stands out as one of Great Britain's first gay novels, but in its titular allusion to the allegory of the charioteer in Plato's *Phaedrus*, it already transitions to the past. *The King Must Die* (1958) and its sequel *The Bull from the Sea* (1962) deal with the mythological adventures of Theseus and their rich texture, including the Minotaur, Ariadne in Naxos, Oedipus in Colonus, the Amazons, Phaedra's adulterous passion and Hippolytus' chastity, and Theseus' return to his father Poseidon.

The Praise Singer (1978) begins at a crucial time in Athens' history. After Draco's institution of harsh legislation, Solon becomes archon and abolishes serfdom. He is followed by the tyrant Pisistratus, who favours the promotion and expansion of Athenian interests. In 508 BC, Cleisthenes instigates democracy, with all freemen enjoying the right to vote – a tremendous *Aufbruch*, the most visible sign of which is the rebuilding of the Acropolis. It is a time of artistic flowering embodied by the rhapsodist Simonides: 'I praise and love every man who does nothing base from free will. Against necessity, even gods do not fight' (epigraph). In the course of the novel, Simonides follows a sign from Apollo to travel the Greek world – Keos, Samos, Athens, the Sacred Way, and Sicily – in pursuit of his poetic apprenticeship, to find a voice that is pure praise, uncontaminated by flattery: 'Praise-singing is like love . . . You do it from the heart, or you're a whore.'[5] On his travels, Simonides meets such illustrious figures as his fellow poet Anakreon (but not his greatest rival, Pindar), the tragedian Aeschylus, the obscure artists Hipponax and Ibykos, the tyrant Polykrates, and 'mad' Pythagoras.

The Last of the Wine (1956) is set against another climax in Athenian history, the reign of Pericles. The Parthenon added yet another monument to the city's greatness. However, to use Renault's metaphor, the grape is beginning to rot, the wine about to turn to sour vinegar. The Peloponnesian War marks the end of Athens' preponderance. Alexias, a fictional noble Athenian, and his lover Lysis fall under Socrates' spell and narrate their views of justice, imperialism or *paiderastia*, all issues that are subtly linked to the experience of military annihilation and post-war disillusionments. Renault uses the starkest measure possible to underline Athens' decline. When the Thirty, Sparta's puppet regime, pass a law prohibiting the teaching of logic, Alexias cannot believe it: 'Who can forbid logic? Logic is.'[6]

The Mask of Apollo (1966) once again underlines fragility and dissolution. After Socrates' execution, several wars diminish Athens' prevalence,

[5] 1978: 95.   [6] 1956: 339.

although the city is able to shake off Spartan hegemony. Nikeratos or 'Niko', an invented actor, never travels without a mask of Apollo, which in the course of the novel takes on the role of his conscience. The mask is a relic of a golden age, a tribute to a heroic past that survives only in art, an evocation of dead heroes:

Once men deserved such gods. And where are they now? They bled to death on battlefields, black with flies; or starved in the siege, being too good to rob their neighbors. Or they sailed off to Sicily singing paeans, and left their bones there in sunken ships, or in the fever swamps or the slave-quarries. If they got home alive, the Thirty Tyrants murdered them. Or if they survived all that, they grew old in dusty corners, mocked by their grandsons, when to speak of greatness was to be a voice from the dead.[7]

Niko quickly gets enmeshed in the political and cultural turmoil of the day, such as Plato's reservations about *mimesis*, which informed Plato's ban of poets from the ideal city of the *Republic*.

Renault's masterpiece is her trilogy of Alexander the Great. *Fire from Heaven* (1969) relates Alexander's youth and ends with his father Philip of Macedon's assassination by his commander-in-chief in 336 BC, when Alexander ascends to the throne. One of the reasons for Alexander's greatness, no doubt, was his education by Aristotle:

[He and his students] talked of ethics and politics, the nature of pleasure and of justice; of the soul, virtue, friendship and love. They considered the causes of things. Everything must be traced to its cause; and there could be no science without demonstration. Soon a whole room was full of specimens: pressed flowers and plants, seedlings in pots; birds' eggs with their embryos preserved in clear honey; decoctions of medicinal herbs ... At night they observed the heavens; the stars were stuff more divine than any other thing man's eye could reach; a fifth element not to be found on earth. They noted winds and mists and the aspect of the clouds, and learned to prognosticate storms. They reflected light from polished bronze, and measured the angles of refraction.[8]

The Persian Boy (1972) is narrated by Bagoas, a eunuch who first serves Darius, the King of Persia, then Alexander. He conveys a picture of Alexander as a *primus inter pares* and his court with rampant freedom of speech. Bagoas eventually falls in love with Alexander and achieves almost perfect happiness, only clouded by his jealousy at Alexander's similar devotion to his companion Hephaistion. After Alexander's death in Babylon, Bagoas bids farewell with a tearful elegy: 'Go to the gods,

[7] 1966: 42.   [8] 1969: 160–61.

unconquered Alexander. May the River of Ordeal be mild as milk to you, and bathe you in light, not fire. May your dead forgive you; you have given more life to men than you brought death ... You were never without love; where you go, may you find it waiting.'[9] *Funeral Games* (1981) takes up the power vacuum created by Alexander's tragic oversight to designate a clear successor. The novel, with the revealing working title *Hot Embers*, emphasises the chaos and fragmentation of Alexander's world.

4.   Columns of Athens, Capes of Africa

Renault's partner once proudly proclaimed, 'Mary always said her best weapon was the pen – or the typewriter.'[10] We know that Renault indignantly turned down a request from her publisher to write a novel about a Coloured lady librarian and her struggle against apartheid,[11] which forever soured her relationship with Mark Longman. This is Renault's rationale to Longman:

I have really no desire to add one more to the many novels on the colour question. My bent is more for personal relationships and development, and I have often seen the introduction of colour having a paralysing effect on character-drawing, when the author conceives each of his characters as if they were representatives rather than individuals, with whom everyone of that race must be able to identify without offence.[12]

Critic Lisa Moore emphasises South Africa as a place of Mediterranean heroism for Renault, free from Anglo-Saxon repression: 'South Africa may indeed have represented a world in which the privilege of a male Athenian citizen was most closely reproduced in the life of a mid-century white British lesbian freed for professional accomplishment by her refusal of the roles of wife and mother.'[13] Biographer Caroline Zilboorg stresses Renault's ideological aversion to politics: 'the body politic seemed alien,

---

[9] 1972: 411.   [10] Zilboorg 2001: 173.

[11] *Statements after an Arrest under the Immorality Act*, devised by Athol Fugard, John Kani and Winston Ntshona in 1972, eventually dealt with this subject matter (Fugard et al. 1974). Thanks to Roy Sargeant for pointing this out to me.

[12] Mary Renault Papers, St Hugh's College Archive, Oxford (DS/CZ 1), 16 November 1957. Thanks to archivist Amanda Ingram at St Hugh's College, Oxford University for facilitating my research there, and thanks also to the Faculty Scholarship Council at Western Kentucky University for supporting my research.

[13] Moore 2003: 27.

uncomfortable, even immoral to her, as any group would be that was prone to absorbing and obscuring the individual'.[14] She also quotes from an editorial in the *Cape Times* (1968), where Renault justifies her withdrawal from current affairs:

No field of human existence has been more exploited in the world today by the committed writer, whether of the left or right, than has South Africa. A point has been reached when the refusal to write propaganda is itself received by opinion-formers as a propagandist act ... A creative artist cannot transform himself at will into a one-man sanity squad. He turns to the food he can absorb, receive stimulus from, and use.[15]

And in her 1973 essay 'History in Fiction', Renault explains her refusal to use the past as a metaphor for the present: 'if what you are really talking about is Nazi Germany or Vietnam or Texas, why not say so instead of misleading your readers about Nero or Caesar or Troy?'[16]

For the degree of Renault's political engagement, therefore, we will have to turn to her fiction.[17] In *The Mask of Apollo*, Renault metafictionally draws attention to literature as an agent for political change. A play about Thersites, who stands up to Achilles in the *Iliad* (and later was interpreted as a social critic revered by Friedrich Nietzsche, various Marxists in the Soviet Union, and Edward Said), conveys the 'modern' spirit in the struggle against the Sicilian demagogue Dionysios I: 'It's antioligarchical. Let us show the common man rebelling; they can do with that in Syracuse.'[18]

The Last of the Wine, together with *The Mask of Apollo*, offers a detailed view of the Socratic circle, with intimate portraits of the 'traitors' Alcibiades and Critias; the title characters of many Platonic dialogues: Euthydemus, Menexenus, Charmides, Phaedo and Lysis; the playwrights Agathon, Aristophanes and Euripides; the historian Xenophon; the orator Lysias; the star actor Theodoros; the philosopher Aristotle; and Anytus, the chief accuser at Socrates' trial. Socrates, of course, was made to drink the hemlock, but his memory lives on: 'fools killed him; but they could not kill his truth, because he did not destroy without offering something better'.[19] Reviewing *The Last of the Wine* for the *New York Times*, Orville Prescott links Alexias' account to contemporary issues: 'The parallels between his

---

[14] Zilboorg 2001: 163.   [15] Ibid. 172–73.   [16] Renault 1973: 316

[17] A sustained comparison between Renault's Hellenism and South African politics has, to my knowledge, not been made. Bernard Dick (1972) analyses Renault's reception of classical world but draws no comparisons.

[18] 1966: 263.   [19] 1966: 64.

age and ours are deadly – wars and the loss of liberty, political passions and the terrors of dictatorships, atrocities and retaliations.' Socrates remains a timeless and timely figure.

Three great twentieth-century crises in the United States saw widespread appeal to the venerated figure of Socrates, with each epoch fashioning its own 'democratic' man of the people: McCarthyism, civil rights and Vietnam. Socrates embodied the resistance to anti-Communist purges: 'The trial of Socrates is unfinished. When disloyalty or heresy is charged today, the prosecutor's words are different … but … the issues are unchanged', John D. Montgomery (a professor and consultant to the Hiroshima Reconstruction Board) declared in his 1954 essay collection *The State versus Socrates: A Case Study in Civic Freedom*.[20] Via Henry David Thoreau's *Civil Disobedience*, Socrates also represented an advocate of civil disobedience to Mahatma Gandhi during his formative years in South Africa. Martin Luther King, Jr, in his 'Letter from a Birmingham Jail' (1963), invokes Jesus and Socrates:

Just as Socrates felt that it was necessary to create a tension in the mind so that individuals could rise from the bondage of myths and half-truths to the unfettered realm of creative analysis and objective appraisal, we must see the need of having nonviolent gadflies to create the kind of tension in society that will help men to rise from the dark depths of prejudice and racism to the majestic heights of understanding and brotherhood … Too long has our beloved Southland been bogged down in the tragic effort to live in monologue rather than dialogue.[21]

Finally, to the pacifists of the Vietnam War generation, Socrates articulated their resistance because of his famous (pre-Christian) maxim in the *Gorgias* that to suffer wrong is better than to do wrong.

As is well known, Socrates was accused of corrupting the young and failing to honour the established gods. His nemesis was also one of the people he loved the most. In *The Last of the Wine*, Renault focuses on the controversy over Alcibiades, on the eve of the megalomaniac excursion to Sicily, who was accused of mutilating sacred statues of Hermes and profaning the Eleusynian Mysteries. The common denominator about Alcibiades is his failure to value the good of the *polis*, his lack of patriotism and his overbearing *philotimia*. According to the famous verdicts by Thucydides and by Plutarch of *paranomia* and of *hubris*, Alcibiades did not fit into a democratic city. However, as David Gribble explains,

---

[20] Quoted in Lane 2007: 212.   [21] Quoted in Washington 1986: 291–92.

The hostility and envy aroused by a life of luxury is the counterpart of a fascination felt at another level. Thus the average Athenian loathed the figure of the tyrant as the embodiment of tendencies absolutely opposed to the city and its values, but at some private level might have liked to be a tyrant himself, and accepted this as a normal desire in others. Excess, even 'undemocratic' excess could be attractive, and the figure who acts in this way may do so partly out of an awareness that his pursuit of the maximum, both of pleasure and power, arouses the admiration of others.[22]

The city loves Alcibiades and hates him, yet it longs to have him back, Aristophanes muses in his *Frogs*.

Renault brings out this very paradox in Alcibiades' rhetoric:

You wished for me, Athenians; I am here. Do not question me, do not hurt me; I am the wish sprung from your heart, and if you wound me your heart will bleed for it. Your love made me. Do not take it away; for without love I am a temple forsaken by its god, where dark Alastor will enter. It was you, Athenians, who conjured me, a daimon whose food is love. Feed me, then, and I will clothe you with glory, and show you to yourselves in the image of your desire. I am hungry: feed me.[23]

Exhortation and intimidation, feeding and forcing alternate and build up to a rhetorical climax. Nevertheless, as we know from Alcibiades' ignominy, political aspirations, when given the greatest leeway, the freest rein, the blankest check, prove self-defeating in the very act of attaining their objectives. Hitler, Stalin, Mussolini, Franco ... were less than distant memories in the Fifties (or alive and well), and things would get worse. After the Sharpeville massacre, Nigel Worden notes in *The Making of Modern South Africa*, 'wide-ranging arbitrary powers provided a new means of state control, circumventing judicial intervention'.[24] Most disturbingly, Alcibiades' notion contradicts Lysis' concept of democracy: 'We fight for our City, where the mark of a citizen is to have a mind and speak it, and people live their daily lives as they choose, with none to put them in fear.'[25] In racist South Africa, conversely, educational opportunities were deliberately withheld from many of the non-white population. As a result, most of its citizens remained semi-literate, lived enforced daily lives, were unable to speak their minds and were kept in fear of reprisals.

And yet, no political orientation, however repressive or liberal, however stable or fragile, is immune to change. What Renault emphasises repeatedly

---

[22] Gribble 1999: 82.   [23] 1956: 40–41.   [24] Worden 2012: 139.   [25] 1956: 116.

is post-tyrannical turmoil or the transience of any political system. The small miracle of establishing democracy is no easy feat. In *The Bull from the Sea*, the mythological Theseus, after the violent deaths of Antigone, Polynices, Eteocles and Creon, ends the fratricidal strife and restores order:

> The people sang me as judge and lawgiver, and shared the pride of it. And indeed, from that time on wronged folk from all the clans of Attica would come to sit on my threshold: slaves with cruel masters, widows oppressed or orphans disinherited; and not even the chiefs dared murmur when I saw right done. It was called the glory of Athens; for myself, I saw it as an offering to the gods.[26]

The glory of Athens he may be, but the king must die. In *The Mask of Apollo*, not only does Plato fail with the Archon Dionysios I, but after Dionysios' son is ousted (and, against the angry people's wishes, given safe passage) and his right hand Philistos mutilated by a malicious mob, the liberator Dion has second thoughts: 'Such people, he began to think, could not know their own good; if left to fend for themselves, they would suffer worse than under the tyranny, and sink even lower: for he believed what Sokrates had taught Plato, and Plato him, that it is better to suffer evil than to do it.'[27] In *The Last of the Wine*, Lysis qualifies his definition of democracy: 'It is what it says, the rule of the people. It is as good as the people are, or as bad.'[28] In *The Praise Singer*, the great Solon once told his successor Pisistratos, 'Tyranny, my dear, is like one of those mountain climbs which take one up, but not down. One can only fall',[29] yet even this democrat is exiled. And when Harmodius and Aristogiton assassinate the tyrant Hipparchos (but miss Hippias), they did great harm – initially at least: 'Already people say that they set Athens free, though they threw her in a reign of fear, and only the Spartans and the Alkmaionids broke it.'[30]

In *Fire from Heaven*, Demosthenes laments: 'In the Great War with Sparta, the Athenians had fought for glory and for empire; they had ended beaten to the dust and stripped of everything. They had fought for freedom and democracy, and had finished under the most brutal tyranny of their recorded years.'[31] In *The Persian Boy*, even though the Persian sovereign is sacrosanct, Darius is betrayed and deposed: 'Disaster after disaster, failure on failure, shame on shame; friend after friend turned traitor; his troops, to whom he should have been as a god, creeping off like thieves every night.'[32] The same happened after Alexander's demise: 'The wars for the world had started; these people were fighting to possess him, as if he were a thing,

---

[26] 2001: 146.   [27] 1966: 298.   [28] 1956: 236.   [29] 1978: 144.   [30] Ibid., 283.   [31] 1969: 253.
[32] 1972: 84.

a symbol, like the Mitra or the throne.'[33] In *Funeral Games*, Alexander is reported to have foreseen on his deathbed 'great contests at my funeral games' (epigraph), which turn out to be deadly intrigues, blood feuds, perpetual revenge and political assassinations. Unable to agree on a competent successor, the Macedonian Assembly proclaims Alexander's idiot brother Arridaios king. People are torn apart by forces beyond their grasp and control: 'All those great men. When Alexander was alive, they pulled together like one chariot-team. And when he died, they bolted like chariot-horses when the driver falls. And broke their backs like horses, too.'[34] Democrats and demagogues, tyrants and tyrannicides, they come and go.

We find a similar attitude in Renault's correspondence. In a letter to an American friend (4 July 1963), Renault addresses the Civil Rights turmoil in the United States – 'America cannot possibly get *governed* by the Negroes whatever civil rights they have' – and concludes the same about South Africa:

Personally I am all for live and let live, and the removal of all racial segregation and social insults. But nothing I've seen causes me to think that under an African government with universal franchise we would get democracy, justice, or even the kind of standards on which such essentials of civilisation as, say, medical ethics depend. I think the only fair way is to have an educational qualification applied with strict fairness to every race, before giving the vote.[35]

A decade later (25 December 1971), Renault seems to have given up entirely on government by the people, resigning herself to a utopian government by the best: 'The truth is, I no longer believe in democracy, anywhere ... I have no more wish to be governed by a black proletariat here than, as now, by a white one; I should greatly prefer to have the best of both.'[36] At the same time, Renault takes issue with reverse-racism:

But one thing does disturb me – it is the way the concept of anti-racialism is being used, often unconsciously, as a cover for all kinds of evil passions, just as the conception of sexual morality was in our grandparents' day. I mean, it is bad to feel superior to people because of their colour. But the real evil is the hubris, the false sense of status, derived from believing you belong to *any* superior group, and causing you to heighten it by insisting on the inferiority of some other group. Over and over again now I see the hatred and aggression being stirred up by generalisations about 'white South Africans' couched in such racialistic terms, with such contempt for the value of the individual human soul, that you cannot believe the people concerned have so little self-criticism as

[33] Ibid., 411.   [34] 1981: 330.   [35] DS/CZ 3   [36] KA/MC 76 i

not to see that, like people in the old days beating the village whore, they are indulging their own suppressed instincts.[37]

For Renault, there is only one historical character, a pre-modern Nelson Mandela so to speak, who is near flawless. In *Fire from Heaven*, sailing to Pella, Aristotle reflects on Hellas' political past and future:

Two generations had seen each decent form of government decay into its own perversion: aristocracy into oligarchy, democracy to demagogy, kingship to tyranny. With mathematical progression, according to the number who shared the evil[,] the deadweight against reform increased. To change an oligarchy called for power and ruthlessness, destructive to the soul. To change a demagogy, one must become a demagogue and destroy one's mind as well. But to reform a monarchy, one need only mould one man. The chance to be a king-shaper, the prize every philosopher prayed for, had fallen to him.[38]

Aristotle embraces Alexander, while his fellow citizen Demosthenes vociferously opposes Alexander's father. In an encounter between Demosthenes and young Alexander, the orator comes across as ludicrous and lecherous, as virulent and vituperative. Renault, it seems, is rejecting Athenian democratic rhetoric in favour of empire, bombast, children. However, Demosthenes is also a man of the past, and his epithets for King Philip reveal deep-seated racial prejudice. Apartheid, we remember, was notoriously based on the principles that people are grouped into races, that only one race is civilised and therefore superior, and that all Whites are of the same race, while Africans, Coloureds and Indians are subdivided (by means of this fiction, Whites could claim to be in the majority). In the *Third Philippic*, especially, Demosthenes belittles Philip in ethnic terms:

But if some slave or supposititious bastard had wasted and squandered what he had no right to, heavens! how much more monstrous and exasperating all would have called it! Yet they have no such qualms about Philip and his present conduct, though he is not only no Greek, nor related to the Greeks, but not even a barbarian from any place that can be named with honour, but a pestilent knave from Macedonia, whence it was never yet possible to buy a decent slave.[39]

'Slave', 'bastard', 'barbarian', carrier of disease, child-like, lacking in honour and decency ... suggest the derogatory terms of abuse for non-European peoples.

---

[37] DS/CZ 7, 2 February 1961.   [38] 1969: 154.
[39] Demosthenes, *Philippics* 3.31, tr. Vince 1930: 241–42.

In any case, Renault's interest lies in Alexander: 'When his faults (those his own times did not account as virtues) have been considered, we are left with the fact that no other human being has attracted in his lifetime, from so many men, so fervent a devotion. Their reasons are worth examining.'[40] Early on, Alexander accepts, to use a modern term, a multicultural society – or a Rainbow Nation, in Archbishop Desmond Tutu's vision. Visiting Athens and a temple to Eros in the olive groves (where Plato used to teach), Alexander uniquely proclaims: 'What does it matter where a man comes from? It's what he is in himself.'[41] Alexander learns different languages, adopts regional dresses, and consults the oracles of the various denominations. He tames the horse Thunder, the 'word for tyranny and pain', and baptises it 'Oxhead';[42] he reads Herodotus' *Customs of the Persians*, for 'One should understand the kind of man one is going to fight';[43] and he chooses his playmates on the basis of fun and his erotic partners on the basis of love, not expediency. In Troy, Alexander and Hephaistion celebrate their commitment by honouring the tomb of Achilles and Patroclus, whose ashes were mingled in one urn: 'Not even a god could sift the one from the other.'[44] While erotic relationships in ancient Greece were normally hierarchical and asymmetrical (*erastes* and *eromenos*), Renault presents Alexander and Hephaistion as equals. In *The Praise Singer*, Renault similarly develops the political love story between Harmodius and Aristogiton. After Hippias' expulsion in 510 BC, Harmodius and Aristogiton were celebrated as patriots and martyrs. It is also significant that they bridged class barriers: 'The youth [Harmodius] had killed for pride, but the man [Aristogiton] for love: from anger at the hurt to his beloved, and that one man should have the power to do it; from fear that he had the power to take the beloved away.'[45] They represent a particularly democratic mode of sexuality, later to be celebrated by gay writers such as Walt Whitman, Edward Carpenter and E. M. Forster.[46] However, these couples epitomise a model of democratic erotics that Renault embraced only in Athens or Alexandria – not in Africa.

5. Conclusion

Renault makes several veiled references to unjust apartheid legislation, which must have been omnipresent. Yet perhaps apartheid's most

---

[40] 1972: 418. [41] 1969: 288. [42] 1969: 137. [43] 1969: 347. [44] 1969: 55. [45] 1978: 283.
[46] See also Endres 2004: 301–2.

Figure 14.1 Roy Sargeant, Mary Renault and actor Michael Atkinson at Renault's home in Camps Bay, Cape Town. The bust of Apollo Belvedere in the foreground may have originated in the Beit Collection. See Sweetman 1993: 244.

notorious manifestation was the pass-laws, confining non-white Africans to living only in specified areas (the Group Areas Act). In her fiction, on the other hand, people travel freely. Preparing for *The Mask of Apollo*, Renault discovered that actors were free to pass between cities – 'fine free lives we actors lead, able to cross frontiers and go anywhere'[47] – even during the upheavals and wars of the fourth century, and often they embarked on state embassies. In mythology, too, when Theseus brings all Attica under the rule of law, he establishes unparalleled peace: 'Any man, unless he had killed with his own hand and paid no blood-price, could pass through his neighbor's deme unarmed.'[48] Still, Renault's role is more like Ptolemy's, recording great deeds of great men rather than making new things. Renault could have blended two good wines to make a better, could have blended her sophisticated knowledge of classical democracy with dedicated political resistance. Like Socrates, Renault avoided political activity or public affairs as much

[47] 1966: 15.   [48] 2001: 80.

as she could (in Socrates' case at least, to his detriment), but the charge of quietism levelled against Socrates, who failed to speak out at crucial crises in Athenian history (for example, the Melian and the Sicilian debates), continues to stick with Renault as well. For her, democracy remains fictional, not factual.

15 | Antiquity's Undertone: Classical Resonances
in the Poetry of Douglas Livingstone

KATHLEEN M. COLEMAN*

Douglas Livingstone (1932–96) was widely acknowledged in his lifetime
as South Africa's premier poet writing in English. His poetry is deeply
engaged with Africa, both the landscape of what he himself referred to as
'the heart-shaped continent'[1] and its urban culture, and many of the
human impulses that he explores in his poetry are particularised in an
African setting. His collected works – over 400 poems – were published in
a single substantial volume in 2004, *A Ruthless Fidelity* (henceforth abbreviated to *RF*).[2] This includes a selection of 96 of Livingstone's previously
unpublished works, and so it is now possible to get an overview of his
achievement and its contours. The 'classical heritage' plays but a very small
role in his poetry. Nevertheless, his work is a particularly good test-case for
the survival and transmutation of the classical tradition, since the atmosphere of most of his poems is overwhelmingly African, and by his own
admission he did not discover Greek and Roman literature until his early
twenties, and then through the medium of English translation. Nor was
the inspiration that he derived from the ancient world limited to Greece
and Rome; the ancient Near East – specifically Babylon and the epic of
Gilgamesh – prompted an important cycle of ten poems entitled 'Tales

* This project began with an invitation to deliver the Stubbs Lecture at University College,
Toronto, in 2006, which specified that it 'should be based on some subject relating to English
Literature or a Greek or Latin subject', but did not exclude their combination. I have benefitted
considerably from the reactions of that audience, and audiences at the Golden Jubilee
Conference of the Classical Association of South Africa in Cape Town in 2007, the Classical
Association of New England Summer Institute at Dartmouth College in 2009, and McMaster
University, Tufts University, the University of Pennsylvania and the University of Victoria; and
from Grant Parker's editorial suggestions. The entire project would have been impossible were it
not for the archives of the National English Literary Museum in Grahamstown, South Africa,
and its expert, patient and hospitable curators. Margaret Daymond of the Programme of English
Studies at the University of KwaZulu-Natal generously furnished me with a catalogue of Douglas
Livingstone's personal library. I gratefully acknowledge also the permission of the National
English Literary Museum, in its capacity as executor of the literary estates of Douglas
Livingstone and Guy Butler, to reproduce material by Livingstone, both published and
unpublished, and Butler's poem, 'Myths'.

[1] In an interview with Michael Chapman upon receipt of the 1984 CNA Literary Award:
Livingstone 1985: 94.

[2] Hacksley and Maclennan 2004.

from the Tower of Babel' (*RF* 361–70).[3] But the legacy of the Greeks and Romans is visible throughout his corpus, and in sampling their influence we may glimpse the enduring power of the ancient world to elicit a creative response from a profoundly original artist.

Livingstone was born in Kuala Lumpur and attended a French convent.[4] He was evacuated to South Africa, to Durban, when he was ten, and spent all his spare time by and in the sea. When he left school he had two jobs: he was a lifesaver on Durban beach by day and a bench-chemist in a sugar mill by night. In 1951 he moved to the Rhodesias, both Northern and Southern, and trained to be a bacteriologist. From his period in what is now Harare there survives in manuscript at the National English Literary Museum in Grahamstown (henceforth NELM) a four-page typescript of a farce entitled *The Fall of Troy*, characterised by Livingstone's irreverent word-play (notably a remark of Paris, 'I cannot forget that heel Achilles').[5] Yet, his reception of antiquity was far from facetious. In a poignant article about his childhood and youth, he remarked, perhaps not entirely artlessly, 'The longest I ever spent in one place was five years. It was a room in a government hostel in Salisbury, Rhodesia, where I used to swill cheap gin of an evening, lying on the floor reading and re-reading Plato's Socratic dialogues.'[6] And in an interview with the Italian scholar Marco Fazzini nearly a quarter of a century later, he claimed of those years in Rhodesia (now Zimbabwe), 'During this time, perhaps because I missed the sea, I discovered and fell in love with Antiquity – classical Greece and Rome – and read everything I could get hold of from Plato to Horace, from Virgil to Catullus (in English translations, of course).'[7] Livingstone did not, however, remain permanently in exile from maritime climes; he returned to Durban in 1964, and became a very well-respected scientist working on water pollution off the coast of Natal. He earned his PhD in microbiology in 1989; his thesis, entitled *Microbial Studies on Seawater Quality off Durban: 1964–1988*, was published by the Centre for Scientific and Industrial Research in 1990.

The relevance of the classical heritage to a poet writing in and of Africa is a thread running throughout Livingstone's work from the beginning. His first published collection, *The Skull in the Mud* (1960), which takes its title from a poem describing one of his experiences while he was employed as

---

[3] First published in *The Purple Renoster* (Livingstone 1968a).
[4] A five-page timeline of Livingstone's life and career is supplied in the unpaginated section entitled 'Chronology' in Hacksley and Maclennan, *A Ruthless Fidelity*, immediately before the pagination begins. For rich personal detail about his early life, see Livingstone 1966.
[5] NELM 2001.1.8.5, 2.   [6] Livingstone 1966: 61.   [7] Fazzini 1991: 135.

a contract diver during the construction of Lake Kariba, opens with 'Chez Moi in Central Africa', an intricately rhymed poem that obliquely questions the relevance of the classical heritage in the heart of Africa (*RF* 3):

> Within the flaccid gut of this flux land
>   I write, a mucoid Jonah, with my sin
>   behind me, standing sentry in the shade,
>   while unrepentant, toasting in the sun,
>   I sing to every blind unheeding maid
>   a tilt at love I would not care to win
> and watch an ant run fretful on my hand.
>
> Against the sudden schisms and the flow
>   I kick my heels and let the others judge.
>   Without a collar I can crave the heat.
>   (Does Hellas count her battle lost or won?)
>   The sky is blue, the row of crops stands neat,
>   the river's down, old herons hunt the sludge,
> the land will last, the people come and go.

The parenthetic question to 'Hellas', easily overlooked by a reader in a hurry, goes to the heart of an issue that has preoccupied many poets trying to link the dramatic African landscape with the mythologies of the western cultural tradition.

Some of the most awe-inspiring features of the South African landscape (the Drakensberg, the Great Karoo, Cape Point…) are comparable in their grandeur to sites in Greece where some of the most powerful Greek myths are located (Delphi, Mount Helicon, the Hellespont…); and yet, despite this shared topography, the western heritage is inherently alien in Africa south of the Fezzan. Douglas Livingstone's slightly older contemporary, Guy Butler (1918–2001), frames precisely this paradox in his poem 'Myths'.[8] It starts shockingly with the poet crushing a cobra's head against a rock, and by the end of the second stanza the incompatibility of the western heritage and the African landscape is made explicit, with a reference to Keats, the Greeks and the Middle Ages. The answer comes in the poet's encounter with an old couple camping by the side of the road:

> Alone one noon on a sheet of igneous rock
> I smashed a five-foot cobra's head to pulp;
> Then, lifting its cool still-squirming gold
> In my sweating ten separate fingers, suddenly

---

[8] Macnab 1958: 11–12.

Tall aloes were also standing there,
Lichens were mat-red patches on glinting boulders,
Clouds erupted white on the mountain's edge,
All, all insisting on being seen.
Familiar, and terribly strange, I felt the sun
Gauntlet my arms and cloak my growing shoulders.

Never quite the same again
Poplar, oak or pine, no, none
Of the multifarious shapes and scents that breed
About the homestead, below the dam, along the canal,
Or any place where a European,
Making the most of a fistful of water, splits
The brown and grey with wedges of daring green —
Known as invaders now, alien,
Like the sounds on my tongue, the pink on my skin;
And, like my heroes, Jason, David, Robin Hood,
Leaving tentative footprints on the sand between
The aloe and the rock, uncertain if this
Were part of their proper destiny. Reading
Keats's *Lamia* and *Saint Agnes' Eve*
Beneath a giant pear tree buzzing with bloom
I glanced at the galvanized windmill turning
Its iron sunflower under the white-hot sky
And wondered if a Grecian or Medieval dream
Could ever strike root away from our wedges of green,
Could ever belong down there
Where the level sheen on new lucerne stops short:
Where aloes and thorns thrust roughly out
Of the slate-blue shales and purple dolerite.

Yet sometimes the ghosts that books had put in my brain
Would slip from their hiding behind my eyes
To take on flesh, the sometimes curious flesh
Of an African incarnation.

One winter dusk when the livid snow
On Swaershoek Pass went dull, and the grey
Ash-bushes grew dim in smudges of smoke,
I stopped at the outspan place to watch,
Intenser as the purple shades drew down,
A little fire leaping near a wagon,
Sending its acrid smoke into the homeless night.
Patient as despair, eyes closed, ugly,

The woman stretched small hands towards the flames;
But the man, back to an indigo boulder,
Face thrown up to the sky, was striking
Rivers of sorrow into the arid darkness
From the throat of a battered, cheap guitar.

It seemed that in an empty hell
Of darkness, cold and hunger, I had stumbled on
Eurydice, ragged, deaf forever,
Orpheus playing to beasts that would or could not hear,
Both eternally lost to news or rumours of spring.

The poet has seen the incarnation of the archetypal Greek story of love and loss, the tale of Orpheus and Eurydice, where the beasts of the African veld – 'beasts that could or would not hear' – are the node that joins the situation to its mythological exemplar. Butler's own comment on this poem, in his autobiography nearly half a century later, is an important authorial statement: '[This poem] has been misunderstood as supporting the view that the white man and his culture are irredeemably alien to Africa. It is nothing of the kind. Among other things it records a moment when Orpheus and Eurydice find partial African incarnation.'[9]

Butler's question in this poem, whether Greek myth is ever relevant in the southern African context, is implicit in almost every classical allusion in the poetry of Douglas Livingstone, who was his friend.[10] Not every poem, however, has an African setting; 'Amphorae' (also from *The Skull in the Mud*) is apparently set in Greece (*RF* 8):

The yellow beach road writhes its sandy skin
under an arch between the white-washed walls
to the bay where a small brown fishing boat,
lateen-rigged, daubs the blue. With gallantry
the stone arch helps the creepers cross the road.
Open windows hint sultry mysteries —
exciting scents of Aphrodite's hair,
sweet, dusky, warming muliebrity —
with perhaps the dark tints of sandalwood.

On a doorstep, two amphorae, beaded,
slim and black, and obviously wine-cool,
strike an uneven, still, sharp, watchful pose.

[9] Butler 1991: 145.
[10] As the epigraph tells us, 'For G.B.', published in *Selected Poems* (1984), was composed for the recipient's sixty-fifth birthday on 21 January 1983 (*RF* 251).

If you half close your eyes, pulling low
fringed lashes, the man on the down-turned tub,
idly whittling, becomes a valued friend
full of wise and mocking terseness. Trojan,
completely old-Levantic, is his air.

Squinting against the white sun, you can walk,
chequered by shade and shine, down the beach road,
past the houses and the phocine wine jars
and muffled women's whispers from the rooms.
Down – scuffing down – past bollards to the bay.
There, quite alone, enter the dancing, blue
wrinkled waters, and, making of yourself
a libation, merge wetly with the sea.

Swaying, sea-drunkenly on light toe-tips,
dream-striding between the ferny seaweed
and shard of old amphorae, where the winds
cast them, filled once with dates or smoky oils;
down – where the water furls, low, cool and green,
by silently waiting, weightless and deep,
you can meet – arrived with a percheron's
suddenness – a dolphin, smile-snouted, gay,
and very Latin, making strong the wish
to stay submerged in all this palpable sea:
an atavistic hearkening to live
inhaling these slow waters thick with life
you have exchanged for insubstantial air.

This poem is explicitly indebted to classical influences upon the English lexicon, a point apparently overlooked by Michael Chapman, the author of the first book-length work of criticism on Livingstone's poetry, who includes 'muliebrity' and 'phocine' from this poem in the category of words in Livingstone's oeuvre for whose use he finds 'little justification'.[11] But these Latin borrowings – 'muliebrity', 'phocine' and, less arcane, 'libation' and 'atavistic' – support the atmosphere of connection with the past: a past, moreover, that is faintly treacherous. The fisherman you stumble upon becomes instantly 'a valued friend / full of wise and mocking terseness. Trojan, / completely old-Levantic, is his air', and the amphorae at the doorway in the second stanza are matched by shards in the fifth, the detritus of a wreck: 'shard of old amphorae, where the winds / cast them,

[11] Chapman 1981: 18.

filled once with dates or smoky oils'. It is by entering the sea, the agent of
shipwreck, that Livingstone connects with an ancient, less corrupted world,
symbolised by the seductive dolphin, 'smile-snouted, gay, / and very Latin'.

   One of the remarkable features of Livingstone's work is his ability to
evoke an urban atmosphere as authentically as a landscape or a seascape.
A particularly famous example, 'Aphrodite's Saturday Night', which was
included in the collection *Eyes Closed Against the Sun* (1970), is predicated
upon the power of the classical past to provide a psychological escape from
a lonely and humdrum urban reality (*RF* 84–5):[12]

> In the small chaotic bedroom above
> his darkened shop, his scrambled shrine to love,
> up there brightly lit and bedclothed tumbled
> he awakes at fifty-three. His eyes stumbled
> by importunate mirrors, five-foot-six;
> in his naked complexion Europes mix;
> belly swollen and grey, the hairy screws
> of lank, lamp black are scratched; he gropes for shoes.
>
> Dressed, button-holed, he walks down to his shop
> and threads the known and holy maze. A crop
> of hunting prints are dangerously stacked
> on black full-bosomed, generously cracked
> and enormous chests bared to the dark.
> A musty smell swells from the mounted lark,
> blitheless in spirit. Glints glance off cabinets,
> dressmakers' dummies, Georgian bassinets.
>
> He weaves gently intent through walls of knives,
> cutlasses, swords and kukris; Plutarch's *Lives*;
> cold yellowing chessmen sullenly trapped
> in ivory or ebony and the chapped
> Queen Anne tea-sets and fire-cracked Chinese gongs;
> brasses and lanterns; sets of chestnut tongs —
> reaches and opens the door marked ANTIQUES
> and stops for her in the street-lit patina.
>
> She stands, six inches tall, inside the door,
> listening to silence. This divine whore
> is not the hacked, hackneyed one from Mylos,
> but a softer, more slender and guileless
> altogether one; head inclined, one hand

---

[12] First published in *London Magazine* (Livingstone 1964a).

guarding the pubic from the public, and
fixed. He will not sell. Like all superior
courtesans, unpriced. He spurns every offer.

He bows. His moustache respectfully brushes
the top of her semiprecious head. Spruce as
a penguin, elated, key safe, he lets
himself out where the tunnelled night wind frets.
He wheels his stick as he walks, unafraid;
breathes, rinsing soggy lungs, uncreaks vertebrae.
He will march the park, ignore the lovers strewn
on every bench, watch for the errant moon.

This poem has an indeterminate geographical setting (it could as easily be London as Johannesburg[13]), though the provenance of the protagonist, hinted at in the line 'in his naked complexion Europes mix', may suggest an expatriate heritage. 'Classical allusion' in this poem is extremely spare: the title; a casual mention of Plutarch's *Lives*; a disparaging reference to 'the hacked, hackneyed one from Mylos', the Venus de Milo, 'hacked' presumably referring to her arms, lost below the joints (Fig. 15.1), just as the statuette's pose, 'one hand / guarding the pubic from the public', conjures up another characteristic sculptural format for Venus, the so-called Venus Capitolina type, in which the left hand modestly shelters the pudenda (Fig. 15.2). The classical allusions are ostensibly on the same plane as the references to 'dressmakers' dummies, Georgian bassinets... Queen Anne tea-sets and fire-cracked Chinese gongs', the indiscriminate bric-à-brac of the past; and yet the statuette of the title is the redeeming feature of the old antique dealer's life, a small effigy of the erotic charge incarnate in Aphrodite/Venus. The deliberate tension in the title, juxtaposing the goddess' name with the party-night of the modern week, distils the collision of the grand, timeless past with the sordid and ephemeral present.

The erotic is a recurring preoccupation with Livingstone. Like 'Chez Moi in Central Africa', from *The Skull in the Mud*, 'To Make You' is also prefatory, providing the opening to Livingstone's collection of love-poems entitled *A Rosary of Bone*, which was first published in 1975 and enlarged in 1983 (*RF* 135):

To make you, love,
Here's a small book of verse,

[13] The same atmosphere of faded sensuality characterises the Johannesburg neighbourhoods of Braamfontein in Athol Fugard's play, *People are Living There* (Fugard 1970, first performed in 1969), and Hillbrow in the novel by Ivan Vladislavić, *The Restless Supermarket* (2001).

Figure 15.1 Aphrodite called 'Venus de Milo'. Hellenistic, ca. 100 BCE. From the island of Melos. Marble, h. 202 cm. Photograph Hervé Lewandowski.

here's a bough,
a jug (here's how!), a loaf.

To make you live
Here's a handful of sea;
  Here's a fig;
Here's sunshine on the leaf.

To make you laugh
here, now, has become sum
  and substance
of my quickening life.

Figure 15.2 The Capitoline Venus, marble statue, Roman copy of Hellenistic Greek original. Photograph Gianni Dagli Orti/The Art Archive at Art Resource, NY.

> To make you love,
> you live, you laugh, my love,
>   here's how: here's
> my love (jug-jug!): my life.

The quatrains, the book of verse, the bough, the jug, the loaf and the address to the beloved are incontrovertible allusions to the twelfth quatrain of the *Rubáiyát* of Omar Khayyam in the translation of 101 selected verses from the Persian original by Edward FitzGerald, first published in 1859; the edition published by Harrap in 1940 is contained in Livingstone's personal library, which now belongs to the Programme of English Studies at the University of KwaZulu-Natal:[14]

> A Book of Verses underneath the Bough,
> A Jug of Wine, a Loaf of Bread—and Thou

---

[14] FitzGerald 1940.

> Beside me singing in the Wilderness—
> Oh, Wilderness were Paradise enow!

But a classical influence is also present. The Zimbabwean poet Colin Style has explicitly linked Livingstone's love-poetry with the precedent of Catullus, singling out 'the same meticulous detailing of experience, flashes of insight deepening into vision'.[15] 'To Make You' acknowledges Livingstone's Catullan debt not only in its tightness of structure and formulaic repetition, characteristics that Catullus shares with the *Rubáiyát*, but especially by verbal allusion: the actions 'love', 'live', 'laugh' that are distributed among the first three verses and combined in the fourth recall the 'signature' of one of the most famous love affairs of western literature, Catullus' affair with the woman he called 'Lesbia'. Poem 5, one of the most frequently imitated of all Latin poems, begins *Viuamus, mea Lesbia, atque amemus / rumoresque senum seueriorum / omnes unius aestimemus assis* ('Let us live, my Lesbia, and let us love, and value at a single *as* [cent] all the rumours of strict old men'); and Poem 51, a translation of a Greek lyric poem by Sappho, describes in a single two-word phrase, *dulce ridentem* (γελαίσας ἰμέροεν, 'sweetly laughing'), the woman with whom the poet falls instantly in love, in the presence of a third party who may be her husband. While Livingstone may have been familiar with some of the English translations and imitations of the Lesbia poems from the Elizabethan age onwards (several modern versions are included in an anthology that he owned, *Voices from the Past*),[16] he certainly possessed a copy of Peter Whigham's translation of Catullus, published by Penguin in 1966, where a free translation of the opening of Poem 5 incorporates 'laugh' alongside 'live' and 'love':[17]

> Lesbia
>   live with me
> & love me so
> we'll laugh at all
> the sour-faced strict-
> ures of the wise.

Certainly, Christopher Marlowe's bucolic idyll, *The Passionate Shepherd to his Love*, which takes its impetus from Catullus, beginning 'Come live with me and be my Love, / And we will all the pleasures prove', was known to Livingstone, since he published a satirical version entitled 'The Passionate

---

[15] Style 1982: 94.   [16] Maclean Todd and Maclean Todd, 1955–1960.
[17] Whigham 1966: 55.

Bacteriologist to His Love' ('Come live with me & be my love / Up in the lab., first floor above'; etc.: *RF* 327).[18] He also owned *All the collected short poems* by Louis Zukofsky,[19] the celebrated Objectivist poet who, with his wife, rendered all of Catullus in 'homophonic translation'; although Livingstone apparently did not own this latter work,[20] he may have had access to it elsewhere, and so may have encountered Catullus in various renderings in both his own bookshelves and beyond. The laconic sensuousness of Catullus' poetry finds a remarkable responsion in Livingstone's, especially in *A Rosary of Bone.*

While erotic love is a prominent theme in Livingstone's poetry, another passion is also a driving force: a passion for Africa. In 'The Sleep of My Lions', also included in *Eyes Closed Against the Sun*, Africa expresses her revulsion at the damage wrought on her continent by mankind, appealing to the sea to wash away the corrupting influences of civilisation (*RF* 96):[21]

> *O, Mare Atlanticum,*
> *Mare Arabicum et Indicum,*
> *Oceanus Orientalis,*
> *Oceanus Aethiopicus*
>   save me
>   from civilization,
>   my pastory
>   from further violation.
>
> Leave me my magics
> and tribes;
> to the quagga, the dodo,
> the sleep of my lions.
>
> Rust me barbed fences.
> Patrol what remains.
> Accept bricks, hunting rifles
> and realists, telephones
> and diesels
> to your antiseptic main.
>
> Grant me a day of
> moon-rites and rain-dances;
> when rhinoceros

---

18 Livingstone 1962.   19 Zukofsky 1965.   20 Zukofsky and Zukofsky 1969.
21 First published in *Contrast*: Livingstone 1968b: 7.

> root in trained hibiscus borders;
> when hippo flatten, with a smile,
> deck-chairs at the beach resorts.
>
> Accord me a time
> of stick-insect gods, and impala
> no longer crushed by concrete;
> when love poems like this
> can again be written in beads.

The epigraph is striking as an example of Livingstone's use of Latin for an incantatory effect; indeed, in an interview with a schoolteacher, Elizabeth Thompson, in 1986, he said so:[22] 'The Latin was supposed to set the mood for a sort of incantation... I guess there is an echo of the Roman Catholic Mass there in the opening'. This opening invocation, '*O, Mare Atlanticum, / Mare Arabicum et Indicum, / Oceanus Orientalis, / Oceanus Aethiopicus*', is surely meant to evoke the mariners' maps of the pristine seas lapping the African continent before the first settlers arrived (see Fig. 15.3 and Plate 9). In the poem, Latin stands for the irrecoverable past, although, for someone brought up in a French convent, it must also be the language of intercession, mapped – literally – onto the uncharted waters of a precolonial continent.

Latin is rarely quoted by Livingstone, but it has a similarly incantatory effect at the beginning of each of the first three stanzas of a nine-stanza poem entitled 'Lunch-hour and Cestodes', which is set in a laboratory. The Latin phrases become shorter in each successive stanza and are echoed in the technical terms of the fourth and the first half of the fifth describing the 'egg', 'head' and 'beak' of a tapeworm ('ovum', 'scolex', 'rostellum'), while the latter half of the poem contains no Latinate terminology at all (*RF* 480–1):[23]

> *Diphyllobothrium latum* or
> *Dibothriocephalus latus*,
> he said card-punching them into
> his already punch-drunk brain.
>
> *Inermicapsifer cubensis*,
> *Saginata*, in beef, bare.
> *Solium*: pork: hooklets,
> (that second letter an O).

[22] Thompson 1986: 6.   [23] NELM 2001.1.1.1.114.

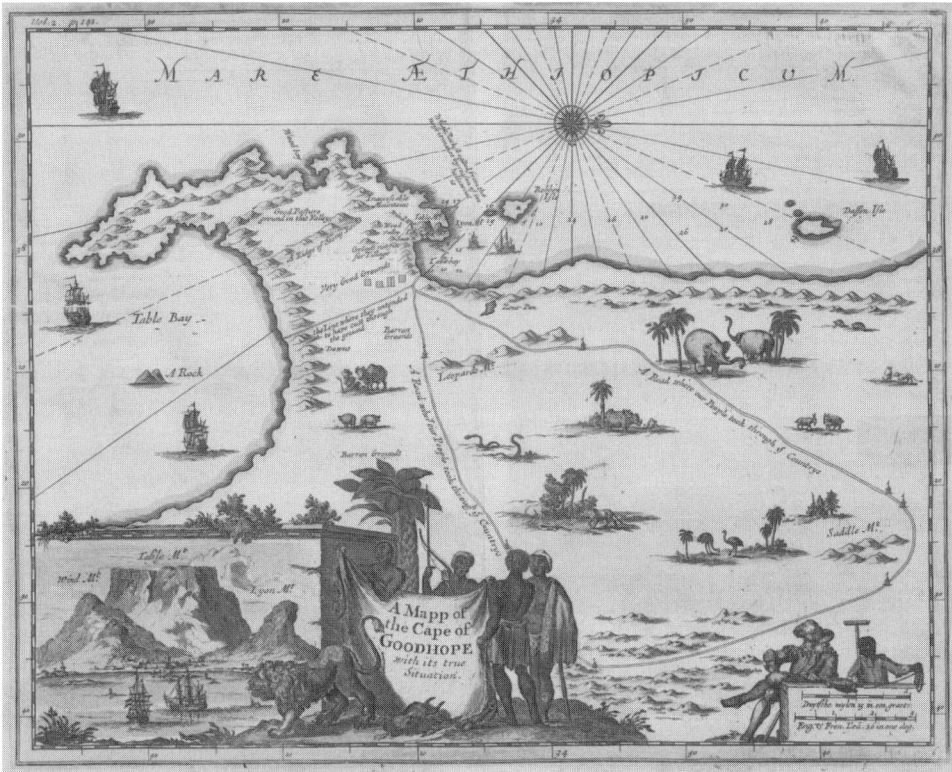

Figure 15.3 'A map of the Cape of Good Hope with its true situation'. Johannes Nieuhof, London, 1703. 27 × 35 cm. (A black and white version of this figure will appear in some formats. For the colour version, please refer to the plate section.)

> *Echinococcus granulosus*:
> daughter cysts in the liver.
> Dropping CLINICAL PARASITOLOGY,
> he lay back on the grass, eyes closed
>
> to swim in his deadly visions.
> Now an ovum, a pig's snout, a cyst;
> a tapeworm piping life
> from his diving-helm of a scolex,
>
> science-fiction rostellum
> hooked into the bowel of his host;
> shaken by alien flushings,
> contracting and spiralling limply
>
> to the sudden moves in the man.
> Now feeling his bowel-wall tearing.

> Now foetal, encysted in muscle;
> a Cuban: fatigue cap and beard.
>
> — Daughter cysts in the liver:
> a fine depiction of Lear.
> A species of water-flea, *Cyclops*,
> is an intermediate host.
>
> The mad escape from the Cyclops
> across the face of the pond:
> blinded he was and roaring
> from his intermediate guest.
>
> And jerked awake to the sun,
> to the trees, the grass and the flowers,
> a butterfly and the friendly stare
> of a basking ginger tom.

By contrast with 'The Sleep of My Lions', here the scientific Latin names, all of them the authentic nomenclature for various types of tapeworm, represent the arcane naming rituals by which Man tries to control his environment; Latin is as much the heritage of Livingstone the scientist as of Livingstone the poet. Similarly, cestodes, the common tapeworm, a class of parasites with an impeccable classical derivation (from Greek κέστος, 'girdle', via Latin *cestus*, 'belt'), worm their way into the title to signal the dual allegiance of the composer. It turns out by the end of the poem that the protagonist has been dreaming: the ordinariness of the final stanza, with its homely vocabulary, suggests that the preceding Latinate diction was the stuff of nightmare, gradually reduced and fading as the protagonist returns to consciousness, lapsing only briefly back into the tyranny of scientific nomenclature with the fleeting mention of the water-flea *Cyclops* in the seventh stanza, which morphs into the monstrous Cyclops of myth in the eighth, precipitating the sequence of flight and pursuit typical of a bad dream.

A different giant is responsible for the special resonance that the classical heritage has for the South African literary tradition, in that, as claimed by the South African critic John Purves more than a century ago, 'the only great figure added to mythology since classical times is a South African figure'.[24] This is Adamastor, an addition to the race of Titans who was invented by Luís de Camões in his great epic poem of Portuguese exploration, the *Lusiadas*. Camões seems to have adopted the name from the

---

[24] Purves 1909: 542.

genealogy of Pantagruel in Rabelais' folk epic, *Gargantua et Pantagruel*.[25]
He created this formidable giant to represent the spirit of the Cape of
Storms, subsequently known as the Cape of Good Hope, Cabo de Bona
Esperança, the Cape which Vasco da Gama took four days to round
in November 1497. Winter storms in Cape Town are notoriously savage,
and although it was early summer when da Gama rounded the Cape,
Camões invented a story to account for raging meteorological conditions
that would match the terrifying magnificence of the landscape, with Table
Mountain rising sheer out of the ocean to a height of 1,084.6 m. In Camões'
myth, Adamastor is a tragic figure, spurned by the goddess Thetis, who
flirted with him and then at the last moment tricked him by escaping from
his embrace. Mortally shamed and disappointed, he became a wild figure
haunting the Cape, sprawling into the sea and menacing sailors, and he
prophesies doom and destruction for the Portuguese invaders in the climax
to his appearance in Camões' poem.

 As essentially a colonial invention, Adamastor poses a challenge to South
African poets, authors and artists coming to terms with South Africa's
colonial past.[26] His legacy in South African literature includes a famous
poem by Roy Campbell (1901–57), the doyen of South African poets in the
first half of the twentieth century, called 'Rounding the Cape', conceived in
1918 but first printed in 1930 in a collection entitled *Adamastor*:

> The low sun whitens on the flying squalls,
> Against the cliffs the long grey surge is rolled
> Where Adamastor from his marble halls
> Threatens the sons of Lusus as of old.
>
> Faint on the glare uptowers the dauntless form,
> Into whose shade abysmal as we draw,
> Down on our decks, from far above the storm,
> Grin the stark ridges of his broken jaw.
>
> Across his back, unheeded, we have broken
> Whole forests: heedless of the blood we've spilled,

---

[25] For the possibility that Rabelais, or even Camões himself, had access to a secret transmission of
Greek magical papyri that contain the name but are otherwise known only from fragments
discovered in the nineteenth century, see Hilton 2006a: 9–10.

[26] The most dramatic artistic interpretation of the myth is the painting 'T'kama-Adamastor' by
Cyril Coetzee, commissioned in 1996 to complete a triptych in the William Cullen Library at
the University of the Witwatersrand (Fig. 1.6), where it joins two paintings that have hung there
since 1936, 'Vasco da Gama – Departure for the Cape', by John Henry Amshewitz, and
'Colonists 1826', by Colin Gill. It is the first South African painting to be the subject of an entire
monograph: Vladislavić 2000.

> In thunder still his prophecies are spoken,
> In silence, by the centuries, fulfilled.
>
> Farewell, terrific shade! though I go free
> Still of the powers of darkness art thou Lord:
> I watch the phantom sinking in the sea
> Of all that I have hated or adored.
>
> The prow glides smoothly on through seas quiescent,
> But where the last point sinks into the deep,
> The land lies dark beneath the rising crescent,
> And Night, the Negro, murmurs in his sleep.

Campbell treats the myth as essentially an allegory of the failure of colonisation; and it is the combined legacy of Camões and subsequent South African adaptations, especially Campbell's, that Livingstone inherited in his verse-drama, *The Sea My Winding-Sheet*, first broadcast in 1971 and subsequently revised in 1978. Eleven poems excerpted from the verse-drama are printed in *A Ruthless Fidelity*. They suffer a little in clarity by being divorced from the narrative of the play, which tells how the 24 Titans, having burst out of Earth's crust to storm Olympus, were repelled by the Olympians and subsequently transformed into the various landmasses on the planet; nevertheless, these poems offer an arresting vision of Camões' creation. A folder in the archive in Grahamstown contains a carbon copy of an appendix that Livingstone affixed to the original version of the play, which he signs with an address in what was then Northern Rhodesia (now Zambia), and which can therefore be dated to the period he spent there between 1959 and 1962. In it he talks about the genesis of the play: 'We have been pretty hard up regarding our share of Greek mythology; I have attempted to promote Adamastor from a minor character to a major one and thus marry this continent firmly into the Greek tradition – no easy task, and of course I may have failed. In the play, Adamastor grows up startlingly, displaying at the end savagery, sentiment and power just as in recent years Africa has grown up startlingly.'[27] He also names his sources: Camões, Campbell, Robert Graves's *Greek Myths*, and Larousse's *Mythology*.

The epigraph to the sequence from the drama in Livingstone's collected poems is spoken by Doris, who encouraged her daughter Thetis first to seduce Adamastor and then to spurn him (*RF* 123):

> Herakles counting corpses, near forgot,
> But searching, found and pulped the Giant's head

---

[27] NELM 2001.1.8.2.4, a.

> As he lay dying, half-submerged by tides.
> This giant, born with travail for his lot,
> Divided, doomed, was in confusion led.
> Around his shores my lovely Thetis rides.
> With thorn and grassy plain his form is draped.
> The continent of Africa is shaped.

The aetiology in the last couplet is an exquisite nod to the aetiological tradition in classical myth and epic. Livingstone has been rebuked for not taking 'his task of explaining Africa in terms of the old Greco-Latin co-ordinates very seriously', treating Adamastor's story as 'a myth of spectacular struggle and elemental action, confused and riotous, yet dynamically contained'.[28] Livingstone's own comment appended to the epigraph is cryptic, dry and ironic: 'Some believe Adamastor is not quite dead yet, but suffered some alteration of personality and temper from the experience' (*RF* 123). Yet, to claim that Livingstone does not take seriously his task of interpreting the myth undervalues his purpose. As Michael Chapman has observed, the sequence ends with a poem that deliberately juxtaposes violent changes of register.[29] It is spoken in the voice of the narrator (*RF* 134):[30]

> When that tough Olympian thug found him and pulped his head
> He fell on parted seas and slept for centuries.
> The thorns and antheaps, embalming him for dead,
> 　　sent foetal dreams of earth's wet glaucous yolk
> 　　until a short in Space or Time was reached that spoke.
>
> Crackling flecks occultly stung his continental stones
> with shocks from out the void. the pumping tocsin chimed.
> Bright gold corpuscles sped to his oily bones.
> 　　In his dimmed soul the early a.m. spark
> 　　was fought, rebuffed; curled and repelled the dark.
>
> A few blades of scrub quivered. The girls on dolphins steered
> about his sandy fringe, hymning his antennae
> with ancient shortwave taunts. Leading them all reared
> 　　the mother of Achilles, laughing; back
> 　　to stretch again this lover on her rack.
>
> Memories of an atomic club dotting him one,
> wrenched to be whirled from some pre-Nordic Yggdrasil —
> if Time's a .38 repeater – he was done:

---

[28] Gray 1977: 10.　　[29] Chapman 1981: 31.
[30] First published in *Sjambok and Other Poems from Africa*: Livingstone 1964b: 6.

> no rifling of his guts by knives impure,
> self-consumption would be slower and more sure.
>
> In the evening we sit quietly as the fireflies pass,
> contemplating the icecubes of the embered day,
> teeth tapping lightly on the sundowning glass,
>   hailing the woman, the tree and the beast,
>   and salivate in foretaste of the feast.

The first stanza is mock-heroic; the second employs scientific and technical
language to wrest Adamastor into the present. The third stanza, returning
to classical symbols with 'girls on dolphins' and Thetis' laughter, puzzles
Chapman by its apparent defiance of chronology; but the sea remains the
constant, primeval element for Livingstone, and the evocation of these
careless nymphs, riding their classical dolphins, paints a sinister picture of
the modern continent ringed by the figures of mythology who treated its
avatar so heartlessly. The last stanza is a devastating cameo of suburban
indifference to the travails of the continent, the 'sundowning glass' capturing the insouciance of the affluent classes. The juxtaposition of the mythological and the banal is perhaps further complicated by what is possibly
a Biblical allusion in the last couplet. The combination of woman, tree
and beast suggests the Garden of Eden, not the innocent paradise with
which nineteenth-century Africa was equated – surely a contrast intended
by Livingstone – but the Paradise Lost to greed and materialism.
Livingstone's Adamastor is a figure of pathos, closer, like Camões', to
Polyphemus mourning the loss of Galatea than to Campbell's vengeful
and threatening hero; and although Livingstone's metre and rhyme-
scheme have a jaunty air, the message is threatening, and the paraphernalia
of classical mythology is deployed to create an atmosphere out of human
reach and beyond human control.

As with Guy Butler's interpretation of the figures of Orpheus and
Eurydice in 'Myths', mythological prototypes also evoke a very personal
response from Livingstone. In his final published collection, *A Littoral
Zone* (1991), which is widely regarded as his masterpiece, one of the 26
bacteriological sampling stations along the seashore outside Durban that
structure the collection prompts a poem, originally composed in 1969, that
is entitled 'Philoctetes at Station X' (*RF* 278):

> About nine months ago I slipped
> right here, slicing my left heel open;
> watched the dark ichor emit from it.

So far, I've used up maybe
three dozen packs of Elastoplast;
have tried to pick the grit from it.

Could be this bloody heel will never heal:
perhaps some noisome venom
that damned day lit on it.

Some nights, soaking the whole foot,
feeling a bit like Achilles, imagined
my small creativity quit through it.

Or that some worse effluvium
anchored in me has taken its final bow,
is planning now a grand exit through it.

The Philoctetes of the title is the Greek hero who was poisoned by a snakebite to his heel on the way to Troy and left behind until, ten years into the war, the Greeks learnt from a Trojan seer that Troy could not be taken unless he were present, whereupon he was summoned and healed, and fought a successful duel against Paris. Although, matching Livingstone's practice elsewhere, the title contains the only explicit reference to Philoctetes in the entire poem and no snake is involved, the suggestion of 'venom' glosses the cause of the mythological Philoctetes' wound, and the arcane vocabulary advertises the poem's classical allegiances through a technique similar to that explored in 'Amphorae' above, also a poem from Livingstone's early period: 'ichor', from ancient Greek ἰχώρ, fundamentally denoting the liquid flowing in the veins of the gods (later simply denoting blood), but also used of a suppurating discharge; 'noisome', deliberately arcane, though from Middle English rather than classical roots; and 'effluvium', from Latin *fluere*, 'flow'. The poet's vulnerability is evoked by the reference to Achilles, whose only weak spot after being dipped into the River Styx was the heel by which his mother held him during the dipping process. This allusion merges with the image of the poet's creativity being sapped through the effluence that he is afraid to see emanating from his wounded heel. It is undoubtedly poignant that this poem was published only five years before Livingstone's death, but to read it, with one of the reviewers of *A Littoral Zone*, as 'contain[ing] his fear of losing creativity as he got older, as well as of death' dilutes the poet's anxiety;[31] this poem was written more than twenty years earlier, when he was only 37.

It is not only Greek myth that stimulated Livingstone; one of his most powerful poems, *After Thermopylae*, which was first published

---

[31] Margaret Lenta, review of Hacksley and Maclennan, *A Ruthless Fidelity*: Lenta 2005: 246.

posthumously, recalls a fabled episode from Greek history, the clash between an alliance of Greek states, led by the Spartan king Leonidas, and the Persians in 480 BCE (*RF* 426–7):[32]

> Years later, limping along
> Some foreign Mainstreet,
> my good eye burning
> from dust and the cataract,
> I saw the sergeant who had broken,
> staring back at me,
> his brow furrowed.
>
> Weeping, he had run,
> stopping to scream back at
> our jerked-about faces,
> surprising our stone-
> set expressions of concentration.
>
> None understood what he shouted;
> disappearing, a crab
> with blooded nails clawing backwards
> over boulders, mouthing.
> Then the foe: right, front.
> An ocean of helmeted beards.
>
> I had forgotten the incident,
> being found, a not-dead man
> under dead men,
> senseless with three wounds:
> my manhood, an open thigh,
> a closed eye – Old Kyklopes.
>
> Two ancient soldiers
> in a strange Mainstreet.
> 'God, gods... Is it really?
> In the name of... A drink.'
> Two sly veterans
> in a complicity of survival.
> I hesitated and looked away
> — a Spartan, he.
> Then I went with him,
> he too having forgotten.

---

[32] NELM 2001.1.1.1.6. For a more detailed version of the discussion that follows, see Coleman 2010: 107–20.

I dot-and-carried to a tavern,
his sword-hand clawed
under my aged, shield bicep.
We drank. He spat,
made libation, recalled
past campaigns, comrades.
I listened, silent,
having also forsaken war.

As with Adamastor, there is a raw juxtaposition of modernity and antiquity in this poem, with the terms 'Mainstreet' (repeated) and 'sergeant' offset by the phrase 'Old Kyklopes' for the wounded eye, a reference to the Spartan ethnicity of the narrator's interlocutor and, in the final stanza, the occurrence of 'tavern', 'shield' and 'libation'. At the end of the third of six stanzas, halfway through the poem, the phrase '[a]n ocean of helmeted beards' conjures up merciless ranks of warriors on a Greek vase (Fig. 15.4). Livingstone does not tell us whether the sergeant who deserted was the traitor who would betray the Greeks by revealing another route over the pass, nor whether the narrator is the survivor who, according to Herodotus, fell subsequently at the battle of Plataea.[33]

But a modern influence is at work, as well: Livingstone had a profound admiration for Constantine Cavafy, whom he described in an interview in 1976 as his 'favourite poet', identifying what was admirable in him as 'a nice touch of erudition and sarcastic gentleness'.[34] The atmosphere of faded sensuality pervading 'Aphrodite's Saturday Night' (discussed above) is one of the points of contact between them. In an unpublished lecture delivered in October 1979 at a conference on 'Writing from Africa', which was organised at the University of Natal by what is now the KwaZulu-Natal branch of the National Professional Teachers' Organisation of South Africa (NAPTOSA KZN), Livingstone identifies Cavafy's voice as a unique blend of 'stoicism, grim humour, deflation of human aspirations, and a way of cynically conveying cameos of history that are true for all time'.[35] To him, Cavafy was especially important because he was from Alexandria; in the same lecture he calls him 'the most magnificent poet the continent of Africa has produced' (later altered on the

---

[33] *Histories* 7.229–31. Herodotus seems less confident about the story of a second survivor, who allegedly hanged himself on his return to Sparta (*Hist.* 7.232).

[34] Ullyatt 1976: 47.

[35] NELM 2001.1.4.18, typescript lecture entitled 'The barbarians: a kind of solution?', 5. For the difficulty of identifying the occasion, see Coleman 2010: 110 n. 9. I am grateful to Mary Johnstone, Principal of Westville Girls' High School in Westville, KwaZulu-Natal, for providing the definitive answer.

Figure 15.4 Black-figured Tyrrhenian amphora (wine-jar). The picture shows the son of Achilles (a little to the left of centre) cutting the throat of Polyxena.

typescript by the hand-written insertion, above the line, of 'one of' in front of 'the most magnificent').[36] Cavafy's poem 'Thermopylae' begins with a tribute to the valiant dead that is predicated upon a famous epigram by Simonides (*Greek Anthology* 7.249); Livingstone may well have known Simonides' poem, because, in addition to the anthology *Voices from the Past*, he owned a translation of selected epigrams from the *Greek Anthology* that includes it.[37] But Cavafy's tribute gives way at the end to a hint of treachery, thereby qualifying it in its own right as a powerful intertext for Livingstone's poem (which, of course, is about all war, and not just the Persian Wars). The title 'After Thermopylae', therefore, while ostensibly chronological, may also convey a subtle tribute to Cavafy.

Livingstone pays a tribute of a different sort to Hadrian. On a sheet from the archive in Grahamstown – a memo obviously intended for other purposes, governed by bureaucratic strictures in two languages, 'Moet nie in hierdie kantspasie skryf nie', 'Do not write in this margin' – he has copied out the famous Latin epigram that the (unreliable) *Historia Augusta* attributes to Hadrian on his deathbed (Fig. 15.5):[38]

> Animula uagula blandula
> hospes comesque corporis
> quae nunc abibis in loca
> pallidula rigida nudula
> nec ut soles dabis iocos.

Since the little Latin that Livingstone had mastered seems to have been self-taught, and he was insecure at spelling (even in English), it is no wonder that his version contains three mistakes: *qui* for *quae* in line 3, and in the final line *et* for *ut* and *dabes* for *dabis*. The first version underneath the transcription, while bristling with smudges and deletions, is faithful to the Latin, presumably translated with the aid of the *Collins gem Latin dictionary* that belongs to his library at the University of KwaZulu-Natal:

> Little vagrant pleasant soul
> Boon companion of the body
> into what places will you now go
> Pallid rigid and naked
> dissporting no longer as before.

---

[36] NELM 2001.1.4.18, p. 3.   [37] Jay 1973: 39, no. 10.
[38] *Scriptores Historiae Augustae, Hadrian* 25.9, NELM GJ INTRO 2001.1.1.12.2.1. See Coleman 2010: 115 n. 11.

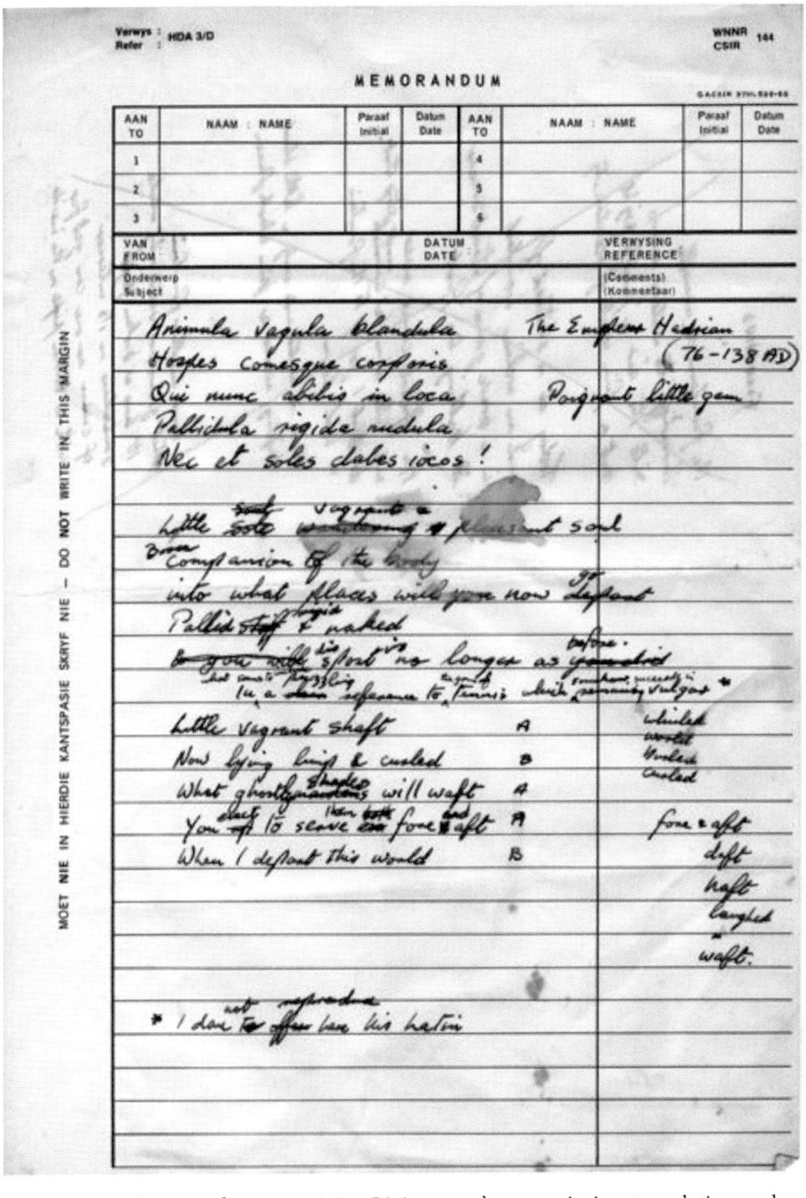

Verwys : Refer : HDA 3/D

WNNR CSIR 144

MEMORANDUM

AAN TO	NAAM : NAME	Paraaf Initial	Datum Date	AAN TO	NAAM : NAME	Paraaf Initial	Datum Date
1				4			
2				5			
3				6			

VAN FROM — DATUM DATE — VERWYSING REFERENCE

Onderwerp Subject — (Comments) (Kommentaar)

Animula vagula blandula — The Emperor Hadrian (76-138 AD)
Hospes comesque corporis
Qui nunc abibis in loca — Poignant little gem
Pallidula rigida nudula
Nec ut soles dabis iocos!

Little soul vagrant pleasant soul
Companion of the body
into what places will you now go
Pallid stiff naked
you will no longer as before
In a puzzling reference to Tennis which somehow succeeds in seeming vulgar *

Little vagrant shaft A
Now lying limp & curled B
What ghostly shadows will waft A
You used to serve fore & aft A
When I depart this world B

whirled, wafted, hurled, curled

fore & aft, daft, haft, tangled, waft.

* I dare not reproduce here his Latin

MOET NIE IN HIERDIE KANTSPASIE SKRYF NIE – DO NOT WRITE IN THIS MARGIN

Figure 15.5 Memorandum containing Livingstone's transcription, translation and parody of an epigram attributed to Hadrian.

To this translation is appended the remark, 'In what seems to include a puzzling reference to the game of tennis which somehow succeeds in seeming vulgar', plus an asterisk, referring to the note at the bottom of page (also subjected to deletions), which reads: 'I dare not reproduce here his Latin.' This annotation suggests that Livingstone intended to include this poem in one of the sequences ostensibly attributed to Giovanni Jacopo, an *alter ego* in whose *persona* he published a number of *jeux d'esprit* (hence the combination 'GJ' in the NELM catalogue number). Below, there follows a distinctly obscene parody of Hadrian's lines, cleverly reflecting something of the diction of the original:

> Little vagrant shaft
> Now lying limp and curled
> What ghostly shades will waft
> You erect to serve them fore and aft
> When I depart this world.

Alongside, we gain a fascinating glimpse of Livingstone's mind at work: his rhyme scheme set out next to the lines (ABAAB, reflecting something of the structure of the original) and, next to that, some candidates for completing the rhymes themselves. The obscene rendering chimes very well with an association between Latin and obscenity that Livingstone makes in his witty response to a question about his *alter ego* from Marco Fazzini:[39]

In the 1970s, there came into my possession about 100 poems in coarse Latin. They were for the most part very earthy and I had a lot of fun trying to translate them into English. They were all titled *Meditations* and were all signed Giovanni Jacopo. I did a lot of detective work and have come to believe they were by G J Casanova – an unmitigated scoundrel and adventurer of excessively low morals, but a very lively and entertaining character nevertheless. Some of the poems are beyond the pale: far too vulgar for publication. The ones I have released, I have tried to clean up a bit and to set in a more or less contemporary context.

Livingstone's choice of Latin as the language in which 'Giovanni Jacopo' ostensibly composed – the historical Casanova wrote in French and Italian – is a nice allusion to the decent obscurity of a 'dead' language and also, perhaps, covert recognition of the bawdy content of such Latin lyrics as the *Carmina Burana*, printed with facing translation in a collection of medieval Latin verse that Livingstone owned.[40] The assertion that his versions are translations of the original is a fiction that matches the reality of Livingstone's own interests, in that his work includes versions of poetry originally composed in other languages – French, German, Hungarian, Shona and Spanish.[41]

[39] Fazzini 1991: 138.   [40] Waddell 1933: 184–273, esp. 222–28, 252–53, 268–71.
[41] 'The Everlasting She' (from Goethe's *Faust*: *RF* 155), 'Ariadne's Crown' (from Luis de Góngora's 'Al tramantor del sol, la nínfa mía': *RF* 156), 'A Presentiment of the Nile', from José-Maria de Hérédia's 'Antoine et Cléopatre': *RF* 166), 'Love' (from the Shona of Wilson Chivaura: *RF* 232), 'Owl' (from the Shona of Noel Kashaya: *RF* 233), 'Dawn' (from the Shona of Joseph

Obscenity is not absent from Livingstone's published work, and much of his urban poetry is concerned with sordid scenarios of cruelty, sex, prostitution and the like. *Penthouse Solo* describes a forlorn whore kept awake by indigestion that finally gives way to a dream (*RF* 352):[42]

> The bedclothes billow, fill, explode:
>> she looks unlovely and no thinner
>>> sitting up: under her gown a spiteful dinner
> has jogged her awake to smoke and think, eyes shut,
> of the terrorised coterie who propitiate her and call her Nina.
>
> She crooks and kneads a pillow.
>> In nervy shreds the daily-brave banner
>>> of her cosmetic youth hangs tattered by night: the manner
> of waspish spearfisher stretched for the sunsparkling hit,
> weapon straight, has fled. She lied creased as a limp nocturnal concertina.
>
> Unarmed, she consoles herself, recalls
>> Port Said where a slim gleaner
>>> of lone tourists almost raped her; fly open; cleaner
> than a cuttlefish his teeth. Her belly, now custard hot,
> digests her back to sleep to dream herself, unbrassiered, Messalina.
>
> The young Empress is nudely tall.
>> Imperiously she struts and knows no finer
>>> marble limbs ever polished the Forum floor, a salt miner,
> sailors, a shepherd stinking of goats in his hide-hung hut
> or half-armoured legionnaires in some slut's Tiber-side cantina.

Even were the presence of Messalina dictated by the strictures of the rhyme-scheme ('Nina', 'concertina', 'Messalina', 'cantina'), her role in this poem would still be transformative, converting realism into fantasy and lowering the tone from sordid to crude: the emperor's wife, laid in every public place or low dive in the city of Rome and beyond. Livingstone's antiquity is as sordid as the present, and – the Roman

Kumbirai: *RF* 234), 'My Garden of Red Soil' (from the Shona of Gibson Mandishona: *RF* 235), 'The Little Beer Pot' (from the Shona of Edgar Musarira: *RF* 236), 'The Hills of Thirst' (from the Shona of Solomon Mutswairo: *RF* 237), 'The Sun Goes Up and Up' (from the Shona of Henry Pote: *RF* 238), 'You Cannot Escape' (from the Hungarian of Gyula Illyés: *RF* 239–40), 'Your stockings, my sister!' (from the Shona of Hapana Memba: *RF* 371), 'Dreams' (from the Shona of Wilson Chivaura: *RF* 377). In translating from Shona, Livingstone was assisted by the Zimbabwean scholar and author, Phillippa Berlyn.

[42] First published in *London Magazine* 5.10: Livingstone 1966b.

part of it, anyway – pervaded by parades of militant authority. This is also the premise of 'Old Mortalities' (*RF* 360):[43]

> They have come and gone, those Caesars
> with their pale Lictors and punctilious Censors,
> obtrusive to their short-lived eras
> as winds bolstered to whales on the roofs of plantations.
>
> Life, really, is all a tree circulates —
> having shrunk, having sprung, and in its springing
> outwhispered clocks, shed Praetorians,
> puncturing the grosser winds with sentences.
>
> Take heart my heart, my springy hearts
> bending your elbowed conifers on bowed hillsides;
> these endure after that which is:
> people, hillsides, trees, a few harpooning words.

The message of this poem is simple: nature and literature outlast governments. *Sic transit gloria mundi* is expressed by the image of Roman authority, prominent in the first stanza (Caesars, Lictors, Censors – the capitals are masterly), still lingering in the second (Praetorians), banished from the third in favour of landscape and words.

One of Livingstone's techniques is to put a spin on a poem that precipitates it into another time and place – what one might call 'universal particularity'. This he sometimes achieves by a classical allusion, as with the poem 'Nereids', noteworthy also for its complete absence of romanticism; for Livingstone, antiquity is faintly menacing and almost always heartless (*RF* 347):[44]

> By water-filtered moonlight
> a cool flicker of white
> if you have on one of the new masks
> with the side pieces;
> if you turn they are gone,
> in a heart beat, beyond.
>
> Once, there was one:
> hair waving like warplumes;
> hands spread like sea asters
> over small breasts and fear;
> tiny gills mouthing and lipping like
> bloodless cuts on the sides of her neck.

---

[43] First published in *New Nation*: Livingstone 1968c: 14.
[44] First published in *New Contrast* and *Outposts*, Livingstone 1965.

She stared at the gun, backing carefully,
her pale flukes flickering forwards,
and just before she dissolved, smiled
with a sharp little mouth
in a sharp little face,
one white breast bare as she beckoned.

I would have followed
but had run out of air;
I go back every night, and the moon up;
fumble on my mask and fins and no gun,
but I never see her: only the flickers
gone, in a heartbeat, beyond.

Five years earlier, in *The Skull in the Mud*, Livingstone published a poem with strong thematic and verbal resemblances to 'Nereids' under the title 'Thalassa Bathing' (*RF* 9):

Lovely, naked as star-spawn, moon-foam girl,
    twisting and backing in the creamy surf,
        sporting as jovial dolphins, sleekly wet,
        sea-aster stark, the moon has paid its debt
    by framing you in silver liquid turf
while breakers tumble limbs awry and whirl.

Thread-lightning on dull thunder, distant, faint,
    your laughter crackles sea-sawing, high-wide
    across the moon-flooded, majestic tide,
faint scream on dark, zig-zag of saffron paint.

Slim star-nymph, catch moonbeams, gaily storm
    strong and spray-brave; thrash from your little fist
        moon dreams, moon-drenched elastic girl of night,
            soles whitely waving and weaving, wave-borne,
            until the chuckling surf relents, love-worn,
        fellow-shipped with wind and water, foam-light,
    ineluctable, limpid as moon-mist,
translucent, terrible, your pagan form.

Come from the clutching surf across the sand
to me, transfixed and moonstruck, where I stand.

This time the title itself makes it clear that the nymph-like apparition is the embodiment of the sea (θάλασσα, *thalassa*, in ancient Greek). The authorial observer – not diving this time, but watching from the beach – is just as much under the spell of the vision as he is in 'Nereids', and the apparition is similarly heartless and defiant. The scene in both poems is moonlit, and similar features – 'sea-asters', 'backing' and 'little' – characterise the apparition. As in 'Amphorae' and 'When that tough Olympian thug', both analysed above, dolphins evoke the ancient Mediterranean world.

In 'Nereids', the title itself is the only explicit allusion to antiquity; indeed, it is noteworthy that the title of a poem may distil a classical essence that is latent rather than prominent in the poem itself, as with 'Amphorae', 'Philoctetes at Station X' and 'After Thermopylae', all discussed above. By choosing a title that evokes antiquity, Livingstone suggests an interpretation of individual details that are not themselves explicitly classical: in 'Nereids', for example, the phrase 'hair waving like warplumes' evokes, most immediately, the way hair spreads out in water; but it also joins 'one white breast bare' as a hint of the Amazonian about this seductive, frightened, tricky mermaid. The encounter between modernity and antiquity, Livingstone seems to be saying, can never be comfortable, and classical allusion cannot spirit us to an idealised world of heroism and doughty deeds. His empathy is too acute for such simplistic idealisation: fear and the instinct for self-preservation would trump the surrender of past to present.

Such ambivalence is also the atmosphere that inhabits 'A Memory', from Livingstone's unpublished Nachlaß (the third stanza containing an example of insecure spelling, where 'fawns' should clearly be spelled 'fauns') (*RF* 482):[45]

> It must have been
> In far off scented glades & colonnades of dim cypresses,
> Within the bastions of heady drugging fumes & colours
> With drowsy bees booming a smooth low accolade
> Of velvet sound.
>
> It must have been
> In some pre-Hellenic grove turfed with caressive grass
> And throbbing dappled sunlight through the leaves
> Etching & limning a blatant bright, then calmer, green
> On fecund ground.
>
> It must have been
> Furtively witnessed by shy & silent fawns, tip-toeing,
> And creeping, apprehensive satyrs with shadowed eyes

---

[45] NELM 2001.1.1.13.43.

> Skirting & yearning, whispering fearfully in the fragrant jasmine bushes
> About that mound.
>
> It must have been
> Here I saw you first so slim & robed in suave white flame
> Chanting the incantations, performing mystic rites, hair swaying,
> And in your eyes the blind & holy light by which the dedicated
>
> After proven bound.
> It must have been
> A moment owned by God wherein, in the brilliance of his sharp white
>   smile,
> He felt a moment's impulse to preserve the scene:
> Priestess & stricken pryer through the leaves,
> Before He frowned.

Here we encounter the archetype who violates mysteries, a mortal spying on a priestess: Actaeon the prurient and Diana in virginal priestly role. The antiquity of the setting is conveyed by the cypresses, the 'pre-Hellenic grove' and the satyrs; and perhaps Yeats's 'bee-loud glade' from 'The Lake Isle of Innisfree' is part of the Memory as well. Livingstone, probably most renowned for his poems about animals and ecological themes, imagines the creatures of mythology fearful in the presence of a mortal: if they are closer to Nature, they have, in his ecological view, every reason to be apprehensive in the presence of humanity.

Among his contemporaries, reverence for Livingstone was not unanimous; he endured scathing criticism from people who believed that the writing of poetry in an un-free society has to be a political activity.[46] But the political battle that he waged in his poetry was against everyone, regardless of colour or creed, who contributes to the degradation of the planet and self-destruction. In an interview in 1991, he was asked which of the following entities post-apartheid South Africa would need: politics, art or individual common sense. He replied: 'South Africa is the world's laboratory: it represents the world's nations and preoccupations in microcosm. If it fails – and the divergences are enormous – there is no future for humanity at large except the ugly spread of racial and religious wars, the final triumph of evil in pursuit of the devils of materialism, power and mindless destructivity. In which case we deserve to go, allowing the planet to recover from our

---

[46] Interviewed by Michael Chapman after receiving the 1984 CNA Literary Award, Livingstone acknowledged this criticism and gave crisp reasons for not capitulating to it: Livingstone 1985: 91–92.

hubris, gather its resources to prepare for a more symbiotic and less quarrel-some species.'[47] Our insouciant waste of the world's resources is a crime that Livingstone, as a biologist, could never forgive, and it is his awareness of the fragility of the planet and his disillusionment with Man as a bellicose and selfish animal that ultimately keeps him from a strident political manifesto; he sees even greater evils than apartheid threatening Africa.

Livingstone was eclectic in accommodating influences, and unselfcon-scious about employing them. He said so to Marco Fazzini: '[T]racking back from the poem, the finished artefact to its origins, I see an immensely long meandering cord threading through all sorts of misted internal land-scapes and seas, libraries of knowledge and vast swamps of intuition'.[48] Within his work, antiquity resonates as an undertone, a faintly perceived but haunting echo.[49] Classical allusion plays a small part in his achieve-ment, but it is a part that is almost never predictable. He himself says something about this at the end of a lecture that he delivered in 1975 entitled 'A poet speaks of his craft'. The lecture is illustrated by a selection of 11 twentieth-century poems by poets as various as Marianne Moore and the Bengali poet Nissim Ezekiel. The last poem that Livingstone discusses, and then quotes in full, is Cavafy's *Ithaka*, in the translation by Edmund Keeley and Philip Sherrard.[50] His prefatory remarks confront the issue of classical allusion head on:[51]

The poem carries some classical references: Laistrygonians, Cyclops, Poseidon—I know, as I presume you do, who or what the last pair are. But if any of you do not know who or what the Laistrygonians were, I'm not going to tell you for one excellent reason: it doesn't matter. . . The point with a great poem. . . is that what it says is clear and unequivocal and powerful, despite regional, classical or other reference. This I think is one of the tests of a poem—a real one.

Clearly, in this lecture Livingstone was trying to convert his audience to the reading of poetry, and so he had a strategic reason for downplaying the potential complexity of classical allusion; his own use of such allusion is always very particular, precise and startling. His knack as a wordsmith

---

[47] Fazzini 1991: 145.   [48] Fazzini 1991: 137.

[49] Livingstone published a collection entitled *The Anvil's Undertone* in 1978, between *A Rosary of Bone* and *A Littoral Zone*. He took care that the titles of these collections should rhyme with his name, which he pronounced with the emphasis on the final syllable (personal communication from Mariss Stevens of NELM, passing on a detail that she learned from Monica Fairall, who was Livingstone's literary executor until her own death in 2009).

[50] Keeley and Sherrard 1966: 15–16.

[51] Livingstone 1975: 26. On Livingstone's misattribution of the translation to Rae Dalven, see Coleman 2010: 117 n. 15.

enables the very slightest of allusions to colour a poem or turn it in a new direction. His profession as a microbiologist, studying damage to the ecology of the seas off the coast of Natal, must have given him a unique sensitivity to a lost past. The connection between the past and now, whether a mythical past or a real past, is one of the features of his poetry that gives it, African and contemporary as it is, universality.

PART VII

After Apartheid

In one of its first pieces of legislation after coming to power in April 1994, the ANC-led government removed the Latin requirement for legal studies. This inevitably reduced the role of Latin in tertiary and even secondary education. Nonetheless, the long-term impact of Greek and Roman concepts of justice runs deeper than that and is reflected in the new constitution of 1996 (see Van Zyl above). A different, much more overt use of antiquity has been seen in contemporary Johannesburg architecture (see Freschi above). The essays in this final section suggest very particular kinds of continuity between pre- and post-1994 South Africa; indeed, they show how the links between the cultural and political domains are complex. For example, whereas Greek mythology had been used on Robben Island and elsewhere as expressions of protest against apartheid (see Parker above), after apartheid many of the same myths have been deployed by artists trying to make sense of social change. The Truth and Reconciliation Commission is one such context, linked by Yaël Farber with the *Oresteia* (**Steinmeyer**). The Kirstenbosch Botanical Garden has provided the setting of the Dionysos Festival, where classical and classically inspired plays continue to be performed. In **Sargeant**'s personal reflection on the festival, the influence of Mary Renault turns out to be formative (see Endres above). While the concept of heritage has predominated contemporary discourse about the curation of ancient cultures, particularly in their material form, classical antiquity has remained largely outside the discussion. One way to make sense of the place of classical pasts in relation to others is through the idea of the collage (**Parker**). The purview could be widened to include, for example, the paintings *Narcissus* (after Caravaggio) and *Encounters* (the Rape of Europa, both 2009) by the Swaziland-born Nandipha Mntambo; or the daring reconceptualisation of Monteverdi's opera, *Il ritorno d'Ulisse in patria*, in which William Kentridge and the Handspring Puppet

Company collaborated (Plates 10–11). All the artists mentioned are based in South Africa but have enjoyed significant international success. In this final section, the emphasis falls on contemporary creative responses to ancient Greece and Rome. Here we glimpse the still-evolving character of classical antiquity.

Bacchus at Kirstenbosch: Reflections of a Play Director

ROY SARGEANT

1. On the Road to the Kirstenbosch *Bacchae*

The *Bacchae* by Euripides is a play that had long rested within my creative imagination as a play director. I first read it while adding Classical Culture to my list of BA credits at the University of Cape Town (UCT). In fact, the androgynous seductiveness of the god Dionysos in Euripides' play and Hesiod's advice to males not to pee into the wind were, until recent years, all I could recall from that popular filler course.

And then in the early 1960s I began one of the most remarkable friendships of my life: a friendship with Mary Challans who, as Mary Renault, wrote those extraordinary novels of Ancient Greece. She lived in Cape Town in the coastal suburb of Camps Bay, overlooking Glen Beach, in a wooden home called *Delos* with her lifelong companion and lover, Julie Mullard (Fig. 14.1).

As her biographer, David Sweetman, has pointed out, Camps Bay, which extends along the Atlantic coast, is a narrow stretch of land moving south down the western side of the Cape Peninsula dominated by towering mountains that branch off from Table Mountain. On arriving in Camps Bay, Renault was instantly reminded of the Phaidriades peaks that cradle Delphi in their arms in western Greece.

Cape Town, as is well known, enjoys a Mediterranean climate and with the Cape's famed wine farms together with the growth of olive farms it was a most natural choice for a novelist (who first of all made a bypass to Durban) wishing to escape the rigours of post-World War II Britain and with kindling ambitions to write about the Ancient Greeks. The Cape's Atlantic Sea can be as 'wine-dark' as the Aegean.

When I used to lunch with Mary and Julie on hot summer days, the beach just below their cottage (in front of which there stood a large bust of the Apollo Belvedere), was packed with blonde, bronzed surfers. Their physicality, fine physiques and semi-nakedness would stir various imaginations (and in certain circumstances this could prove a form of 'outing' of any new guests depending on how long they hovered at the picture window overlooking the beach), making me think of the palaestra, of the sculptured and powerful bodies reflected in the statuary of warriors and athletes of Ancient Greece.

In 1966 Renault published her novel concerning the life and challenges faced by Nikeratos, a professional actor living in fourth-century Greece. The novel is called *The Mask of Apollo*. I lay in bed one night in 1966 reading a proof copy of the book. (I finished the novel at dawn, a time of day that would prove, many years later, to be very special to me.)

I had been given the proof to read by Renault as, at that time, I was a radio drama producer with the South African Broadcasting Corporation's English Service and had proposed the possibility of producing Renault's next novel as a radio drama serial. The passages in the book describing a fourth-century production of the *Bacchae* in the theatre at Syracuse clinched it for me. Renault had cunningly woven the production into her plot and shown an acute understanding of the mind of Euripides, extraordinarily evoking the professional world of the Ancient Greek actor. Her editor at Longmans, John Guest, would speak of her 'psychic vision of life in Ancient Greece'.[1]

I believe there are times in the study of the past or from imaginative involvement with the past that you stand back for a moment and say, simply: 'Yes, that is precisely how it was. I know.' Colin Renfrew puts it this way: 'Sometimes when one visits a great museum or a major excavation, there comes a moment of intense, almost personal contact with the past.'[2] That was my experience with *The Mask of Apollo* throughout the night in 1966.

We did the radio drama serial production of *Mask*. The years passed. Mary died in 1983.

In 2001 a legendary South African playwright and director, Fatima Dike, invited me to direct a graduation production of one of her plays with her students at the New Africa Theatre Association (NATA) training school. The play, *The Sacrifice of Kreli*, is one of the few, if only, plays by a black South African playwright to deal with an eccentric moment in the history of the Xhosa people. It tells of a nineteenth-century Xhosa leader, King Kreli, who became so demoralised by the endless and devastating defeats he and his men suffered at the hands of the British army in the Eastern Cape that he led his warriors in retreat high up in the mountains. Kreli and

[1] Sweetman 1993: 156.   [2] Colin Renfrew in his general editor's foreword to Camp 1992: 8.

his warriors left their wives, children and parents behind them in their village.

This was Dike's first play and originated at the legendary Space Theatre in Cape Town, a bastion against the apartheid theatre of the 1970s. The play then transferred to the equally legendary Market Theatre in Johannesburg.

I arrived at NATA to be faced with the usual drama school predicament: many female students and a handful of males. But with the inclusion of two professional actors in the cast, Joko Scott as Kreli, the protagonist, and Tshamano Sebe as Mlanjeli, the antagonist, we could cover all the male roles. But what would we do with the twenty or so young women? Dike and I hit on the solution together. 'Supply me with a whole new strand to your play,' I proposed, 'a Chorus of Wives and Children, write it in the Greek manner!' And Dike did just that, giving to her already powerful play a dark and fascinating new dimension. Using song (lyrics in isiXhosa), dance, speech and formalised movement the Chorus commented on the action, pitied themselves at being deprived of their men, and grew angry at their problems.

My study of the piece brought me to realise that Dike's writing, the language of the dialogue, poetic and heightened, bore an uncanny resemblance to the writing of the ancient Greek dramatists, Sophocles in particular.

The play begins with a description of a meeting a white journalist, Southey, had with Kreli up in the mountains,

SOUTHEY
. . . But first I must describe the place into which Kreli and his defeated warriors had crept after our forces conquered them . . . It is a deep depression about twelve miles long by two and a half wide . . . it is a fortress: the bottom of it is only reached by a series of ridges that abruptly rise now and again into steep *krantzes*.[3] Upon one of these *krantzes* the lion, Kreli, has built his den and a wonderful stronghold he has. We rode down steep declivities that threw our horses on their haunches at every step. The ridges were so narrow that a slip to the right or left would have meant a fall of hundreds of feet. Quite a thousand feet below us we saw the bleached bones of a native and his horse. A week or so ago he slipped off the ridge, and what remains of him seems to say that the way to the lion's den is still the way to death.

A song of defeat is heard as Mr Southey goes and the Chorus enters together with the other actors. After the song:

---

[3] *Krantzes*, overhanging sheer cliff-faces or crags: originally Afrikaans: Branford 1978: 127.

CHORUS

Then, the cloud of death,
After splitting our heads,
And breaking our spears,
Drove us out of our home
And flung us into the arms of Ama-Bomvana.[4]
They painfully said goodbye to their
Children, their wives and their parents.
They gathered their spears and crawled into this hole,
Where men put their hands on their heads,
Where crying is the only music,
And owls hoot on the roofs they made in haste,
Where men look at the soil that does not give them any food.
Bawooo, bawooo, bawooo, where are you our father? where are you
   Ntaba?

The tone of deep mourning, this Chorus of women and children crying out against cruel, inexorable death, death that has distorted the natural order of things where *men* 'put their hands on their heads' as African *women* do when they weep, the fruitless calling to the Father ('bawo') and to the African god Ntaba with which the opening chorus ends are vividly reminiscent of Ancient Greek tragedy. Compare this to a chorus in *Oedipus the King* by Sophocles:

CHORUS

With a voice sweet as music from the house of god
The priestess speaks to sunlit Thebes,
And the god speaks through her. But his meaning's obscure.
My hands are shaking, my heart is cold,
On the rack with fear.
From your island of Delos, supreme physician,
Send us your antidote to ease these plagues.[5]

As the Counsellors of ancient Thebes speak of their fear and call out to Apollo to lift their burdens, so do the Xhosa women of South Africa call out to their patriarchs and their god.

Dike's text drew me into staging the play in a lightly formalised manner, a manner I would heighten with the Kirstenbosch Greek productions. This manner of staging *The Sacrifice of Kreli* pointed the way for me when I came to imagine the world of Euripides' *Bacchae*.

---

[4] This is a sub-tribe of AmaGcaleka, Kreli's tribe.
[5] Sophocles, *Oedipus the King*, tr. Taylor 1998: 12.

2.   An Amphitheatre at Kirstenbosch

There is in Cape Town a glorious and wonderful garden, the Kirstenbosch National Botanical Garden. Alice Notten says,

It is acclaimed as one of the great botanic gardens of the world. Few gardens can match the sheer grandeur of the setting of Kirstenbosch, against the eastern slopes of Cape Town's Table Mountain. Kirstenbosch was established in 1913 to promote, conserve and display the extraordinarily rich and diverse flora of southern Africa, and was the first botanic garden in the world to be devoted to a country's indigenous flora. The Garden covers 36 hectares in a 528 hectare estate that contains protected mountainside supporting natural forest and *fynbos*[6] along with a variety of animals and birds. Kirstenbosch lies in the heart of the Cape Floristic Region, also known as the Cape Floral Kingdom. In 2004 the Cape Floristic Region, including Kirstenbosch, was declared a UNESCO World Heritage Site – another first for Kirstenbosch, it is the first botanic garden in the world to be included within a natural World Heritage Site.[7]

My eye was caught by Notten's use of the word 'grandeur' in describing Kirstenbosch because I am reminded of Mary Renault's praise for Robert Fagles's translation of Aeschylus' *The Oresteia*. She wrote, 'How satisfying to read at last a translation which is rooted in Greek feeling and Greek thought, and is not intimidated by grandeur.'[8]

Here is some connective tissue, and the connection was stitched fast when in early 2002 Sarah Struys experienced an epiphany. She says:

I was appointed as Events Manager for Kirstenbosch in December 2001, and the most exciting part of my portfolio was to come up with new events that would attract visitors to the garden. Kirstenbosch already had a successful outdoor music concert programme for summer as well as an indoor winter concert series. There were also plenty of fine art exhibitions. I started my brainstorming by looking for the things that were missing. There was music and fine art, but no theatre. There were summer and winter festivals, but nothing to celebrate spring, and spring is the most important season in a garden. Having an Honours degree in Drama, it didn't take me long to make the connection between theatre, spring, the garden and Dionysos and ancient Greek theatre. At the end of that first month in my new job, at the Kirstenbosch New Year's Eve concert, I was introduced to Francois Adriaan, who was the Marketing Manager

---

[6] *Fynbos* refers to the species of narrow-leaved indigenous shrubs common to South Africa's winter rainfall areas: Branford 1978: 72.

[7] Information provided by Alice Notten, Interpretation Officer, Kirstenbosch National Botanical Garden.

[8] Aeschylus, *The Oresteia*, tr. Fagles 1984, quoted on the back cover.

of the Artscape Theatre Centre in Cape Town.[9] I mentioned my idea to him that night and that is how the planning of the Dionysos Festival started.

Artscape took up the proposed collaboration with Kirstenbosch with enthusiasm. I was, and still am, Drama Consultant to Artscape and so, inevitably, I was drawn into the plot.

And there, slightly to the north of the main visitors' centre in the garden stands a small, stone amphitheatre. A set of wide, sweeping stone steps leads up from the garden on the south side, going north to a perfect circular paved place, which in turn leads to another smaller sweep of steps, curving and holding the circular place directly in its view. We tested the acoustic. It was perfect. It had to be, we were surrounded by stone. As we stood, Sarah and I, marvelling at this gift, I told her I could feel Dionysos breathing down my neck. There would be no *skene*,[10] but there would be an *orchestra*,[11] a perfect one in miniature, and there would be an auditorium seating about two-hundred people. And towering over the amphitheatre there are the majestic slopes of Table Mountain, this time on the eastern side of the Cape Peninsular. The similarity in atmosphere with the Theatre at Delphi, which looks down onto the fertile valley below, is uncanny as you look down from the Kirstenbosch Theatre to the 'valley' of the gardens lying below. And far to the west across the plains lie the vineyards and olive groves of the Boland and Constantia.

Sarah and I chose the *Bacchae* for the first Dionysos Festival in 2002 for the obvious reason that it is the only Ancient Greek tragedy in which the god appears as a character.

3. The Kirstenbosch Bacchae in Preparation and Rehearsal

There is general agreement that the statues of Ancient Greece (other than the known portrait busts) represent idealised portraits of the

---

[9] Artscape Theatre Centre is one of the major theatre complexes in Cape Town and it is state funded.

[10] *Skene*: by the fifth century this was a permanent stone building that closed off the back of the acting area in an ancient Greek theatre, built to accommodate various mechanical devices like the *mechane*, a large crane which allowed characters either an entrance from heaven or into heaven; used with a great flourish, no doubt, at the end of *Medea*, when Medea flies off in her chariot; on stage level the *skene* contained three doors through which the principal characters could enter onto their raised acting area, which backed the orchestra.

[11] *Orchestra*: not a musical band, but known originally as the dancing-place, it was a circular performance space in front of the *skene* and in the centre of which, in ancient times, there stood the altar of Dionysos, around which the Chorus performed.

philosophers, athletes, statesmen, and so on, of the time. As art historian Kenneth Clarke put it in his book *The Nude*, '. . . in our Diogenes search for physical beauty, our instinctive desire is not to imitate but to perfect. This is part of our Greek inheritance, and it was formulated by Aristotle with his usual deceptive simplicity. "Art", he says, "completes what nature cannot bring to a finish. The artist gives us knowledge of nature's unrealised ends."'[12]

The mystery of the use of masks in productions of Ancient Greek plays is still a tantalising one. There is so little contemporary written discussion of their use and, worse, so little iconography that to unmask the masks is, in scholarly terms, I suspect, frustrating. Inspired and/or well-reasoned assumptions seem to be the best that can be laid out, and when this is yoked to capturing the experiences of twentieth-century and contemporary theatre practitioners who explore the mysterious world of acting masked, then it would seem we can come as close as is possible to 'feeling' and 'seeing' what might have happened.

In contrast, there is the fact that in the mature flowering of Ancient Greek tragedy the producers employed a Chorus and three principal actors. These three actors played many parts and so the masks provided infinite and visually imaginative solutions for doubling, trebling and quadrupling of role playing. But it seems to me that in purely aesthetic terms the use of the actors' masks can be related to the Greeks' ideal for bodying forth that perfection of 'nature's unrealised ends', of which Aristotle speaks. This would, naturally, be limited to the use of masks in the tragedies. Comic masks would have had their own grotesque, satirical goals.

I am only going to deal with the Kirstenbosch *Bacchae* at any length, as it was the first play we produced in the garden and the beginning of our exciting journey into what emerged eventually as a highly stylised form of theatrical presentation. We followed the *Bacchae* (Figs 16.1–2) with *Oedipus the King* by Sophocles in 2003 and with Aristophanes' *The Birds* in 2004/5. After that year we ran out of funding.[13]

How to do the play? I am not a classicist, but in the world of Ancient Greece I am a determined *amateur*. And I determined to try and recreate

---

[12] Clark 1956: 9.

[13] The Siyasanga Cape Town Theatre Company, of which Fatima Dike is Managing Director and I am Artistic Director, revived the Greek plays at Kirstenbosch in the summer of 2011/12 with a production of Aristophanes' *Birds* (see Figs 16.3–4), and is planning to present Dike's *The Sacrifice of Kreli* there as well.

Figure 16.1 Scene from Roy Sargeant's production of Euripides' *Bacchae* at Kirstenbosch, as part of the Dionysos Festival, 2002.

Figure 16.2 Scene from Roy Sargeant's production of Euripides' *Bacchae* at Kirstenbosch, as part of the Dionysos Festival, 2002.

Figure 16.3 Scene from Roy Sargeant's production of Aristophanes' *The Birds* at Kirstenbosch, 2011/12. Photographs by Nellis Rietmann. See footnote 13.

something of the sense of the Ancient Greek theatrical experience with the Kirstenbosch *Bacchae*.

There had been no serious, sustained attempt to do the plays of Ancient Greece in South Africa (fitful drama school productions, possibly, to take care of all those girls!) since the early 1960s when the on-campus Dramatic Society (as against the Drama School) at UCT used to present the plays on the stone steps and against the Greek columns of its graduation hall, the Jameson Hall, with the audience sitting on the road below. I played Orestes in what we entitled *The Revenge of Orestes* (*The Libation Bearers*) by Aeschylus there in 1961. Jameson Hall is a huge, imposing pseudo-Greek building and when the audience was seated on the road down below, they could just catch a glimpse of a forbidding, dark Table Mountain. The contrast with Kirstenbosch in 2002 was that the audience looked up at actors dwarfed by the Hall and the Mountain; the plays were presented at night using floodlights; acoustics were perfect; no masks were used. Conversely, at Kirstenbosch the audience sat very close to the actors, looking down on the action. The demographics of the audiences for these two Greek experiences was identical: that is to say, 98 per cent white.

Decades had passed since any of the Greek plays had been produced professionally in South Africa. Acting in masks, other than in specialised classes at South African drama schools, was non-existent. But in general terms the South African actor is exposed to a lot of work in physical theatre and dance, and, as with most responsible professionals throughout the world, keeps his body supple, powerful and keenly tuned. It would, I believed, be most important to have a company of energetic actors who would not rely simply on the verse to embody idea and image but would also employ their bodies in a vivid way to lay out emotional subtext. Total acting (derived from total theatre) would be needed. This use of total means would be something fresh for South African actors in 2002 as would the reading and reception of those means by the South African audiences.

I cannot claim there was any careful planning in the selection of the three plays that we produced at Kirstenbosch. The choice of the *Bacchae* was motivated by the known popularity of the play and, as I have noted, its connection to Struys' Dionysos Festival and my personal devotion to it. The choice of *Oedipus the King* was, once again, driven by the play's popularity and because there is a black actor named Dumisane Mbebe who is a man of extraordinary beauty, height and strength, who simply had to take on the doomed King. Whenever I worked with Mbebe I was reminded of Renault describing to a group of us how she and Julie had driven through the Transkei (in the east of South Africa) and they had seen a young, half-naked, magnificently built Xhosa man, *knobkierie*[14] in hand, running alongside the road with his dog at his heels and how this man brought into her imagination a vision of a young Ancient Greek warrior. Finally, *The Birds* was chosen in order to produce a comedy after two tragedies.

As I have noted, in the later Greek classical tragedies the speaking parts were sustained all through by three adult men, who doubled and trebled roles, male and female, with the aid of the masks, as we know, and, probably, an astonishing range of voice-production. The Choruses were played by boys. The approach in Cape Town in 2002 that I chose would mean employing an all-male cast but no boys, as spring and summer here are the times schoolchildren are involved in final examinations. The chorus of Oriental Women, devotees of Dionysos and Agave, Pentheus' mother, in the *Bacchae*, would be played by men and young men. I felt instinctively that in playing the women, the actors should in no circumstances attempt to alter the pitch of their voices radically. Only the subtlest change of pitch, I felt, would assist in the transformation. What would be essential would be to live the women from the inside out. The spirit of the Oriental Women, the spirit of Agave bred from the instinctive woman the actor has at his command

[14] *Knobkierie*, war club: Branford 1978: 121.

personally. The actor would need to capitalise on his latent performance bisexuality (as Laurence Olivier described it). If these two ideas came together I hoped that the actors would enter the lives of the women of the *Bacchae* convincingly. It would not then be a drag stunt. Rather, the sound of the women would be distinguished partially by the very physicality of their performances, the assumption of the utter nature of the female body, an athletic female body, a body articulating many physical details. This was most stunningly created by a young actor, Niall Griffin, in his performance as Jocasta in *Oedipus the King*. His discovery of the use of his bare feet, toes and tops of his feet brushing the stage floor as he walked set off a reaction all the way up his limbs to his hips, which swayed gently and provocatively.

The Chorus of Oriental Women in the *Bacchae* drew a lot of praise, even from rather angry actresses who, justifiably, felt left out. One elderly, 'lay' female member of our audience said to me at the end of a performance of the *Bacchae*, 'Dearie, I've never been sexy, but I've learnt a lot this morning about *being* sexy as a lady from those young men.'

Knowing of the development of Ancient Greek theatrical perfor-mance from the one reciter, to the two actors, to the three principal actors, a glance at the character list of the *Bacchae* indicated that there are eight principal roles, other than the Chorus-Leader, the Chorus and the extras. Thirty-eight years of experience of theatre budgeting led me to realise that one of the eight characters could be merged into another, giving us seven leading, speaking characters. And so began the stimulat-ing task of seeing which actors could play which parts. The Dionysos–Tiresias double was obvious, as was the Pentheus–Agave double. So, First and Second Actor were accounted for, leaving the Third Actor to take on Kadmos, together with Pentheus' Servant, moulded into an army officer so that the same character could report the death of Pentheus at the end, while at the same time command the soldiers, and this actor would also play the Herdsman who reports the rampage of the maenads on Mount Cithaeron. We had a Chorus-Leader in position, a Chorus of five other Oriental Woman (we did not have the financial resources of an Ancient Greek *choregos*[15] to pay for a Chorus of 12 or 15), two soldiers as extras, and we had at a very realistic salary budget for actors. The Ancient Greek theatre producers were, clearly, excellent businessmen.

---

[15] *Choregos*, a wealthy citizen who, by virtue of his superior financial situation, would be required by the city-state to finance the employment of the chorus members for the production of a play.

Figure 16.4 Scene from Roy Sargeant's production of Aristophanes' *The Birds* at Kirstenbosch, 2011/12. Photograph by Nellis Rietmann. See footnote 13.

But doubling and trebling roles does come at a price, if not a financial one. How to continue maintaining the audience's suspension of disbelief as one actor returns in two or more roles?

Once again the Greek producers provided the well-known answer: the masks (Fig. 16.5). But now the question in twenty-first-century Cape Town was: should we use masks? And, if we were to do so, what kind of masks? And so, the Kirstenbosch *Bacchae* company set out on a journey, which was for us into the unknown.

The Ancient Greek tragedies treat of the good, the bad, and the un-ugly:[16] kings and princes, queens and princesses, heroes and heroines; the great and powerful who often fall into despair and death. In *Oedipus The King* Sophocles describes this fall vividly (874–77):

Insolence breeds the tyrant, insolence
   if it is glutted with a surfeit, unseasonable, unprofitable,
   climbs to the rooftop and plunges
   sheer down to the ruin that must be . . .

---

[16] I am reminded of one of Renault's delightful insights into ancient Greek actors and acting. On his first tour as a young actor, Nikeratos, the hero of the novel, has to work with a mean-spirited fellow, Meidias. Nikeratos comments, 'Some mocking god has given him a handsome face, the one beauty an actor can do without . . .': Renault 1966: 13.

Figure 16.5 Tragic mask attributed to the Primato Painter, depicted on a Lucanian red-figured squat lekythos (oil flask), ca. 350–330 BC, British Museum. Sketch by Kenney Mencher.

Working with the designer of the production, Michael Mitchell, and then later with the actors, we turned to the visual records at the prompting of the classical scholars who set up the clues. We began our discoveries by studying the faces of some key statues. In terms of the statues, our journey of discovery took us from the *Doryphoros* of Polykleitos through the agony of the *Laokoön* of Rhodes to the *Dying Trumpeter* and the *Dead Gaul* (both figures from the bronze dedication of Attalos I at Pergamum) to the *Head of a Dead Persian* (also from the victory monument at Pergamum). With the *Head of the Dead Persian* we felt we were, visually, in dramatic mask territory. Imagine the closed, dead eyes as open spaces. The lightly closed mouth wide open. The corners of the lips either drawn up in the ironic smile of the triumphant Dionysos in the *Bacchae* or the angry, discontented, downwards smirk of the hubristic Pentheus in the play.

Kenneth Clarke in *The Nude* points out three important aspects of Ancient Greek athletics, which he says are,

. . . so like and yet so unlike [their] 19th-century Anglo-Saxon counterpart. In our study of the nude it is the unlikeness which is significant: not simply because Greek athletes wore no clothes, although this is of real importance, but because of two powerful emotions which dominated the Greek games and are largely absent from our own: religious dedication and love. These give the cult of physical perfection a solemnity and a rapture which have not been experienced since.[17]

Three of the four ideas about Greek athletics and the idealisation of Greek athletes through the nude celebratory statues set out by Clarke struck me as similar within the realm of Greek tragedy: 'religious dedication', 'solemnity' and 'rapture'. The three ideas are there in the plays and most certainly must have been there in the performances. 'Solemnity' and 'rapture' must, in terms of our experience with the Kirstenbosch *Bacchae*, have been there in those great open-air stone theatres of Ancient Greece. While not underestimating the talents of the Greek costume designers and makers and the gorgeous clothes they provided for the actors, all eyes were probably mainly on the masks and some information, visually in terms of character, was probably read from the masks. Once again the idea of 'grandeur' emerges. David Wiles says, after arguing the possibility that the masks emerged from the experience of the Eleusinian mysteries, that the masks were 'wholly saturated in the idea of grandeur and Eternity',[18] though Wiles feels the masks did not delineate character but were 'impassive'.[19]

The decision was taken to make use of full masks for the Kirstenbosch *Bacchae*.

Much of the glory of Euripides's text lies in the fact that the tension of the play comes from the use of irony by this cynical playwright. Actors relish seeking out these ambiguities, these contradictions and contrasts within poetic drama. A play such as this, so full of fascinating contrasts and contradictions, provides the most thrilling dramatic tension when acted out. The *Bacchae* is about east and west, about order and freedom, reason and emotion, faith and instinct, male and female, life and death. Very soon in rehearsal we became aware that the play presents a very real danger of trivialisation if its meaning is understood in black and white terms as purely yet one more battle between Dionysian Man and Apollonian Man, or worse as a sudden deathbed conversion to a belief in the gods by a formerly rigorous, cynical atheist, the man called Euripides. The play cannot be played as propaganda.

Guided by some inspiring informal talks given to us by Professors Richard Whitaker and Clive Chandler of UCT's Department of Classics,[20] we strove

[17] Clarke 1956: 29.   [18] Wiles 2007: 90.   [19] Ibid.

[20] This Department's staff would present a lecture series during the season of *The Bacchae* and playwright Fatima Dike gave one lecture entitled 'Beliefs without borders: the strange synchronicity of ancient Greek and African beliefs', in which she spoke of the similarities

to play out the contradictions of the play. We attempted to present all the arguments with equal force. We tried to find that balance of argument and idea that is so nicely judged by the dramatist.

In rehearsal, at first the masks are inhibiting. An actor, peripheral vision gone, feels disorientated and panics. When he rips the mask off there is genuine fear in his eyes, sweat on his face. We dispense with the text. We work in masks using only gestures, of hands, arms and bodies. And all the while behind that: thought. What is the character thinking in those ten lines we've chosen to explore silently? Slowly the actor gains confidence, articulating hands, arms, fingers, bare feet, hips, waists, shoulders, the whole body. There is a major breakthrough when the actor articulates not only those but the mask as well. Neck and head are used to provide movement and life to the mask. Add the dialogue, and the actor, in total command of the mask and his body now, breathes vivid life into the mask. It seems we had come close to what Wiles describes as Nietzsche's and Ariane Mnouchkine's understanding of the masks, that they 'combine a notion of critical distance and a notion of inner transformation' for the actor.[21]

In production, this is nowhere more movingly revealed than when Agave turns from upstage to downstage at the moment of recognition of the terrible deed she has committed. The Agave mask breathes pathos, terror and stoicism all at once, gathering up so many of the play's contradictions into one single, insightful theatrical moment. I cannot argue that a great actor's bare face would not achieve the same thrilling moment. But what the mask does do is to allow the actor to deal with the most intense emotions in a controlled and disciplined way. The mask in Greek tragedy, as many scholars have written, imposes form on the deepest and most terrible of emotions.

The masks now dictate all to our company. Every facet of the style of playing. Every facet of the nature of the costume designs and the prop designs. The masks are the controlling factor. Brilliantly designed by Michael Mitchell, the masks flow physically into neck, into shoulders, metaphorically across the trunk, down the legs to the feet. The mask is the defining glory of the actor's presence on our small stage. The logical conclusion of the physical presence of the character. Stillness within the groupings of the characters onstage seems to grow in importance. Stillness especially if the character is not directly involved in the action or is receiving information. The mask wrongly moved becomes a terrible distraction.

between ancient Greek mythology, religious beliefs and worship and their African counterparts.
[21] Wiles 2007: 101.

We soon learn that the natural hand cannot be held to touch the mask-as-face. A hand gesture to the mask-as-face must be kept at a distance from the image. And judging that means the actor moves his hand in a slow, controlled manner. That is a thrilling development because now there is emerging on the rehearsal room floor a distinctive style of acting. It seems to us that the play will need a dignified, formal physical life contrasted by handling the verse in an energetic and supple manner. This will be especially so for the Chorus as they are there to tell the story, whether in words through speech and song or dance and movement. The slow physical life grows more and more fascinating as rehearsals develop and a broadness of physical and vocal style, anathema in this age of Method acting, appears to sit on each actor's shoulders with grace and ease. And that was the manner of the play's acting out at Kirstenbosch. That word 'grandeur', as Renault had used it in her advocacy of Fagles's translation, had become enlivened.

4. The Kirstenbosch Bacchae in Performance

The Chorus of Oriental Women is the most important 'character' in Euripides' play.[22] A constant presence after the Prologue, they are a group of Dionysian disciples. He, the god, has led them to Thebes from Lydia. Their being strange and from other lands is important. By choosing a group of young men to play the ladies I think we found an important part of the way towards representing their being different, alien. But the contributions of Andrew Michau, composer, and Andrew Gilder, choreographer, made this presentation of the foreignness of the Chorus so much more exotic and dazzling. Song and dance, recitative, spoken passages were carefully selected so that weightier pronouncements would be spoken, recitative would help the building of tension and emotional climaxes in the Chorus's speeches would be sung.

Everything, for all the tightly controlled grandeur of the performing style, is conspiring to lead us to represent the meaning of the play in the simplest manner possible, without distortions and spurious relevance. Part of this simplicity is that all sound effects, all the music must be made onstage by the actors. And the use of a range of percussion instruments and particularly the drum lend themselves to this aspect of the production.

---

[22] I was amused when speaking to one young actor's agent with a view to hiring him as a Chorus member. She told me, 'No, So-and-So doesn't appear as part of a chorus.'

Early in rehearsal we stumble on the fact that at no time in the play can the Chorus be a backdrop to any main action between principal characters. At all times the Chorus has to be totally engaged in the unfolding action, commenting silently, if needs be, but there all the time, woven in. An example of this is the Messenger's speech, the Herdsman's description of the behaviour of the maenads out on the mountainside, for as he speaks in lyrical terms of the beauty of the women, the Chorus needs to reflect this physically; as the Herdsman speaks of the horrific elements, the slaughter of the cattle by the maenads, the Chorus, once again, needs to reflect this; later in the play when the second messenger, played as a captain of the guard in our production, tells the story of Pentheus's awful death with terror and wonder, the Chorus needs to reflect this. Now by 'reflect' I do not mean that they tumble into imitative action, demonstrating what is being spoken. That would be a serious lapse of taste. The reflection we discover is in hearing very intently what is being narrated and using sparing body and head gestures to comment on what is being told and, even more sparingly, vocal reactions.

These reflections are important onstage because Euripides brings off something of a hidden *coup de theatre*. The audience never sees the Theban maenads out there on that mountainside and yet, from the beginning of the play to the end, the audience does 'see' them, not only in the talk about them or the final ghastly appearance of Agave, but because the Chorus enlivens the unseen maenads for us, making them ever present.

At the same time the six young men move, react, at times speak as one character. At other times chorus lines are shared out for speaking/reciting/ singing singly, in pairs, and so on. Their masks are identical. Using these principles, the Chorus is performing its key function: binding the meaning of the play together, focusing the central conflict of the principal characters for the audience, bringing on to stage what is not on stage. It is fascinating to observe how the Chorus even-handedly expresses Pity and Terror. Fear of Dionysos; Pity for Pentheus, for Agave.

Something very rewarding about the Kirstenbosch *Bacchae* was the way the audience enjoyed the wisdom of the Chorus, the wisdom of Euripides.[23] There was, from the reactions received, a revelling in the truths and wisdom of the play. The insights of the Ancient Greek

[23] Nelson Mandela, when he was imprisoned on Robben Island, was eventually allowed the luxury of books for study, and one of the collections he was given was a set of Greek tragedies. He found them very instructive, providing sensitive instruction on caring for others, he said. 'Reading of Greek tragedy is one of the greatest experiences you can have,' he stated on a BBC World Service documentary, *Nelson Mandela in his own words*, broadcast on 23 October 2010.

dramatists, long forgotten in Cape Town, rang out loud and clear for that audience in 2002. A fundamental, even if complex, morality was being brought home again. And what was even more gratifying was that the dreary perception of Ancient Greek tragedy as turgid and boring, a challenge thrown at me by a radio interviewer, was defied by this outing with Euripides' play. Above all the warm audience responses to all the Kirstenbosch Greeks gave proof to the argument Mary Renault made in an article published in 1979. Answering the question of why we go to the past, she argued:

> One can say, 'Because it is there.' But unlike Everest, not only is it there, but we are its products. We go, perhaps, to find ourselves; perhaps to free ourselves. It is certain we shall never know ourselves, till we have broken out of the brittle capsule of the Megalopolis, and taken a long look back along the rocky road which brought us to where we are.[24]

The performance of the *Bacchae* is contained within the circle of the Kirstenbosch amphitheatre. It is a beautiful circle and it looks out over the gardens to the garden suburb of Bishopscourt and to Wynberg Hill. To the left and east, some 50 kilometres or more away, lies the Hottentots Holland mountain range. The sun rises over those mountains. To the right and west, and close by, as I have noted, there towers the splendour and majesty of Table Mountain.

Once again we become aware that the staging of the play, the plotting of the movement of the characters is being controlled by two elements: the mask and the stage space, the circle, in which we will act. Both elements bring out a formality in the staging. Movement gains an almost dance-like flow and patterning, with moments of reality being severely limited. But these limitations of 'real' gesture gain a thousandfold in significance and import. Their impact visually being to underscore like a cymbal beat in a piece of music. Never in my career has the theatrical truism, 'less is more', been so manifest. Yet over the spare-ness of the movement, of the music, of the songs, of the dance, there soars the richness of the text. And it seemed to us that we might have caught as much of the truth of Euripides' play as we lesser mortals were capable of uncovering at that time and in that place.

Once the major turning point of the play reveals some unexpected riches. It is the moment when protagonist (Dionysos) and antagonist (Pentheus) lay down their ideological weapons and Dionysos woos Pentheus into a kind

---

[24] Renault 1979: 57.

of sinister intimacy. Pentheus tells Dionysos that he wishes to see the Bacchae rampaging on the mountainside. There is an embrace between Matthew Wild (Dionysos) and Tauriq Jenkins (Pentheus); it is sexual, intimate, and Pentheus is trapped. Now, in preparation for his departure for Mount Cithaeron, the Chorus will encircle him. We break with Ancient Greek tradition for one moment in our production, by having Pentheus ceremonially robed *onstage* by the Chorus in the dress he will wear to go out to the mountains disguised as a young woman. The robing seems to gain in symbolic weight, in terror, by being seen by the audience and an added bonus is gained: a dimension of ridicule, of comedic mockery levelled against Pentheus. He is firmly set on his doom-laden path. Yet his prancing and simpering gains us laughter from the audience. In the earlier Tiresias/Kadmos scene we had also mined some good laughs at the ridiculous cavorting of the old men preparing for their Bacchic revels. I was reminded of the Elizabethan/Jacobean scholar, Muriel Bradbrook's phrase concerning the development of tragi-comedy during the mid-1500s, as she referred to it as a 'coarsening of the fibre'.[25] But, surprisingly, here the coarsened fibre was written during the last decade of the fourth century BC, perching unexpectedly within what many people have imagined as the pristine purity of the Ancient Greek tragic mode.

We take the hymn-like and sonorous final tag of the play from Mary Renault's novel:

In vain man's expectation;
  God brings the unthought to be,
  As here we see.[26]

Did she translate this herself?[27] She had only a rudimentary knowledge of Ancient Greek, but no credit is given for the translation in the novel. Anyway, the tag thunders out across the hills of Kirstenbosch with such power. Its implications of the inexplicable and man's mystification are so tantalising that there is a noticeable pause at each performance before the applause begins.

This mingling of the Chorus with the principal characters marks a great difference, of course, between the work at Kirstenbosch and

---

[25] These were words used by Bradbrook during a dinner at which I was a guest in Professor Guy Butler's house in Grahamstown during one of the Grahamstown National Arts Festivals when Bradbrook was a guest lecturer.

[26] Euripides, *Bacchae*, 1390–92, at Renault 1966: 199.

[27] Renault, *Mask of Apollo*, on the copyright page of the novel published in 1966 the only credits given for translations are for the quotations from Euripides' *The Trojan Women* and from *Plato's Epitaph for Dion*. No credit is given for this translation.

what happened – and still, on occasions, does happen – in the Ancient Greek theatres. Ours is a small, intimate space in contrast to the gigantism of the original theatres where it was usual, but not invariable, we believe, to keep the Chorus (in the *orchestra*) and Principals (on the *skene*) in separate spaces. Where an audience member at the back of the Theatre of Dionysos in Athens might have beheld the mask as something of a blur, at Kirstenbosch the eyes could see the mask in continual, sharp focus.

5.   Sargeant Touched by a Moment of Madness

Stage lighting at night can effectively light the even, geometric beauty of the Kirstenbosch *orchestra*. But stage lighting can really only light a few trees in the background at night. A mad idea entered my head as we approached the *Bacchae* performances. I recalled this sentence from Renault's *The Mask of Apollo*, 'they doused the cressets which had lit the audience to their seats'.[28] Of course, the ancient Greeks went to the theatre in the early morning, arriving just before dawn. Now to get Cape Town audiences to any play at the usual times of theatrical performances is hard enough, let alone hoping they will go to a theatre at dawn. The god had touched Sargeant with a stroke of madness. But I persisted and slowly the idea took root. We would give two so-called dawn performances on Saturday mornings. It was decided that a six o'clock start was too rigorous and so a compromise was reached: we would start at seven o'clock.

With the 2003 production of *Oedipus* we included more morning performances than evening ones. All the performances were packed, but there was an especial excitement about the dawn shows and so when it came to *The Birds* in 2005 we *only* did morning performances. Once again we played to full houses. Seeing an Ancient Greek play in the South African dawn had become an 'outing'. Culture, followed by a picnic or restaurant breakfast.

I remember the Greek Consul coming to *The Birds* in his business suit and then heading off to the Consulate at the end of the play for a day's work. Other than being a little bothered about getting up at six o'clock, he told me that being transported away from the usual tensions of facing the working day was truly therapeutic as his imagination was stimulated to gather up information of a time that was truly once upon a time.

---

[28] Ibid., 188.

To the eastern side of the stage there stands a large tree, which shades and cools the stage as the sun rises over the Hottentots Holland Mountains. This tree provides a dappled light over the actors, over the masks, ever-changing as the play moves on its inexorable course, bringing more distinctive, flickering life to the masks.

How to characterise the magic of those first two morning performances of the *Bacchae*? A strange and bitterly cold November. Dull, dirty, grey light. A weak sun coming up over the Hottentots Holland range. The threat of rain. A brisk, early morning breeze. Bird-chorus resounding all about. As Matthew begins the Prologue as Dionysos, slowly, snuffling, the breeze dies down. The Prologue mounts, reaching its emotional and vocal climax at 'And I will go to the folds of Mount Cithaeron, where/The Bacchants are, and join them in their holy dance',[29] and at that very moment the clouds part and sunlight breaks across the stage. I recall another quotation from *The Mask of Apollo* – the leading character, the actor Nikeratos, is narrating, and Menekrates is the actor playing Pentheus in the production of the *Bacchae* at Syracuse: 'Menekrates started his shouting off, denouncing the Bacchae and their rites. Just at his entrance-cue, the first sunbeams struck the stage, one falling on the very door, all ready. I thought, some god loves us today.'[30] What Renault had imagined about a fourth-century performance of the *Bacchae* in her study in Camps Bay, Cape Town, in the early 1960s was something, in variation, we were to experience, thrillingly, onstage at Kirstenbosch in 2002.

The performance of the play, made even simpler now by not using stage lighting, grows in clarity and definition. Two packed houses lean forward, savouring every line of Euripides, every twist in the plot. Eagles soar across auditorium and stage. Hadedahs crunch out their dreadful cries.[31] Guinea fowl, firmly set in their pathways, teeter up from down below the acting area, across the stage towards the audience and only once they get to the first row of seats do they realise that their usual path is blocked. Peeved, they turn and skitter off back again down into the gardens. And Euripides' play moves on, oblivious, in the early morning light and gaining from that light a unique clarity – a clarity that no theatrical box-of-tricks can disguise

---

[29] *Bacchae*, 62–63.   [30] Ibid., 189.

[31] *Hadedah*: large ibis with a harshly strident call. Curiously, Jean Branford in her *Dictionary of South African English* (1978: 82–83) uses this quotation to illustrate the use of the word. 'Overhead a ragged formation of Hadedahs tacked against the wind and hurled volleys of oaths at those below in high-pitched voices.' The quotation is taken from Fulton (1970). Naturally, we had lots of fun with the birds in the Kirstenbosch Garden during our production of *The Birds*, with improvised dialogue and squawked replies being bandied between actors and our feathered friends.

or embellish. Gaining an honesty and openness of purpose that I have seldom witnessed on the stages of the world. And this is not because our production was so great, but simply because our predecessors had set the space, the time and the pace. We had to find our way into that space, that time, and feel the heartbeat. In Renault's terms both the acting company and the audience were helped to find themselves, to free themselves. We were able to break out of 'the brittle capsule of the Megalopolis' as we all took 'a long look back along the rocky road which brought us to where we are'.

ELKE STEINMEYER

The ancient Greek myth of Electra can probably be considered as the epitome of a tale of pain, mourning, hatred, the desire for revenge and the impossibility of forgiveness. This might be one explanation for why this particular myth has been very popular among authors and playwrights in South Africa, especially after the abolition of apartheid in 1994 and the establishment of the Truth and Reconciliation Commission (TRC) in 1995.[1] For years afterwards, media reports and footage of the TRC hearings would generate public debate and even controversy among South Africans concerning the very questions that were already the core of the ancient Electra myth. In the same way that the ancient Greek tragedians struggled to come to terms with the underlying problems of the myth and offered different, tentative solutions, modern South African writers have proposed other possible interpretations, one of which will be investigated in this essay.

Five South African adaptations of the Electra myth can be identified, of which three make extensive use of the TRC hearings and findings:[2] Mark Fleishman's *In the City of Paradise* (1998); Mervyn McMurtry's *Electra* (2000); and Yaël Farber's *Molora*, which had its premiere in 2003 at the Grahamstown National Festival of the Arts and has subsequently played to several overseas audiences (Figs 17.1–2).

At the end of Fleishman's play,[3] Orestes and Electra have been given amnesty by the judges and celebrate this amnesty with an opulent feast to which they also invite Clytemnestra's parents, Tyndareus and Leda, as a gesture of reconciliation. But Clytemnestra's parents cannot come to terms with the fact that the murderers of their own daughter walk free and that the murder remains unatoned. Tyndareus even spits in Orestes' face

---

[1] It appears that only South Africa, among African countries, has produced an adaptation of the Electra myth.

[2] The remaining two adapt the Electra myth to different contexts: Tug Yourgrau, *The Song of Jacob Zulu* (1993, Fig. 17.3), and Mervyn McMurtry et al., *Family* (2007). Compare also Athol Fugard's *Orestes*, in Gray (1978).

[3] See my article: Steinmeyer 2007: 102–18, with further references.

Figure 17.1 Scene from Yaël Farber, *Molora*.

before he and Leda leave the stage. Their position symbolises the one of so many parents and family members in South Africa who, during or after the TRC hearings, were not able to forgive the perpetrators for crimes committed under apartheid.

McMurtry, taking a post-modern approach, questions the validity of truth.[4] He inserts quotations from the TRC hearings into the choral odes and depicts women as eternal victims of male violence. His play ends in a sort of Platonic *aporia* with the chorus uttering in different languages: 'I do not know.'

Farber's adaptation of the Electra myth, *Molora*, is an adaptation of Aeschylus' *Oresteia* (including elements from other source texts) set in a South African context and with particular reference to the TRC. It recreates the atmosphere of a TRC hearing, while at the same time being firmly rooted in Xhosa culture. There is constant code-switching between English and Xhosa. The Xhosa chorus, consisting of six women and one man (who often acts as translator), represents the TRC commissioners.

In this chapter I shall focus on the performative nature of the TRC hearings and the similarities between the Greek myth and several aspects of Xhosa

---

[4] See my article: Steinmeyer 2009: 111–24, with further references.

Figure 17.2 Scene from Yaël Farber, *Molora*.

culture. I shall propose that there is particular significance in the use of so-called 'split-tone singing', a salient feature of Xhosa culture. Performed on stage during the play by the women of the chorus, it reflects the situation of the TRC hearings, where historical truth and individual story were performed simultaneously, and even informs the structure of *Molora* with its interplay between macro- and micro-historical levels, between public and personal.

Farber was born in 1971 in Johannesburg, where she was educated and graduated in 1993 with a BA (Hons) in Dramatic Art from the University of the Witwatersrand. In her Director's Note for the production of *Molora* at the Oxford Playhouse in 2007, Farber says:

I long wanted to create a work that explores the cycle of violence and the compelling human impulse for revenge. It was on reading the ancient *Oresteia* Trilogy that I felt the potency of the classic texts as metaphorical vehicles for expressing complex contemporary reality.

And in the foreword of the printed version of the text in 2008, she says:

The premise of this ancient story was striking to me as a powerful canvas on which to explore the history of dispossession, violence and human-rights violations in the country I grew up in. I had long been interested in creating a work that explores the journey back from the dark heart of unspeakable trauma and pain – and the choices facing those shattered by the past.

The setting of the play is already reminiscent of the hearings of the TRC. The flyer for the Oxford production states: 'Molora is set in one of the many South African halls where people gathered to testify at the Truth and Reconciliation Commission'; Farber refines the stage directions further by stating that,

[t]he ideal venue is a bare hall or room – much like the drab, simple venues in which most of the testimonies were heard during the course of South Africa's Truth and Reconciliation Commission: Two large, old tables – each with a chair – face one another on opposite ends . . . Upon each table is a microphone on a stand. Between these two tables is a low platform which demarcates the area in which the past / memory will be re-enacted.[5]

In the back there are seven chairs for the chorus, whose important function will be discussed below. According to the flyer, the audience should ideally be seated around the performance, perhaps even on stage, so that they become part of the story and turn into witnesses and participants rather than simple spectators or 'voyeurs'. In this way they are aligned with people present at the TRC hearings. The situation in the play is the confrontation between Clytemnestra and Electra, mirroring the standard *agon* between mother and daughter in the Greek tragedies, and cast here as a fictional TRC hearing. Clytemnestra must account for her murder of Agamemnon before Electra and the audience.

Farber exhibits two common features of South African theatre practice: first there is a multi-racial cast, which is frequently used in South African theatre productions, but here the skin colour of the actors

---

[5] Farber 2008: 19.

actually has a significance: Clytemnestra, the murderer of Agamemnon and ruler of Mycenae, is played by a white actor, her victims, Electra and Orestes, and the chorus are played by black actors and actresses, representing the hierarchy under the apartheid regime, in which a white minority ruled over an oppressed majority of black people. Or, as van Zyl Smit puts it: 'The ancient Greek tragedy becomes a metaphor for revisiting the suffering of the black majority under apartheid.'[6] Second, the plot of the play draws on all major ancient sources of the Electra myth. Although the subtitle of the play reads 'Based on the *Oresteia* by Aeschylus', it actually contains elements and quotations also from the *Electra* plays by Sophocles and Euripides, Euripides' *Iphigeneia in Aulis*, Sartre's modern adaptation *Les Mouches* plus Shakespeare's *The Merchant of Venice* and the biblical book of *Genesis*. Farber dutifully references as many of the quotations as possible in footnotes. This procedure of appropriating existing material in a new version is common in modern theatre, especially in South Africa.

The plot consists of 19 scenes of different lengths plus a prologue and an epilogue. There are only three characters on stage: Clytemnestra, Electra and Orestes, plus the members of the chorus. Aegisthus, who is called Ayesthus in the play, is represented only by an oversized overall hanging on a washing line; Agamemnon features only as a corpse played by the same actor who later plays the part of Orestes. The play is framed by two testimonies of Clytemnestra. The main narrative is the fictional TRC hearing, and the past is re-enacted in numerous flashbacks from their personal histories. Clytemnestra's testimonies illustrate another important aspect of the TRC findings: the fact that the supposedly clear-cut binary between perpetrator and victim was in fact often blurred so that one and the same person could turn out to be a victim and perpetrator at the same time. Clytemnestra has murdered Agamemnon, but at the same time 'has her own stories of injustice to tell',[7] which makes her a much more ambivalent character than in the ancient Greek myth. Also, the re-enactment of scenes from the past bears a strong resemblance to the TRC hearings. Van Weyenberg states, with reference to Cole's article: 'Farber's use of the metatheatrical device of the play-within-the-play points to the theatrical nature of the TRC hearings, hearings that . . . were highly performative events in terms of their "theatrical and dramatic emotional displays, improvisational storytelling, singing, weeping, and ritualistic lighting of candles"'.[8] Cole later makes the following comparison:

---

[6] Van Zyl Smit 2008: 379.   [7] Van Weyenberg 2008: 35.   [8] Cole 2010: 167, 174.

'The TRC toured like a travelling road show.'[9] And she makes an explicit link between the TRC and storytelling: 'For all their innate theatricality, the TRC proceedings were driven more by storytelling than by action.'[10] I will come back to the importance of storytelling later, bearing in mind that to tell the South African stories was part of the mandate of the TRC.

Farber's version includes most of the standard elements of the myth: Agamemnon's murder by Clytemnestra is symbolised by the act of smashing an axe on the table; Electra steals the infant Orestes and hands him over to the women of the chorus; Clytemnestra tries to extract information about Orestes' whereabouts from Electra; Orestes returns as an unknown young man with the tin of Orestes' supposed ashes and the lie about his own death; the recognition scene between brother and sister and the invocation of Agamemnon's spirit are included; the murder of Aegisthus is also a stylised action; the confrontation with the mother leads to a surprising turn of events, which will be discussed shortly. Scene ii, 'murder', is of particular interest. It is a flashback to Electra's childhood: Electra is seven years old and her mother washes her with a cloth and water from a pot while Electra is singing. Then her mother stops, wraps Electra in a blanket, embraces her, and goes to kill Agamemnon. Electra is devastated, clings to her father's corpse and screams, but is pulled away by her mother. This scene illustrates that there was once a genuine affection between mother and daughter which has been destroyed by the murder, but which returns time and again in the play. Ironically, it will be this same pot of water linked with this affectionate memory that Clytemnestra will use as an instrument of torture in scenes iii, 'exile', and iv, 'interrogation'. Since Electra refuses to divulge any information, her mother pushes her head several times into the pot of water, almost drowning her. Other methods of torture include Clytemnestra putting a cloth into Electra's mouth and burning her neck and palm with a lit cigarette in the same scenes, and most importantly, the use of the so-called 'wet bag method', sometimes also referred to as 'black bag', in scene viii, a method which 'was common knowledge to members of the anti-terrorist unit'[11] in the South African Police Force. It became notorious during the TRC amnesty hearing of Jeffrey Theodore Benzien, captain in the South African Police in Cape Town, on 14 July 1997, when the police officer explained this method in detail and re-enacted it in person at the special request of one of his former

[9] Cole 2010: 5.   [10] Ibid., 13.

[11] South African Truth and Reconciliation Commission, AC/99/0027, Jeffrey Theodore Benzien Applicant AM 5314/97, Decision, www.justice.gov.za/trc/decisions%5C1999/99_benzien.html.

victims, Tony Sitembiso Yengeni.[12] A prominent ANC activist, Yengeni later became a member of parliament and was convicted of fraud and corruption, one of the cases involving the subsequent state president, Jacob Zuma.

The following description of this method was included in the Amnesty Committee's decision (1999) to uphold Benzien's application for amnesty for crimes committed in the period June 1986 to June 1990:[13]

Benzien's favourite method of torture, was what has been described as the 'wet bag' method. It is a cloth bag normally used in police stations for keeping loose articles of a prisoner's property. The procedure described by Benzien was as follows:

The suspect is made to lie on the ground on his stomach, with his hands handcuffed behind his back. Benzien then sits on the small of his back, with his feet between the victim's arms. A bag soaked in water is then pulled over the head of the victim and twisted tightly around his neck, cutting off the air supply to the victim. The suspect is then questioned. From time to time, the bag is released to avoid the victim losing consciousness. The bag is only removed when the victim shows signs of wanting to talk.

According to the evidence of Benzien, his technique was so effective that he invariably got the desired results within a matter of thirty minutes. The suspect was usually undressed and sometimes he was blindfolded before the wet bag was put over his head. This was done to disorientate the suspect. The wet bag was held tightly over the victim's head but released in time to prevent suffocation. The victim was usually in considerable distress. Benzien admits threatening his victims with torture if they did not co-operate with the interrogation.[14]

In Farber's play Electra asks her mother in scene viii, 'wet bag method': 'Please, demonstrate for this commission how you tried to get information out of me as to my brother's whereabouts.'[15] Clytemnestra re-enacts the torture with Electra, but in the performances I have seen she uses a plastic bag instead of a wet cloth bag. Still, the effect is very similar and is probably the most dramatic link to the TRC hearings.

The end of Farber's play takes a surprising turn: Clytemnestra pleads with her children in scene xvii, 'truth', and warns them not

---

[12] South African Truth and Reconciliation Commission Amnesty Hearing, 14 July 1997, Jeffery T. Benzien Day 1, www.justice.gov.za/trc/amntrans/capetown/capetown_benzien.htm.

[13] TRC, Benzien decision.   [14] www.justice.gov.za/trc/decisions/1999/99_benzien.html.

[15] Farber 2008a: 47. At the TRC hearing it was Yengeni that asked Benzien to demonstrate the use of the bag.

to become like her. She says: 'Nothing … nothing is written. Do not choose to be me.'[16] Orestes still wants to kill his mother but he cannot do it. Electra, however, takes an axe and runs screaming towards Clytemnestra, but she is overpowered by the women of the chorus who hold her back until she breaks down and weeps in scene xix, 'rises'. Finally, she and Orestes crawl towards their mother and help her to get up. The cycle of vengeance has been broken and the end of the myth has been rewritten on a positive note. One critic observes about this unexpected turn of events: 'Farber suggests that victims have agency. Revenge is such a tempting action for victims because it appears to furnish them with what they have lost: power. But Farber suggests that the choice afforded to victims automatically confers upon them influence – they have the power to halt the cycle of violence.'[17] In my opinion, however, it is the chorus that is most instrumental in preventing the matricide, since the bloodshed is avoided only by the interference of the women of the chorus who are present throughout the whole play, simultaneously representing the commission and the people and those who turn the action around. As Farber states in the foreword of the printed version of the text:

In the epic eye of South Africa's storm, it was not the god – not any *deus ex machina* – that delivered us from ourselves. It was the common everyman and everywoman who, in the years following democracy, gathered in modest halls across the country to face their perpetrators across a table, and find a way forward for us all.[18]

And she adds in the Director's note for the Oxford production: '*Molora* is an attempt to grapple with the drive for revenge – and a celebration of the breaking of the cycles of vengeance by the courage of the "ordinary" man.' Farber's attempt succeeds very well. Her ordinary people, the members of the chorus, represent the countless historical people who were present at the TRC hearings and in whose hands the destiny of the new South Africa was placed. It was undoubtedly in the power of the South African population to start a full-blown civil war and start an ongoing cycle of exacting vengeance in response to decades of injustice. But instead a (predominantly) peaceful alternative prevailed, widely known as the 'Rainbow Nation', under the charismatic and conciliatory leadership of Nelson Mandela. The same goes for Farber's play: it was ultimately the intervention of the chorus that opened up an alternative

---

[16] Farber 2008a: 82. [17] Corrigal 2007: 11. [18] Farber 2008a: 7.

solution for the endless cycle of vengeance and an avenue for a peaceful future. This gives the chorus in Farber a more active role than in Greek tragedy, where the chorus hardly acts independently.

Farber believes that the purpose of the chorus in Greek tragedy is to 'represent the weight and conscience of the community', and she adds: 'In *Molora* the device of the ancient Greek chorus is radically reinvented in the form of a deeply traditional, rural Xhosa aesthetic.'[19] The chorus consists of 'Xhosa tribeswomen from the Ngqoko Cultural Group'[20] from the Transkei, which 'is a body of men and women committed to the indigenous music, songs and traditions of the rural Xhosa communities.'[21] This is confirmed by the critic de Beer, who also describes Farber's chorus as 'the conscience … which thrusts the Greek tragedy powerfully into an African context'.[22]

The Xhosa people mainly live in the south-east of South Africa and were close neighbours to the Khoisan people, also known as Bushman or Hottentots, who are the oldest indigenous culture in South Africa. Historical evidence shows their presence in the Eastern Cape at least as early as 1593, but recent excavations and the oral tradition suggest that they might have lived there already since the seventh century AD.[23] The Xhosa culture is strongly influenced by the Khoisan culture in which many of the San traditions have been preserved. Farber rewrites the European myth in an African context by placing it firmly in the framework of Xhosa culture. The whole play is interspersed with elements of Xhosa culture, some of which are contextualised below.

Orestes' return from exile in scene ix, 'initiation', is described as the return of a young Xhosa man (*umkhwetha*) from the mountains after the initiation ceremony. In scene iii, 'exile', Electra describes how she stole the baby Orestes from his bed the night their father was murdered and gave him 'to the women of our tribe to grow him like a tree in the mountains, until he became a man'.[24] She has been awaiting his return for 17 years. This is an interesting parallel between the Greek myth and the Xhosa custom, since in both, the boy (or baby, in Orestes' case) leaves home as a child and returns as a man. This initiation ceremony plays an important part in Xhosa culture as a rite of passage into adulthood, during which the act of circumcision is performed under rudimentary medical conditions that each year cost the lives of many young men. Hirst says the following about this initiation:

---

[19] Farber 2008a: 12.   [20] Ibid., 10.   [21] Ibid., 12.   [22] De Beer 2007.   [23] Hirst 1998: 12.
[24] Farber 2008a: 31.

Some 150 years ago or more, all southern African chiefdoms and Khoisan peoples observed initiation practices to prepare the youth, male and female, for their future roles in adult society. At some unknown date in the past, the Xhosa chiefdom adopted circumcision as the principal form of male initiation, possibly from a Sotho source, and it has become closely associated with them ever since.[25]

He assumes that 'circumcision originally had a militaristic significance, as a worthy ordeal for the young men who were to serve as warriors before being eligible to marry'.[26] Mgqolozana in his autobiographical novel offers the following argument:

The circumcision process is a physical and tangible manifestation of what manhood is really about. It teaches you how to endure, how to manoeuvre your way through and out of the difficult situations that life presents to you. It trains you in the lessons of patience, for it is something that cannot be rushed through but can only be completed step by step.[27]

In addition W. D. Hammond-Tooke makes an explicit connection between the act of circumcision and the role of cattle in Zulu and Xhosa cultures, where (castrated) oxen are held in higher esteem than (uncastrated) bulls, the former being considered as 'reliable, tractable and responsible',[28] while the latter is feared for his aggressiveness and unpredictability. He says: 'In some Bantu-speaking societies in South Africa a common metaphor for circumcision is to "castrate the young bulls", referring to the maturation that coming-of-age rituals bring about.'[29] After the circumcision the initiates have to stay in seclusion for eight days in the mountains or in the bush, not being allowed to sleep or to lie down, to eat only special, very simple food and to smear their faces with white clay. After this period of time, the initiates come back to their village, where a special ceremony takes place to celebrate their passage into adulthood. In scene ix, 'initiation', in Farber's play, when Orestes comes back as an initiated man, he is wearing the typical blanket of an initiate in white with red stripes,[30] and he carries with him a special black stick (*umnqayi*) 'traditionally carried by all circumcised men as a symbol of manhood'.[31] He also has a clean-shaven

---

[25] Hirst 1998: 33.

[26] Ibid. It is interesting to note that in the eighteenth century the Zulu kings Dingiswayo and Shaka abolished circumcision among the Zulus: Hirst 1998: 33–34, and Hammond-Tooke 2008: 65.

[27] Mgqolozana 2009: 65.   [28] Hammond-Tooke 2008: 65.   [29] Ibid.

[30] See Mgqolozana 2009: 81.

[31] Ibid., 185; see also 104. 'The *iminqayi* symbolize peace and the initiates' newly acquired ability to settle disputes with words rather than resorting to blows': Hirst 1998: 15.

head. He then drops the old blanket and puts on a new brown one to signal his newly acquired manhood.[32] He has to fight his way back into his village against the women of the chorus who, while singing and ululating, obstruct his way in order to test his strength. They also perform stick-fighting, which is normally practised by the men who guide the initiates home, but since Orestes is returning alone, this task has been taken over by the women of the chorus. Orestes performs the 'Dance of the Bull',[33] an interesting link to the above-mentioned connection between circumcision and bulls. The women of the chorus sing traditional songs that are performed to welcome the young men returning to their village, reminding them that they are men now and expected to execute manly tasks.[34]

   In both Zulu and Xhosa culture, the cult and worship of the ancestors (*amadlozi* or *abaphansi*), the spirits of the dead, play a very important role. The ancestors are always present and have a great influence on the life of the living; therefore, it is important to respect them (*ukuhlonipha*) and perform certain rituals and ceremonies in order to communicate with them and in order to request their support. Normally, people who would like to communicate with the ancestors go to the graveyard and the tombs of the deceased. They burn a special herb, a dried plant called *imphepho* (*Helicrysum odoratissimum / cymosum* or *rugulosum*),[35] which creates a very distinctive smell. The ancestors particularly like freshly slaughtered meat (preferably beef, but often also goat) and freshly brewed Zulu sorghum beer (*utshwala*). It is brewed and fermented in a large clay pot called *imbiza* and drunk from a smaller clay pot called *ukhamba*, which has a dark black colour through a second carbonised firing (normal vessels receive only one firing). Armstrong gives the following explanation:

The second firing is a customary ritual to honor the ancestors (*amadlozi*). Zulu traditionalists say that the *amadlozi* are enticed to beer ceremonies by the presence of black vessels. The *amadlozi* prefer dark cool places; the shiny *ukhamba* with incised designs, for example, can serve as a welcoming beacon for the ancestors called to protect the living.[36]

---

[32] Ibid., 159.   [33] Farber 2008a: 50.   [34] Ibid., 49.

[35] Armstrong 2008: 416, note 6. This specific herb is also used by some Zulu diviners, because 'this is supposed to allow for greater clarity in the visions she [the Zulu diviner] experiences': Kirby-Hirst 2004: 84. Berglund translates it as Helichrysum miconiaefolium. The plant resembles the shades, because both do not wither. Its sweet smell cannot be forgotten or confused with other odours: Berglund 1976: 113–14.

[36] Armstrong 2008: 415.

In scene xi, 'found', Orestes approaches his father's grave and invokes the ancestors, requesting their support for his important task by spitting traditional beer on the grave and burning *imphepho*. After Electra and Orestes recognise each other, each sibling invokes Agamemnon's spirit with increasing intensity, remembering how he was killed by Clytemnestra and her lover, how she buried him without funeral rites and mutilated his corpse, and request Agamemnon's support. Electra dances around the grave while Orestes repeatedly spits beer on the grave. At the end of the scene Electra compares herself and her brother to wolves 'whose savage hearts do not relent'[37] in the same manner as in Aeschylus' *Choephoroi* or *Libation Bearers*, where she says: 'We are savage, just like wolves' (420).[38] It is interesting to observe that there is another use of the wolf metaphor in Aeschylus' *Agamemnon*, when Cassandra describes Aegisthus as the wolf in bed with the double-footed lioness (Clytemnestra) in the absence of the noble lion (Agamemnon) (1258–59). Therefore, the same animal serves a two-fold purpose in Aeschylus: a negative connotation as cowardly and ignoble on the one hand, but on the other standing for perseverance in revenge – the latter used by Farber. In scene xvii, 'truth', Clytemnestra describes herself as 'the two-footed lioness that bore these wanting wolves (i.e. Electra and Orestes)'.[39] Another difference between Greek and Xhosa/Zulu ritual can be found in the liquids which are used to appease the spirits of the dead. While the traditional libations in ancient Greek funeral rites consisted of wine, milk, honey and water,[40] Zulu culture uses traditional sorghum beer.

There is an interesting link between the function of dreams in the cult of the ancestors and Clytemnestra's dream in scene v, 'dreams'. Farber has adopted this version of Clytemnestra's dream from Aeschylus' *Libation Bearers* (527–50). Clytemnestra dreams that she gives birth to a snake, which she puts on her breast, but together with the milk, the snake sucks out clots of Clytemnestra's blood. In Orestes' interpretation of this dream he is this very snake (549–50). In *Molora*, this dream is acted out on stage with Clytemnestra giving birth to a snake and the women of the chorus acting as midwives. Clytemnestra later refers twice again to Orestes as 'that serpent sucking out my heart's red wine' in scene x, 'ash',[41] and scene xii, 'plan'.[42] In Zulu and Xhosa culture the spirits of the ancestors are often believed to appear in the form of a snake

[37] Farber 2008a: 64.   [38] Aeschylus, *The Oresteia*, tr. Ewans (1995).   [39] Farber 2008a: 81.
[40] Homer, *Odyssey* 11.27–28. Odysseus sprinkles on this barley meal as well.
[41] Farber 2008a: 55.   [42] Ibid., 65. See also 66.

called *itongo*.[43] Depending on the colour and the behaviour of the snake, the ancestor is either harmless or angry. The ancestors can also haunt a particular person via dreams, if they feel neglected or are angry. According to Berglund: 'Dreams are the channel of communication between survivors and the shades.'[44] The afflicted person is supposed to appease the angry spirit with sacrifices, mainly freshly slaughtered meat. In Aeschylus' play, the chorus describes the situation as follows (32–44):

> A piercing cry rang out,
> it made our hair stand up!
> At dead of night shrill Fear, the dream-interpreter,
> roared out its anger from her sleep
> deep in the house,
> and fell in fury on the women's rooms.
> Then those who judge the meaning of such dreams
> swore oaths before the gods to tell the truth
> and said it meant the dead below the earth
> were furiously angry, held us all to blame
> and raged against their murderers.
> The godless woman sent me here
> to ward off torment from herself.

One can also see here in Aeschylus the anger of the dead [Agamemnon], which needs to be appeased through offerings and libations in order to prevent further haunting. The chorus describes Clytemnestra's reaction thus: 'Then she sent these offerings, hoping to find a cure that would cut through her torments' (538–39). This creates a strong parallel between the perception of the dead in the Greek myth and Xhosa and Zulu cultures. Also in Clytemnestra's dream itself, an interesting link can be found. According to Zulu belief, the birth of a child resembles a snake changing its skin, as Berglund reports:

When people speak of a snake that changes its skin, then you must know that it is a shade . . . The snake is like a child when it (the snake) changes its skin. When it (the child) is ready, it leaves the womb. The shades drive it out. It leaves the mother and the womb, gliding out of it. The shade-snake does the same thing. It is like the child that glides out. It glides out of its old skin. The shade and the child are the same in this aspect.[45]

---

[43] Callaway 1970: 140.   [44] Berglund 1976: 98.

[45] Berglund 1976: 94. Berglund compares the old skin of the snake with the placenta in the mother's womb (ibid.).

Berglund states further that the child is already a shade before it is born.[46] If one applies this theory to Clytemnestra's dream, the snake she gave birth to is at the same time the spirit of the dead Agamemnon and the son Orestes. This merging of father and son into one is illustrated in Farber's play through the fact that the same actor plays the corpse of Agamemnon and later Orestes.

Another link between Farber's play and Xhosa culture can be found in the way in which the women of the chorus are dressed. Wearing traditional blankets, they smoke long pipes in scene xiii ('home'), the traditional accessory for married Xhosa women who have given birth.[47] Elliott observed: 'The women's pipes are much longer than those of menfolk, and for a good reason – their impressive length ensures that ash doesn't fall on the babies on their laps or at their breasts.'[48]

But probably the most powerful element is the use of traditional musical instruments and the famous split-tone or overtone singing, called *umngqokolo* in Xhosa, which literally means 'rough noise'. This specific art of singing consists of an ability to produce two notes at the same time through a special technique, a sort of *basso continuo* or *Generalbass* and overtones, which constitute the melody. The ethnomusicologist Dargie describes the technique as follows:

Now it is the singer who attempts to reproduce the bows' method of following the *izicabo* (text-lines) of the song ... In 'ordinary' *umngqokolo*, the singer – always a woman or girl – artificially forces the voice down into the bass register ... The forced bass fundamental, very rough in tone, is well suited to the production of overtones. The singer lifts the tip of the tongue over the teeth, holding the lips in a position as when pronouncing the vowel u̱ as in u̱lulate, but with the lips thrust out a bit more than normal. The tongue touches the inside of the under lip. By lifting and lowering the tongue slightly, by shaping it and by shaping the lips, the singer is able to resonate chosen overtones of each particular fundamental tone ... Because of this close harmony relation of fundamentals and melody tones, the overtone singing fits perfectly into the harmony patterns of bow and singers using normal voice. From a distance, the overtone singer, once she has got her music going well, sounds not unlike an *umrhubhe* being well played.[49]

There is also a similar kind of overtone singing called *umngqokolo ngomqangi* (split tone singing by means of a bow, *umqangi* being an old

[46] Ibid., 94 and 100.
[47] According to Hirst 1998: 20, this applies only to women after menopause, who are by then considered to be almost equal to men.
[48] Elliott 2005: 2.   [49] Dargie 1993: 4–5.

name for *umrhube*), which differs from the former insofar as the overtones are louder and clearer.[50] According to the critic Zvomuya, in *Molora* 'the group's singing and chanting creates a surreal atmosphere . . . to propel the soul of the play'.[51]

This singing is accompanied by various instruments, such as a calabash bow called *uhadi*, a mouth bow called *umrhubhe*, a mouth harp called *isitolotolo*, the milking drum called *umasengwana*, and the traditional drum called *igubu*. Xhosa music uses very complicated rhythms. It accompanies traditional story telling in Xhosa oral poetry. For oral poetry, storytelling and music are inseparable. Scheub observes: 'Dance is part of storytelling, music is the essence of storytelling: it is not possible to divorce stories and their tellers from dances and their dancers, from music and its musicians',[52] and 'stories, like music, consist of melody and rhythm, the essence of poetry'.[53] The interplay between storytelling and music mirrors the structure of the above-mentioned split-tone singing, where the fusion of the two simultaneous voices creates the melody. It is also mirrored in the structure of traditional oral poetry, where there is no clear-cut distinction between story and history and where, according to Scheub, 'storyteller, historian, epic-performer, poet: all create their works in much the same way, in the sense that each manipulates and patterns relations between images of the past and those of the present'.[54] Scheub adds later: 'truth, meaning, occurs in the nexus of history and the imaginative tradition',[55] and 'if the poet adds metaphor to history, the historian adds story to names, facts, time-lines. Each has the effect of theatricalising history, giving it an artistic dimension that seems inattentive to fact but is moving to a conception of truth.'[56] One can see here that, according to Scheub's definition, truth is an interplay between individual story and factual history in the same way as it was witnessed in the hearings of the TRC.[57] This is confirmed by Cole: 'We also see how individuals performed within the commission the particular truths they were trying to achieve.'[58] Music, storytelling, history and performance are the interwoven facets of truth.

In her introduction to Farber's book *Theatre as Witness*, Amanda Stuart Fisher uses the term 'testimonial theatre' in order to characterise

---

[50] Ibid., 7.   [51] Zvomuya 2007, 8.   [52] Scheub 2002: 3.   [53] Ibid., 203.   [54] Scheub 1996: 51.
[55] Ibid., 57.   [56] Ibid., 205.
[57] Cole lists four truths, 'factual / forensic, personal / narrative, social / dialogue and healing / restorative truths' (2010: 163).
[58] Ibid., xvii.

a fundamental 'concept that permeates throughout Yaël Farber's body of theatrical work'.[59] She explains this concept as follows:

Personal testimony of this kind plays a crucial role in the process of history-making, because through testimony we can bear witness to what has actually been lived through. The witness, in other words, does not merely add to the weight of factual evidence of what happened, rather he or she gives voice to that which the objective narrative of history tends to overlook and even suppress.[60]

Here again one can see that the structure of the TRC and the concept of the *umngqokolo* split-tone singing mirror the concept of Farber's storytelling.[61] The structure of her plot in this 'split-tone drama' with her re-working of an ancient myth into a contemporary context resembles Jacobs's analysis of Zakes Mda's novel *Heart of Redness* as *Umngqokolo*: 'The two stories blend into a seamless narrative of the past and of the present, and the two voices combine into a single, split-tone song.'[62] Also the critic Zvomuya emphasises the mutual links between the TRC, the *umngqokolo*, and the plot of *Molora* by stating:

What makes the play relevant to a contemporary audience is the music and acting from the Ngqoko Cultural Group, who are trained in the ancient art of split-tone singing. They make use of what the playmakers have termed a 'rural Xhosa aesthetic', and this helps render the play an artistically authentic depiction of the South African reconciliation process.[63]

And Cole remarks: 'the TRC served as a literal and figurative stage for South Africa's political transition'.[64]

In conclusion, the title of the play, *Molora*, is the seSotho word for 'ash'. Again, one can find here a link to Xhosa and Zulu cultures and especially to the ancestors. Berglund relates a conversation between him and a Zulu diviner:[65]

N: The ash comes from the hearth in my hut. That is where I take it. It must be from this place. From no other place.

B: Why do you use ash?

N: Because the ash is white. It comes from the hearth, the place of the hearth-stones. It is this ash. It must be this very ash.

B: So the important thing is the ash. Not the colour of the ash?[66]

---

[59] Amanda Stuart Fisher, 'Introduction', in Farber 2008b: 11.   [60] Ibid., 10.
[61] In an interview with Stuart Fisher, Farber states: 'We are storytellers. Our task is simply to tell a story well' (ibid., 24). This links the story of the play 'Molora' even more closely to the practice of traditional Xhosa storytelling and the performative nature of the TRC hearings.
[62] Jacobs 2002: 236.   [63] Zvomuya 2007: 8.   [64] Cole 2010: xvi.   [65] Berglund 1976: 205–6.
[66] The shades of the ancestors are believed to be white, despite being shades (ibid., 90).

Figure 17.3 Scene from Tug Yourgrau, *The Song of Jacob Zulu* (1993). Photograph by Michael Brosilow.

N: That is so. It is the ash that is important. It must be the ash from the hearth.

B: Why must there be ash? Is there some connection between ash and the shades?

N: There is a connection. The shades are there, in the place of the ash.

B: Are the shades in the ash?

N: No. They are not in the ash. But they are near the place of the ash (i.e. the hearth). The ash is the thing of the hearth. It comes from that place. The hearth is the place of the shades. That is the point of connection. The ash comes from the place of the shades in the hut.

The word 'ash' features several times prominently in the play. For Farber 'ash' symbolises the eternal *condition humaine*. In her Director's Note for the Oxford production she explains: 'In the long nights following the attack on the World Trade Center, a fine white residue floated gently down on devastated Manhattan.' In the epilogue of the play Clytemnestra says: 'It falls softly the residue of revenge ... like rain'.[67] The stage direction indicates that 'A fine powdery substance gently floats down on' the actors and audience.[68] Farber concludes her Director's Note: 'Our story begins with Orestes returning home with a tin full of ash. It is the state from which we all come, from the concentration camps of Europe, the ruins of Baghdad, Palestine, Northern Ireland and Rwanda ... to the ash around the fire after the storytelling is done – it is the state to which we must all humbly return.'

[67] Farber 2008a: 87.   [68] Ibid.

18 | Classical Heritage? By Way of an Afterword

GRANT PARKER

> Heritage . . . is culture named and projected into the past, and, simultaneously, the past congealed into culture. . . . It is identity in tractable, alienable form, identity whose found objects and objectifications may be consumed by others and, therefore, be delivered to the market.[1]

1.   From Monuments to Heritage

Heritage can mean many different things, whether as a legacy, in the sense of an enriching survival or bequest, or as a burden, either on the lines of inheriting a debt or of traumatic collective memory.[2] Let us begin by outlining specific institutional senses of heritage in South Africa before considering its relation to ancient Greece and Rome.

   The Bushman Relics Protection Act (1911), passed one year after Union, was the earliest legislation intended to protect South African cultural phenomena.[3] In 1923 the Historical Monuments Commission was founded by a further act of parliament, which was revised and expanded in 1934 as the Natural and Historical Monuments, Relics and Antiquities Act (1934) (Fig. 18.1). Some three hundred monuments were established in this framework. Further revision took place in 1969 with the passing of the National Monuments Act, which would remain in force until the end of the millennium. Under the National Monuments Council, as it was known from 1969 to 2000, roughly one-half of the declared national monuments were in the Western Cape, and the organisation was based in Cape Town rather than the executive capital, Pretoria. This geographic inequality reflects the preponderance of early Dutch structures in what is now the Western Cape province, the site of the earliest European colonial presence. Thus, although the South African state initially focused on San rock art – vulnerable by virtue of its dispersed rural locations – it was instead Dutch and British colonial sites and artefacts that would predominate in the

---

[1] Comaroff and Comaroff 2009: 10.   [2] Meskell 2002.
[3] For a critical overview, see Shepherd 2008.

Figure 18.1 National Monuments Council plaque: see also Fig. 1.11.

curation of monuments in the twentieth century. From 1960, European artefacts, which had been housed within the hugely varied collection of the South African Museum, were displayed in their own location, the South African Cultural History Museum. The naming of this new museum in the Verwoerd era seems especially pointed given that the building had once housed the Dutch East India Company's slaves (and would accordingly be renamed the Slave Lodge in 1998). In 1960 the impetus to bracket off colonial culture from indigenous nature could not have been more obvious, even if it was undermined at a different level by the deep history of its physical setting.

   This is the dispensation that has been, to one degree or another, subject to redress since the political transition of the 1990s. As a vital first measure, ACTAG – the Arts and Culture Task Group established by the ANC-led government, bringing together practitioners, adminis-trators and educators in heritage and the arts – produced the White Paper on Arts, Culture and Heritage (1996). This document proposed a more inclusive approach that would embrace South Africa's ethnic and cultural diversity, and would distinguish itself from grand apartheid and its essentialised notion of cultures as discrete entities or 'own affairs' (*eiesake* in Afrikaans). The White Paper paved the way for the South African Heritage Resources Act (1999), which sought to reconstitute the heritage sector from the ground up. With this legislation the National Monuments Council was superseded by the South African Heritage Resources Agency (SAHRA), while part of its functioning was devolved to provincial heritage resources authorities (PHRAs). Within a tripartite division of heritage resources, SAHRA was responsible for the highest, national grade of heritage resources, whereas the different PHRAs would deal with the second, provincial grade, and usually also the third, local one as well, given that few municipalities have the capacity to fulfil this function. The Act also established the National Heritage Council, based in Pretoria, intended to complement SAHRA, and which has often focused on the twentieth-century struggle against apartheid.[4] By the time of these developments, international practices of UNESCO and other organisations had broadened so as to include and even emphasise intangible heritage.[5]

Most recently, the Department of Arts and Culture released a new version of its White Paper (June 2013). The revised version adapts its 1996 predecessor by aligning it with the 'outcomes-based approach' of prevailing ANC policy, and indicates intensified efforts to make heritage resources self-sustaining via job creation. Within this vision, Cultural and Creative Industries receive emphasis as 'the foundation of socio-economic development'. Here heritage is defined anew as

the sum total of wildlife and scenic parks, sites of scientific and historical impor-tance, national monuments, historic buildings, works of art, literature and music, oral traditions and museum collections and their documentation which provides the basis for a shared culture and creativity in the arts.[6]

The order of items is instructive: in this conception of heritage, the physical environment, including flora and fauna, receives pride of place. As suggested in the Comaroffs' provocative comment above, and as many others have pointed out, economic viability has gone a long way towards redefining heritage for the neoliberal world order. This tendency has been fuelled by the ever-growing significance of tourism in the national economy, by the rise of consumerism, and by the ANC-led government's commitment to market-friendly neoliberal economic policies from the

[4] On heritage in a human rights framework, see Weiss 2014. Weiss focuses on plans for a Liberation Heritage Trail and the resultant clashes between cosmopolitan, national and local interests.

[5] Ahmad 2006.

[6] Department of Arts and Culture, *Revised White Paper on Arts, Culture and Heritage* (4 June 2013), 17.

early 1990s onwards.[7] It is thus not surprising that natural heritage has grown in prominence within recent policy-making. The selection of the country's eight World Heritage sites further reflects this.[8]

Where does classical antiquity fit into all this, if at all? Barely, it would appear, and then only incidentally. Nor should that cause surprise, if we bear in mind, firstly, that the classical components of European colonial cultures have often been indirect and, secondly, that the rise of Afrocentric and traditionalist elements have predominated in public discourse since the 1990s. To be sure, the foregoing chapters have revealed classical elements, often unexpected, in some of the country's most famous sites. Robben Island, selected a World Heritage site by virtue of its lengthy penal use, contains the prison in which *Antigone* was performed and where Ahmed Kathrada studied classics via the University of South Africa. At Groot Constantia, famous for its wine culture, the Cloete Cellar contains a relief by Anton Anreith, depicting the Rape of Ganymede (Fig. 1.10) – a grim if unintended reminder that slave labour sustained the estate for more than a century. Herbert Baker's subsequent Cape Dutch structure of Groote Schuur Estate contains several hundred classical translations commissioned by Cecil John Rhodes, an elaborate indication of the embrace of classics and colonialism. And a classicising frieze fills the anti-classical Voortrekker Monument in Pretoria. The last three are merely the most traditional, monumental, Eurocentric examples of heritage. On the other hand, Graeco-Roman slave names live on in South Africa's 'Coloured' population, as we have seen. In these cases, a classical element is more implicit than explicit.

As many scholars have noted, heritage in the new South Africa has shown divergent tendencies in practice. On the one hand, it has sometimes expressed group identities and interests, notably the District Six Museum in Cape Town, which tells the story of the racial zoning of Coloured people out of District Six. On the other hand, it has been a matter of nation building, as seen in some of Gauteng province's most prominent new memorials: Johannesburg's Apartheid Museum

---

[7] A landmark was the Mandela government's unveiling of GEAR (Growth, Employment and Redistribution Programme) in 1996, in a clear departure from previous policy. Among the many assessments of the first two decades after apartheid, Bundy 2014; Mangcu 2014; Saul and Bond 2014: 145–210; and Turok 2014 contain especially important insights.

[8] Four (including Robben Island) are designated cultural sites – three natural and one mixed: http://whc.unesco.org/en/list/. Lynn Meskell shows the eclipsing of cultural heritage in favour of conservation and the natural environment: Meskell 2012.

and Constitutional Hill, and Pretoria's Freedom Park.[9] These three were conceived and generously funded as visible symbols of a new dispensation, located in South Africa's main financial centre and political centre, respectively. Each of these is a reflective memorial rather than a triumphalist monument:[10] they tell the post-1994 story of a nation forged in the furnace of adversity, a master narrative of ANC-led liberation that highlights the plight of apartheid's victims. Such an agenda presumably contributed to the choice of non-classical architecture as a symbolic attempt to escape colonial mindsets.

In these divergent senses the 'shared culture' mentioned in the *Revised White Paper* quoted above remains ambiguous: who is sharing and who is excluded in effect? In neither the narrower nor the broader sense of heritage have ancient Greece and Rome had an obvious role. Nor have they played any part in the market so emphasised by the Comaroffs above. Nonetheless, it is possible to outline three different scenarios for the relation of classical antiquity and heritage in South Africa. This typology is not absolute, but reflects different emphases. First, there are parallel streams, in which classical (indeed all European) and African traditions have been conceived in isolation from one another. This conforms most obviously with apartheid's 'own affairs' policy, but in fact an even longer durée of South Africa's museum history reflects it. Second, a few instances suggest that the two phenomena may be overtly at odds with each other, and that mutually exclusive choices have been made. Masters' story of competition for museum space is one such case, with its overt choice between Greek ceramics and the vernacular African art of Bonnie Ntshalintshali. In the changed political landscape, museum curators, here and elsewhere, have asserted their political relevance, by implication seeking the support of the new decision-makers within the ANC establishment.[11] Indigenous traditions have needed new prominence, and classical antiquity has been an easy victim. Third, the classical may be considered part of South African heritage, deeply embedded. In this scenario, choices are not mutually exclusive but coexist in a dynamic relation. This involves creative recontextualisation and juxtaposition, often in innovative settings. South African theatre continues to show the creative use of Greek myths. The country's premier art museum, the Iziko South African National Gallery, in 1995 had a Ndebele design painted into the twin alcoves of the façade, each flanked by the original Greek columns (see Figs 18.2–3). This was presumably intended by the curators as a means to claim relevance within the rapidly changing political

---

[9] Rankin 2013.   [10] Danto 1998: 153–58.   [11] Herwitz 2012; Coombes 2003.

Figure 18.2 Iziko South African National Gallery, Cape Town, with Devil's Peak in the background.

Figure 18.3 Iziko South African National Gallery, detail of façade. The niches were painted in 1995 by artists from KwaNdebele in preparation for the exhibit, *IGugu lamaNdebele* ('Pride of the Ndebele') inside the Gallery. Photograph by Terence Parker.

landscape. While the gesture seems like a Band-Aid solution to challenges relating to the rapid political transition, the contents of the museum reveal more radical changes: a recent exhibit, '1910–2010: from Pierneef to Gugulective', offered an overview of South African art, starting with Union in 1910 and continuing, in the style of a grand narrative of nation-building, into the twenty-first century.[12] Three further examples will round out this book, at the same time underlining the sense of deeply embedded, recontextualised classicism manifested both before and after the end of apartheid.

2.   Heritage as Collage

At Burgersdorp in the Eastern Cape, a classicising statue of a female figure honours the Dutch language (1893) (Fig. 18.4).[13] The figure, suggesting a Muse and modelled on a local girl, carries and points to a large inscribed tablet. During the South African War the statue was intentionally damaged, and was removed at the behest of Lord Milner in keeping with his policy of Anglicisation. Soon after the War, local Afrikaners prevailed on the British government to replace it (1907). The original was found in 1939 at King William's Town some three hundred kilometres away and re-erected in its broken state, placed slightly behind the replica. There it forms a triangle with an obelisk commemorating the centenary of the 'Great Trek' (1938).[14] This ensemble is a case of reiterated commemoration in the face of adversity, a monument to steadfast resolve, and is matched in at least one other site linked to the South African War.[15] Here an unmistakably classical form is used (and reused) in the cause of Afrikaans nationalism, focused on language.

---

[12] Pierneef (1886–1957), who specialised in landscapes, was the doyen of (white) South African painters of his age. The Gugulective began in 2006 as a multi-media collective of young, politically engaged (mostly black) artists who took their name from the black township of Gugulethu, where it first exhibited in a shebeen or speakeasy. The SANG exhibit was intended in part to indicate the change of leadership and priorities at the renamed museum: www.iziko .org.za/calendar/event/1910-2010-from-pierneef-to-gugulective.

[13] The inscription on the tablet reads: 'Vrijhijd voor de Hollandsche Taal' (freedom for the Dutch language). Afrikaans was not fully recognised as a separate language until 1925.

[14] Goldblatt 1998: 223. Goldblatt's inimitable photography adds another level of memorialisation, for it is via his photograph of 1990 that the place has been viewed from far afield.

[15] The Paardekraal Monument in Krugersdorp, designed by W. Y. Veitsch, was originally built in 1890 in the shape of an obelisk atop a pedestal. It is placed on the same spot where stones had been piled up into a cairn to honour the Boer Republic's successful resistance to British incursions. During the South African War the stones were removed by the British on Lord Roberts' instructions and thrown into the Vaal River, but the monument was reconstituted after the end of the war. Indeed, obelisks have often been used in Afrikaner monuments, including those marking the route of the Great Trek on the occasion of its centenary (1938).

Figure 18.4 A whole and a headless monument to the 'triumph of the Dutch language' together with other Afrikaner monuments, Burgersdorp, Cape. 29 September 1990. Photograph by David Goldblatt.

The Iziko Social History Centre, which includes the warehouses of the Iziko Museum system, is housed in the Old Mutual Building at Church Square in the heart of Cape Town. It is here that we turn to consider the multiple valences of place, and in fact it transpires that classicism has played a considerable if incidental role. In front of the Old Mutual building stands a statue of Onze Jan Hofmeyr (1845–1909), a founding father of the Afrikaner nation and grandfather of Jan Hendrik Hofmeyr (see Allen above). In 2008, Church Square was used to commemorate slavery by the installation of Wilma Cruise and Gavin Younge's 11 granite blocks engraved with slave names (Fig. 1.13)[16] – some of them classicising, as we have seen. Indeed, the Slave Lodge adjoins Church Square. In the early

---

[16] Wilma Cruise and Gavin Younge, http://wilmacruise.com/site-specific/the-memorial-to-the-slaves/. Rankin discusses the importance of displaying names, e.g. at Freedom Park (2013: 83, 87 and 94–95).

1990s a rally was held in this area: Chris Hani led a march towards the nearby Houses of Parliament. Press photographs of the march show Hani with both the Old Mutual Building and the Slave Lodge (then Cultural History Museum) in the background (see Fig. 1.2). Ancient Greece and Rome per se may be only a small part of the background to the political transition, but both here and in the Burgersdorp language monument they have added to the density of historical memory, much of it centred on intergroup conflict. This notion of heritage would seem to go beyond the Comaroffs' insistence on commodification.

Finally, we have already seen that both the Voortrekker Monument frieze in Pretoria and Cyril Coetzee's *T'kama Adamastor* in Johannesburg adapt classical media and themes to narrate South Africa's history – each from its own point of view. Taken together, these two monuments in Gauteng's main cities well characterise the term 'classical confrontations'. The recently deceased artist and poet Peter Clarke (1929–2014) created a work that is more abstract but no less telling in this respect. In his collage *Annunciation* (1987), Clarke juxtaposes different components (Fig. 18.5 and Plate 12). The figure on the left is based on the Winged Victory (Nike) of Samothrace: this famous statue once stood at the front of a ship, celebrating a victory of the Rhodians (second century BC), and is now at the Louvre. A photograph of the broken statue is supplemented on its wings with gold plate and on its head with a female African (Nigerian) figure. As if kneeling reverentially before it is a black man, his head under a cloth covering that suggests a nun, with hands and feet that do not match by virtue of their size and colour. Above right is a medieval book manuscript that depicts the Adoration of the Magi, the first of them kneeling before the baby Jesus. The manuscript contains the opening lines of Psalm 70, which have been part of Christian liturgy since early medieval times: 'Deus in adiutorium meum intende. Domine ad adiuvandum me festina.' ('Make haste, O God, to deliver me. Make haste to help me, O Lord.')

There appears to be a connection between the two kneeling figures, both kneeling in anticipation of a message. By the artist's own account, there is a substantial element of chance in the realisation of the work: he saw the Nike statue while visiting Paris and was struck by both its command of space and its fragmentary nature, and he used materials that happened to be available in his home studio. (The Adoration scene in the top right is provided by a Christmas card.)[17] This combination would in the end

---

[17] Rolf Michael Schneider, interview with Peter Clarke, Ocean View (Western Cape), 1 January 2013. I thank Professor Schneider for making a transcript available to me. For a somewhat different account, see Hobbs and Rankin 2011: 181–83.

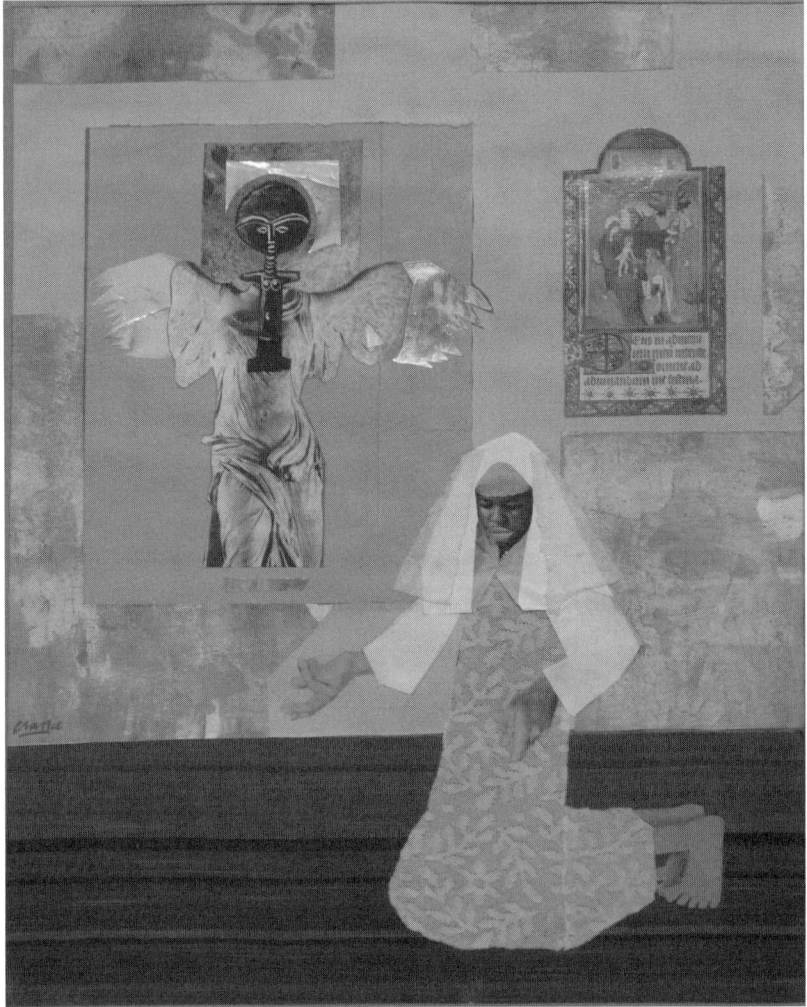

Figure 18.5 Peter Clarke, *Annunciation* (1987). (A black and white version of this figure will appear in some formats. For the colour version, please refer to the plate section.)

juxtapose different traditions and simultaneously bring different identities into dialogue: African and European, Christian and pagan, male and female, black and white, the sublime and the mundane. The work thus represents the result of chance collecting, which for Peter Clarke nonetheless had 'a purpose' beyond clear-cut definitions. Within this ensemble, the classical is visibly transformed: in Clarke's hands it is decentred from the cultural and political priority that it has so often received in South Africa's colonial history, from what Mudimbe calls the 'colonial library', yet it continues in a new setting. The classical is not privileged but one element of a multifarious collage.[18] The same can be said of Cyril Coetzee's juxtaposition of elements in *T'kama Adamastor* (Fig. 1.6).

In this sense the collage may be taken as a compelling metaphor for South Africa's varied manifestations of ancient Greece and Rome. Different elements come together in new ways, implicitly defying the apartheid mould of racial and cultural purity. The classical is present and resonant without dominating. Indeed, heritage does not necessarily have to be a conservative phenomenon of preservation, as it has often been in practice, and as is sometimes implied by the notion of cultural property.[19] Rather, it is as well to make provision for the creative component of heritage as well. While it is true that classicism has been a means by which the colonial elite has articulated and manipulated its identity, examples like Clarke's *Annunciation* tell a different story: that in South Africa, Greece and Rome have provided the basis for a wide range of artistic and political expression, and – though often close to power – they have in various media also enabled the critique of power. In this very South African sense of collage, classical heritage is not an oxymoron after all.

---

[18] Compare Laurence Wright's pointed comments on Shakespeare in South Africa: 'From a sober Africanist perspective, Shakespeare in South Africa is a sideshow to a sideshow, just one significant strand in a marginal story of colonial drama and its heritage.' But Wright goes on to emphasise the creativity with which Shakespeare's plays have been adapted in South African settings (Wright 2004: 63).

[19] Herwitz 2012: 3.

Bibliography

Aeschylus (1979), *The Oresteia*, tr. Robert Fagles, Harmondsworth: Penguin.

Aeschylus (1995), *The Oresteia*, tr. Michael Ewans, London: Everyman.

Ahmad, Y. (2006), 'The scope and definitions of heritage: from tangible to intangible', *International Journal of Heritage Studies* 12.3: 292–300.

Akkerman, A. (2003), 'Harmonies of urban design and discords of city form', in A. R. Cuthbert, ed., *Designing Cities: Critical Readings in Urban Design*, Oxford: Blackwell, 76–98.

Albertyn, C. F., ed. (1953), *Die Afrikaanse Kinderensiklopedie*, 10 vols, 2nd edition, Cape Town: Nasionale Boekhandel.

Alexander, E. (1953), *Morris Alexander: A Biography*, Cape Town: Juta.

Alföldy, G. (1999), *Das Imperium Romanum. Ein Vorbild für das vereinte Europa?*, Basel: Schwabe.

Amery, C., M. Richardson and G. Stamp (1982), 'Catalogue', in C. Amery, ed., *Lutyens: The Work of the English Architect Sir Edwin Lutyens (1869–1944)*, London: Arts Council of Great Britain.

Amery, L. (1953), *My Political Life*, vol. 1: *England Before the Storm, 1896–1914*, London: Hutchinson.

Amptelike program en gedenkboek van die fees inwyding van die Voortrekkermonument 13 to 16 Desember 1949, Pretoria: Voortrekkermonument-inwydingskomitee, 1949.

Anagnostopoulos, G., ed. (2009), *A Companion to Aristotle*, Malden: Wiley-Blackwell.

Anderson, M. J. (1997), *The Fall of Troy in Early Greek Poetry and Art*, Oxford: Oxford University Press.

Anouilh, J. (1960 [1943]), *Antigone: A Tragedy*, tr. L. Galantière, London: Methuen.

Arendt, H. (1946), 'Expansion and the philosophy of power', *The Sewanee Review* 54: 601–16.

Arendt, H. (1973), *The Origins of Totalitarianism*, New York: Harcourt Brace Jovanovich.

Armstrong, J. (2008), 'Ceremonial beer pots and their uses', in B. Carton, J. Laband and J. Sithole, eds, *Zulu Identities: Being Zulu, Past and Present*, Pietermaritzburg: University of KwaZulu-Natal Press, 414–17.

Arnheim, M. T. W. (1972), *The Senatorial Aristocracy in the Later Roman Empire*, Oxford: Clarendon.

496

Arnheim, M. T. W. (1977), *Aristocracy in Greek Society*, London: Thames and Hudson.

Arnheim, M. T. W. (1979), *South Africa after Vorster*, Cape Town: Howard Timmins.

Arnold, T. (1848), *History of Rome*, London: B. Fellowes.

Arnold, T. A. and W. T. Arnold (1886), *The Second Punic War, Being Chapters in the History of Rome by the Late Thomas Arnold*, London: Macmillan.

Arnott, P. D. (1971), *An Introduction to the Greek Theatre*, London: St Martin's Press.

Arnott, P. D. (1997), *Public and Performance in the Greek Theatre*, London: Routledge.

Artefacts (A). 'Baker, Sir Herbert', No date. Retrieved 28 February 2011 from Artefacts.co.za: www.artefacts.co.za/main/Buildings/archframes.php?archid=60&countadd=0.

Artefacts (B). 'Pretoria Regionalism', No date. Retrieved 25 February 2011 from Artefacts.co.za: www.artefacts.co.za/main/Buildings/style_det.php?styleid=185.

Artthrob, 'Bonnie Ntshalintshali dies', *Artthrob* 27, November 1999, www.artthrob.co.za/99nov/news.html.

Ashby, T. (1904), 'Recent excavations in Rome', *The Classical Review* 18.2: 137–41.

Atkinson, J. (2000), 'Originality and its limits in the Alexander sources of the early empire', in A. B. Bosworth and E. Baynham, eds, *Alexander the Great in Fact and Fiction*, Oxford: Oxford University Press, 307–25.

Atkinson, J. (2010), 'Benjamin Farrington: Cape Town and the shaping of a public intellectual', *South African Historical Journal* 62.4: 671–92.

Atkinson, J. (2012), Review of Lambert 2011, *Acta Classica* 55: 178–82.

Atkinson, J. (2014), 'Alexander and the unity of mankind: some Cape Town perspectives', in P. R. Bosman, ed., *Alexander in Africa*, *Acta Classica* supplement 5: 170–84.

Axelson, E. (1961), 'Prince Henry the Navigator and the discovery of the sea route to India', *Geographical Journal* 127.2: 145–55.

Badian, E. (1958), 'Alexander the Great and the unity of mankind', *Historia* 7: 425–44, reprinted in G. T. Griffith, ed., *Alexander the Great: The Main Problems*, Cambridge: Heffer, 1966, 287–306.

Bailey, C. (1928), 'Karl Marx on Greek atomism', *Classical Quarterly* 22: 205–6.

Bailey, C., ed. (1947), *Titi Lucreti Cari De Rerum Natura Libri Sex*, 3 vols., Oxford: Clarendon.

Baker, H. (1909), 'The architectural needs of South Africa', *The State* 1.5: 512–24.

Baker, H. (1934), *Cecil Rhodes by His Architect*, Oxford: Oxford University Press.

Baker, H. (1944), *Architecture and Personalities*, London: Country Life.

Baker, H. and W. T. Stead (1977), *Cecil Rhodes: The Man and His Dream*, Bulawayo: Books of Rhodesia.

Banchich, T. M. and E. N. Lane, tr. (2009), *The History of Zonaras*, London: Routledge.

Baring, E. (Lord Cromer) (1910), *Ancient and Modern Imperialism*, London: John Murray.

Bartlett, R., ed. (2006), *Halala Madiba: Nelson Mandela in Poetry*, Laverstock: Aflame Books.

Baumer, L. E., T. Hölscher and L. Winkler (1991), 'Narrative Systematik und politisches Konzept in den Reliefs der Traianssäule. Drei Fallstudien', *Jahrbuch des Deutschen Archäologischen Instituts* 106: 261–95.

Baumgart, W. (1982), *Imperialism: The Idea and Reality of British and French Colonial Expansion, 1880–1914*, Oxford: Oxford University Press, first published 1975.

Beard, M. and J. Henderson (1995), *Classics: A Very Short Introduction*, Oxford: Oxford University Press.

Belich, J. (2004), 'Grey, Sir George (1812–1894)', *Oxford Dictionary of National Biography*, Oxford: Oxford University Press, online edition.

Bell, D. S. A. (2006), 'Empire and international relations in Victorian political thought', *The Historical Journal* 49: 281–98.

Benn, A. W. (1882), *The Greek Philosophers*, London: Paul, Trench and co.

Benson, H. H., ed. (2009), *A Companion to Plato*, Malden: Wiley-Blackwell.

Bent, J. T. (1893), *The Ruined Cities of Mashonaland, Being a Record of Excavation and Exploration in 1891*, new edition, London: Longmans.

Berggren, J. L., and A. Jones (2000), *Ptolemy's Geography: An Annotated Translation of the Theoretical Chapters*, Princeton: Princeton University Press.

Berglund, A.-I. (1976), *Zulu Thought-Patterns and Symbolism*, Bloomington and Indianapolis: Indiana University Press.

Betts, R. F. (1971), 'The allusion to Rome in British imperialist thought of the late nineteenth and early twentieth centuries', *Victorian Studies* 15: 149–59.

Beukes, W. D., ed. (1992), *Boekewêreld: Die Nasionale Pers in die Uitgewersbedryf Tot 1990*, Cape Town: Nasionale Boekhandel.

Bickford-Smith, V. (2009), 'Creating a city of the tourist imagination: "The fairest Cape of them all"', *Urban Studies* 46.9: 1763–85.

Bignamini, I. and C. Hornsby (2010), *Digging and Dealing in Eighteenth-Century Rome*, New Haven: Yale University Press.

Bilbey, D. and M. Trusted (2010), '"The question of casts": collecting and later reassessment of the cast collections at South Kensington', in Frederiksen and Marchand (2010), 465–83.

Blanshard, A. (2010), *Sex: Vice and Love from Antiquity to Modernity*, Oxford: Wiley-Blackwell.

Blum, P. (1955), *Steenbok tot Poolsee*, Cape Town: Tafelberg.

Boardman, J. and M. Pope (1961), *Greek Vases in Cape Town*, South African Museum Guide no. 6, Haarlem: J. Enschede.

Boehmer, E., ed. (1998), *Empire Writing: An Anthology of Colonial Literature, 1870–1918*, Oxford: Oxford University Press.

Boot, M. (2001), 'The case for American empire', *Weekly Standard* 7, 15 October 2001.

Booyens, B. (1966), 'Studentelewe – die jongste tydperk', in Thom et al., *Stellenbosch*, 359–405.

Borman, M. (1989), *The Cape Education Department, 1839–1939*, tr. A. Clarkson, Cape Town: Cape Education Department.

Boshoff, A. (1995), *The Early Dynastic Egyptian Ceramics of Kafr-Tarkhan (3000–2800 BC)*, Masters thesis, University of Stellenbosch.

Bottini, A., ed. (2006), *Musa pensosa. L'immagine dell'intellettuale nell'antichità*, mostra Roma, Colosseo 19 febbraio – 20 agosto 2006, Rome: Electa.

Boyer, M. C. (1994), *The City of Collective Memory: Its Historical Imagery and Architectural Entertainments*, Cambridge, Mass.: MIT Press.

Branford, J. (1978), *A Dictionary of South African English*, Cape Town: Oxford University Press.

Bredekamp, H. C. (Jatti) (2001), *The Cultural Heritage of Democratic South Africa: An Overview*, Library and Information Association of South Africa.

Bredenkamp, F., tr. (2007), *Meditasies van Marcus Aurelius Antoninus*, Pretoria: Protea.

Breytenbach, B. (1998), *Boklied: 'n vermaaklikheid in drie bedrywe*, Cape Town: Human & Rousseau.

Brink, A. (2003), 'English and the Afrikaner writer', in S. G. Kellman, ed., *Switching Languages: Translingual Writers Reflect on their Craft*, Lincoln: University of Nebraska Press, 201–22.

Brinkmann, V., O. Primavesi and M. Hollein, eds (2010), *Circumlitio: The Polychromy of Antique and Mediaeval Sculpture*, Proceedings of the Johann David Passavant Colloquium, 10–12 December 2008, Munich: Hirmer.

Brits, J. P. (1994), *Op die Vooraand van Apartheid: die rassevraagstuk en die blanke politiek in Suid-Afrika, 1939–1948*. Pretoria: UNISA Press.

Brooke Simons, P. (1996), *Groote Schuur: From Granary to Stately Home*, Vlaeberg: Fernwood Press.

Brookes, E. (1924), *The History of the Native Policy in South Africa from 1830 to the Present Day*, Cape Town: Nasionale Pers.

Brookes, E. (1974), *White Rule in South Africa 1830–1910*, Pietermaritzburg: University of Natal Press.

Brookes, E. (1977), *A South African Pilgrimage*, Johannesburg: Ravan Press.

Brownlee, F. (1970), *The Transkeian Native Territories: Historical Records*, Westport Connecticut: Negro University Press.

Bryant, A. T. (1967), *The Zulu People as They Were Before the White Man Came*, 2nd edition, Pietermaritzburg: Shuter and Shooter.

Bryce, J. (1897), *Impressions of South Africa*, London: Macmillan.

Bryce, J. (1914), *The Ancient Roman Empire and the British Empire in India: The Diffusion of Roman and English Law Throughout the World. Two Historical Studies*, London; New York: H. Milford, Oxford University Press.

Buchan, J. (1903), *The African Colony: Studies in the Reconstruction*, Edinburgh: W. Blackwood and Sons.

Buchan, J. (1937), *Augustus*, London: Hodder & Stoughton.

Buchan, J. (1940), *Memory Hold-the-Door*, London: Hodder & Stoughton.

Bull, M. (1975), *A Study of Some Aspects of the Life and Work of Abraham de Smidt, Surveyor-General of the Cape Colony*, Masters thesis, University of Cape Town.

Bundy, C. (2014), *Short-Changed: South Africa Since Apartheid*, Auckland Park: Jacana.

Bunn, D. (1998), 'Whited sepulchres: On the reluctance of monuments', in H. Judin and I. Vladislavić, eds, *Blank ___ Architecture, Apartheid and After*, Cape Town: David Philip, 93–177.

Burckhardt, J. (1990), *The Civilization of the Renaissance in Italy*, tr. S. G. C. Middlemore, Harmondsworth: Penguin; German original 1860.

Burke, E. E., V. W. Hiller and J. P. R. Wallis (1953), *The Story of Cecil Rhodes Set Out in a Series of Historical Pictures and Objects to Commemorate the Centenary of his Birth 1853–1953*, Bulawayo: Central African Rhodes Centenary Exhibition.

Burton, A. (1972), *Diodorus Siculus Book 1: A Commentary*, Leiden: Brill.

Buruma, I. and A. Margalit (2004), *Occidentalism: The West in the Eyes of Its Enemies*, Penguin: New York.

Butler, G. (1991), *A Local Habitation: An Autobiography, 1945–90*, Cape Town: David Philip.

Butler, S. (1922), *The Authoress of the Odyssey*, London: Jonathan Cape, first published 1897.

Byala, S. (2013), *A Place That Matters Yet: John Gubbins's Museum Africa in the Postcolonial World*, Chicago: University of Chicago Press.

Callaway, H. (1970), *The Religious System of the amaZulu*, Cape Town: Struik.

Cameron, D., C. Christov-Bakargiev and J. M. Coetzee (1999), *William Kentridge*, London: Phaidon Press.

Camões, L. V. (1997), *The Lusíads*, tr. L. White, Oxford: Oxford University Press.

Camp, J. McK., II (1992), *The Athenian Agora: Excavations in the Heart of Classical Athens*, revised edition, London: Thames and Hudson.

Campana, R. (1998), 'Lo studio Bartolini-Romanelli in San Frediano', in R. P. Ciardi, ed., *Case di artisti in Toscana*, Florence: Silvana Editoriale, 167–253.

Cape Argus (1948), 'The fairy godfather of South African Galleries', 2 July 1948.

Carman, J. (2006), *Uplifting the Colonial Philistine: Florence Phillips and the Making of the Johannesburg Art Gallery*, Johannesburg: Wits University Press.

CASA, *P&SP* = The Classical Association of South Africa: *Proceedings and Selected Papers* 1 (1929).

Chapman, M. (1981), *Douglas Livingstone: A Critical Study of His Poetry*. Johannesburg: Ad Donker.

Chipkin, C. M. (1993), *Johannesburg Style: Architecture and Society, 1880s–1960s*, Cape Town: David Philip.

Church, J. (1996), 'The future of the Roman-Dutch legal heritage', *Fundamina* 2: 308–19.

Claassen, J.-M. (1997), 'A conference that could have changed our world: Fort Hare 1930', *Alternation* 4.2: 136–61.

Claassen, J.-M. (1999), *Displaced Persons: The Literature of Exile from Cicero to Boethius*, Madison: University of Wisconsin Press.

Claassen, J.-M. (2009), '"Yonder lies your hinterland": Rhodes, Baker and the twisted strands of the South African architectural tradition', *Akroterion* 54: 69–86.

Claassen, J.-M. (2012), Review of Lambert 2011, *Acta Classica* 55: 172–78.

Claassen, J.-M. (2013), *N. P. van Wyk Louw: Germanicus*, translated with introduction, Dragonfly eBooks.

Clark, D. L., ed. (1954), *Shelley's Prose, or The Trumpet of a Prophecy*, Albuquerque: University of New Mexico Press.

Clark, K. (1947), *Ruskin at Oxford: Inaugural Lecture Delivered Before the University of Oxford, 14 November 1946*, Oxford: Clarendon.

Clark, K. (1956), *The Nude: A Study of Ideal Art*, Harmondsworth: Penguin Books.

Clark, N. L. and W. H. Worger (2004), *South Africa: The Rise and Fall of Apartheid*, Pearson: Harlow.

Coarelli, F. (2000), *The Column of Trajan*, Rome: Colombo.

Coarelli, F. (2008), *The Column of Marcus Aurelius*, Rome: Colombo.

Coetzee, J. M. (2001), *Stranger Shores: Literary Essays, 1986–1999*, New York: Viking.

Coetzee, N. J. (1988), 'Die voorstelling van die Voortrekkers in die kuns', in J. J. Bergh, ed., *Herdenkingsjaar 1988: Portugese, Hugenote en Voortrekkers*, Pretoria: de Jager Haum, 177–89.

Coetzee, N. J. (1992) *Pierneef, Land and Landscape: The Johannesburg Station Panels in Context*, Johannesburg: CBM Publishing.

Coetzer, W. H. (1947), *My Kwas Vertel*, Johannesburg: L & S Boek en Kunssentrum.

Coetzer, W. H. (1980), *W. H. Coetzer 80*, Roodepoort: CUM Boeke.

Cole, C. M. (2010), *Performing South Africa's Truth Commission: Stages of Transition*, Bloomington and Indianapolis: Indiana University Press.

Coleman, K. M. (2010), 'C. P. Cavafy and Douglas Livingstone: an African legacy', in P. Roilos, ed., *Imagination and Logos: Essays on C. P. Cavafy*, Cambridge, MA: Department of Classics, Harvard University, 107–20.

Colonial Office of the Cape of Good Hope, Government Notice (No. 25 of 1855), 25 June 1855.

Comaroff, J. L. (1989), 'Images of empire, contests of conscience: models of Domination in South Africa', *American Ethnologist* 16: 661–85.

Comaroff, J. L. and J. Comaroff (2009), *Ethnicity, Inc.*, Chicago: University of Chicago Press.

Connor, P. (1989), 'Cast collecting in the nineteenth century: scholarship, aesthetics, connoisseurship', in G. W. Clarke, ed., *Rediscovering Hellenism:*

The Hellenic Inheritance and the English Imagination, Cambridge: Cambridge University Press, 187–235.

Conradie, P. J. (1976), *Niks is in sy tyd Gesluit*, Pretoria: Academica.

Constant, B. (1988), *Political Writings*, tr. and ed. B. Fontana, Cambridge: Cambridge University Press.

Cooke, I. (2010), 'Colonial contexts: the changing meanings of the cast collection of the Auckland War Memorial Museum', in Frederiksen and Marchand (2010), 577–93.

Cooke, L. (2001), 'Mundus inversus, mundus perversus', in M. Sittenfeld, ed., *William Kentridge*, Chicago: Museum of Contemporary Art, 39–57.

Coombes, A. (2003), *History after Apartheid: Visual Culture and Public Memory in a Democratic South Africa*, Durham, NC: Duke University Press.

Cooper, A. A. (1986), *The Freemasons of South Africa*, Cape Town: Human & Rousseau.

Corbett, M. M. (1987), 'Aspects of the role of policy in the evolution of our Common Law', *South African Law Journal* 104: 52–69.

Cornelius, I. (2001), 'Van Karnak tot Kakamas: die naleef van ou Egipte in die Suid-Afrikaanse boukuns', *Akroterion* 46: 75–91.

Cornelius, I. (2003), 'Egyptianizing motifs in South African architecture', in J.-M. Humbert and C. Price, eds, *Imhotep Today: Egyptianizing Architecture*, London: UCL Press, 247–55.

Cornford, F. M. (1967), 'The Marxist view of ancient philosophy' (first published 1942), reprinted in his *The Unwritten Philosophy and Other Essays*, ed. W. K. C. Guthrie, Cambridge: Cambridge University Press, 117–37.

Corrigal, M. (2007), 'Breaking a cycle of violence gives us hope', *Sunday Independent* 27 May 2007, 11.

Crais, C. C. (1992), *White Supremacy and Black Resistance in Pre-Industrial South Africa: The Making of the Colonial Order, 1770–1865*, Cambridge: Cambridge University Press.

Cramb, J. A. (1915), *The Origins and Destiny of Imperial Britain: Nineteenth Century Europe*, London: J. Murray.

Crampton, A. (2001), 'The Voortrekker Monument, the birth of apartheid, and beyond', *Political Geography* 20: 221–46.

Crewe, J. (1999), 'Recalling Adamastor: literature as cultural memory in "white" South Africa', in M. Bal et al., eds, *Acts of Memory: Cultural Recall in the Present*, Hanover, NH: University Press of New England, 171–90.

Crinson, M. (2003), *Modern Architecture and the End of Empire*, Aldershot: Ashgate.

Cross, M. (1999), *Imagery of Identity in South African Education, 1880–1990*, Durham, NC: Carolina Academic Press.

Cummings, E. E. (1963), *Selected Poems, 1923–1958*, Harmondsworth: Penguin.

Cummings, E. E. (1971), *Six Non-Lectures*, New York: Atheneum.

Curtis, L. (1938), *Civitas Dei*, London: Allen and Unwin.

Dalby, A. (2006), *Rediscovering Homer: Inside the Origins of the Epic*, New York: Norton.

Dallman, P. R. (1998), *Plant Life in the World's Mediterranean Climates: California, Chile, South Africa, Australia, and the Mediterranean Basin*, Berkeley: University of California Press.

Daniel, T. K. (1991), 'The scholars and the saboteurs: the wrecking of a South African Irish scheme, Paris 1922', *Southern African-Irish Studies* 1: 162–75.

Danto, A. C. (1998), *The Wake of Art: Criticism, Philosophy and the Ends of Taste*, ed. G. Horowitz and T. Huhn, Abingdon: Routledge.

Dargie, D. (1993), 'Umngqokolo: Thembu Xhosa Umngqokolo overtone singing: the use of the human voice as a type of "musical bow"', unpublished conference paper, Berlin, 4–5.

Davidson, A. (2003), *Cecil Rhodes and His Time*, Pretoria: Protea Book House.

Davis, R. H. (1979), 'School vs. blanket and settler: Elijah Makiwane and the leadership of the Cape school community', *African Affairs* 78.310: 12–31.

Davis, S. (1951), *Race-Relations in Ancient Egypt: Greek, Egyptian, Hebrew, Roman*, London: Methuen.

Davison, P. (2000), 'Museums, memorials and public memory', in S. Nuttall and C. Coetzee, eds, *Negotiating the Past: The Making of Memory in South Africa*, Oxford: Oxford University Press, 143–60.

De Beer, A. (1969), *Die lewe en werk van die skilder W. H. Coetzer en sy kultuur-historiese betekenis*, MA thesis, University of Pretoria (http://upetd.up.ac.za/thesis/available/etd-12072011-110708/; accessed 23 June 2014).

De Beer, D. (2007), 'Everything remains raw', *Star* 22 May 2007, 1.

De Klerk, F. W. (2005), 'The effect of great changes and the role of leadership in social conditions' (Athens, 19 May 2005), F. W. de Klerk Foundation.

De Kock, J. M. (1987), 'Grobbelaar, Coert Smit', in C. J. Beyers and J. L. Basson, eds, *Dictionary of South African Biography* Vol. V. Pretoria: RGN, 307.

De Smidt, A. (1871), 'An art gallery for South Africa', *Cape Monthly Magazine*, April 1871.

Delmont, E. (1987), 'The Voortrekker Monument: monolith to myth', *South African Historical Journal* 29 (November 1993), 76–101.

Demosthenes (1930), *Olynthiacs, Philippics, Minor Public Speeches, Speech Against Leptines I–XVII, XX*, trans. J. H. Vince, Loeb Classical Library, Cambridge, Mass.: Harvard University Press.

Department of Arts, Culture, Science and Technology (1996), 'All our legacies, our common future', *White Paper on Arts, Culture and Heritage*, Pretoria, 4 June 1996.

Department of Arts and Culture (2013), *Revised White Paper on Arts, Culture and Heritage*, Pretoria, 4 June 2013.

Derbyshire, J. (2003), 'An empire like no other', *National Review* 55, 1 September 2003, 33–35.

Dick, A. L. (2013), *The Hidden History of South Africa's Book and Reading Cultures*, Scottsville: University of KwaZulu-Natal Press.

Dick, B. F. (1972), *The Hellenism of Mary Renault*, Carbondale and Edwardsville: Southern Illinois University Press.

Dietrich, B. C. (1971), 'New vases in the Rhodes Museum', *Acta Classica* 14: 119–22.

Dietrich, B. C. (1972), 'Two new Rhodes University vases', *Acta Classica* 15: ix, 1–2.

Dietrich, B. C. (1975), 'Two kylikes in the Rhodes Collection', *Acta Classica* 18: 5–7.

Dietrich, B. C. and A. C. Dietrich (1966), 'The Rhodes University vases', *Acta Classica* 9: 1–13.

Dircksen, M. (2010), 'Latyn en die opleiding van regstudente in Suid-Afrika: 'n nuwe relevansie', *De Jure* 43: 117–28.

Distiller, N. (2006), 'Mourning the African Renaissance', *Shakespeare in Southern Africa* 18: 49–56.

Dodds, E. R. (1977), *Missing Persons: An Autobiography*, Oxford: Oxford University Press.

Dominik, W. J. (2007), 'Africa', in C. W. Kallendorf, ed., *A Companion to the Classical Tradition*, Malden, MA: Blackwell, 117–31.

Doordan, D. P. (2001), *Twentieth-Century Architecture*. London: Laurence King.

Douglas Livingstone Collection, Grahamstown: National English Literary Museum.

Dowling, L. (1985), 'Roman decadence and Victorian historiography', *Victorian Studies* 28.4: 579–607.

Dowling, L. C. (1994), *Hellenism and Homosexuality in Victorian Oxford*, Ithaca: Cornell University Press.

Drew, A. (2002), *Discordant Comrades: Identities and Loyalties on the South African Left*, Pretoria: UNISA Press.

Drummond, H. (1894), *The Lowell Lectures on the Ascent of Man*, London: Hodder and Stoughton.

Dubow, S. (1991), *Afrikaner Nationalism, Apartheid, and the Conceptualisation of 'Race'*, Johannesburg: African Studies Institute, University of the Witwatersrand.

Dubow, S. (1997), 'Colonial nationalism, the Milner Kindergarten and the rise of "South Africanism"', *History Workshop Journal* 43: 53–85.

Duff Gordon, L. (1927), *Letters from the Cape*, ed. D. Fairbridge, London: Oxford University Press.

Duffey, A. E. (1993), 'Laurika Postma', in A. Werth and F. Harmsen, eds, *Our Art 4*, Pretoria: Foundation for Education, Science and Technology, 50–57.

Duffey, A. (2005), ''n Egte lugkasteel: Moerdijk, Van Wouw en die Voortrekkermonument', *2de Moerdijk gedenklesing*, Pretoria: Voortrekkermonument Komitee.

Duffey, A. E. (2008), 'Dr Peter Kirchhoff (1893–1978)', *Africana Society Pretoria Yearbook* 22: 150–51.

Du Toit, A. (2005), 'The legacy of Daantjie Oosthuizen: revisiting the liberal defence of academic freedom', *African Sociological Review* 9: 40–61.

Du Toit, A. (2011), 'The "dark sides" of humanism in South Africa', in J. W. de Gruchy, ed., *The Humanist Imperative in South Africa*, Stellenbosch: Sun Press and STIAS, 117–32.

Du Toit, P. S. (1966), 'Verdere fakulteite wat in 1918 ontstaan het', in Thom et al., *Stellenbosch*, 98–124.

Duvenage, G. D. J. (1988), *Die Gedenktrek van 1938: 'n edevaart en 'n kruistog*. Pretoria: Gutenberg Boekdrukkers.

Dyson, S. L. (2010) 'Cast collecting in the United States', in Frederiksen and Marchand (2010), 557–75.

Edelstein, L. and I. G. Kidd, eds (1972) *Posidonius*, vol. 1: *the fragments*, Cambridge: Cambridge University Press.

Elliott, A. (2005), *The Xhosa and Their Traditional Way of Life*, Cape Town and Singapore: Struik Publishers.

Endres, N. (2004), 'Subjects of the visual arts: Harmodius and Aristogeiton', in C. J. Summers, ed., *The Queer Encyclopedia of the Visual Arts*, San Francisco: Cleis, 301–2.

Englert, W. G. (1987), *Epicurus on the Swerve and Voluntary Action*, Atlanta: Scholars Press.

Enwezor, O. and R. Bester, eds (2013), *Rise and Fall of Apartheid: Photography and the Bureaucracy of Everyday Life* (exhibition catalogue, September 14, 2012 – January 6, 2013), New York: International Center of Photography and Prestel.

Etherington, N. (2001), *The Great Treks: The Transformation of Southern Africa, 1815–1854*, London et al: Pearson Education.

Euripides (1954), *The Bacchae and Other Plays*, translated by P. Vellacott, Harmondsworth: Penguin Books.

Euripides (1963), *Medea and Other Plays*, translated by P. Vellacott, Harmondsworth: Penguin Books.

Evans, R. (2007), 'Perspectives on post-colonialism in South Africa: the Voortrekker Monument's classical heritage', in L. Hardwick and C. Gillespie, eds, *Classics in Post-Colonial Worlds*, Oxford: Oxford University Press, 141–56.

Fabbri, P. (1994), *Monteverdi*, tr. T. Carter, Cambridge and New York: Cambridge University Press.

Fagan, E. (1996), 'Roman-Dutch Law in its South African historical context', in R. Zimmermann and D. Visser, eds, *Southern Cross: Civil and Common Law in South Africa*, Oxford: Clarendon Press, 33–64.

Fagles, R., tr. (1982), *Sophocles: The Three Theban Plays*, New York: Viking.

Fairbridge, D. (1913), *Piet of Italy*, Cape Town: J. C. Juta.

Fairbridge, D. (1915), *The Torch Bearer*, Cape Town: J. C. Juta.

Fairbridge, D. (1918), *A History of South Africa*, London: Oxford University Press.

Fairbridge, D. (1926), *The Uninvited*, London: Edward Arnold.

Fairbridge, D. (1928), *The Pilgrims' Way in South Africa*, Oxford: Oxford University Press.

Fan, K. S. (2009), 'Culture for sale: western classical architecture in China's recent building boom', *Journal of Architectural Education* 63.1: 64–74.

Farber, Y. (2008a), *Molora*, London: Oberon Books.

Farber, Y. (2008b), *Theatre as Witness: Three Testimonial Plays from South Africa*, London: Oberon Books.

Farrington, B. (1927), *Primum Graius Homo: An Anthology of Latin Translations from the Greek*, Cambridge: Cambridge University Press.

Farrington, B. (1929), *Samuel Butler and the Odyssey*, London: Jonathan Cape.

Farrington, B., tr. (1932), *The Preface of Andreas Vesalius to De Fabrica Corporis Humani*, Cape Town: n. p.

Farrington, B., tr. (1933), W. ten Rhyne, *Schediasma de Promonotorio Bonae Spei ejusve tractus incolis Hottentotis* and J.G. (de) Grevenbroek, *Elegans et accurata gentis Africanae circa Promontorium Capitis Bonae Spei, vulgo Hottentotten nuncupatae, descriptio* in I. Schapera, ed., *The Early Cape Hottentots*, Cape Town: The Van Riebeeck Society, 82–299.

Farrington, B. (1937), *Diodorus Siculus, Universal Historian: Inaugural Lecture Delivered at the University College of Swansea, November 1936*, University of Wales Press Board.

Farrington, B. (1947a), *Head and Hand in Ancient Greece*, London: Watts.

Farrington, B. (1947b), *Science in Antiquity*, revised edition, London: Home University Library, first published 1936.

Farrington, B. (1949), *Francis Bacon: Philosopher of Industrial Science*, New York: Henry Schuman, reprinted London, 1951.

Farrington, B. (1953a), 'On misunderstanding the philosophy of Francis Bacon', *Science, Medicine and History* 1: 439–50.

Farrington, B. (1953b), 'Second thoughts on Epicurus', *Science and Society* 17: 326–39.

Farrington, B. (1963), 'Polemical allusions to the *de rerum natura* of Lucretius in the works of Vergil', in L. Varcl and R. F. Willetts, eds, *Geras: Studies Presented to George Thomson*, Prague: Charles University, 87–94.

Farrington, B. (1965), *Science and Politics in the Ancient World*, 2nd edition, London: Allen and Unwin, first published 1939.

Farrington, B. (1967), *The Faith of Epicurus*, London: Weidenfeld and Nicolson.

Farrington, B. (1971), review of Stanford and McDowell, Mahaffy (1971), *Journal of Hellenic Studies* 91: 217.

Fassler, J. (1952), 'Some aspects of the future planning of Johannesburg', *South African Architectural Record* 37.1: 6–10.

Fazzini, M. (1991), 'Interviewing Douglas Livingstone', *New Contrast* 19: 135–45.

Ferguson, N. (2003a), *Empire: How Britain Made the Modern World*, London: Allen Lane.

Ferguson, N. (2003b), 'Hegemony or empire?', *Foreign Affairs* (September/October 2003).

Ferguson, N. (2006), 'Empire falls: lessons unlearned', *Vanity Fair* (October 2006).

Ferguson, W. S. (1918), 'The Zulus and the Spartans', *Harvard African Studies* 2: 197–234, repr. E. L. Wheeler, ed., *The Armies of Classical Greece*, Aldershot: Ashgate, 2007.

Ferreira, O. J. O., ed. (2008), *Adamastor: Spirit of the Cape of Storms*, Pretoria: University of Pretoria.

Fisher, R. C. (1997), 'Norman Eaton: some influences on his insights', *South African Journal of Cultural History* 11.2: 68–83.

Fisher, R. (2003), 'Gerard Moerdijk: the formative years', *South African Journal of Art History* 18: 28–37.

Fisher, R. C. (2006), 'Baker and Moerdijk: a shared legacy apart', *South African Journal of Art History* 21.2: 124–36.

Fisher, R. C. and N. J. Clarke (2010), 'Gerard Moerdijk: death and memorializing in his architecture for the Afrikaner nationalist project', *South African Journal of Art History* 25.2: 151–60.

FitzGerald, E. tr. (1940), *The Rubáiyát of Omar Khayyam*, London: Harrap.

Flanders, J. (2002), *A Circle of Sisters: Alice Kipling, Georgiana Burne-Jones, Agnes Poynter and Louisa Baldwin*, London: Penguin.

Fletcher, B. (1897), *A History of Architecture on the Comparative Method*, London et al.: B. T. Batsford.

Flint, J. (1974), *Cecil Rhodes*. Boston: Little Brown.

Foster, J. (2004), 'Creating a temenos, positing "South Africanism": material memory, landscape practice and the circulation of identity at Delville Wood', *Cultural Geographies* 11: 250–90.

Foster, R. F. (2003), *The Archpoet, 1915–1939*. Vol. 2 of *W. B. Yeats: A Life*, Oxford: Oxford University Press.

Foucault, M. (2001), *Fearless Speech*, tr. J. Pearson, Los Angeles: Semiotext(e).

Fowler, W. W. (1892), *Julius Caesar and the Foundation of the Roman Imperial System*, London: G. P. Putnam's Sons.

Frederiksen, R. and E. Marchand, eds (2010), *Plaster Casts: Making, Collecting and Displaying from Classical Antiquity to the Present*, Berlin: Walter de Gruyter.

Frendo, J. D., tr. (1975), *Agathias: The Histories*, Berlin: De Gruyter.

Freschi, F. (2004), 'Imagining Fusion: the politics of South Africanism as reflected in the decorative programme of the Pretoria City Hall (1935)', *De Arte* 69: 4–25.

Freschi, F. (2005), 'The fine art of Fusion: race, gender, and the politics of South Africanism in the decorative programme of South Africa House, London (1933)', *De Arte* 71: 14–34.

Freschi, F. (2009), 'The business of belonging: Volkskapitalisme, modernity and the imaginary of national belonging in the decorative programmes of selected commercial buildings in Cape Town, South Africa, 1930–1940', *South African Historical Journal* 61.3: 67–95.

Frischer, B. (1982), *The Sculpted Word: Epicureanism and Philosophical Recruitment in Ancient Greece*, Berkeley: University of California Press.

Fugard, A. (1970), *People are Living There: A Play in Two Acts*, London: Oxford University Press.

Fugard, A., J. Kani and W. Nshona (1974), *Statements: Two Workshop Productions Devised by Athol Fugard, John Kani and Winston Nshona*, Oxford: Oxford University Press.

Fugard, A. (2002), 'Antigone in Africa', in M. McDonald and J. M. Watson eds, *Amid Our Troubles: Irish Versions of Greek Tragedy*, London: Methuen, 128–47.

Fuller, Sir T. E. (1910), *The Right Honourable Cecil John Rhodes: A Monograph and a Reminiscence*, London: Longmans Green and Co.

Fussell, P. (1980), *Abroad: British Travelling Between the Wars*, Oxford: Oxford University Press.

Galbally, A. (1988), 'The lost museum: Redmond Barry and Melbourne's "Musée des Copies"', *Australian Journal of Art* 7: 28–49.

Galla, A. (1996), 'Shifting the paradigm: a plan to diversify heritage practice in South Africa', discussion document, Cape Town: South African Museum.

Gandhi, M. (1958–), *Collected Works*, Delhi: Ministry of Information and Broadcasting.

Garlake, P. (2002), *Early Art and Architecture of Africa*, Oxford: Oxford University Press.

Giliomee, H. (2003), *The Afrikaners: Biography of a People*, Cape Town: Tafelberg Publishers Press (2nd edition 2009).

Giliomee, H. (2012), *The Last Afrikaner Leaders: A Supreme Test of Power*, Cape Town: Tafelberg.

Gill, E. L. (1934), *Catalogue of the De Pass Collection*, Cape Town: South African Museum.

Glenn, I. and E. Rybicki (2006), 'Douglas Livingstone's two cultures', *Current Writing* 18.1: 78–89.

Gluckman, M. (1940), 'The kingdom of the Zulu of South Africa', in M. Fortes and E. E. Evans-Pritchard, eds, *African Political Systems*, Oxford: Oxford University Press, 25–55.

Goff, B., ed. (2005), *Classics and Colonialism*, London: Duckworth.

Goff, B. (2007), 'No man's island: Fugard, Kani and Ntshona's The Island', in B. Goff and M. Simpson (2007), 271–320.

Goff, B. and M. Simpson (2007), *Crossroads in the Black Aegean: Oedipus, Antigone and Dramas of the African Diaspora*, Oxford: Oxford University Press.

Goldblatt, D. (1998), *South Africa: The Structure of Things Then*, Cape Town: Oxford University Press.

Goldsmith, O. (1860), *A History of Rome from the Earliest Times with an Introduction to the Study of Roman History, Also, Chapters on the Literature, Art, Manners, Institutions, and Antiquities of the Romans*, London: Simkin, Marshall & Co.

Gooch, G. P. (1952), *History and Historians in the Nineteenth Century*, with new introduction, London and New York: Longmans, Green, first published 1913.

Gosling, A. (1989), *Museum of Classical Archaeology Special Exhibition of Ancient Coins May 1989: Greek, Roman and Byzantine*, Durban: University of Natal.

Gradidge, R. (1981), *Edwin Lutyens: Architect Laureate*, London: George Allen & Unwin.

Grafton, A. (1992), *New Worlds, Ancient Texts: The Power of Tradition and the Shock of Discovery*, Cambridge, MA: Harvard University Press.

Grafton, A., G. W. Most and S. Settis, eds (2010), *The Classical Tradition*, Cambridge, MA: Harvard University Press.

Graßhoff, G., M. Heinzelmann and M. Wäfler, eds (2009), *The Pantheon in Rome: Contributions to the Conference, Bern, November 9–12, 2006, Pantheon I*, Bern: Bern Studies in the History and Philosophy of Science.

Gray, J. (2004), 'Ever the Twain', *Times Literary Supplement*, 8 October 2004, 25.

Gray, S. (1977), 'The myth of Adamastor in South African literature', *Theoria* 48: 1–23.

Gray, S., ed. (1978), *Theatre One: New South African Drama*, Johannesburg: Ad Donker.

Greenhalgh, M. (1990), *What Is Classicism?* London: Academy Editions.

Greenwood, E. (2010), *Afro-Greeks: Dialogues Between Afro-Caribbean Literature and Classics in the Twentieth Century*, Oxford: Oxford University Press.

Gregorovius, F. (1898), *The Emperor Hadrian: A Picture of the Graeco-Roman World in His Time*, tr. M. E. Robinson, London: Macmillan.

Greig, D. E. (1970), *Herbert Baker in South Africa*, Cape Town: Purnell.

Greig, D. E. (1978), 'The work of Edwin Lutyens in Johannesburg', *The Mafeking Mail, Journal of Africana* 1.5: 1–2.

Gribble, D. (1999), *Alcibiades and Athens: A Study in Literary Presentation*, Oxford: Clarendon Press.

Griebel, J. (2013), *Der Kaiser im Krieg: die Bilder der Säule des Marc Aurel*, Berlin and Boston: De Gruyter.

Grobbelaar, E. (1988), 'The Davis Collection of Chinese ceramics in the South African Cultural History Museum', *Bulletin of the South African Cultural History Museum* 9: 39–52.

Grobler, E. (2005), *Collections Management Practices at the Transvaal Museum, 1913–1964, Anthropological, Archaeological and Historical*, DPhil thesis, Pretoria: University of Pretoria. http://repository.up.ac.za/handle/2263/24550?show=full

Grobler, J. (2001), *Ontdek die Voortrekkermonument – Discover the Voortrekker Monument*, Pretoria: Grourie Entrepreneurs.

Grobler, J. (2008), 'The impact of politics on heritage and cultural tourism in South Africa', *South African Journal of Cultural History* 22.1: 163–85.

Grobler, J. (2011), 'The Retief massacre of 6 February 1938 revisited', *Historia: official organ of the Historical Association of South Africa* 56.2: 113–32.

Grundlingh, A. (2009), 'A cultural conundrum? Old monuments and new regimes. The Voortrekker Monument as symbol of Afrikaner power in a postapartheid

South Africa', in D. J. Walkowitz and L. Maya Knauer, eds, *Contested Histories in Public Space: Memory, Race, and Nation*, Durham: Duke University Press, 157–77.

Grundlingh, A. and H. Sapire (1989), 'From feverish festival to repetitive ritual? The changing fortunes of Great Trek mythologies in an industrializing South Africa, 1938–1988', *South African Historical Journal* 21: 19–37.

Gutsche, T. (1966), *No Ordinary Woman: The life and Times of Florence Phillips*, Cape Town: Howard Timmins.

Haarhoff, T. J. (1920), 'Principles and practice of the Roman empire', in J. H. Hofmeyr and T. J. Haarhoff, eds *Studies in Ancient Imperialism*, Johannesburg: Council of Education.

Haarhoff, T. J. (1948), *The Stranger at the Gate: Aspects of Exclusiveness and Co-operation in Ancient Greece and Rome, With Some Reference to Modern Times*, Boston: Beacon Press.

Haarhoff, T. J. (1949), *Vergil, the Universal*, Oxford: Basil Blackwell.

Haarhoff, T. J. (1970), *Smuts, the Humanist*, Oxford: Basil Blackwell.

Haarhoff, T. J., and C. M. van den Heever (1934), *The Achievement of Afrikaans*, Johannesburg: Central News Agency.

Habermas, J. (1985), *Philosophical-Political Profiles*, Cambridge, MA: MIT Press.

Hacksley, M. and D. Maclennan, eds (2004), *A Ruthless Fidelity: Collected Poems of Douglas Livingstone*, Johannesburg and Cape Town: Ad Donker.

Hadot, P. (1995), *Philosophy as a Way of Life: Spiritual Exercises from Socrates to Foucault*, tr. A. I. Davidson, Oxford: Blackwell.

Hagg, G. (1989), 'Coert Steynberg en die opkoms van die Afrikaner-Nasionalisme: 1930–40', *South African Journal of Art History* 4.1&2: 12–19.

Hahlo, H. R. and E. Kahn (1960), *The Union of South Africa: The Development of its Laws and Constitution*, London: Stevens.

Hahlo, H. R. and E. Kahn (1968), *The South African Legal System and Its Background*, Cape Town: Juta.

Hall, M. (1984), 'The burden of tribalism: the social context of Southern African iron Age studies', *American Antiquity* 49.3: 455–67.

Hall, M. and P. Bombardella (2005), 'Las Vegas in Africa', *Journal of Social Archaeology* 5.1: 5–24.

Hammerton, J. (1946), *Child of Wonder: An Intimate Biography of Arthur Mee*, London: Hodder & Stoughton.

Hammond-Tooke, W. D. (2008), 'Cattle symbolism in Zulu culture', in B. Carton, J. Laband and J. Sithole, eds, *Zulu Identities: Being Zulu, Past and Present*, Pietermaritzburg: University of KwaZulu-Natal Press, 62–68.

Hanson, N. (1952), 'Symposium: notes for an address on man-made Johannesburg', *South African Architectural Record* 37.1: 3–6.

Hanson, V. D. (2007), 'Armies for democracy – past, present, and future', *American Spectator* (July/August 2007).

Harber, R. (1992), 'Union style architecture', *NIA: Journal of the Natal Institute of Architects* 3.4: 7–8.

Hardwick, L. (2003), *Reception Studies*, Oxford: Oxford University Press.

Hardwick, L. (2008), 'Translated classics around the millennium: vibrant hybrids or shattered icons?', in A. Lianeri and V. Zajko, eds, *Translation and the Classic: Identity as Change in the History of Culture*, Oxford: Oxford University Press, 341–66.

Hardwick, L. and C. Gillespie, eds (2007), *Classics and Post-Colonial Worlds*, Oxford: Oxford University Press.

Harris, J. and G. Stamp (1977), *Silent Cities: An Exhibition of the Memorial and Cemetery Architecture of the Great War*, London: Royal Institute of British Architects.

Haskell, F. and N. Penny (1982), *Taste and the Antique: The Lure of Classical Sculpture, 1500–1900*, New Haven: Yale.

Hauman, R. ed. (1978), *Kennis: Die Eerste Afrikaanse Ensiklopedie in Kleur*, Kaapstad: Kennis-Uitgewers.

Haverfield, F. (1905), 'The Romanization of Roman Britain', *Proceedings of the British Academy* 2: 185–217.

Haverfield, F. (1915), *The Romanization of Roman Britain*, Oxford: Clarendon.

Hearn, F. (2003), *Ideas that Shaped Buildings*, Cambridge, MA: MIT Press.

Heathcote, E. (2010), 'Meaning from Floor to Ceiling', *Financial Times: House and Home*, 26 June 2010.

Heese, J. de V. (1947), 'Ons groot kinderboek', *Die Huisgenoot*, 19 September 1947, 21.

Hegel, G. W. F. (1872), *Lectures on the Philosophy of History*, tr. J. Sibree, London: Bell and Deldy.

Hemmy, G. (1998), *Dissertatio juridica inauguralis de testimoniis Aethiopum, Chinensium aliorumque paganorum in India orientali*, tr. M. L. Hewett, Cape Town: privately published, original 1770.

Henderson, W. J. (2004), 'The Classical Association of South Africa: April 1956–January 1961', *Akroterion* 49: 89–109.

Henderson, W. J. (2005), 'The Classical Association of South Africa: February 1961–July 1966', *Akroterion* 50: 109–23.

Henderson, W. J. (2006), 'The Classical Association of South Africa: July 1966–January 1971', *Akroterion* 51: 135–56.

Henderson, W. J. (2007), 'The Classical Association of South Africa: January 1971–January 1975', *Akroterion* 52: 99–114.

Henderson, W. J. (2008), 'The Classical Association of South Africa: January 1975–January 1979', *Akroterion* 53: 81–98.

Henderson, W. J. (2010), 'The Classical Association of South Africa: February 1979–January 1981', *Akroterion* 55: 87–115.

Henderson, W. J. (2013), 'The Classical Association of South Africa, 1908–1956', *Akroterion* 58: 123–50.

Henderson, W. J. (2014), 'The Classical Association of South Africa: February 1981-January 1983', *Akroterion* 59: 123–40.

Herbert, G. (1975), *Martienssen and the International Style: The Modern Movement in South Africa*, Cape Town: Balkema.

Hersey, G. L. (1988), *The Lost Meaning of Classical Architecture: Speculations on Ornament from Vitruvius to Venturi*, Cambridge, MA: MIT Press.

Herwitz, D. (2012), *Heritage, Culture, and Politics in the Postcolony*, New York: Columbia University Press.

Heymans, R. and S. Theart-Peddle (2009), *The Voortrekker Monument: Visitor's Guide and Souvenir*, Pretoria: Voortrekker Monument and Nature Reserve (1st edition 1986).

Higgins, D. (1987), *Pattern Poetry: Guide to an Unknown Literature*, Albany: State University of New York Press.

Higgs, C. (1997), *The Ghost of Equality: The Public Lives of D. D. T. Jabavu of South Africa, 1885–1959*, Athens, OH: Ohio University Press.

Hills, H. (2005), 'Architecture and affect: Leon Battisti Alberti and edification', in P. Gouk and H. Hills, eds, *Representing Emotions: New Connections in the Histories of Art, Music and Medicine*, Aldershot: Ashgate, 89–108.

Hilton, J. (1993), 'Peoples of Azania', *Electronic Antiquity* 1.5 http://scholar.lib.vt .edu/ejournals/ElAnt/V1N5/hilton.html

Hilton, J. (2004), 'The classical names given to slaves at the Western Cape in the eighteenth century', *Nomina Africana* 18.1–2: 18–36.

Hilton, J. L. (2005), 'Lucian and the Great Moon Hoax of 1835', *Akroterion* 50: 87–108.

Hilton, J. L. (2006a), '"Chamei-me Adamastor": naming the spirit of the Cape in Luis Vaz de Camões' Lusiads', *Nomina Africana* 20: 3–15.

Hilton, J. (2006b), 'The Herschel obelisk, classics, and Egyptomania at the Cape', *Akroterion* 51: 117–34.

Hilton, J. (2007a), 'The influence of Roman law on the practice of slavery at the Cape of Good Hope (1652–1834)', *Acta Classica* 50: 1–14.

Hilton, J. (2007b), 'Introduction', in J. Hilton and A. Gosling (2007), 11–40.

Hilton, J. (2009), 'Adamastor, gigantomachies, and the literature of exile in Camões' Lusíads', *AUMLA* 112: 1–23.

Hilton, J. (2011), 'The influence of classical ideas on the anti-slavery debate at the Cape of Good Hope, South Africa (1795–1834)', in E. Hall, R. Alston and J. McConnell, eds, *Ancient Slavery and Abolition: From Hobbes to Hollywood*, Oxford: Oxford University Press, 103–24.

Hilton, J. (2013), 'A democratic turn in the reception of Roman-Dutch law of treason in South Africa?', L. Hardwick and S. Harrison, eds, *Classics in the Modern World: A Democratic Turn?* Oxford: Oxford University Press, 47–61.

Hilton, J. and A. Gosling, eds (2007), *Alma Parens Originalis? The Reception of Classical Ideas in Africa, Europe, Cuba, and the United States*, Oxford: Peter Lang.

Hingley, R. (2000), *Roman Officers and English Gentlemen: The Imperial Origins of Roman Archaeology*, London: Routledge.

Hingley, R. (2001), 'Images of Rome', in R. Hingley, ed., *Images of Rome: Perceptions of Ancient Rome in Europe and the United States in the Modern Age*, Portsmouth, RI: Journal of Roman Archaeology, 7–22.

Hingley, R. (2005), *Globalizing Roman Culture: Unity, Diversity and Empire*, London: Routledge.

Hirson, B. (2001), *The Cape Town Intellectuals: Ruth Schechter and her Circle, 1907–1934*, Johannesburg: Witwatersrand University Press.

Hirst, M. (1998), 'The Xhosa', in P. Magubane, ed., *Vanishing Cultures of South Africa: Changing Customs in a Changing World*, London et al.: Struik, 12–33.

Hobbs, P. and E. Rankin (2011), *Listening to Distant Thunder: The Art of Peter Clarke*, Johannesburg: Standard Bank.

Hobsbawm, E. and T. Ranger, eds (1983), *The Invention of Tradition*, Cambridge: Cambridge University Press.

Hoffmann, S.-L. (1994), 'Sakraler Monumentalismus um 1900: Das Leipziger Völkerschlachtdenkmal', in R. Koselleck and M. Jeismann, eds, *Der politische Totenkult, Kriegerdenkmäler in der Moderne*, Munich: Wilhelm Fink Verlag, 249–80.

Hofmeyr, J. H. (1920), 'Imperialism and liberty in ancient Rome', in J. H. Hofmeyr and T. J. Haarhoff, *Studies in Ancient Imperialism*, Johannesburg: Council of Education.

Hofmeyr, J. H. (1929a), 'The achievement of Roman imperialism', *CASA P&SP* 1: 5–14.

Hofmeyr, J. H. (1929b), 'South Africa after the elections', *Foreign Affairs* 8: 130–34.

Hofmeyr, J. H. (1937), 'The approach to the Native Problem', *Journal of the Royal African Society* 36: 270–97.

Hogben, L. (1998), *Lancelot Hogben, Scientific Humanist: An Unauthorized Autobiography*, ed. A. and A. Hogben, Woodbridge: Merlin Press.

Holland, B. (1901), *Imperium et Libertas: A Study in History and Politics*, London: Edward Arnold.

Houston, G. F. and J. Ngculu (2014), *Chris Hani: Voices of Liberation*, Cape Town: HSRC Press.

Hölscher, T. (2003), 'Images of war in Greece and Rome: between military practice, public memory and cultural symbolism', *Journal of Roman Studies* 93: 1–17.

Huber, U. (1939), *Heedendaegse Rechtsgeleertheyt as The Jurisprudence of my Time*, tr. P. Gane, 5th edition, Durban: Butterworth.

Hussey, C. (1950), *The Life of Sir Edwin Lutyens*, London: Country Life.

Hutter, P. (1990), *Die feinste Barbarei: das Völkerschlachtdenkmal bei Leipzig*, Mainz am Rhein: Philipp von Zabern.

Huyssen, H. (2006), Remember Dido, Così Facciamo, Ensemble für alte und neue Musik, Mucavi Records.

Inglis, K. S. (2005), *Sacred Places: War Memorials in the Australian Landscape*, Melbourne: Melbourne University Press (1st edition 1998).

Irving, R. G. (1981), *Indian Summer: Lutyens, Baker and Imperial Delhi.* New Haven: Yale University Press.

Irving, R. G. (1982), 'Architecture for empire's sake: Lutyens's Palace for Delhi', *Perspecta* 18: 7–23.

Isaac, B. (2004), *The Invention of Racism in Classical Antiquity*, Princeton: Princeton University Press.

Iziko Museums of Cape Town, 'Our name'. www.iziko.org.za/iziko/ourname.html

Iziko Museums of Cape Town (2006), 'Transformation of Iziko Slave Lodge under way', press release, issued 25 May 2006.

van Jaarsveld, F. A. (1961), *The Awakening of Afrikaner Nationalism, 1868–1881*, tr. F. R. Metrowich, Cape Town: Human & Rousseau.

Jabavu, D. D. T. (1920), *The Black Problem: Papers and Addresses on Various Native Problems*, Lovedale: The Book Department.

Jabavu, D. D. T. (1922), *John Tengu Jabavu, A Great Bantu Patriot*, Alice: Lovedale Institution Press.

Jabavu, D. D. T. (1928), *The Segregation Fallacy and Other Papers: A Native View of Some South African Inter-Racial Problems*, Alice: Lovedale Institution Press.

Jabavu, D. D. T. (1929), 'Higher education and the professional training of Bantu', *South African Journal of Science* 26: 934–36.

Jabavu, D. D. T. (1937), 'The child as he comes to school', in E. G. Malherbe, ed., *Educational Adaptations in a Changing Society*, Cape Town and Johannesburg: Juta, 432–35.

Jabavu, D. D. T. (n. d.), *The Influence of English on Bantu Literature*, Alice: Lovedale Press (1943?).

Jabavu, N. (1960), *Drawn in Colour: African Contrasts*, London: John Murray.

Jabavu, N. (1963), *The Ochre People: Scenes from a South African Life*, London: John Murray.

Jacobs, J. U. (2002), 'Zakes Mda's The Heart of Redness: the novel as Umngqokolo', *Kunapipi* 24: 224–36.

Jansen, J. and P. Vale, eds (2011), *Consensus Study on the Study of the Humanities in South Africa: Status, Prospects and Strategies*, Pretoria: Academy of Science of South Africa.

Jay, P., ed. (1973), *The Greek Anthology and Other Ancient Greek Epigrams*, London: Allen Lane.

Jencks, C. (1991), *Post-Modern Triumphs in London*, London: Academy Editions.

Jenkins, I. (1990), 'The acquisition and supply of casts of the Parthenon sculptures by the British Museum, 1835–1939', *Annual of the British School of Athens* 85: 89–114.

Jenkins, I. (1992), *Archaeologists and Aesthetes in the Sculpture Galleries of the British Museum, 1800–1939*, London: The British Museum Press.

Jenkyns, R. (1980), *The Victorians and Ancient Greece*, Oxford: Blackwell.

Jenkyns, R. (1991), *Dignity and Decadence: Victorian Art and the Classical Inheritance*, London: HarperCollins.

Jeppesen, K. (2002), *The Maussolleion at Halikarnassos: Reports of the Danish Archaeological Expedition to Bodrum*, vol. 5, *The Superstructure, A Comparative Analysis of the Architectural, Sculptural, and Literary Evidence*, Aarhus: Aarhus University Press.

Johns, S. (1973), Protest and Hope, 1882–1934, in T. Karis and G. M. Carter, eds *From Protest to Challenge: A Documentary History of African Politics in South Africa, 1882–1990*, vol. I: Stanford: Hoover Institution Press.

Johnson, B. (2006), *The Dream of Rome*, London: HarperPress.

Johnson Barker, B. (2003), *The Castle of Good Hope from 1666*, Cape Town: The Castle Military Museum.

Jones, P. R. (2006), 'The sociology of architecture and the politics of building: the discursive construction of Ground Zero', *Sociology* 40.3, 549–65.

Jourdan, P. (1910), *Cecil Rhodes: His Private Life by his Private Secretary*, London: The Bodley Head.

Joyce, J. (1968), *Ulysses*, Harmondsworth: Penguin, new edition (original published 1922).

Judd, D. (2001), *Empire: The British Imperial Experience from 1765 to the Present*, London: Phoenix.

Juta, J. (1972), *Background in Sunshine: Memories of South Africa*, New York: Charles Scribner's Sons.

Juta, R. (1909), *The Masque of the Silver Trees*, Cape Town: Juta.

Juta, R. (1924), *Cannes and the Hills*, London: Martin Secker.

Kateb, G. (2006), 'Socratic integrity', in *Patriotism and Other Mistakes*, New Haven: Yale University Press, 215–44.

Katkov, G. (1969), *The Trial of Bukharin*, New York: Stein and Day.

Kathrada, A. M. (2004), *Memoirs*, Cape Town: Zebra Press.

Kathrada, A. (2006), *Ahmed Kathrada's Notebook from Robben Island*, ed. S. Venter, Cape Town: Jacana.

Kathrada, A. M., H. Deacon, et al. (1996), *Esiqithini: The Robben Island Exhibition*, Cape Town: South African Museum.

Kaufmann, T. DaC. (1997), *Court, Cloister, and City: The Art and Culture of Central Europe, 1450–1800*, Chicago: University of Chicago Press.

Keath, M., 'The Baker School: a continuing tradition, 1902–1940', in R. C. Fisher, S. le Roux, and E. Maré, eds, *Architecture of the Transvaal*, Pretoria: University of South Africa, 1998, 79–97.

Keeley, E. and P. Sherrard, tr. (1966), *Four Greek Poets: C. P. Cavafy, George Seferis, Odysseus Elytis, Nikos Gatsos*, Harmondsworth: Penguin.

Keller, K. and H.-D. Schmidt (1995), *Vom Kult zur Kulisse: das Völkerschlachtdenkmal als Gegenstand der Geschichtskultur*, Leipzig: Leipziger Universitäts-Verlag.

Kennedy, R. F. (1971), *Catalogue of Pictures in the Africana Museum*, vol. 6, Johannesburg: Africana Museum.

Keown, G. (2001), 'The Irish Race Conference, 1922, reconsidered', *Irish Historical Studies* 32 (127): 365–76.

Kingsley, C. (1864), *The Roman and the Teuton: A Series of Lectures Delivered Before the University of Cambridge*, London: Macmillan and Co.

Kirby-Hirst, M. A. (2004), *The Future in the Past: Belief in Magical Divination and Other Methods of Prophecy Among the Archaic and Classical Greeks and Among the Zulu in South Africa During the Late Nineteenth and Early Twentieth Centuries*, unpublished MA dissertation, University of KwaZulu-Natal, Durban.

Kirk, G. E. (1939), review of Farrington 1939 (1965), *Journal of Hellenic Studies* 59: 298–99.

Kitto, H. D. F. (1959), *Form and Meaning in Drama*, London: Methuen.

Kitto, H. D. F. (1973), *Greek Tragedy*, London: Methuen.

Kluppels, A. (2009), *'The Struggle to Become South African'. National Identity and Collective Memory in South Africa: Reconciliation Day*, MA thesis, Rotterdam: Erasmus Universiteit. http://hdl.handle.net/2105/6402.

Kohler, A. (2009), 'Thinking through puppets', in J, Taylor, ed., *Handspring Puppet Company*, Johannesburg: David Krut Publishing, 42–49.

Kondlo, K. (2009), *In the Twilight of the Revolution: The Pan Africanist Congress of Azania (South Africa), 1959–1994*, Basel: Basler Afrika Bibliographien.

Kriel, D. (2009), 'In memoriam G. van N. Viljoen (11.09.1926–29.03.2009)', *Acta Classica* 52: vii–x.

Krikler, J. (2005), *The Rand Revolt*, Johannesburg and Cape Town: Jonathan Ball (first published as *White Rising: The 1922 Insurrection and Social Killing in South Africa*, Manchester: Manchester University Press, 2005).

Kruger, C. and E. Pretorius (2009), 'Alternative narrative of the Voortrekker Monument: the contribution of black labour to the construction of the Voortrekker Monument (1931-1949)', unpublished manuscript, Voortrekker Monument Heritage Site, Pretoria.

Kytzler, B. (2000), 'Gysbert Hemmys Hamburger *Oratio vom Kap der Guten Hoffnung*', in A. Haltenhoof and F. H. Mutschler, eds, *Hortus Litterarum Antiquarum. Festschrift für Hans Armin Gärtner zum 70. Geburtstag*, Heidelberg: Winter, 323–32.

L. R. (1947), 'Loosening the fetters: two significant new trends in Afrikaans literature: D. R. Church's losing fight', *The Forum*, 8 November 1947, 25–28.

Laing, S. (1892), *Human Origins*, London: Watts & Co.

Lambert, M. (2011), *The Classics and South African Identities*, London: Duckworth.

Lane, M. (2007), '"Gadfly in God's own country": Socrates in twentieth-century America', in M. Trapp, ed., *Socrates in the Nineteenth and Twentieth Centuries*, Aldershot: Ashgate, 205–26.

Lashbrook, A. M. (1960), *Lucius Ampelius, Liber Memorialis*, dissertation University of Pennsylvania.

Laski, M. (1987), *From Alm to Pine: Rudyard Kipling Abroad and at Home*, London: Sidgwick and Jackson.

Lechtman, H. and L. Hobbs (1986), 'Roman concrete and Roman architectural revolution, ceramics and civilization', in W. D. Kingery, ed., *High Technology Ceramics: Past, Present, Future*, Westerville, OH: American Ceramics Society, 81–128.

Lenta, M. (2005), review of Hacksley and Maclennan 2004, *English in Africa* 32.2: 243–6.

van Leeuwen, S. (1881–86), *Het Roomsch-Hollandsch Recht as Commentaries on Roman-Dutch Law*, tr. J. G. Kotzé, London: Stevens.

Lexicon Iconographicum Mythologiae Classicae II, Zurich and Munich: Artemis & Winkler, 1984.

van Lill, D., ed. (2010), Britannica Junior: Ensiklopedie vir Suidelike Afrika, 10 vols., Parklands: Jacklin.

Livingstone, D. (1962), 'The Passionate Bacteriologist to His Love', *A Medical Bulletin* 10.1: 28.

Livingstone, D. (1964a), 'Aphrodite's Saturday Night', *London Magazine* 4.8: 20–21.

Livingstone, D. (1964b), *Sjambok and Other Poems from Africa*, London: Oxford University Press.

Livingstone, D. (1965), 'Nereids', *New Contrast* 4.1: 44 = *Outposts* 66: 9.

Livingstone, D. (1965–66), 'Four poems', London Magazine 5.10: 35–38.

Livingstone, D. (1966), 'Leaving school—XII', *London Magazine* 6.7: 51–62.

Livingstone, D. (1968a), 'Tales from the Tower of Babel', *The Purple Renoster* 8: 52–60.

Livingstone, D. (1968b), 'The sleep of my lions', *Contrast* 5.3: 7.

Livingstone, D. (1968c), 'Old mortalities', *New Nation*, January 1968: 14.

Livingstone, D. (1975), 'A poet speaks of his craft', *Natal Education Department Bulletin* 13: 5–27.

Livingstone, D. (1978), *The Anvil's Undertone*, Johannesburg: Ad Donker.

Livingstone, D. (1984), *Selected Poems*, Craighall: Ad Donker.

Livingstone, D. (1985), 'The science of poetry and the poetry of science', *English Academy Review* 3: 89–101.

Lloyd, C. (1985), review of Haskell and Penny 1982, *English Historical Review* 100 (395): 415.

Lockhart, J. G. and C. M. Woodhouse (1963), *Cecil Rhodes: The Colossus of Southern Africa*, London: Hodder and Stoughton.

Lodge, T. (1983), *Black Politics in South Africa Since 1945*, New York: Longman.

Lodge, T. (2006), *Mandela: A Critical Life*, Oxford: Oxford University Press.

Louw, B. and F. van Rensburg, eds (1997), *Bestendige Binnevuur: Perspektiewe op Gerrit Viljoen*, Cape Town: Tafelberg.

Lucas, C. P. (1912), *Greater Rome and Greater Britain*, Oxford: Clarendon Press.

Lulat, Y. G.-M. (2005), *A History of African Higher Education from Antiquity to the Present: A Critical Synthesis*, Westport, CT: Prager.

Lyotard, J.-F. (1984), *The Postmodern Condition: A Report on Knowledge*, tr. G. Bennington, Minneapolis: University of Minnesota Press (French original 1979).

McCracken, D. P., ed. (1996), *Ireland and South Africa in Modern Times (Southern African-Irish Studies 3)*, Durban, 1996, including his papers, 'Irish identity in twentieth-century South Africa', 7–45; 'The Irish Republican Association of South Africa, 1920–2', 46–66.

MacIntyre, A. (1998), 'Politics, philosophy, and the common good', in K. Knight, ed., *The MacIntyre Reader*, Oxford: Polity Press, 235–54.

Mackay, E. A. (1992), 'In the museum: Museum of Classical Archaeology, University of Natal', *Scholia* 1: 140–141.

Mackay, E. A., (1993a), 'A fragment attributed to the Centaur Painter', *Scholia* 2: 149–52.

Mackay, E. A. (1993b), 'The oral shaping of culture', *Scholia* 2 104–14.

Mackay, E. A. (1995), 'In the museum: Museum of Classical Archaeology, University of Natal', *Scholia* 4: 160–61.

Mackay, E. A. (1998), 'In the museum: Museum of Classical Archaeology, University of Natal', *Scholia* 7: 171–72.

Mackenzie, C. (2009), 'Thanking and creating: issues in the translation of ancient Greek literature into isiZulu', unpublished seminar paper, University of KwaZulu-Natal Pietermaritzburg.

Mackenzie, J. M. (2009), *Museums and Empire: Natural History, Human Cultures and Colonial Identities*, Manchester: Manchester University Press.

McKnight, T. L. and D. Hess (2000), *Physical Geography: A Landscape Appreciation*, Upper Saddle River, NJ: Prentice Hall.

Maclean Todd, J. and J. Maclean Todd, eds (1955–1960), *Voices from the Past: A Classical Anthology for the Modern Reader*, 2 vols, London: Arrow Books.

MacMillan, H. (2014), *Chris Hani*, Auckland Park: Jacana.

Macnab, R., ed. (1958), *Poets in South Africa: An Anthology*, Cape Town: Maskew Miller.

McNutt, J. K. (1990), 'Plaster casts after antique sculpture: their role in the elevation of public taste and in American art instruction', *Studies in Art Education: A Journal of Issues and Research* 31.3: 158–67.

Madden, F. and D. K. Fieldhouse, eds (1982), *Oxford and the Idea of Commonwealth: Essays Presented to Sir Edgar Williams*, London: Croom Helm.

Maguire, M. (2012), *Southern Myths*, Christchurch: PaperGraphica.

Mahaffy, J. P. (1879), *Social Life in Greece*, 4th edition, London (n. p.).

Mahaffy, J. P. (1887), *Alexander's Empire*, New York: G. P. Putnam (digital reprint 2014).

Mahaffy, J. P. (1892), *Problems in Greek History*, London (n. p.).

Mahaffy, J. P. (1897), *A Survey of Greek Civilization*, London (n. p.).

Makgoba, M. W. (1999), ed., *African Renaissance: The New Struggle*, Cape Town: Mafube and Tafelberg.

Malan, R. (1991), *My Traitor's Heart*, London: Vintage.

Malherbe, E. G., ed. (1937), *Educational Adaptations in a Changing Society*, Cape Town and Johannesburg: Juta.

Mandela, N. (1994a), *Long Walk to Freedom: The Autobiography of Nelson Mandela*, Boston: Little Brown, 1994.

Mandela, N. (1994b), 'Statement by President Nelson Mandela at the OAU meeting of heads of state and governments, Tunis, 13 June 1994', www.anc.org.za/show.php?id=4888

Mangcu, X. (2014), *The Arrogance of Power: South Africa's Leadership Meltdown*, Cape Town: Tafelberg.

Mare, E. A. (2002), 'The aesthetics of ideology: the vicissitude of monuments', *South African Journal of Cultural History* 16.2: 15–24.

Markell, A., M. Hall and C. Schrire (1995), 'The historical archaeology of Vergelegen, an early farmstead at the Cape of Good Hope', *Historical Archaeology* 29.1: 10–34.

Markoe, G. E. (2001), *The Phoenicians*, Berkeley: University of California Press.

Marks, S. and S. Trapido (1979), 'Lord Milner and the South African state', *History Workshop* 8: 50–80.

Marks, S. and S. Trapido (2004), 'Cecil John Rhodes', in L. Goldman, ed., *Oxford Dictionary of National Biography*, Oxford: Oxford University Press, 592–603.

Marlowe, J. (1972), *Cecil Rhodes: The Anatomy of Empire*, London: Elek.

Marschall, S. (2001), 'The search for essence: "Africanness" in 20th century South African architecture', *South African Humanities* 13: 139–54.

Martienssen, R. D. (1964), *The Idea of Space in Greek Architecture, With Special Reference to the Doric Temple and its Setting*, 2nd edition, Johannesburg: Witwatersrand University Press.

Marx, C. (1998), *Im Zeichen des Ochsenwagen. Der radikale Afrikaaner-Nationalismus in Südafrika und die Geschichte der Ossewabrandweg*, Berlin: Lit.

Masters, S. (2008), 'In the museum: Containing Antiquity – an exhibition in the Sasol Art Museum, Stellenbosch', *Akroterion* 53: 99–109.

Matthaeus, A. (1987–1994), *On Crimes*, tr. M. L. Hewett, Cape Town: Juta.

Matthews, J. (1975), *Western Aristocracies and Imperial Court, AD 364–425*, Oxford: Clarendon.

Matthews, L. (2012), review of Lambert 2011, *Bryn Mawr Classical Review* 2012.01.10, http://bmcr.brynmawr.edu/2012/2012-01-10.html.

Matthews, Z. K. (1946), 'Native education in South Africa during the last twenty-five years', *South African Outlook* 76 (905): 138–41.

Matthews, Z. K. (1950), 'Race relations and the universities', *South African Outlook* 80 (955): 164–65.

Matthews, Z. K. (1959), 'Professor D. D. T. Jabavu', *Race Relations Journal* 26: 83–85.

Matthews, Z. K. (1981), *Freedom for My People: The Autobiography of Z. K. Matthews, Southern Africa, 1901 to 1968*, ed. M. Wilson, Cape Town and Johannesburg: David Philip.

Maylam, P. (2005), *The Cult of Rhodes: Remembering an Imperialist in Africa*, Cape Town: David Philip.

Mbeki, T. (1996), 'I am an African', speech at the adoption of the The Republic of South Africa Constitution Bill, 8 May 1996, Cape Town www.anc.org.za/show.php?id=4322

Mbeki, T. (2005), 'The African Renaissance: challenges of development and security in the new millennium', *Distinguished Lecture Series, National War College*, no. 5, Abuja: African Centre for Strategic Research and Training.

Mbembe, A. (2008), 'Aesthetics of superfluity', in S. Nuttall and A. Mbembe, eds, *Johannesburg: The Elusive Metropolis*, Johannesburg: Witwatersrand University Press, 37–67.

Mdudumane, K. (2005), *The Historical Productions of Cecil John Rhodes in Twentieth-Century Cape Town*, MA thesis, University of the Western Cape.

Mee, A., ed. (1908–25), *The Children's Encyclopedia*, 8 vols., London: Educational Book Co. (2nd edition, 10 vols., 1925).

Meier, C. (2010), *Das Gebot zu vergessen und die Unabweisbarkeit des Erinnerns. Vom öffentlichen Umgang mit schlimmer Vergangenheit*, München: Siedler.

Merivale, C. (1865), *History of the Romans Under the Empire*, London: Longman.

Merrington, P. (1995), 'Pageantry and primitivism: Dorothea Fairbridge and the "Aesthetics of Union"', *Journal of Southern African Studies* 21.4: 643–56.

Merrington, P. (2001), 'A staggered orientalism: the Cape-to-Cairo imaginary', *Poetics Today*, 22.2: 323–42.

Merrington, P. (2006), 'Cape Dutch Tongaat: a case study in "heritage"', *Journal of Southern African Studies* 32.4: 683–700.

Meskell, L. (2002), 'Negative heritage and past mastering in archaeology', *Anthropological Quarterly* 75.3: 557–74.

Meskell, L. (2012), *The Nature of Heritage: The New South Africa*, Malden, MA: Wiley-Blackwell.

Meskell, L. and L. Weiss (2006), 'Coetzee on South Africa's past: remembering in the time of forgetting', *American Anthropologist* 108.1: 88–99.

Metcalf, T. (1980), 'Architecture and empire', *History Today* 30.12 (December 1980), 7–12.

Mgqolozana, T. (2009), *A Man Who Is Not a Man*, Pietermaritzburg: University of KwaZulu-Natal Press.

Michell, Sir L. Ll. (1910), *The Life and Times of the Right Honourable Cecil John Rhodes, 1853–1902*, 2 vols., London: Edward Arnold.

Miller, M. (2002), 'City beautiful on the Rand: Lutyens and the planning of Johannesburg', in A. Hopkins and G. Stamp, eds, *Lutyens Abroad*, London: British School and Rome, 159–68.

Moerdijk, G. (1917), 'Greek history and Greek temples', *Journal of the Association of Transvaal Architects* 8.2 (December 1917): 109–10.

Moerdijk, G. (1919), *Kerkgeboue vir Suidafrika*, Johannesburg: privately published.

Moerdyk, G. (1935), *Die geskiedenis van boukuns*, Pretoria: J. L. van Schaik.

Molora (2007), Programme and Flyer for a production at the Oxford Playhouse (12–16 June 2007).

Momigliano, A. (1941), review of Farrington 1939 (1965), *Journal of Roman Studies* 31: 149–57.

Montaigne, M. de (1965), 'Of vanity', in *The Complete Essays of Montaigne*, Stanford: Stanford University Press, 721–66.

Montesquieu, C. de S. (1965), *Considerations on the Causes of the Greatness of the Romans and their Decline*, tr. D. Lowenthal, New York: Free Press.

Moore, L. L. (2003), 'Lesbian migrations: Mary Renault's South Africa', *GLQ* 10: 23–46.

Morrison, D. R. ed. (2011), *The Cambridge Companion to Socrates*, Cambridge: Cambridge University Press.

Mostert, D. (1940), *Gedenkboek van die ossewaens op die pad van Suid-Afrika: eeufees: 1838–1939*, Cape Town: Nasionale Pers.

Muller, C. F. J. (1987), *Die Oorsprong van die Groot Trek*, Pretoria: UNISA Press (1st edition 1974).

Muller, C. F. J. (1990), *Sonop in die Suide: geboorte en groei van die Nasionale Pers 1915–1948*, Kaapstad: Nasionale Boekhandel.

Muller, T. (1925), *'n Inspirasie vir Jong Suid-Afrika*, Kaapstad: Nasionale Pers.

Mulligan, G. A. (1952), 'Bellum Juridicum (3): purists, pollutionists and pragmatists', *South African Law Journal* 69: 25–32.

Murphy, J. P. (1977), *Rufus Festus Avienus: Ora Maritima*, Chicago: Ares.

Murray, B. K. (1997), *Wits, the 'Open' Years: A History of the University of the Witwatersrand, Johannesburg, 1939–1959*, Johannesburg: Witwatersrand University Press.

Murray, J. (2014), '"These are our jewels": women and Classical education at Huguenot College', *Acta Classica* 57: 105–26.

Nagy, G. (1996), *Homeric Questions*, Austin: University of Texas Press.

Naidoo, J., 'Was the Retief-Dingane Treaty a fake?', *History in Africa* 12 (1985), 187–210.

Nash, A. (1985), *Colonialism and Philosophy: R. F. Alfred Hoernlé in South Africa, 1908–11*, MA thesis, University of Stellenbosch.

Nash, A. (2009), *The Dialectical Tradition in South Africa*, New York and London: Routledge.

Neander, A. (1850), *The Emperor Julian and His Generation: An Historical Picture*, tr. G. Valentine Cox, New York: J. C. Riker.

Neumeister, A. and E. Haeberle, eds (1897), *Völkerschlacht-Denkmal bei Leipzig: Deutsche Konkurrenzen*, vol. 7.1, Leipzig: Seemann.

Niebuhr, B. G., et al. (1835), *The History of Rome*, London: Taylor and Walton.

Nimmocks, W. (1968), *Milner's Young Men: The 'Kindergarten' in Edwardian Imperial Affairs*, London: Hodder & Stoughton.

Noodt, G. (2009), *The Three Books on Interest-bearing Loans and Interest*, tr. D. M. Kriel, Pretoria: Pulp.

Notopoulos, J. A. (1949), *The Platonism of Shelley*, Durham, NC: Duke University Press.

Notule van 20ste S.V.K. – Vergadering gehou in die Parlementshuis, Kaapstad, op Saterdag, 25 Januarie 1935 (also earlier incomplete minutes, undated).

O'Brien, T. H. (1979), *Milner: Viscount Milner of St James and Cape Town, 1854–1925*, London: Constable.

Official Guide: The Voortrekker Monument, Pretoria (1970), Pretoria: The Board of Control of the Voortrekker Monument, 7th edition (1st edition 1954).

Olivier, M. (1992), 'The Humphrey John Talbot collection in Cape Town', *Annals of the South African Cultural History Museum* 5.2: 3.

O'Meara, D. (1996), *Forty Lost Years: The Apartheid State and the Politics of the National Party, 1948–94*, Randburg: Ravan.

Otten, K., *Kate Otten Architects: profile*. Retrieved 17 January 2012 from Kate Otten Architects: www.kateottenarchitects.com/profile_main.html

Pagden, A. (2005), 'Fellow citizens and imperial subjects: conquest and sovereignty in Europe's overseas empires', *History and Theory* 44.4: 28–46.

Pagden, A. (2006), 'The empire's new clothes: from empire to federation, yesterday and today', *Common Knowledge* 12: 36–46.

Papenfus, T. (2010), *Pik Botha and His Times*, Pretoria: Litera.

Parker, G. (2010), 'Heraclitus on the highveld: the universalism (ancient and modern) of T. J. Haarhoff', in P. Vasunia and S. A. Stephens, eds, *Classics and National Cultures*, Oxford: Oxford University Press, 217–34.

Parker, H. N., tr. (2007), *Censorinus: The Birthday Book*, Chicago: University of Chicago Press.

Paton, A. (1965), *South African Tragedy: The Life and Times of Jan Hofmeyr*, New York: Scribner.

Peffer, J. (2005), 'Censorship and iconoclasm – unsettling monuments', *Res* 48 (Autumn 2005), 45–60.

Pelzer, A. N. (1979), *Die Afrikaner-Broederbond: Eerste 50 Jaar*, Kaapstad: Tafelberg.

Pemble, J. (1987), *The Mediterranean Passion: Victorians and Edwardians in the South*, Oxford: Oxford University Press.

Penn, N. (2005), *The Forgotten Frontier: Colonist and Khoisan on the Cape's Northern Frontier in the 18th Century*, Cape Town: Double Storey Books.

Percy, C. and J. Ridley, eds (1985), *The Letters of Edwin Lutyens to His Wife Lady Emily*, London: Collins.

Perrin, N. (1970), *Dr Bowdler's Legacy: A History of Expurgated Books in England and America*, London: Macmillan.

Philips, J. A. S. (1981), 'Alfred A. de Pass: benefactor of Groot Constantia', *Bulletin of the South African Cultural History Museum* 2: 5–13.

Phillips, H. (1993), *The University of Cape Town, 1918–1948: The Formative Years*, Cape Town: University of Cape Town Press.

Pillman, N. (1984), *Laurika Postma: 'n biografie*, Pretoria: De Jager-HAUM.

Pirro, R. C. (2011), *The Politics of Tragedy and Democratic Citizenship*, New York: Continuum.

Pitts, J. (2010), 'Hobson and the critique of liberal empire', *Raritan* 29: 8–22.

Plato (1975), *The Laws*, translated by T. J. Saunders, Harmondsworth: Penguin Books.

Plomer, W. C. F. (1933), *Cecil Rhodes*, London: Peter Davies.

Plotz, J. A. (1993), 'Latin for empire: Kipling's "Regulus" as a classics class for the ruling class', *The Lion and the Unicorn* 17: 152–67.

Pont, D. (1971–72), 'The transplantation of the Roman-Dutch law into South Africa', *Speculum Juris* 7: 3–17.

Pope, M. W. M. (1986), 'Epicureanism and the atomic swerve', *Symbolae Osloenses* 61: 77–97.

Porter, J. I., ed. (2006), *Classical Pasts: The Classical Traditions of Greece and Rome*, Princeton: Princeton University Press.

Potgieter, H. (1987), *Voortrekker Monument Pretoria*, Pretoria: Hennie's Secretarial Services.

Pottinger, B. (1988), *The Imperial Presidency: P. W. Botha, The First Ten Years*, Johannesburg: Southern Book Publishers.

Preller, G. S. (1917), *Piet Retief: lewensgeskiedenis van die Grote Voortrekker*, Pretoria: J.L. van Schaik, facsimile reprint *Scripta Africana Reeks II, Die Groot Trek* (1988).

Preller, G. S., ed. (1928), *Hoe ons aan Dingaansdag kom: Jan Bantjes se dagverhaal van die Winkommado*, Bloemfontein: Nasionale Pers.

Preller, G. S. (1937), *Andries Pretorius: lewensbeskrywing van die Voortrekker Kommandant-Generaal*, Johannesburg: The Afrikaans Press, facsimile reprint Scripta Africana Reeks II, Die Groot Trek (1988).

Prescott, O. (1956), 'Books of The Times', *New York Times* (17 October 1956), 33.

Pretorius, E. (2003), 'The Italians and the Voortrekker Monument', Paper presented to the Northern Transvaal GSSA branch on 18th August 2003 www.eggsa .org/articles/italians_and_voortrekker_monument_e.htm

Proculus Redivivus (1965), 'South African law at the crossroads, or What is our Common Law?', *South African Law Journal* 82: 17–25.

Purves, J. (1909), 'Camoens and the epic of Africa', *The State* 542–55 and 734–45.

Randall-MacIver, D. (1906), 'The Rhodesia Ruins: their probable origins and significance', *The Geographical Journal* 27.4: 325–36.

Rankin, E. (1991), 'Training and trading: the influence of tuition and the art market on some South African sculptors', *De Arte* 43 (April 1991), 5–25.

Rankin, E. (2013), 'Creating/curating cultural capital: monuments and museums for post-apartheid South Africa', *Humanities* 2.1: 72–98 www.mdpi.com/2076-0787/2/1/72

Reade, W. W. (1934), *The Martyrdom of Man*, London: Watts & Co.

Reich, E. (1890), *Graeco-Roman Institutions: From Anti-Evolutionist Points of View: Roman Law, Classical Slavery, Social Conditions*, Oxford: Parker.

Renault, M. (1956), *The Last of the Wine*, New York: Pantheon.

Renault, M. (1958), *The King Must Die*, New York: Pantheon.

Renault, M. (1966), *The Mask of Apollo*, New York: Pantheon.

Renault, M. (1969), *Fire from Heaven*, New York: Pantheon.

Renault, M. (1972), *The Persian Boy*, New York: Pantheon.

Renault, M. (1973), 'History in fiction', *Times Literary Supplement* 23 (March 1973), 315–16.

Renault, M. (1978), *The Praise Singer*, New York: Pantheon.

Renault, M. (1979), 'The fiction of history', *London Magazine* 18.12 (March 1979).

Renault, M. (1981), *Funeral Games*, New York: Pantheon.

Renault, M. (1988), *The Mask of Apollo*, New York: Vintage.

Renault, M. (1993), *The Charioteer*, New York: Harvest.

Renault, M. (2001), *The Bull from the Sea*, New York: Vintage.

Rich, P., Peter Rich Architects: Practice. Retrieved 17 January 2012 from Peter Rich Architects: www.peterricharchitects.co.za/practice.php

Ridley, J. (1998), 'Edwin Lutyens, New Delhi, and the architecture of imperialism', in P. Burroughs and A. J. Stockwell, eds, *Managing the Business of Empire: Essays in Honour of David Fieldhouse*, London: Frank Cass Publishers, 67–83.

Rist, J. M. (1972), *Epicurus: An Introduction*, Cambridge: Cambridge University Press.

Ritchie, David G. (1891), *Darwinism and Politics*, 2nd edition, London: Swan Sonnenschein.

Robert, Carl (1919), *Die antiken Sarkophag-Reliefs III. Einzelmythen*, Dritte Abteilung. *Niobiden – Triptolemos. Ungedeutet*, Berlin: G. Grote'sche Verlagsbuchhandlung.

Robertson, H. M. (1984), *A History of the University of Cape Town*, unpublished manuscript, UCT Libraries, Department of Manuscripts and Archives.

Rodekamp, V., ed. (2009), *Völkerschlachtdenkmal*: Stadtgeschichtliches Museum Leipzig, 3rd edition, Altenburg: Druckerei zu Altenburg.

Romanes, G. J. (1888), *Mental Evolution in Man: Origin of Human Faculty*, London: Kegan Paul, Trench & Co.

Romm, J. S. (1992), *The Edges of the Earth in Ancient Thought*, Princeton: Princeton University Press.

Ronca, I. (1992), 'Semper aliquid novi Africam adferre: philological afterthoughts on the Plinian reception of a pre-Aristotelian saying', *Akroterion* 37.3–4: 146–58.

Ross, M. H. (2007), *Cultural Contestations in Ethnic Conflict*, Cambridge: Cambridge University Press.

Ross, R. (1999), *A Concise History of South Africa*, Cambridge: Cambridge University Press.

Ross, R., A. K. Mager and B. Nasson, eds (2011), *The Cambridge History of South Africa*, vol. 2, Cambridge: Cambridge University Press.

Rotberg, R. I. (1988), *The Founder: Cecil Rhodes and the Pursuit of Power*, with the collaboration of M. F. Shore, Johannesburg & Cape Town: Jonathan Ball.

Roux, E. (1964), *Time Longer than Rope: A History of the Black Man's Struggle for Freedom in South Africa*, 2nd edition, Wisconsin: Wisconsin University Press.

Rowland, I. D. (2006), 'Raphael, Angelo Colocci, and the architectural orders', in M. W. Cole, ed., *Sixteenth-Century Italian Art*, Oxford: Blackwell, 511–31.

Ryan, A. J. and A. Gosling (2003), 'In the museum', *Akroterion* 48: 123–28.

Ryback, T. W. (2009), *Hitler's Private Library: The Books that Shaped His Life*, London: Bodley Head.

Sachs, A. (1996), *The Jail Diary of Albie Sachs*, New York: McGraw-Hill.

SACS = South African Communists Speak: Documents from the History of the South African Communist Party 1915–1980, London: Inkululeko, 1980.

Saddington, D. B. (1987), 'Some unpublished Hispano-Roman coins in the Mann Collection in the Cultural History Museum in Cape Town', *Akroterion* 32.3–4: 94–98.

Said, E. W. (1978), *Orientalism: Western Conceptions of the Orient*, New York: Vintage.

Said, E. W. (1993), *Culture and Imperialism*, London: Chatto & Windus.

Salazar, P.-J. (2002), *An African Athens: Rhetoric and the Shaping of Democracy in South Africa*, Mahwah, NJ: L. Erlbaum.

Sampson, A. (1999), *Mandela: The Authorized Biography*, London: HarperCollins.

Saul, J. S. and P. Bond (2014), *South Africa: The Present as History, from Mrs Ples to Mandela and Marikana*, Johannesburg: Jacana.

Schellekens, J. (1997), 'A note on the Dutch origins of South African colonial architecture', *Journal of the Society of Architectural Historians* 56.2: 204–6.

Scheub, H. (1996), *The Tongue is Fire: South African Storytellers and Apartheid*, Madison, WI: University of Wisconsin Press.

Scheub, H. (2002), *The Poem in the Story: Music, Poetry and Narrative*, Madison, WI: University of Wisconsin Press.

Schmitz, B. (1900), *Drei Kaiserdenkmäler: Ausgeführte Architekturwerke*, vols. 1–3, Berlin: Wasmuth.

Schneider, M. (2005), 'The Roman coin collection at Stellenbosch: a sequel', *Akroterion* 50: 67–85.

Schoeman, B. M. (1982), *Die Broederbond in die Afrikaner-Politiek*. Pretoria: Aktuele Publikasies.

Schoonees, P. (1991), *Inscriptions on Padrões, Postal Stones, Tombstones and Beacons*, South African Cultural History Museum: Cape Town.

Schoonraad, M. (1988), 'Suid-Afrikaanse kunstenaars se siening van die Groot Trek', *Lantern: Tydskrif vir Kennis en Kultur* 37.4 (October 1988), 75–82.

Schwenke, A. (2009), 'Die historiese marmerfries in die Voortrekkermonument', *Plus 50* 4/5 (October/November 2009), 16–17.

Scott, J. (1993), 'The future of Roman-Dutch Law: reflections and a suggestion', *De Jure* 26: 394–400.

Scruton, R. (1994), *The Classical Vernacular: Architectural Principles in an Age of Nihilism*, Manchester: Carcanet.

Seeley, J. R. (1870), *Lectures and Essays*, London: MacMillan.

Shaw, G. B. (1932) *The Adventures of the Black Girl in Her Search for God*, London: Constable.

Shell, R. C.-H. (1994), *Children of Bondage: A Social History of the Slave Society at the Cape of Good Hope, 1652–1838*, Johannesburg: Wits University Press.

Shelley, J. P. see Notopoulos.

Shepherd, N. (2008), 'Heritage', in N. Shepherd and S. Robins, eds, *New South African Keywords*, Auckland Park: Jacana, 116–28.

Sheppard, J. G. (1861), *The Fall of Rome, and the Rise of the New Nationalities: A Series of Lectures on the Connection Between Ancient and Modern History*, London: Routledge, Warne and Routledge.

Sitas, A. et al. (2011), *Charter for the Humanities and Social Sciences: Report Commissioned by the Minister of Higher Education*, Pretoria: Department of Higher Education and Training.

Smith, C. (1899), 'The "Tomb of Romulus"', *The Classical Review* 13.1: 87–88.

Smith, J. and B. Tromp (2009), *Hani: A Life Too Short: A Biography*, Johannesburg: Ball.

Smith, M. F. (1993), *Diogenes of Oinoanda: The Epicurean Inscription*, Naples: Bibliopolis.

Smith, N. (2009), *Die Afrikaner Broederbond: Belewinge van die Binnekant*, Pretoria: LAPA Uitgewers.

Smuts, F. (1960), 'Classical scholarship and the teaching of Classics at Cape Town and Stellenbosch', *Acta Classica* 3: 7–31.

Smuts, F. (1976), 'Die Klassieke in Suid-Afrika, 1930–1976', *Akroterion* 21.4: 11–21.

Snowball, J. D. and W. D. Snowball (2005), 'Five unpublished coins of Alexander the Great and his successors in the Rhodes University Collection', *Akroterion* 50: 13–26.

Soldevilla, R. M. (2006), *Martial Book IV: A Commentary*, Leiden: Brill.

Sophocles (1970), *Oedipus the Tyrant*, tr. L. Berkowitz and T. F. Brunner, New York: W. W. Norton and Company, Inc.

Sophocles (1982), *Three Theban Plays: Antigone, Oedipus the King, Oedipus at Colonus*, tr. R. Fagles, New York: Penguin.

Sophocles (1998), *Oedipus the King*, tr. D. Taylor, London: Methuen Drama.

South African Cultural History Museum, *Bulletin of the South African Cultural History Museum* 14 (1993).

South African Museum, *Annual Report to the Trustees of the South African Museum*, 1906.

South African Museum, *Annual Report to the Trustees*, 1890.

South African Museum, *Minutes of the South African Museum*, 1911.

South African Museum, *Minutes of the South African Museum*, 1929.

South African Museum, *Report to the Trustees of The South African Museum*, 1855 (1).

South African Museum, *Report to the Trustees of The South African Museum*, 1855 (2).

South African Museum. *Report to the Trustees of the South African Museum*, 1856, published as Government Notice no 24.

Souvenir of the Pageant in Commemoration of the Union of South Africa (1910), Cape Town: The Pageant Committee.

Sparks, A. (1994), *Tomorrow Is Another Country: The Inside Story of South Africa's Negotiated Revolution*, Sandton: Struik.

Spoerri, W. (1959), *Späthellenische Berichte über Welt, Kultur und Götter. Untersuchungen zu Diodor von Sizilien*, Basel: Friedrich Reinhardt.

Stamp, G. (1981), 'New Delhi', in C. Amery, M. Richardson and G. Stamp, eds, *Lutyens: The Work of the English Architect Sir Edwin Lutyens (1869–1944)*, London: Arts Council of Great Britain.

Stanford, W. B., and R. B. McDowell (1971), *Mahaffy: A Biography of an Anglo-Irishman*, London: Routledge.

Stead, W. T. (1902), *The Last Will and Testament of Cecil John Rhodes with Elucidatory Notes, To Which Are Appended Some Chapters Describing the Political and Religious Ideas of the Testator*, London: The Review of Reviews Office.

Steenkamp, A. C. (2006), 'Apartheid to democracy: representation and politics in the Voortrekker Monument and Red Location Museum', *Architectural Research Quarterly* 10: 249–54.

Steenkamp, A. C. (2008a), *Space, Power and the Body: The Civil and Uncivil as Represented in the Voortrekker Monument and the Native Township Model*, PhD thesis, Delft: Technische Universiteit.

Steenkamp, A. (2008b), 'Architecture rethought in relation to space, power and the body: a concise critical history of the Voortrekker Monument', *Journal of the South African Institute of Architects* (November/December 2008), 60–68.

Steenkamp, A. (2009a), 'Ambiguous associations: monuments referred to in the design of the Voortrekker Monument', *South African Journal of Art History* 26.3: 79–89.

Steenkamp, A. (2009b), 'A shared spatial symbolism: the Voortrekker Monument, the Völkerslachtdenkmal (sic) and Freemasonry', *South African Journal of Art History* 24.1: 150–60.

Steinmeyer, E. (2007), 'Post-apartheid Electra: In the City of Paradise', in L. Hardwick and C. Gillespie, eds., *Classics in Post-Colonial Worlds*, Oxford: Oxford University Press, 103–18.

Steinmeyer, E. (2009), 'Post-traumatic and post-modern: A South African Electra', *Akroterion* 54: 111–24.

Stevenson, M. (1997), *Old Masters and Aspirations: The Randlords, Art and South Africa*, PhD thesis, University of Cape Town.

Stevenson, M. (2002), *Art and Aspirations: The Randlords of South Africa and Their Collections*, Vlaeberg: Fernwood.

Steyn, J. C. (1998), *Van Wyk Louw: 'n lewensverhaal*, 2 vols., Kaapstad: Tafelberg.

Steynberg, C. (1982), *Coert Steynberg: 'n Outobiografie*, Roodepoort: CUM Boeke.

Steytler, F. A. (1958), ''n Voortrekkermonument te Pretoria: voorstel van pres. Kruger op 16 Desember 1888', *Historia: Official Organ of the Historical Association of South Africa* 3.1 3–7.

Style, C. (1982), 'The poetry of Douglas Livingstone', *London Magazine* 22.5/6: 92–96.

Suckau, E. de (1857), *Étude sur Marc-Aurèle. Sa vie et sa doctrine*, Paris: Durand.

le Sueur, G. (1913), *Cecil Rhodes: The Man and His Work*, London: John Murray.

Summers, R. F. H. (1975), *A History of the South African Museum, 1825–1975*, Cape Town: A. A. Balkema.

SVK see Sentrale Volksmonumente-Komitee.

Sweetman, D. (1993), *Mary Renault: A Biography*, New York: Harcourt Brace.

Taplin, O. (2003), *Greek Tragedy in Action*, 2nd edition. London: Routledge.

Tarapor, M. (1980), 'John Lockwood Kipling and British art education in India', *Victorian Studies* 24.1 (Autumn 1980): 53–81.

Tarn, W. W. (1933), Alexander the Great and the Unity of Mankind, London: Milford = 'Alexander the Great and the unity of mankind', *Proceedings of the British Academy* 19: 123–66; also reprinted in G. T. Griffith, ed., *Alexander the Great: The Main Problems*, Cambridge: Heffer, 1966, 243–86.

Tarn, W. W. (1948), *Alexander the Great*, 2 vols., Cambridge: Cambridge University Press.

Taylor, B. B. (1984), 'Rethinking colonial architecture: demythologising colonial architecture, forms and models', *MIMAR: Architecture in Development* 13: 16–25.

Taylor, B. B. (1986), 'Perspectives and limits on regionalism and architectural identity', *MIMAR: Architecture in Development* 19: 19–21.

Thacker, A. (2003), *Moving Through Modernity: Space and Geography in Modernism*, Manchester: Manchester University Press.

The Cape of Good Hope: Official Handbook of the City of Cape Town, Cape Town: Corporation of the City, 1911.

The Voortrekker Monument, Pretoria: Official Guide, Pretoria: Board of Control of the Voortekker Monument, 1954.

Thom, H. B., et al., eds (1966), *Stellenbosch 1866–1966: Honderd Jaar Hoër Onderwys*, Kaapstad: Nasionale Boekhandel Beperk.

Thomas, A. (1996), *Rhodes: The Race for Africa*, Johannesburg: Jonathan Ball.

Thompson, E. (1986), 'An interview with Douglas Livingstone', *Crux* 20.4: 3–12.

Thompson, L. (2001), *A History of South Africa*, 3rd edition, New Haven: Yale University Press.

Thomson, G. (1932), *Aeschylus, The Prometheus Bound*, edited with introduction, commentary and translation, Cambridge: Cambridge University Press.

Thomson, G. (1941), *Aeschylus and Athens: A Study in the Social Origins of Drama*, London: Lawrence and Wishart.

Tietze, A. (1995), *The Alfred de Pass Presentation to the South African National Gallery*, Cape Town: South African National Gallery.

Tillyard, K. (1988), *The Impact of Modernism: The Visual Arts in Edwardian England*, London: Routledge.

Topfstedt, T. (2009), '"Erhaben, von jeglicher persönlicher Beziehung und von jedem kleinen Zweck entbunden, steht das Werk in ruhiger Schönheit da": das Völkerschlachtdenkmal als Gesamtkunstwerk', in V. Rodekamp, ed., *Völkerschlachtdenkmal, Stadtgeschichtliches Museum Leipzig*, 3rd edition, Altenburg: Druckerei zu Altenburg, 8–43.

Tracy, M. (2008), *The World of the Edwardian Child, As Seen in Arthur Mee's Children's Encyclopædia, 1908–1910.* London: Hermitage.

Truth and Reconciliation Commission, Human Rights Violations, Submissions, Questions and Answers, Ebrahim Rassool, 2 June 1997, www.justice.gov.za/trc/special/trojan/rasool.htm

Turok, B., ed. (2010), *The Historical Roots of the ANC*, Auckland Park: Jacana.

Turok, B. (2014), *With My Head Above the Parapet: An Insider's Account of the ANC in Power*, Auckland Park: Jacana.

Tzonis, A. and L. Lefaivre (1987), *Classical Architecture: The Poetics of Order*, Cambridge, MA: MIT Press.

Ullyatt, A. G. (1976), 'An interview with Douglas Livingstone', *UNISA English Studies* 14.1: 45–49.

Van der Merwe, D. (1994), 'Es läßt sich nicht lesen: reflections on the status and continued relevance of the South African common law', *Tydskrif vir die Suid-Afrikaanse Reg* 1994.4: 660–81.

Van der Poel, J. (1951), *The Jameson Raid*, Oxford: Oxford University Press.

Van der Watt, L. (1997), '"Savagery and civilisation": race as a signifier of difference in Afrikaner nationalist art', *De Arte* 55 (April 1997): 36–47.

Van der Westhuysen, P. J. (1984), *Hennie Potgieter: Volkskunstenaar*, MA thesis, Pretoria: University of Pretoria. http://upetd.up.ac.za/thesis/available/etd-12072011-081616/

Van Reenen, T. P. (1996), 'The relevance of Roman (Dutch) law for legal integration in South Africa (with some lessons to be learnt from the African and European experiences)', *Fundamina* 2: 65–102.

Van Sittert, L. (2004), 'The nature of power: Cape environmental history, the history of ideas and neo-liberal historiography', *Journal of African History*, 45.2: 305–13.

Van Stekelenburg, A. V. (1988), 'Ex Africa semper aliquid novi: a proverb's pedigree', *Akroterion* 33.4: 114–20.

Van Stekelenburg, A. V. (2003), 'The Cape in Latin and Latin in the Cape in the 17th and 18th centuries', *Akroterion* 48: 89–109.

Van Stekelenburg, B. (1978), 'Coins of the Roman Republic from the collection of the University of Stellenbosch: a historical description', *Akroterion* 23.3: 9–23.

Van Weyenberg, A. (2008), '"Rewrite this ancient end!" staging transition in post-apartheid South Africa', *New Voices in Classical Reception Studies* 3 www2.open .ac.uk/ClassicalStudies/GreekPlays/newvoices/issue%203/Weyenberg.pdf

Van Wyk Louw, N. P. (1988), *Germanicus*, Cape Town: Nasionale Boekhandel, 1956. (Cf. Claassen 2013)

Van Wyk Smith, M., ed. (1988), *Shades of Adamastor: Africa and the Portuguese Connection: An Anthology of Poetry*, Grahamstown: Institute for the Study of English in Africa.

Van Wyk Smith, M. (2009), *The First Ethiopians: The Image of Africa and Africans in the Early Mediterranean World*, Johannesburg: Wits University Press.

Van Zyl, D. H. (1972), 'Die Regshistoriese Metode', *Tydskrif vir Hedendaagse Romeins-Hollandse Reg* 35: 19–37.

Van Zyl, D. H. (1979), *Geskiedenis van die Romeins-Hollandse Reg*, Durban: Butterworth.

Van Zyl, D. H. (1983), *History and Principles of Roman Private Law*, Durban: Butterworths.

Van Zyl, D. H. (1991a), *Justice and Equity in Cicero: A Critical Evaluation in Contextual Perspective*, Pretoria: Academica.

Van Zyl, D. H. (1991b), *Justice and Equity in Greek and Roman Legal Thought*, Pretoria: Academica.

Van Zyl, D. H. (2000), 'Roman-Dutch law: a South African perspective', in J. E. Spruit, W. J. Kamba and M. O. Hinz, eds, *Roman Law at the Crossroads*, Kenwyn: Juta, 169–82.

Van Zyl Smit, B. (2003), 'The reception of Greek tragedy in the "old" and the "new" South Africa', *Akroterion* 48: 3–20.

Van Zyl Smit, B. (2007), 'Medea in Afrikaans', in Hilton and Gosling (2007), 73–91.

Van Zyl Smit, B. (2008), 'Multicultural reception: Greek drama in South Africa in the late twentieth and early twenty-first centuries', in L. Hardwick and C. Stray, eds, *A Companion to Classical Receptions*, Malden and Oxford: Blackwell, 373–85.

Van Zyl Smit, B. (2014), 'Black Medeas', in D. Stuttard, ed., *Looking at Medea*, London: Bloomsbury, 157–66.

Vance, N. (1997), *The Victorians and Ancient Rome*, Oxford: Blackwell Publishers.

Varley, H. L. (1953), 'Imperialism and Rudyard Kipling', *Journal of the History of Ideas* 14: 124–35.

Vasunia, P. (2005), 'Greater Rome and Greater Britain', in B. Goff, ed., *Classics and Colonialism*, London: Duckworth, 38–64.

Vasunia, P. (2008), 'Greek, Latin, and the Indian civil service', in J. P. Hallett and C. Stray, eds, *British Classics Outside England: The Academy and Beyond*, Waco, TX: Baylor University Press, 61–93.

Venter, C. (1991), 'Die Voortrekker en die ingeboekte slawe wat die Groot Trek meegemaak het, 1835–1838', *Historia: Official Organ of the Historical Association of South Africa* 36: 14–29.

Vermeulen, I. (1999), *Man en Monument: die lewe en werk van Gerard Moerdijk*, Pretoria: J. L. van Schaik.

Versfeld, M. (1958), *A Guide to the City of God*, London & New York: Sheed & Ward.

Versfeld, M. (1960), *The Mirror of Philosophers*, London & New York: Sheed & Ward.

Versfeld, M. (1962), 'The nature of the tragic', *English Studies in Africa* 5: 129–50.

Versfeld, M. (1969), 'Moraliteit en moralisme', in W. A. de Klerk, M. Versfeld and J. J. Degenaar, eds, *Beweging Uitwaarts*, Cape Town: John Malherbe, 67–108.

Versfeld, M. (1972), 'The Socratic spirit', *Modern Age*, 16: 237–45.

Versfeld, M. (1979), *Our Selves*, Cape Town: David Philip.

Versfeld, M. (1988), 'Vandag se Hugenote', *De Kat* 3: 40–42.

Versfeld, M. (1992), *Sum: Selected Works*, Cape Town: Carrefour Press.

Vickers, B. (1973), *Towards Greek Tragedy: Drama, Myth, Society*, London: Longman.

Viljoen, G. van N. (1955), *Pindaros se Tiende en Twaalfde Olimpiese Odes*, Leiden: Luctor et Emergo.

Viljoen, J. M. H. (1943), 'Die Afrikaanse Kinderensiklopedie', *Die Huisgenoot*, 24 September 1943.

Viljoen, L. (2004), 'Playing the poet in *Boklied* and *Die Toneelstuk*', in J. L. Coullie and J. U. Jacobs, eds, *a.k.a. Breyten Breytenbach: Critical Approaches to his Writings and Paintings*, Amsterdam: Rodopi, 329–36.

Villa, D. (2001), *Socratic Citizenship*, Princeton: Princeton University Press.

Vindex (= F. Verschoyle) (1900), *Cecil Rhodes: His Political Life and Speeches, 1881–1900*, London: Chapman & Hall.

Visagie, G. G. (1969), *Regspleging en Reg aan die Kaap van 1652 tot 1806*, PhD thesis, University of Cape Town.

Vladislavić, I., ed. (2000), *T'kama-Adamastor: Inventions of Africa in a South African Painting*, Johannesburg: University of the Witwatersrand.

Vladislavić, I. (2001), *The Restless Supermarket*, Cape Town: David Philip.

Vlastos, G. ed. (1971), *The Philosophy of Socrates: A Collection of Critical Essays*, Notre Dame: University of Notre Dame Press.

Voet, J. (1955–1958), *The Selective Voet, Being the Commentary on the Pandects by Johannes Voet (1647–1713) and the Supplement to that Work by Johannes van der Linden (1756–1835)*, tr. Percival Gane, Durban: Butterworth.

'Voortrekker monument now a national heritage site', *South African Government News Agency*, 16 March 2012 www.sanews.gov.za/south-africa/voortrekker-monument-now-national-heritage-site

Waddell, H., tr. (1933), *Mediaeval Latin Lyrics*, 4th edition, revised, London: Constable.

Walker, E. A. (1929), *The South African College and the University of Cape Town, 1829–1929, Written for the University Centenary Celebrations*, Cape Town: Cape Times.

Walshe, P. (1970), *The Rise of African Nationalism in South Africa, 1912–1952*, London: Hurst.

Walton, J. M. (1984), *The Greek Sense of Theatre: Tragedy Reviewed*, London: Methuen.

Ward, S. (2006), 'Echoes of empire', *History Workshop Journal* 62: 264–78.

Wardle, D. (1993), 'The Rhodes Collection: a national asset', *Akroterion* 38: 86–91.

Wardle, D., ed. (2006), *Cicero On Divination, Book 1*, Oxford: Clarendon Press.

Washington, J. M., ed. (1986), *A Testament of Hope: The Essential Writings of Martin Luther King, Jr*, San Francisco: Harper & Row.

Weinthal, L. (1922), *The Story of the Cape to Cairo Railway and River Route, 1887–1922*, London: The Pioneer Publishing Co. and The African World.

Weiss, L. M. (2014), 'Informal settlements and urban heritage landscapes in South Africa', *Journal of Social Archaeology* 41.1: 3–25.

Wêreldspektrum (1983–1994) Johannesburg: Ensiklopedie Afrikana.

Wessels, J. W. (1908), *History of the Roman-Dutch Law*, Grahamstown: African Book Company.

Wessels, J. W. (1920), 'The future of Roman-Dutch law in South Africa', *South African Law Journal* 37: 265–67.

Wheen, Francis (2004), *How Mumbo-Jumbo Conquered the World: A Short History of Modern Delusions*, London: Fourth Estate.

Whigham, P., tr. (1966), *The Poems of Catullus*, Harmondsworth: Penguin.

Whitaker, R. (1997), 'The Classics in South African society: past, present and future', *Acta Classica* 40: 5–14.

Whitaker, R. (2002), 'Translating Homer in an African context', in F. Montanari et al., eds, *Omero Tremila Anni Dopo*, Rome: Edizioni di Storia e Letteratura, 523–53.

Whitaker, R., tr. (2012), *The Iliad of Homer: A Southern African Translation*, Cape Town: New Voices.

Wiles, D. (2007), *Mask and Performance in Greek Tragedy*, Cambridge: Cambridge University Press.

Williams, B. (1921), *Cecil Rhodes*, London: Constable.

Wilson Jones, M. (2000), *Principles of Roman Architecture*, London and New Haven: Yale University Press.

Windschuttle, K. (1998), 'Liberalism and imperialism', *New Criterion* 17: 4–14.

Wittenberg, H. (1993), 'Rhodes Memorial: on the aesthetics and politics of colonial culture', *Inter Action* 2: 217–30.

Wolff, E. (2010), 'Selfkennis, verstandigheid, en inkarnasie: 'n interpretasie van Martin Versfeld se Oor gode en afgode', *LitNet Akademies* 7: 257–79, www .oulitnet.co.za/akademies_geestes/pdf/LA_7_2_wolff.pdf

Wood, C. W. (1894), letters published in *The Argosy*, 57–58: 48–50, 144.

Wood, G. (1969), *The Creation of the American Republic, 1776–1787*, New York & London: Norton.

Woodbridge, S. B. (1991), *Details: The Architect's Art*, San Francisco: Chronicle Books.

Woodward, D. (2007), 'Cartography and the Renaissance: continuity and change', in D. Woodward, ed., *History of Geography, vol. 3.1: Cartography in the European Renaissance*, Chicago: University of Chicago Press, 3–23.

Worden, N. (2012), *The Making of Modern South Africa: Conquest, Apartheid, Democracy*, 5th edition, Malden: Blackwell.

Wright, L. (2004), 'Shakespeare in South Africa: alpha and "omega"', *Postcolonial Studies* 7.1: 63–81,

Wright, T. (2008), *Oscar's Books: A Journey Through the Library of Oscar Wilde*, London: Chatto and Windus.

Yoashida, K. and J. Mack (2008), *Preserving the Cultural Heritage of Africa: Crisis or Renaissance?*, Muckleneuk: UNISA Press.

Zanker, P. (2004), *Mit Mythen Leben: Die Bilderwelt der Römischen Sarkophage*, Munich: Hirmer.

Zilboorg, C. (2001), *The Masks of Mary Renault: A Literary Biography*, Columbia: University of Missouri Press.

Zimmermann, R., D. Visser and K. Reid, eds (2004), *Mixed Legal Systems in Comparative Perspective: Property and Obligations in Scotland and South Africa*, Oxford: Oxford University Press.

Zukofsky, C. and L. Zukofsky, trans. (1969), *Catullus (Gai Valeri Catulli Veronensis liber)*, London: Cape Goliard Press.

Zukofsky, L. (1965), *All the Collected Short Poems, 1923–1958*, New York: Norton.

Zuma, J. (2013), 'Address by President Jacob Zuma to the Joint Sitting of Parliament on the occasion of marking Heritage Month, National Assembly, Cape Town', *The Presidency, Republic of South Africa*, 10 September 2013 www .thepresidency.gov.za/pebble.asp?relid=16075

Zvomuya, P. (2007), 'Relevant revelations on reconciliation', *Mail and Guardian*, 31 May 2007, 8.

Index